MICROSOFT
Excel 2000

Comprehensive Concepts and Techniques

Gary B. Shelly
Thomas J. Cashman
James S. Quasney

Contributing Authors
Jeffrey J. Quasney
Joy L. Starks

COURSE
TECHNOLOGY

COURSE TECHNOLOGY
ONE MAIN STREET
CAMBRIDGE MA 02142

Thomson Learning™

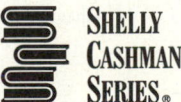
SHELLY
CASHMAN
SERIES®

Australia • Canada • Denmark • Japan • Mexico • New Zealand • Philippines
Puerto Rico • Singapore • South Africa • Spain • United Kingdom • United States

"Microsoft and the Microsoft Office User Specialist Logo are registered trademarks of Microsoft Corporation in the United States and other countries. Course Technology is an independent entity from Microsoft Corporation, and not affiliated with Microsoft Corporation in any manner. This textbook may be used in assisting students to prepare for a Microsoft Office User Specialist Exam. Neither Microsoft Corporation, its designated review company, nor Course Technology warrants that use of this textbook will ensure passing the relevant Exam.

"Use of the Microsoft Office User Specialist Approved Courseware Logo on this product signifies that it has been independently reviewed and approved in complying with the following standards: 'Acceptable coverage of all content related to the Microsoft Office Exam entitled "Microsoft Excel 2000 Core Exam" or "Microsoft Excel 2000 Expert Exam;" and sufficient performance-based exercises that relate closely to all required content, based on sampling of text."

PHOTO CREDITS: Microsoft Excel 2000 *Project 1, pages E 1.4-5* Background swirls, building doorway, business man photo, circuit board, hand, library, man at ATM, man talking on telephone, people with groceries, stack of books, student on steps, student with books, woman at computer, woman holding garment, Courtesy of PhotoDisc, Inc.; parking meter, Courtesy of KPT MetaTools; *Project 2, pages E 2.2-3* Bike helmet, coffee cup, moon, mountain bike, Courtesy of Corel Corporation; *Project 3, pages E 3.2-3* Money, stacks of bills, house, Courtesy of PhotoDisc, Inc.; *Project 4, pages E 4.2-3* Couple reviewing notes, mortgage printout, home, hand on keyboard, Courtesy of PhotoDisc, Inc.; *page E 4.5* Pig, money, Courtesy of Corel Corporation; *Project 5, pages E 5.2-3* Senior citizen pool players, man, woman, group of people working, Courtesy of PhotoDisc, Inc.; *page E 5.5* Skates, hockey equipment, Courtesy of MetaTools; *Project 6, pages E 6.2-3* Ambulance, women praying, emergency medics, family, Courtesy of PhotoDisc, Inc.; Country Companies Insurance Group brochure, Courtesy of Country Life Insurance Company; *page E 6.5* Sound systems, conductor, globe, Courtesy of Corel Corporation; *Project 7, pages E 7.2-3* Two couples, Courtesy of PhotoDisc, Inc.; *Project 8, pages E 8.2-3* Woman in cafeteria, chef, boy with lunch tray, people in cafeteria, Courtesy of PhotoDisc, Inc.; *Project 9, pages E 9.2-3* Chester Carlson, Courtesy of Bettmann/Corbis.

ISBN 0-7895-5609-X

4 5 6 7 8 9 10   BC   04 03 02 01

MICROSOFT

Excel 2000

Comprehensive Concepts and Techniques

C O N T E N T S

Microsoft Excel 2000

● PROJECT 1

CREATING A WORKSHEET AND EMBEDDED CHART

● PROJECT 2

FORMULAS, FUNCTIONS, FORMATTING, AND WEB QUERIES

Preface

The Shelly Cashman Series® offers the finest textbooks in computer education. We are proud of the fact that our *Microsoft Excel 5*, *Microsoft Excel 7*, and *Microsoft Excel 97* textbooks have been the most widely used spreadsheet books in education. Each edition of our Excel textbooks has included innovations, many based on comments made by the instructors and students who use our books. The *Microsoft Excel 2000* books continue with the innovation, quality, and reliability that you have come to expect from the Shelly Cashman Series.

In our *Excel 2000* books, you will find an educationally sound and easy-to-follow pedagogy that combines a step-by-step approach with corresponding screens. All projects and exercises in this book are designed to take full advantage of the Excel 2000 enhancements. The popular Other Ways and More About features offer in-depth knowledge of Excel 2000. The project openers provide a fascinating perspective of the subject covered in the project. The project material is developed carefully to ensure that students will see the importance of learning Excel 2000 for future course work.

Objectives of This Textbook

Microsoft Excel 2000: Comprehensive Concepts and Techniques is intended for a three-unit course that presents Microsoft Excel 2000. No experience with a computer is assumed, and no mathematics beyond the high school freshman level is required. The objectives of this book are:

- To teach the fundamentals of Microsoft Excel 2000
- To expose students to practical examples of the computer as a useful tool
- To acquaint students with the proper procedures to create worksheets suitable for course work, professional purposes, and personal use
- To develop an exercise-oriented approach that allows learning by example
- To encourage independent study, and help those who are working alone
- To demonstrate the Microsoft Excel 2000 Expert level skill set for the Microsoft Office User Specialist Exam

Approved by Microsoft as Courseware for the Microsoft Office User Specialist Program – Expert Level

This book has been approved by Microsoft as courseware for the Microsoft Office User Specialist (MOUS) program. After completing the projects and exercises in this book, students will be prepared to take the Expert level examination for the Microsoft Office User Specialist Exam for Microsoft Excel 2000. By passing the certification exam for a Microsoft software application, students demonstrate their proficiency in that application to employers. This exam is offered at participating centers, participating corporations, and participating employment agencies. See Appendix D for additional information on the MOUS program and for a table that includes the Microsoft Excel 2000 MOUS skill sets for both Core level and Expert level and corresponding page numbers where a skill is discussed in the book, or visit the Web site at www.mous.net.

The Shelly Cashman Series Microsoft Office User Specialist Center Web page (Figure 1) has more than fifteen Web pages you can visit to obtain additional information on the MOUS Certification program. The Web page (www.scsite.com/off2000/cert.htm) includes links to general information on certification, choosing an application for certification, preparing for the certification exam, and taking and passing the certification exam.

FIGURE 1

The Shelly Cashman Approach

Features of the Shelly Cashman Series *Microsoft Excel 2000* books include:

- **Project Orientation:** Each project in the book presents a practical problem and complete solution in an easy-to-understand approach.

- **Step-by-Step, Screen-by-Screen Instructions:** Each of the tasks required to complete a project is shown using a step-by-step, screen-by-screen approach. The screens are shown in full color.

- **Thoroughly Tested Projects:** Every screen in the book is correct because it is produced by the author only after performing a step, resulting in unprecedented quality.

- **Other Ways Boxes and Quick Reference Summary:** Excel 2000 provides a variety of ways to carry out a given task. The Other Ways boxes displayed at the end of most of the step-by-step sequences specify the other ways to do the task completed in the steps. Thus, the steps and the Other Ways box make a comprehensive reference unit. A Quick Reference Summary, available in the back of this book and on the Web, summarizes the ways specific tasks can be completed.

- **More About Feature:** These marginal annotations provide background information that complements the topics covered, adding depth and perspective.

- **Integration of the World Wide Web:** The World Wide Web is integrated into the Excel 2000 learning experience by (1) More Abouts that send students to Web sites for up-to-date information and alternative approaches to tasks; (2) a MOUS information Web page and a MOUS map Web page so students can better prepare for the Microsoft Office Use Specialist (MOUS) Certification examinations; (3) an Excel 2000 Quick Reference Summary Web page that summarizes the ways to complete tasks (mouse, menu, shortcut menu, and keyboard); and (4) project reinforcement Web pages in the form of true/false, multiple choice, and short answer questions, and other types of student activities.

FIGURE 6-1

More About 2000

Showing Scenarios

You can add a list of scenarios to your toolbar by using the Customize command on the Toolbars submenu of the View menu. Click the Commands tab and select Tools. Drag the Scenario command with the drop-down arrow up to the toolbar. You then can quickly switch between scenarios on the worksheet.

Other Ways

1. Click Record Macro button on Visual Basic toolbar
2. Press ALT+T, press M, press R

Organization of This Textbook

Microsoft Excel 2000: Comprehensive Concepts and Techniques provides detailed instruction on how to use Excel 2000. The material is divided into nine projects, two Web Features, an Integration Feature, four appendices, and a Quick Reference Summary.

Project 1 – Creating a Worksheet and Embedded Chart In Project 1, students are introduced to Excel terminology, the Excel window, and the basic characteristics of a worksheet and workbook. Topics include starting and quitting Excel; entering text and numbers; selecting a range; using the AutoSum button; copying using the fill handle; changing font size; formatting in bold; centering across columns; using the AutoFormat command; charting using the ChartWizard; saving and opening a workbook; editing a worksheet; using the AutoCalculate area; and using the Excel Help system.

Project 2 – Formulas, Functions, Formatting, and Web Queries In Project 2, students use formulas and functions to build a worksheet and learn more about formatting and printing a worksheet. Topics include entering formulas; using functions; verifying formulas; formatting text and numbers; conditional formatting; drawing borders; changing the widths of columns and rows; spell checking; previewing a worksheet; printing a section of a worksheet; and displaying and printing the formulas in a worksheet. This project also introduces students to accessing real-time data using Web Queries and sending the open workbook as an e-mail attachment directly from Excel.

Project 3 – What-If-Analysis, Charting, and Working with Large Worksheets In Project 3, students learn how to work with larger worksheets, how to create a worksheet based on assumptions, how to use the IF function and absolute cell references, charting techniques, and how to perform what-if analysis. Topics include assigning global formats; rotating text; using the fill handle to create a series; deleting, inserting, copying, and moving data on a worksheet; displaying and formatting the system date; displaying and docking toolbars; creating a 3-D Pie chart on a chart sheet, enhancing a 3-D Pie chart; freezing titles; changing the magnification of worksheets; displaying different parts of the worksheet using panes; and simple what-if analysis and goal seeking.

Web Feature – Creating Static and Dynamic Web Pages Using Excel In the Web Feature, students are introduced to creating static Web pages (noninteractive pages that do not change) and dynamic Web pages (interactive pages that offer Excel functionality). Topics include saving and previewing an Excel workbook as a Web page; viewing and manipulating a Web page created in Excel using a browser; and using the Spreadsheet Property Toolbox.

Project 4 – Financial Functions, Data Tables, Amortization Schedules, and Hyperlinks In Project 4, students learn how to use financial functions and learn more about analyzing data in a worksheet. Topics include applying the PMT function to determine a monthly payment; the PV function to determine the amount due on a loan at the end of a year; adding a hyperlink to a Web page; using names to reference cells; protecting a worksheet; and analyzing data by (1) goal seeking, (2) creating a data table, and (3) creating an amortization schedule.

Project 5 – Creating, Sorting, and Querying a Worksheet Database In Project 5, students learn how to create, sort, and filter a database. Topics include using a data form to create and maintain a database; creating subtotals; finding, extracting, and deleting records that pass a test; outlining a worksheet; and applying database and lookup functions.

Project 6 – Creating Templates and Working with Multiple Worksheets and Workbooks In Project 6, students learn to create a template and consolidate data into one worksheet. Topics include building and copying a template; multiple worksheets; 3-D cell references; customized formats; styles; charting; WordArt; adding notes to a cell; adding a header and footer; creating and modifying lines and objects; changing page setup characteristics; and finding and replacing data.

Integration Feature – Linking an Excel Worksheet to a Word Document In the Integration Feature, students are introduced to linking a worksheet to a Word document. Topics include a discussion of the differences among copying and pasting, copying and embedding, and copying and linking; opening multiple applications; saving and printing a document with a linked worksheet; and editing a linked worksheet in a Word document.

Project 7 – Using Visual Basic for Applications (VBA) with Excel In Project 7, students learn how to automate tasks by incorporating VBA into their workbooks. Topics include protecting worksheets with passwords; using the macro recorder; executing macros; security; adding buttons to toolbars and commands to menus; creating a user interface by adding controls to a worksheet; setting properties; writing VBA code; using the Visual Basic Editor; validating incoming data; and using event-driven programs.

Project 8 – Auditing, Data Validation, and Solving Complex Problems In Project 8, students learn how to go about solving complex problems. Topics include using the Auditing toolbar; using data validation; goal seeking; using Solver to solve multiple problems; saving multiple scenarios with Scenario Manager; analysis of Solver answers and multiple scenarios; and workbook properties.

Project 9 – Importing External Data, Tracking and Routing Changes, and Creating Data Maps, PivotCharts, and PivotTables In Project 9, students learn how to import data into an Excel workbook, collaboration techniques, and advanced data analysis techniques. Topics include importing data from a text file, an Access database, and a Web page; turning Track Changes on and off; accepting and rejecting changes; serially routing a workbook to recipients; creating a data map; creating a PivotChart and PivotTable; analyzing a worksheet database using a PivotChart and PivotTable; and sharing and merging workbooks.

Web Feature – Creating a PivotTable List Web Page Using Excel In this Web Feature, students learn how to create and manipulate a PivotTable list. Topics include saving a worksheet database as a PivotTable list; viewing the PivotTable list using a browser; changing the view of the PivotTable list; adding summary totals; sorting columns of data; filtering techniques; removing fields and adding fields to a PivotTable list; and improving the appearance of a PivotTable list.

Appendices

Appendix A presents a detailed step-by-step introduction to the Microsoft Excel Help system. Students learn how to use the Office Assistant and the Contents, Answer Wizard, and Index sheets in the Excel Help window. Appendix B describes how to publish Excel Web pages to a Web server. Appendix C shows students how to reset the menus and toolbars. Appendix D introduces students to the Microsoft Office User Specialist (MOUS) Certification program and includes a MOUS map that lists a page number in the book for each of the MOUS activities for Core level and Expert level.

Quick Reference Summary

In Excel, you can accomplish a task in a number of ways, such as using the mouse, menu, shortcut menu, and keyboard. The Quick Reference Summary at the back of this book provides a quick reference to the different ways to complete each task presented in this textbook. The Quick Reference Summary also is available on the Web at www.scsite.com/off2000/qr.htm.

End-of-Project Student Activities

A notable strength of the Shelly Cashman Series *Microsoft Excel 2000* books is the extensive student activities at the end of each project. Well-structured student activities can make the difference between students merely participating in a class and students retaining the information they learn. The activities in the Shelly Cashman Series *Excel 2000* books include the following.

- **What You Should Know** A listing of the tasks completed within a project together with the pages where the step-by-step, screen-by-screen explanations appear. This section provides a perfect study review for students.

- **Project Reinforcement on the Web** Every project has a Web page (www.scsite.com/off2000/reinforce.htm). The Web page includes true/false, multiple choice, and short answer questions, and additional project-related reinforcement activities that will help students gain confidence in their Excel 2000 abilities. The Project Reinforcement exercises also are included on the Shelly Cashman Series Teaching Tools CD-ROM.

- **Apply Your Knowledge** This exercise requires students to open and manipulate a file on the Data Disk. To obtain a copy of the Data Disk, follow the instructions on the inside back cover of this book.

- **In the Lab** Three in-depth assignments per project require students to apply the knowledge gained in the project to solve problems on a computer.

- **Cases and Places** Up to seven unique case studies that require students to apply their knowledge to real-world situations.

Shelly Cashman Series Teaching Tools

A comprehensive set of Teaching Tools accompanies this textbook in the form of a CD-ROM. The CD-ROM includes an Instructor's Manual and teaching and testing aids. The CD-ROM (ISBN 0-7895-4636-1) is available through your Course Technology representative or by calling one of the following telephone numbers: Colleges and Universities, 1-800-648-7450; High Schools, 1-800-824-5179; Career Colleges, 1-800-477-3692; Canada, 1-800-268-2222; and Corporations and Government Agencies, 1-800-340-7450.

- **Instructor's Manual** The Instructor's Manual is made up of Microsoft Word files. The files include lecture notes, solutions to laboratory assignments, and a large test bank. The files allow you to modify the lecture notes or generate quizzes and exams from the test bank using your own word processing software. Where appropriate, solutions to laboratory assignments are embedded as icons in the files. When an icon appears, double-click it and the application will start and the solution will display on the screen. The Instructor's Manual includes the following for each project: project objectives; project overview; detailed lesson plans with page number references; teacher notes and activities;

answers to the end-of-project exercises; test bank of 110 questions for every project (25 multiple-choice, 50 true/false, and 35 fill-in-the-blank) with page number references; and transparency references. The transparencies are available through the Figures in the Book. The test bank questions are numbered the same as in Course Test Manager. Thus, you can print a copy of the project test bank and use the printout to select your questions in Course Test Manager.

○ **Figures in the Book** Illustrations for every screen and table in the textbook are available in JPEG format. Use this ancillary to create a slide show from the illustrations for lecture or to print transparencies for use in lecture. You also may create your own PowerPoint presentations and insert these illustrations.

○ **Course Test Manager** Course Test Manager is a powerful testing and assessment package that enables instructors to create and print tests from the large test bank. Instructors with access to a networked computer lab (LAN) can administer, grade, and track tests online. Students also can take online practice tests, which generate customized study guides.

○ **Course Syllabus** Any instructor who has been assigned a course at the last minute knows how difficult it is to come up with a course syllabus. For this reason, sample syllabi are included for each of the Excel 2000 products that can be customized easily to a course.

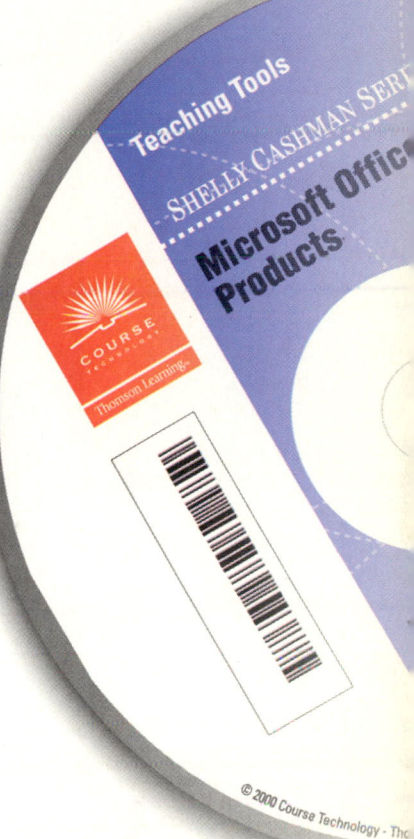

○ **Lecture Success System** Lecture Success System files are for use with the application software, a personal computer, and projection device to explain and illustrate the step-by-step, screen-by-screen development of a project in the textbook without entering large amounts of data.

○ **Instructor's Lab Solutions** Solutions and required files for all the In the Lab assignments at the end of each project are available.

○ **Lab Tests/Test Outs** Tests that parallel the In the Lab assignments are supplied for the purpose of testing students in the laboratory on the material covered in the project or testing students out of the course.

○ **Project Reinforcement** True/false, multiple choice, and short answer questions, and additional project-related reinforcement activities for each project help students gain confidence in their Excel 2000 abilities.

○ **Student Files** All the files that are required by students to complete the Apply Your Knowledge exercises are included.

○ **Interactive Labs** Eighteen hands-on interactive labs that take students from ten to fifteen minutes each to step through help solidify and reinforce mouse and keyboard usage and computer concepts. Student assessment is available.

○ **WebCT Content** This ancillary includes book-related content that can be uploaded to your institution's WebCT site. The content includes a sample syllabus, practice tests, a bank of test questions, a list of book-related links, and lecture notes from the Instructor's Manual.

Acknowledgments

The Shelly Cashman Series would not be the leading computer education series without the contributions of outstanding publishing professionals. First, and foremost, among them is Becky Herrington, director of production and designer. She is the heart and soul of the Shelly Cashman Series, and it is only through her leadership, dedication, and tireless efforts that superior products are made possible. Becky created and produced the award-winning Windows series of books.

Under Becky's direction, the following individuals made significant contributions to these books: Doug Cowley, production manager; Ginny Harvey, series specialist and developmental editor; Ken Russo, senior Web designer; Mike Bodnar, associate production manager; Stephanie Nance, graphic artist and cover designer; Mark Norton, Web designer; Meena Mohtadi, production editor; Marlo Mitchem, Chris Schneider, Hector Arvizu, Kenny Tran, Kathy Mayers, and Dave Bonnewitz, graphic artists; Jeanne Black and Betty Hopkins, Quark experts; Nancy Lamm, Lyn Markowicz, Margaret Gatling, and Laurie Sullivan, copyeditors; Marilyn Martin, Kim Kosmatka, Cherilyn King, Mary Steinman, and Pat Hadden, proofreaders; Cristina Haley, indexer; Sarah Evertson of Image Quest, photo researcher; Susan Sebok and Ginny Harvey, contributing writers; and Bill Daley, technical reviewer.

Special thanks go to Richard Keaveny, managing editor; Jim Quasney, series consulting editor; Lora Wade, product manager; Erin Bennett, associate product manager; Francis Schurgot, Web product manager; Marc Ouellette, associate Web product manager; Scott Wiseman, online developer; Rajika Gupta, marketing manager; and Erin Runyon, editorial assistant.

Gary B. Shelly
Thomas J. Cashman
James S. Quasney

Excel 2000

Microsoft **Excel 2000**

Microsoft Excel 2000

Creating a Worksheet and Embedded Chart

OBJECTIVES

You will have mastered the material in this project when you can:

- Start Excel
- Describe the Excel worksheet
- Reset menus and toolbars
- Select a cell or range of cells
- Enter text and numbers
- Use the AutoSum button to sum a range of cells
- Copy a cell to a range of cells using the fill handle
- Change the size of the font in a cell
- Bold cell entries
- Apply the AutoFormat command to format a range
- Center cell contents across a series of columns
- Use the Name box to select a cell
- Create a Column chart using the Chart Wizard
- Save a workbook
- Print a worksheet
- Quit Excel
- Open a workbook
- Use the AutoCalculate area to determine totals
- Correct errors on a worksheet
- Use the Office Assistant and other online Help tools to answer your questions

Get Smart

Smart Cards Open Convenience Doors

What can pay for your laundry, open your dorm door, feed the parking meter, and withdraw money from an automatic teller machine? Need a hint? It is smart, but it never went to college. It is a smart card, and it is coming soon to your wallet.

This ingenious card resembles a credit card in size, but instead of a magnetic strip on the back, it has a microprocessor chip inside. This chip gives the card its brains, while it gives its owner convenience and security.

University of Michigan and University of Illinois students are familiar with the card, as are students at 25 other schools across the United States and Canada. They use it for everything from calling Mom back home to checking out library books to debiting their checking accounts.

The nonprofit Smart Card Forum (www.smartcardforum.org) has helped bring this technology to education. The 200 members of this organization represent a cross-section of technology experts and smart card users who are working to increase multiple-application smart cards in the government, private, and education sectors.

Some visionaries predict 3.75 billion smart cards will be issued by 2005, with owners using them to make 25 billion transactions yearly. The cost to manufacture one card ranges from 80 cents to 15 dollars depending on the application and complexity.

Two types of smart cards are available. One is a memory card. The memory card contains a stored value that the owner can spend on transactions such as paying bus fare or making a call from a public telephone. When the value is depleted, the card is useless.

The second is an intelligent card. The intelligent card contains a central processing unit that can store data and make decisions. Owners begin with a set monetary value, such as $100, and then they can make a purchase that does not exceed this figure. If the amount is insufficient, they can add money to the balance. These functions are similar to the activities you will perform using Microsoft Excel in this project for the Fun-N-Sun Sojourn company, where you will enter numbers in predefined storage areas, or cells, and then calculate a sum.

The smart card originated in 1974 when Roland Moreno, a reporter and self-taught inventor, secured a chip on an epoxy card. His vision was for merchants to accept electronic payments by inserting three cards in his Take the Money and Run (TMR) machine. One card identified the merchant, the second contained the customer's electronic money, and the third had a list of deadbeat accounts that could not be used to make a transaction. Pictures and descriptions of Moreno's invention and other smart card developments are found in the Smart Card Museum (www.cardshow.com/museum).

Today, chips for the cards are manufactured by such industry leaders as Motorola, Gemplus, and Schlumberger. These companies are working to meet the demand for the cards, which is increasing at a rate of 30 percent annually. With an ever-growing global marketplace, smart cards are a smart way of doing business.

Microsoft Excel 2000

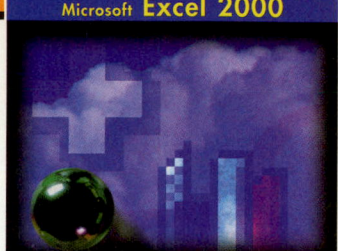

Creating a Worksheet and Embedded Chart

C A S E   P E R S P E C T I V E

While on spring break in the Bahamas four years ago, Kylie Waiter and three of her friends came up with the idea of creating a worldwide travel agency that catered to young adults. After graduation, they invested $3,000 each and started their dream company, Fun-N-Sun Sojourn. Thanks to their market savvy and the popularity of personal computers and the World Wide Web, the company has become the premier provider of student vacations.

As sales continue to grow, the management at Fun-N-Sun Sojourn has realized they need a better tracking system for first quarter sales. As a result, they have asked you to prepare a first quarter sales worksheet that shows the sales for the first quarter.

In addition, Kylie has asked you to create a graphical representation of the first quarter sales because she has little tolerance for lists of numbers.

What Is Microsoft Excel 2000?

Microsoft Excel is a powerful spreadsheet program that allows you to organize data, complete calculations, make decisions, graph data, develop professional looking reports, publish organized data to the Web, and access real-time data from Web sites. The four major parts of Excel are:

▶ **Worksheets** Worksheets allow you to enter, calculate, manipulate, and analyze data such as numbers and text. The term worksheet means the same as spreadsheet.

▶ **Charts** Charts pictorially represent data. Excel can draw a variety of two-dimensional and three-dimensional charts.

▶ **Databases** Databases manage data. For example, once you enter data onto a worksheet, Excel can sort the data, search for specific data, and select data that meets a criteria.

▶ **Web Support** Web support allows Excel to save workbooks or parts of a workbook in HTML format so they can be viewed and manipulated using a browser. You also can access real-time data using Web queries.

Project One — Fun-N-Sun Sojourn First Quarter Sales

From your meeting with Fun-N-Sun Sojourn's management, you have determined the following needs, source of data, calculations, and chart requirements.

Need: An easy-to-read worksheet (Figure 1-1) that shows Fun-N-Sun Sojourn's first quarter sales for each key vacation package (Bahamas Repose, Daytona Delight, Key West Haven, and South Padre Del Sol) by sales channel (Mail, Campus, Telephone, and Web). The worksheet also should include total sales for each vacation package, each sales channel, and total company sales for the first quarter.

FIGURE 1-1

Source of Data: The data for the worksheet is available at the end of the first quarter from Eric Jacobs, chief financial officer (CFO) of Fun-N-Sun Sojourn.

Calculations: You have determined that the following calculations must be made for the worksheet: (a) total first quarter sales for each of the four vacation packages; (b) total first quarter sales for each of the four sales channels; and (c) total company first quarter sales.

Chart Requirements: Below the worksheet, construct a 3-D Column chart that compares the amount of sales to the four sales channels for each vacation package.

Starting Excel

To start Excel, Windows must be running. Perform the following steps to start Excel.

 To Start Excel

1 Click the Start button on the taskbar and then point to New Office Document.

The Start menu displays (Figure 1-2).

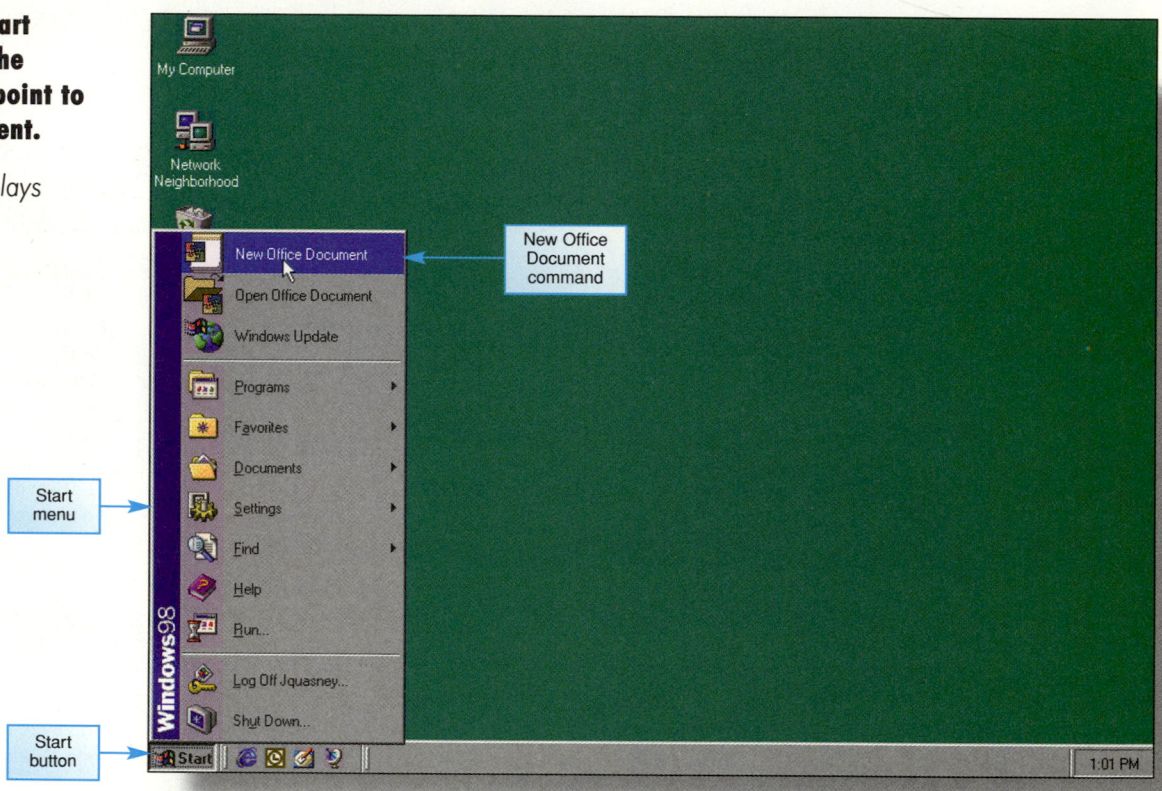

FIGURE 1-2

2 Click New Office Document. If necessary, click the General tab, and then point to the Blank Workbook icon.

The New Office Document dialog box displays (Figure 1-3).

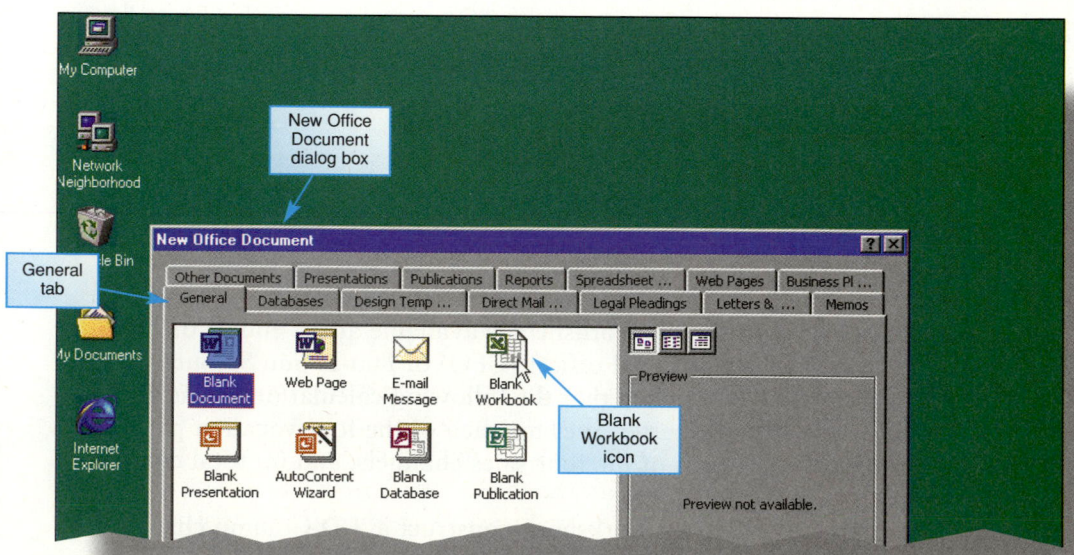

FIGURE 1-3

3 **Double-click the Blank Workbook icon. If necessary, maximize the Excel window by double-clicking its title bar.**

Excel displays an empty workbook titled Book1 (Figure 1-4).

FIGURE 1-4

4 **If the Office Assistant displays (Figure 1-4), click Help on the menu bar and then click Hide the Office Assistant.**

Excel hides the Office Assistant (Figure 1-5). The purpose of the Office Assistant will be discussed later in this project.

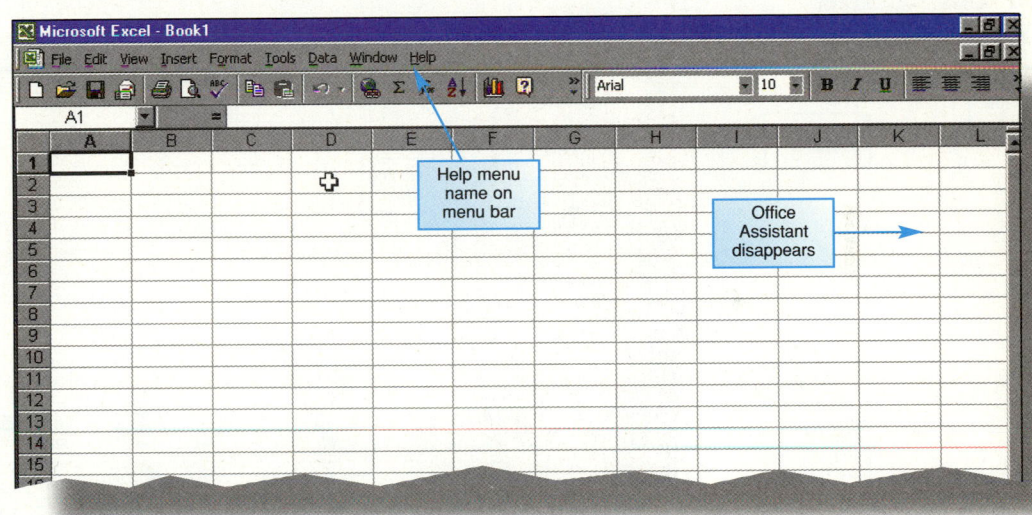

FIGURE 1-5

The Excel Worksheet

When Excel starts, it creates a new empty workbook, called Book1. The **workbook** (Figure 1-6 on the next page) is like a notebook. Inside the workbook are sheets, called **worksheets**. Each sheet name displays on a **sheet tab** at the bottom of the workbook. For example, Sheet1 is the name of the active worksheet displayed in the workbook called Book1. If you click the tab labeled Sheet2, Excel displays the Sheet2 worksheet. A new workbook opens with three worksheets. If necessary, you can add additional worksheets to a maximum of 255. This project uses only the Sheet1 worksheet. Later projects will use multiple worksheets in a workbook.

The Worksheet

The worksheet is organized into a rectangular grid containing columns (vertical) and rows (horizontal). A column letter above the grid, also called the **column heading**, identifies each **column**. A row number on the left side of the grid, also called the **row heading**, identifies each **row**. With the screen resolution set to 800 × 600, twelve columns (A through L) and twenty-five rows (1 through 25) of the worksheet display on the screen when the worksheet is maximized as shown in Figure 1-6 on the next page.

The Office Assistant

In Step 4 you were instructed to hide the Office Assistant. You may want to have it remain on the screen because it can be helpful. For example, the Office Assistant tracks your work. If you complete a task and the Office Assistant knows a better, alternative way to carry out the task, it will add the alternative to its tips list. You can view the most recent tip by clicking the light bulb when it displays above the Office Assistant.

Sheet1 worksheet

Name box with active cell reference

up to 255 worksheets available

worksheet window

status bar

heavy border surrounds active cell

indicates cell A1 is active

mouse pointer

gridlines

cell C5

column heading letters

row heading numbers

scroll boxes

tab scrolling buttons

sheet tabs

Excel taskbar button

tab split box

scroll bars

scroll arrows

FIGURE 1-6

The intersection of each column and row is a cell. A **cell** is the basic unit of a worksheet into which you enter data. Each worksheet in a workbook has 256 columns and 65,536 rows for a total of 16,777,216 cells. The column headings begin with A and end with IV. The row headings begin with 1 and end with 65,536. Only a small fraction of the active worksheet displays on the screen at one time.

A cell is referred to by its unique address, or **cell reference**, which is the coordinates of the intersection of a column and a row. To identify a cell, specify the column letter first, followed by the row number. For example, cell reference C5 refers to the cell located at the intersection of column C and row 5 (Figure 1-6).

One cell on the worksheet, designated the **active cell**, is the one in which you can enter data. The active cell in Figure 1-6 is A1. Cell A1 is identified in three ways. First, a heavy border surrounds the cell; second, the **active cell reference** displays immediately above column A in the **Name box**; and third, the column heading A and row heading 1 light up so it is easy to see which cell is active (Figure 1-6).

The horizontal and vertical lines on the worksheet itself are called **gridlines**. Gridlines make it easier to see and identify each cell in the worksheet. If desired, you can turn the gridlines off so they do not display on the worksheet, but it is recommended that you leave them on.

The mouse pointer in Figure 1-6 has the shape of a block plus sign. The mouse pointer displays as a **block plus sign** whenever it is located in a cell on the worksheet. Another common shape of the mouse pointer is the block arrow. The mouse pointer turns into the **block arrow** whenever you move it outside the worksheet or when you drag cell contents between rows or columns. The other mouse pointer shapes are described when they display on the screen during this and subsequent projects.

Worksheet Window

You view the portion of the worksheet displayed on the screen through a **worksheet window** (Figure 1-6). Below and to the right of the worksheet window are **scroll bars**, **scroll arrows**, and **scroll boxes** that you can use to move the window around to view different parts of the active worksheet. To the right of the sheet tabs at the bottom of the screen is the **tab split box**. You can drag the tab split box (Figure 1-6) to increase or decrease the view of the sheet tabs. When you decrease the view of the sheet tabs, you increase the length of the horizontal scroll bar; and vice versa.

The menu bar, Standard toolbar, and Formatting toolbar display at the top of the screen just below the title bar (Figure 1-7a). The Standard toolbar and Formatting toolbar display on one row. Because both of these toolbars cannot fit entirely on a single row, a portion or all of the Standard toolbar displays on the left of the row and a portion or all of the Formatting toolbar displays on the right.

(a) Menu Bar and Toolbars

(b) Short Menu

(c) Full Menu

FIGURE 1-7

More About 2000

The Worksheet Window

If the buttons and toolbars on your screen are distracting to you, you can increase the number of rows and columns displayed by clicking Full Screen on the View menu. Excel immediately will hide the buttons and bars, thus increasing the size of the window. Excel also displays a small toolbar with the Full Screen button on it. Click the Full Screen button to return to the previous view.

Menu Bar

The menu bar is a special toolbar that includes the Excel menu names (Figure 1-7a on the previous page). The menu bar that displays when you start Excel is the **Worksheet menu bar**. Each menu name represents a menu of commands that you can use to retrieve, store, print, and manipulate data on the worksheet. When you point to a menu name on the menu bar, the area of the menu bar containing the name changes to a button. To display a menu, such as the Edit menu, click the Edit menu name on the menu bar (Figures 1-7b and 1-7c on the previous page). If you point to a command with an arrow on the right, a submenu displays from which you can choose a command.

When you click a menu name on the menu bar, a **short menu** displays listing the most recently used commands (Figure 1-7b). If you wait a few seconds or click the arrows at the bottom of the short menu (Figure 1-7b), the full menu displays. The **full menu** lists all the commands associated with a menu (Figure 1-7c). You also can display a full menu immediately by double-clicking the menu name on the menu bar. In this book, when you display a menu, always display the full menu using one of the following techniques.

1. Click the menu name on the menu bar and then wait a few seconds.
2. Click the menu name and then click the arrows at the bottom of the short menu.
3. Click the menu name and then point to the arrows at the bottom of the short menu.
4. Double-click the menu name.

When a full menu displays, some of the commands are recessed into a shaded gray background and others are dimmed. A recessed command is called a **hidden command** because it does not display on the short menu. As you use Excel, it automatically personalizes the short menus for you based on how often you use commands. That is, as you use hidden commands, Excel unhides them and places them on the short menu. A **dimmed command** displays in a faint type, which indicates it is not available for the current selection.

The menu bar can change to include other menu names depending on the type of work you are doing in Excel. For example, if you are working with a chart sheet rather than a worksheet, the **Chart menu bar** displays with menu names that reflect charting commands.

Standard Toolbar and Formatting Toolbar

The Standard toolbar (Figure 1-8a) and the Formatting toolbar (Figure 1-8b) contain buttons and list boxes that allow you to perform frequent tasks more quickly than when using the menu bar. For example, to print a worksheet, you click the Print button on the Standard toolbar. Each button has a picture on the button face that helps you remember the button's function. Also, when you move the mouse pointer over a button or box, the name of the button or box displays below it in a **ScreenTip**.

FIGURE 1-8a Standard Toolbar

FIGURE 1-8b Formatting Toolbar

Figures 1-8a and 1-8b illustrate the Standard and Formatting toolbars and describe the functions of the buttons. Each of the buttons and list boxes will be explained in detail when they are used in the projects.

Both the Standard and Formatting toolbars are preset to display on the same row, immediately below the menu bar. To display the entire Standard toolbar, double-click the move handle on the left. Excel slides the Formatting toolbar to the right so the toolbars appear as shown in Figure 1-9a.

(a) Complete Standard Toolbar and Partial Formatting Toolbar

(b) Partial Standard Toolbar and Complete Formatting Toolbar

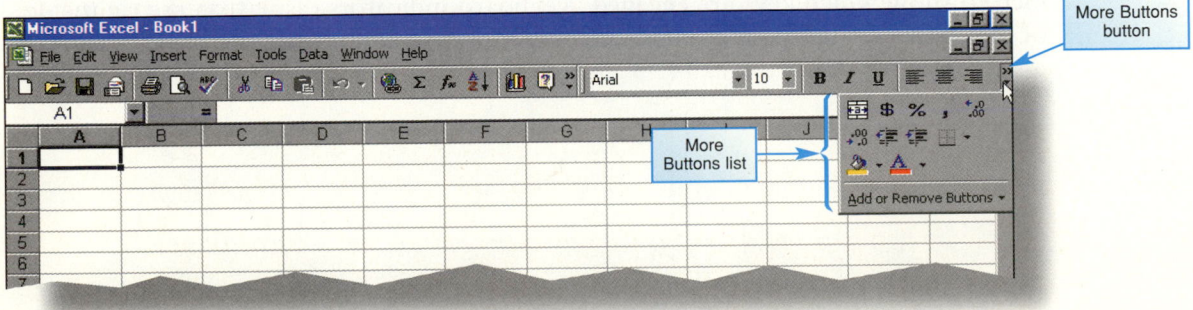

(c) More Buttons List

FIGURE 1-9

To display the entire Formatting toolbar, double-click the move handle on its left edge or drag the move handle to the left. When you display the complete Formatting toolbar, a portion of the Standard toolbar is hidden (Figure 1-9b on the previous page).

An alternative to sliding one toolbar over another is to use the **More Buttons button** on a toolbar to display the buttons that are hidden (Figure 1-9c on the previous page).

As with the menus, Excel will personalize the toolbars. That is, if you use a hidden button on a partially displayed toolbar, Excel will remove the button from the More Buttons list (Figure 1-9c) and promote it to the toolbar. For example, if you click the Bold button and then the Italic button on the Formatting toolbar in Figure 1-9c, Excel will promote these buttons to the Formatting toolbar and remove buttons from the Standard or Formatting toolbars to make room on the row.

Resetting Menus and Toolbars

Each project in this book begins with resetting the menus and toolbars to the settings as they were at the initial installation of the software. To reset your menus and toolbars so they display exactly as shown in this book, follow the steps outlined in Appendix C.

Formula Bar

Below the Standard and Formatting toolbars is the formula bar (Figure 1-10). As you type, the data displays in the **formula bar**. Excel also displays the active cell reference on the left side of the formula bar in the **Name box**.

Status Bar

Immediately above the Windows taskbar at the bottom of the screen is the status bar. The **status bar** displays a brief description of the command selected (highlighted) in a menu, the function of the button the mouse pointer is pointing to, or the current activity (mode) in progress (Figure 1-10). **Mode indicators**, such as Enter and Ready, display on the status bar and specify the current mode of Excel. When the mode is **Ready**, Excel is ready to accept the next command or data entry. When the mode indicator reads **Enter**, Excel is in the process of accepting data through the keyboard into the active cell.

In the middle of the status bar is the AutoCalculate area. The **AutoCalculate area** can be used in place of a calculator to view the sum, average, or other types of totals of a group of numbers on the worksheet. The AutoCalculate area is discussed in detail later in this project.

Keyboard indicators, such as NUM (Num Lock), CAPS (Caps Lock), and SCRL (Scroll) show which keys are engaged. Keyboard indicators display on the right side of the status bar within the small rectangular boxes (Figure 1-10).

FIGURE 1-10

Selecting a Cell

To enter data into a cell, you first must select it. The easiest way to **select a cell** (make it active) is to use the mouse to move the block plus sign to the cell and then click.

An alternative method is to use the **arrow keys** that are located just to the right of the typewriter keys on the keyboard. An arrow key selects the cell adjacent to the active cell in the direction of the arrow on the key.

You know a cell is selected (active) when a heavy border surrounds the cell (cell A1 in Figure 1-10) and the active cell reference displays in the Name box on the left side of the formula bar.

Entering Text

In Excel, any set of characters containing a letter, hyphen (as in a telephone number), or space is considered **text**. Text is used to place titles on the worksheet, such as worksheet titles, column titles, and row titles. In Project 1 (Figure 1-11 on the next page), the worksheet title, Fun-N-Sun Sojourn 1st Qtr Sales, identifies the worksheet. The column titles in row 2 (Mail, Campus, Telephone, Web, and Total) identify the data in each column. The row titles in column A (Bahamas Repose, Daytona Delight, Key West Haven, South Padre Del Sol, and Total) identify the data in each row.

More *About*

Selecting a Cell

You can select any cell by typing the cell reference, such as B4, in the Name box on the left side of the formula bar.

More *About*

Text

A text entry in a cell can contain from 1 to 32,767 characters. Although text entries are used primarily to identify parts of the worksheet, other applications exist in which text entries are data that you dissect, string together, and manipulate using text functions.

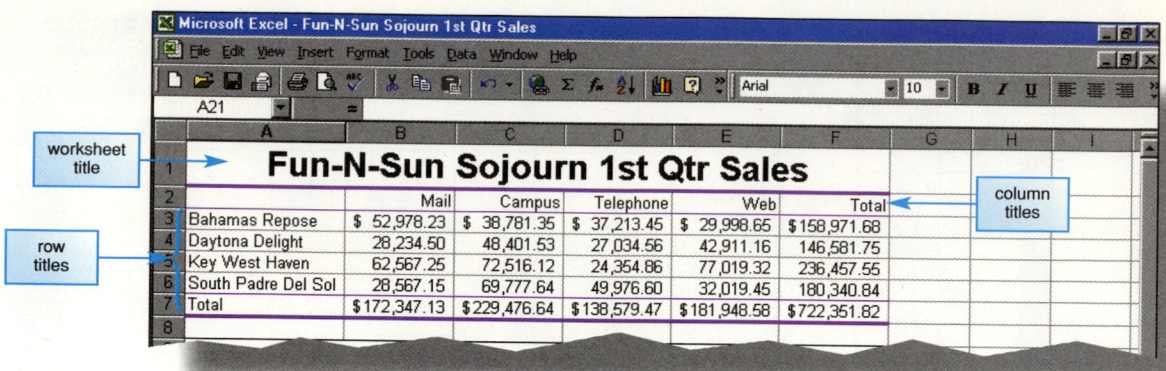

FIGURE 1-11

Entering the Worksheet Title

The following steps show how to enter the worksheet title in cell A1. Later in this project, the worksheet title will be formatted so it displays as shown in Figure 1-11.

 To Enter the Worksheet Title

1   **Click cell A1.**

Cell A1 becomes the active cell and a heavy border surrounds it (Figure 1-12).

FIGURE 1-12

2   **Type** Fun-N-Sun Sojourn 1st Qtr Sales **in cell A1.**

*The title displays in the formula bar and in cell A1. The text in cell A1 is followed by the insertion point (Figure 1-13). The **insertion point** is a blinking vertical line that indicates where the next character typed will display.*

FIGURE 1-13

3 **Point to the Enter box (Figure 1-14).**

When you begin typing a cell entry, Excel displays two boxes in the formula bar: the Cancel box and the Enter box.

FIGURE 1-14

4 **Click the Enter box to complete the entry.**

Excel enters the worksheet title in cell A1 (Figure 1-15).

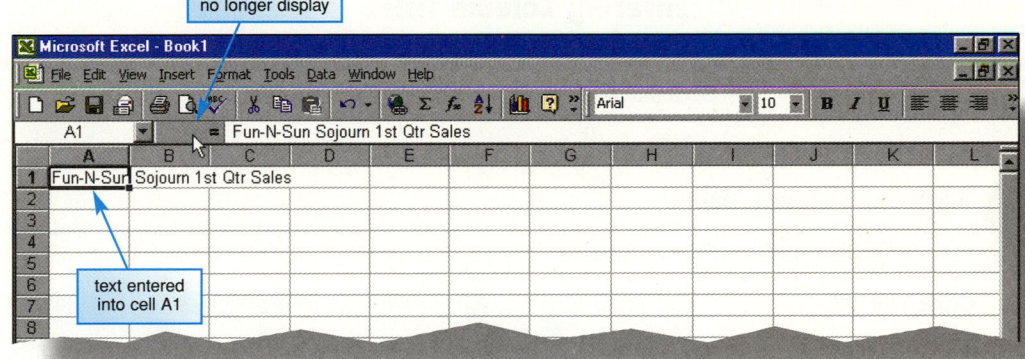

FIGURE 1-15

In Step 3, clicking the **Enter box** completes the entry. Clicking the **Cancel box** cancels the entry.

When you complete a text entry into a cell, a series of events occurs. First, Excel positions the text left-aligned in the cell. **Left-aligned** means the cell entry is positioned at the far left in the cell. Therefore, the F in the worksheet title, Fun-N-Sun Sojourn 1st Qtr Sales, begins in the leftmost position of cell A1.

Second, when the text is longer than the width of a column, Excel displays the overflow characters in adjacent cells to the right as long as these adjacent cells contain no data. In Figure 1-15, the width of cell A1 is approximately nine characters. The text consists of 31 characters. Therefore, Excel displays the overflow characters from cell A1 in cells B1, C1, and D1 because these cells are empty. If cell B1 contained data, only the first nine characters in cell A1 would display on the worksheet. Excel would hide the overflow characters, but they still would remain stored in cell A1 and display in the formula bar whenever cell A1 is the active cell.

Third, when you complete an entry by clicking the Enter box, the cell in which the text is entered remains the active cell.

Correcting a Mistake While Typing

If you type the wrong letter and notice the error before clicking the Enter box or pressing the **ENTER key**, use the **BACKSPACE key** to erase all the characters back to and including the one that is wrong. To cancel the entire entry before entering it into the cell, click the Cancel box in the formula bar or press the **ESC key**. If you see an error in a cell, select the cell and retype the entry. Later in this project, additional error-correction techniques are covered.

Other Ways

1. Click any cell other than active cell
2. Press ENTER
3. Press an arrow key
4. Press HOME, PAGE UP PAGE DOWN, or END

More About 2000

Entering Data

Unless you are entering large amounts of data into a worksheet, you probably will want to set the ENTER key to complete an entry without changing the active cell location. If pressing the ENTER key changes the active cell location, you can change it by clicking Options on the Tools menu, clicking the Edit tab, removing the check mark from the Move Selection after Enter check box, and then clicking the OK button. If you want the ENTER key to change the active cell location, click the desired direction in the Move Selection after Enter list box and then click the OK button.

The IntelliSense Technology

Microsoft's IntelliSense technology is built into all the Office 2000 applications. It tries to understand what you are doing and helps you do it. The smart toolbars, adaptive menus, Office Assistant, and AutoCorrect are part of the IntelliSense technology. For example, Excel can correct common misspellings automatically. When you press the ENTER key, the corrected text is entered in the cell.

AutoCorrect

The **AutoCorrect feature** of Excel works behind the scenes, correcting common mistakes when you complete a text entry in a cell. AutoCorrect makes three types of corrections for you:

1. Corrects two initial capital letters by changing the second letter to lowercase.
2. Capitalizes the first letter in the names of days.
3. Replaces commonly misspelled words with their correct spelling. For example, it will change the misspelled word *recieve* to *receive* when you complete the entry. AutoCorrect will correct the spelling automatically of more than 400 commonly misspelled words.

Entering Column Titles

To enter the column titles, select the appropriate cell and then enter the text, as described in the following steps.

 To Enter Column Titles

 Click cell B2.

Cell B2 becomes the active cell. The active cell reference in the Name box changes from A1 to B2 (Figure 1-16).

FIGURE 1-16

 Type `Mail` **in cell B2.**

Excel displays Mail in the formula bar and in cell B2 (Figure 1-17).

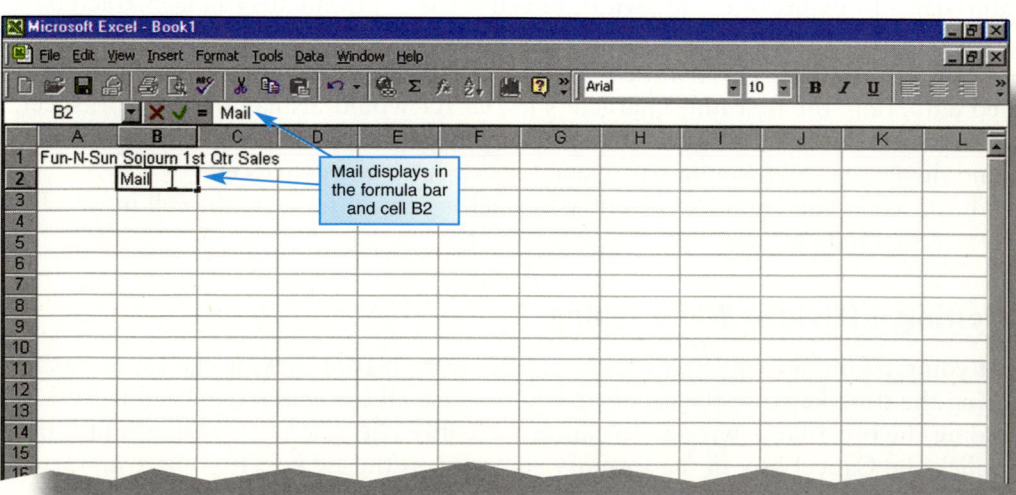

FIGURE 1-17

3 **Press the RIGHT ARROW key.**

Excel enters the column title, Mail, in cell B2 and makes cell C2 the active cell (Figure 1-18).

FIGURE 1-18

4 **Repeat Steps 2 and 3 for the remaining column titles in row 2. That is, enter** Campus **in cell C2,** Telephone **in cell D2,** Web **in cell E2, and** Total **in cell F2. Complete the last entry in cell F2 by pressing the ENTER key.**

The column titles display left-aligned as shown in Figure 1-19.

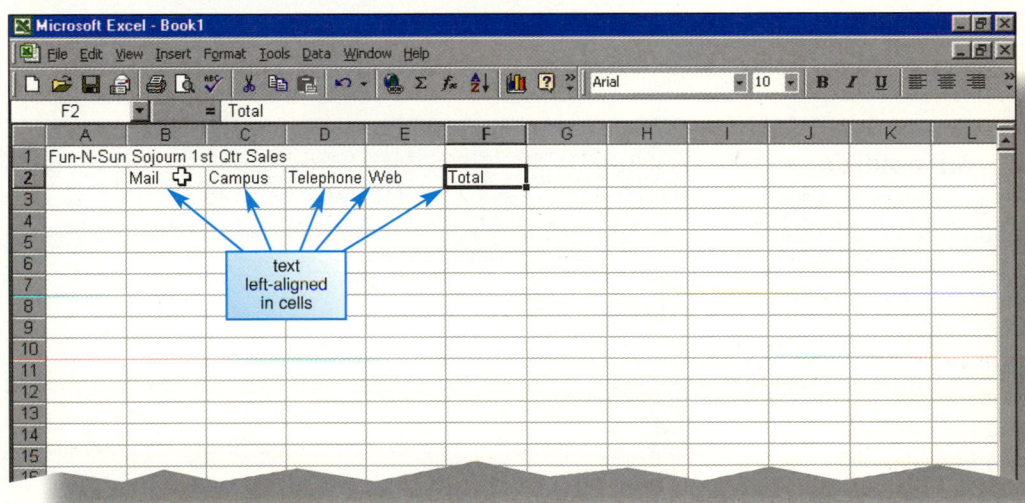

FIGURE 1-19

If the next entry is in an adjacent cell, use the arrow keys to complete the entry in a cell. When you press an arrow key to complete an entry, the adjacent cell in the direction of the arrow (up, down, left, or right) becomes the active cell. If the next entry is in a non-adjacent cell, click the next cell in which you plan to enter data, or click the Enter box, or press the ENTER key and then click the appropriate cell for the next entry.

Entering Row Titles

The next step in developing the worksheet in Project 1 is to enter the row titles in column A. This process is similar to entering the column titles and is described in the steps on the next page.

Steps To Enter Row Titles

1 **Click cell A3. Type** Bahamas Repose **and then press the DOWN ARROW key.**

Excel enters the row title Bahamas Repose in cell A3 and cell A4 becomes the active cell (Figure 1-20).

FIGURE 1-20

2 **Repeat Step 1 for the remaining row titles in column A. Enter** Daytona Delight **in cell A4,** Key West Haven **in cell A5,** South Padre Del Sol **in cell A 6, and** Total **in cell A7.**

The row titles display as shown in Figure 1-21.

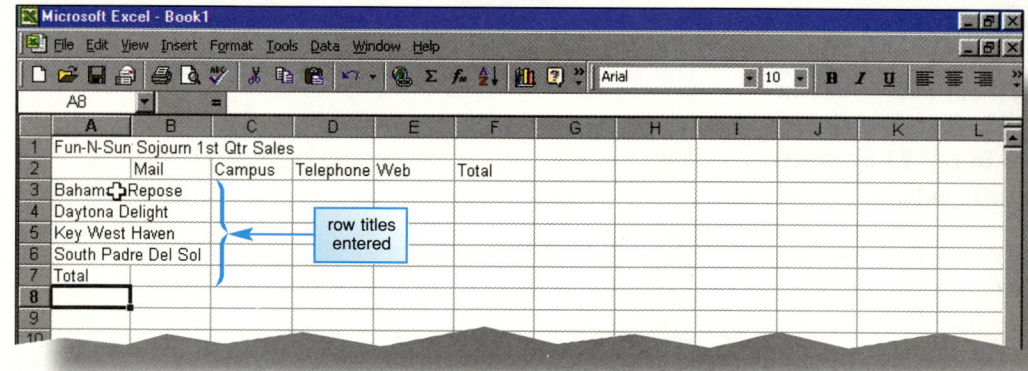

FIGURE 1-21

In Excel, text is left-aligned in a cell, unless you change it by realigning it. Excel treats any combination of numbers, spaces, and nonnumeric characters as text. For example, the following entries are text:

401AX21, 921-231, 619' 321, 883XTY

Entering Data

When you type the first few letters of an entry in a cell, Excel can complete the entry for you, based on the entries already in that column. This is called the AutoComplete feature. If you want to pick an entry from a list of column entries, right-click a cell in the column and then click Pick from List on the shortcut menu.

Entering Numbers

In Excel, you can enter numbers into cells to represent amounts. **Numbers** can contain only the following characters:

0 1 2 3 4 5 6 7 8 9 + - ( ) , / . $ % E e

If a cell entry contains any other keyboard character (including spaces), Excel interprets the entry as text and treats it accordingly. The use of the special characters is explained when they are used in a project.

In Project 1, the Fun-N-Sun first quarter numbers are summarized in Table 1-1.

Table 1-1   Fun-N-Sun First Quarter Data

	MAIL	CAMPUS	TELEPHONE	WEB
Bahamas Repose	52978.23	38781.35	37213.45	29998.65
Daytona Delight	28234.50	48401.53	27034.56	42911.16
Key West Haven	62567.25	72516.12	24354.86	77019.32
South Padre Del Sol	28567.15	69777.64	49976.60	32019.45

More About 2000

Entering Numbers as Text

Some times, you will want Excel to treat numbers, such as ZIP codes, as text. To enter a number as text, start the entry with an apostrophe (').

These numbers, which represent first quarter sales for each of the sales channels and vacation packages, must be entered in rows 3, 4, 5, and 6. The following steps illustrate how to enter these values one row at a time.

 To Enter Numeric Data

1 Click cell B3. Type 52978.23 **and then press the RIGHT ARROW key.**

Excel enters the number 52978.23 in cell B3 and changes the active cell to cell C3 (Figure 1-22). The numbers are formatted with dollar signs and commas later in this project.

FIGURE 1-22

2 Enter 38781.35 **in cell C3,** 37213.45 **in cell D3, and** 29998.65 **in cell E3.**

Row 3 now contains the first quarter sales by sales channel for the vacation package Bahamas Repose (Figure 1-23). The numbers in row 3 are **right-aligned**, which means Excel displays the cell entry to the far right in the cell.

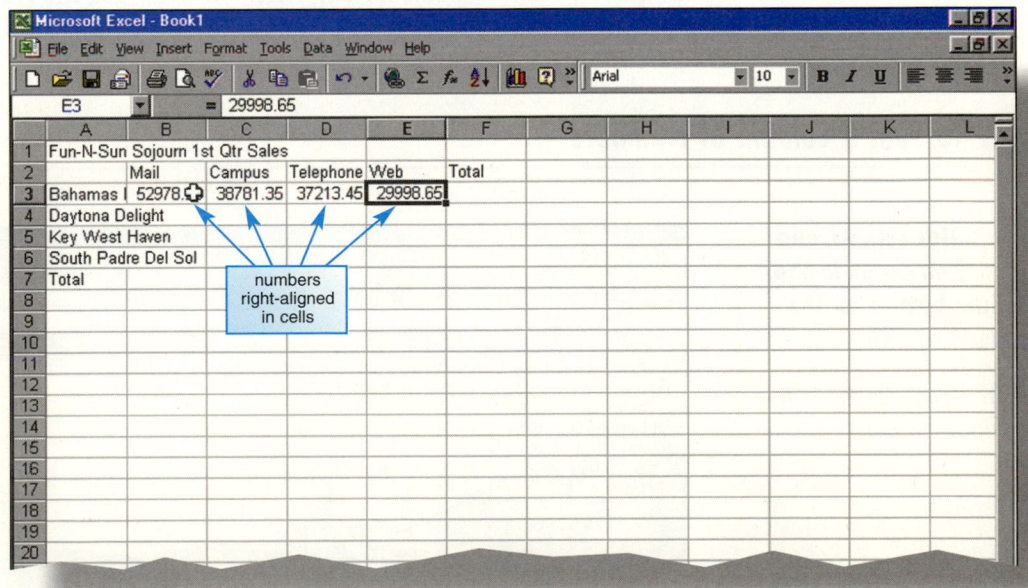

FIGURE 1-23

3 Click cell B4. Enter the remaining first quarter sales provided on the previous page in Table 1-1 by sales channel for each of the three remaining vacation packages in rows 4, 5, and 6.

The first quarter sales display as shown in Figure 1-24.

FIGURE 1-24

As you can see in Figure 1-24, when you enter data into the cell in column B, the row titles in column A partially display. Later when the worksheet is formatted, the row titles will display in their entirety.

Steps 1 through 3 complete the numeric entries. You are not required to type dollar signs, commas, or trailing zeros. As you can see in Figure 1-24, if you typed the trailing zeros, as indicated in Table 1, they do not display. When you enter a number that has cents, however, you must add the decimal point and the numbers representing the cents when you enter the number. Later in this project, dollar signs, commas, and trailing zeros will be added to improve the appearance of the numbers.

Calculating a Sum

The next step in creating the first quarter sales worksheet is to determine the total first quarter sales by Mail in column B. To calculate this value in cell B7, Excel must add the numbers in cells B3, B4, B5, and B6. Excel's **SUM function** provides a convenient means to accomplish this task.

To use the SUM function, first you must identify the cell in which the sum will be stored after it is calculated. Then, you can use the **AutoSum button** on the Standard toolbar to enter the SUM function as shown in the following steps.

Steps To Sum a Column of Numbers

1 Click cell B7 and then point to the AutoSum button on the Standard toolbar.

Cell B7 becomes the active cell (Figure 1-25).

FIGURE 1-25

② Click the AutoSum button.

Excel responds by displaying = SUM(B3:B6) in the formula bar and in the active cell B7 (Figure 1-26). The B3:B6 within parentheses following the function name SUM is Excel's way of identifying the cells B3 through B6. Excel also surrounds the proposed cells to sum with a moving border, called a **marquee**.

FIGURE 1-26

③ Click the AutoSum button a second time.

Excel enters the sum of the first quarter sales in cell B7 (Figure 1-27). The SUM function assigned to cell B7 displays in the formula bar when cell B7 is the active cell.

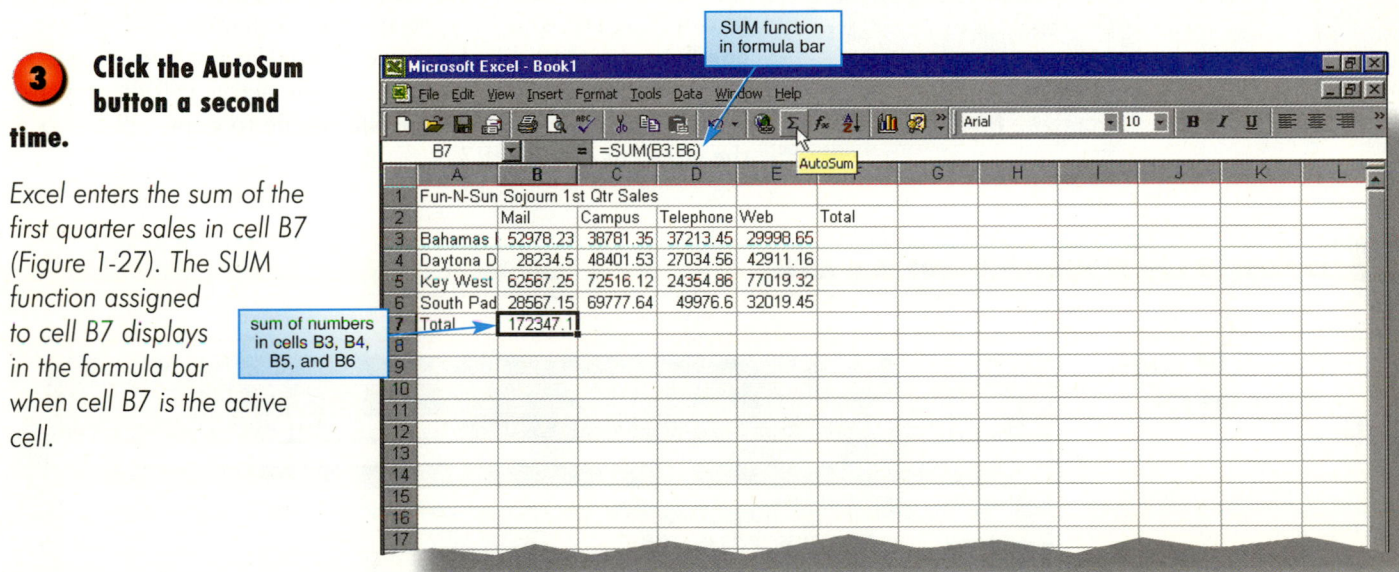

FIGURE 1-27

When you enter the SUM function using the AutoSum button, Excel automatically selects what it considers to be your choice of the group of cells to sum. The group of adjacent cells B3, B4, B5, and B6 is called a range. A **range** is a series of two or more adjacent cells in a column or row or a rectangular group of cells. Many Excel operations, such as summing numbers, take place on a range of cells.

When proposing the range to sum, Excel first looks for a range of cells with numbers above the active cell and then to the left. If Excel proposes the wrong range, you can drag through the correct range anytime prior to clicking the AutoSum button a second time. You also can enter the correct range by typing the beginning cell reference, a colon (:), and the ending cell reference.

1. Press ALT+EQUAL SIGN (=) twice
2. Click Edit Formula (=) box in formula bar, select SUM in Functions list, click OK button

Using the Fill Handle to Copy a Cell to Adjacent Cells

Excel also must calculate the totals for Campus in cell C7, Telephone in cell D7, and for Web in cell E7. Table 1-2 illustrates the similarities between the entry in cell B7 and the entries required for the totals in cells C7, D7, and E7.

To place the SUM functions in cells C7, D7, and E7, you can follow the same steps shown previously in Figures 1-25 through 1-27. A second, more efficient method is to copy the SUM function from cell B7 to the range C7:E7. The cell being copied is called the **copy area**. The range of cells receiving the copy is called the **paste area**.

Although the SUM function entries are similar in Table 1-2, they are not exact copies. The range in each SUM function entry to the right of cell B7 uses cell references that are one column to the right of the previous column. When you copy cell references, Excel automatically adjusts them for each new position, resulting in the SUM function entries illustrated in Table 1-2. Each adjusted cell reference is called a **relative reference**.

The easiest way to copy the SUM formula from cell B7 to cells C7, D7, and E7 is to use the fill handle. The **fill handle** is the small black square located in the lower-right corner of the heavy border around the active cell. Perform the following steps to use the fill handle to copy cell B7 to the adjacent cells C7:E7.

Table 1-2	**SUM Function Entries in Row 7**	
CELL	**SUM FUNCTION ENTRIES**	**REMARK**
B7	=SUM(B3:B6)	Sums cells B3, B4, B5, and B6
C7	=SUM(C3:C6)	Sums cells C3, C4, C5, and C6
D7	=SUM(D3:D6)	Sums cells D3, D4, D5, and D6
E7	=SUM(E3:E6)	Sums cells E3, E4, E5, and E6

Steps **To Copy a Cell to Adjacent Cells in a Row**

1 **With cell B7 active, point to the fill handle.**

The mouse pointer changes to a cross hair (Figure 1-28).

cross hair indicates fill handle is selected

FIGURE 1-28

2 Drag the fill handle to select the paste area, range C7:E7.

Excel displays a shaded border around the paste area, range C7:E7, and the copy area, cell B7 (Figure 1-29).

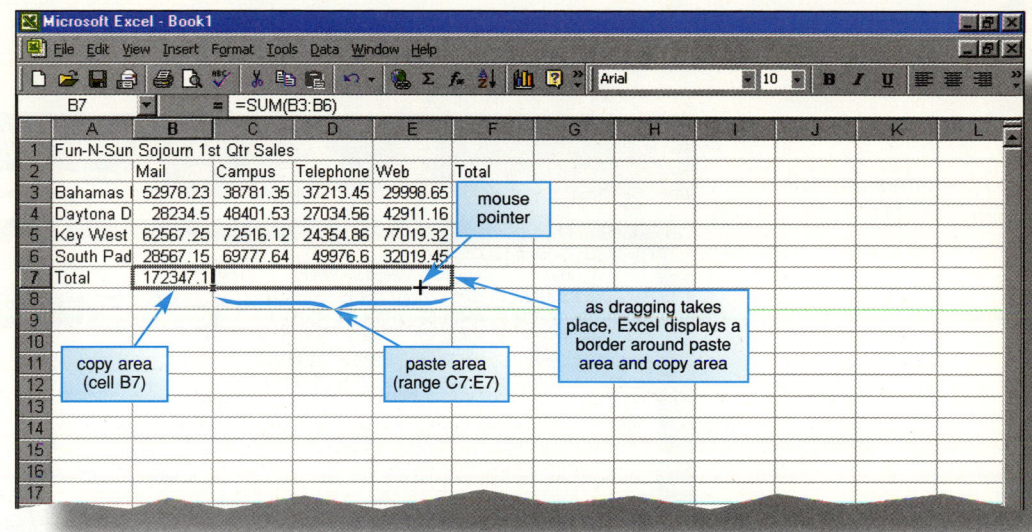

FIGURE 1-29

3 Release the mouse button.

Excel copies the SUM function in cell B7 to the range C7:E7 (Figure 1-30). In addition, Excel calculates the sums and enters the results in cells C7, D7, and E7.

FIGURE 1-30

Once the copy is complete, Excel continues to display a heavy border and transparent (blue) background around cells B7:E7. The heavy border and transparent background indicate a selected range. Cell B7, the first cell in the range, does not display with the transparent background because it is the active cell. If you click any cell, Excel will remove the heavy border and transparent background. The heavy border and transparent (blue) background is called **see-through view**.

Determining Row Totals

The next step in building the worksheet is to determine totals for each vacation package and total first quarter sales for the company in column F. Use the SUM function in the same manner as you did when the sales by sales channel were totaled in row 7. In this example, however, all the rows will be totaled at the same time. The steps on the next page illustrate this process.

More About

Using the Mouse to Copy

Another way to copy a cell or range of cells is to select the copy area, point to the border of the copy area, and then, while holding down the CTRL key, drag the copy area to the paste area. If you drag without holding down the CTRL key, Excel moves the data, rather than copying it.

To Determine Multiple Totals at the Same Time

 Click cell F3.

Cell F3 becomes the active cell (Figure 1-31).

FIGURE 1-31

With the mouse pointer in cell F3 and in the shape of a block plus sign, drag the mouse pointer down to cell F7.

Excel highlights the range F3:F7 (Figure 1-32).

FIGURE 1-32

Click the AutoSum button on the Standard toolbar.

Excel assigns the appropriate SUM functions to cell F3, F4, F5, F6, and F7, and then calculates and displays the sums in the respective cells (Figure 1-33).

 Select cell A8 to deselect the range F3:F7.

FIGURE 1-33

If each cell in the selected range is next to a row of numbers, Excel assigns the SUM function to each cell in the selected range when you click the AutoSum button. Thus, five SUM functions with different ranges were assigned to the selected range, one for each row. This same procedure could have been used earlier to sum the columns. That is, rather than selecting cell B7, clicking the AutoSum button twice, and then copying the SUM function to the range C7:E7, you could have selected the range B7:E7 and then clicked the AutoSum button once.

More About 2000

Summing Columns and Rows

A quick way to determine all of the totals in row 7 and column F shown in Figure 1-33 at once is to select the range (B3:F7) and then click the AutoSum button. The range B3:F7 includes the numbers to sum plus an additional row (row 7) and an additional column (column F), in which the totals will display.

Formatting the Worksheet

The text, numeric entries, and functions for the worksheet now are complete. The next step is to format the worksheet. You **format** a worksheet to emphasize certain entries and make the worksheet easier to read and understand.

Figure 1-34a shows the worksheet before formatting. Figure 1-34b shows the worksheet after formatting. As you can see from the two figures, a worksheet that is formatted not only is easier to read, but also looks more professional.

(a) Before Formatting

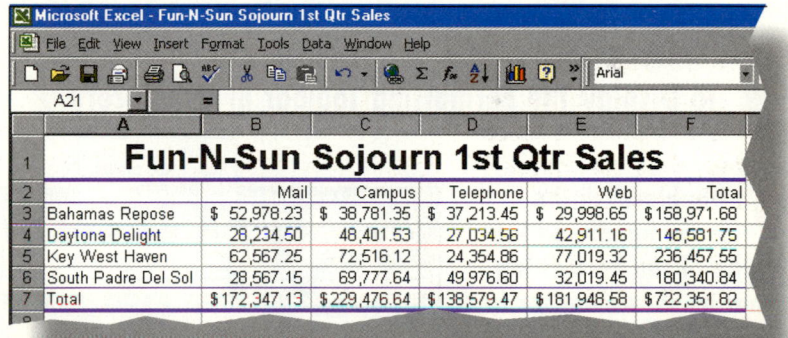

(b) After Formatting

FIGURE 1-34

To change the unformatted worksheet in Figure 1-34a to the formatted worksheet in Figure 1-34b, the following tasks must be completed:

1. Bold the worksheet title in cell A1.
2. Enlarge the worksheet title in cell A1.
3. Format the body of the worksheet. The body of the worksheet, range A2:F7, includes the column titles, row titles, and numbers. Formatting the body of the worksheet results in numbers represented in a dollars-and-cents format, dollar signs in the first row of numbers and the total row, underlines that emphasize portions of the worksheet, and modified column widths.
4. Center the worksheet title in cell A1 across columns A through F.

The process required to format the worksheet is explained in the remainder of this section. Although the format procedures will be carried out in the order described above, you should be aware that you can make these format changes in any order.

More About

Changing Fonts

In general, use no more than two font types and font styles in a worksheet to maintain balance and simplicity.

Fonts, Font Size, and Font Style

Characters that display on the screen are a specific shape, size, and style. The **font type** defines the appearance and shape of the letters, numbers, and special characters. The **font size** specifies the size of the characters on the screen. Font size is gauged by a measurement system called points. A single **point** is about 1/72 of one inch in height. Thus, a character with a **point size** of 10 is about 10/72 of one inch in height.

Font style indicates how the characters are formatted. Common font styles include regular, bold, underlined, or italicized.

When Excel begins, the preset font type for the entire workbook is Arial with a size and style of 10-point regular. Excel allows you to change the font characteristics in a single cell, a range of cells, the entire worksheet, or the entire workbook.

Displaying the Formatting Toolbar in Its Entirety

Most of the formatting you will do in Excel can be accomplished using the buttons on the Formatting toolbar. Thus, before starting the formatting process display the Formatting toolbar in its entirety as shown in the following steps.

Steps To Display the Formatting Toolbar in Its Entirety

1 Double-click the move handle on the left side of the Formatting toolbar as shown earlier in Figure 1-33 on page E1.26.

The entire Formatting toolbar displays and only a portion of the Standard toolbar displays (Figure 1-35).

FIGURE 1-35

Other Ways

1. Drag move handle to left
2. Click More Buttons button on Standard toolbar to display hidden buttons

Bolding a Cell

You **bold** an entry in a cell to emphasize it or make it stand out from the rest of the worksheet. Perform the following steps to bold the worksheet title in cell A1.

Steps To Bold a Cell

1 Click cell A1 and then point to the Bold button on the Formatting toolbar.

The ScreenTip displays immediately below the Bold button to identify the function of the button (Figure 1-36).

FIGURE 1-36

2 Click the Bold button.

Excel applies a bold format to the worksheet title *Fun-N-Sun Sojourn 1st Qtr Sales* (Figure 1-37).

FIGURE 1-37

When the active cell is bold, the Bold button on the Formatting toolbar is recessed, or dimmed (Figure 1-37). Clicking the Bold button a second time removes the bold format.

Other Ways

1. Press CTRL+B
2. Right-click cell, click Format Cells on shortcut menu, click Font tab, click Bold, click OK button
3. On Format menu click Cells, click Font tab, click Bold, click OK button

Increasing the Font Size

Increasing the font size is the next step in formatting the worksheet title. You increase the font size of a cell so the entry stands out and is easier to read.

Steps **To Increase the Font Size of a Cell Entry**

1 **With cell A1 selected, click the Font Size box arrow on the Formatting toolbar and then point to 20 in the Font Size list (Figure 1-38).**

FIGURE 1-38

2 **Click 20.**

The font size of the characters in the worksheet title in cell A1 increase from 10 point to 20 point (Figure 1-39).

FIGURE 1-39

Other Ways

1. Press CTRL+1, click Font tab, select font size, click OK button

2. Right-click cell, click Format Cells on shortcut menu, click Font tab, select font size, click OK button

3. On Format menu click Cells, click Font tab, select font size, click OK button

An alternative to clicking a font size in the Font Size list is to type the font size in the Font Size box and then press the ENTER key. With cell A1 selected (Figure 1-39), the Font Size box shows the new font size 20 and the recessed Bold button shows the active cell is bold.

According to the requirements, the worksheet title must be centered across columns A through F. Because the increased font size causes the worksheet title to exceed the length of the combined columns (Figure 1-39), the centering will be done after the body of the worksheet is formatted.

Using AutoFormat to Format the Body of a Worksheet

Excel has several customized format styles called **table formats** that allow you to format the body of the worksheet. Using table formats can give your worksheet a professional appearance. Follow these steps to format the range A2:F7 automatically using the **AutoFormat command** on the Format menu.

Steps: To Use AutoFormat to Format the Body of a Worksheet

1 Select cell A2, the upper-left corner cell of the rectangular range to format. Drag the mouse pointer to cell F7, the lower-right corner cell of the range to format.

Excel highlights the range to format with a heavy border and blue background (Figure 1-40).

FIGURE 1-40

2 Click Format on the menu bar and then point to AutoFormat.

The Format menu displays (Figure 1-41).

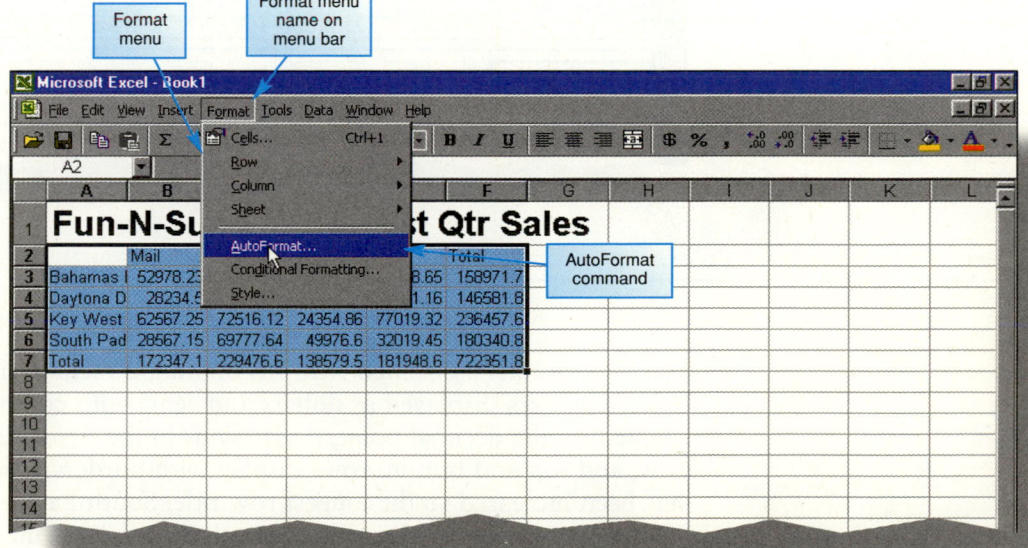

FIGURE 1-41

3 **Click AutoFormat. Click the Accounting 2 format (column 2, row 3) in the AutoFormat dialog box. Point to the OK button.**

The AutoFormat dialog box displays with a list of customized formats (Figure 1-42). Each format illustrates how the body of the worksheet will display if it is chosen.

FIGURE 1-42

4 **Click the OK button. Select cell A9 to deselect the range A2:F7.**

Excel displays the worksheet with the range A2:F7 using the customized format, Accounting 2 (Figure 1-43).

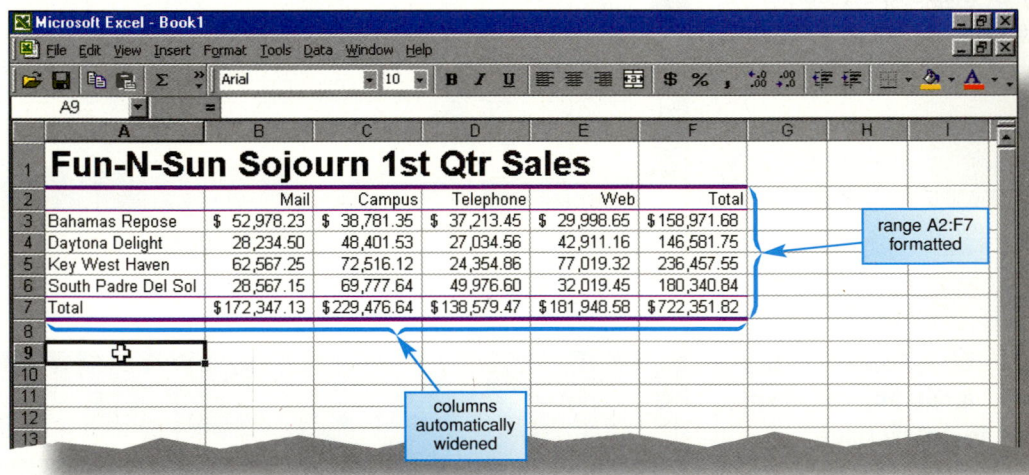

FIGURE 1-43

The formats associated with Accounting 2 include right-alignment of column titles, numbers displayed as dollars and cents with comma separators, numbers aligned on the decimal point, dollar signs in the first row of numbers and in the total row, and top and bottom rows display with borders. The width of column A also has been increased so the longest row title, South Padre Del Sol, just fits in the column. The widths of columns B through F have been increased so that the formatted numbers will fit in the cells.

The AutoFormat dialog box shown in Figure 1-42 includes 17 customized formats and five buttons. Use the scroll bar to view the 11 customized formats that do not display in the dialog box. Each one of these customized formats offers a different look. The one you choose depends on the worksheet you are creating.

The five buttons in the dialog box allow you to cancel, complete the entries, get Help, and adjust a customized format. The **Close button** terminates current activity without making changes. You also can use the **Cancel button**, immediately below the **OK button**, for this purpose. Use the **Question Mark button**, to obtain Help on any box or button located in the dialog box. The **Options button** allows you to select additional formats to assign as part of the selected customized format.

Centering the Worksheet Title Across Columns

With the column widths increased, the final step in formatting the worksheet title is to center it across columns A through F. Centering a worksheet title across the columns used in the body of the worksheet improves the worksheet's appearance.

More About 2000

Customizing the AutoFormat

It is not uncommon to apply two or more of the customized formats shown in Figure 1-42 to the same range. If you assign two customized formats to a range, Excel does not remove the original format from the range; it simply adds the second customized format to the first. Thus, if you decide to change a customized format, first select the range, and then, in the AutoFormat dialog box, assign it the customized format titled None.

 Steps ## To Center a Cell's Contents Across Columns

1 **Click cell A1. Drag the block plus sign to the rightmost cell (F1) of the range to center (A1:F1). Point to the Merge and Center button on the Formatting toolbar.**

When you drag through the range A1:F1, Excel highlights the cells (Figure 1-44).

FIGURE 1-44

2 Click the Merge and Center button.

Excel merges the cells A1 through F1 to create a new cell A1 and centers the contents of cell A1 across columns A through F (Figure 1-45). After the merge, cells B1 through F1 no longer exist on the worksheet.

3 Click cell A9 to deselect cell A1.

FIGURE 1-45

The Name Box

If you repeatedly select certain cells in a worksheet, consider naming the cells in the Name box. Select the cells one at a time and then type a name in the Name box for each, such as Company Total, for cell F7 shown in Figure 1-48. Then, when you want to select one of the named cells, click the Name box arrow and click the cell name in the Name box list.

Excel not only centers the worksheet title, but also merges cells A1 through F1 into one cell, cell A1. Thus, the heavy border that defines the active cell in Figure 1-45 covers what originally was cells A1 through F1. For the Merge and Center button to work properly, all the cells except the leftmost cell in the range of cells must be empty.

Most formats assigned to a cell will display on the Formatting toolbar when the cell is selected. For example, the font type and font size display in their appropriate boxes. Recessed buttons indicate an assigned format. To determine if less frequently used formats are assigned to a cell, point to the cell and right-click. Next, click Format Cells, and then click each of the tabs in the Format Cells dialog box.

The worksheet now is complete. The next step is to chart the first quarter sales for the four vacation packages by sales channel. To create the chart, you must select the cell in the upper-left corner of the range to chart (cell A2). Rather than clicking cell A2 to select it, the next section describes how to use the Name box to select the cell.

Using the Name Box to Select a Cell

The **Name box** is located on the left side of the formula bar. To select any cell, click the Name box and enter the cell reference of the cell you want to select. Perform the following steps to select cell A2.

To Use the Name Box to Select a Cell

1 **Click the Name box in the formula bar. Type** a2 **in the Name box.**

Even though cell A9 is the active cell, the Name box displays the typed cell reference a2 (Figure 1-46).

FIGURE 1-46

2 **Press the ENTER key.**

Excel changes the active cell from cell A9 to cell A2 (Figure 1-47).

FIGURE 1-47

As you will see in later projects, besides using the Name box to select any cell in a worksheet, you also can use it to assign names to a cell or range of cells.

Excel supports several additional ways to select a cell, as summarized on the next page in Table 1-3.

Table 1-3 Selecting Cells in Excel	
KEY, BOX, OR COMMAND	**FUNCTION**
ALT+PAGE DOWN	Selects the cell one window to the right and moves the window accordingly.
ALT+PAGE UP	Selects the cell one window to the left and moves the window accordingly.
ARROW	Selects the adjacent cell in the direction of the arrow on the key.
CTRL+ARROW	Selects the border cell of the worksheet in combination with the arrow keys and moves the window accordingly. For example, to select the rightmost cell in the row that contains the active cell, press CTRL+RIGHT arrow. You also can press the END key, release it, and then press the arrow key to accomplish the same task.
CTRL+HOME	Selects cell A1 or the cell one column and one row below and to the right of frozen titles and moves the the window accordingly.
Find command on Edit menu	Finds and selects a cell that contains specific contents that you enter in the Find dialog box. If necessary, Excel moves the window to display the cell. You can press SHIFT+F5 or CTRL+F to display the Find dialog box.
F5 or Go To command on Edit menu	Selects the cell that corresponds to the cell reference you enter in the Go To dialog box and moves the window accordingly. You can press CTRL+G to display the Find dialog box.
HOME	Selects the cell at the beginning of the row that contains the active cell and moves the window accordingly.
Name box	Selects the cell in the workbook that corresponds to the cell reference you enter in the Name box.
PAGE DOWN	Selects the cell down one window from the active cell and moves the window accordingly.
PAGE UP	Selects the cell up one window from the active cell and moves the window accordingly.

Navigation

For more information on selecting cells that contain certain entries, such as constants or formulas, visit the Excel 2000 More About Web page (www.scsite.com/ex2000/more.htm) and click Using Go To Special.

Adding a 3-D Column Chart to the Worksheet

The 3-D Column chart (Figure 1-48) is called an **embedded chart** because it is drawn on the same worksheet as the data.

FIGURE 1-48

For the sales channel Mail, the light blue column represents the first quarter sales for the Bahamas Repose vacation package ($52,978.23); the purple column represents the first quarter sales for Daytona Delight ($28,234.50); the light yellow column represents the first quarter sales for Key West Haven ($62,567.25); and the turquoise column represents the first quarter sales for South Padre Del Sol ($28,567.15). For the sales channels Campus, Telephone, and Web, the columns follow the same color scheme to represent the comparable first quarter sales. The totals from the worksheet are not represented because the totals were not in the range specified for charting.

Excel derives the scale along the vertical axis (also called the **y-axis** or **value axis**) of the chart on the basis of the values in the worksheet. For example, no value in the range B3:E6 is less than zero or greater than $80,000.00. Excel also determines the $20,000.00 increments along the y-axis automatically. The format used by Excel for the numbers along the y-axis includes representing zero (0) with a dash (Figure 1-48).

With the range to chart selected, you click the **Chart Wizard button** on the Standard toolbar to initiate drawing the chart. The area on the worksheet where the chart displays is called the **chart location**. The chart location is the range A9:F19, immediately below the worksheet data.

Follow the steps below to draw a 3-D Column chart that compares the first quarter sales by vacation package for the four sales channels.

Steps To Add a 3-D Column Chart to the Worksheet

1 Double-click the move handle on the left side of the Standard toolbar to display the entire toolbar. With cell A2 selected, position the block plus sign within the cell's border and drag the mouse pointer to the lower-right corner cell (cell E6) of the range to chart (A2:E6). Point to the Chart Wizard button on the Standard toolbar.

Excel highlights the range to chart (Figure 1-49).

FIGURE 1-49

2 Click the Chart Wizard button.

The Chart Wizard – Step 1 of 4 – Chart Type dialog box displays.

3 With Column selected in the Chart type list, click the 3-D Column chart sub-type (column 1, row 2) in the Chart sub-type area. Point to the Finish button.

Column is highlighted in the Chart type list and Clustered column with a 3-D visual effect is highlighted in the Chart sub-type area (Figure 1-50).

FIGURE 1-50

4 Click the Finish button.

Excel draws the 3-D Column chart (Figure 1-51). The chart displays in the middle of the window in a selection rectangle. The small sizing handles at the corners and along the sides of the selection rectangle indicate the chart is selected.

FIGURE 1-51

5 Point to an open area in the lower-right section of the Chart Area so the ScreenTip, Chart Area, displays (Figure 1-51). The ScreenTip defines the area of the chart that the mouse pointer is pointing to. Drag the chart down and to the left to position the upper-left corner of the dotted line rectangle over the upper-left corner of cell A9 (Figure 1-52).

Excel displays a dotted line rectangle showing the new chart location. As you drag the selected chart, the mouse pointer changes to a cross hair with four arrowheads.

FIGURE 1-52

6 Release the mouse button. Point to the middle sizing handle on the right edge of the selection rectangle.

The chart displays in a new location (Figure 1-53). The mouse pointer changes to a horizontal line with two arrowheads when it points to a sizing handle.

FIGURE 1-53

Microsoft **Excel 2000**

7 While holding down the ALT key, drag the sizing handle to the right edge of column F. Release the mouse button.

While you drag, the dotted line rectangle shows the new chart location (Figure 1-54). Holding down the ALT key while you drag a chart snaps (aligns) the new border to the worksheet gridlines.

FIGURE 1-54

8 If necessary, hold down the ALT key and drag the lower-middle sizing handle up to the lower edge of row 19. Click cell A21 to deselect the chart.

The new chart location extends from the top of cell A9 to the bottom of cell F19 (Figure 1-55).

FIGURE 1-55

Other Ways

1. Select range, press F11
2. Select range, on Insert menu click Chart

The embedded 3-D Column chart in Figure 1-55 compares the first quarter sales for the four vacation packages within each sales channel. It also allows you to compare first quarter sales among the sales channels.

Excel automatically selects the entries in the topmost row of the range (row 2) as the titles for the horizontal axis (also called the **x-axis** or **category axis**) and draws a column for each of the 16 cells in the range containing numbers. The small box to the right of the column chart in Figure 1-55 contains the legend. The **legend** identifies each bar in the chart. Excel automatically selects the leftmost column of the range (column A) as titles within the legend. As indicated earlier, it also automatically scales the y-axis on the basis of the magnitude of the numbers in the chart range.

Excel offers 14 different chart types (Figure 1-50 on page E 1.38). The **default chart type** is the chart Excel draws if you click the Finish button in the first Chart Wizard dialog box. When you install Excel on a computer, the default chart type is the 2-D (two-dimensional) Column chart.

Saving a Workbook

While you are building a workbook, the computer stores it in memory. If the computer is turned off or if you lose electrical power, the workbook is lost. Hence, you must save on a floppy disk or hard disk any workbook that you will use later. A saved workbook is referred to as a **file** or **workbook**. The following steps illustrate how to save a workbook on a floppy disk in drive A using the Save button on the Standard toolbar.

More About

Changing the Chart Type

Excel has fourteen chart types from which to choose. You can change the embedded 3-D Column chart to another type by double-clicking the chart location. When a heavy gray border surrounds the chart location, right-click the chart and then click Chart Type on the shortcut menu. You also can use the shortcut menu to format the chart to make it look more professional. Subsequent projects will discuss changing charts, sizing charts, adding text to charts, and drawing a chart on a chart sheet.

Steps To Save a Workbook

1 **With a floppy disk in drive A, click the Save button on the Standard toolbar.**

The Save As dialog box displays (Figure 1-56). The preset Save in folder is My Documents, the preset file name is Book1, and the file type is Microsoft Excel Workbook. The buttons on the top and on the side are used to select folders and change the display of file names and other information.

FIGURE 1-56

2 **Type** Fun-N-Sun Sojourn 1st Qtr Sales **in the File name text box.**

The new file name replaces Book1 in the File name text box (Figure 1-57). A file name can be up to 255 characters and can include spaces.

FIGURE 1-57

3 **Click the Save in box arrow and then point to 3½ Floppy (A:).**

A list of available drives and folders displays (Figure 1-58).

FIGURE 1-58

4 **Click 3½ Floppy (A:) and then point to the Save button in the Save As dialog box.**

Drive A becomes the selected drive (Figure 1-59).

FIGURE 1-59

5 **Click the Save button.**

Excel saves the workbook on the floppy disk in drive A using the file name Fun-N-Sun Sojourn 1st Qtr Sales. Excel automatically appends the extension .xls to the file name you entered in Step 2, which stands for Excel workbook. Although the workbook is saved on a floppy disk, it also remains in memory and displays on the screen (Figure 1-60). Notice the file name in the title bar.

FIGURE 1-60

Other Ways

1. Press CTRL+S, type file name, select drive or folder, click OK button

2. Right-click workbook Control-menu icon on menu bar, click Save As on shortcut menu, type file name, select drive of folder, click OK button

3. On File menu click Save As, type file name, select drive of folder, click OK button

Saving a Worksheet as a Web Page

Excel allows you to save a worksheet in HTML format so you can publish it to the World Wide Web. Click Save as Web Page on the File menu. You have the option to save the worksheet as a static Web page or as a dynamic Web page. A static Web page means you can view the worksheet on the World Wide Web, but you cannot change cell contents. A dynamic Web page means you can modify the worksheet using a browser.

While Excel is saving the workbook, it momentarily changes the word Ready on the status bar to Saving. It also displays a horizontal bar on the status bar indicating the amount of the workbook saved. After the save operation is complete, Excel changes the name of the workbook in the title bar from Book1 to Fun-N-Sun Sojourn 1st Qtr Sales (Figure 1-60 on the previous page).

When you click the **Tools button** in the Save As dialog box (Figure 1-59 on the previous page), a list box displays. The **General Options command** in the list allows you to save a backup copy of the workbook, create a password to limit access to the workbook, and carry out other functions that will be discussed later. Saving a **backup workbook** means that each time you save a workbook, Excel copies the current version of the workbook on disk to a file with the same name, but with the words, Backup of, appended to the front of the file name. In the case of a power failure or some other problem, use the backup version to restore your work.

You also can use the General Options command on the Tools list to assign a **password** to a workbook so others cannot open it. A password is case sensitive and can be up to 15 characters long. **Case sensitive** means Excel can differentiate between uppercase and lowercase letters. If you assign a password and forget the password, you cannot access the workbook.

The seven buttons at the top and to the right in the Save As dialog box (Figure 1-59) and their functions are summarized in Table 1-4.

AutoSave

Are you worried about losing your work because your computer might crash? If so, you can use the AutoSave command on the Tools menu. The AutoSave command automatically saves your work every 10 minutes. If you prefer to change the time between saves, you can do so through the AutoSave dialog box that displays when you invoke the AutoSave command. AutoSave is an add-in program. If the AutoSave command does not display on your Tools menu, use the Add-Ins command on the Tools menu to add it.

Table 1-4	Save As Dialog Box Toolbar Buttons	
BUTTON	**BUTTON NAME**	**FUNCTION**
⬅	Default File Location	Displays contents of default file location
🔼	Up One Level	Displays contents of next level up folder
🔍	Search the Web	Starts browser and displays search engine
✕	Delete	Deletes selected file or folder
📁	Create New Folder	Creates new folder
▦	Views	Changes view of files and folders
Tools ▾	Tools	Lists commands to print or modify file names and folders

The five buttons on the left of the Save As dialog box in Figure 1-59 allow you to select frequently used folders. The **History button** displays a list of shortcuts (pointers) to the most recently used files in a folder titled Recent. You can not save workbooks to the Recent folder.

Printing the Worksheet

Once you have created the worksheet and saved it on a floppy disk or hard disk, you might want to print it. A printed version of the worksheet is called a **hard copy** or **printout**.

You might want a printout for several reasons. First, to present the worksheet and chart to someone who does not have access to a computer, it must be in printed form. A printout, for example, can be handed out in a management meeting about first quarter sales. In addition, worksheets and charts often are kept for reference by people other than those who prepare them. In many cases, worksheets and charts are printed and kept in binders for use by others. This section describes how to print a worksheet and an embedded chart.

More About 2000

Saving Paper

If you are an environmentalist interested in saving trees, you can preview the printout on your screen, make adjustments to the worksheet, and then print it only when it appears exactly as you desire. The Print Preview button is immediately to the right of the Print button on the Standard toolbar. Clicking it displays an onscreen image of how the printout will appear. Each time you preview rather than print, you save paper destined for the wastepaper basket, which, in turn, saves trees.

 To Print a Worksheet

1 **Ready the printer according to the printer instructions. Point to the Print button on the Standard toolbar (Figure 1-61).**

FIGURE 1-61

② Click the Print button. When the printer stops printing the worksheet and the chart, retrieve the printout (Figure 1-62).

Excel displays the Printing dialog box that allows you to cancel the print job while the system is sending the work-sheet and chart image to the printer.

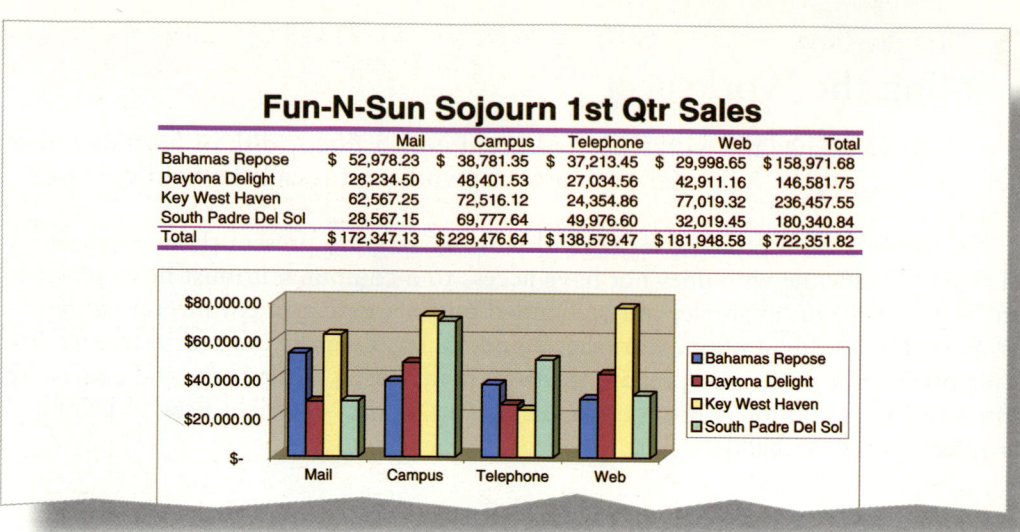

FIGURE 1-62

Prior to clicking the Print button, you can select which columns and rows in the worksheet to print. The range of cells you choose to print is called the **print area**. If you do not select a print area, as was the case in the previous set of steps, Excel automatically selects a print area on the basis of used cells. As you will see in future projects, Excel has many different print options, such as allowing you to preview the printout on the screen to see if the printout is satisfactory prior to sending it to the printer. Several of these print options are discussed in Project 2.

Quitting Excel

After you build, save, and print the worksheet and chart, Project 1 is complete. To quit Excel, complete the following steps.

To Quit Excel

① Point to the Close button on the right side of the title bar (Figure 1-63).

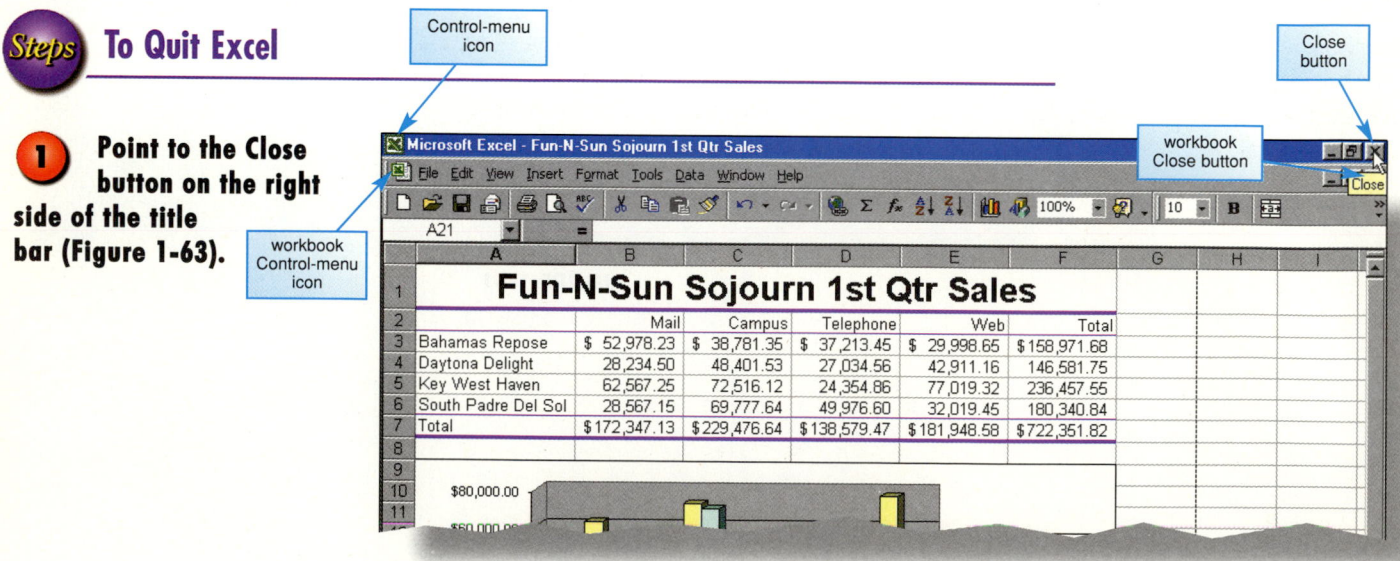

FIGURE 1-63

2 **Click the Close button.**

If you made changes to the workbook, the Microsoft Excel dialog box displays the question, Do you want to save the changes you made to 'Fun-N-Sun Sojourn 1st Qtr Sales.xls'? (Figure 1-64). Clicking the Yes button saves the changes before quitting Excel. Clicking the No button quits Excel without saving the changes. Clicking the Cancel button stops the Exit command and returns to the worksheet.

3 **Click the No button.**

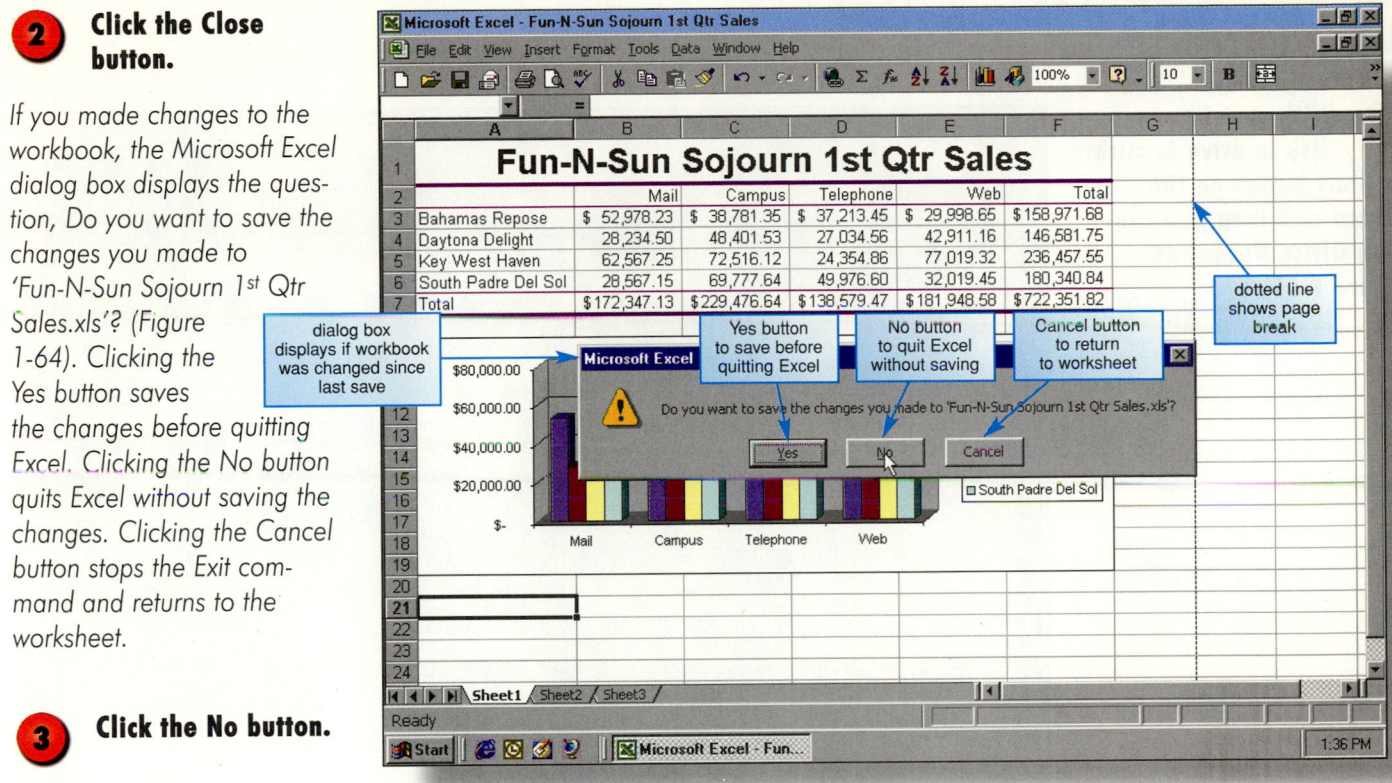

FIGURE 1-64

In Figure 1-63, you can see that two Close buttons and two Control-menu icons display. The Close button and Control-menu icon on the title bar close Excel. The Close button and Control-menu icon on the menu bar close the workbook.

Starting Excel and Opening a Workbook

Once you have created and saved a workbook, you often will have reason to retrieve it from a floppy disk. For example, you might want to review the calculations on the worksheet and enter additional or revised data on it. The steps on the next page assume Excel is not running.

Other Ways

1. Double-click Control-menu icon
2. Right-click Microsoft Excel button on taskbar, click Close on shortcut menu
3. On File menu click Exit

To Start Excel and Open a Workbook

1 With your floppy disk in drive A, click the Start button on the taskbar and then point to Open Office Document (Figure 1-65).

FIGURE 1-65

2 Click Open Office Document. If necessary, click the Look in box arrow and then click 3½ Floppy (A:).

The Open Office Document dialog box displays (Figure 1-66).

FIGURE 1-66

③ Double-click the file name Fun-N-Sun Sojourn 1st Qtr Sales.

Excel starts, opens the work-book Fun-N-Sun Sojourn 1st Qtr Sales.xls from drive A, and displays it on the screen (Figure 1-67). An alternative to double-clicking the file name is to click it and then click the Open button in the Open Office Document dialog box.

FIGURE 1-67

AutoCalculate

You easily can obtain a total, an average, or other information about the numbers in a range by using the **AutoCalculate area** on the status bar (bottom of Figure 1-67). All you need do is select the range of cells containing the numbers you want to check. Next, right-click the AutoCalculate area to display the shortcut menu (Figure 1-68 on the next page). The recessed check mark to the left of the active function (Sum) indicates that the sum of the selected range displays. The function commands on the AutoCalculate shortcut menu are described in Table 1-5.

Table 1-5	AutoCalculate Shortcut Menu Commands
COMMAND	**FUNCTION**
Average	Displays the average of the numbers in the selected range
Count	Displays the number of nonblank cells in the selected range
Count Nums	Displays the number of cells containing numbers in the selected range
Max	Displays the highest value in the selected range
Min	Displays the lowest value in the selected range
Sum	Displays the sum of the numbers in the selected range

The following steps show how to display the average first quarter sales by sales channel for the Bahamas Repose vacation package.

Steps: To Use the AutoCalculate Area to Determine an Average

1 Select the range B3:E3. Right-click the AutoCalculate area on the status bar.

The sum of the numbers in the range B3:E3 displays ($158,971.68) as shown in Figure 1-68 because Sum is active in the AutoCalculate area (you may see a total other than the Sum in your AutoCalculate area). The shortcut menu listing the various types of functions displays over the AutoCalculate area.

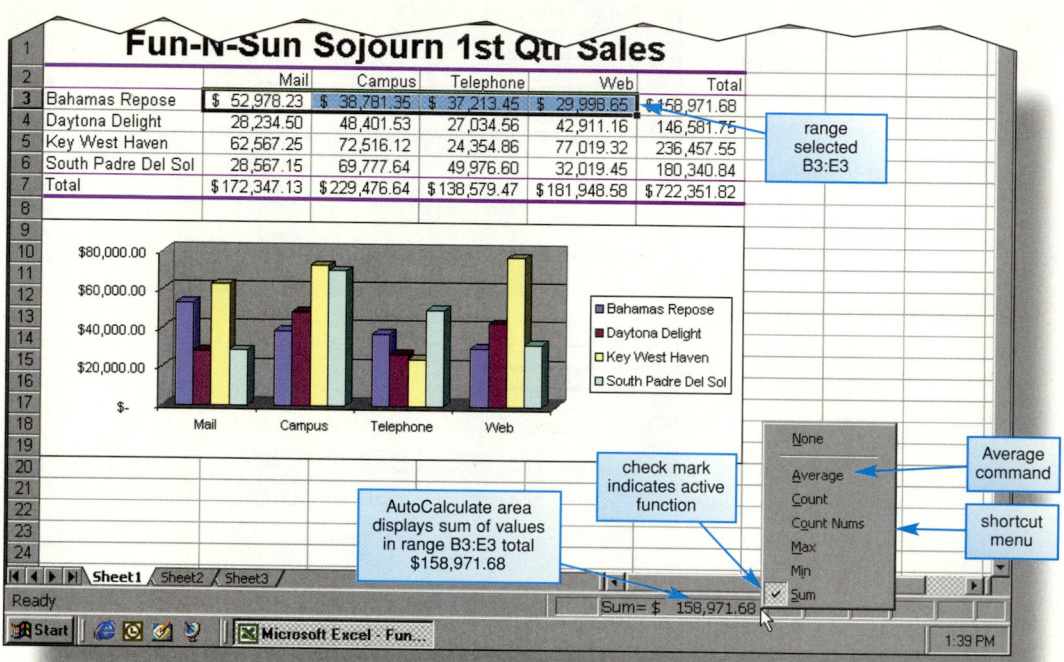

FIGURE 1-68

2 Click Average on the shortcut menu.

The average of the numbers in the range B3:E3 displays in the AutoCalculate area (Figure 1-69).

3 Right-click the AutoCalculate area and then click Sum on the shortcut menu.

FIGURE 1-69

To change to any one of the other five functions for the range B3:E3, right-click the AutoCalculate area. Then click the desired function.

Correcting Errors

You can correct errors on a worksheet using one of several methods. The one you choose will depend on the extent of the error and whether you notice it while typing the data or after you have entered the incorrect data into the cell.

Correcting Errors While You Are Typing Data into a Cell

If you notice an error while you are typing data into a cell, press the BACKSPACE key to erase the portion in error and then type the correct characters. If the error is a major one, click the Cancel box in the formula bar or press the ESC key to erase the entire entry and then reenter the data from the beginning.

In-Cell Editing

If you find an error in the worksheet after entering the data, you can correct the error in one of two ways:

1. If the entry is short, select the cell, retype the entry correctly, and click the Enter box or press the ENTER key. The new entry will replace the old entry.
2. If the entry in the cell is long and the errors are minor, the **Edit mode** may be a better choice. Use the Edit mode as described below.
    a. Double-click the cell containing the error. Excel switches to Edit mode, the active cell contents display in the formula bar, and a flashing insertion point displays in the active cell (Figure 1-70). This editing procedure is called **in-cell editing** because you can edit the contents directly in the cell. The active cell contents also display in the formula bar.

FIGURE 1-70

b. Make your changes, as specified below.
    (1) To insert between two characters, place the insertion point between the two characters and begin typing. Excel inserts the new characters at the location of the insertion point.
    (2) To delete a character in the cell, move the insertion point to the left of the character you want to delete and then press the DELETE key, or place the insertion point to the right of the character you want to delete and then press the BACKSPACE key. You also can use the mouse to drag through the character or adjacent characters you want to delete and then press the DELETE key or click the **Cut button** on the Standard toolbar.

Editing the Contents of a Cell

Rather than using in-cell editing, you can select the cell and then click the formula bar to edit the contents.

(3) When you are finished editing an entry, click the Enter box or press the ENTER key.

When Excel enters the Edit mode, the keyboard usually is in Insert mode. In **Insert mode**, as you type a character, Excel inserts the character and moves all characters to the right of the typed character one position to the right. You can change to Overtype mode by pressing the INSERT key. In **Overtype mode**, Excel overtypes the character to the right of the insertion point. The INSERT key toggles the keyboard between Insert mode and Overtype mode.

While in Edit mode, you may have reason to move the insertion point to various points in the cell, select portions of the data in the cell, or switch from inserting characters to overtyping characters. Table 1-6 summarizes the most common tasks used during in-cell editing.

Table 1-6 Summary of In-Cell Editing Tasks

TASK	MOUSE	KEYBOARD
Move the insertion point to the beginning of data in a cell	Point to the left of the first character and click	Press HOME
Move the insertion point to the end of data in a cell	Point to the right of the last character and click	Press END
Move the insertion point anywhere in a cell	Point to the appropriate position and click the character	Press RIGHT ARROW or LEFT ARROW
Highlight one or more adjacent characters	Drag the mouse pointer through adjacent characters	Press SHIFT+RIGHT ARROW or SHIFT+LEFT ARROW
Select all data in a cell	Double-click the cell with the insertion point in the cell	
Delete selected characters	Click the Cut button on the Standard toolbar	Press DELETE
Toggle between Insert and Overtype modes		Press INSERT

Undoing the Last Entry

Excel provides the **Undo command** on the Edit menu and the **Undo button** on the Standard toolbar (Figure 1-71) that you can use to erase the most recent cell entry. Thus, if you enter incorrect data in a cell and notice it immediately, click the Undo command or Undo button and Excel changes the cell contents to what they were prior to entering the incorrect data.

FIGURE 1-71

If Excel cannot undo an action, then the Undo button is inoperative. Excel remembers the last 16 actions you have completed. Thus, you can undo up to 16 previous actions by clicking the Undo box arrow to display the Undo list and clicking the action to be undone (Figure 1-71). You also can click Undo on the Edit menu rather than using the Undo button.

Next to the Undo button on the Standard toolbar is the Redo button. The **Redo button** allows you to repeat previous actions. You also can click Redo on the Edit menu rather than using the Redo button.

Clearing a Cell or Range of Cells

If you enter data into the wrong cell or range of cells, you can erase, or clear, the data using one of several methods. **Never press the** SPACEBAR **to clear a cell.** Pressing the SPACEBAR enters a blank character. A blank character is text and is different from an empty cell, even though the cell may appear empty.

Excel provides four methods to clear the contents of a cell or a range of cells.

TO CLEAR CELL CONTENTS USING THE FILL HANDLE

1 Select the cell or range of cells and point to the fill handle so the mouse pointer changes to a cross hair.

2 Drag the fill handle back into the selected cell or range until a shadow covers the cell or cells you want to erase. Release the mouse button.

TO CLEAR CELL CONTENTS USING THE SHORTCUT MENU

1 Select the cell or range of cells to be cleared.

2 Right-click the selection.

3 Click Clear Contents on the shortcut menu.

TO CLEAR CELL CONTENTS USING THE DELETE KEY

1 Select the cell or range of cells to be cleared.

2 Press the DELETE key.

TO CLEAR CELL CONTENTS USING THE CLEAR COMMAND

1 Select the cell or range of cells to be cleared.

2 Click Edit on the menu bar and then click Clear.

3 Click All on the submenu.

You also can select a range of cells and click the Cut button on the Standard toolbar or click Cut on the Edit menu. Be aware, however, that the **Cut button** or **Cut command** not only deletes the contents from the range, but also copies the contents of the range to the Office Clipboard.

The Undo Button

The Undo button can undo far more complicated worksheet activities than just removing the latest entry from a cell. In fact, most commands can be undone if you click the Undo button before you make another entry or issue another command. You cannot undo a save or print command, but, as a general rule, the Undo button can restore the worksheet data and settings to their same state as the last time Excel was in Ready mode. With Excel 2000, multiple-level undo and redo capabilities are available.

Clearing Formats

If you accidentally assign unwanted formats to a range of cells, you can use the Clear command on the Edit menu to delete the formats of a selected range. Doing so changes the format to normal. To view the characteristics of the normal format, click Style on the Format menu or press ALT+APOSTROPHE (').

Quick Reference

For a table that lists how to complete the tasks covered in this book using the mouse, menu, shortcut menu, and keyboard, visit the Shelly Cashman Series Office Web page (www.scsite.com/off2000/qr.htm), and then click Microsoft Excel 2000.

Clearing the Entire Worksheet

Sometimes, everything goes wrong. If this happens, you may want to clear the worksheet entirely and start over. To clear the worksheet, follow these steps.

TO CLEAR THE ENTIRE WORKSHEET

1 Click the Select All button on the worksheet (Figure 1-71 on page E 1.52).

2 Press the DELETE key or on the Edit menu click Clear and then click All on the submenu.

The **Select All button** selects the entire worksheet. Instead of clicking the Select All button, you also can press CTRL+A. You also can clear an unsaved workbook by clicking the workbook's Close button or by clicking **Close** on the File menu. If you close the workbook, click the **New button** on the Standard toolbar or click **New** on the File menu to begin working on the next workbook.

TO DELETE AN EMBEDDED CHART

1 Click the chart to select it.

2 Press the DELETE key.

Excel Help System

At any time while you are using Excel, you can get answers to questions by using the **Excel Help system**. Used properly, this form of online assistance can increase your productivity and reduce your frustrations by minimizing the time you spend learning how to use Excel.

The following section shows how to get answers to your questions using the Office Assistant. For additional information on using the Excel Help system, see Appendix A and Table 1-7 on page E1.57.

The Office Assistant

The Office Assistant unifies Excel Help, allows users to ask questions in their own words, and interactively provides tips and suggestions to let users discover the power of Excel 2000.

Using the Office Assistant

The **Office Assistant** answers your questions and suggests more efficient ways to complete a task. With the Office Assistant active, for example, you can type a question, word, or phrase in a text box and the Office Assistant provides immediate help on the subject. Also, as you create a worksheet, the Office Assistant accumulates tips that suggest more efficient ways to do the tasks you completed while building a worksheet, such as formatting, printing, and saving. This tip feature is part of the **IntelliSense™ technology** that is built into Excel, which understands what you are trying to do and suggests better ways to do it. When the light bulb displays above the Office Assistant, click it to see a tip.

The following steps show how to use the Office Assistant to obtain information on formatting a worksheet.

To Obtain Help Using the Office Assistant

1 If the Office Assistant is not on the screen, click Help on the menu bar and then click Show the Office Assistant. With the Office Assistant on the screen, click it. Type formatting in the What would you like to do? text box in the Office Assistant balloon. Point to the Search button (Figure 1-72).

FIGURE 1-72

2 Click the Search button. Point to the topic About worksheet formatting in the Office Assistant balloon.

The Office Assistant displays a list of topics relating to the question, how do i format. The mouse pointer changes to a hand indicating it is pointing to a link (Figure 1-73).

FIGURE 1-73

3 **Click About worksheet formatting. When Excel displays the Microsoft Excel Help window, double-click its title bar to maximize it.**

The Office Assistant displays a Microsoft Excel Help window that provides Help information about worksheet formatting (Figure 1-74).

4 **Click the Close button on the Microsoft Excel Help window title bar.**

The Microsoft Excel Help window closes and the worksheet is active.

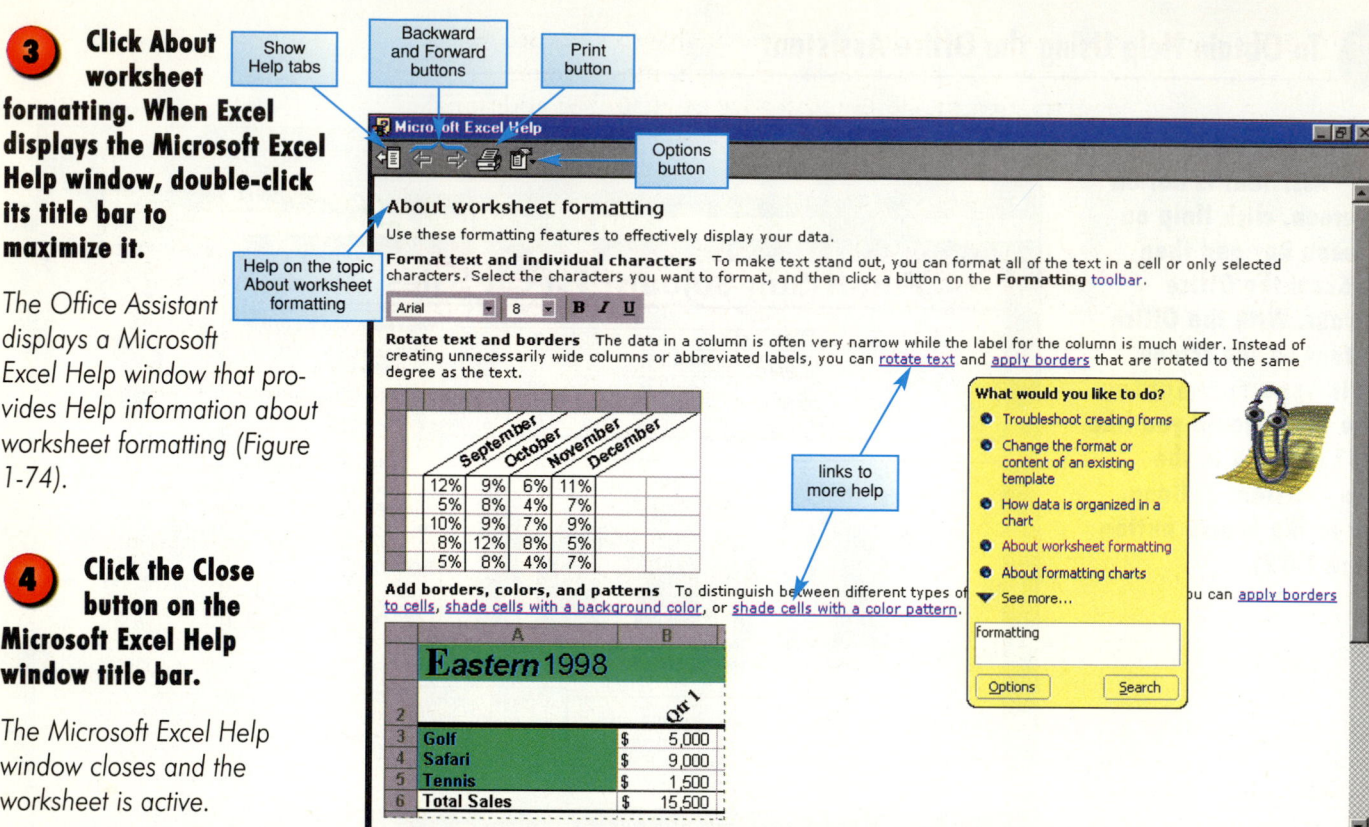

FIGURE 1-74

Use the buttons in the upper-left corner of the Microsoft Excel Help window (Figure 1-74) to navigate through the Help system, change the display, and print the contents of the window.

Table 1-7 summarizes the nine categories of Help available to you. Because of the way the Excel Help system works, please review the right most column of Table 1-7 if you have difficulties activating the desired category of Help. For additional information on using the Excel Help system, see Appendix A.

Table 1-7	Excel Help System		
TYPE	DESCRIPTION	HOW TO ACTIVATE	TURNING THE OFFICE ASSISTANT ON AND OFF
Answer Wizard	Similar to the Office Assistant in that it answers questions that you type in your own words.	Click the Microsoft Excel Help button on the Standard toolbar. If necessary, maximize the Help window by double-clicking its title bar. Click the Answer Wizard tab.	If the Office Assistant displays, right-click it, click Options on the shortcut menu, click Use the Office Assistant to remove the check mark, click the OK button.
Contents sheet	Groups Help topics by general categories. Use when you know only the general category of the topic in question.	Click the Microsoft Excel Help button on the Standard toolbar. If necessary, maximize the Help window by double-clicking its title bar. Click the Contents tab.	If the Office Assistant displays, right-click it, click Options, click Use the Office Assistant to remove the check mark, click the OK button.
Detect and Repair	Automatically finds and fixes errors in the application.	Click Detect and Repair on the Help menu.	
Hardware and Software Information	Shows Product ID and allows access to system information and technical support information.	Click About Microsoft Excel on the Help menu and then click the appropriate button.	
Help for Lotus 1-2-3 Users	Used to assist Lotus 1-2-3 users who are learning Microsoft Excel.	Click Lotus 1-2-3 Help on the Help menu.	
Index sheet	Similar to an index in a book. Use when you know exactly what you want.	Click the Microsoft Excel Help button on the Standard toolbar. If necessary, maximize the Help window by double-clicking its title bar. Click the Index tab.	If the Office Assistant displays, right-click it, click Options, click Use the Office Assistant to remove the check mark, click the OK button.
Office Assistant	Answers questions that you type in your own words, offers tips, and provides Help for a variety of Excel features.	Click the Microsoft Excel Help button on the Standard toolbar or double-click the Office Assistant icon. Some dialog boxes also include the Microsoft Excel Help button.	If the Office Assistant does not display, click Show the Office Assistant on the Help menu.
Office on the Web	Used to access technical resources and download free product enhancements on the Web.	Click Office on the Web on the Help menu.	
Question Mark button and What's This? command	Used to identify unfamiliar items on the screen.	In a dialog box, click the Question Mark button and then click an item in the dialog box. Click What's This? on the Help menu, and then click an item on the screen.	

Quitting Excel

To quit Excel, complete the following steps.

TO QUIT EXCEL

1 Click the Close button on the right side of the title bar (see Figure 1-63 on page E 1.46).

2 If the Microsoft Excel dialog box displays, click the No button.

More About 2000

Quitting Excel 2000

Do not forget to remove the floppy disk from drive A after quitting Excel, especially if you are working in a laboratory environment. Nothing can be more frustrating than leaving all of your hard work behind on a floppy disk for the next user.

C A S E   P E R S P E C T I V E   S U M M A R Y

The worksheet created in this project (Figure 1-1 on page E 1.7) allows the management of the Fun-N-Sun Sojourn company to examine the first quarter sales for the four key vacation packages. Furthermore, the 3-D Column chart should meet the needs of Kylie Waiter, who as you recall, has little tolerance for lists of numbers.

Project Summary

In creating the Fun-N-Sun Sojourn 1st Quarter Sales worksheet and chart in this project, you gained a broad knowledge about Excel. First, you were introduced to starting Excel. You learned about the Excel window and how to enter text and numbers to create a worksheet. You learned how to select a range and how to use the AutoSum button to sum numbers in a column or row. Using the fill handle, you learned how to copy a cell to adjacent cells.

Once the worksheet was built, you learned how to change the font size of the title, bold the title, and center the title across a range using buttons on the Formatting toolbar. Using the steps and techniques presented in the project, you formatted the body of the worksheet using the AutoFormat command, and you used the Chart Wizard to add a 3-D Column chart. After completing the worksheet, you saved the workbook on disk and printed the worksheet and chart. You learned how to edit data in cells. Finally, you learned how to use the Excel Help system to answer your questions.

What You Should Know

Having completed this project, you now should be able to perform the following tasks:

- Add a 3-D Column Chart to the Worksheet *(E 1.37)*
- Bold a Cell *(E 1.29)*
- Center a Cell's Contents Across Columns *(E 1.33)*
- Clear Cell Contents Using the Clear Command *(E 1.53)*
- Clear Cell Contents Using the DELETE Key *(E 1.53)*
- Clear Cell Contents Using the Fill Handle *(E 1.53)*
- Clear Cell Contents Using the Shortcut Menu *(E 1.53)*
- Clear the Entire Worksheet *(E 1.54)*
- Copy a Cell to Adjacent Cells in a Row *(E 1.24)*
- Delete an Embedded Chart *(E 1.54)*
- Determine Multiple Totals at the Same Time *(E 1.26)*
- Display the Formatting Toolbar in Its Entirety *(E 1.28)*
- Enter Column Titles *(E 1.18)*
- Enter Numeric Data *(E 1.21)*
- Enter Row Titles *(E 1.20)*
- Enter the Worksheet Title *(E 1.16)*
- Increase the Font Size of a Cell Entry *(E 1.30)*
- Obtain Help Using the Office Assistant *(E 1.55)*
- Print a Worksheet *(E 1.45)*
- Quit Excel *(E 1.46, E 1.57)*
- Save a Workbook *(E 1.41)*
- Start Excel *(E 1.8)*
- Start Excel and Open a Workbook *(E 1.48)*
- Sum a Column of Numbers *(E 1.22)*
- Use AutoFormat to Format the Body of a Worksheet *(E 1.31)*
- Use the AutoCalculate Area to Determine an Average *(E 1.50)*
- Use the Name Box to Select a Cell *(E 1.35)*

More *About* **2000**

Microsoft Certification

The Microsoft Office User Specialist (MOUS) Certification program provides an opportunity for you to obtain a valuable industry credential — proof that you have the Excel 2000 skills required by employers. For more information, see Appendix D or visit the Shelly Cashman Series MOUS Web page at www.scsite.com/off2000/cert.htm.

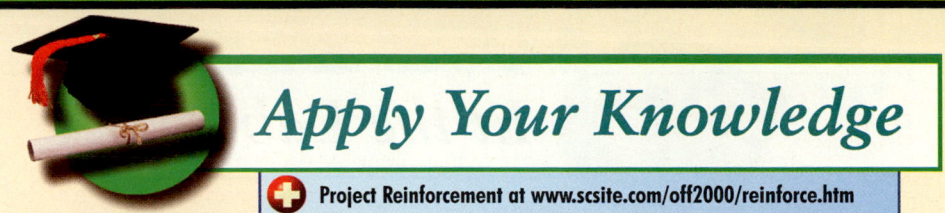

Apply Your Knowledge

➕ Project Reinforcement at www.scsite.com/off2000/reinforce.htm

1 Changing Data in a Worksheet

Instructions: Start Excel. Open the workbook Trevor's Shady Tree Service from the Data Disk. See the inside back cover of this book for instructions for downloading the Data Disk or see your instructor for information on accessing the files required in this book.

Make the changes to the worksheet described in Table 1-8 so it appears as shown in Figure 1-75. As you edit the values in the cells containing numeric data, watch the values in the total income (row 6), the total expenses (row 11), and the profit (row 12). The

FIGURE 1-75

numbers in these three rows are based on formulas. When you enter a new value, Excel automatically recalculates the formulas. After you have successfully made the changes listed in the table, the profits in cells C12 through F12 should equal $18,580.17, $45,452.34, $44,101.35, and $26,996.44, respectively.

Save the workbook. Use the file name, Eric's Arborescent Service. Print the revised worksheet in landscape orientation and hand in the printout to your instructor. Use the Excel Help system to learn how to print in landscape orientation.

Table 1-8 New Worksheet Data

CELL	CHANGE CELL CONTENTS TO
A1	Eric's Arborescent Service
C3	62,613.25
D4	31,721.97
E5	42,982.90
F5	14,213.75
C8	54,430.00
E10	30,793.20
F10	43,645.25

In the Lab

1 Marvin's Music & Movie Mirage Sales Analysis Worksheet

Problem: The chief financial officer (CFO) of Marvin's Music & Movie Mirage needs a sales analysis worksheet similar to the one shown in Figure 1-76. Your task is to develop the worksheet. Table 1-9 provides the sales figures for the worksheet.

Instructions: Perform the following tasks.

1. Create the worksheet shown in Figure 1-76 using the title, sales amounts, and categories in Table 1-9.

2. Determine the totals for the types of products, sales channels, and company totals.

3. Format the worksheet title, Marvin's Music & Movie Mirage, in 18-point Arial, bold font, centered across columns A through F.

4. Format the range A2:F8 using the AutoFormat command on the

FIGURE 1-76

Format menu as follows: (a) Select the range A2:F8 and then apply the table format Accounting 1; and (b) with the range A2:F8 still selected, apply the table format List 2. Excel 2000 appends the formats of List 2 to the formats of Accounting 1.

5. Select the range A2:E7 and then use the Chart Wizard button on the Standard toolbar to draw a Clustered column with a 3-D visual effect chart (column 1, row 2 in Chart sub-type list). Move the chart to the upper-left corner of cell A10 and then drag the lower-right corner of the chart location to cell F20.

6. Enter your name, course, laboratory assignment number, date, and instructor name in cells A24 through A28.

7. Save the workbook using the file name Marvin's Music & Movie Mirage.

8. Print the worksheet.

9. Make the following two corrections to the sales amounts: $35,987.99 for DVDs sold in a store and $36,498.33 for Videos sold over the telephone. After you enter the corrections, the company totals should equal $157,390.58 in cell C8 and $111,876.00 in cell D8.

10. Print the revised worksheet. Close the workbook without saving the changes.

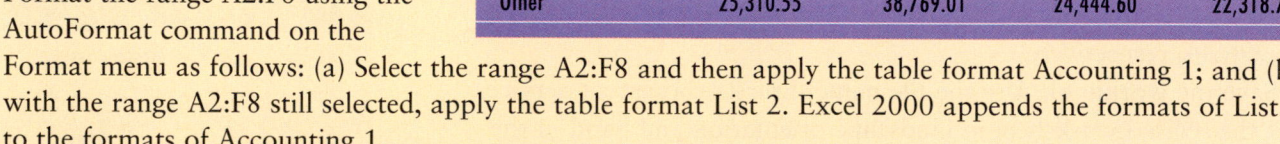

Table 1-9	Marvin's Music & Movie Mirage Data			
	MAIL ORDER	**STORE**	**TELEPHONE**	**WEB**
CDs	$23,789.34	$24,897.12	$34,612.89	$16,410.51
DVDs	35,912.54	23,908.23	9,219.42	29,900.32
Tapes	23,719.32	23,823.90	7,100.76	16,758.45
Videos	8,313.10	33,912.56	24,200.87	29,126.71
Other	25,310.55	38,769.01	24,444.60	22,318.75

In the Lab

2 Dollar Bill's Annual Software Sales Worksheet

Problem: As the assistant financial manager for Dollar Bill's Software, Inc., your supervisor has asked you to create a workbook to analyze the annual sales for the company by product group and store location. The software sales for the year are shown in Table 1-10.

Table 1-10	Dollar Bill's Data			
	SAN ANTONIO	SAN FRANCISCO	CLEVELAND	CHARLOTTE
Business	35,102.15	18,231.56	31,012.40	12,012.00
Database	42,970.50	57,210.00	29,089.12	29,765.23
Education	21,892.70	18,329.34	26,723.15	22,914.50
Graphics	9,312.45	12,923.21	9,012.56	8,910.32
Games	13,453.30	22,134.45	13,908.55	9,143.75

Instructions: Perform the following tasks.

1. Create the worksheet shown in Figure 1-77 using the sales amounts in Table 1-10.

2. Direct Excel to determine the totals for the four store locations, the product categories, and the company.

3. Format the worksheet title, Dollar Bill's Annual Software Sales, in 18-point Arial bold font, and centered across columns A through F.

4. Use the AutoFormat command on the Format menu to format the range A2:F8. Use the table format Accounting 2.

FIGURE 1-77

5. Use the ChartWizard button on the Standard toolbar to draw the 3-D Stacked Cylinder chart (column 3, row 1 in the Chart sub-type list), as shown in Figure 1-77. Chart the range A2:E7 and use the chart location A9:H22. Extend the chart location to the right, if necessary.

6. Enter your name in cell A25. Enter your course, computer laboratory assignment number, date, and instructor name in cells A26 through A29.

7. Save the workbook using the file name, Dollar Bill's Annual Software Sales. Print the worksheet.

8. Two corrections to the sales amounts were sent in from the accounting department. The correct sales amounts are $16,453.21 for Games in San Antonio and $42,781.50 for Database software in Charlotte. Enter the two corrections. After you enter the two corrections, the company total should equal $460,067.42 in cell F8. Print the revised worksheet.

9. Use the Undo button to change the worksheet back to the original numbers in Table 1-10.

10. Use the Redo button to change the worksheet back to the revised state.

11. Hand in all printouts to your instructor. Close the workbook without saving the changes.

In the Lab

3 Projected College Cash Flow Analysis

Problem: Attending college is an expensive proposition and your resources are limited. To plan for your four-year college career, you have decided to organize your anticipated expenses and resources in a worksheet. The data required to prepare your worksheet is shown in Table 1-11.

Part 1 Instructions: Using the numbers in Table 1-11, create the worksheet shown in Figure 1-78. Enter the worksheet title in cell A1 and the section titles, Expenses and Resources, in cells A2 and A10, respectively. Use the AutoSum button to calculate the totals in rows 9 and 16 and column F.

To format the worksheet, use the table format Accounting 1 for the range A3:F9 and again for the range A11:F16. Increase the font size of the worksheet title to 18 point and the section titles to 16 point. Bold the entire worksheet by first clicking the Select All button on the worksheet and then clicking the Bold button on the Formatting toolbar. Center the title across columns A through F. Enter your name in cell A19 and your course, laboratory assignment number, date, and instructor name in cells A20 through A23. Use Help to determine how to use the Font Color button on the Formatting toolbar to change the font color of the worksheet title and section titles as shown in Figure 1-78.

Save the workbook using the file name, College Expenses and Resources. Print the worksheet. Use the Office Assistant to learn how to print only a specific area of a worksheet and then print the selection A1:F9 of the worksheet.

Table 1-11	College Expenses and Resources			
EXPENSES	**FRESHMAN**	**SOPHOMORE**	**JUNIOR**	**SENIOR**
Room & Board	$3,290.00	$3,454.50	$3,627.23	$3,808.59
Tuition & Books	4,850.00	5,092.50	5,347.13	5,614.48
Clothes	490.00	514.50	540.23	567.24
Entertainment	635.00	666.75	700.09	735.09
Miscellaneous	325.00	341.25	358.31	376.23
RESOURCES	**FRESHMAN**	**SOPHOMORE**	**JUNIOR**	**SENIOR**
Savings	$1,600.00	$1,680.00	$1,764.00	$1,852.20
Parents	2,340.00	2,457.00	2,579.85	2,708.84
Job	1,450.00	1,522.50	1,598.64	1,678.56
Financial Aid	4,200.00	4,410.00	4,630.50	4,862.03

FIGURE 1-78

In the Lab

Increment all Junior-year expenses in column D by $500. Increment the financial aid for the Junior year by the amount required to cover the increase. The totals in cells F9 and F16 should equal $43,834.12. Print the worksheet. Close the workbook without saving changes. Hand in the three printouts to your instructor.

Part 2 Instructions: Open the workbook College Expenses and Resources created in Part 1. A close inspection of Table 1-11 shows a 5% increase each year over the previous year. Use the Office Assistant to determine how to enter the data for the last three years using a formula and the Copy command. For example, the formula to enter in cell C4 is =B4 * 1.05. Enter formulas to replace all the numbers in the range C4:E8 and C12:E15. If necessary, reformat the tables using Accounting 1 as you did in Part 1. The worksheet should appear as shown in Figure 1-78, except that some of the totals will be off by 0.01 due to round-off errors. Save the worksheet using the file name, College Expenses and Resources2. Print the worksheet. Press CTRL+` (left single quotation mark) to display the formulas. Print the formulas version. Hand in both printouts to your instructor.

Cases and Places

The difficulty of these case studies varies:
▶ are the least difficult; ▶▶ are more difficult; and ▶▶▶ are the most difficult.

1 ▶ You just started as a summer intern at the Blue Suede Music Company. Your manager, Elma Presley, has asked you to prepare a worksheet and chart to help her analyze the yearly guitar sales by region and by guitar type (Table 1-12). Use the concepts and techniques presented in this project to create the worksheet and chart.

Table 1-12	Blue Suede Music Company Data			
	NORTH	EAST	WEST	SOUTH
Classical	6734	7821	4123	7989
Steel String	5423	2134	6574	3401
Electric	3495	6291	7345	7098
Bass	5462	2923	8034	5135

2 ▶ The number of new cars and trucks has increased each year from 1996 through 2000, as indicated in Table 1-13. Create a worksheet and 3-D Column chart that illustrates these increases. Show model year and type car and truck totals. Use the concepts and techniques presented in this project to create the worksheet and chart.

Table 1-13	1996 - 2000 New Cars and Trucks Data			
YEAR	DOMESTIC CARS*	IMPORT CARS*	DOMESTIC TRUCKS*	IMPORT TRUCKS*
1996	7,323	2,231	6,125	225
1997	7,498	2,356	6,315	257
1998	7,615	2,489	6,727	313
1999	7,734	2,501	6,501	407
2000	7,944	2,578	6,623	661
* in thousands				

Cases and Places

3 ▶ You are a teaching assistant for the Computer Information Systems department. The department head has asked you to take her grade ledger (Table 1-14), which shows her grade distributions for all her spring classes, and separate them into categories based on the class and the grade. She wants a worksheet and 3-D Column chart to make it easier to view the grades as well as the totals at a glance. Use the concepts and techniques presented in this project to create the worksheet and chart.

Table 1-14	Semester Grade Summary			
GRADE	CIS 104	CIS 205	CIS 299	CIS 331
A	2	1	4	2
B	22	7	2	3
C	15	10	11	9
D	20	5	15	6
F	11	8	19	3

4 ▶ The CheeseHeads restaurant in Green Bay, Wisconsin is trying to decide whether it is feasible to open another restaurant in the neighboring community of Oshkosh, Wisconsin. The owner, G. B. Pack, has asked you to develop a worksheet totaling all the revenue received last year. The revenue by quarter is: Quarter 1, $94,342.98; Quarter 2, $81,500.65; Quarter 3, $158,220.09; and Quarter 4, $225,435.50. Create a 3-D Pie chart to illustrate revenue contribution by quarter. Use the AutoCalculate area to find the average quarterly revenue.

5 ▶▶ The Palace Theater is a small movie house that shows almost-current releases at weekday evening, weekend matinee, and weekend evening screenings. Three types of tickets are sold at each presentation: general admission, senior citizen, and children. The theater management has asked you to prepare a worksheet, based on the revenue from a typical week, that can be used in reevaluating its ticket structure. During an average week, weekday evening shows generate $7,540 from general admission ticket sales, $3,575 from senior citizen ticket sales, and $1,375 from children ticket sales. Weekend matinee shows make $5,500 from general admission ticket sales, $1,950 from senior citizen ticket sales, and $2,500 from children ticket sales. Weekend evening shows earn $8,540 from general admission ticket sales, $7,350 from senior citizen ticket sales, and $1,100 from children ticket sales. Use the concepts and techniques presented in this project to prepare a worksheet that includes total revenues for each type of ticket and for each presentation time, and a Bar chart illustrating ticket revenues.

6 ▶▶▶ Some academic disciplines appear to attract more students of one gender than the other. Visit the Registrar's office at your school and find out how many males and how many females have declared majors in five disciplines. Using this information, create a worksheet showing the number of male, female, and total number of majors in each discipline. Include totals for each numeric column. Include a Column chart to illustrate your data.

Microsoft Excel 2000

2

Formulas, Functions, Formatting, and Web Queries

OBJECTIVES

You will have mastered the material in this project when you can:

- Enter multiple lines of text in the same cell
- Enter a formula using the keyboard
- Enter formulas using Point mode
- Identify the arithmetic operators +, −, *, /, %, and ^
- Apply the AVERAGE, MAX, and MIN functions
- Determine a percentage
- Verify a formula
- Change the font of a cell
- Color the characters and background of a cell
- Add borders to a range
- Format numbers using the Format Cells dialog box
- Add conditional formatting to a range of cells
- Align text in cells
- Change the width of a column and height of a row
- Check the spelling of a worksheet
- Preview how a printed copy of the worksheet will look
- Distinguish between portrait and landscape orientation
- Print a partial or complete worksheet
- Display and print the formulas version of a worksheet
- Print to fit
- Use a Web query to get real-time data from a Web site
- Rename sheets
- E-mail the active workbook from within Excel

Windy City Pedal Pushers

Riding L.A.T.E. into the Morning

Mountain bikes, helmets, and reflectors ready, very early morning cyclists do whatever it takes to prepare themselves to pedal their bikes 25 miles in Chicago during the annual Friends of the Parks' L.A.T.E. Ride. The event is aptly named. L.A.T.E. is an acronym for Long After Twilight Ends. The moonstruck ride occurs from 1:30 A.M. to sunrise and weaves through Chicago's downtown and north side neighborhoods and parks.

Friends of the Parks' mission is to preserve and improve Chicago's neighborhood, regional, and lakefront parks in addition to children's playlots. Every year, volunteers contribute time, funds, and effort to clean and maintain the park grounds. Friends of the Parks' has been representing Chicago citizens since 1975, and the L.A.T.E. Ride is one event, in addition to the annual Earth Day clean-up, that promotes its causes.

So how does the Friends of the Parks' organization attempt to manage and organize information about the more than 9,000 participants who take part in the L.A.T.E. Ride event each year? Staff, many of whom volunteer their time and expertise, use worksheets to organize, chart, and present all types of

NUMBER OF CYCLISTS

1989	350
1990	750
1991	1,800
1992	3,200
1993	4,500
1994	6,500
1995	
1996	
1997	
1998	

PEDAL PUSHERS: 1998 DEMOGRAPHICS

Residence

Chicago Suburbs (55%)
City of Chicago (34%)
Northwest Indiana (3%)
Other States (5%)
Other Areas in Illinois (3%)

Age

40-49yrs.
30-39yrs. (30%)
(5%)
60+ yrs.
Age not given (2.5%)
9 and younger (2.5%)
10-14 yrs. (3%)
15-18 yrs. (4%)
19-22 yrs. (6%)

Chicago Suburbs (55% of total riders)

North and Northwest (42%)
Southwest (8%)
South (13%)
West and Far West (37%)

City of Chicago (34% of total riders)

Downtown and North Side (66%)

WGN-TV Children's Charities Presents
Friends of the Parks'
L.A.T.E. Ride
July 11 1999

WGN-TV Children's Charities Presents
Friends of the Parks'
L.A.T.E. Ride
July 11 1999
Saturday Night/Sunday Morning July 11
RIDER GUIDE

data with relative ease. They analyze and manipulate data; specifically, they input numbers and enter formulas to determine averages and percentages, as well as find the minimum and maximum numbers in a series. In addition, they create traditional Pie charts, Column charts, and other chart forms to represent the data visually.

If they want to determine, for example, the demographics of the L.A.T.E. bike riders, they can input participants' ages taken from a Friends of the Parks' survey and then allow the worksheet to generate Pie charts depicting the age breakdowns in a matter of seconds. Moreover, they can create a Column chart showing the number of participants from year to year. The Friends of the Parks' also can track how many participants live in Chicago, the suburbs, or other states and the number of male and female cyclists.

You will perform similar tasks in this project when you create a worksheet for the BetNet Stock Club. You will enter formulas, use the

AVERAGE, MAX, and MIN functions, and then verify the formulas for accuracy.

The L.A.T.E. Ride was established in 1989 with 350 cyclists; most recently nearly 10,000 bike riders have participated. It is not by sheer coincidence that the numbers have escalated dramatically. Once the staff at the Friends of the Parks' collects survey data, they then input the numbers into worksheets using ranges of numbers, enter formulas, and apply formats for appropriate charts. Such data is important to determine marketing strategies or finalize the total number of glow-in-the-dark T-shirts and number tags needed for the participants to don for the ride.

So, if you are up for a challenge in the middle of the night in mid-July in the Windy City, grab your bike and head to the shores of Lake Michigan for the start of a L.A.T.E. night, pedal-pushing experience.

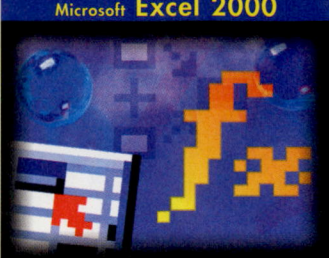

Microsoft Excel 2000

Formulas, Functions, Formatting, and Web Queries

P R O J E C T
2

C A S E   P E R S P E C T I V E

During their Freshman year in college, Michael Santos and six classmates began playing the Investment Challenge game on the Yahoo! Web site (quote.yahoo.com). In the game, each contestant is given $100,000 in fantasy money to make fantasy trades for a period of one month. Yahoo! awards the top finisher a $5,000 cash prize.

Recently, Michael and his classmates won the contest. With their newly gained confidence in investing, they used the prize money to start the BetNet Stock Club. They decided to invest in only the high-flying Internet stocks.

Each month, Michael summarizes the month-end financial status. As the club members approach graduation from college, the value of the club's portfolio has grown to nearly $900,000. As a result, the members voted to buy a new computer and Microsoft Office 2000 for Michael. With Office 2000, he plans to create a worksheet summarizing the club's stock activities that he can e-mail to the members. Michael has asked you to show him how to create the workbook and access real-time stock quotes over the Internet using Excel 2000.

Introduction

In Project 1, you learned how to enter data, sum values, make the worksheet easier to read, and draw a chart. You also learned about online Help and saving, printing, and loading a workbook from a floppy disk into memory. This project continues to emphasize these topics and presents some new ones.

The new topics include formulas, verifying formulas, changing fonts, adding borders, formatting numbers, conditional formatting, changing the widths of columns and heights of rows, spell checking, e-mailing from within an application, and alternative types of worksheet displays and printouts. One alternative display and printout shows the formulas rather than the values in the worksheet. When you display the formulas in the worksheet, you see exactly what text, data, formulas, and functions you have entered into it. Finally, this project covers Web queries to obtain real-time data from a Web site.

Project Two — BetNet Stock Club

The summary notes from your meeting with Michael include the following: need, source of data, calculations, and Web requirements.

Need: An easy-to-read worksheet that summarizes the club's investments (Figure 2-1a). For each stock, the worksheet is to include the name, symbol, date acquired, number of shares, initial price, initial cost, current price, current value, gain/loss, and percent gain/loss. Michael also has requested that the worksheet include totals and the average, highest value, and lowest value for each column of numbers. Finally, Michael wants to use Excel to access real-time stock quotes using Web queries (Figure 2-1b).

(a) Worksheet

(b) Web Query

FIGURE 2-1

Source of Data: The data supplied by Michael includes the stock names, symbols, dates acquired, number of shares, initial prices, and current prices. This data is shown in Table 2-1.

Calculations: The following calculations must be made for each of the stocks:

1. Initial Cost = Shares × Initial Price
2. Current Value = Shares × Current Price
3. Gain/Loss = Current Value – Initial Cost
4. Percentage Gain/Loss = $\dfrac{\text{Gain/Loss}}{\text{Initial Cost}}$
5. Compute the totals for initial cost, current value, and gain/loss.
6. Use the AVERAGE function to determine the average for the number of shares, initial price per share, initial stock cost, current stock price, current stock value, and gain/loss for each stock.
7. Use the MAX and MIN functions to determine the highest and lowest values for the number of shares, initial price per share, initial stock cost, current stock price, current stock value, gain/loss for each stock, and percent gain/loss.

Web Requirements: Use the Web query feature of Excel to get real-time stock quotes for stocks being reviewed by the BetNet Stock Club members as they consider a flight to safety (Figure 2-1b).

Starting Excel and Resetting the Toolbars

To start Excel, Windows must be running. Perform the following steps to start Excel. Once Excel displays, steps 4 through 6 reset the toolbars to their default. Step 6 is necessary only if you added or deleted new buttons on the toolbars.

TO START EXCEL AND RESET THE TOOLBARS

1 Click the Start button on the taskbar.

2 Click New Office Document on the Start menu. If necessary, click the General tab in the New Office Document dialog box.

3 Double-click the Blank Workbook icon.

4 When the blank worksheet displays, click View on the menu bar, point to Toolbars, and then click Customize on the Toolbars submenu.

5 When the Customize dialog box displays, click the Options tab, make sure the top three check boxes have check marks, click the Reset my usage data button, and then click the Yes button.

6 Click the Toolbars tab. Click Standard, click the Reset button, and then click the OK button. Click Formatting, click the Reset button, and the click the OK button. Click the Close button.

The Standard and Formatting toolbars display as shown in Figure 2-1a on the previous page.

An alternative to Steps 1 through 3 is to click the Start button, point to Programs, and then click Microsoft Excel on the Programs submenu.

More About

Web Queries

Thinking about being a day trader of stocks? If so, you will find Excel's Web Queries to be an invaluable tool. The Excel Web Query titled, Microsoft Investor Stock Quotes, can return near real-time stock quotes and links to breaking news for up to 20 stocks almost instantaneously. And you can refresh the results as often as you want.

More About

Starting Excel

An alternative way to start Excel when you want to open a workbook is to start Explorer, display the contents of the folder containing the workbook, and then double-click the workbook name.

Entering the Titles and Numbers into the Worksheet

The worksheet title in Figure 2-1a is centered across columns A through J in row 1. Because the centered text first must be entered into the leftmost column of the area across which it is centered, it will be entered into cell A1.

TO ENTER THE WORKSHEET TITLE

1 Select cell A1. Type `BetNet Stock Club` in the cell.

2 Press the DOWN ARROW key.

The worksheet title displays in cell A1 as shown in Figure 2-2 on the next page.

The column titles in row 2 begin in cell A2 and extend through cell J2. As shown in Figure 2-1a, the column titles in row 2 include multiple lines of text. To start a new line in a cell, press ALT+ENTER after each line, except for the last line, which is completed by clicking the Enter box, pressing the ENTER key, or pressing one of the arrow keys. When you see ALT+ENTER in a step, while holding down the ALT key, press the ENTER key and then release both keys.

The stock names and the row titles Total, Average, Highest, and Lowest in column A begin in cell A3 and continue down to cell A14.

The stock club's investments are summarized in Table 2-1. These numbers are entered into rows 3 through 10. The steps required to enter the column titles, stock names and symbols, total row titles, and numbers as shown in Figure 2-2 are explained in the remainder of this section.

Table 2-1	BetNet Stock Club Portfolio				
STOCK	SYMBOL	DATE ACQUIRED	SHARES	INITIAL PRICE	CURRENT PRICE
Amazon.com	AMZN	10/14/97	800	15.875	172.00
America Online	AOL	12/14/98	720	93.50	128.688
Broadcast.com	BCST	2/2/99	610	85.25	121.5
EarthLink	ELNK	3/1/99	500	63.125	65.25
eBay	EBAY	4/13/99	920	200.50	162.50
Infoseek	SEEK	2/12/98	750	12.875	50.563
UBid	UBID	12/21/98	400	151.375	44.25
Yahoo	YHOO	5/12/98	700	21.00	171.00

TO ENTER THE COLUMN TITLES

1 With cell A2 active, type `Stock` and then press the RIGHT ARROW key.

2 Type `Symbol` and then press the RIGHT ARROW key.

3 Type `Date` and then press ALT+ENTER. Type `Acquired` and then press the RIGHT ARROW key.

4 Type `Shares` and then press the RIGHT ARROW key.

5 Type `Initial` and then press ALT+ENTER. Type `Price` and then press the RIGHT ARROW key.

6 Type `Initial` and then press ALT+ENTER. Type `Cost` and then press the RIGHT ARROW key.

7 Type `Current` and then press ALT+ENTER. Type `Price` and then press the RIGHT ARROW key.

Formatting a Worksheet

With early spreadsheet packages, users often skipped rows to improve the appearance of the worksheet. With Excel, it is not necessary to skip rows because you can increase the height of rows to add white space between information.

Entering Two-Digit Years

When you enter a two-digit year value, Excel interprets the year as follows: (1) 00 through 29 as the years 2000 through 2029 and (2) 30 through 99 as the years 1930 through 1999. You may use four-digit years to ensure that Excel interprets year values the way you intend.

Entering Numbers into a Range

An efficient way to enter data into a range of cells is first to select the range. Enter the number that you want to assign to the upper-left cell. Excel responds by entering the value and moving the active cell selection down one cell. When you enter the last value in the first column, Excel moves to the top of the next column.

8 Type Current and then press ALT+ENTER. Type Value and then press the RIGHT ARROW key.

9 Type Gain/Loss and press the RIGHT ARROW key.

10 Type % Gain/Loss and then click cell A3.

The column titles display as shown in row 2 of Figure 2-2 below. When you press ALT+ENTER to add more lines to a cell, Excel automatically increases the height of the entire row.

The stock data in Table 2-1 on the previous page includes a date on which each stock was acquired. Excel considers a date to be a number and, therefore, displays it right-aligned in the cell. When you enter a date, Excel automatically formats the date so it resembles the way you entered it. For example, if you enter May 20, 1999, Excel displays it as 20-May-99. If you enter the same date in the format 5/20/99, then Excel displays it as 5/20/99. The following steps describe how to enter the stock data shown in Table 2-1, which includes dates.

TO ENTER THE STOCK DATA

1 With cell A3 selected, type Amazon.com and then press the RIGHT ARROW key. Type AMZN and then press the RIGHT ARROW key.

2 With cell C3 selected, type 10/14/97 and then press the RIGHT ARROW key. Type 800 and then press the RIGHT ARROW key.

3 With cell E3 selected, type 15.875 and then press the RIGHT ARROW key twice. Type 172 and then press the ENTER key.

4 Click cell A4. Enter the data in Table 2-1 for the seven remaining stocks in rows 4 through 10.

The stock data displays in rows 3 through 10 as shown in Figure 2-2.

TO ENTER THE TOTAL ROW TITLES

1 Click cell A11. Type Total and then press the DOWN ARROW key. With cell A12 selected, type Average and then press the DOWN ARROW key.

2 With cell A13 selected, type Highest and then press the DOWN ARROW key. With cell A14 selected, type Lowest and then press the ENTER key. Click cell F3.

The total row titles display as shown in Figure 2-2.

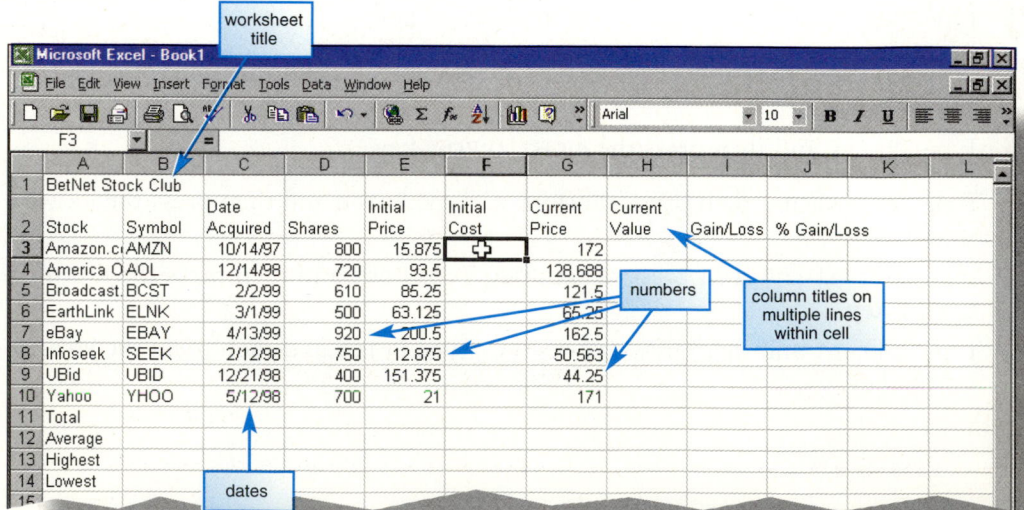

FIGURE 2-2

Entering Formulas

The initial cost for each stock, which displays in column F, is equal to the number of shares in column D times the initial price in column E. Thus, the initial cost for Amazon.com in row 3 is obtained by multiplying 800 (cell D3) times 15.875 (cell E3).

One of the reasons Excel is such a valuable tool is that you can assign a **formula** to a cell and Excel will calculate the result. Consider, for example, what would happen if you had to multiply 800 × 15.875 and then manually enter the result, 12700, in cell F3. Every time the values in cells D3 and E3 changed, you would have to recalculate the product and enter the new value in cell F3. By contrast, if you enter a formula in cell F3 to multiply the values in cells D3 and E3, Excel recalculates the product whenever new values are entered into those cells and displays the result in cell F3. Complete the following steps to enter the formula using the keyboard.

More About

Recalculation of Formulas

Every time you enter a value into a cell in the worksheet, Excel recalculates all formulas. It makes no difference whether the worksheet contains one formula or hundreds of formulas. Excel recalculates the formulas instantaneously. This is one of the reasons why a spreadsheet package, such as Excel, is so powerful.

 To Enter a Formula Using the Keyboard

1 **With cell F3 selected, type =d3*e3 in the cell.**

The formula displays in the formula bar and in cell F3 (Figure 2-3).

FIGURE 2-3

2 **Press the RIGHT ARROW key twice to select cell H3.**

Instead of displaying the formula in cell F3, Excel completes the arithmetic operation indicated by the formula and displays the result, 12700 (Figure 2-4).

FIGURE 2-4

The equal sign (=) preceding d3*e3 is an important part of the formula, it alerts Excel that you are entering a formula or function and not text. The asterisk (*) following d3 is the arithmetic operator that directs Excel to perform the multiplication operation. The valid Excel arithmetic operators are described in Table 2-2.

Table 2-2	Summary of Arithmetic Operators		
ARITHMETIC OPERATOR	**MEANING**	**EXAMPLE OF USAGE**	**MEANING**
–	Negation	–10	Negative 10
%	Percentage	=30%	Multiplies 30 by 0.01
^	Exponentiation	=2 ^ 3	Raises 2 to the third power, which in this example is equal to 8
*	Multiplication	=6.1 * A1	Multiplies the contents of cell A1 by 6.1
/	Division	=H3 / H5	Divides the contents of cell H3 by the contents of cell H5
+	Addition	=4 + 8	Adds 4 and 8
–	Subtraction	=D34 – 35	Subtracts 35 from the contents of cell D34

You can enter the cell references in formulas in uppercase or lowercase, and you can add spaces before and after arithmetic operators to make the formulas easier to read. That is, =d3*e3 is the same as =d3 * e3, =D3 * e3, or =D3 * E3.

Order of Operations

When more than one operator is involved in a formula, Excel follows the same basic order of operations that you use in algebra. Moving from left to right in a formula, the **order of operations** is as follows: first negation (–), then all percentages (%), then all exponentiations (^), then all multiplications (*) and divisions (/), and finally, all additions (+) and subtractions (–).

You can use **parentheses** to override the order of operations. For example, if Excel follows the order of operations, 10 * 6 – 3 equals 57. If you use parentheses, however, to change the formula to 10 * (6 – 3), the result is 30, because the parentheses instruct Excel to subtract 3 from 6 before multiplying by 10. Table 2-3 illustrates several examples of valid formulas and explains the order of operations.

Table 2-3	Examples of Excel Formulas
FORMULA	**REMARK**
=F6	Assigns the value in cell F6 to the active cell.
=6 + – 3^2	Assigns the sum of 6 + 9 (or 15) to the active cell.
=2 * K4 or =K4 * 2 or =(2 * K4)	Assigns two times the contents of cell K4 to the active cell.
=50% * 16	Assigns the product of 0.5 times 16 (or 8) to the active cell.
=– (J12 * S23)	Assigns the negative value of the product of the values contained in cells J12 and S23 to the active cell.
=5 * (L14 – H3)	Assigns the product of five times the difference between the values contained in cells H3 and L14 to the active cell.
=D1 / X6 – A3 * A4 + A5 ^ A6	From left to right: first exponentiation (A5 ^ A6), then division (D1 / X6), then multiplication (A3 * A4), then subtraction (D1 / X6) – (A3 * A4), and finally addition (D1 / X6 – A3 * A4) + (A5 ^ A6). If cells D1 = 10, A3 = 6, A4 = 2, A5 = 5, A6 = 2, and X6 = 2, then Excel assigns the active cell the value 18 (10 / 2 - 6 * 2 + 5 ^ 2 = 18).

The first formula (=d3*e3) in the worksheet was entered into cell F3 using the keyboard. The next section shows you how to enter the formulas in cells H3 and I3 using the mouse to select cell references in a formula.

Entering Formulas Using Point Mode

In the worksheet shown in Figure 2-1a on page E 2.5, the current value of each stock displays in column H. The current value for Amazon.com in cell H3 is equal to the number of shares in cell D3 times the current price in cell G3. The gain/loss for Amazon.com in cell I3 is equal to the current value in cell H3 minus the initial cost in cell F3. The percentage gain loss for Amazon.com in cell J3 is equal to the gain/loss in cell I3 divided by the initial cost in cell F3.

Instead of using the keyboard to enter the formulas =D3*G3 in cell H3, =H3 – F3 in cell I3, and =I3/F3 in cell J3, you can use the mouse and Point mode to enter these three formulas. **Point mode** allows you to select cells for use in a formula by using the mouse.

More About

Using Point Mode

Point mode allows you to create formulas using the mouse. Rather than typing a cell reference in a formula, simply click a cell and Excel appends the corresponding cell reference at the location of the insertion point. You also can use the Customize command on the shortcut menu that displays when you right-click a toolbar to create a Custom toolbar consisting of buttons that represent the operators. Thus, with Excel, you can enter entire formulas without ever touching the keyboard.

 ## To Enter Formulas Using Point Mode

1 **With cell H3 selected, type = (equal sign) to begin the formula and then click cell D3.**

Excel surrounds cell D3 with a marquee and appends D3 to the equal sign (=) in cell H3 (Figure 2-5).

FIGURE 2-5

2 **Type * (asterisk) and then click cell G3.**

Excel surrounds cell G3 with a marquee and appends G3 to the asterisk (*) in cell H3 (Figure 2-6).

FIGURE 2-6

3 Click the Enter box. Click cell I3. Type = (equal sign) and then click cell H3. Type − (minus sign) and then click cell F3.

Excel determines the product of =D3*G3 and displays the result, 137600, in cell H3. The formula =H3 − F3 displays in cell I3 and in the formula bar (Figure 2-7).

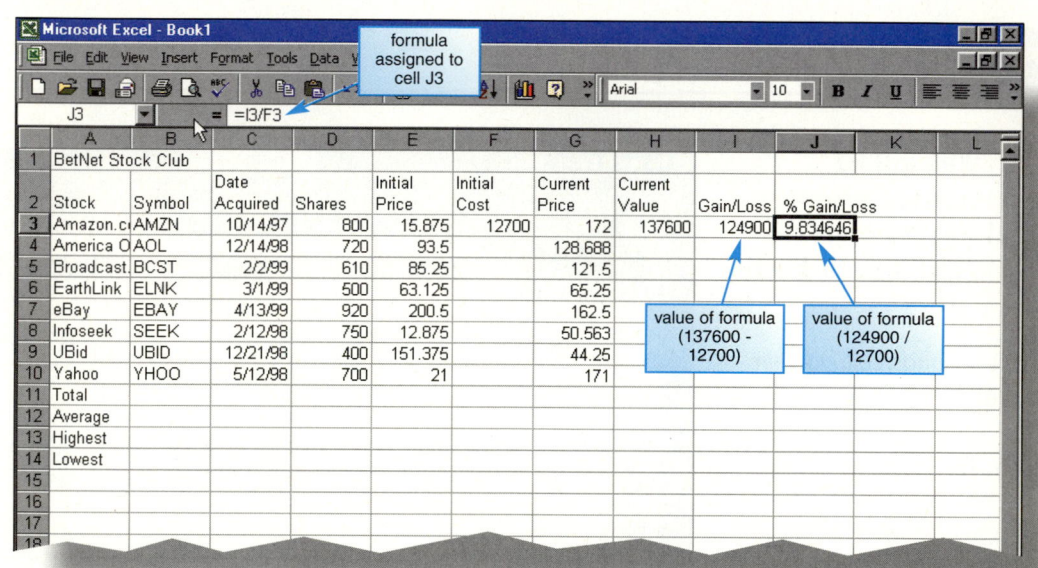

FIGURE 2-7

4 Click the Enter box. Click cell J3. Type = (equal sign) and then click cell I3. Type / (division sign) and then click cell F3. Click the Enter box.

The Gain/Loss for Amazon.com, 124900, displays in cell I3 and the % Gain/Loss for Amazon.com, 9.834646, displays in cell J3 (Figure 2-8). The 9.834646 represents 983.4646%.

FIGURE 2-8

Formulas

To change a formula to a number (constant), select the cell, click the Copy button on the Standard toolbar, on the Edit menu click Paste Special, click Values, and click the OK button.

Depending on the length and complexity of the formula, using Point mode to enter formulas often is faster and more accurate than using the keyboard. As shown later in the project, in some instances, you may want to combine the keyboard and mouse when entering a formula in a cell. You can use the keyboard to begin the formula, for example, and then use the mouse to select a range of cells.

Copying the Formulas Using the Fill Handle

The four formulas for Amazon.com in cells F3, H3, I3, and J3 now are complete. You could enter the same four formulas one at a time for the seven remaining stocks, America Online, Broadcast.com, EarthLink, eBay, Infoseek, UBid, and Yahoo. A much easier method of entering the formulas, however, is to select the formulas in row 3 and then use the fill handle to copy them through row 10. Recall from Project 1 that the fill handle is a small rectangle in the lower-right corner of the active cell. Perform the following steps to copy the formulas.

To Copy Formulas Using the Fill Handle

1 Click cell F3 and then point to the fill handle. Drag the fill handle down through cell F10 and continue to hold down the mouse button.

A border surrounds the copy and paste areas (range F3:F10) and the mouse pointer changes to a cross hair (Figure 2-9).

FIGURE 2-9

2 Release the mouse button. Select the range H3:J3 and then point to the fill handle.

Excel copies the formula =D3*E3 to the range F4:F10 and displays the initial costs for the remaining seven stocks. The range H3:J3 is selected (Figure 2-10).

FIGURE 2-10

3 **Drag the fill handle down through the range H4:J10.**

Excel copies the three formulas =D3*G3 in cell H3, =H3-F3 in cell I3, and =I3/F3 in cell J3 to the range H4:J10 and displays the current value, gain/loss, and percentage gain/loss for the remaining seven stocks (Figure 2-11).

FIGURE 2-11

1. Select copy area, right-click copy area, click Copy on shortcut menu, select paste area, right-click paste area, click Paste on shortcut menu

2. Select copy area, click Copy button on Standard toolbar, select paste area, click Paste button on Standard toolbar

3. Select copy area, on Edit menu click Copy, select paste area, on Edit menu click Paste

4. Select copy area, press CTRL+C, select paste area, press CTRL+V

Recall that when you copy a formula, Excel adjusts the cell references so the new formulas contain references corresponding to the new location and performs calculations using the appropriate values. Thus, if you copy downward, Excel adjusts the row portion of cell references. If you copy across, then Excel adjusts the column portion of cell references. These cell references are called **relative references**.

Determining the Totals Using the AutoSum Button

The next step is to determine the totals in row 11 for the initial cost in column F, current value in column H, and gain/loss in column I. To determine the total initial cost in column F, you must sum cells F3 through F10. To do so, you can enter the function =sum(f3:f10) in cell F11, or you can select cell F11 and then click the Auto-Sum button on the Standard toolbar twice. Similar SUM functions or the AutoSum button can be used in cells H11 and I11 to determine total current value and total gain/loss, respectively. Recall from Project 1 that when you select one cell and use the AutoSum button, you must click the button twice. If you select a range, then you need only click the AutoSum button once.

TO DETERMINE TOTALS USING THE AUTOSUM BUTTON

1 Select cell F11. Click the AutoSum button twice. (Do not double-click.)

2 Select the range H11:I11. Click the AutoSum button.

The three totals display in row 11 as shown in Figure 2-12.

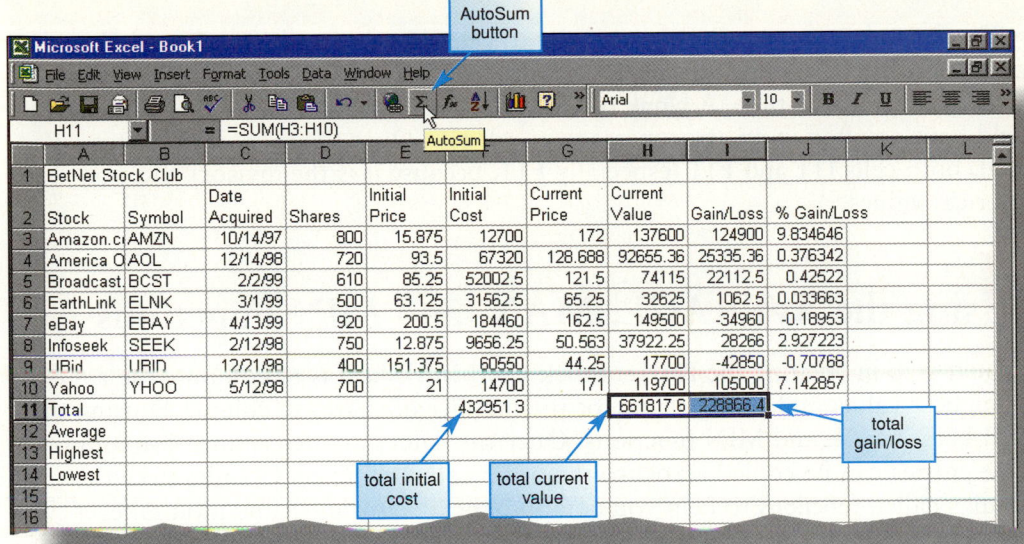

FIGURE 2-12

Rather than using the AutoSum function to calculate column totals individually, you can select all three cells before clicking the AutoSum button to calculate all three column totals at one time. To select the nonadjacent range F11, H11, and I11, select cell F11, and then, while holding down the CTRL key, drag through the range H11:I11. Next, click the AutoSum button.

Determining the Total Percentage Gain/Loss

With the totals in row 11 determined, you can copy the percentage gain/loss formula in cell J10 to cell J11 as shown in the following steps.

TO DETERMINE THE TOTAL PERCENTAGE GAIN/LOSS

1. Select cell J10 and then point to the fill handle.

2. Drag the fill handle down through cell J11.

The formula, =I10/F10, is copied to cell J11. The resultant formula in cell J11 is =I11/F11, which shows a total club gain on the club's holdings of 0.528619 or 52.8619% (Figure 2-13).

More About 2000

Selecting a Range

If you dislike dragging to select a range, press F8 and use the arrow keys to select one corner of the range and then the cell diagonally opposite it in the proposed range. Make sure you press F8 to turn the selection off after you are finished with the range or you will continue to select ranges.

FIGURE 2-13

Formulas and Functions

For more information on entering formulas and functions, visit the Excel 2000 More About Web page (www.scsite.com/ex2000/more.htm) and click Using Formulas and Functions.

The formula was not copied originally to cell J11 when cell J3 was copied to the range J4:J10 because both cells involved in the computation (I11 and F11) were blank, or zero, at the time. A **blank cell** in Excel has a numerical value of zero, which would have resulted in an error message in cell J11. Once the totals were determined, both cells I11 and F11 (especially F11, because it is the divisor) had non-zero numerical values.

Using the AVERAGE, MAX, and MIN Functions

The next step in creating the BetNet Stock Club worksheet is to compute the average, highest value, and lowest value for the number of shares in column D using the AVERAGE, MAX, and MIN functions. Once the values are determined for column D, the entries can be copied across to the other columns. Excel includes prewritten formulas called **functions** to help you compute these statistics. A function takes a value or values, performs an operation, and returns a result to the cell. The values that you use with a function are called **arguments**. All functions begin with an equal sign and include the arguments in parentheses after the function name. For example, in the function =AVERAGE(D3:D10), the function name is AVERAGE and the argument is the range D3:D10.

With Excel, you can enter functions using one of three methods: (1) the keyboard or mouse; (2) the Edit Formula box and Functions box; and (3) the Paste Function button on the Standard toolbar. The method you choose will depend on whether you can recall the function name and required arguments. In the following pages, each of the three methods will be used. The keyboard and mouse will be used to determine the average number of shares (cell D12). The Edit Formula box and Functions box will be used to determine the highest number of shares (cell D13). The Paste Function button will be used to determine the lowest number of shares (cell D14).

Determining the Average of a Range of Numbers

The **AVERAGE function** sums the numbers in the specified range and then divides the sum by the number of non-zero cells in the range. To determine the average of the numbers in the range D3:D10, use the AVERAGE function as shown in the following steps.

The AVERAGE Function

A blank cell usually is considered to be equal to zero. The statistical functions, however, ignore blank cells. Thus, in Excel, the average of three cells with values of 2, blank, and 4 is 3 or (2 + 4) / 2, and not 2 or (2 + 0 + 4) / 3.

Steps To Determine the Average of a Range of Numbers Using the Keyboard and Mouse

1 Select cell D12. Type =average(in the cell. Click cell D3, the first endpoint of the range to average. Drag through cell D10, the second endpoint of the range to average.

A marquee surrounds the range D3:D10. When you click cell D3, Excel appends cell D3 to the left parenthesis in the formula bar and surrounds cell D3 with a marquee. When you begin dragging, Excel appends to the argument a colon (:) and the cell reference of the cell where the mouse pointer is located (Figure 2-14).

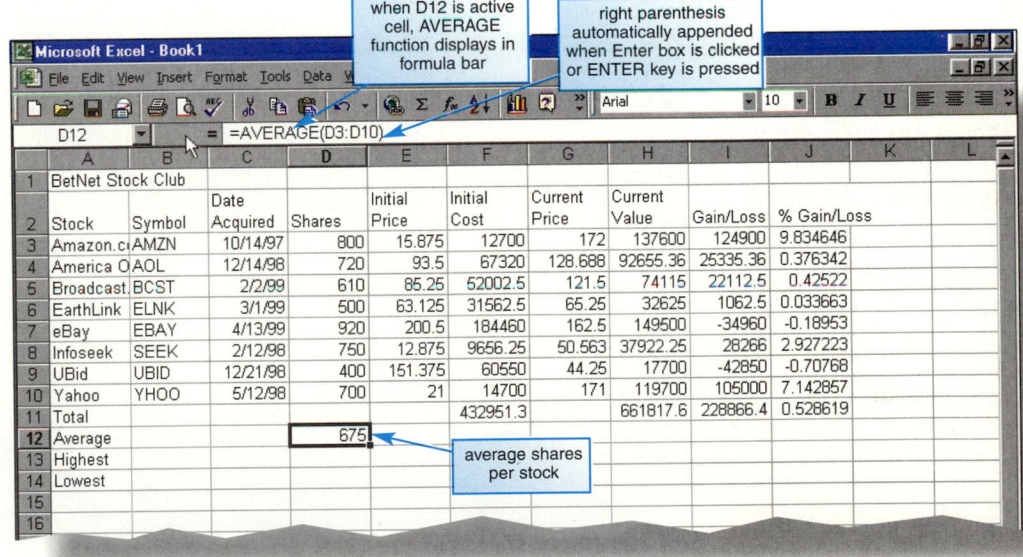

Enter box

AVERAGE function with range to average shows in active cell and formula bar

marquee surrounds selected range D3:D10

FIGURE 2-14

2 Click the Enter box.

Excel computes the average of the eight numbers in the range D3:D10 and displays the result, 675, in cell D12 (Figure 2-15). Thus, the average number of shares owned in the eight companies is 675.

when D12 is active cell, AVERAGE function displays in formula bar

right parenthesis automatically appended when Enter box is clicked or ENTER key is pressed

average shares per stock

FIGURE 2-15

Other Ways

1. Click Edit Formula box in formula bar, click AVERAGE in Functions box

2. Click Paste Function button on Standard toolbar, click AVERAGE function

The AVERAGE function requires that the range (the argument) be included within parentheses following the function name. Excel thus automatically appends the right parenthesis to complete the AVERAGE function when you click the Enter box or press the ENTER key. When you use Point mode, as in the previous steps, you cannot use the arrow keys to complete the entry. While in Point mode, the arrow keys change the selected cell reference in the formula you are creating.

Determining the Highest Number in a Range of Numbers

The next step is to select cell D13 and determine the highest (maximum) number in the range D3:D10. Excel has a function called the **MAX function** that displays the highest value in a range. Although you could enter the MAX function using the keyboard and Point mode as you did in the previous steps, an alternative method to entering the function is to use the Edit Formula box and Functions box.

 To Determine the Highest Number in a Range of Numbers Using the Edit Formula Box and Functions Box

1 **Select cell D13. Click the Edit Formula box in the formula bar. Click the Functions box arrow and then point to MAX.**

*The Name box in the formula bar changes to the **Functions box**. The Formula Palette displays immediately below the formula bar (Figure 2-16). An equal sign displays in the formula bar and the active cell, D13.*

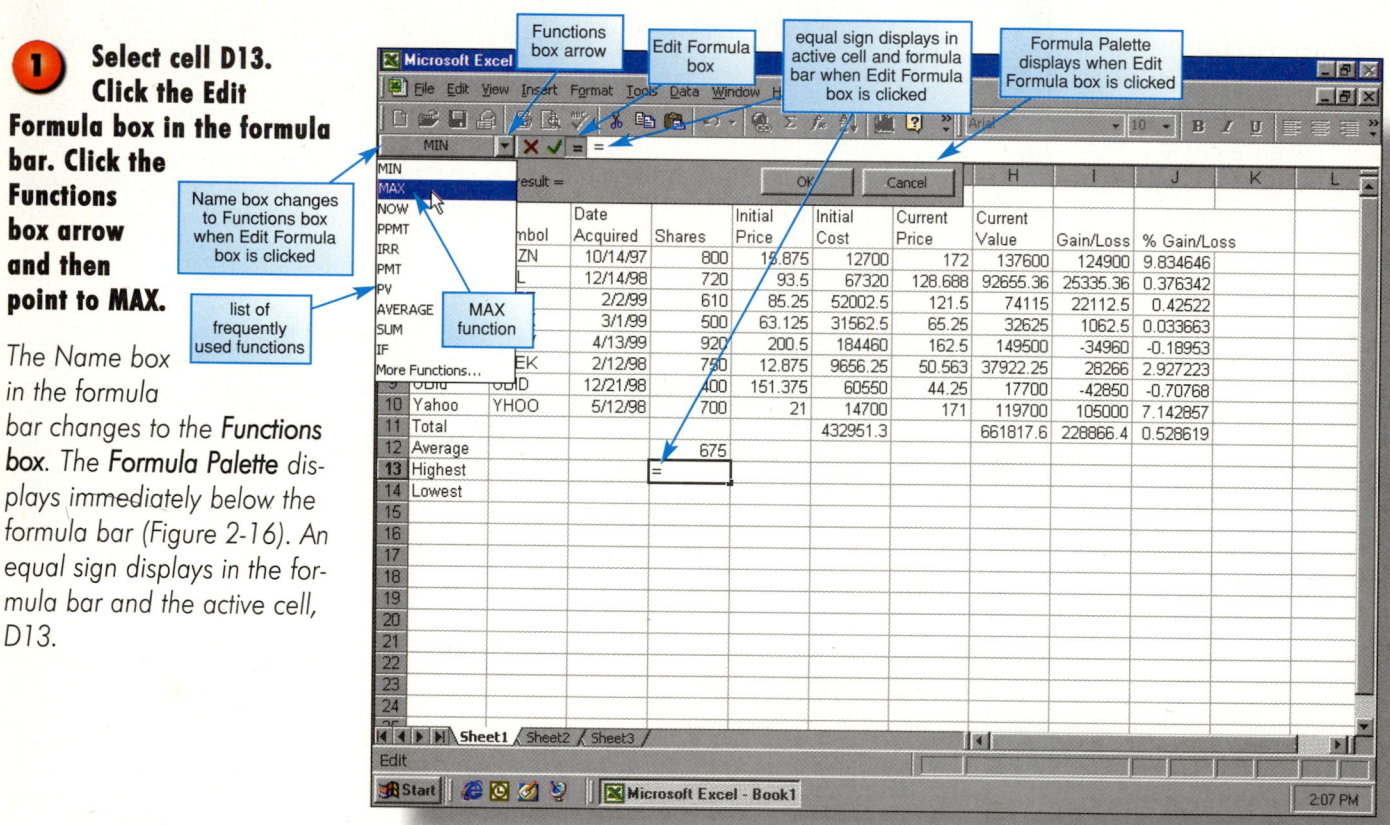

FIGURE 2-16

2 **Click MAX. When the MAX Formula Palette displays, type d3:d10 in the Number 1 edit box. Point to the OK button.**

The MAX Formula Palette displays with the range d3:d10 entered in the Number 1 edit box (Figure 2-17). The completed MAX function displays in the formula bar, and the end of the function displays in the active cell, D13.

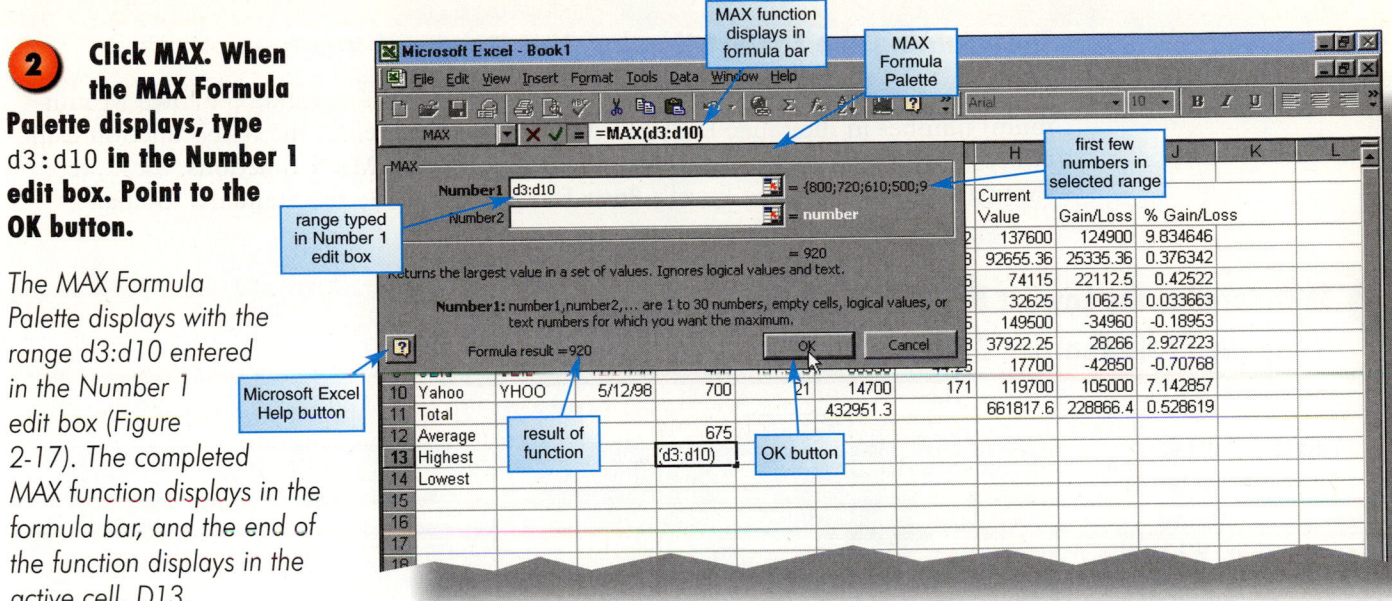

FIGURE 2-17

3 **Click the OK button.**

Excel determines that the highest value in the range D3:D10 is 920 (cell D7) and displays it in cell D13 (Figure 2-18).

FIGURE 2-18

As shown in Figure 2-17, the MAX Formula Palette displays the value the MAX function will return to cell D13. It also lists the first few numbers in the selected range, next to the Number 1 edit box.

In this example, rather than entering the MAX function, you easily could scan the range D3:D10, determine that the highest number of shares is 920, and enter the number as a constant in cell D13. The display would be the same as Figure 2-18. Because it contains a constant, cell D13 will continue to display 920, even if the values in the range D3:D10 change. If you use the MAX function, however, Excel will recalculate the highest value in the range D3:D10 each time a new value is entered into the worksheet. Manually determining the highest value in the range also would be more difficult if the club owned more stocks.

Other Ways

1. Click Paste Function button on Standard toolbar, click MAX function
2. Type MAX function in cell

Determining the Lowest Number in a Range of Numbers

Next, you will enter the **MIN function** in cell D14 to determine the lowest (minimum) number in the range D3:D10. Although you can enter the MIN function using either of the methods used to enter the AVERAGE and MAX functions, these steps show an alternative using Excel's **Paste Function button** on the Standard toolbar.

To Determine the Lowest Number in a Range of Numbers Using the Paste Function Button

1 Select cell D14. Click the Paste Function button on the Standard toolbar. When the Paste Function dialog box displays, click Statistical in the Function category list. Scroll down and click MIN in the Function name list. Point to the OK button.

The Paste Function dialog box displays (Figure 2-19). Statistical and MIN are selected. An equal sign displays in the formula bar and in the active cell, D14.

FIGURE 2-19

2 Click the OK button. When the MIN Formula Palette displays, drag it to the bottom of the screen. Click cell D3 and then drag through cell D10.

The MIN Formula Palette displays at the bottom of the screen (Figure 2-20). The range D3:D10 displays in the Number 1 edit box. The MIN function displays in the formula bar and the end of the MIN function displays in the active cell, D14.

FIGURE 2-20

Click the Enter box.

Excel determines that the lowest value in the range D3:D10 is 400 and displays it in cell D14 (Figure 2-21).

FIGURE 2-21

You can see from the previous example that using the Paste Function button on the Standard toolbar allows you to enter a function into a cell easily without requiring you to memorize its name or the required arguments. Anytime you desire to enter a function, but cannot remember the function name or the required arguments, simply click the Paste Function button on the Standard toolbar, select the desired function, and enter the arguments in the Formula Palette.

Thus far, you have learned to use the SUM, AVERAGE, MAX, and MIN functions. In addition to these four functions, Excel has more than 400 additional functions that perform just about every type of calculation you can imagine. These functions are categorized as shown in the Function category list box shown in Figure 2-19. To obtain a description of a selected function, select the Function name in the Paste Function dialog box. The description displays below the two list boxes in the dialog box.

Copying the AVERAGE, MAX, and MIN Functions

The next step is to copy the AVERAGE, MAX, and MIN functions in the range D12:D14 to the range E12:J14. The fill handle again will be used to complete the copy. The steps on the next page illustrate this procedure.

1. Click Edit Formula box in formula bar, click MIN function in Functions box
2. Type MIN function in cell

The Formula Palette

Rather than dragging the Formula Palette out of the way to use Point mode to select a range as was done in Step 2 on the previous page, you can click the Collapse Dialog button to the right of the Number 1 or Number 2 boxes to hide the Formula Palette. Once you select the range, click the button a second time to re-display the Formula Palette.

To Copy a Range of Cells Across Columns to an Adjacent Range Using the Fill Handle

1 Select the range D12:D14. Drag the fill handle in the lower-right corner of the selected range through cell J14 and continue to hold down the mouse button.

Excel displays an outline around the paste area (range D12:J14) as shown in Figure 2-22.

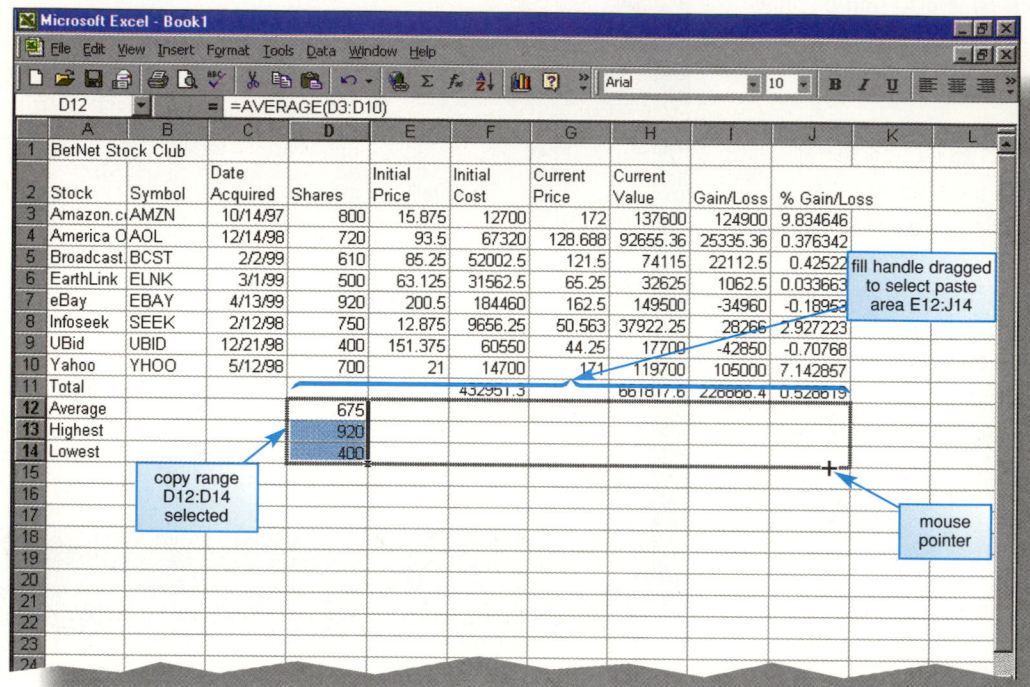

FIGURE 2-22

2 Release the mouse button.

Excel copies the three functions to the range E12:J14 (Figure 2-23).

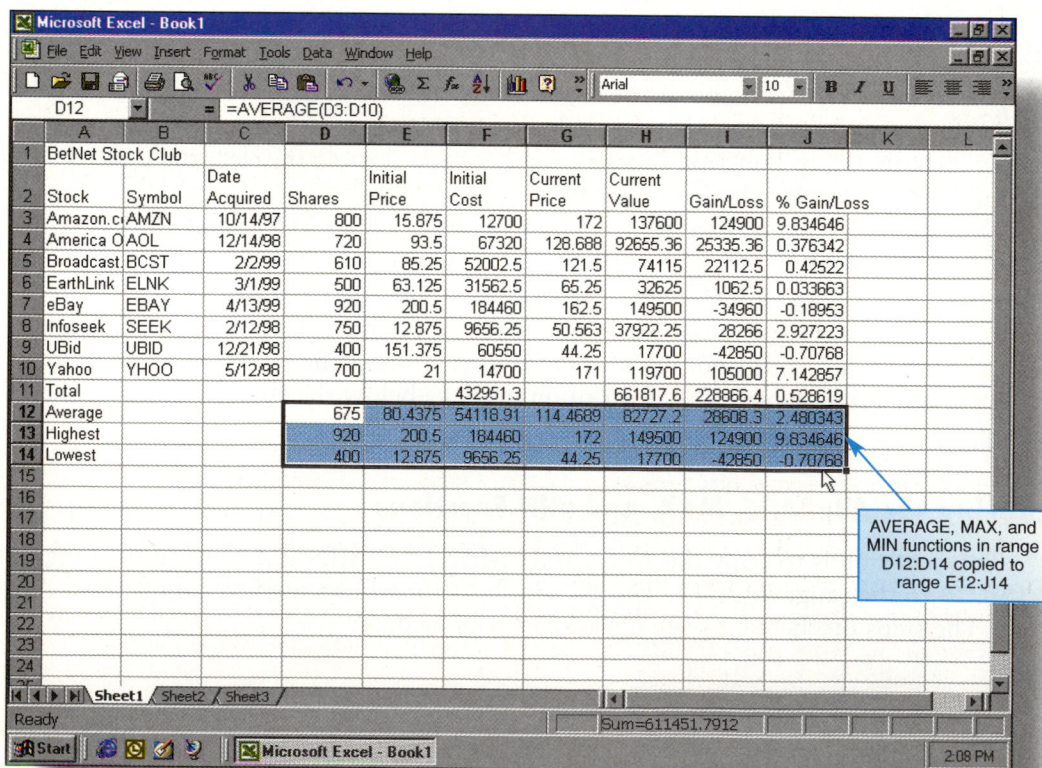

FIGURE 2-23

3 Select cell J12 and press the DELETE key to delete the average of the percentage gain/loss.

Cell J12 is blank (Figure 2-24).

4 Click the Save button on the Standard toolbar. Type BetNet Stock Club in the File name text box. If necessary, click 3½ Floppy (A:) in the Save in box. Click the Save button in the Save As dialog box.

The file name in the title bar changes to BetNet Stock Club (Figure 2-24).

Save button

BetNet Stock Club in title bar

percents in range J3:J10 cannot be averaged

	A	B	C	D	E	F	G	H	I	J	K
1	BetNet Stock Club										
2	Stock	Symbol	Date Acquired	Shares	Initial Price	Initial Cost	Current Price	Current Value	Gain/Loss	% Gain/Loss	
3	Amazon.c	AMZN	10/14/97	800	15.875	12700	172	137600	124900	9.834646	
4	America O	AOL	12/14/98	720	93.5	67320	128.688	92655.36	25335.36	0.376342	
5	Broadcast.	BCST	2/2/99	610	85.25	52002.5	121.5	74115	22112.5	0.42522	
6	EarthLink	ELNK	3/1/99	500	63.125	31562.5	65.25	32625	1062.5	0.033663	
7	eBay	EBAY	4/13/99	920	200.5	184460	162.5	149500	-34960	-0.18953	
8	Infoseek	SEEK	2/12/98	750	12.875	9656.25	50.563	37922.25	28266	2.927223	
9	UBid	UBID	12/21/98	400	151.375	60550	44.25	17700	-42850	-0.70768	
10	Yahoo	YHOO	5/12/98	700	21	14700	171	119700	105000	7.142857	
11	Total					432951.3		661817.6	228866.4	0.528619	
12	Average			675	80.4375	54118.91	114.4689	82727.2	28608.3		
13	Highest			920	200.5	184460	172	149500	124900	9.834646	
14	Lowest			400	12.875	9656.25	44.25	17700	-42850	-0.70768	

Ready

Start Microsoft Excel - Bet... 2:09 PM

FIGURE 2-24

The average of the percentage gain/loss in cell J12 was deleted in Step 3 because an average of percents of this type is mathematically invalid.

Remember that Excel adjusts the ranges in the copied functions so each function refers to the column of numbers above it. Review the numbers in rows 12 through 14 in Figure 2-24. You should see that the functions in each column return the appropriate values, based on the numbers in rows 3 through 10 of that column.

This concludes entering the data and formulas into the worksheet. After saving the file, the worksheet remains on the screen with the file name, BetNet Stock Club, in the title bar. You immediately can continue with the next activity.

Verifying Formulas

One of the most common mistakes made with Excel is to include a wrong cell reference in a formula. Excel has two methods, the Auditing commands and Range Finder, to verify that a formula references the cells you want it to reference. The **Auditing commands** allow you to trace precedents and trace dependents. The **Trace Precedents command** highlights the cells in the worksheet that are referenced by the formula in the active cell. The **Trace Dependents command** highlights the cells with formulas in the worksheet that reference the active cell. The **Remove all Arrows command** removes the highlights.

As with the Trace Precedents command, **Range Finder** can be used to check which cells are being referenced in the formula assigned to the active cell. One of the advantages of Range Finder is that it allows you to make immediate changes to the cells referenced in a formula.

More About

Verifying Formulas

If you lack confidence in your mathematical abilities, then you will find Range Finder and the Auditing commands to be useful to ensure the formulas you enter reference the correct cells.

Verifying a Formula Using Range Finder

To use Range Finder to verify that a formula contains the intended cell references, double-click the cell with the formula you want to check. Excel responds by highlighting the cells referenced in the formula so you can check that the correct cells are being used. The following steps use Range Finder to check the formula in cell J3.

To Verify a Formula Using Range Finder

1 **Double-click cell J3.**

Excel responds by displaying the cells in the worksheet referenced by the formula in cell J3 using different color borders (Figure 2-25). The different colors allow you to see easily which cells are being referenced by the formula in cell J3.

2 **Click any cell or press the ESC key to quit Range Finder.**

cells referenced in formula in active cell are highlighted with corresponding colors

color of cell references corresponds to color of highlighted cells

	A	B	C	D	E	F	G	H	I	J	K
1	BetNet Stock Club										
2	Stock	Symbol	Date Acquired	Shares	Initial Price	Initial Cost	Current Price	Current Value	Gain/Loss	% Gain/Loss	
3	Amazon.c	AMZN	10/14/97	800	15.875	12700	172	137600	124900	=I3/F3	
4	America O	AOL	12/14/98	720	93.5	67320	128.688	92655.36	25335.36	0.376342	
5	Broadcast	BCST	2/2/99	610	85.25	52002.5	121.5	74115	22112.5	0.42522	
6	EarthLink	ELNK	3/1/99	500	63.125	31562.5	65.25	32625	1062.5	0.033663	
7	eBay	EBAY	4/13/99	920	200.5	184460	162.5	149500	-34960	-0.18953	
8	Infoseek	SEEK	2/12/98	750	12.875	9656.25	50.563	37922.25	28266	2.927223	
9	UBid	UBID	12/21/98	400	151.375	60550	44.25	17700	-42850	-0.70768	
10	Yahoo	YHOO	5/12/98	700	21	14700	171	119700	105000	7.142857	
11	Total					432951.3		661817.6	228866.4	0.528619	
12	Average			675	80.4375	54118.91	114.4689	82727.2	28608.3		
13	Highest			920	200.5	184460	172	149500	124900	9.834646	
14	Lowest			400	12.875	9656.25	44.25	17700	-42850	-0.70768	

FIGURE 2-25

Not only does Range Finder show you the cells referenced in the formula in cell J3, but you can drag the colored borders to other cells and Excel will change the cell references in the formula to the newly selected cells. If you use Range Finder to change cells referenced in a formula, press the ENTER key to complete the edit.

Verifying a Formula Using the Auditing Commands

The following steps show how to use the Trace Precedent and Trace Dependent commands to verify a formula is referencing the correct cells and to determine the cells that reference the active cell.

To Verify a Formula Using the Auditing Commands

1 If necessary, click cell J3. Click Tools on the menu bar and then click the down arrows at the bottom of the Tools menu to display the full menu. Point to Auditing. When the Auditing submenu displays, point to Trace Precedents.

The Auditing submenu displays as shown in Figure 2-26.

FIGURE 2-26

Click Trace Precedents.

Blue rounded tracer arrows that point upward display along a blue line in the cells (F3 and I3) that are used by the formula in the active cell, J3 (Figure 2-27). The horizontal arrow in cell J3 at the right end of the blue line indicates the active cell. You can use the blue line and arrows to verify that the correct cells are being used in the formula.

FIGURE 2-27

3 **Click Tools on the menu bar and then point to Auditing. When the Auditing submenu displays, click Trace Dependents.**

A blue rounded tracer arrow that points upward displays in the active cell, J3. A blue line extends downward to the two cells, J13 and J14 that depend on the value in cell J3. Cells J13 and J14 have arrowheads (Figure 2-28).

4 **Click Tools on the menu bar and then point to Auditing. When the Auditing submenu displays, click Remove All Arrows. Click cell A16.**

FIGURE 2-28

To change the active cell to the one at the other end of the blue line, double-click the blue line. This technique gives you a quick way to move from the active cell to one that provides data to the active cell. This is especially helpful in large worksheets.

If you click the Trace Precedents command a second time, Excel displays tracer arrows that show a second level of cells that are indirectly supplying data to the active cell. The same applies to the Trace Dependents command, only it shows the next level of cells that are dependent on the active cell.

Formatting the Worksheet

Although the worksheet contains the appropriate data, formulas, and functions, the text and numbers need to be formatted to improve their appearance and readability.

In Project 1, you used the AutoFormat command to format the majority of the worksheet. This section describes how to change the unformatted worksheet in Figure 2-29a to the formatted worksheet in Figure 2-29b using the Formatting toolbar and Format Cells command.

(a) Unformatted Worksheet

(b) Formatted Worksheet

FIGURE 2-29

Labels in figure:
- blue background
- 36-point Bookman Old Style white font
- heavy border surrounds worksheet title
- thick bottom border
- column titles centered
- negative numbers display in bold with red background
- row height increased
- thick bottom border
- data centered in cells
- numbers formatted
- Currency style format
- Comma style format
- Percentage style format
- column width changed

The following outlines the type of formatting that is required in Project 2:

1. Worksheet title
   a. Font type — bold Bookman Old Style
   b. Font size — 36
   c. Font style — bold
   d. Alignment — center across columns A through J
   e. Background color (range A1:J1) — dark blue
   f. Font color — white
   g. Border — thick box border around range A1:J1
2. Column titles
   a. Font style — bold
   b. Alignment — center
   c. Border — thick bottom border on row 2
3. Data
   a. Alignment — center data in column B
   b. Numbers in top row (columns E through I in row 3) — Currency style
   c. Numbers below top row (rows 4 through 10) — Comma style
   d. Border — thick bottom border on row 10

More About 2000

Choosing Colors

Knowing how people perceive colors helps you emphasize parts of your worksheet. Warmer colors (red and orange) tend to reach toward the reader. Cooler colors (blue, green, and violet) tend to pull away from the reader. Bright colors jump out of a dark background and are easiest to see. White or yellow text on a dark blue, green, purple, or black background is ideal.

4. Total line
   a. Numbers — Currency style
5. Function lines
   a. Numbers — Currency style in columns E through I
6. Percentages in column J
   a. Numbers — Percentage style; if a cell in range J3:J10 is less than zero, then bold font and color background of cell red
7. Column widths
   a. Columns A through E — best fit
   b. Columns F, H through J — 12.00 characters
   c. Column G — 8.71 characters
8. Row heights
   a. Row 1 — 61.50 points
   b. Rows 2 — 36.00 points
   c. Row 12 —24.00 points
   d. Remaining rows — default

Except for the Currency style assigned to the functions in rows 12 through 14 and the conditional formatting in column J, all of the listed formats can be assigned to cells using the Formatting toolbar and mouse.

Changing the Font and Centering the Worksheet Title

When developing presentation-quality worksheets, different fonts often are used in the same worksheet. Excel allows you to change the font of individual characters in a cell or all the characters in a cell, in a range of cells, or in the entire worksheet. To emphasize the worksheet title in cell A1, the font type, size, and style are changed and the worksheet title is centered as described in the following steps.

To Change the Font and Center the Worksheet Title

1 Click cell A1. Double-click the move handle on the left side of the Formatting toolbar to display it in its entirety. Click the Font box arrow on the Formatting toolbar and then point to Bookman Old Style (or Courier New if your system does not have Bookman Old Style).

The Font list displays with Bookman Old Style highlighted (Figure 2-30).

FIGURE 2-30

2 **Click Bookman Old Style (or Courier New). Click the Font Size box arrow on the Formatting toolbar and then point to 36.**

The characters in cell A1 display using Bookman Old Style (or Courier New). The font size 36 is highlighted in the Font Size list (Figure 2-31).

FIGURE 2-31

3 **Click 36. Click the Bold button on the Formatting toolbar.**

The text in cell A1 displays in 36-point Bookman Old Style bold font. Excel automatically increases the height of row 1 so that the larger characters fit in the cells (Figure 2-32).

FIGURE 2-32

4 Select the range A1:J1. Click the Merge and Center button on the Formatting toolbar.

Excel merges the cells A1 through J1 to create a new cell A1 and centers the worksheet title across columns A through J (Figure 2-33).

FIGURE 2-33

You can change a font type, size, or style at any time while the worksheet is active. Some Excel users prefer to change fonts before they enter any data. Others change the font while they are building the worksheet or after they have entered all the data.

Changing the Worksheet Title Background and Font Colors and Applying an Outline Border

The final formats to be assigned to the worksheet title are the dark blue background color, white font color, and thick box border (Figure 2-29b on page E 2.27). Perform the following steps to complete the formatting of the worksheet title.

 To Change the Title Background and Font Colors and Apply an Outline Border

1 With cell A1 selected, click the Fill Color button arrow on the Formatting toolbar and then point to the color Dark Blue (column 6, row 1) on the Fill Color palette.

The Fill Color palette displays (Figure 2-34).

FIGURE 2-34

2 **Click the color Dark Blue. Click the Font Color button arrow on the Formatting toolbar. Point to the color White (column 8, row 5) on the Font Color palette.**

The background color of cell A1 changes from white to dark blue. The Font Color palette displays (Figure 2-35).

FIGURE 2-35

3 **Click the color White. Click the Borders button arrow on the Formatting toolbar and then point to the Thick Box Border button (column 4, row 3) on the Borders palette.**

The font in the worksheet title changes from black to white. The Borders palette displays (Figure 2-36).

FIGURE 2-36

4 **Click the Thick Box Border button. Click cell A2 to deselect cell A1.**

Excel displays a thick box border around cell A1 (Figure 2-37).

	A	B	C	D	E	F	G	H	I	J	K	L
1					**BetNet Stock Club**							
2	Stock	Symbol	Date Acquired	Shares	Initial Price	Initial Cost	Current Price	Current Value	Gain/Loss	% Gain/Loss		
3	Amazon.c	AMZN	10/14/97	800	15.875	12700	172	137600	124900	9.834646		
4	America O	AOL	12/14/98	720	93.5	67320	128.688	92655.36	25335.36	0.376342		
5	Broadcast.	BCST	2/2/99	610	85.25	52002.5	121.5	74115	22112.5	0.42522		
6	EarthLink	ELNK	3/1/99	500	63.125	31562.5	65.25	32625	1062.5	0.033663		
7	eBay	EBAY	4/13/99	920	200.5	184460	162.5	149500	-34960	-0.18953		
8	Infoseek	SEEK	2/12/98	750	12.875	9656.25	50.563	37922.25	28266	2.927223		
9	UBid	UBID	12/21/98	400	151.375	60550	44.25	17700	-42850	-0.70768		
10	Yahoo	YHOO	5/12/98	700	21	14700	171	119700	105000	7.142857		
11	Total					432951.3		661817.6	228866.4	0.528619		
12	Average			675	80.4375	54118.91	114.4689	82727.2	28608.3			
13	Highest			920	200.5	184460	172	149500	124900	9.834646		
14	Lowest			400	12.875	9656.25	44.25	17700	-42850	-0.70768		

thick box border surrounds worksheet title in cell A1

FIGURE 2-37

You can remove borders, such as the thick box border around cell A1, by selecting the range and clicking the No Border button on the Borders palette. You can remove a background color by selecting the range, clicking the Fill Color button arrow on the Formatting toolbar, and clicking No Fill on the Fill Color palette. The same technique allows you to change the font color back to Excel's default, except you use the Font Color button arrow and click Automatic.

Applying Formats to the Column Titles

According to Figure 2-29b on page E 2.27, the column titles are bold, centered, and have a thick bottom border (underline). The following steps assign these formats to the column titles.

Steps **To Bold, Center, and Underline the Column Titles**

 Select the range A2:J2. Click the Bold button on the Formatting toolbar. Click the Center button on the Formatting toolbar. Click the Borders button arrow on the Formatting toolbar and then point to the Thick Bottom Border button (column 2, row 2) on the Borders palette.

The column titles in row 2 are bold and centered. The Borders palette displays (Figure 2-38).

2 **Click the Thick Bottom Border button.**

Excel adds a thick bottom border to the range A2:J2.

FIGURE 2-38

You can align the contents of cells in several different ways. Left alignment, center alignment, and right alignment are the more frequently used alignments. In fact, these three alignments are used so often that Excel has Left Align, Center, and Right Align buttons on the Formatting toolbar. In addition to aligning the contents of a cell horizontally, you also can align the contents of a cell vertically. You even can rotate the contents of a cell to various angles. For more information on alignment, on the Format menu click Cells and then click the Alignment tab.

Centering the Stock Symbols and Formatting the Numbers in the Worksheet

With the column titles formatted, the next step is to center the stock symbols in column B and format the numbers. If a cell entry is short, such as the stock symbols in column B, centering the entries within their respective columns improves the appearance of the worksheet. The following steps center the data in cells B3 to B10.

TO CENTER DATA IN CELLS

1 Select the range B3:B10. Click the Center button on the Formatting toolbar.

The stock symbols in column B are centered (Figure 2-39 on the next page).

Other Ways

1. Right-click cell, click Format Cells on shortcut menu, click Alignment tab, click Center in Horizontal list, click Font tab, click Bold in Font style list, click Border tab, click desired border, click OK button

2. On Format menu click Cells, click Alignment tab, click Center in Horizontal list, click Font tab, click Bold in Font style list, click Border tab, click desired border, click OK button

3. Press CTRL+1, click Alignment tab, click Center in Horizontal list, click Font tab, click Bold in Font style list, click Border tab, click desired border, click OK button

FIGURE 2-39

**Aligning
and Rotating
Text in Cells**

Besides aligning text horizontally in a cell, you can align text vertically (top, center, bottom, or justify). You can also rotate text. To align vertically or rotate the text, click Format Cells on the shortcut menu, click the Alignment tab, and then select the type of alignment you want.

Rather than selecting the range B3:B10 in the previous step, you could have clicked the column B heading immediately above cell B1, and then clicked the Center button on the Formatting toolbar. In this case, all cells in column B down to cell B65536 would have been assigned center alignment.

When using Excel, you can use the buttons on the Formatting toolbar to format numbers as dollar amounts, whole numbers with comma placement, and percentages. Customized numeric formats also can be assigned using the **Cells command** on the Format menu or the **Format Cells command** on the shortcut menu.

As shown in Figure 2-29b on page E 2.27, the worksheet is formatted to resemble an accounting report. For example, in columns E through I, the first row of numbers (row 3), the totals (row 11), and the rows below the totals (rows 13 and 14) display with dollar signs, while the remaining numbers (rows 4 through 10) in these columns do not. To display a dollar sign in a number, you should use the Currency style format.

The **Currency style format** displays a dollar sign to the left of the number, inserts a comma every three positions to the left of the decimal point, and displays numbers to the nearest cent (hundredths place). The **Currency Style button** on the Formatting toolbar will assign the desired Currency style format. When you use the Currency Style button, Excel displays a **fixed dollar sign** to the far left in the cell, often with spaces between it and the first digit. To assign a **floating dollar sign** that displays immediately to the left of the first digit with no spaces, you must use the Cells command on the Format menu or the Format Cells command on the shortcut menu. The project specifications call for a fixed dollar sign to be assigned to the numbers in columns E through I in rows 3 and 11, and a floating dollar sign to be assigned to the monetary amounts in columns E through I in rows 12 through 14.

To display monetary amounts with commas and no dollar signs, you will want to use the Comma style format. The **Comma style format** inserts a comma every three positions to the left of the decimal point and displays numbers to the nearest hundredths (cents).

The remainder of this section describes how to format the numbers as shown in Figure 2-29b on page E 2.27.

Formatting Numbers Using the Formatting Toolbar

The following steps show how to assign formats using the Currency Style button and the Comma Style button on the Formatting toolbar.

 Steps To Apply a Currency Style Format and Comma Style Format Using the Formatting Toolbar

1 Select the range E3:I3. While holding down the CTRL key, select the nonadjacent range F11:I11. Point to the Currency Style button on the Formatting toolbar.

The nonadjacent ranges display as shown in Figure 2-40.

2 Click the Currency Style button. Select the range E4:I10 and then point to the Comma Style button on the Formatting toolbar.

Excel automatically increases the width of columns F, H, and I to best fit, so the numbers assigned the Currency style format will fit in the cells (Figure 2-41). The range E4:I10 is selected.

FIGURE 2-40

FIGURE 2-41

3 Click the Comma Style button. Select the range A10:J10 and then click the Borders button on the Formatting toolbar.

Excel assigns the Comma style format to the range E4:I10 and a thick bottom border to row 10.

4 Click cell E3. Click the Increase Decimal button on the Formatting toolbar. Do the same to cell G3. Select the range E4:E10. Click the Increase Decimal button on the Formatting toolbar. Do the same to the range G4:G10. Click cell E12 to deselect the range G4:G10.

The initial prices and current prices display with three decimal positions (Figure 2-42).

FIGURE 2-42

Other Ways

1. Right-click range, click Format Cells on shortcut menu, click Number tab, click Currency in Category list, click OK button

2. On Format menu click Cells, click Number tab, click Currency in Category list, click OK button

The **Increase Decimal button** on the Formatting toolbar is used to display additional decimal places in a cell. Each time you click the Increase Decimal button, Excel adds a decimal place to the selected cell. The **Decrease Decimal button** removes a decimal place from the selected cell each time it is clicked.

In Step 3, you clicked the Borders button on the Formatting toolbar because the Borders button is set to the thick bottom border that was assigned earlier to row 2.

The Currency Style button assigns a fixed dollar sign to the numbers in the ranges E3:I3 and F11:I11. In each cell in these ranges, the dollar sign displays to the far left with spaces between it and the first digit in the cell. Excel automatically rounds a number to fit the selected format.

Formatting Numbers Using the Format Cells Command on the Shortcut Menu

Thus far, you have been introduced to two ways of formatting numbers in a worksheet. In Project 1, you formatted the numbers using the AutoFormat command on the Format menu. In the previous section, you used the Formatting toolbar as a means of applying a format style. A third way to format numbers is to use the Cells command on the Format menu or the Format Cells command on the shortcut menu. Using either command allows you to display numbers in almost any format you want. The following steps show you how to use the Format Cells command to apply the Currency style format with a floating dollar sign to the totals in the range E12:I14.

Steps: To Apply a Currency Style Format with a Floating Dollar Sign Using the Format Cells Command

1 Select the range E12:I14. Right-click the selected range. Point to Format Cells on the shortcut menu.

The shortcut menu displays (Figure 2-43).

FIGURE 2-43

2 Click Format Cells. Click the Number tab in the Format Cells dialog box. Click Currency in the Category list, click the third style ($1,234.10) in the Negative numbers list, and then point to the OK button.

The Format Cells dialog box displays (Figure 2-44).

FIGURE 2-44

3 **Click the OK button.**

The worksheet displays with the totals in rows 12 through 14 assigned the Currency style format with a floating dollar sign (Figure 2-45).

FIGURE 2-45

Formatting Numbers as You Enter Them

You can format numbers when you enter them by entering a dollar sign ($), comma (,), or percent sign (%) as part of the number. For example, if you enter 1500, Excel displays 1500. If you enter $1500, however, Excel displays $1,500.

Recall that a floating dollar sign always displays immediately to the left of the first digit, and the fixed dollar sign always displays on the left side of the cell. Cell E3, for example, has a fixed dollar sign, while cell E12 has a floating dollar sign. Also recall that, while cells E3 and E12 both were assigned a Currency style format, the Currency style was assigned to cell E3 using the Currency Style button on the Formatting toolbar. The result is a fixed dollar sign. The Currency style was assigned to cell E12 using the Format Cells dialog box and the result is a floating dollar sign.

As shown in Figure 2-44 on the previous page, 12 categories of formats are available from which you can choose. Once you select a category, you can select the number of decimal places, whether or not a dollar sign should display, and how negative numbers should display.

Selecting the appropriate negative numbers format in Step 2 is important, because doing so adds a space to the right of the number (as do the Currency Style and Comma Style buttons). Some of the available negative number formats do not align the numbers in the worksheet on the decimal points.

The negative number format selected in the previous set of steps displays in cell I14, which has a negative entry. The third selection in the Negative numbers list box (Figure 2-44) purposely was chosen to agree with the negative number format assigned to cell I9 using the Comma Style button.

Formatting Numbers Using the Percent Style Button and Increase Decimal Button

The last entry in the worksheet that needs to be formatted is the percent gain/loss in column J. Currently, the numbers in column J display as a decimal fraction (9.834646 in cell J3). Follow these steps to change to the Percent style format with two decimal places.

 To Apply a Percent Style Format

1 **Select the range J3:J14. Click the Percent Style button on the Formatting toolbar.**

The numbers in column J display as a rounded whole percent.

2 **Click the Increase Decimal button on the Formatting toolbar twice.**

The numbers in column J display with two decimal places (Figure 2-46).

FIGURE 2-46

The **Percent Style button** on the Formatting toolbar is used to display a value determined by multiplying the cell entry by 100, rounding the result to the nearest percent, and adding a percent sign. For example, when cell J3 is formatted using the Increase Decimal button, the value 9.834646 displays as 983.46%. While they do not display, Excel does maintain all the decimal places for computational purposes. Thus, if cell J3 is used in a formula, the value used for computational purposes is 9.834646.

The last formatting requirement is to display the negative percents in column J in bold with a red background so they stand out. The **Conditional Formatting command** on the Format menu will be used to complete this task.

 More About

Rounding Numbers

When you instruct Excel to display a certain number of digits, it does maintain all the decimal places for computational purposes. For this reason, you may find a column sum to be off by a penny, because it is displaying data rounded to a specified number of digits, but it is using all the decimal places in the computation.

More About 2000

Conditional Formatting

You can conditionally assign any format to a cell, a range of cells, the worksheet, or an entire workbook. If the value of the cell changes and no longer meets the specified condition, Excel temporarily suppresses the formats that highlight that condition.

Conditional Formatting

Excel lets you apply formatting that appears only when the value in a cell meets conditions that you specify. This type of formatting is called **conditional formatting**. You can apply conditional formatting to a cell, a range of cells, the entire worksheet, or the entire workbook. Usually, you apply it to a range of cells that contains values you want to highlight if conditions warrant. For example, you can instruct Excel to bold and change the color of the background of a cell if the value in the cell meets a condition, such as being less than zero. For example, assume you assign the range J3:J10 the following condition:

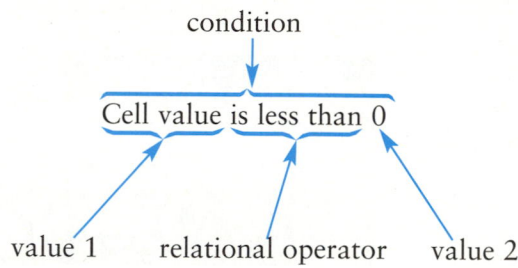

A **condition,** which is made up of two values and a relational operator, is true or false for each cell in the range. If the condition is true, then Excel applies the formatting. If the condition is false, then Excel suppresses the formatting. What makes conditional formatting so powerful is that the cell's appearance can change as you enter new values in the worksheet.

The following steps show how to assign conditional formatting to the range J3:J10. In this case, any cell value less than zero will cause the number in the cell to display in bold with a red background.

To Apply Conditional Formatting

1 Select the range J3:J10. Click Format on the menu bar and then point to Conditional Formatting.

The Format menu displays (Figure 2-47).

FIGURE 2-47

2 Click Conditional Formatting. If necessary, click the leftmost text box arrow and then click Cell Value is. Click the middle text box arrow and then click less than. Type 0 in the rightmost text box. Point to the Format button.

The Conditional Formatting dialog box displays as shown in Figure 2-48.

FIGURE 2-48

3 Click the Format button. When the Format Cells dialog box displays, click the Font tab and then click Bold in the Font style list. Click the Patterns tab. Click the color red (column 1, row 3). Point to the OK button.

The Patterns sheet in the Format Cells dialog box displays as shown in Figure 2-49.

FIGURE 2-49

4 **Click the OK button. When the Conditional Formatting dialog box displays, point to the OK button.**

The Conditional Formatting dialog box displays as shown in Figure 2-50.

FIGURE 2-50

5 **Click the OK button. Click cell A16 to deselect the range J3:J10.**

Excel assigns the conditional format to the range J3:J10. Any negative value in this range displays in bold with a red background (Figure 2-51).

FIGURE 2-51

In Figure 2-50, the **Preview window** in the Conditional Formatting dialog box shows the format that will be assigned to any cells in the range J3:J10 that have a value less than zero. This preview allows you to modify the format before you click the OK button. The **Add button** in the Conditional Formatting dialog box allows you to add up to two additional conditions. The **Delete button** allows you to delete one or more active conditions.

The middle text box in the Conditional Formatting dialog box contains the relational operator. The eight different relational operators from which you can choose are summarized in Table 2-4.

Table 2-4 Summary of Conditional Formatting Relational Operators	
RELATIONAL OPERATOR	DESCRIPTION
Between	Cell value is between two numbers
Not between	Cell value is not between two numbers
Equal to	Cell value is equal to a number
Not equal to	Cell value is not equal to a number
Greater than	Cell value is greater than a number
Less than	Cell value is less than a number
Greater than or equal to	Cell value is greater than or equal to a number
Less than or equal to	Cell value is less than or equal to a number

With the number formatting complete, the next step is to change the column widths and row heights to make the worksheet easier to read.

Changing the Widths of Columns and Heights of Rows

When Excel starts and the blank worksheet displays on the screen, all of the columns have a default width of 8.43 characters, or 64 pixels. A **character** is defined as a letter, number, symbol, or punctuation mark in 10-point Arial font, the default font used by Excel. An average of 8.43 characters in this font will fit in a cell. Another measure is **pixels**, which is short for picture element. A pixel is a dot on the screen that contains a color. The size of the dot is based on your screen's resolution. At a common resolution of 800 × 600, 800 pixels display across the screen and 600 pixels display down the screen for a total of 480,000 pixels. It is these 480,000 pixels that form the font and other items you see on the screen.

The default row height in a blank worksheet is 12.75 points (or 17 pixels). Recall from Project 1 that a point is equal to 1/72 of an inch. Thus, 12.75 points is equal to about one-sixth of an inch. You can change the width of the columns or height of the rows at any time to make the worksheet easier to read or to ensure that an entry displays properly in a cell.

Changing the Widths of Columns

When changing the column width, you can set the width manually or you can instruct Excel to size the column to best fit. **Best fit** means that the width of the column will be increased or decreased so the widest entry will fit in the column. When the format you assign to a cell causes the entry to exceed the width of a column, Excel automatically changes the column width to best fit. This happened earlier when the Currency style format was used (Figure 2-41 on page E 2.35). If you do not assign a cell in a column a format, the width will remain 8.43 characters as is the case in columns A through D. To set a column width to best fit, double-click the right boundary of the column heading above row 1.

Sometimes, you may prefer more or less white space in a column than best fit provides. Excel thus allows you to change column widths manually. The following changes will be made to the column widths: columns A through E to best fit; column F to 12.00 characters, column G to 8.71 characters; and columns H through J to 12.00 characters.

More About

Painting Formats

Painting is not an envious chore. In Excel, however, if you know how to paint, you can save yourself time and effort when formatting a worksheet. For example, if you see a cell that has the format you want to assign to another cell or range of cells, click the cell with the desired format, click the Format Painter button on the Standard toolbar, and then click the cell or drag through the cells you want to paint the format with.

More About

Best Fit

Although Excel automatically increases the width of a column or the height of a row when you assign a format to a cell, it will not increase the column width or row height when a cell contains a formula and you change the value of a cell that is referenced in the formula. For example, if you change the number of shares in cell D3 from 800 to 10,0000, Excel will recalculate the formulas and display number signs (#) for the initial cost and gain/lost because the results of the formulas have more digits than can fit in the cell. You can fix the problem by double-clicking the right boundary of the column heading to change to best fit.

To Change the Widths of Columns

1 **Drag through column headings A through E above row 1. Point to the boundary on the right side of column heading E.**

The mouse pointer becomes a split double arrow (Figure 2-52).

FIGURE 2-52

2 **Double-click the right boundary of column heading E. Click cell A16 to deselect columns A through E. Point to the boundary on the right side of the column F heading above row 1. Drag to the right until the ScreenTip, Width: 12.00 (89 pixels), displays.**

A dotted line shows the proposed right border of column F (Figure 2-53).

FIGURE 2-53

3 **Release the mouse button. Point to the boundary on the right side of the column G heading above row 1. Drag to the left until the ScreenTip, Width: 8.71 (66 pixels), displays.**

A dotted line shows the proposed right border of column G (Figure 2-54).

FIGURE 2-54

4 **Release the mouse button. Drag through column headings H through J above row 1. Point to the boundary on the right side of column J. Drag to the right until the ScreenTip, Width: 12.00 (89 pixels), displays.**

A dotted line shows the proposed right border of columns H through J (Figure 2-55).

FIGURE 2-55

5 **Release the mouse button. Click cell A16 to deselect columns H through J.**

The worksheet displays with the new columns widths (Figure 2-56).

| width of columns A through E set to best fit | width of column F set to 12.00 | width of column G set to 8.71 | width of columns H through J set to 12.00 |

FIGURE 2-56

If you want to increase or decrease the column width significantly, you can use the Column Width command on the shortcut menu to change a column's width. To use this command, however, you must select one or more entire columns. As shown in the previous set of steps, you select entire columns by dragging through the column headings above row 1.

A column width can vary from zero (0) to 255 characters. If you decrease the column width to zero, the column is hidden. **Hiding** is a technique you can use to hide data that might not be relevant to a particular report or sensitive data that you do not want others to see. When you print a worksheet, hidden columns do not print. To display a hidden column, position the mouse pointer to the left of the column heading boundary where the hidden column is located and then drag to the right.

Changing the Heights of Rows

When you increase the font size of a cell entry, such as the title in cell A1, Excel automatically increases the row height to best fit so the characters display properly. Recall that Excel did this earlier (Figure 2-2 on page E 2.8) when you entered multiple lines in a cell in row 2.

You also can increase or decrease the height of a row manually to improve the appearance of the worksheet. The following steps show how to improve the appearance of the worksheet by increasing the height of row 1 to 61.50 points, row 2 to 36.00 points, and row 12 to 24.00 points. Perform the following steps to change the heights of these three rows.

To Change the Height of a Row by Dragging

1 **Point to the boundary below row heading 1. Drag down until the ScreenTip, Height: 61.50 (82 pixels), displays.**

The mouse pointer changes to a split double arrow (Figure 2-57). The distance between the dotted line and the top of row 1 indicates the proposed row height for row 1.

FIGURE 2-57

2 **Release the mouse button. Point to the boundary below row heading 2. Drag down until the ScreenTip, Height: 36.00 (48 pixels), displays.**

Excel displays a horizontal dotted line (Figure 2-58). The distance between the dotted line and the top of row 2 indicates the proposed height for row 2.

FIGURE 2-58

3 Release the mouse button. Point to the boundary below row heading 12. Drag down until the ScreenTip, **Height: 24.00 (32 pixels)**, displays. Release the mouse button.

The Total row and the Average row have additional white space between them, which improves the appearance of the worksheet. The formatting of the worksheet is complete (Figure 2-59).

row height is 36.00 points

added white space improves appearance of worksheet

formatting of worksheet complete

BetNet Stock Club

Stock	Symbol	Date Acquired	Shares	Initial Price	Initial Cost	Current Price	Current Value	Gain/Loss	% Gain/Loss
Amazon.com	AMZN	10/14/97	800	$ 15.875	$ 12,700.00	$172.000	$ 137,600.00	$ 124,900.00	983.46%
America Online	AOL	12/14/98	720	93.500	67,320.00	128.688	92,655.36	25,335.36	37.63%
Broadcast.com	BCST	2/12/99	610	85.250	52,002.50	121.500	74,115.00	22,112.50	42.52%
EarthLink	ELNK	3/1/99	500	63.125	31,562.50	65.250	32,625.00	1,062.50	3.37%
eBay	EBAY	4/13/99	920	200.500	184,460.00	162.500	149,500.00	(34,960.00)	-18.95%
Infoseek	SEEK	2/12/98	750	12.875	9,656.25	50.563	37,922.25	28,266.00	292.72%
Ubid	UBID	12/21/98	400	151.375	60,550.00	44.250	17,700.00	(42,850.00)	-70.77%
Yahoo	YHOO	5/12/98	700	21.000	14,700.00	171.000	119,700.00	105,000.00	714.29%
Total					$ 432,951.25		$ 661,817.61	$ 228,866.36	52.86%
Average			675	$80.44	$54,118.91	$114.47	$82,727.20	$28,608.30	
Highest			920	$200.50	$184,460.00	$172.00	$149,500.00	$124,900.00	983.46%
Lowest			400	$12.88	$9,656.25	$44.25	$17,700.00	($42,850.00)	-70.77%

FIGURE 2-59

The row height can vary between zero (0) and 409 points. As with column widths, when you decrease the row height to zero, the row is hidden. To display a hidden row, position the mouse pointer just below the row heading boundary where the row is hidden and then drag down. To set a row height to best fit, double-click the bottom boundary of the row heading.

The task of formatting the worksheet is complete. The next step is to check the spelling of the worksheet.

Checking Spelling

Excel has a spell checker you can use to check the worksheet for spelling errors. The spell checker looks for spelling errors by comparing words on the worksheet against words contained in its standard dictionary. If you often use specialized terms that are not in the standard dictionary, you may want to add them to a custom dictionary using the Spelling dialog box.

When the spell checker finds a word that is not in either dictionary, it displays the word in the Spelling dialog box. You then can correct it if it is misspelled.

To illustrate how Excel responds to a misspelled word, the word, Stock, in cell A2 is misspelled purposely as the word, Stpck, as shown in Figure 2-60.

Steps: To Check Spelling on the Worksheet

1 **Double-click the move handle on the left side of the Standard toolbar to display the toolbar in its entirety. Select cell A2 and enter Stpck to misspell the word Stock. Select cell A1. Click the Spelling button on the Standard toolbar. When the spell checker stops on BetNet, click the Ignore button. When the spell checker stops on cell A2, click the word Stock in the Suggestions list.**

When the spell checker identifies the misspelled word, Stpck, the Spelling dialog box displays (Figure 2-60).

FIGURE 2-60

2 **Click the Change button. As the spell checker checks the remainder of the worksheet, click the Ignore and Change buttons as needed.**

The spell checker changes the misspelled word, Stpck, to the correct word, Stock, and continues spell checking the worksheet. When the spell checker is finished, it displays the Microsoft Excel dialog box with a message indicating that the spell check is complete for the entire sheet (Figure 2-61).

FIGURE 2-61

3 **Click the OK button.**

Other Ways

1. On the Tools menu click Spelling
2. Press F7

Checking Spelling

Always take the time to check the spelling of a worksheet before submitting it to your supervisor or instructor. Nothing deflates an impression more than a professional looking report with misspelled words.

When the spell checker identifies that a cell contains a word not in its standard or custom dictionary, it selects that cell as the active cell and displays the Spelling dialog box. The Spelling dialog box (Figure 2-60 on the previous page) lists the word not in the dictionary, a suggested correction, and a list of alternative suggestions. If you agree with the suggested correction in the **Change to box**, click the **Change button**. To change the word throughout the worksheet, click the **Change All button**.

If one of the words in the **Suggestions list** is correct, click the correct word in the Suggestions list and then click the Change button, or double-click the word in the Suggestions list. If none of the suggestions is correct, type the correct word in the Change to box and then click the Change button. To skip correcting the word, click the **Ignore button**. To have Excel ignore the word for the remainder of the worksheet, click the **Ignore All button**.

Consider these additional guidelines when using the spell checker:

▶ To check the spelling of the text in a single cell, double-click the cell to make the formula bar active and then click the Spelling button on the Standard toolbar.

▶ If you select a single cell so that the formula bar is not active and then start the spell checker, Excel checks the entire worksheet, including notes and embedded charts.

▶ If you select a range of cells before starting the spell checker, Excel checks only the spelling of the words in the selected range.

▶ To check the spelling of all the sheets in a workbook, click Select All Sheets on the sheet tab shortcut menu and then start the spell checker. To display the sheet tab shortcut menu, right-click the sheet tab.

▶ If you select a cell other than cell A1 before you start the spell checker, a dialog box will display when the spell checker reaches the end of the worksheet, asking if you want to continue checking at the beginning.

▶ To add words to the dictionary, click the **Add button** in the Spelling dialog box (Figure 2-60) when Excel identifies the word as not in the dictionary.

▶ Click the **AutoCorrect button** (Figure 2-60) to add the misspelled word and the correct version of the word to the AutoCorrect list. For example, suppose you misspell the word, do, as the word, dox. When the Spelling dialog box displays the correct word, do, in the Change to box, click the AutoCorrect button. Then, anytime in the future that you type the word, dox, Excel will change it to the word, do.

Saving the Workbook a Second Time Using the Same File Name

Saving

If you want to save the workbook under a new name, click the Save As command on the File menu. Some Excel users feel better if they save workbooks on two different drives. They use the Save button on the Standard toolbar to save the latest version of the workbook on the default drive. Then, they use the Save As command to save a second copy on another drive.

Earlier in this project, you saved an intermediate version of the workbook using the file name, BetNet Stock Club. To save the workbook a second time using the same file name, click the Save button on the Standard toolbar. Excel automatically stores the latest version of the workbook using the same file name, BetNet Stock Club. When you save a workbook a second time using the same file name, Excel will not display the Save As dialog box as it does the first time you save the workbook. You also can click **Save** on the File menu or press SHIFT+F12 or CTRL+S to re-save a workbook.

If you want to save the workbook using a new name or on a different drive, click **Save As** on the File menu. Some Excel users, for example, use the Save button to save the latest version of the workbook on the default drive. Then, they use the Save As command to save a copy on another drive.

Previewing and Printing the Worksheet

In Project 1, you printed the worksheet without previewing it on the screen by clicking the Print button on the Standard toolbar. You can print the BetNet Stock Club worksheet the same way. By previewing the worksheet, however, you see exactly how it will look without generating a printout. Previewing allows you to see if the worksheet will print on one page in portrait orientation. **Portrait orientation** means the printout is printed across the width of the page. **Landscape orientation** means the printout is printed across the length of the page. Previewing a worksheet using the **Print Preview command** on the File menu or **Print Preview button** on the Standard toolbar can save time, paper, and the frustration of waiting for a printout only to discover it is not what you want.

More About 2000

Print Preview

A popular button in the preview window (Figure 2-63) is the Margins button. The Margins button allows you to drag the top, bottom, left, and right margins to center a worksheet or add room to fit a wide or long worksheet on a page. You even can change the column widths.

 To Preview and Print a Worksheet

1 Point to the Print Preview button on the Standard toolbar (Figure 2-62).

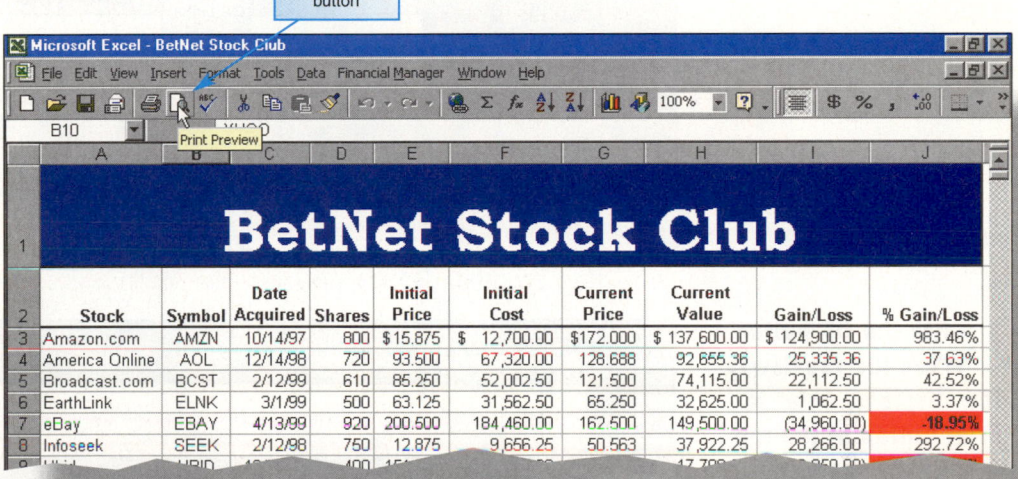

FIGURE 2-62

2 Click the Print Preview button. When the Preview window displays, point to the Setup button.

Excel displays a preview of the worksheet in portrait orientation. In portrait orientation, the worksheet does not fit on one page (Figure 2-63).

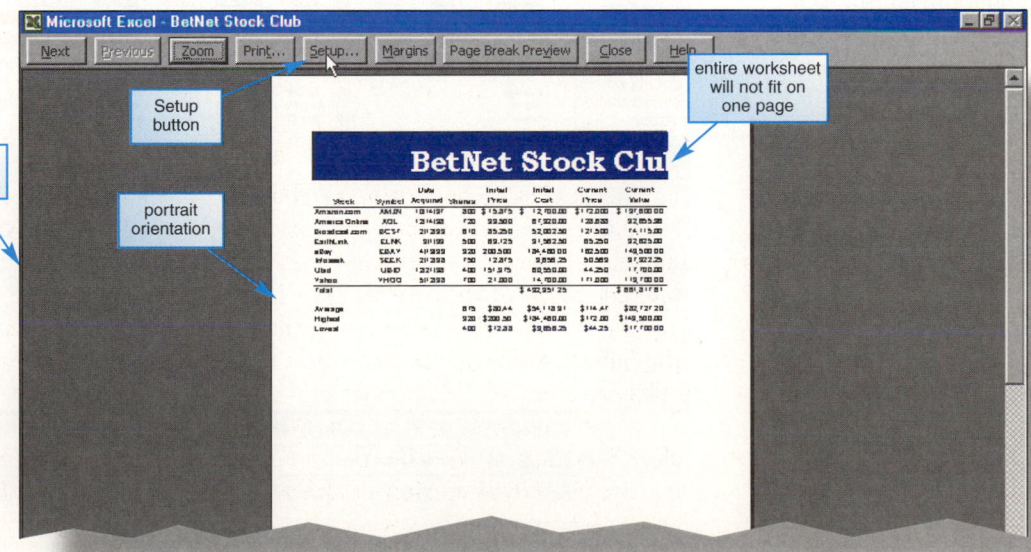

FIGURE 2-63

3 Click the Setup button. When the Page Setup dialog box displays, click the Page tab and then click Landscape. Point to the OK button.

The Page Setup dialog box displays. You have two choices in the Orientation area, Portrait or Landscape (Figure 2-64).

FIGURE 2-64

4 Click the OK button. When the Preview window displays, point to the Print button at the top of the Preview window.

The worksheet displays in the Preview window in landscape orientation (Figure 2-65)

FIGURE 2-65

5 Click the Print button. When the Print dialog box displays, point to the OK button.

The Print dialog box displays as shown in Figure 2-66.

FIGURE 2-66

6 Click the OK button. Click the Save button on the Standard toolbar.

Excel prints the worksheet (Figure 2-67). The workbook is saved with the landscape orientation.

FIGURE 2-67

Once you change the orientation and save the workbook, it will remain until you change it. Excel sets the orientation for a new workbook to portrait.

There are several buttons at the top of the Preview window (Figure 2-65). The functions of these buttons are summarized in Table 2-5 on the next page.

Rather than click the Next and Previous buttons to move from page to page as described in Table 2-5, you can press the PAGE UP and PAGE DOWN keys. You also can click the previewed page in the Preview window when the mouse pointer shape is a magnifying glass to carry out the function of the Zoom button.

Other Ways

1. On the File menu click Print Preview

2. On the File menu click Page Setup, click Print Preview button

3. On File menu click Print, click Preview button

Table 2-5 Print Preview Buttons	
BUTTON	**FUNCTION**
Next	Previews the next page
Previous	Previews the previous page
Zoom	Magnifies or reduces the print preview
Print...	Prints the worksheet
Setup...	Displays the Print Setup dialog box
Margins	Changes the print margins
Page Break Preview	Previews page breaks
Close	Closes the Preview window
Help	Displays Help about the Preview window

The Page Setup dialog box in Figure 2-64 on page E 2.52 allows you to make changes to the default settings for a printout. For example, on the Page tab, you can set the orientation as was done in the previous set of steps, scale the printout so it fits on one page, set the page size, and print quality. Scaling is an alternative to changing the orientation to fit a wide worksheet on one page. This technique will be discussed shortly. The Margins tab, Header/Footer tab, and Sheet tab in the Page Setup dialog box allow even more control of the way the printout will appear. These tabs will be discussed in later projects.

The Print dialog box shown in Figure 2-66 on the previous page displays when you use the Print command on the File menu or a Print button in a dialog box or Preview window. It does not display when you use the Print button on the Standard toolbar as was the case in Project 1. The Print dialog box allows you to select a printer, instruct Excel what to print, and indicate how many copies of the printout you want.

Printing a Section of the Worksheet

You might not always want to print the entire worksheet. You can print portions of the worksheet by selecting the range of cells to print and then clicking the Selection option button in the Print what area in the Print dialog box. The following steps show how to print the range A2:F11.

 To Print a Section of the Worksheet

1 **Select the range A2:F11. Click File on the menu bar and then click Print. Click Selection in the Print what area. Point to the OK button.**

The Print dialog box displays (Figure 2-68). Because the Selection option button is selected, Excel will print only the selected range.

FIGURE 2-68

2   **Click the OK button. Click cell A16 to deselect the range A2:F11.**

Excel prints the selected range of the worksheet on the printer (Figure 2-69).

Stock	Symbol	Date Acquired	Shares	Initial Price	Initial Cost
Amazon.com	AMZN	10/14/97	800	$15.875	$ 12,700.00
America Online	AOL	12/14/98	720	93.500	67,320.00
Broadcast.com	BCST	2/12/99	610	85.250	52,002.50
EarthLink	ELNK	3/1/99	500	63.125	31,562.50
eBay	EBAY	4/13/99	920	200.500	184,460.00
Infoseek	SEEK	2/12/98	750	12.875	9,656.25
Ubid	UBID	12/21/98	400	151.375	60,550.00
Yahoo	YHOO	5/12/98	700	21.000	14,700.00
Total					$ 432,951.25

only selected range prints

FIGURE 2-69

Three option buttons display in the Print what area in the Print dialog box (Figure 2-68). As shown in the previous steps, the **Selection option button** instructs Excel to print the selected range. The **Active sheet(s) option button** instructs Excel to print the active sheet (the one displaying on the screen) or the selected sheets. Finally, the **Entire workbook option button** instructs Excel to print all the sheets with content in the workbook.

Displaying and Printing the Formulas Version of the Worksheet

Thus far, you have been working with the **values version** of the worksheet, which shows the results of the formulas you have entered, rather than the actual formulas. Excel also allows you to display and print the **formulas version** of the worksheet, which displays the actual formulas you have entered, rather than the resulting values. You can toggle between the values version and formulas version by pressing CTRL+LEFT SINGLE QUOTATION MARK (` to the left of the number 1 key).

The formulas version is useful for debugging a worksheet. **Debugging** is the process of finding and correcting errors in the worksheet. Because the formula version displays and prints formulas and functions, rather than the results, it makes it easier to see if any mistakes were made in the formulas.

When you change from the values version to the formulas version, Excel increases the width of the columns so the formulas and text do not overflow into adjacent cells on the right. The formulas version of the worksheet thus usually is significantly wider than the values version. To fit the wide printout on one page, you can use landscape orientation and the **Fit to option** on the Page tab in the Page Setup dialog box. To change from the values version to the formulas version of the worksheet and print the formulas on one page, perform the steps on the next page.

Other Ways

1. Select range to print, on File menu click Print Area, click Set Print Area, click Print button on Standard toolbar; on File menu click Print Area, click Clear Print Area

More About 2000

Printing

A dark font on a dark background, such as a red font on a blue background, will not print properly on a black and white printer. For black and white printing, use a light colored font on a dark background and a dark font on a light colored background.

More About 2000

Values versus Formulas

When completing class assignments, do not enter numbers in cells that require formulas. Most instructors require their students to hand in both the values version and formulas version of the worksheet. The formulas version verifies that you entered formulas, rather than numbers in formula-based cells.

To Display the Formulas in the Worksheet and Fit the Printout on One Page

1 Press CTRL+LEFT SINGLE QUOTATION MARK (`). Click the right horizontal scroll arrow until column J displays.

Excel changes the display of the worksheet from values to formulas (Figure 2-70). The formulas in the worksheet display showing unformatted numbers, formulas, and functions that were assigned to the cells. Excel automatically increases the column widths.

FIGURE 2-70

2 Click File on the menu bar, and then click Page Setup. When the Page Setup dialog box displays, click the Page tab. If necessary, click Landscape, and then click Fit to. Point to the Print button in the Page Setup dialog box.

Excel displays the Page Setup dialog box with the Landscape and Fit to option buttons selected (Figure 2-71).

FIGURE 2-71

3 Click the Print button. When the Print dialog box displays, click the OK button. When you are done viewing and printing the formulas version, press CTRL + LEFT SINGLE QUOTATION MARK (`) to display the values version.

Excel prints the formulas in the worksheet on one page in landscape orientation (Figure 2-72).

BetNet Stock Club

Stock	Symbol	Date Acquired	Shares	Initial Price	Initial Cost	Current Price	Current Value	Gain/Loss
Amazon.com	AMZN	35717	800	15.875	=D3*E3	172	=D3*G3	=H3-F3
America Online	AOL	36143	720	93.5	=D4*E4	128.688	=D4*G4	=H4-F4
Broadcast.com	BCST	36203	610	85.25	=D5*E5	121.5	=D5*G5	=H5-F5
EarthLink	ELNK	36220	500	63.125	=D6*E6	65.25	=D6*G6	=H6-F6
eBay	EBAY	36263	920	200.5	=D7*E7	162.5	=D7*G7	=H7-F7
Infoseek	SEEK	35838	750	12.875	=D8*E8	50.563	=D8*G8	=H8-F8
Ubid	UBID	36150	400	151.375	=D9*E9	44.25	=D9*G9	=H9-F9
Yahoo	YHOO	35927	700	21	=D10*E10	171	=D10*G10	=H10-F10
Total					=SUM(F3:F10)		=SUM(H3:H10)	=SUM(I3:I10)
Average			=AVERAGE(D3:D10)	=AVERAGE(E3:E10)	=AVERAGE(F3:F10)	=AVERAGE(G3:G10)	=AVERAGE(H3:H10)	=AVERAGE(I3:I10)
Highest			=MAX(D3:D10)	=MAX(E3:E10)	=MAX(F3:F10)	=MAX(G3:G10)	=MAX(H3:H10)	=MAX(I3:I10)
Lowest			=MIN(D3:D10)	=MIN(E3:E10)	=MIN(F3:F10)	=MIN(G3:G10)	=MIN(H3:H10)	=MIN(I3:I10)

formulas instead of values printed

font size automatically reduced so worksheet fits on one page

FIGURE 2-72

Although the formulas version of the worksheet was printed in the previous example, you can see from Figure 2-72 that the display on the screen also can be used for debugging the worksheet.

Changing the Print Scaling Option Back to 100%

Depending on your printer driver, you may have to change the Print Scaling option back to 100% after using the Fit to option. Complete the following steps to reset the Print Scaling option so future worksheets print at 100%, instead of being squeezed on one page.

TO CHANGE THE PRINT SCALING OPTION BACK TO 100%

1 Click File on the menu bar and then click Page Setup.

2 Click the Page tab in the Page Setup dialog box. Click Adjust to in the Scaling area.

3 If necessary, type 100 in the Adjust to box.

4 Click the OK button.

The print scaling is set to normal.

The **Adjust to box** allows you to specify the percentage of reduction or enlargement in the printout of a worksheet. The default percentage is 100%. When you click the Fit to option, this percentage automatically changes to the percentage required to fit the printout on one page.

The Fit To Option

Do not take the Fit To option lightly. Most applications involve worksheets that extend well beyond the 8½-by-11-inch page. Most users, however, want the information on one page, at least with respect to the width of the worksheet. Thus, the Fit To option is a common choice among Excel users.

Getting External Data from a Web Source Using a Web Query

One of the major features of Excel 2000 is its capability of obtaining external data from sites on the World Wide Web. To get external data from a World Wide Web site, you must have access to the Internet. You then can run a **Web query** to retrieve data stored on a World Wide Web site. When you run a Web query, Excel returns the external data in the form of a worksheet. As described in Table 2-6, four Web queries are available when you first install Excel. Three of the four Web queries available relate to investment and stock market activities.

Table 2-6 Excel Web Queries	
QUERY	EXTERNAL DATA RETURNED
Get More Web	Download additional Web queries
Microsoft Investor Currency Rates	Currency rates
Microsoft Investor Major Indices	Major Indices
Microsoft Investor Stock Quotes	Up to 20 stocks of your choice

The data returned by the stock-related Web queries is real-time in the sense that it is no more than 20 minutes old during the business day. The steps below show how to get the most recent stock quotes for the following six stocks being reviewed by the BetNet Stock Club members as they consider a flight to safety — Exxon Mobil (XOM), General Electric (GE), Merck (MRK), Pfizer (PFE), Proctor & Gamble (PG), and Walgreen (WAG). Although you can have a Web query return data to a blank workbook, the following steps have the data returned to a blank worksheet in the BetNet Stock Club workbook.

Steps **To Get External Data from a Web Source Using a Web Query**

1 **With the BetNet Stock Club workbook open, click the Sheet2 tab at the bottom of the window. Click cell A1. Click Data on the menu bar, point to Get External Data and then point to Run Saved Query on the Get External Data submenu.**

The Get External Data submenu displays as shown in Figure 2-73.

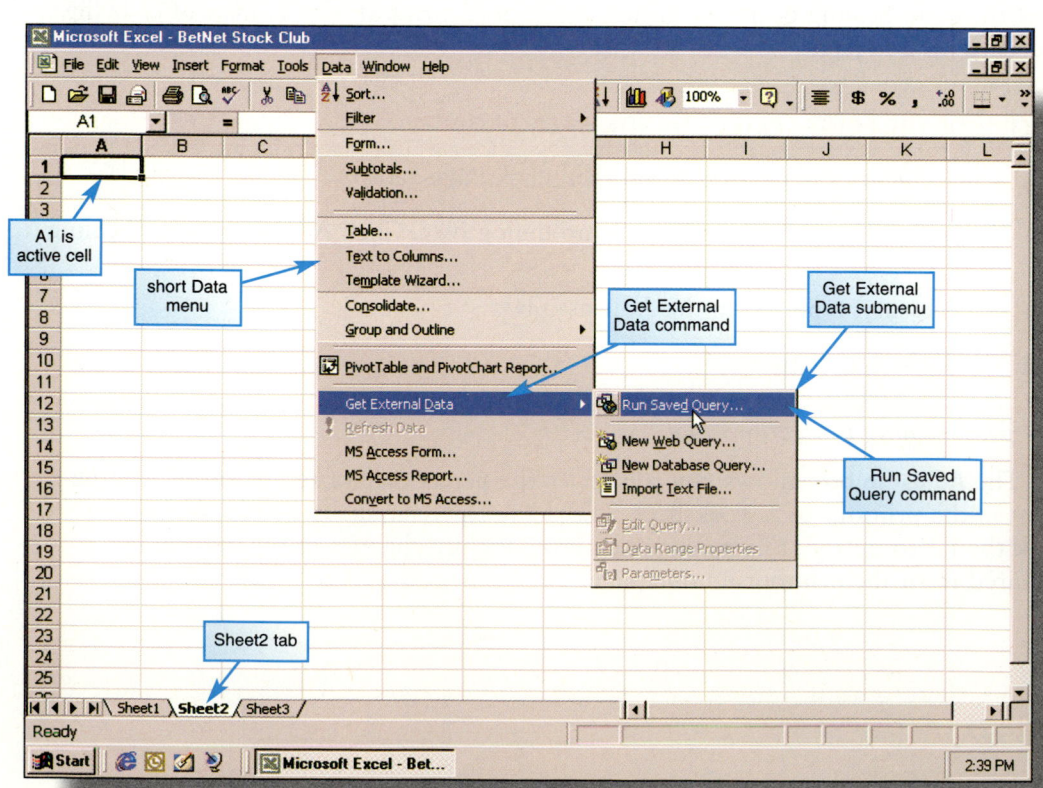

FIGURE 2-73

2 Click Run Saved Query. When the Run Query dialog box displays, click Microsoft Investor Stock Quotes. Point to the Get Data button.

The Run Query dialog box displays (Figure 2-74). If your display is different, ask your instructor for the folder location of the Web queries.

FIGURE 2-74

3 Click the Get Data button. When the Returning External Data to Microsoft Excel dialog box displays, click Existing worksheet, if necessary, to select it. Point to the OK button.

The Returning External Data to Microsoft Excel dialog box displays (Figure 2-75).

FIGURE 2-75

4 Click the OK button. When the Enter Parameter Value dialog box displays, type the stock symbols xom, ge, mrk, pfe, pg, wag, in the text box. Click Use this value/reference for future refreshes to select it. Point to the OK button.

The Enter Parameter Value dialog box displays (Figure 2-76). You can enter up to 20 stock symbols separated by commas (or spaces).

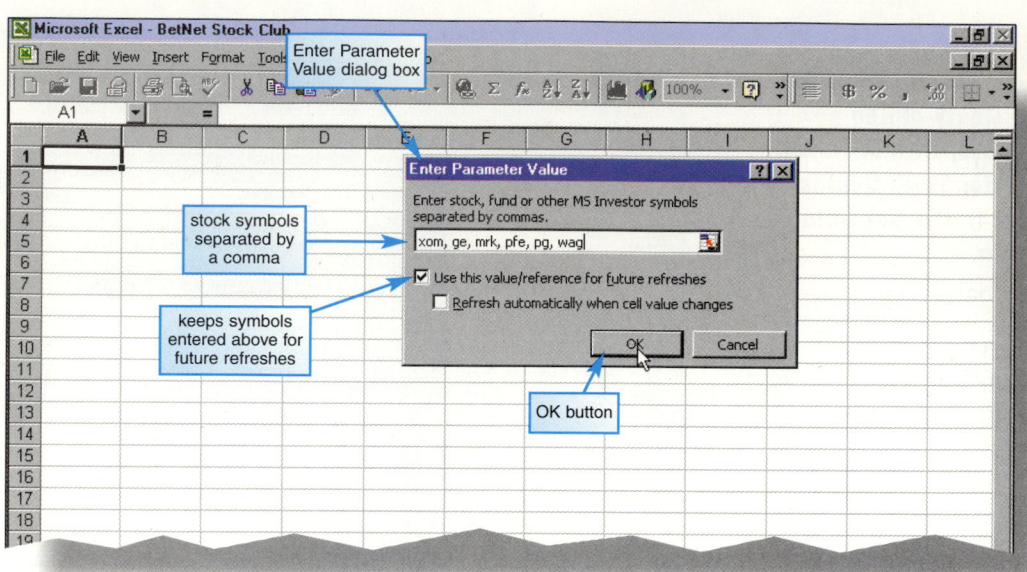

FIGURE 2-76

5 Click the OK button.

Once your computer connects to the Internet, a message displays to inform you that Excel is getting external data. After a short period, Excel displays a new worksheet with the desired data (Figure 2-77).

FIGURE 2-77

As shown in Figure 2-77, Excel displays the data returned from the Web query in an organized, formatted worksheet, which has a worksheet title, column titles, and a row of data for each stock symbol entered. Other than the first column, which contains the stock name and stock symbol, you have no control over the remaining columns of data returned. The latest price of each stock displays in column D.

Once the worksheet displays, you can refresh the data as often as you want. To refresh the data for all the stocks, click the **Refresh All button** on the **External Data toolbar** (Figure 2-78). Because the Use this value/reference for future refreshes check box was selected (Figure 2-76), Excel will continue to use the same stock symbols each time it refreshes. You can change the symbols by clicking the **Query Parameters button** on the External Data toolbar.

If the External Data toolbar does not display, right-click any toolbar and then click External Data. You also can invoke any Web query command by right-clicking the returned worksheet to display a shortcut menu.

This section gives you an idea of the potential of Web queries by having you use just one of Excel's many available Web queries. To reinforce the topics covered here, work through In the Lab 3 at the end of this project.

The workbook is nearly complete. The final step is to change the names of the sheets located on the sheet tabs at the bottom of the Excel window.

FIGURE 2-78

Changing the Sheet Names

At the bottom of the window (Figure 2-79) are the tabs that allow you to display any sheet in the workbook. You click the tab of the sheet you want to display. The names of the sheets are preset to Sheet1, Sheet2, and so on. These names become increasingly important as you move towards more sophisticated workbooks, especially those in which you reference cells between sheets. The following steps show how to rename sheets by double-clicking the sheet tabs.

 To Rename the Sheets

1 **Double-click the tab labeled Sheet2 in the lower-left corner of the window. Type** Real-Time Stock Quotes **as the sheet name and then click a cell on the worksheet.**

The new sheet name displays on the tab (Figure 2-79).

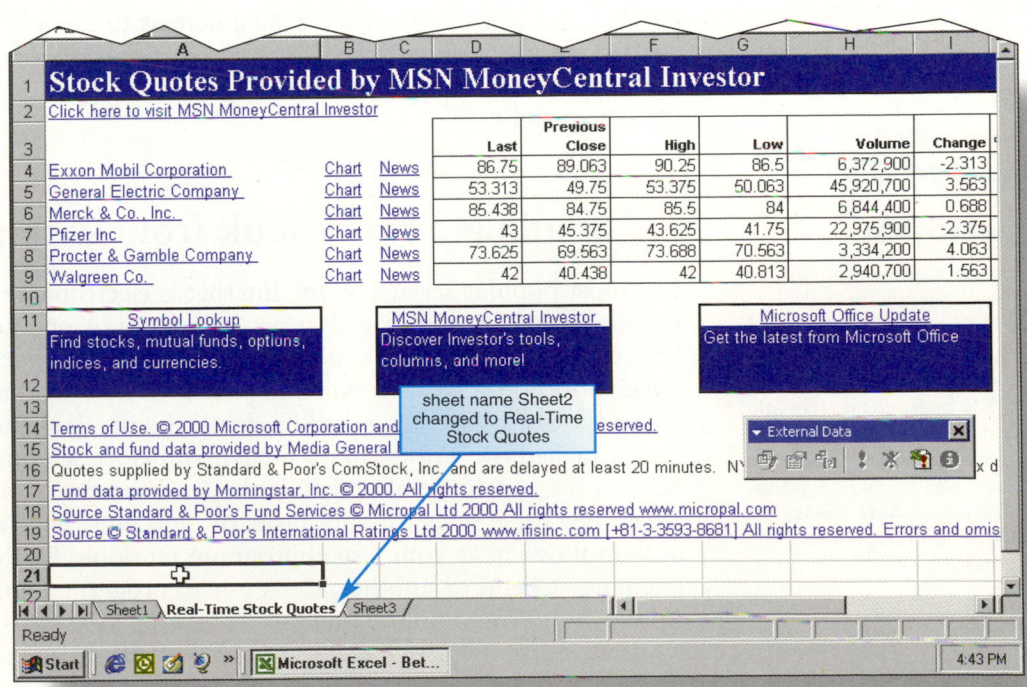

FIGURE 2-79

2 Double-click the tab labeled Sheet1 in the lower-left corner of the window. Type `Investment Analysis` as the sheet name and then press the ENTER key.

The sheet name changes from Sheet1 to Investment Analysis (Figure 2-80).

3 Click the Save button on the Standard toolbar.

BetNet Stock Club

Stock	Symbol	Date Acquired	Shares	Initial Price	Initial Cost	Current Price	Current Value	Gain/Loss	% Gain/Loss
Amazon.com	AMZN	10/14/97	800	$15.875	$ 12,700.00	$172.000	$ 137,600.00	$ 124,900.00	983.46%
America Online	AOL	12/14/98	720	93.500	67,320.00	128.688	92,655.36	25,335.36	37.63%
Broadcast.com	BCST	2/12/99	610	85.250	52,002.50	121.500	74,115.00	22,112.50	42.52%
EarthLink	ELNK	3/1/99	500	63.125	31,562.50	65.250	32,625.00	1,062.50	3.37%
eBay	EBAY	4/13/99	920	200.500	184,460.00	162.500	149,500.00	(34,960.00)	-18.95%
Infoseek	SEEK	2/12/98	750	12.875	9,656.25	50.563	37,922.25	28,266.00	292.72%
Ubid	UBID	12/21/98	400	151.375	60,550.00	44.250	17,700.00	(42,850.00)	-70.77%
Yahoo	YHOO	5/12/98	700	21.000	14,700.00	171.000	119,700.00	105,000.00	714.29%
Total					$ 432,951.25		$ 661,817.61	$ 228,866.36	52.86%
Average			675	$80.44	$54,118.91	$114.47	$82,727.20	$28,608.30	
Highest			920	$200.50	$184,460.00	$172.00	$149,500.00	$124,900.00	983.46%
Lowest				$12.88	$9,656.25	$44.25	$17,700.00	($42,850.00)	-70.77%

sheet name Sheet1 changed to Investment Analysis

tab split box

Investment Analysis / Real-Time Stock Quotes / Sheet3 /

Ready

Start | Microsoft Excel - Bet... | 2:43 PM

tab scrolling buttons

FIGURE 2-80

Other Ways

1. To rename, right-click sheet tab, click Rename on shortcut menu
2. To move, right-click sheet tab, click Move or Copy on shortcut menu
3. To move, on Edit menu click Move or Copy

More About

Sheets Tabs

To move from sheet to sheet in a workbook, you click the sheet tabs at the bottom of the window. The name of the active sheet always is bold on a white background. Through the shortcut menu, you can rename the sheets, reorder the sheets, add and delete sheets, and move or copy sheets within a workbook or to another workbook.

Sheet names can contain up to 31 characters (including spaces) in length. Longer sheet names, however, mean that fewer tabs will display. To display more sheet tabs, you can drag the **tab split box** (Figure 2-80) to the right. This will reduce the size of the scroll bar at the bottom of the screen. Double-click the tab split box to reset it to its normal position.

You also can use the **tab scrolling buttons** to the left of the sheet tabs (Figure 2-80) to move between sheets. The leftmost and rightmost scroll buttons move to the first or last sheet in the workbook. The two middle scroll buttons move one sheet to the left or right.

E-mailing a Workbook from within Excel

The most popular service on the Internet is electronic mail, or e-mail. Using **e-mail**, you can converse with friends across the room or on another continent. One of the features of e-mail is the ability to attach Office files, such as Word documents or Excel workbooks to an e-mail and send it to a co-worker. In the past, if you wanted to send a workbook you saved it, closed the file, launched your e-mail program, and then attached the workbook to the e-mail before sending it. A new feature of Office 2000 is the capability of e-mailing the worksheet or workbook directly from within Excel. For these steps to work properly, you must have an e-mail address and one of the following as your e-mail program: Outlook, Outlook Express, Microsoft Exchange Client, or another 32-bit e-mail program compatible with Messaging Application Programming Interface. The following steps show how to e-mail the workbook from within Excel to Michael Santos. Assume his e-mail address is michael_santos@hotmail.com.

Steps **To E-mail a Workbook from within Excel**

1 **With the BetNet Stock Club workbook open, click File on the menu bar, point to Send To, and then point to Mail Recipient (as Attachment).**

The File menu and Send To submenu display as shown in Figure 2-81.

FIGURE 2-81

2 **Click Mail Recipient (as Attachment). When the e-mail Message window displays, type** michael_santos @hotmail.com **in the To text box. Type** BetNet Stock Club workbook **in the Subject text box. Point to the Send button.**

Excel displays the e-mail Message window (Figure 2-82).

3 **Click the Send button.**

The e-mail with the attached workbook is sent to michael_santos @hotmail.com.

FIGURE 2-82

 Other Ways

1. Click E-mail button on Standard toolbar

More About

E-mail

Several Web sites are available that allow you to sign up for free e-mail. For more information on signing up for free e-mail, visit the Excel 2000 More About Web page (www.scsite.com/ex2000/more.htm) and click Signing Up for E-mail.

More About

Quick Reference

For a table that lists how to complete the tasks covered in this book using the mouse, menu, shortcut menu, and keyboard, visit the Office 2000 Web page (www.scsite.com/off2000/qr.htm), and then click Microsoft Excel 2000.

Because the workbook was sent as an attachment, Michael Santos can save the attachment and then open the workbook in Excel. The alternative in the E-mail dialog box in Figure 2-81 on the previous page is to send a copy of the worksheet in HTML format. In this case, Michael would be able to read the worksheet in the e-mail message, but would not be able to open it in Excel.

Many more options are available that you can choose when you send an e-mail from within Excel. For example, the Bcc and From buttons on the toolbar in the Message window give you the same capabilities as an e-mail program. The Options button on the toolbar allows you to send the e-mail to a group of people in a particular sequence and get responses along the route.

Quitting Excel

After completing the workbook and related activities, you can quit Excel by performing the following steps.

TO QUIT EXCEL

1 Click the Investment Analysis tab.

2 Click the Close button on the upper-right corner of the title bar.

3 When the Microsoft Excel dialog box displays, click the Yes button.

CASE PERSPECTIVE SUMMARY

The worksheet and Web query (Figure 2-1 on page E 2.5) you created for Michael Santos will serve his purpose well. The worksheet, which he plans to e-mail to the club members, contains valuable information in an easy-to-read format. Finally, the Web query allows Michael to obtain the latest stock prices to keep the workbook as up to date as possible.

Project Summary

In creating the BetNet Stock Club workbook, you learned how to enter formulas, calculate an average, find the highest and lowest numbers in a range, audit formulas, change fonts, draw borders, format numbers, change column widths and row heights, and add conditional formatting to a range of numbers. You learned how to spell check a worksheet, preview a worksheet, print a worksheet, print a section of a worksheet and display and print the formulas in the worksheet using the Fit to option. You also learned how to complete a Web query to generate a worksheet using external data obtained from the World Wide Web and rename sheet tabs. Finally, you learned how to send an e-mail directly from within Excel with the opened workbook attached.

What You Should Know

Having completed this project, you now should be able to perform the following tasks:

- Apply a Currency Style Format and Comma Style Format Using the Formatting Toolbar *(E 2.35)*
- Apply a Currency Style Format with a Floating Dollar Sign Using the Format Cells Command *(E 2.37*
- Apply a Percent Style Format *(E 2.39)*
- Apply Conditional Formatting *(E 2.40)*
- Bold, Center, and Underline the Column Titles *(E 2.33)*
- Center Data in Cells *(E 2.33)*
- Change the Title Background and Font Colors and Apply an Outline Border *(E 2.30)*
- Change the Font and Center the Worksheet Title *(E 2.28)*
- Change the Height of a Row by Dragging *(E 2.47)*
- Change the Print Scaling Option Back to 100% *(E 2.57)*
- Change the Widths of Columns *(E 2.44)*
- Check Spelling on the Worksheet *(E 2.49)*
- Copy a Range of Cells Across Columns to an Adjacent Range Using the Fill Handle *(E 2.22)*
- Copy Formulas Using the Fill Handle *(E 2.13)*
- Determine the Average of a Range of Numbers Using the Keyboard and Mouse *(E 2.17)*
- Determine the Highest Number in a Range of Numbers Using the Edit Formula Box and Function Box *(E 2.18)*

- Determine the Lowest Number in a Range of Numbers Using the Paste Function Button *(E 2.20)*
- Determine the Total Percentage Gain/Loss *(E 2.15)*
- Determine Totals Using the AutoSum Button *(E 2.14)*
- Display the Formulas in the Worksheet and Fit the Printout on One Page *(E 2.56)*
- Enter a Formula Using the Keyboard *(E 2.9)*
- Enter Formulas Using Point Mode *(E 2.11)*
- Enter the Column Titles *(E 2.7)*
- Enter the Stock Data *(E 2.8)*
- Enter the Total Row Titles *(E 2.8)*
- Enter the Worksheet Title *(E 2.7)*
- E-mail a Workbook from within Excel *(E 2.63)*
- Get External Data from a Web Source Using a Web Query *(E 2.58)*
- Preview and Print a Worksheet *(E 2.51)*
- Print a Section of the Worksheet *(E 2.54)*
- Quit Excel *(E 2.64)*
- Rename the Sheets *(E 2.61)*
- Start Excel and Reset the Toolbars *(E 2.6)*
- Verify a Formula Using the Auditing Commands *(E 2.25)*
- Verify a Formula Using Range Finder *(E 2.24)*

Microsoft Certification

The Microsoft Office User Specialist (MOUS) Certification program provides an opportunity for you to obtain a valuable industry credential — proof that you have the Excel 2000 skills required by employers. For more information, see Appendix D or visit the Shelly Cashman Series MOUS Web page at www.scsite.com/off2000/cert.htm.

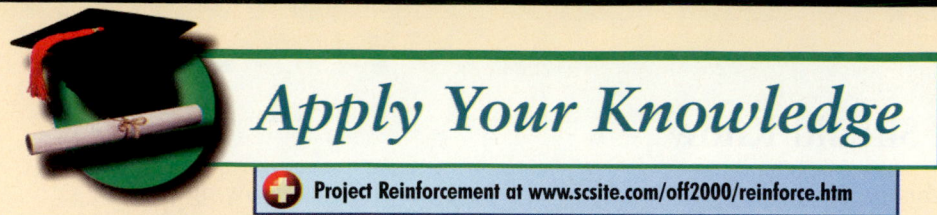

Apply Your Knowledge

⊕ **Project Reinforcement at www.scsite.com/off2000/reinforce.htm**

1 Sizes Galore and Much More Profit Analysis Worksheet

Instructions: Start Excel. Open the workbook Sizes Galore and Much More from the Data Disk. See the inside back cover of this book for instructions for downloading the Data Disk or see your instructor. The purpose of this exercise is to have you open a partially completed workbook, enter formulas and functions, copy the formulas and functions, and then format the numbers. As shown in Figure 2-83, the completed worksheet analyzes profits by product.

FIGURE 2-83

Perform the following tasks.

1. Complete the following entries in row 3:
   a. Total Sales (cell F3) = Units Sold * (Cost + Profit) or =E3 * (C3+D3)
   b. Profit (cell G3) = Units Sold * Profit or = E3 * D3
      % Profit (cell H3) = Profit / Total Sales or = G3 / F3
2. Use the fill handle to copy the three formulas in the range F3:H3 to the range F4:H12.
3. Determine the Total Sales, and Profit column totals in row 13.
4. In the range C14:C16, determine the lowest value, highest value, and average value, respectively for the range C3:C12. Use the fill handle to copy the three functions to the range D14:H16. Delete the average from cell H16, because you can not average percents.
5. Use the Currency Style button on the Formatting toolbar to format the numbers in the ranges C3:D3, F3:G3, and F13:G13. Use the Comma Style button on the Formatting toolbar to format the numbers in cell E3 and the range C4:G12. Use the Decrease Decimal button on the Formatting toolbar to display the numbers in the range E3:E16 as whole numbers. Use the Percent Style and the Increase Decimal buttons on the Formatting toolbar to format the range H3:H15. Increase the decimal positions in this range to 3. Use the Format Cells command on the shortcut menu to format the numbers in the ranges C14:D16 and F14:G16 to a floating dollar sign.

Apply Your Knowledge

➕ Project Reinforcement at www.scsite.com/off2000/reinforce.htm

6. Use Range Finder and then the Auditing commands to verify the formula in cell G3. Check both precedents and dependents (Figure 2-83) using the Auditing commands. Use the Remove Arrows command on the Auditing submenu to remove the arrows.

7. Enter your name, course, laboratory assignment number (Apply 2-1), date, and instructor name in the range A20:A24.

8. Preview and print the worksheet in landscape orientation. Save the workbook. Use the file name, Sizes Galore and Much More 2.

9. Print the range A1:H13. Print the formulas version (press CTRL+LEFT QUOTATION MARK) of the worksheet in landscape orientation (Figure 2-84) using the Fit to option on the Page tab in the Page Setup dialog box.

10. In column D, use the keyboard to add manually $1.00 to the profit of each product whose profit is less than $10.00, or else add $2.00. You should end up with $5,909,676.16 in cell G13. Print the worksheet. Do not save the workbook. Hand in the printouts to your instructor.

Report

Sizes Galore and Much More
Profit Analysis

Product	Description	Cost	Profit	Units Sold	Total Sales	Profit	
T211	Sweater	92.95	9.25	52435	=E3*(C3+D3)	=E3*D3	
C215	Dress	175.99	15.65	16534	=E4*(C4+D4)	=E4*D4	
D212	Jacket	110.6	11.58	32102	=E5*(C5+D5)	=E5*D5	
K214	Coat	160.5	26.82	43910	=E6*(C6+D6)	=E6*D6	
Q213	Suit	121.35	13.21	34391	=E7*(C7+D7)	=E7*D7	
X216	Custom	200.23	38.35	23910	=E8*(C8+D8)	=E8*D8	
D342	Sleepwear	50.65	8.45	45219	=E9*(C9+D9)	=E9*D9	
H567	Hat	34.2	5.83	63213	=E10*(C10+D10)	=E10*D10	
C289	Shirt	43	6.75	52109	=E11*(C11+D11)	=E11*D11	
K451	Slacks	38.25	7.25	76145	=E12*(C12+D12)	=E12*D12	
Totals				=SUM(E3:E12)	=SUM(F3:F12)	=SUM(G3:G12)	
Lowest		=MIN(C3:C12)	=MIN(D3:D12)	=MIN(E3:E12)	=MIN(F3:F12)	=MIN(G3:G12)	
Highest		=MAX(C3:C12)	=MAX(D3:D12)	=MAX(E3:E12)	=MAX(F3:F12)	=MAX(G3:G12)	
Average		=AVERAGE(C3:C12)	=AVERAGE(D3:D12)	=AVERAGE(E3:E12)	=AVERAGE(F3:F12)	=AVERAGE(G3:G12)	

Page 1

FIGURE 2-84

In the Lab

1 Stars and Stripes Automotive Weekly Payroll Worksheet

Problem: The Stars and Stripes Automotive Company has hired you as a summer intern in its software applications area. Because you took an Excel course last semester, the assistant manager has asked you to prepare a weekly payroll report for the six employees listed in Table 2-7.

Instructions: Perform the following tasks to create a worksheet similar to the one shown in Figure 2-85.

1. Enter the worksheet title Stars and Stripes Automotive Weekly Payroll in cell A1. Enter the column titles in row 2, the row titles in column A, and the data from Table 2-7 in columns B through D as shown in Figure 2-85.

2. Use the following formulas to determine the gross pay, federal tax, state tax, and net pay for the first employee
   a. Gross Pay (cell E3) = Rate*Hours or =B3*C3.
   b. Federal Tax (cell F3) = 20% * (Gross Pay – Dependents * 38.46) or =20% *(E3 – D3 * 38.46)
   c. State Tax (cell G3) = 3.2% * Gross Pay or =3.2% * E3
   d. Net Pay (cell H3) = Gross Pay – (Federal Tax + State Tax) or =E3 – (F3 + G3)
   Copy the formulas for the first employee to the remaining employees.

3. Calculate totals for hours, gross pay, federal tax, state tax, and net pay in row 9.

4. Use the appropriate functions to determine the average, highest, and lowest values of each column in rows 10 through 12.

5. Use Range Finder and then the Auditing commands to verify the formula entered in cell F3. Check both precedents and dependents with the Auditing commands. Remove all arrows.

FIGURE 2-85

Table 2-7	Payroll Data		
EMPLOYEE	**RATE**	**HOURS**	**DEPENDENTS**
Breeze, Linus	27.50	40.25	4
Santiago, Juan	18.75	56.00	1
Webb, Trevor	28.35	38.00	3
Sabol, Kylie	21.50	46.50	6
Ali, Abdul	19.35	17.00	2
Goldstein, Kevin	17.05	28.00	5

In the Lab

6. Bold the worksheet title. Use buttons on the Formatting toolbar to assign the Comma style with two decimal places to the range B3:H12. Bold, italicize, and assign a thick bottom border (column 4, row 3 on the Borders palette) to the range A2:H2. Right-align the column titles in the range B2:H2. Italicize the range A9:A12. Assign a top border and double-line bottom border to the range A9:H9.

7. Change the width of column A to 15.00 characters. If necessary, change the widths of columns B through H to best fit. Change the height of rows 2 and 10 to 24.00 points.

8. Use the Conditional Formatting command on the Format menu to display bold font on a green background for any gross pay greater than $1,050.00 in the range E3:E8.

9. Enter your name, course, laboratory assignment number (Lab 2-1), date, and instructor name in the range A14:A18.

10. Save the workbook using the file name Stars and Stripes Automotive.

11. Preview and then print the worksheet.

12. Press CTRL+LEFT SINGLE QUOTATION MARK (`) to change the display from the values version to the formulas version. Print the formulas version of the worksheet in landscape orientation using the Fit to option on the Page tab in the Page Setup dialog box. After the printer is finished, press CTRL+LEFT SINGLE QUOTATION MARK (`) to reset the worksheet to display the values version. Reset the Scaling option to 100% by clicking the Adjust to option button in the Page sheet in the Page Setup dialog box and then setting the percent value to 100%.

13. Use the keyboard to increase manually the number of hours worked for each employee by 8 hours. The total net pay in cell H9 should equal $4,846.54. If necessary, increase the width of column F to best fit to view the new federal tax total. Preview and print the worksheet with the new values. Close the workbook without saving the changes. Hand in the printouts to your instructor.

2 Mortimer's Seaside Emporium Monthly Accounts Receivable Balance Sheet

Problem: You were recently hired as a part-time assistant in the Accounting department of Mortimer's Seaside Emporium, a popular Biloxi-based general merchandise company with several outlets along the Gulf coast. You have been asked to use Excel to generate a report (Figure 2-86 on the next page) that summarizes the monthly accounts receivable balance. A graphic breakdown of the data also is desired. The customer accounts receivable data in Table 2-8 is available for test purposes.

Table 2-8 Accounts Receivable Data					
CUSTOMER NUMBER	*CUSTOMER NAME*	*BEGINNING BALANCE*	*PURCHASES*	*PAYMENTS*	*CREDITS*
27839	Patel, Nipul	$2,356.15	$739.19	$175.00	$435.10
31982	Jaworski, Stanley	6,291.74	1,098.35	250.00	0.00
45012	Portugal, Juanita	4,103.75	620.75	4,000.00	25.00
56341	Country, James	5,691.45	4,352.12	250.00	35.25
76894	Santiago, Carlos	1,045.23	542.10	750.00	189.95

(continued)

In the Lab

Mortimer's Seaside Emporium Monthly Accounts Receivable Balance Sheet *(continued)*

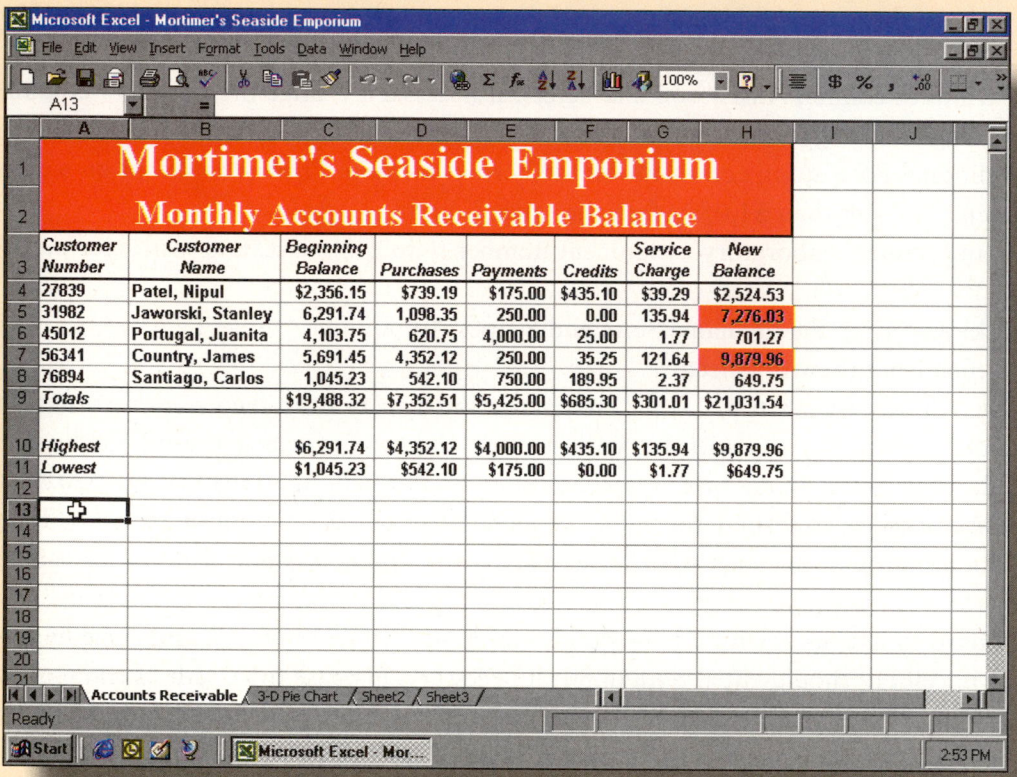

FIGURE 2-86

Instructions Part 1: Create a worksheet similar to the one shown in Figure 2-86. Include all six items in Table 2-8 on the previous page in the report, plus a service charge and a new balance for each customer. Assume no negative unpaid monthly balances. Perform the following tasks.

1. Click the Select All button (to the left of column heading A) and then click the Bold button on the Standard toolbar to bold the entire worksheet.
2. Assign the worksheet title, `Mortimer's Seaside Emporium`, to cell A1. Assign the worksheet subtitle, `Monthly Accounts Receivable Balance`, to cell A2.
3. Enter the column titles in the range A3:H3 as shown in Figure 2-86. Change the width of column A to 9.57. Change the widths of columns B through H to best fit.
4. Enter the customer numbers and row titles in column A. Enter the customer numbers as text, rather than numbers. To enter the customer numbers as text, begin each entry with an apostrophe ('). Enter the remaining data in Table 2-8.
5. Use the following formulas to determine the monthly service charge in column G and the new balance in column H for customer 27839. Copy the two formulas down through the remaining customers.
   a. Service Charge = 2.25% * (Beginning Balance – Payments – Credits)
   b. New Balance = Beginning Balance + Purchases – Payments – Credits + Service Charge

In the Lab

6. Calculate totals for beginning balance, purchases, payments, credits, service charge, and new balance in row 9.

7. Assign cell C10 the appropriate function to calculate the maximum value in the range C4:C8. Copy cell C10 to the range D10:H10.

8. Assign cell C11 the appropriate function to calculate the minimum value in the range C4:C8. Copy cell C11 to the range D11:H11.

9. Change the worksheet title in cell A1 to 28-point CG Times font. Format the worksheet subtitle in cell A2 to 20-point CG Times font. Center the worksheet titles in cells A1 and A2 across column A through H. Change the heights of rows 1 through 3 and row 10 to 27.75. Add a heavy outline to the range A1:H2 using the Borders button on the Formatting toolbar.

10. Select the range A1:H2 and then change the background color to Orange (column 2, row 2) on the Fill Color palette. Change the font color in the range A1:H2 to White (column 8, row 5) on the Font Color palette.

11. Italicize the column titles in row 3. Use the Borders button to add a thick bottom border to the column titles in row 3. Center the column titles in the range B3:H3. Italicize the titles in rows 9, 10, and 11. Use the Borders button to add a single top border and double-line bottom border to the range A9:H9 (column 4, row 2) on the Borders palette.

12. Use the Format Cells command on the shortcut menu to assign the Currency style with a floating dollar sign to the cells containing numeric data in row 4 and rows 9 through 11. Use the same command to assign the Comma style (currency with no dollar sign) to the range C5:H8. The Format Cells command is preferred over the Comma Style button because the worksheet specifications call for displaying zero as 0.00 rather than as a dash (-), as shown in Figure 2-86.

13. Use the Conditional Formatting command on the Format menu to bold the font and color the background orange of any cell in the range H4:H8 that contains a value greater than or equal to 3000.

14. Change the widths of columns B through H again to best fit, if necessary.

15. Rename the sheet Accounts Receivable.

16. Enter your name, course, laboratory assignment number (Lab 2-2), date, and instructor name in the range A13:A17.

17. Save the workbook using the file name Mortimer's Seaside Emporium. Preview and then print the worksheet. Print the range A3:C9.

18. Press CTRL+LEFT SINGLE QUOTATION MARK (`) to change the display from the values version to the formulas version and then print the worksheet to fit on one page in landscape orientation. After the printer is finished, press CTRL+LEFT SINGLE QUOTATION MARK (`) to reset the worksheet to display the values version. Reset the Scaling option to 100% by clicking the Adjust to option button on the Page tab in the Page Setup dialog box and then setting the percent value to 100%. Hand in the printouts to your instructor.

(continued)

In the Lab

Mortimer's Seaside Emporium Monthly Accounts Receivable Balance Sheet *(continued)*

Instructions Part 2: This part requires that you use the Chart Wizard button on the Standard toolbar to draw a Pie chart. If necessary, use the Office Assistant to obtain information on drawing a Pie chart.

Draw the 3-D Pie chart showing the contribution of each customer to the total new balance as shown in Figure 2-87. Select the nonadjacent chart ranges B4:B8 and H4:H8. That is, select the range B4:B8 and then hold down the CTRL key and select the range H4:H8. The category names in the range B4:B8 will identify the slices, while the data series in the range H4:H8 will determine the size of the slices. Click the Chart Wizard button on the Standard toolbar. Draw the 3-D Pie chart on a new chart sheet. Use the 3-D Pie chart sub-type (column 2, row 1). Add the chart title Contributions to Accounts Receivable.

Rename the Chart1 sheet 3-D Pie Chart. Drag the Accounts Receivable tab to the left of the 3-D Pie Chart tab. Save the workbook using the same file name as in Part 1. Preview and print the chart.

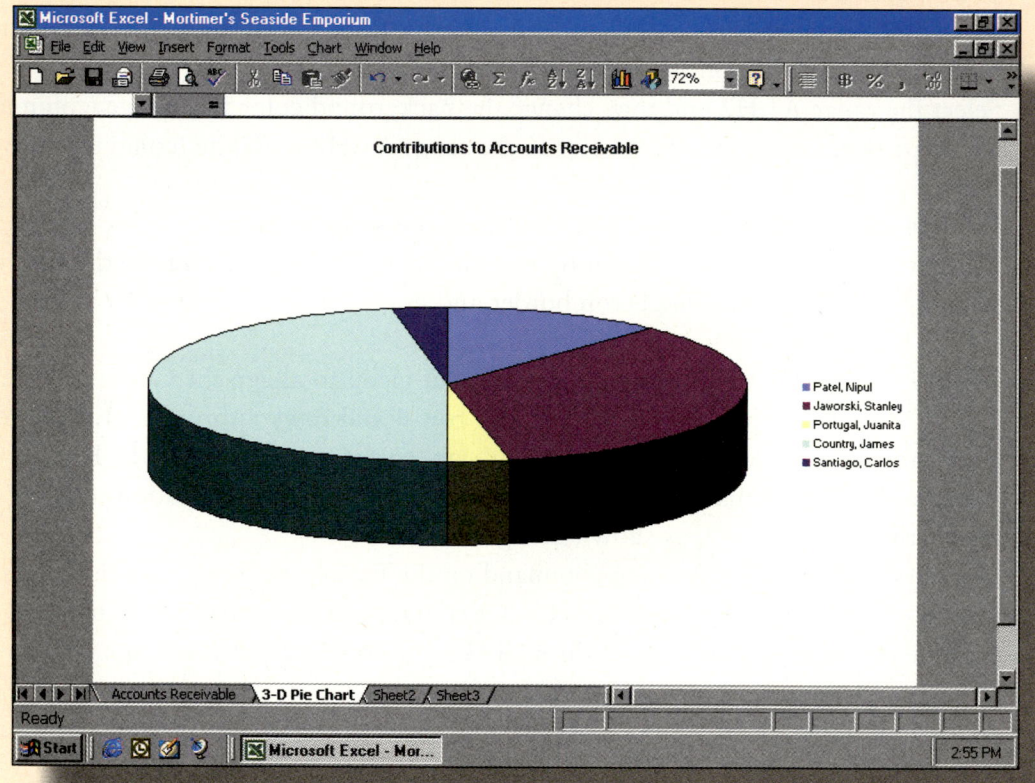

FIGURE 2-87

Instructions Part 3:
Change the following purchases: account number 31982 to $3000.00; account number 76894 to $2500.00. The total new balance in cell H9 should equal $24,891.09. Select both sheets by holding down the SHIFT key and clicking the 3-D Pie Chart tab. Preview and print the selected sheets. Hand in the printouts to your instructor.

Instructions Part 4: With your instructor's permission, e-mail the workbook as an attachment to your instructor. Close the workbook without saving the changes.

In the Lab

3 Equity Web Queries

Problem: The chief accountant at Rhine.com recently attended a Microsoft seminar and learned that Microsoft Excel 2000 can connect to the World Wide Web, download real-time stock data into a worksheet, and then refresh the data as often as needed. Because you have had courses in Excel and the Internet, she has hired you as a consultant to develop a stock analysis workbook. Her portfolio is listed in Table 2-9.

Table 2-9	Portfolio
COMPANY	*STOCK SYMBOL*
Dell	DELL
IBM	IBM
Caterpillar	CAT
Wal-Mart	WMT

Instructions Part 1: If necessary, connect to the Internet. Open a new Excel workbook and select cell A1. Perform the following steps to run a Web query to obtain multiple stock quotes, using the stock symbols in Table 2-9.

1. Point to Get External Data on the Data menu and then click Run Saved Query.
2. Double-click Microsoft Investor Stock Quotes in the Run Query dialog box. If the Queries folder does not display, see your instructor for its location.
3. Click the OK button in the Returning External Data to Microsoft Excel dialog box.
4. When the Enter Parameter Value dialog box displays, enter the stock symbols in Table 2-9 into the text box, being sure to separate them by a comma or space. Click the Use this value/reference for future refreshes check box, click the Refresh automatically when cell value changes, and then click the OK button. After several seconds, the stock data returned by the Web query displays in a worksheet as shown in Figure 2-88 on the next page. Because the stock data returned is real-time, the numbers on your worksheet may be different.
5. Enter your name, course, laboratory assignment number (Lab 2-3a), date, and instructor name in the range A20:A24.
6. Rename the sheet Multiple Quotes. Save the workbook using the file name Equities Online. Preview and then print the worksheet in landscape orientation using the Fit to option.
7. Click the following links and print each: Microsoft Investor, Dell Computer Corporation, Dell Chart, and Dell News. After printing each Web page, close the browser and click the Microsoft Excel button on the taskbar to activate Excel. Hand in the printouts to your instructor.

(continued)

Microsoft **Excel 2000**

In the Lab

Equity Web Queries *(continued)*

FIGURE 2-88

Instructions Part 2: Do the following to create a worksheet listing the major indices and their current values as shown in Figure 2-89.

1. With the workbook created in Part 1 open, click the Sheet2 tab. Point to Get External Data on the Data menu and then click Run Saved Query.
2. Double-click Microsoft Investor Major Indices in the Run Query dialog box.
3. Click the OK button in the Returning External Data to Microsoft Excel dialog box, starting the data in cell A1 of the existing worksheet.
4. The Web query returns the worksheet shown in Figure 2-89. Your results may differ.
5. Enter your name, course, laboratory assignment number (Lab 2-3b), date, and instructor name in the range A24:A28.
6. Rename the sheet Major Indices. Save the workbook using the same file as in Part 1. Preview and then print the worksheet in landscape orientation using the Fit to option. Hand in the printouts to your instructor.

In the Lab

FIGURE 2-89

Instructions Part 3: Create a worksheet showing the latest commodity prices (Figure 2-90 on the next page). The Web query for commodity prices is not one of the queries available in the Queries folder by default. Thus, you must download it from the World Wide Web.

Perform the following tasks.

1. With the workbook Equities Online created in Parts 1 and 2 open, click Sheet3. Rename the Sheet3 tab Get More Queries.

2. Point to Get External Data on the Data menu, and then click Run Saved Query. Double-click Get More Web Queries in the Run Query dialog box.

3. Click the OK button in the Returning External Data to Microsoft Excel dialog box, starting the data in cell A1 of the existing worksheet.

4. When the worksheet titled Microsoft Excel Web Queries displays, scroll down and click the link DBC Major Markets under Stock Market Reports.

5. If the File in Use dialog box displays, click the Notify button. If the File Now Available dialog box displays, click the Read-Write button. The query creates a Read-Only workbook (Book2) and a Read-Write workbook (Book3).

6. With Book3 active, scroll down and over so cell B5 displays in the top left corner of your screen (Figure 2-90).

(continued)

In the Lab

Equity Web Queries *(continued)*

7. Enter your name, course, laboratory assignment number (Lab 2-3c), date, and instructor name in the range B1:B4.

8. After viewing the DBC Major Markets worksheet, preview and print the range B1:H33. On the Windows menu, click Equities Online. Click the Multiple Quotes tab and then save the workbook using the same name as in Part 1. Hand in the printout to your instructor.

FIGURE 2-90

Instructions Part 4: Click the Multiple Quotes tab. Right-click a toolbar and click External Data on the shortcut menu. Refresh the data by clicking the Refresh All button on the External Data toolbar. Click the Click here to visit Microsoft Investor link. When the MSN Money Central investor page displays, find the latest prices for the following symbols: MSFT, INTC, YHOO, and GE. Print the Web page for each. Hand in the printouts to your instructor.

Cases and Places

The difficulty of these case studies varies:
▶ are the least difficult; ▶▶ are more difficult; and ▶▶▶ are the most difficult.

1 ▶ The household electric bill has just arrived in the mail, and you have been accused of driving up the total by burning the midnight oil. You are convinced your late-night studying has little effect on the total amount due. You obtain a brochure from the electric company that lists the typical operating costs of appliances based on average sizes and local electricity rates (Figure 2-91).

With this data, you produce a worksheet to share with your family. Use the concepts and techniques presented in this project to create and format the worksheet.

APPLIANCE	COST PER HOUR	HOURS USED DAILY	TOTAL COST PER DAY	TOTAL COST PER MONTH (30 DAYS)
Clothes dryer	$0.5331	2		
Iron	$0.1173	0.5		
Light bulb (150 watt)	$0.0160	5		
Personal computer	$0.0213	3		
Radio	$0.0075	2		
Refrigerator	$0.0113	24		
Stereo	$0.0053	4		
Television	$0.0128	6		
VCR	$0.0032	2		

FIGURE 2-91

2 ▶ In order to determine the effectiveness of their endangered species recovery plan, the Fish and Wildlife Department traps and releases red wolves in selected areas and records how many are pregnant. To obtain a representative sample, the department tries to trap approximately 20% of the population. The sample for 5 sections is shown in Table 2-10.

Use the following formula to determine the total red wolf population for each section:

Table 2-10	Red Wolf Catch Data		
SECTION	WOLVES CAUGHT	WOLVES PREGNANT	ANNUAL DEATH RATE
1	55	21	19%
2	32	7	22%
3	26	8	32%
4	29	17	8%
5	72	28	29%

Wolves in a Section = 5 * (Total Catch + Pregnant Wolves) – 5 * Death Rate * (Total Catch + Pregnant Wolves)

Use the concepts and techniques presented in this project to create the worksheet. Determine appropriate totals. Finally, estimate the total state red wolf population if 898 sections are in the state.

Cases and Places

3 ▶ The Student Loan Office has a special assistance program that offers emergency short-term loans at simple interest. The five types of emergency loans, end-of-year principal, rate, and time are shown in Table 2-11.

Create a worksheet that includes the information in Table 2-11, the interest, and amount due. Use the following formulas:

Interest = Principal x Rate x Time

Amount Due = Principal + Interest

Also include a total, maximum value, and minimum value for Principal, Interest, and Amount Due. Format the worksheet using the techniques presented in this project.

Table 2-11	Emergency Loans		
LOAN TYPE	*PRINCIPAL*	*RATE*	*TIME IN YEARS*
Tuition Assistance	$96,000	9%	0.4
Academic Supplies	$32,000	11%	0.3
Room and Board	56,250	8%	0.2
Personal Emergency	$7,500	7%	0.17
Travel Expenses	$6,275	15%	0.33

4 ▶ Rich's Oil Production Company drills oil in six states. The management has asked you to develop a worksheet for the company's next meeting from the data in Table 2-12. The worksheet should determine the gross value of the oil, the taxes, and the net value for each state, as well as the net value for all the states. Use these formulas:

Gross Value = Barrels of Oil Produced × Price Per Barrel

Taxes = Gross Value * 7%

Net Value = Gross Value – Taxes

Include appropriate totals, averages, minimums, and maximums. Draw a pie chart on a separate sheet that shows the barrels of oil contribution of each state.

Table 2-12	Oil Production Data	
STATE	*BARRELS OF OIL PRODUCED*	*PRICE PER BARREL*
Alaska	12,890	$14.25
California	4,321	$13.50
Louisiana	8,500	$15.25
Montana	4,250	$13.50
Oklahoma	9,705	$11.75
Texas	7,543	$14.25

5 ▶▶ Use the concepts and techniques described in this project to run the Web queries titled Microsoft Investor Dow30 and Microsoft Investor Currency Rates on separate worksheets shortly after the stock market opens. Print each worksheet to fit on one page in landscape orientation. Refresh the worksheets later in the day near the stock market close. Print the worksheets and compare them.

Run Get More Web Queries through the Run Saved Query command. Print the list on queries available on the Web. Download three of the queries. Run each one and print the results. For more information, see In the Lab Part 3 on page E 2.75.

Cases and Places

6 ▶▶ The Woodbridge Furniture Company has decided to pay a 5% commission to its salespeople to stimulate sales. The company currently pays each employee a base salary. The management has projected each employee's sales for the next quarter. This information - employee name, employee base salary, and projected sales - follows: Baker, Tim, $6,000.00, $225,456.00; Learner, Joseph, $7,500.00, $264,888.00; Albright, Barbara, $8,500.00, $235,250.00; Mourissee, Lynn, $7,250.00, $258,450.00; Noble, Richard, $4,250.00, $325,456.00.

With this data, you have been asked to develop a worksheet calculating the amount of commission and the quarterly salary for each employee. The following formulas can be used to obtain this information:

Commission Amount = 5% x Projected Sales

Quarterly Salary = Employee Base Salary + Commission Amount

Include a total, Average Value, Highest Value, and Lowest Value for Employee Base Salary, Commission Amount, and Quarterly Salary. Create an appropriate chart illustrating the portion each employee's quarterly salary contributes to the total quarterly salary. Use the concepts and techniques presented in this project to create and format the worksheet and chart.

7 ▶▶▶ Regular, moderate exercise lowers cholesterol and blood pressure, reduces stress, controls weight, and increases bone strength. Fitness experts recommend individuals who need to lose weight do so at the rate of 1½ to 2 pounds per week. If an individual maintains a regular, sensible diet and burns 750 extra calories each day, he or she will lose about 1½ pounds of fatty tissue a week. Visit a fitness center at your school or in your community to discuss various exercise options. Find out the types of activities offered (for example, aerobics, swimming, jogging, tennis, racquetball, and basketball). Then, list how many calories are burned per hour when performing each of these activities. Using this information, create a worksheet showing the activities offered, the number of calories burned per hour performing these activities, the number of calories burned and pounds lost if you exercise two hours, four hours, and seven hours a week while performing each of these activities.

Microsoft Excel 2000

3

What-If Analysis, Charting, and Working with Large Worksheets

O B J E C T I V E S

You will have mastered the material in this project when you can:

- Rotate text in a cell
- Use the fill handle to create a series of month names
- Copy a cell's format to another cell using the Format Painter button
- Copy a range of cells to a nonadjacent paste area
- Freeze column and row titles
- Insert and delete cells
- Format numbers using format symbols
- Use the NOW function to display the system date
- Format the system date
- Use absolute cell references in a formula
- Use the IF function to enter one value or another in a cell on the basis of a logical test
- Copy absolute cell references
- Display and dock toolbars
- Add a drop shadow to a range of cells
- Create a 3-D Pie chart on a separate chart sheet
- Format a 3-D Pie chart
- Rearrange sheets in a workbook
- Preview and print multiple sheets
- Use the Zoom box to change the appearance of the worksheet
- View different parts of the worksheet through window panes
- Use Excel to answer what-if questions
- Use the Goal Seek command to analyze worksheet data

10^{12}

What If You Had to Manage This Kind of Money?

Try to imagine counting one trillion dollars. One trillion is equal to 10 to the twelfth power or 10 times 100 billion. In any case, it is hard even to imagine what a trillion dollars is. If you were given a trillion $1 bills, just counting them would take you 32,000 years at a rate of one per second, twenty-four hours a day. You would break several records if you accomplished that feat.

The world is still waiting for its first trillionaire — speculated to be America's Bill Gates, Asia's Richard Li, or Brunei's Sultan Hassanal Bolkiah.

The current U.S. national debt exceeds five trillion dollars ($5,000,000,000,000) with projected annual interest payments of $235 billion. Italy, Japan, and Australia also face debts in trillions of dollars. It is no wonder that financial counselors encourage sound fiscal control and budgeting to avoid deficit spending or debt. People who borrow are expected both to be able and willing to pay back what they owe along with an appropriate amount of interest.

U.S. National Debt Clock

The Outstanding Public Debt as of 06/22/99 at 09:16:21 PM PDT is:

$5,608,965,261,367.73

When working with any sum of money — whether an individual's thousands, the more than 125 American billionaires' billions, or even the nation's trillions — creating a realistic budget indeed can be difficult. Budgets provide a sense of perspective that makes it possible to keep debt at a minimum. Although you are not responsible for preparing a national $1.64 trillion budget, knowing where your money goes is the first step in planning a sound personal budget.

Budgeting using worksheets helps reconcile income and expenses. For example, based on a loan calculation and a budget, you can determine a reasonable monthly car payment. Your living expenses may include rent, food, utilities, car and loan payments, credit card payments, and entertainment. Developing a solid budget for these expenses can help you determine if you will be able to buy a future home. Budgets track your income, expenses, net worth, and cash flow, while organizing your financial data in a logical format. Using electronic spreadsheet software makes it easy to show exactly how you spend money.

In this project, you will use Excel's automatic recalculation feature to complete what-if analysis. It is a powerful tool used to analyze worksheet data. It allows you to scrutinize the impact of changing values in cells that are referenced by a formula in another cell. What if you need to know how much money to put down on a home loan in order to find a manageable monthly payment? What if your income changes or you add a new expense or pay a final payment? These questions and more can be answered easily with Excel's what-if capabilities. Excel not only recalculates all the formulas in a worksheet when new data is entered, it also redraws any associated charts.

Just as the nation must examine line by line how its money is spent, personal budget calculations allow you to do the same. Appearing somewhat restrictive, a personal budget is a necessity to avoid the alternative — if you exceed the average debt-to-asset ratio of 30 percent, you could end up joining the world's trillionaire debt club.

Microsoft Excel 2000

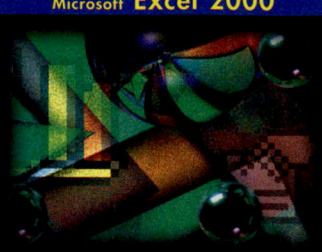

What-If Analysis, Charting, and Working with Large Worksheets

P R O J E C T
3

CASE PERSPECTIVE

Hyperlink.com is a global provider of routers, LAN switches, dial-up access servers, and network management software for the Internet. These products link geographically dispersed networks. Each June and December, the chief executive officer (CEO) of Hyperlink.com, Frances Collins, submits a plan to the board of directors to show projected revenues, expenses, and net income for the next six months.

Last December, Frances used pencil, paper, and a calculator to complete the report and draw a 3-D Pie chart. When she presented her report, the directors asked for the effect on the projected net income if the administrative expense allocation was changed. While the directors waited impatiently, Frances took several minutes to calculate the answers. Once she changed the projected expenses, the 3-D Pie chart no longer matched the projections. Frances now wants to use a computer and spreadsheet software to address what-if questions so she can take advantage of its instantaneous recalculation feature. As lead spreadsheet specialist for Hyperlink.com, you are to meet with Frances, determine her needs, and create the worksheet and chart.

Introduction

This project introduces you to techniques that will enhance your abilities to create worksheets and draw charts. You will learn about other methods for entering values in cells and formatting these values. You also will learn how to use absolute cell references and how to use the IF function to assign a value to a cell based on a logical test.

In the previous projects, you learned how to use the Standard and Formatting toolbars. Excel has several other toolbars that can make your work easier. One such toolbar is the **Drawing toolbar**, which allows you to draw shapes and arrows and add drop shadows to cells you want to emphasize.

Worksheets normally are much larger than those created in the previous projects, often extending beyond the size of the window. Because you cannot see the entire worksheet on the screen at one time, working with a large worksheet can be difficult. For this reason, Excel provides several commands that allow you to change the display on the screen so you can view critical parts of a large worksheet at one time. One command lets you freeze the row and column titles so they always display on the screen. Another command splits the worksheet into separate window panes so you can view different parts of a worksheet.

From your work in Project 1, you are aware of how easily charts can be created. This project covers additional charting techniques that allow you to convey your message in a dramatic pictorial fashion.

When you set up a worksheet, you should use as many cell references in formulas as possible, rather than constant values. The cell references in a formula often are called assumptions. **Assumptions** are values in cells you can change to determine new values for formulas. This project emphasizes the use of assumptions and introduces you to answering what-if questions such as, what if you decrease the marketing expenses assumption (cell B18 in Figure 3-1a) by 1% — how would the decrease affect the projected six-month net income (cell H14 in Figure 3-1a)? Being able to quickly analyze the effect of changing values in a worksheet is an important skill in making business decisions.

Hyperlink.com

Six-Month Projected Revenue, Expenses, and Net Income   11/26/2001

	July	August	September	October	November	December	Total
Revenue	$8,754,250.00	$4,978,200.00	$5,250,000.00	$7,554,875.00	$4,768,300.00	$6,550,700.00	$37,856,325.00
Expenses							
Administrative	$1,159,938.13	$659,611.50	$695,625.00	$1,001,020.94	$631,799.75	$867,967.75	$5,015,963.06
Marketing	831,653.75	472,929.00	498,750.00	717,713.13	452,988.50	622,316.50	3,596,350.88
Commission	153,199.38	87,118.50	91,875.00	132,210.31	83,445.25	114,637.25	662,485.69
Bonus	75,000.00	0.00	75,000.00	75,000.00	0.00	75,000.00	300,000.00
Technical Support	2,516,846.88	1,431,232.50	1,509,375.00	2,172,026.56	1,370,886.25	1,883,326.25	10,883,693.44
Equipment	2,735,703.13	1,555,687.50	1,640,625.00	2,360,898.44	1,490,093.75	2,047,093.75	11,830,101.56
Total Expenses	$7,472,341.25	$4,206,579.00	$4,511,250.00	$6,458,869.38	$4,029,213.50	$5,610,341.50	$32,288,594.63
Net Income	$1,281,908.75	$771,621.00	$738,750.00	$1,096,005.63	$739,086.50	$940,358.50	$5,567,730.38

Assumptions	
Administrative	13.25%
Marketing	9.50%
Commission	1.75%
Bonus	75,000.00
Revenue for Bonus	5,000,000.00
Technical Support	28.75%
Equipment	31.25%

(a) Worksheet

Microsoft Excel - Hyperlink

File   Edit   View   Insert   Format   Tools   Chart   Window   Help

Projected Net Income

October 20%
November 13%
December 17%
July 23%
August 14%
September 13%

Six-Month Plan / **3-D Pie Chart** / Sheet2 / Sheet3

Ready

Start   Microsoft Excel - Hyp...   3:01 PM

(b) 3-D Pie Chart

FIGURE 3-1

Project Three — Hyperlink.com Six-Month Projected Revenue, Expenses, and Net Income

You took the following notes about the required worksheet and chart in your meeting with the CEO, Frances Collins.

Need: A worksheet (Figure 3-1a on the previous page) and 3-D Pie chart (Figure 3-1b on the previous page) are required. The worksheet is to show Hyperlink.com's projected monthly revenue, expenses, and net income for a six-month period. The 3-D Pie chart is to show the contribution of each projected month's net income to the projected seven-month total net income.

Source of Data: The six projected monthly revenues (row 4 of Figure 3-1a) and the seven assumptions (range B17:B23) that are used to determine the projected monthly expenses are based on the company's historical data. All the remaining numbers in Figure 3-1a are determined from these twelve numbers using formulas.

Calculations: Each of the projected monthly expenses in the range B7:G12 of Figure 3-1a — administrative, marketing, commission, bonus, technical support, and equipment — is determined by taking an assumed percentage of the corresponding projected monthly revenue in row 4. The assumptions in the range B17:B23 are as follows:

1. The projected monthly administrative expenses (row 7) are 13.25% of the projected monthly revenue (row 4).
2. The projected monthly marketing expenses (row 8) are 9.50% of the projected monthly revenue (row 4).
3. The projected monthly commission expenses (row 9) are 1.75% of the projected monthly revenue (row 4).
4. The projected monthly bonus (row 10) is $75,000.00, if the projected monthly revenue (row 4) exceeds the revenue for bonus to be awarded, otherwise the projected monthly bonus is zero. The revenue for bonus value is in cell B21 ($5,000,000.00).
5. The projected monthly technical support expenses (row 11) are 28.75% of the projected monthly revenue (row 4).
6. The projected monthly equipment expenses (row 12) are 31.25% of the projected monthly revenue (row 4).

The projected total monthly expenses in row 13 of Figure 3-1a are the sum of the corresponding projected monthly expenses in rows 7 through 12. The projected monthly net income in row 14 is equal to the corresponding projected monthly revenue (row 4) minus the projected monthly total expenses (row 13).

Because the projected expenses in rows 7 through 12 are dependent on the assumptions in the range B17:B23, you can use the what-if capability of Excel to determine the impact of changing these assumptions on the projected monthly total expenses in row 13.

Chart Requirements: A 3-D Pie chart is required on a separate sheet (Figure 3-1b) that shows the contribution of each month to the projected net income for the six-month period.

Starting Excel and Resetting Toolbars and Menus

To start Excel, Windows must be running. Perform the following steps to start Excel. Once Excel displays, Steps 4 through 6 reset the toolbars and menus to their original settings.

More *About* 2000

Garbage In Garbage Out

Studies have shown that more than 25 percent of all business worksheets have errors. If your data or formulas are in error, then the results are in error. You can ensure accuracy of your formulas by using the Auditing command on the Tools menu. The Auditing command indicates relationships among formulas.

More *About* 2000

Formulas and Recalculation

Excel automatically recalculates all formulas in the workbook when you enter a value in a cell. If a workbook has many formulas, you can grow impatient waiting for the recalculation to take place, even though it seldom takes more than a few seconds with hundreds of formulas in a workbook. You can switch Excel to manual recalculation by clicking Tools on the menu bar, clicking Options, clicking the Calculation tab, and then clicking the Manual option button. You press F9 to recalculate when you have entered all of the values.

TO START EXCEL AND RESET TOOLBARS AND MENUS

1 Click the Start button on the taskbar.

2 Click New Office Document. If necessary, click the General tab in the New Office Document dialog box.

3 Double-click the Blank Workbook icon.

4 When the blank worksheet displays, click View on the menu bar, click the arrows at the bottom of the menu to display the full menu, point to Toolbars, and click Customize on the Toolbars submenu.

5 When the Customize dialog box displays, click the Options tab, make sure the top three check boxes contain check marks, click the Reset my usage data button, and then click the Yes button.

6 Click the Toolbars tab. Click Standard, click the Reset button, and then click the OK button. Click Formatting, click the Reset button, and the click the OK button. Click the Close button.

7 Double-click the move handle on the far left side of the Formatting toolbar so it displays in its entirety.

The Standard and Formatting toolbars should display as shown in Figure 3-2 on the next page.

See Appendix B for additional information on resetting the toolbars and menus.

Changing the Font of the Entire Worksheet to Bold

After starting Excel, the next step is to change the font of the entire worksheet to bold so all entries will be emphasized.

TO BOLD THE FONT OF THE ENTIRE WORKSHEET

1 Click the Select All button immediately above row heading 1 and to the left of column heading A.

2 Click the Bold button on the Formatting toolbar.

No immediate change takes place on the screen. As you enter text and numbers into the worksheet, however, Excel will display them in bold.

Entering the Worksheet Titles

The worksheet contains two titles, one in cell A1, and another in cell A2. In the previous projects, titles were centered across the worksheet. With large worksheets that extend beyond the size of a window, it is best to enter titles in the upper-left corner as shown in Figure 3-1a on page E 3.5.

TO ENTER THE WORKSHEET TITLES

1 Select cell A1 and then type Hyperlink.com to enter the title.

2 Select cell A2 and then type Six-Month Projected Revenue, Expenses, and Net Income to enter the second title.

3 Select cell B3.

Excel responds by displaying the worksheet titles in cells A1 and A2 in bold (Figure 3-2).

More *About*

Rotating Text

If you enter 90° in the Degrees box in the Alignment tab of the Format Cells dialog box, the text will display vertically and read from bottom to top in the cell. You can rotate the text clockwise by entering a number between -1° and -90°. If you enter -90°, the text will display vertically and read from top to bottom in the cell.

Rotating Text and Using the Fill Handle to Create a Series

When you first enter text, its angle is zero degrees (0°), and it reads from left to right in a cell. You can **rotate text** counterclockwise by entering a number between 1° and 90° on the Alignment sheet in the Format Cells dialog box. An example of rotating the text is shown in the next set of steps.

In Projects 1 and 2, you used the fill handle to copy a cell or a range of cells to adjacent cells. You also can use the fill handle to create a series of numbers, dates, or month names automatically. Perform the following steps to enter the month name, July, in cell B3, format cell B3 (including rotating the text), and then enter the remaining month names in the range C3:G3 using the fill handle.

Steps: To Rotate Text and Use the Fill Handle to Create a Series of Month Names

1 **With cell B3 active, type** July **and then press the ENTER key. On the Formatting toolbar, click the Font Size box arrow and then click 11 in the Font Size list. Click the Borders button arrow and then click the Thick Bottom Border button on the Borders palette. Right-click cell B3 and then point to Format Cells on the shortcut menu.**

The text, July, displays in cell B3 using the assigned formats (Figure 3-2). The shortcut menu displays.

FIGURE 3-2

2 Click Format Cells. When the Format Cells dialog box displays, click the Alignment tab. Click the 45° point in the Orientation area and point to the OK button.

The Alignment sheet in the Format Cells dialog box displays. The Text hand in the Orientation area points to the 45° point and 45 displays in the Degrees box (Figure 3-3).

FIGURE 3-3

3 Click the OK button. Point to the fill handle on the lower-right edge of cell B3.

The text, July, in cell B3 displays at a 45° angle (Figure 3-4). Excel automatically increases the height of row 3 to best fit to display the rotated text. The mouse pointer changes to a cross hair.

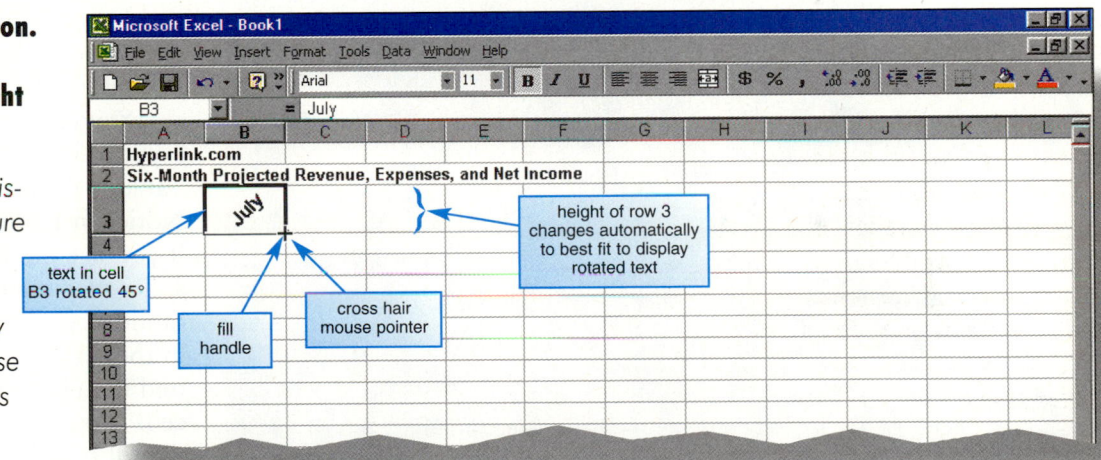

FIGURE 3-4

4 Drag the fill handle to the right to select the range C3:G3.

Excel displays a light border that surrounds the selected range (Figure 3-5).

FIGURE 3-5

Microsoft **Excel 2000**

5 Release the mouse button.

Using July in cell B3 as the basis, Excel creates the month name series August through December in the range C3:G3 (Figure 3-6). The formats assigned to cell B3 earlier in Step 1 (11-point font, thick bottom border, text rotated 45°) also are copied to the range C3:G3.

FIGURE 3-6

1. Enter start month in cell, right-drag fill handle in direction to fill, click Fill Months on shortcut menu

Besides creating a series of values, the fill handle also copies the format of cell B3 (11-point font, thick bottom border, text rotated 45°) to the range C3:G3. You can use the fill handle to create longer series than the one shown in Figure 3-6. If you drag the fill handle past cell G3 in Step 4, Excel continues to increment the months and logically will repeat July, August, and so on, if you extend the range far enough to the right.

You can create several different types of series using the fill handle. Table 3-1 illustrates several examples. Notice in Examples 4 through 7 that, if you use the fill handle to create a series of numbers or non-sequential months, you must enter the first item in the series in one cell and the second item in the series in an adjacent cell. Next, select both cells and drag the fill handle through the paste area.

Table 3-1	Examples of Series Using the Fill Handle	
EXAMPLE	CONTENTS OF CELL(S) COPIED USING THE FILL HANDLE	NEXT THREE VALUES OF EXTENDED SERIES
1	3:00	4:00, 5:00, 6:00
2	Qtr3	Qtr4, Qtr1, Qtr2
3	Quarter 1	Quarter 2, Quarter 3, Quarter 4
4	Jul-2001, Oct-2001	Jan-2002, Apr-2002, Jul-2002
5	2000, 2001	2002, 2003, 2004
6	1, 2	3, 4, 5
7	600, 580	560, 540, 520
8	Sun	Mon, Tue, Wed
9	Saturday, Monday	Wednesday, Friday, Sunday
10	1st Section	2nd Section, 3rd Section, 4th Section
11	-99, -101	-103, -105, -107

Copying a Cell's Format Using the Format Painter Button

Because it is not part of the series, the last column title, Total, must be entered separately in cell H3 and formatted to match the other column titles. Imagine how many steps it would take, however, to assign the formatting of the other column titles to this cell — first, you have to change the font to 11 point, then add a thick bottom border, and finally, rotate the text 45°. Using the **Format Painter button** on the Standard toolbar, however, you can format a cell quickly by copying a cell's format to another cell. The following steps enter the column title, Total, in cell H3 and format the cell using the Format Painter button.

Steps: To Copy a Cell's Format Using the Format Painter Button

1 Double-click the move handle on the Standard toolbar to display it in its entirety. Click cell H3. Type Total and then press the LEFT ARROW key. With cell G3 selected, click the Format Painter button on the Standard toolbar. Point to cell H3.

The mouse pointer changes to a block plus sign with a paint brush (Figure 3-7).

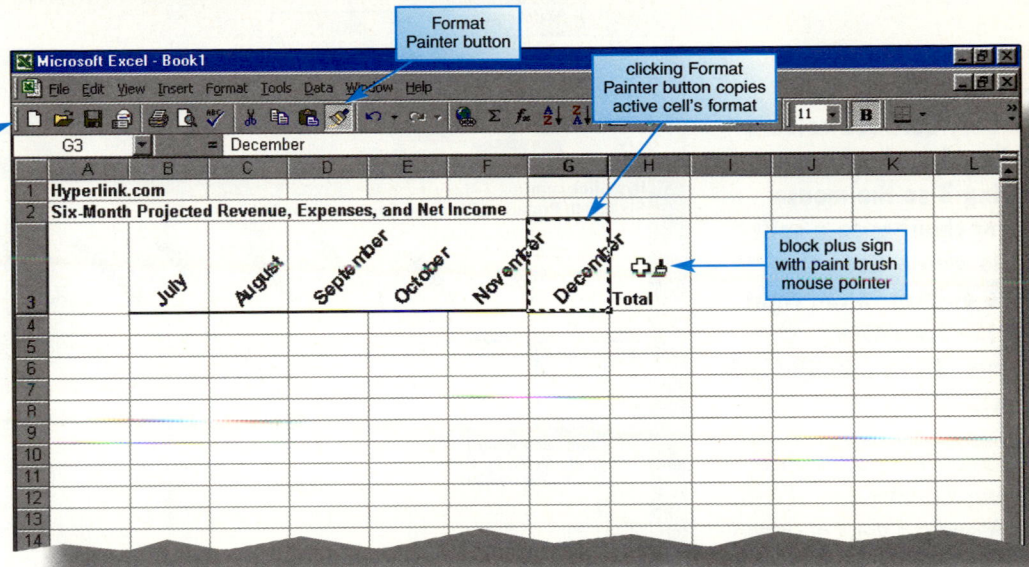

FIGURE 3-7

2 Click cell H3 to assign the format of cell G3 to cell H3. Click cell A4.

Excel copies the format of cell G3 (11-point font, thick bottom border, text rotated 45°) to cell H3 (Figure 3-8).

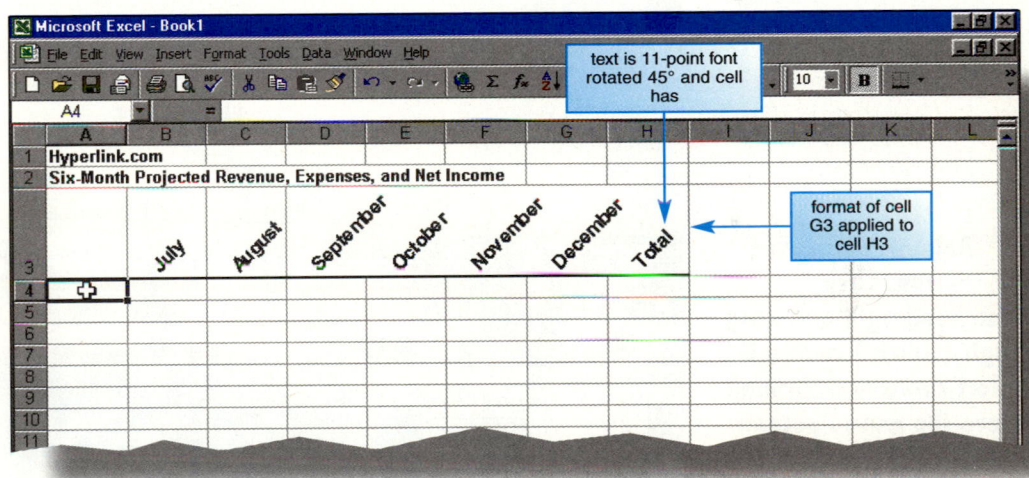

FIGURE 3-8

The Format Painter button also can be used to copy the formats of a cell to a range of cells. To copy formats to a range of cells, select the cell or range with the desired format, click the Format Painter button on the Standard toolbar, and then drag through the range to which you want to paste the formats.

Increasing the Column Widths and Entering Row Titles

In Project 2, the column widths were increased after the values were entered into the worksheet. Sometimes, you may want to increase the column widths before you enter the values and then, if necessary, adjust them later. The steps on the next page increase the column widths and add the row titles in column A down to the Assumptions in cell A16.

Other Ways

1. Click Copy button, on Edit menu click Paste Special, click Formats, click OK button

More About 2000

The Format Painter Button

Double-click the Format Painter button on the Standard toolbar to copy the formats to nonadjacent ranges. Click the Format Painter button to deactivate it.

Steps To Increase Column Widths and Enter Row Titles

1 Move the mouse pointer to the boundary between column heading A and column heading B so the mouse pointer changes to a split double arrow. Drag the mouse pointer to the right until the ScreenTip displays, Width: 25.00 (180 pixels).

The ScreenTip and distance between the left edge of column A and the vertical dotted line below the mouse pointer shows the proposed column width (Figure 3-9).

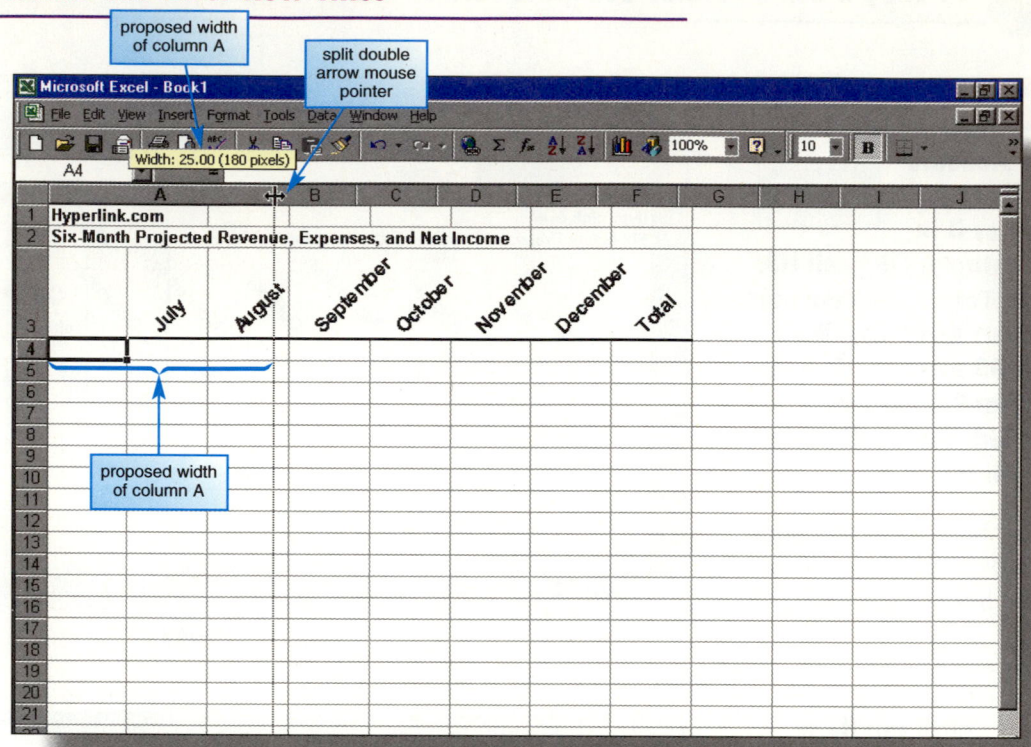

FIGURE 3-9

2 Release the mouse button. Click column heading B and drag through column heading G to select columns B through G. Move the mouse pointer to the boundary between column headings B and C and then drag the mouse to the right until the ScreenTip displays, Width: 13.00 (96 pixels).

The distance between the left edge of column B and the vertical line below the mouse pointer shows the proposed width of columns B through G (Figure 3-10).

FIGURE 3-10

3 **Release the mouse button. Use the technique described in Step 1 to increase the width of column H to 15.00. Enter** Revenue **in cell A4,** Expenses **in cell A6,** Administrative **in cell A7,** Marketing **in cell A8, and** Commission **in cell A9. Enter** Bonus **in cell A10,** Technical Support **in cell A11,** Equipment **in cell A12,** Total Expenses **in cell A13,** Net Income **in cell A14, and** Assumptions **in cell A16. Select the range A7:A12. Double-click the move handle on the Formatting toolbar to display it in its entirety. Click the Increase Indent button on the Formatting toolbar. Click cell A17.**

The row titles display as shown in Figure 3-11.

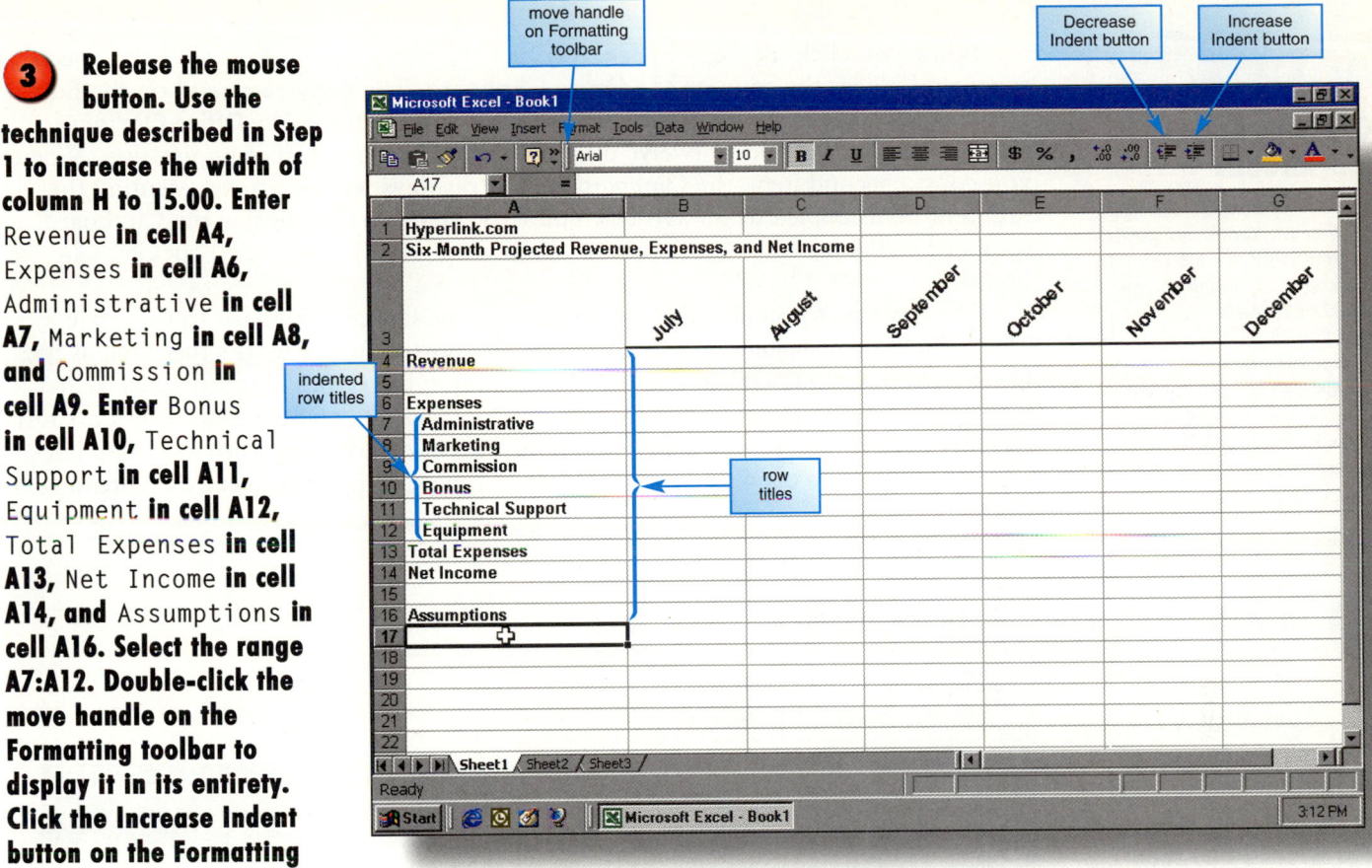

FIGURE 3-11

The **Increase Indent button** indents the contents of a cell to the right by three spaces each time you click it. The **Decrease Indent button** decreases the indent by three spaces each time you click it.

Copying a Range of Cells to a Nonadjacent Paste Area

As shown in Figure 3-1a on page E 3.5, the row titles in the Assumptions table in the range A17:A23 are the same as the row titles in the range A7:A12, with the exception of the additional entry in cell A21. Hence, you can create the Assumptions table row titles by copying the range A7:A12 to the range A17:A23 and inserting the additional entry in cell A21. The range to copy (range A7:A12) is not adjacent to the paste area (range A17:A22). In the first two projects, you used the fill handle to copy a range of cells to an adjacent paste area. To copy a range of cells to a nonadjacent paste area, however, you cannot use the fill handle.

A more versatile method of copying a cell or range of cells is to use the Copy button and Paste button on the Standard toolbar. You can use these two buttons to copy a range of cells to an adjacent or nonadjacent paste area.

Other Ways

1. Right-click range, click Format cells, click Alignment tab, click Left (Indent) in Horizontal list, type number of spaces to indent in Indent text box, click OK button

More About 2000

Shrink to Fit

An alternative to increasing the column widths is to shrink the characters in the cell to fit the current width of the column. To shrink to fit, click Format on the menu bar, click Cells, click the Alignment tab, and click the Shrink to fit check box in the Text control area.

Copying Across Workbooks

If you have a range of cells in another workbook that you want to copy into the current workbook, open the source workbook, select the range, and then click the Copy button to place the range of cells on the Office Clipboard. Next, activate the destination workbook by clicking its file name on the Window menu. Finally, select the paste area and then click the Paste button.

When you click the **Copy button**, it copies the contents and format of the selected range and places the copy on the Office Clipboard. The **Copy command** on the Edit menu or shortcut menu works the same as the Copy button. The **Office Clipboard** allows you to collect up to twelve different items from any Office application. When you copy a second item, the **Clipboard toolbar** displays with icons representing the different items copied to the Office Clipboard. You also can display the Clipboard toolbar by clicking View on the menu bar, pointing to Toolbars, and clicking Clipboard.

The **Paste button** copies the newest item on the Office Clipboard to the paste area. The **Paste command** on the Edit menu or shortcut menu works the same as the Paste button. If you want to copy an older item on the Office Clipboard, click the icon representing the item on the Clipboard toolbar. When you are copying the most recently copied item to more than one nonadjacent cell or range, use the Paste button. When you are copying to a single cell or range, complete the copy by pressing the ENTER key.

 To Copy a Range of Cells to a Nonadjacent Paste Area

1 **Double-click the move handle on the Standard toolbar to display it in its entirety. Select the range A7:A12 and then click the Copy button on the Standard toolbar. Click cell A17, the top cell in the paste area.**

Excel surrounds the range A7:A12 with a marquee when you click the Copy button (Figure 3-12). Excel also copies the values and formats of the range A7:A12 onto the Office Clipboard.

FIGURE 3-12

2 **Press the ENTER key to complete the copy.**

Excel copies the contents of the Office Clipboard (range A7:A12) to the paste area A17:A22 (Figure 3-13).

FIGURE 3-13

In Step 1 and Figure 3-12, you can see that you are not required to select the entire paste area (range A17:A22) before pressing the ENTER key to complete the copy. Because the paste area is exactly the same size as the range you are copying, you have to select only the top left cell of the paste area. In the case of a single column range such as A17:A22, the top cell of the paste area (cell A17) also is the upper-left cell of the paste area.

When you complete a copy, the values and formats in the paste area are replaced with the values and formats on the Office Clipboard. Any data contained in the paste area prior to the copy and paste is lost. If you accidentally delete valuable data, immediately click the Undo button on the Standard toolbar or click the **Undo Paste command** on the Edit menu to undo the paste.

When you press the ENTER key to complete a copy, the contents on the Office Clipboard are not available unless you display the Clipboard toolbar. When you paste using the Paste button or the Paste command on the Edit menu or shortcut menu, the contents of the Office Clipboard remain available for additional copying via the Paste button or Paste command. Hence, if you plan to copy the cells to more than one paste area, click the Paste button or click Paste on the Edit menu or shortcut menu instead of pressing the ENTER key. Then, select the next paste area and invoke the Paste command again. If you paste using the Paste button or the Paste command on the Edit menu or shortcut menu, the marquee remains around the copied range to remind you that this range is still on the Office Clipboard. To remove the marquee, press the ESC key.

Using Drag and Drop to Move or Copy Cells

You also can use the mouse to move or copy cells. First, you select the copy area and point to the border of the cell or range. You know you are pointing to the border of the cell or range when the mouse pointer changes to a **block arrow**. To move the selected cell or cells, drag the selection to its new location. To copy a selection, hold down the CTRL key while dragging the selection to its new location. Be sure to release the mouse button before you release the CTRL key. Using the mouse to move or copy cells is called **drag and drop**.

Other Ways

1. Select copy area and point to border of range; while holding down CTRL key, drag copy area to paste area
2. Right-click copy area, click Copy on shortcut menu, right-click paste area, click Paste
3. Select copy area, on Edit menu click Copy, select paste area, on Edit menu click Paste
4. Select copy area, press CTRL+C, select paste area, press CTRL+V

More About 2000

Copying versus Moving

You may hear someone say, "move it or copy it, it is all the same." No, it is not the same! When you move cells, the original location is blanked and the format is reset to the default. When you copy cells, the copy area remains intact. In short, copy cells to duplicate and move cells to rearrange.

Using the Cut Command

When you cut a cell or range of cells using the Cut command or Cut button on the Standard toolbar, it is copied to the Office Clipboard. It is not removed from the worksheet until you paste it in its new location by clicking the Paste button or pressing the ENTER key.

Another way to move cells is to select them, click the Cut button on the Standard toolbar (Figure 3-12 on page E 3.14) to remove them from the worksheet and copy them to the Office Clipboard, select the new area, and then click the Paste button on the Standard toolbar or press the ENTER key. You also can use the Cut command on the Edit menu or shortcut menu.

Inserting and Deleting Cells in a Worksheet

At any time while the worksheet is on the screen, you can insert cells to enter new data or delete cells to remove unwanted data. You can insert or delete individual cells, a range of cells, entire rows, entire columns, or entire worksheets.

Inserting Rows

The **Rows command** on the Insert menu or the **Insert command** on the shortcut menu allows you to insert rows between rows that already contain data. In the Assumptions table at the bottom of the worksheet, a row must be inserted between rows 20 and 21 so the Revenue for Bonus assumption can be added (see Figure 3-1a on page E 3.5). The following steps show how to accomplish the task of inserting a new row into the worksheet.

 ## To Insert Rows

1 **Right-click row heading 21 and then point to Insert on the shortcut menu.**

Row 21 is selected, and the shortcut menu displays (Figure 3-14).

FIGURE 3-14

2 **Click Insert.**
Click cell A21.

Excel inserts a new row by shifting down all rows below and including row 21, the one originally selected (Figure 3-15).

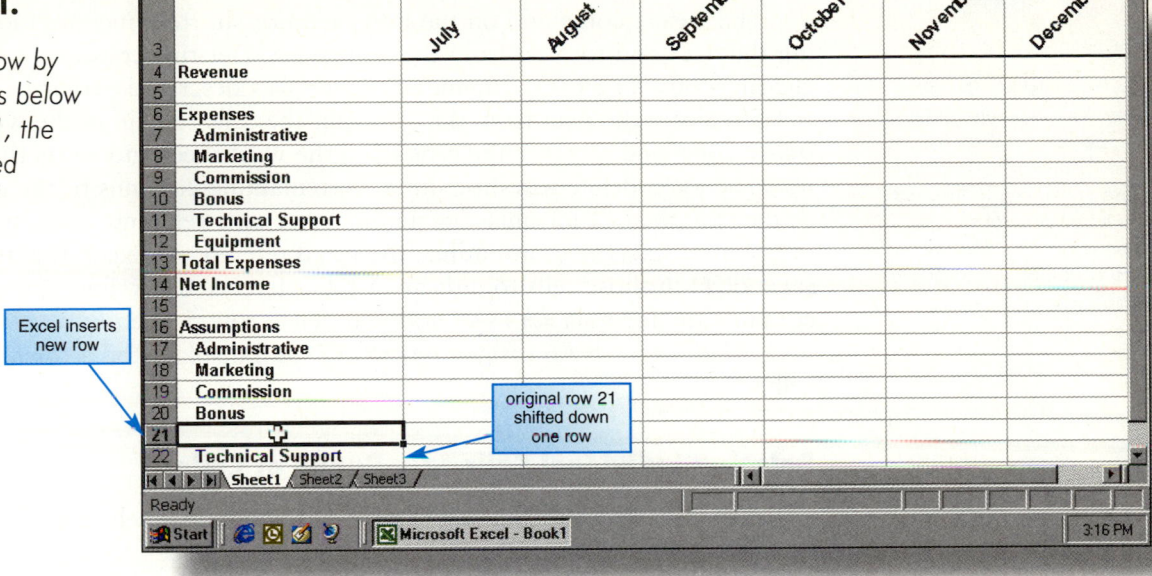

FIGURE 3-15

If the rows that are shifted down include any formulas, Excel adjusts the cell references to the new locations. Thus, if a formula in the worksheet references a cell in row 21 before the insert, then the cell reference in the formula is adjusted to row 22 after the insert.

The primary difference between the Insert command on the shortcut menu and the Rows command on the Insert menu is this: The Insert command on the shortcut menu requires that you select an entire row (or rows) in order to insert a row (or rows). The Rows command on the Insert menu requires that you select a single cell in a row to insert one row or a range of cells to insert multiple rows.

Inserting Columns

You insert columns into a worksheet in the same way you insert rows. To insert columns, begin your column selection immediately to the right of where you want Excel to insert the new blank columns. Select the number of columns you want to insert. Next, click Columns on the Insert menu or click Insert on the shortcut menu. Again, the primary difference between these two commands is this: The **Columns command** on the Insert menu requires that you select a single cell in a column to insert one column or a range of cells to insert multiple columns. The Insert command on the shortcut menu, however, requires that you select an entire column (or columns) to insert a column (or columns).

Inserting Individual Cells or a Range of Cells

The Insert command on the shortcut menu or the **Cells command** on the Insert menu allows you to insert a single cell or a range of cells. You should be aware that if you shift a single cell or a range of cells, however, they no longer may be lined up with their associated cells. To ensure that the values in the worksheet do not get out of order, it is recommended that you insert only entire rows or entire columns.

Other Ways

1. On the Insert menu click Rows
2. Press CTRL+SHIFT+PLUS SIGN, click Entire Row, click OK button

More About 2000

Moving and Inserting

You can move and insert between existing cells by holding down the SHIFT key while you drag the selection to the gridline where you want to insert. You also can copy and insert by holding down the CTRL and SHIFT keys while you drag the selection to the desired gridline.

Undo

Copying, deleting, inserting, and moving have the potential to render a worksheet useless. Carefully review these actions before continuing to the next task. If you are not sure the action is correct, click the Undo button on the Standard toolbar.

Deleting Columns and Rows

The Delete command on the Edit menu or shortcut menu removes cells (including the data and format) from the worksheet. Deleting cells is not the same as clearing cells. The Clear command, which was described earlier in Project 1 on page E 1.53, clears the data from the cells, but the cells remain in the worksheet. The **Delete command** removes the cells from the worksheet and shifts the remaining rows up (when you delete rows) or shifts the remaining columns to the left (when you delete columns). If formulas located in other cells reference cells in the deleted row or column, Excel does not adjust these cell references. Excel displays the error message **#REF!** in those cells to indicate a cell reference error. For example, if cell A7 contains the formula =A4+A5 and you delete row 5, then Excel assigns the formula =A4+#REF! to cell A6 (originally cell A7) and displays the error message #REF! in cell A6.

Deleting Individual Cells or a Range of Cells

Although Excel allows you to delete an individual cell or range of cells, you should be aware that if you shift a cell or range of cells on the worksheet, they no longer may be lined up with their associated cells. For this reason, it is recommended that you delete only entire rows or entire columns.

Entering Numbers with a Format Symbol

The next step in creating the Six-Month Projected Revenue, Expenses, and Net Income worksheet is to enter the row title, Revenue for Bonus, in cell A21 and enter the assumption values in the range B17:B23. You can enter the assumption numbers with decimal places and then format them later, as you did in Projects 1 and 2, or you can enter them with format symbols. When you enter a number with a **format symbol**, Excel immediately displays the number with the assigned format. Valid format symbols include the dollar sign ($), comma (,), and percent sign (%).

If the number entered is a whole number, then it displays without any decimal places. If the number entered with a format symbol has one or more decimal places, then Excel displays the number with two decimal places. Table 3-2 illustrates several examples of numbers entered with format symbols. The number in parentheses in column 4 indicates the number of decimal places.

Table 3-2	Numbers Entered with Format Symbols		
FORMAT SYMBOL	*TYPED IN FORMULA BAR*	*DISPLAYS IN CELL*	*COMPARABLE FORMAT*
,	2,934	2,934	Comma (0)
	7,912.5	7,912.50	Comma (2)
$	$777	$777	Currency (0)
	$9281.12	$9,281.12	Currency (2)
	$48,103.6	$48,103.60	Currency (2)
%	32%	32%	Percent (0)
	89.2%	89.20%	Percent (2)
	16.31%	16.31%	Percent (2)

The following steps describe how to complete the entries in the Assumptions table and save an intermediate version of the workbook.

To Enter a Number with a Format Symbol

1 **Click cell A21 and enter** Revenue for Bonus **in the cell. Enter** 13.25% **in cell B17,** 9.5% **in cell B18,** 1.75% **in cell B19,** 75,000.00 **in cell B20,** 5,000,000.00 **in cell B21,** 28.75% **in cell B22, and** 31.25% **in cell B23.**

The entries display in a format based on the format symbols entered with the numbers (Figure 3-16).

2 **With a floppy disk in drive A, click the Save button on the Standard toolbar. Type** Hyperlink **in the File name text box. Click the Save in box arrow and then click 3½ Floppy (A:). Click the Save button in the Save As dialog box.**

The workbook name in the title bar changes from Book1 to Hyperlink.

FIGURE 3-16

Freezing Worksheet Titles

Freezing worksheet titles is a useful technique for viewing large worksheets that extend beyond the window. For example, when you scroll down or to the right, the column titles in row 3 and the row titles in column A that define the numbers no longer display on the screen. This makes it difficult to remember what the numbers represent. To alleviate this problem, Excel allows you to freeze the titles so they display on the screen no matter how far down or to the right you scroll.

Complete the steps on the next page to freeze the worksheet title and column titles in rows 1, 2, and 3, and the row titles in column A using the **Freeze Panes command** on the **Window menu**.

Other Ways

1. Enter numbers without format symbols, right-click range, click Format cells on shortcut menu

2. Enter numbers without format symbols, on Format menu click Cells

To Freeze Column and Row Titles

1 Click cell B4, the cell below the column headings you want to freeze and to the right of the row titles you want to freeze. Click Window on the menu bar and then point to Freeze Panes (Figure 3-17).

FIGURE 3-17

2 Click Freeze Panes.

Excel splits the window into two parts. The right border of column A changes to a thin black line indicating the split between the frozen row titles in column A and the rest of the worksheet. The bottom border of row 3 changes to a thin black line indicating the split between the frozen column titles in rows 1 through 3 and the rest of the worksheet (Figure 3-18).

FIGURE 3-18

Once frozen, the row titles in column A will remain on the screen even when you scroll to the right to display column H.

The titles remain frozen until you unfreeze them. You unfreeze the titles by clicking the **Unfreeze Panes command** on the Window menu. Later steps in this project show you how to use the Unfreeze Panes command.

Entering the Projected Revenue

The next step is to enter the projected monthly revenue and projected six-month total revenue in row 4. Enter these numbers without any format symbols as shown in the following steps.

TO ENTER THE PROJECTED REVENUE

1 Enter 8754250 in cell B4, 4978200 in cell C4, 5250000 in cell D4, 7554875 in cell E4, 4768300 in cell F4, and 6550700 in cell G4.

2 Click cell H4 and then click the AutoSum button on the Standard toolbar twice.

The projected six-month total revenue (37856325) displays in cell H4 (Figure 3-19). Columns B and C have scrolled off the screen, but column A remains because it was frozen earlier.

FIGURE 3-19

Recall from Projects 1 and 2 that if you select a single cell below or to the right of a range of numbers, then you must click the AutoSum button twice to display the sum. If you select a range of cells below or to the right of a range of numbers, then you only have to click the AutoSum button once to display the sums.

Displaying the System Date

The worksheet in Figure 3-1a on page E 3.5 includes a date stamp in cell H2. A **date stamp** shows the system date of which your computer keeps track. If the computer's system date is set to the current date, which normally it is, then the date stamp is equivalent to the current date.

In information processing, a report often is meaningless without a date stamp. For example, if a printout of the worksheet in this project was distributed to the company's analysts, the date stamp would show when the six-month projections were made.

To enter the system date in a cell in the worksheet, use the **NOW function**. The NOW function is one of twenty date and time functions available in Excel. When assigned to a cell, the NOW function returns a number that corresponds to the date and time for the days January 1, 1900 through December 31, 9999. Excel automatically formats the date stamp to the date and time format, m/d/yy h:mm, where the first m is the month, d is the day of the month, yy is the last two digits of the year, h is the hour of the day, and mm is the minutes past the hour.

The following steps show how to enter the NOW function and change the from m/d/yy h:mm to m/d/yyyy, where m is the month number, d is the day of the month, and yyyy is the year. With the recent turn of the century, it is recommended that you display all dates with a four-digit year.

 Steps

To Enter and Format the System Date

1 Click cell H2 and then click the Paste Function button on the Standard toolbar. When the Paste Function dialog box displays, click Date & Time in the Function category list box. Scroll down in the Function name list box and then click NOW. Point to the OK button.

Excel displays an equal sign in the active cell and in the formula bar. The Paste Function dialog box displays (Figure 3-20).

FIGURE 3-20

2 **Click the OK button. When the NOW Formula Palette displays, click the OK button. Right-click cell H2 and point to Format Cells.**

Excel displays the system date and time in cell H2 using the default date and time format m/d/yy h:mm. The date on your computer may be different. The shortcut menu displays (Figure 3-21).

FIGURE 3-21

3 **Click Format Cells on the shortcut menu. If necessary, click the Number tab in the Format Cells dialog box. Click Date in the Category list box. Scroll down in the Type list box and then click 3/14/1998. Point to the OK button.**

Excel displays the Format Cells dialog box with Date and 3/14/1998 (m/dd/yyyy) highlighted (Figure 3-22). A sample of the format using the data in the active cell (H2) displays in the Sample area.

FIGURE 3-22

4 **Click the OK button.**

Excel displays the system date in the form m/d/yyyy (Figure 3-23). The date on your computer may be different.

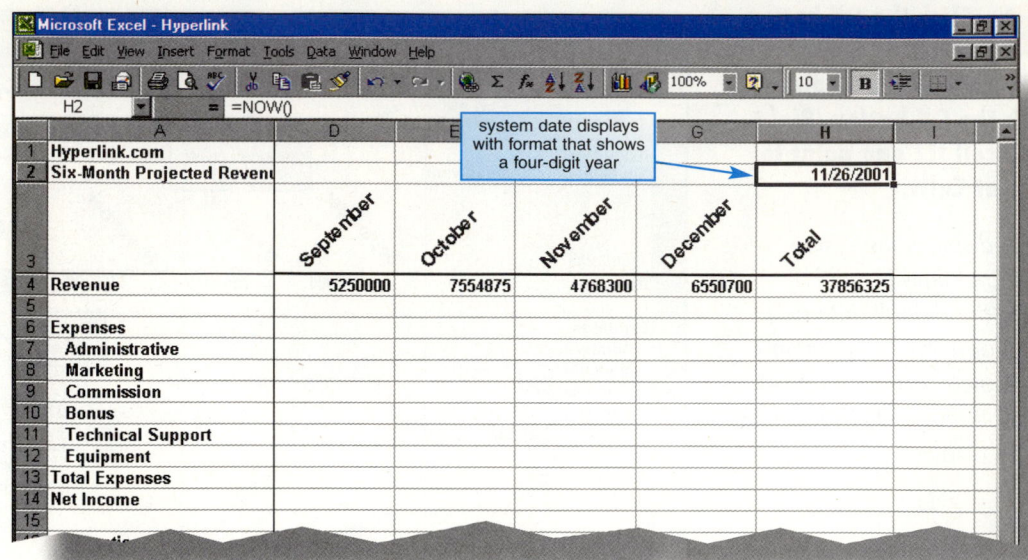

FIGURE 3-23

Other Ways

1. On Insert menu click Function, click Date & Time, click NOW, click Next button, click OK button
2. Press CTRL+SEMICOLON (not a volatile date)
3. Press CTRL+SHIFT+POUND SIGN to format date to day-month-year

In Figure 3-23, the date displays right-aligned in the cell because Excel treats a date as a number. If you assign the **General format** (Excel's preset, or default, format for numbers) to a date in a cell, the date displays as a number. For example, if the system time and date is 6:00 P.M. on June 29, 2001 and the cell containing the NOW function is assigned the General format, then Excel displays the following number in the cell:

$$37071.75$$

number of days since December 31, 1899   time of day is 6:00 P.M. (¾ of day complete)

The whole number portion of the number (37071) represents the number of days since December 31, 1899. The decimal portion .75 represents the time of day (6:00 P.M.). To assign the General format to a cell, click General in the Category list box in the Format Cells dialog box.

Date Manipulation

How many days have you been alive? Enter today's date (i.e., 12/5/2001) in cell A1. Next, enter your birth date (i.e., 6/22/1982) in cell A2. Select cell A3 and enter the formula =A1 - A2. Format cell A3 to the General style. Cell A3 will display the number of days you have been alive.

Absolute Versus Relative Addressing

The next step is to enter the formulas that calculate the projected monthly expenses in the range B7:G13 and the net incomes in row 14 (Figure 3-1a on page E 3.5). The projected monthly expenses are based on the projected monthly revenue in row 4 and the assumptions in the range B17:B23. The formulas for each column are the same, except for the reference to the projected monthly revenues in row 4, which varies according to the month (B4 for July, C4 for August, and so on). Thus, the formulas can be entered for July in column B and copied to columns C through G. The formulas for determining the projected July expenses and net income in column B are shown in Table 3-3.

If you enter the formulas shown in the third column in Table 3-3 in column B for July and then copy them to columns C through G (August through December) in the worksheet, Excel will adjust the cell references for each column automatically. Thus, after the copy, the August administrative expense in cell C7 would be =C17*C4. While the cell reference C4 (August Revenue) is correct, the cell reference C17 references an empty cell. The formula for cell C7 should read =B17*C4 rather than =C17*C4. In this instance, you need a way to keep a cell reference in a formula the same when it is copied.

To keep a cell reference constant when it copies a formula or function, Excel uses a technique called **absolute referencing**. To specify an absolute reference in a formula, enter a dollar sign ($) before any column letters or row numbers you want to keep constant in formulas you plan to copy. For example, $B$17 is an absolute reference, while B17 is a relative reference. Both reference the same cell. The difference shows when they are copied. A formula using the absolute reference $B$17 instructs Excel to keep the cell reference B17 constant (absolute) as it copies the formula to a new location. A formula using the relative cell reference B17 instructs Excel to adjust the cell reference as it copies. Table 3-4 gives some additional examples of absolute references. A cell reference with only one dollar sign before either the column or the row is called a **mixed cell reference**.

Table 3-3	Formulas for Determining July Expenses and Net Income		
CELL	EXPENSE/INCOME	FORMULA	COMMENT
B7	Administrative	=B17 * B4	Administrative % times July Revenue
B8	Marketing	=B18 * B4	Marketing % times July Revenue
B9	Commission	=B19 * B4	Commission % times July Revenue
B10	Bonus	=IF(B4 >= B21, B20, 0)	Bonus equals value in B20 or zero
B11	Technical Support	=B22 * B4	Technical Support % times July Revenue
B12	Equipment	=B23 * B4	Equipment % times July Revenue
B13	Total Expenses	=SUM(B7:B12)	Sum of July expenses
B14	Net Income	=B4 - B13	July Revenue minus July Expenses

Absolute Referencing

Absolute referencing is one of the more difficult worksheet concepts to understand. One point to keep in mind is that the Copy command is the only command affected by an absolute cell reference. An absolute cell reference instructs Excel to keep the same cell reference as it copies a formula from one cell to another.

Table 3-4	Additional Examples of Absolute References	
CELL REFERENCE	TYPE OF REFERENCE	MEANING
$B$17	Absolute reference	Both column and row references remain the same when you copy this cell reference because they are absolute.
B$17	Mixed reference	This cell reference is mixed. The column reference changes when you copy this cell reference to another column because it is relative. The row reference does not change because it is absolute.
$B17	Mixed reference	This cell reference is mixed. The row reference changes when you copy this cell reference to another row because it is relative. The column reference does not change because it is absolute.
B17	Relative reference	Both column and row references are relative. When copied to another row and column, both the row and column in the cell reference are adjusted to reflect the new location.

Entering the July Administrative, Marketing, and Commission Formulas

The following steps show how to enter the Administrative formula (=$B$17*B4) in cell B7, the Marketing formula (=$B$18*B4) in cell B8, and the Commissions formula (=$B$19*B4) in cell B9 for the month of July using Point mode. To enter an absolute reference, you can type the dollar sign ($) or you can place the insertion point in or to the right of the cell reference you want to change to absolute and press then F4.

Microsoft **Excel 2000**

Steps To Enter Formulas Containing Absolute Cell References

1 Click cell B7. Type = (equal sign) and then click cell B17. Press F4 to change B17 to an absolute reference in the formula. Type * (asterisk) and then click cell B4.

The formula =$B$17*B4 displays in cell B7 and in the formula bar (Figure 3-24). A marquee surrounds cell B4.

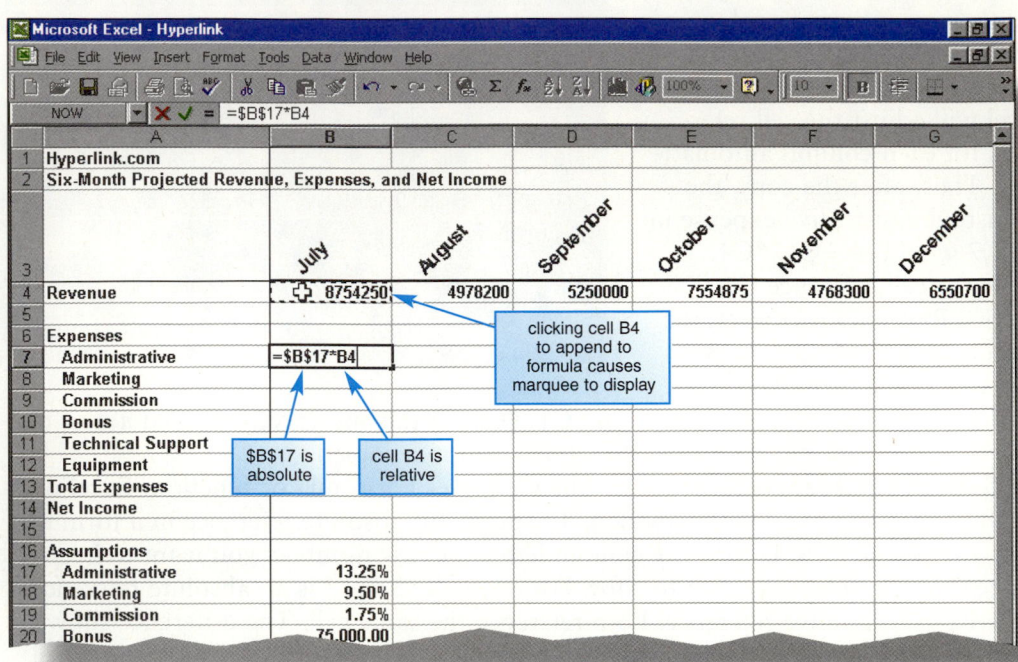

FIGURE 3-24

2 Click the Enter box.

3 Click cell B8. Type = (equal sign) and then click cell B18. Press F4 to change B18 to an absolute reference in the formula. Type * (asterisk) and then click cell B4. Click the Enter box. Click cell B9. Type = (equal sign) and then click cell B19. Press F4 to change B19 to an absolute reference in the formula. Type * (asterisk) and then click cell B4. Click the Enter box.

Excel displays the results in cells B7, B8, and B9 as shown in Figure 3-25.

FIGURE 3-25

Other Ways

1. Enter formulas using keyboard

Making Decisions – The IF Function

If the projected July revenue in cell B4 is greater than or equal to the revenue for bonus in cell B21 (5,000,000.00), then the projected July bonus in cell B10 is equal to the amount in cell B20 (75,000.00); otherwise, cell B10 is equal to zero. One way to assign the projected monthly bonus in row 10 is to check each month individually to see if the projected revenue in row 4 equals or exceeds the revenue for bonus amount in cell B21 and, if so, then to enter 75,000.00 in row 10 for the corresponding month. Because the data in the worksheet changes each time you prepare the report or adjust the figures, however, you will find it preferable to have Excel assign the projected monthly bonus to the entries in the appropriate cells automatically. To do so, you need a formula or function in cell B10 that displays 75,000.00 or 0.00 (zero), depending on whether the projected July revenue in cell B4 is greater than or equal to or less than the number in cell B21.

The Excel **IF function** is useful when the value you want to assign to a cell is dependent on a logical test. For example, assume you assign cell B10 the IF function:

=IF(B4>=$B$21,$B$20,0)

logical_test   value_if_true   value_if_false

If the projected July revenue in cell B4 is greater than or equal to the value in cell B21, then the value in cell B20, 75000, displays in cell B10. If the projected July revenue in cell B4 is less than the value in cell B21, then cell B10 displays 0 (zero).

The general form of the IF function is:

=IF(logical_test, value_if_true, value_if_false)

The argument, value_if_true, is the value you want displayed in the cell when the logical test is true. The argument, value_if_false, is the value you want displayed in the cell when the logical test is false.

The leftmost entry in the general form of the IF function, **logical_test**, is made up of two expressions and a comparison operator. Each expression can be a cell reference, a number, text, a function, or a formula. Valid **comparison operators**, their meaning, and examples of their use in IF functions are shown in Table 3-5.

Table 3-5 Comparison Operators		
COMPARISON OPERATOR	MEANING	EXAMPLE
=	Equal to	=IF(A4 = G6, S12 ^ R3, J4 + K3)
<	Less than	=IF(C23 * Q2 < 534, $F$3, U23 - 3)
>	Greater than	=IF(=AVERAGE(F3:F5) > 70, 1, 0)
>=	Greater than or equal to	=IF(V4 >= $D$2, K8 * P4, 7)
<=	Less than or equal to	=IF(Y6 + H2 <= 25, $K13, 10 * L2)
<>	Not equal to	=IF(H4 <> C$3, "No", "Yes")

The steps on the next page assign the IF function =IF(B4>=$B$21,$B$20,0) to cell B10. This IF function will determine whether or not the worksheet assigns a bonus for July.

Steps: To Enter an IF Function

1 **Click cell B10. Type**
`=if(b4>=$b$21,`
`$b$20,0` **in
the cell.
Click the
Edit Formula
box in the formula bar to
display the IF Formula
Palette to view the function
arguments.**

*The IF function displays in the
formula bar and in the active
cell B10. The IF Formula
Palette displays that shows
the logical_test, value_if_true,
value_if_false, results of each
part of the IF function, and
the value that will be
assigned to the cell based on
the logical test (Figure 3-26).*

FIGURE 3-26

2 **Click the OK button.**

*Excel displays 75000 in cell
B10 because the value in cell
B4 (8754250) is greater than
or equal to the value in cell
B21 (5,000,000.00) (Figure
3-27).*

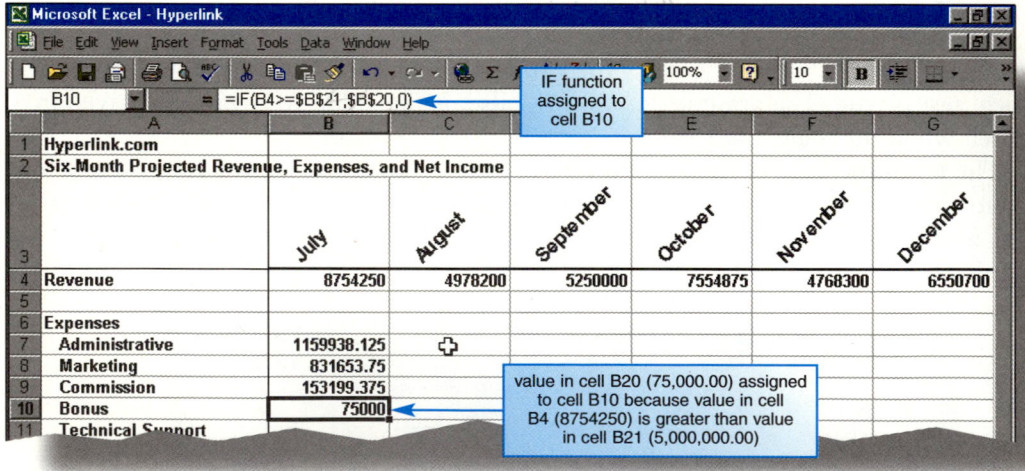

FIGURE 3-27

Other Ways

1. Click Paste Function button on Standard toolbar, click Logical category, click IF
2. Click Edit Formula box, click Functions box arrow, click IF

In Step 1, you could have clicked the Enter box or pressed the ENTER key to complete the entry rather than clicking the Edit Formula box. The Edit Formula box was clicked so you could see the IF function arguments on the IF Formula Palette before assigning the function to cell B10.

The value that Excel displays in cell B10 depends on the values assigned to cells B4, B20, and B21. For example, if the projected revenue in cell B4 is reduced below 5,000,000.00, then the IF function in cell B10 will change the display to zero. Increasing the revenue for bonus in cell B21 so that it exceeds the projected monthly revenue has the same effect.

Entering the Remaining Projected Expense and Net Income Formulas for July

The projected July technical support expense in cell B11 is equal to the technical support assumption in cell B22 (28.75%) times the projected July revenue in cell B4. Likewise, the projected July equipment expense in cell B12 is equal to the equipment assumption in cell B23 (31.25%) times the projected July revenue in cell B4. The projected total expenses for July in cell B13 is equal to the sum of the July expenses in the range B7:B12. The projected July net income in cell B14 is equal to the projected July revenue in cell B4 minus the projected July expenses in cell B13. The formulas are short and therefore they will be typed in, rather than entered using Point mode.

More About 2000

Changing a Formula to Its Result

You can replace a formula with its result so it remains constant. Do the following: (1) click the cell with the formula; (2) press F2 or click in the formula bar; (3) press F9 to display the value in the formula bar; and (4) press the ENTER key.

TO ENTER THE REMAINING PROJECTED JULY EXPENSE AND NET INCOME FORMULAS

1 Click cell B11. Type =b22*b4 and then press the DOWN ARROW key.

2 Type =b23*b4 and then press the DOWN ARROW key.

3 With cell B13 selected, click the AutoSum button on the Standard toolbar twice.

4 Click cell B14. Type =b4-b13 and then press the ENTER key.

The projected July technical support, manufacturing, total expenses, and net income display in cells B11, B12, B13, and B14, respectively (Figure 3-28a).

You can view the formulas in the worksheet by pressing CTRL+LEFT QUOTATION MARK (`). The display shown in Figure 3-28a changes to the display shown in Figure 3-28b. You can see that Excel converts all the formulas to uppercase. Press CTRL+LEFT QUOTATION MARK (`) to display the values again.

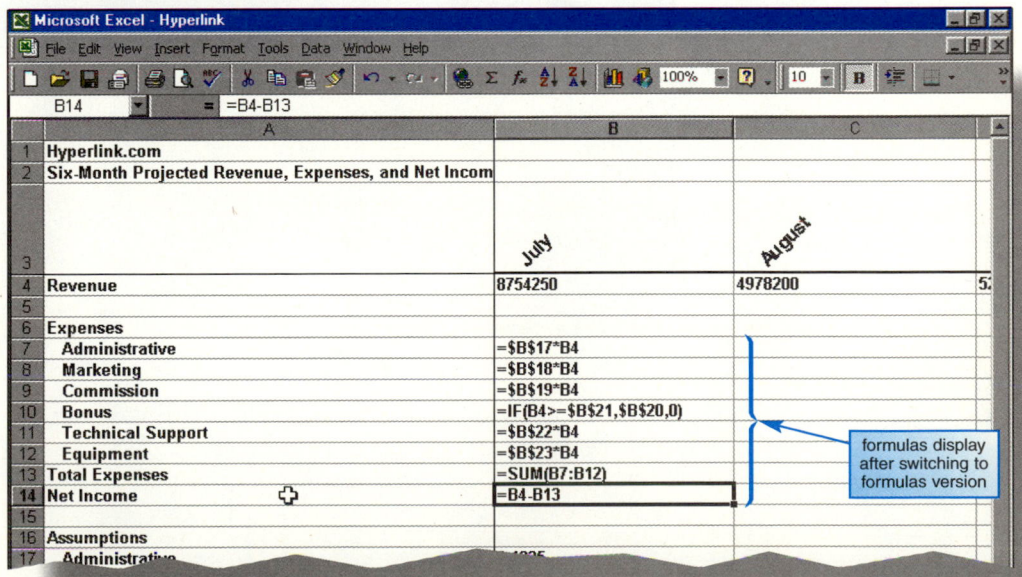

(a) Values Version

(b) Formulas Version

FIGURE 3-28

Copying the Projected July Expenses and Net Income Formulas to the Other Months

To copy the projected expenses and totals for July to the other five months, complete the following steps using the fill handle.

Steps To Copy the Projected July Expenses and Net Income Using the Fill Handle

1 Select the range B7:B14. Point to the fill handle in the lower-right corner of cell B14.

The range B7:B14 is selected and the mouse pointer changes to a cross hair (Figure 3-29).

FIGURE 3-29

(2) Drag the fill handle to select the paste area range C7:G14.

Excel copies the formulas in the range B7:B14 to the paste area range C7:G14 and displays the calculated amounts (Figure 3-30).

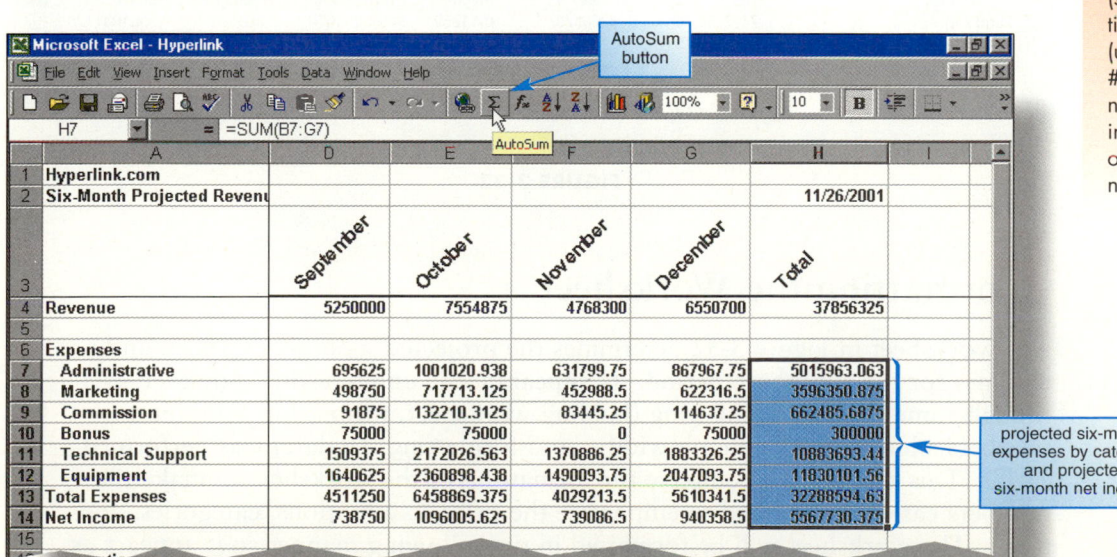

FIGURE 3-30

Determining the Projected Total Expenses by Category and Total Net Income

Follow the steps below to determine the total projected expenses by category and net income in the range H7:H14.

TO DETERMINE THE PROJECTED EXPENSES BY CATEGORY AND NET INCOME

(1) Select the range H7:H14.

(2) Click the AutoSum button on the Standard toolbar.

The projected total expenses by category and total net income display in the range H7:H14 (Figure 3-31).

FIGURE 3-31

More About 2000

Error Values

Excel displays an error value in a cell when it cannot calculate the formula. Error values always begin with a number sign #. The more common occurring error values are: #DIV/0! (trying to divide by zero); #NAME? (use of a name Excel does not recognize); #N/A (refers to a value not available); #NULL! (specifies an invalid intersection of two areas); #NUM! (uses a number incorrectly); #REF (refers to a cell that is not valid); #VALUE! (uses an incorrect argument or operand); and ##### (cell not wide enough).

Unfreezing Worksheet Titles and Saving the Workbook

All the text, data, and formulas have been entered into the worksheet. The next step is to improve the appearance of the worksheet. Before modifying the worksheet's appearance, complete the following steps to unfreeze the titles and save the workbook under its current file name, Hyperlink.

TO UNFREEZE THE WORKSHEET TITLES AND SAVE THE WORKBOOK

1 Click cell B4 to clear the range selection from the previous steps.

2 Click Window on the menu bar and then point to Unfreeze Panes (Figure 3-32).

3 Click Unfreeze Panes.

4 Click the Save button on the Standard toolbar.

Excel unfreezes the titles so that column A scrolls off the screen when you scroll to the right and the first three rows scroll off the screen when you scroll down. The latest changes to the workbook are saved on disk using the file name Hyperlink.

FIGURE 3-32

Formatting the Worksheet

The worksheet in Figure 3-32 determines the projected monthly expenses and net incomes for the six-month period. Its appearance is uninteresting, however, even though some minimal formatting (bolding worksheet, formatting assumptions' numbers, changing the column widths, and formatting the date) was performed earlier. This section will complete the formatting of the worksheet to make the numbers easier to read and to emphasize the titles, assumptions, categories, and totals. The worksheet will be formatted in the following manner so it appears as shown in Figure 3-33: (1) format the numbers; (2) format the worksheet title, column title, row titles, and net income row; and (3) format the assumptions table.

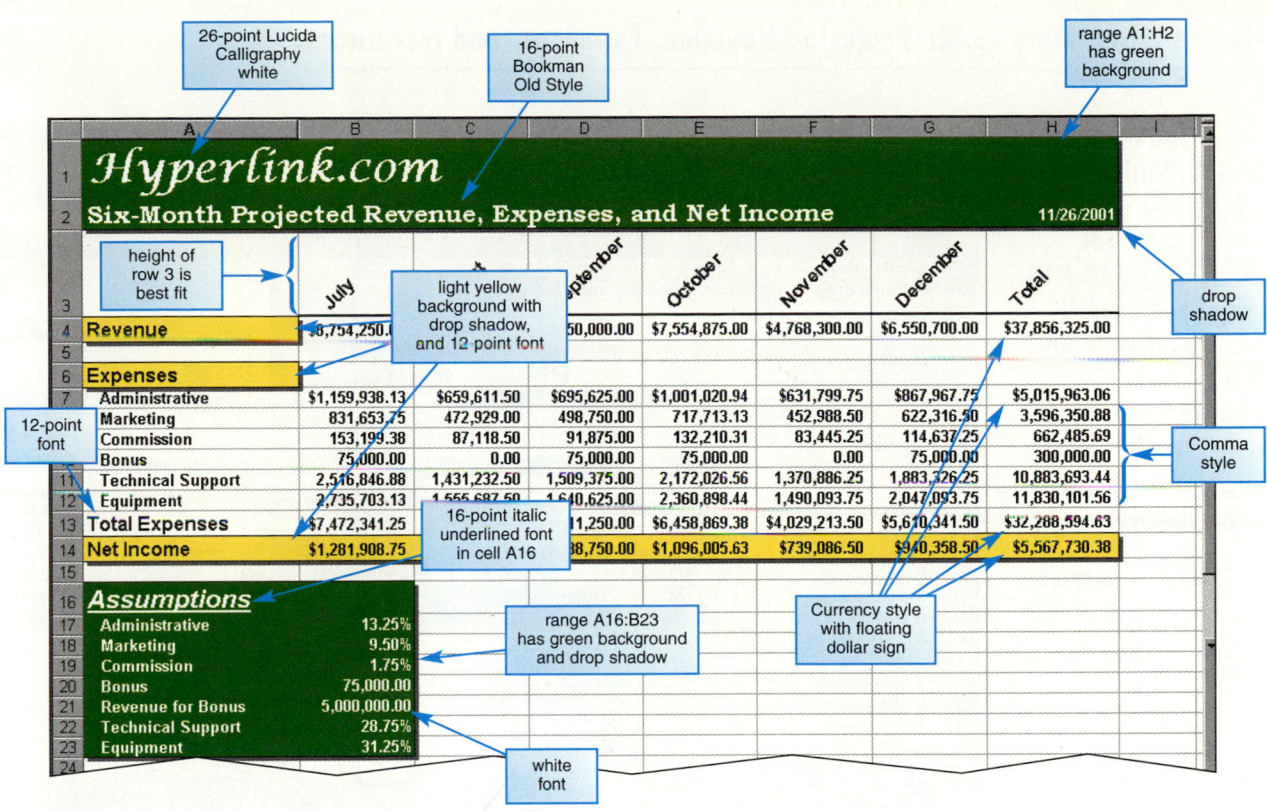

26-point Lucida Calligraphy white

16-point Bookman Old Style

range A1:H2 has green background

height of row 3 is best fit

light yellow background with drop shadow, and 12-point font

drop shadow

12-point font

Comma style

16-point italic underlined font in cell A16

Currency style with floating dollar sign

range A16:B23 has green background and drop shadow

white font

FIGURE 3-33

Formatting the Numbers

Format the projected monthly revenue and expenses in the range B4:H13 as follows:

1. Assign the Currency style with a floating dollar sign to rows 4, 7, 13, and 14.
2. Assign a customized Comma style to rows 8 through 12.

To assign a Currency style with a floating dollar sign, you must use the **Format Cells command** rather than the Currency Style button on the Formatting toolbar, which assigns a fixed dollar sign. The Comma style also must be assigned using the Format Cells command, because the Comma Style button on the Formatting toolbar displays a dash (-) when a cell has a value of zero. The specifications for this worksheet call for displaying a value of zero as 0.00 (see cell C10 in Figure 3-33), rather than as a dash. To create a Comma style using the Format Cells command, you can assign a Currency style with no dollar sign. The steps on the next two pages format the numbers in rows 4 and 7 through 14.

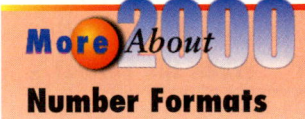

Number Formats

To view all the number formats available with Excel, click Custom in the Category list in the Number tab of the Format Cells dialog box.

Steps To Assign Formats to the Projected Revenue, Expenses, and Net Income

1 Select the range B4:H4. While holding down the CTRL key, select the nonadjacent ranges B7:H7 and B13:H14. Use the horizontal scroll button to display cells to select, if necessary. Release the CTRL key. Right-click the selected range and then point to Format Cells on the shortcut menu.

Excel highlights the selected nonadjacent ranges and the shortcut menu displays as shown in Figure 3-34.

FIGURE 3-34

2 Click Format Cells. When the Format Cells dialog box displays, click the Number tab, click Currency in the Category list, select 2 in the Decimal places box, click $ in the Symbol list to ensure a dollar sign displays, and click ($1,234.10) in the Negative numbers list. Point to the OK button.

The cell format settings display in the Number sheet of the Format Cells dialog box (Figure 3-35).

FIGURE 3-35

3 Click the OK button. Select the range B8:H12. Right-click the selected range. Click Format Cells on the shortcut menu. Click Currency in the Category list, click 2 in the Decimal places box, click None in the Symbol list so a dollar sign does not display, click (1,234.10) in the Negative numbers list. Point to the OK button.

The format settings display in the Format Cells dialog box as shown in Figure 3-36.

FIGURE 3-36

4 Click the OK button. Select cell A1 to deselect the range B8:H12.

The cell formats display as shown in Figure 3-37.

FIGURE 3-37

In accounting, negative numbers often are displayed with parentheses surrounding the value rather than with a negative sign preceding the value. Thus, in Step 3 the format (1,234.10) in the Negative numbers list box was clicked. With the data being used in this project there are no negative numbers. You must, however, select a format for negative numbers and you must be consistent if you are choosing different formats in a column or the decimal points may not line up.

Instead of selecting Currency in the Category list in Step 3 (Figure 3-36), you could have selected Accounting to generate the same format. You should review the formats available below each category title. Thousands of combinations of format styles can be created using the options in the Format Cells dialog box.

Formatting the Worksheet Titles

To emphasize the worksheet titles in cells A1 and A2, the font type, size, and color are changed as described in the following steps.

Steps To Format the Worksheet Titles

1 Double-click the move handle on the Formatting toolbar to display it in its entirety. Click cell A1. Click the Font box arrow on the Formatting toolbar. Scroll down and point to Lucida Calligraphy (or a similar font in the Font list).

The Font list displays as shown in Figure 3-38. The names of the fonts in the Font list display in the font style they represent, allowing you to view the style before you assign it to a cell or range of cells.

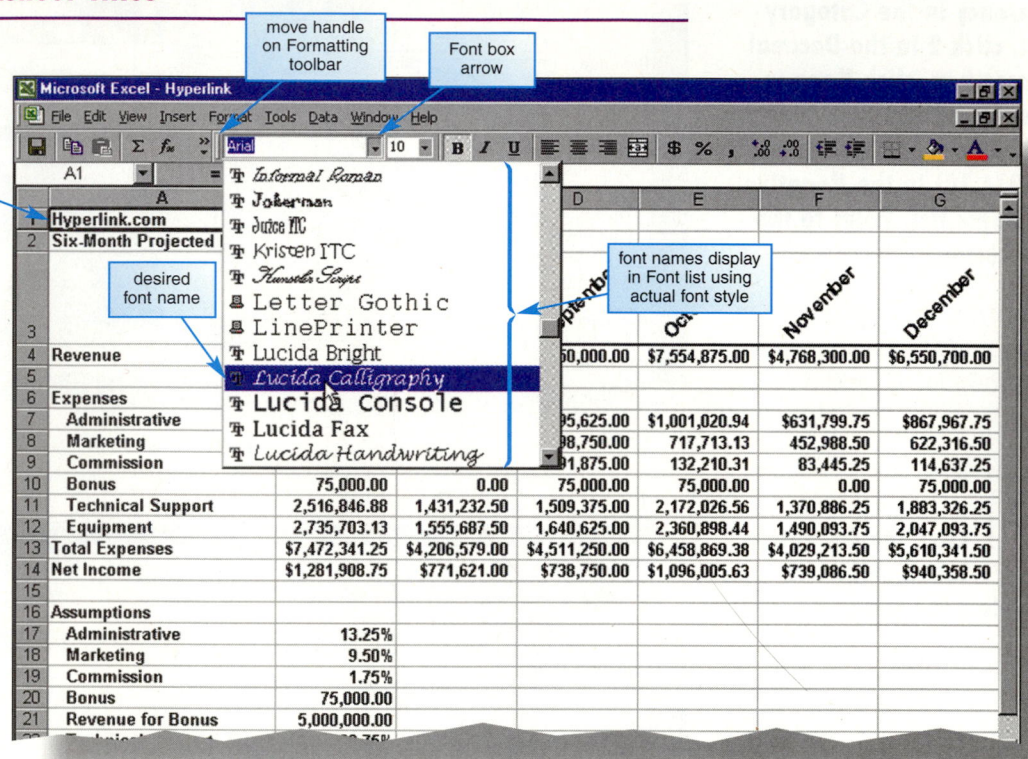

FIGURE 3-38

2 Click Lucida Calligraphy. Click the Font Size box arrow on the Formatting toolbar and then click 26.

3 Click cell A2. Click the Font box arrow. Scroll down and click Bookman Old Style (or a similar font). Click the Font Size box arrow and then click 16.

The worksheet titles in cells A1 and A2 display (Figure 3-39).

FIGURE 3-39

4 Select the range A1:H2. Click the Fill Color button arrow on the Formatting toolbar. Click Green (column 4, row 2) on the Fill Color palette. Click the Font Color button arrow on the Formatting toolbar. Point to White (column 8, row 5) on the Font Color palette).

Excel assigns a green background to the selected range and the Font Color palette displays (Figure 3-40).

5 Click White.

Excel changes the color of the font in the range A1:H2 from black to white (see Figure 3-33 on page E 3.33).

FIGURE 3-40

The next step is to add a drop shadow to the selected range A1:H2 using the Shadow button on the Drawing toolbar. First, the Drawing toolbar must display on the screen. The following section describes how to display and dock an inactive (hidden) toolbar.

Displaying the Drawing Toolbar

Excel has more than 200 toolbar buttons, most of which display on sixteen built-in toolbars. Two of these sixteen built-in toolbars are the Standard toolbar and Formatting toolbar, which usually display at the top of the screen. Another built-in toolbar is the Drawing toolbar. The **Drawing toolbar** provides tools that can simplify adding lines, boxes, and other geometric figures to a worksheet. You also can create customized toolbars containing the buttons that you use often.

You can use the shortcut menu or the **Toolbars command** on the View menu to display or hide any one of the sixteen toolbars. The Drawing toolbar also can be displayed or hidden by clicking the Drawing button on the Standard toolbar. Perform the steps on the next page to display the Drawing toolbar.

Other Ways

1. Right-click range, click Format cells on shortcut menu, click Patterns tab to color background or click Font tab to color font
2. On Format menu click Cells, click Patterns tab to color background or click Font tab to color font

More About 2000

Color Palettes

If your Color palette contains fewer colors than shown on the Color palette in Figure 3-40, then your system is using a different Color palette setting. The figures in this book were created using High Color (16 bit). To check your Color palette setting, return to the desktop, right-click the desktop, click Properties on the shortcut menu, click the Settings tab, and locate the Color palette box.

To Display the Drawing Toolbar

1 Double-click the move handle on the Standard toolbar to display it in its entirety.

2 Click the Drawing button on the Standard toolbar.

The Drawing toolbar displays (Figure 3-41). Excel displays the Drawing toolbar on the screen in the same location and with the same shape as it displayed the last time it was used.

FIGURE 3-41

Other Ways

1. Right-click Standard or Formatting toolbar, click Drawing or shortcut menu
2. On View menu point to Toolbars, click Drawing

More About 2000

Docking Toolbars

If you dock a toolbar on the left or right edge of the window that includes a box or a button with a list associated with it, the list will not be available.

Moving and Docking a Toolbar

The Drawing toolbar in Figure 3-41 is called a **floating toolbar** because it displays in its own window with a title bar and can be moved anywhere in the Excel window. You move the toolbar by pointing to the toolbar title bar or to a blank area within the toolbar window (not on a button) and then dragging the toolbar to its new location. As with any window, you also can resize the toolbar by dragging the toolbar window borders. To hide a floating toolbar, click the Close button on the toolbar title bar. Sometimes a floating toolbar gets in the way no matter where you move it or how you resize it. Hiding the toolbar is one solution. At times, however, you will want to keep the toolbar available for use. For this reason, Excel allows you to position toolbars on the edge of its window. If you drag the toolbar close to the edge of the window, Excel positions the toolbar in a **toolbar dock**.

Excel has four toolbar docks, one on each of the four sides of the window. You can add as many toolbars to a dock as you want. Each time you dock a toolbar, however, the Excel window slightly decreases in size to compensate for the room taken up by the toolbar. The following steps show how to dock the Drawing toolbar at the bottom of the screen below the scroll bar.

Steps ## To Dock a Toolbar at the Bottom of the Screen

1 **Point to the Drawing toolbar title bar or to a blank area in the Drawing toolbar.**

2 **Drag the Drawing toolbar over the status bar at the bottom of the screen.**

Excel docks the Drawing toolbar at the bottom of the screen (Figure 3-42).

		$1,159,938	659,611.50	.00	$1,001,	$631,799.75	$867,967.
8	Marketing	831,653.75	472,929.00	498,750.00	717,713.13	452,988.50	622,316.50
9	Commission	153,199.38	87,118.50	91,875.00	132,210.31	83,445.25	114,637.25
10	Bonus	75,000.00	0.00	75,000.00	75,000.00	0.00	75,000.00
11	Technical Support	2,516,846.88	1,431,232.50	1,509,375.00	2,172,026.56	1,370,886.25	1,883,326.25
12	Equipment	2,735,703.13	1,555,687.50	1,640,625.00	2,360,898.44	1,490,00	2,047,093.75
13	Total Expenses	$7,472,341.25	$4,206,579.00	$4,511,250.00	$6,458,869.38	$4,029,2	
14	Net Income	$1,281,908.75	$771,621.00	$738,750.00	$1,096,005.63	$739,0	
15							
16	Assumptions						
17	Administrative	13.25%					
18	Marketing	9.50%					

Drawing toolbar docked horizontally across bottom of screen

Draw ▾ ⤾ ⟳ AutoShapes ▾ \ ↘ □ ○ ▣ ◢ ⭐ ▧ · ⧸ · A · ≡ ≡ ⇄ ▉ ▤ ▾

Ready — Sum=37221.65768

Start | Microsoft Excel - Hyp... | 3:54 PM

FIGURE 3-42

Compare Figure 3-42 with Figure 3-41. Excel automatically resizes the Drawing toolbar to fit across the window and between the scroll bar and status bar. Also notice that the heavy window border that surrounded the floating toolbar has changed to a light border. To move a toolbar to any of the other three docks, drag the toolbar from its current position to the desired side of the window.

Adding a Drop Shadow to the Title Area

With the Drawing toolbar docked at the bottom of the screen, the next step is to add the drop shadow to the range A1:H2.

More About
2000

Toolbars

You can create your own toolbar and assemble the buttons you want on it by using the Customize command on the shortcut menu that displays when you right-click a toolbar.

 Steps ## To Add a Drop Shadow

1 **With the range A1:H2 selected, click the Shadow button on the Drawing toolbar. Point to Shadow Style 14 (column 2, row 4) on the Shadow palette.**

Excel displays the Shadow palette of drop shadows with varying shadow depths (Figure 3-43).

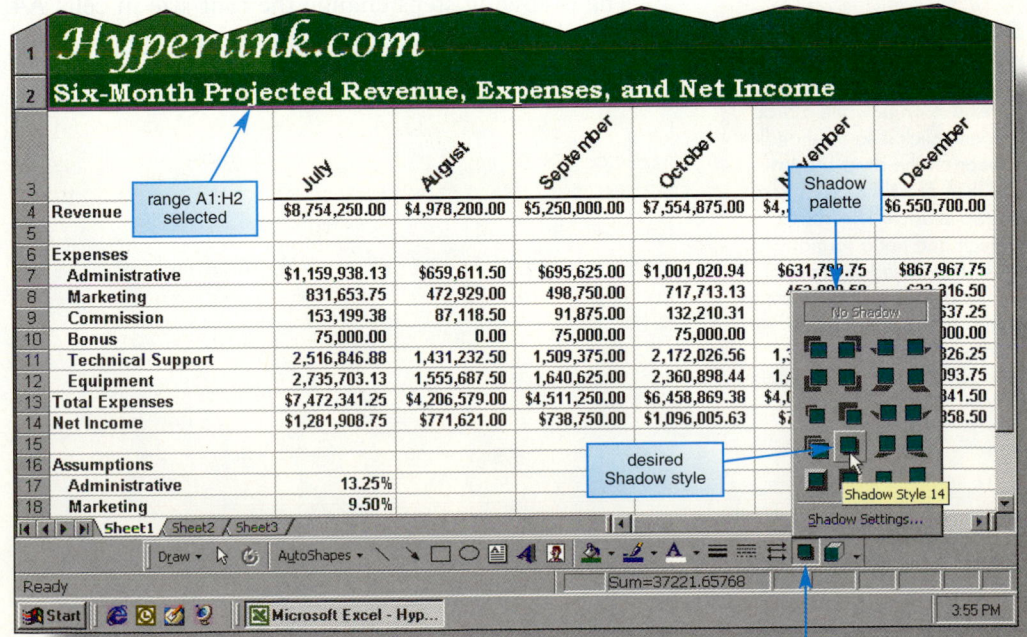

FIGURE 3-43

2 **Click Shadow Style 14. Click cell A4 to deselect the range A1:H2.**

Excel adds a drop shadow to the range A1:H2 (Figure 3-44).

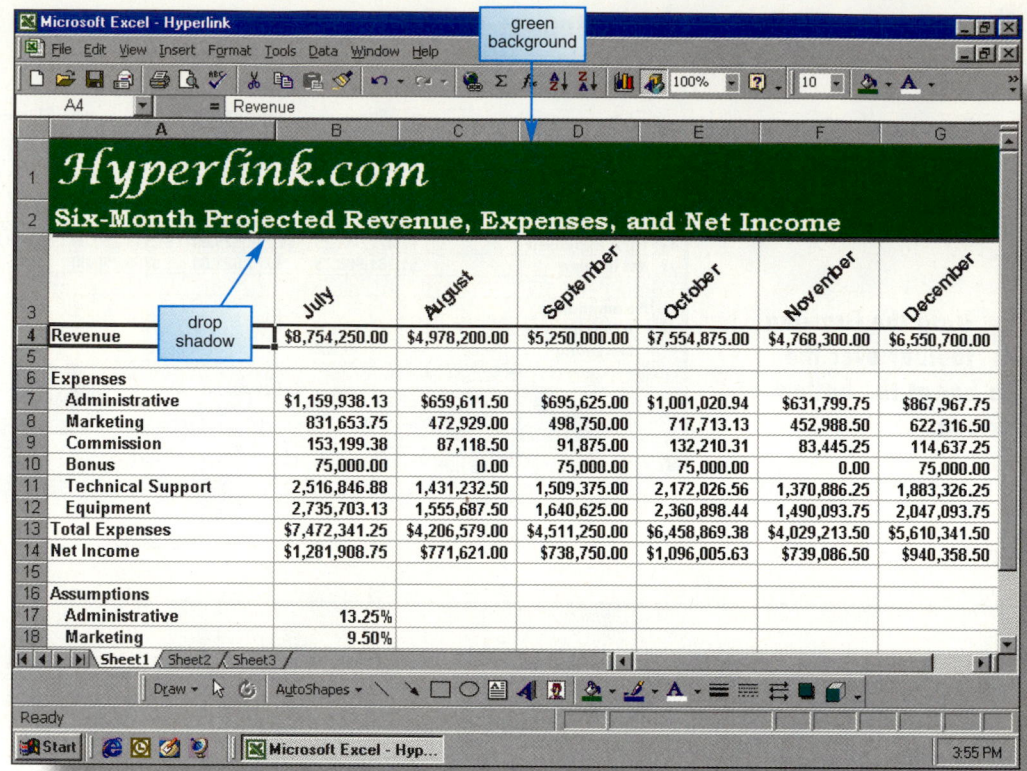

FIGURE 3-44

When you add a drop shadow to a range of cells, Excel also selects the drop shadow and surrounds it with handles. To deselect the drop shadow, select any cell, as described in Step 2 above.

Formatting the Category Row Titles and Net Income Row

The following steps change the font size in cells A4, A6, A13, and A14 to 12 point; and then adds the light yellow background color and drop shadows to cells A4, A6, and the range A14:H14.

To Change Font Size, Add Background Colors, and Add Drop Shadows to Nonadjacent Selections

1 Double-click the move handle on the Formatting toolbar to display it in its entirety. With cell A4 selected, hold down the CTRL key, click cells A6, A13, and A14. Click the Font Size box arrow on the Formatting toolbar and then click 12.

The font size in cells A4, A6, A13, and A14 changes to 12 point.

2 Click cell A4. While holding down the CTRL key, click cell A6 and then select the range A14:H14. Click the Fill Color button arrow on the Formatting toolbar. Click Yellow (column 3, row 5) on the Fill Color palette. Click the Shadow button on the Drawing toolbar and point to Shadow Style 14 (column 2, row 4) in the Shadow palette.

The nonadjacent ranges are selected and the background color is changed to yellow (Figure 3-45). The Shadow palette displays.

3 Click Shadow Style 14.

Excel adds a drop shadow to cells A4, A6, and the range A14:H14 (Figure 3-46).

FIGURE 3-45

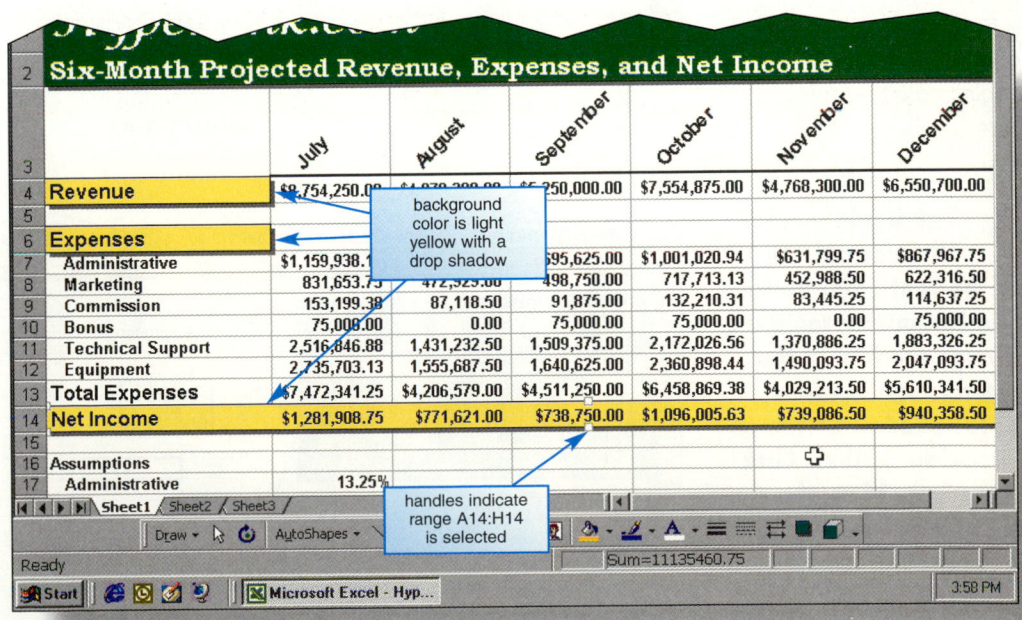

FIGURE 3-46

An alternative to formatting all three areas (cell A4, cell A6, and the range A14:H14) at once is to select each one separately and apply the formats.

Formatting the Assumptions Table

The last step to improving the appearance of the worksheet is to format the Assumptions table in the range A16:B23. The specifications in Figure 3-33 on page E 3.33 require a 16-point italic underlined font for the title in cell A16. The range A16:B23 has a green background color, white font, and a drop shadow that surrounds it. The following steps format the Assumptions table.

Steps **To Format the Assumptions Table**

1 Scroll down so rows 16 through 23 display. Click cell A16. Click the Font Size box arrow on the Formatting toolbar and then click 16. Click the Italic button and then the Underline button on the Formatting toolbar. Select the range A16:B23. Click the Fill Color button arrow on the Formatting toolbar. Point to Green (column 4, row 2) on the Fill Color palette.

The Assumptions table heading displays with the new formats. The range A16:B23 is selected and the Fill Color palette displays (Figure 3-47).

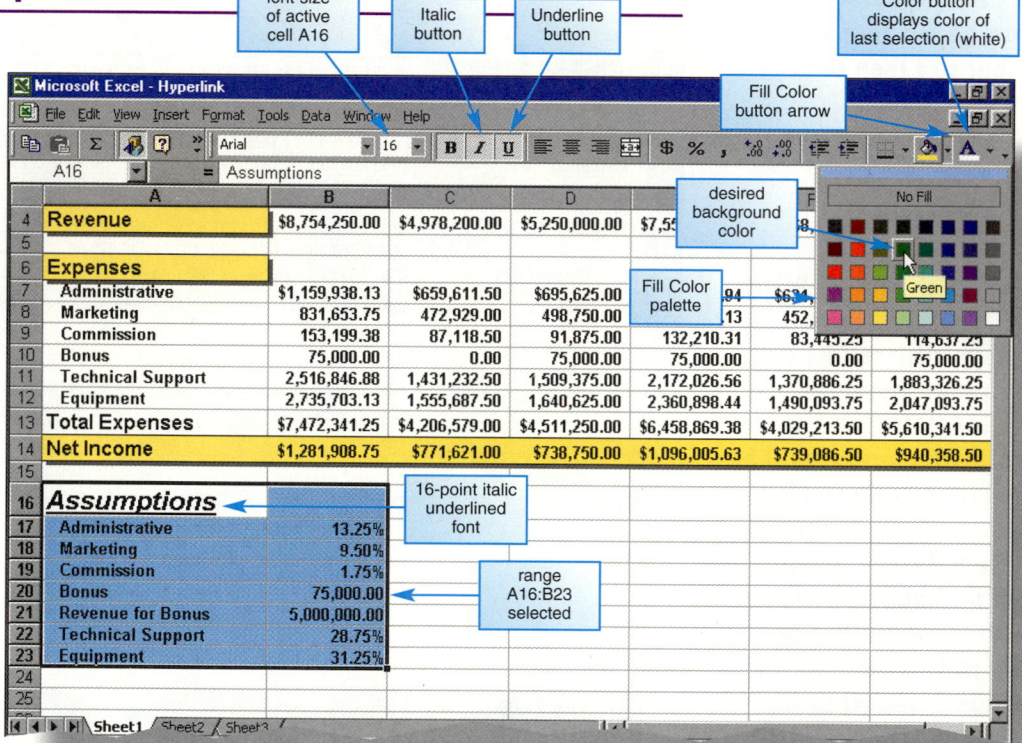

FIGURE 3-47

2 Click Green on the Fill Color palette. Click the Font Color button on the Formatting toolbar to change the font in the selected range to white. Click the Shadow button on the Drawing toolbar. Click Shadow Style 14 on the Shadow palette. Select cell D23 to deselect the range A16:B23.

The Assumptions table displays as shown in Figure 3-48.

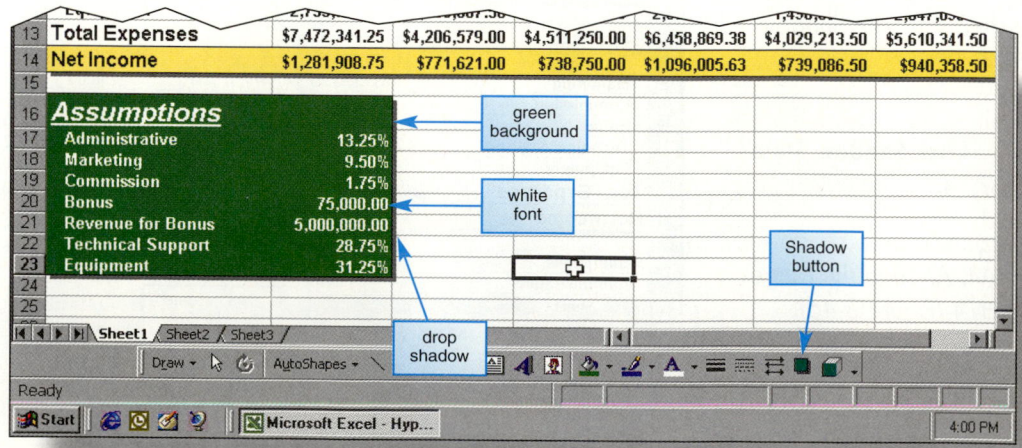

FIGURE 3-48

3 Double-click the move handle on the Standard toolbar to display it in its entirety. Click the Drawing button on the Standard toolbar. Click the Save button on the Standard toolbar.

Excel hides the Drawing tool-bar and saves the workbook using the file name Hyperlink.

FIGURE 3-49

Other Ways

1. Right-click toolbar, click toolbar name on shortcut menu
2. On View menu click Toolbars, click toolbar name

The previous steps introduced you to two new formats, italic and underline. When you assign the **italic** font style to a cell, Excel slants the characters slightly to the right as shown in cell A16 in Figure 3-49. The **underline** format underlines only the characters in the cell rather than the entire cell as is the case when you assign a cell a bottom border.

The formatting of the worksheet is complete.

Adding a 3-D Pie Chart to the Workbook

The next step in the project is to draw the 3-D Pie chart on a separate sheet in the workbook Hyperlink, as shown in Figure 3-50 on the next page. A **Pie chart** is used to show the relationship or proportion of parts to a whole. Each slice (or wedge) of the pie shows what percent that slice contributes to the total (100%). The 3-D Pie chart in Figure 3-50 shows the contribution of each projected month's net income to the projected six-month net income. The Pie chart makes it easy to see that the month of July represents the largest contribution to the projected six-month net income.

Chart Selection

Line chart, Bar chart, Pie chart – which chart will best describe my worksheet data? For answers, click the Contents tab in the Microsoft Excel Help window. Double click the Changing the Type of Chart book. Click the Examples of chart types link, and then click the graphic.

FIGURE 3-50

Nonadjacent Ranges

One of the more difficult tasks to learn is selecting nonadjacent ranges. To complete this task, do not hold down the CTRL key when you select the first range because Excel will consider the current active cell to be the first selection. Once the first range is selected, then hold down the CTRL key and drag through the ranges. If a desired range is not in the window, use the scroll arrows to move the window over the range. It is not necessary to hold down the CTRL key while you move the window.

Unlike the 3-D Column chart in Project 1, the 3-D Pie chart in Figure 3-50 is not embedded in the worksheet. This Pie chart resides on a separate sheet called a **chart sheet**.

The ranges in the worksheet to chart are the nonadjacent ranges B3:G3 and B14:G14 (Figure 3-51). The month names in the range B3:G3 will identify the slices; these entries are called **category names**. The range B14:G14 contains the data that determines the size of the slices in the pie; these entries are called the **data series**. Because there are six months, the 3-D Pie chart contains six slices.

This project also calls for emphasizing the month with the greatest contribution to the total projected net income (July) by offsetting its slice from the main portion. A Pie chart with one or more slices offset is called an **exploded Pie chart**.

As shown in Figure 3-50, the default 3-D Pie chart also has been enhanced by rotating and tilting the pie forward, changing the colors of the slices, and modifying the chart title and labels that identify the slices.

Drawing a 3-D Pie Chart on a Separate Chart Sheet

To draw the 3-D Pie chart on a separate chart sheet, select the nonadjacent ranges and then click the Chart Wizard button on the Standard toolbar. Once the chart is created, you can format it as shown in Figure 3-50.

To Draw a 3-D Pie Chart on a Separate Chart Sheet

1 **Select the range B3:G3. While holding down the CTRL key, select the range B14:G14. Point to the Chart Wizard button on the Standard toolbar.**

The nonadjacent ranges are selected (Figure 3-51).

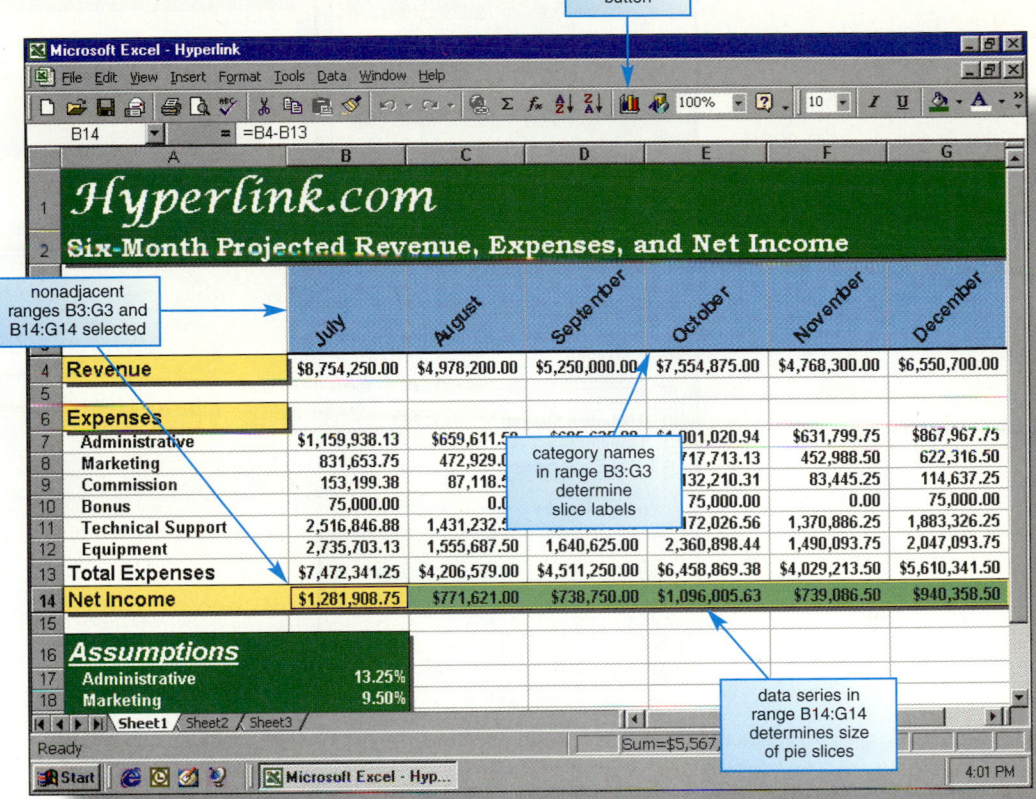

FIGURE 3-51

2 **Click the Chart Wizard button. When the Chart Wizard – Step 1 of 4 – Chart Type dialog box displays, click Pie in the Chart type list and then click the 3-D Pie chart (column 2, row 1) in the Chart sub-type box. Point to the Next button.**

The Chart Wizard—Step 1 of 4—Chart Type dialog box displays, which allows you to select one of the fourteen types of charts available in Excel (Figure 3-52).

FIGURE 3-52

Click the Next button.

The Chart Wizard—Step 2 of 4—Chart Source Data dialog box displays showing a sample of the 3-D Pie chart and the chart data range. A marquee surrounds the nonadjacent ranges on the worksheet (Figure 3-53).

FIGURE 3-53

Click the Next button. When the Chart Wizard – Step 3 of 4 – Chart Options dialog box displays, type Projected Net Income in the Chart title text box. Point to the Legend tab.

Excel redraws the sample 3-D Pie chart with the chart title, Projected Net Income (Figure 3-54).

FIGURE 3-54

5 Click the Legend tab and then click Show legend to remove the check mark. Point to the Data Labels tab.

The Legend tab displays. Excel redraws the sample 3-D Pie chart without the legend. (Figure 3-55).

FIGURE 3-55

6 Click the Data Labels tab. Click Show label and percent in the Data labels area. Point to the Next button.

The Data Labels sheet displays. Excel redraws the sample 3-D Pie chart with data labels and percents (Figure 3-56).

FIGURE 3-56

Microsoft **Excel 2000**

7 Click the Next button. When the Chart Wizard – Step 4 of 4 – Chart Location dialog box displays, click As new sheet. Point to the Finish button.

The Chart Wizard Step 4 of 4 Chart Location dialog box gives you two chart location options: to draw the chart on a new sheet in the workbook or to draw it as an object in a worksheet (Figure 3-57).

FIGURE 3-57

8 Click the Finish button.

Excel draws the 3-D Pie chart on a separate chart sheet (Chart1) in the Hyperlink workbook (Figure 3-58).

9 Click the Save button on the Standard toolbar.

FIGURE 3-58

1. Select range to chart, press F11

Each slice of the 3-D Pie chart in Figure 3-58 represents one of the six months — July, August, September, October, November, and December. The names of the months and the percent contribution to the total value display outside the slices. The chart title, Projected Net Income, displays immediately above the 3-D Pie chart.

Excel determines the direction of the data series range (down a column or across a row) on the basis of the selected range. Because the selection for the 3-D Pie chart is across the worksheet (ranges B3:G3 and B14:G14), Excel automatically selects the Rows option button in the Data Range sheet as shown in Figure 3-53 on page E 3.46.

In any of the four Chart Wizard dialog boxes (Figure 3-53 through Figure 3-57), you can click the Back button to return to the previous Chart Wizard dialog box. You also can click the Finish button in any of the dialog boxes to create the chart with the options selected thus far.

Formatting the Chart Title and Chart Labels

The next step is to format the chart title and labels that identify the slices. Before you can format a **chart item**, such as the chart title or labels, you must select it. Once a chart item is selected, you can format it using the Formatting toolbar, shortcut menu, special keys, or the Format menu. In the following sections, you will use the Formatting toolbar to format chart items much like you formatted the cell entries earlier. Complete the following steps to format the chart title and labels.

Steps To Format the Chart Title and Labels

1 Double-click the move handle on the Formatting toolbar to display it in its entirety. Click the chart title. On the Formatting toolbar, click the Font Size box arrow, click 36, click the Underline button, click the Font Color button arrow, and then point to Red (column 1, row 3) on the Font Color palette.

Excel displays a box with han-dles around the chart title, increases the font size of the chart title, and underlines the chart title (Figure 3-59). The Font Color palette displays.

FIGURE 3-59

2 Click Red. Right-click one of the five data labels that identify the slices. On the Formatting toolbar, click the Font Size box arrow, click 12, click the Bold button, and then click the Font Color button to change the font to the color red.

The chart title and data labels display in red as shown in Figure 3-60. The data labels are selected.

FIGURE 3-60

If you compare Figure 3-60 with Figure 3-58 on page E 3.48, you can see that the labels and chart title are easier to read and make the chart sheet look more professional.

Changing the Colors of the Slices

The next step is to change the colors of the slices of the pie. The colors shown in Figure 3-61 are the default colors Excel uses when you first create a Pie chart. Project 3 requires that the colors be changed to those shown in Figure 3-50 on page E 3.44. To change the colors of the slices, select them one at a time and use the Fill Color button on the Formatting toolbar as shown in the following steps.

Steps **To Change the Colors of the Pie Slices**

1 **Click the July slice twice, once to select all the slices and once to select the individual slice. (Do not double-click.) Click the Fill Color button arrow on the Formatting toolbar and then point to Red (column 1, row 3) on the Fill Color palette.**

Excel displays resizing handles around the July slice and the Fill Color palette displays (Figure3-61).

FIGURE 3-61

2 **Click Red. One at a time, click the remaining slices and then use the Fill Color palette to change each slice to the following colors: December – Green (column 4, row 2); November – Orange (column 2, row 2); October – Yellow (column 3, row 4); September – Blue (column 6, row 2), and August – Plum (column 7, row 4). Click outside the Chart Area.**

The Pie chart displays with colors assigned to the slices as shown in Figure 3-62.

FIGURE 3-62

Other Ways

1. Click slice twice, right-click selected slice, click Format Data Point on shortcut menu, click Patterns tab, click color, click OK button

2. Click slice twice, on Format menu click Selected Data Point, click Patterns tab, click color, click OK button

Exploding a 3-D Pie Chart

If you click the 3-D Pie chart so all the slices are selected, you can drag one of the slices to explode all of the slices.

Exploding the 3-D Pie Chart

The next step is to emphasize the slice representing July by offsetting, or **exploding**, it from the rest of the slices. Of the six months, July represents the greatest net income contributor; by exploding it, you can make this slice stand out from the rest. Perform the following steps to explode a slice of the 3-D Pie chart.

 To Explode the 3-D Pie Chart

1 **Click the slice labeled July twice. (Do not double-click.)**

Excel displays resizing handles around the July slice.

2 **Drag the slice to the desired position and then release the mouse button.**

Excel redraws the 3-D Pie chart with the July slice offset from the rest of the slices (Figure 3-63).

FIGURE 3-63

You can offset as many slices as you want, but remember that the reason for offsetting a slice is to emphasize it. Offsetting multiple slices tends to reduce the impact on the reader and reduces the overall size of the pie chart.

Changing a Pie Chart's Perspective

You can increase or decrease the base height (thickness) of the Pie chart by changing the height to base ratio in the Format 3-D View dialog box.

Rotating and Tilting the 3-D Pie Chart

With a three-dimensional chart, you can change the view to better display the section of the chart you are trying to emphasize. Excel allows you to control the rotation angle, elevation, perspective, height, and angle of the axes by using the **3-D View command** on the Chart menu.

To obtain a better view of the offset July slice, you can rotate the 3-D Pie chart 80° to the left. The rotation angle of the 3-D Pie chart is defined by the line that divides the July and December slices. When Excel initially draws a Pie chart, it always points one of the dividing lines between two slices to twelve o'clock (or zero degrees). Besides rotating the 3-D Pie chart, the following steps also change, or tilt, the elevation so the 3-D Pie chart is at less of an angle to the viewer.

Steps | To Rotate and Tilt the 3-D Pie Chart

1 With the July slice selected, click Chart on the menu bar and then point to 3-D View.

The Chart menu displays (Figure 3-64).

FIGURE 3-64

2 Click 3-D View. When the 3-D View dialog box displays, click the up arrow button in the 3-D View dialog box until 25 displays in the Elevation box.

The 3-D View dialog box displays (Figure 3-65). A sample of the 3-D Pie chart displays in the dialog box. The result of increasing the elevation of the 3-D Pie chart is to tilt it forward.

FIGURE 3-65

3 Rotate the Pie chart by clicking the Left Rotation button until the Rotation box displays 80.

The new rotation setting (80) displays in the Rotation box as shown in Figure 3-66. A sample of the rotated Pie chart displays in the dialog box.

FIGURE 3-66

4 Click the OK button. Click outside the chart area.

Excel displays the 3-D Pie chart tilted forward and rotated to the left, which makes the space between the July slice and the main portion of the pie more prominent (Figure 3-67).

5 Click File on the menu bar and then click Save.

FIGURE 3-67

Compare Figure 3-67 with Figure 3-64 on page E 3.53. The offset of the July slice is more noticeable in Figure 3-67 because the Pie chart has been tilted and rotated to expose the white space between the July slice and the main portion of the 3-D Pie chart.

In addition to controlling the rotation angle and elevation, you also can control the thickness of the 3-D Pie chart by entering a percent smaller or larger than the default 100% in the **Height box** (Figure 3-66).

More *About* **2000**

Charting

Press the ESC key to deselect a chart item.

Adding Leader Lines to the Data Labels

If you drag the data labels away from each slice, Excel draws thin **leader lines** that connect each data label to its corresponding slice. If the leader lines do not display, click Chart Options on the Chart menu and click the Show leader lines option button (see Figure 3-56 on page E 3.47).

 Steps To Add Leader Lines to the Data Labels

1 **Click the July data label twice. (Do not double-click.)**

Excel displays a box with handles around the July data label.

2 **Point to the upper-left handles on the box border and drag the July data label away from the July slice. Select and drag the remaining data labels away from their corresponding slices as shown in Figure 3-68. Click outside the chart area.**

The data labels display with leader lines as shown in Figure 3-68.

FIGURE 3-68

You also can select and format individual labels by clicking a specific data label after all the data labels have been selected. Making an individual data label larger or a different color, for example, helps you emphasize a small or large slice in a Pie chart.

Changing the Names of the Sheets and Rearranging the Order of the Sheets

The final step in creating the workbook is to change the names of the sheets at the bottom of the screen. The following steps show you how to rename the sheets and reorder the sheets so the worksheet comes before the chart sheet.

Steps To Rename the Sheets and Rearrange the Order of the Sheets

1 **Double-click the tab labeled Chart1 at the bottom of the screen. Type** 3-D Pie Chart **as the new tab label. Press the ENTER key.**

The label on the Chart1 tab changes to 3-D Pie Chart (Figure 3-69).

sheet name Chart1 changed to 3-D Pie Chart

FIGURE 3-69

2 **Double-click the tab labeled Sheet1 at the bottom of the screen. Type** Six-Month Plan **as the new tab label and then press the ENTER key. Drag the Six-Month Plan tab to the left in front of the 3-D Pie Chart tab. Click cell D17 to deselect the chart ranges.**

Excel rearranges the sequence of the sheets and displays the worksheet (Figure 3-70).

Revenue	$8,754,250.00	$4,978,200.00	$5,0 .00	$7,554,0 .00	$4,768,300.00	$6,550,700.00
5						
6 **Expenses**						
7 Administrative	$1,159,938.13	$659,611.50	$695,625.00	$1,001,020.94	$631,799.75	$867,967.75
8 Marketing	831,653.75	472,929.00	498,750.00	717,713.13	452,988.50	622,316.50
9 Commission	153,199.38	87,118.50	91,875.00	132,210.31	83,445.25	114,637.25
10 Bonus	0.00	75,000.00	75,000.00	75,000.00	0.00	75,000.00
11 Technical Support	,431,232.50	1,509,375.00	2,172,026.56	1,370,886.25	1,883,326.25
12 Equipment	,555,687.50	1,640,625.00	2,360,898.44	1,490,093.75	2,047,093.75
13 Total Expenses	,206,579.00	$4,511,250.00	$6,458,869.38	$4,029,213.50	$5,610,341.50
14 Net Income	$1,281,908.75	$771,621.00	$738,750.00	$1,096,005.63	$739,086.50	$940,358.50
15						
16 **Assumptions**						
17 Administrative	13.25%					
18 Marketing	9.50%					

Sheet1 sheet renamed Six-Month Plan and moved ahead of 3-D Pie Chart sheet

Six-Month Plan / 3-D Pie Chart / Sheet2 / Sheet3

Ready

Start   Microsoft Excel - Hyp...   4:20 PM

FIGURE 3-70

Other Ways

1. To rename, right-click sheet tab, click Rename on shortcut menu

2. To move, right-click sheet tab, click Move or Copy on shortcut menu

3. To move, on the Edit menu click Move or Copy on shortcut menu

Checking Spelling, Saving, Previewing, and Printing the Workbook

With the workbook complete, the next sequences of steps check spelling, save, preview, and print the workbook. Each sequence of steps concludes with saving the workbook to ensure that the latest changes are saved on disk.

Checking Spelling in Multiple Sheets

The spelling checker checks the spelling only in the selected sheets. It will check all the cells in the selected sheets unless you select a range of two or more cells. Before checking the spelling, select the 3-D Pie Chart sheet as described in the following steps.

TO CHECK SPELLING IN MULTIPLE SHEETS

1 Double-click the move handle on the Standard toolbar to display it in its entirety. With the Six-Month Plan sheet active, hold down the CTRL key and then click the 3-D Pie Chart tab.

2 Click the Spelling button on the Standard toolbar. Correct any errors.

3 Click the Save button on the Standard toolbar.

Previewing and Printing the Workbook

After checking the spelling, the next step is to preview and print the sheets. As with spelling, Excel previews and prints only selected sheets. Also, because the worksheet is too wide to print in portrait orientation, you must change the orientation to landscape. Perform the steps on the next page to preview and print the workbook.

More About 2000

Checking Spelling

Unless a range of cells or an object is selected when you check spelling, Excel checks the selected worksheet, including all cell values, cell comments, embedded charts, text boxes, buttons, and headers and footers.

Printing

Is it taking too long and using too much ink to print colored worksheets? You can speed up the printing process and save ink if you do the following before printing a worksheet with color: click File on the menu bar, click Page Setup, click the Sheet tab, click the Black and white check box, and then click the OK button.

TO PREVIEW AND PRINT THE WORKBOOK IN LANDSCAPE ORIENTATION

1 Ready the printer. If both sheets are not selected, select the inactive one by holding down the CTRL key and then clicking the tab of the inactive sheet.

2 Click File on the menu bar and then click Page Setup. Click the Page tab and then click Landscape.

3 Click the Print Preview button in the Page Setup dialog box. When the preview of the first of the selected sheets displays, click the Next button to view the next sheet. Click the Previous button to redisplay the first sheet.

4 Click the Print button at the top of the Print Preview window. When the Print dialog box displays, click the OK button.

5 Right-click the Six-Month Plan tab. Click Ungroup Sheets on the shortcut menu to deselect the 3-D Pie Chart tab.

6 Click the Save button on the Standard toolbar.

The worksheet and 3-D Pie chart print as shown in Figures 3-71a and 3-71b.

(a) Worksheet

Hyperlink.com
Six-Month Projected Revenue, Expenses, and Net Income

	July	August	September	October	November
Revenue	$8,754,250.00	$4,978,200.00	$5,250,000.00	$7,554,875.00	$4,768,300.00
Expenses					
Administrative	$1,159,938.13	$659,611.50	$695,625.00	$1,001,020.94	$631,799.75
Marketing	831,653.75	472,929.00	498,750.00	717,713.13	452,988.50
Commission	153,199.38	87,118.50	91,875.00	132,210.31	83,445.25
Bonus	75,000.00	0.00	75,000.00	75,000.00	0.00
Technical Support	2,516,846.88	1,431,232.50	1,509,375.00	2,172,026.56	1,370,886.25
Equipment	2,735,703.13	1,555,687.50	1,640,625.00	2,360,898.44	1,490,093.75
Total Expenses	$7,472,341.25	$4,206,579.00	$4,511,250.00	$6,458,869.38	$4,029,213.50
Net Income	$1,281,908.75	$771,621.00	$738,750.00	$1,096,005.63	$739,086.50

Assumptions
Administrative	13.25%
Marketing	9.50%
Commission	1.75%
Bonus	75,000.00
Revenue for Bonus	5,000,000.00
Technical Support	28.75%
Equipment	31.25%

(b) 3-D Pie Chart

Projected Net Income

- November 13%
- December 17%
- October 20%
- July 23%
- September 13%
- August 14%

FIGURE 3-71

An alternative to using the Ungroup Sheets command on the tab shortcut menu is to hold down the SHIFT key and then click the tab of the sheet you want active.

Changing the View of the Worksheet

With Excel, you easily can change the view of the worksheet. For example, you can magnify or shrink the worksheet on the screen. You also can view different parts of the worksheet through **window panes**.

Shrinking and Magnifying the View of a Worksheet or Chart

You can magnify (zoom in) or shrink (zoom out) the display of a worksheet or chart by using the **Zoom box** on the Standard toolbar. When you magnify a worksheet, the characters on the screen become large and fewer columns and rows display. Alternatively, when you shrink a worksheet, more columns and rows display. Magnifying or shrinking a worksheet affects only the view; it does not change the window size or printout of the worksheet or chart. Perform the following steps to shrink and magnify the view of the worksheet.

More About 2000

Zooming

You can type any number between 10 and 400 in the Zoom box on the Standard toolbar.

Steps | To Shrink and Magnify the View of a Worksheet or Chart

1 Click the Zoom box arrow on the Standard toolbar. Point to 75% in the Zoom list.

A list of percentages displays (Figure 3-72).

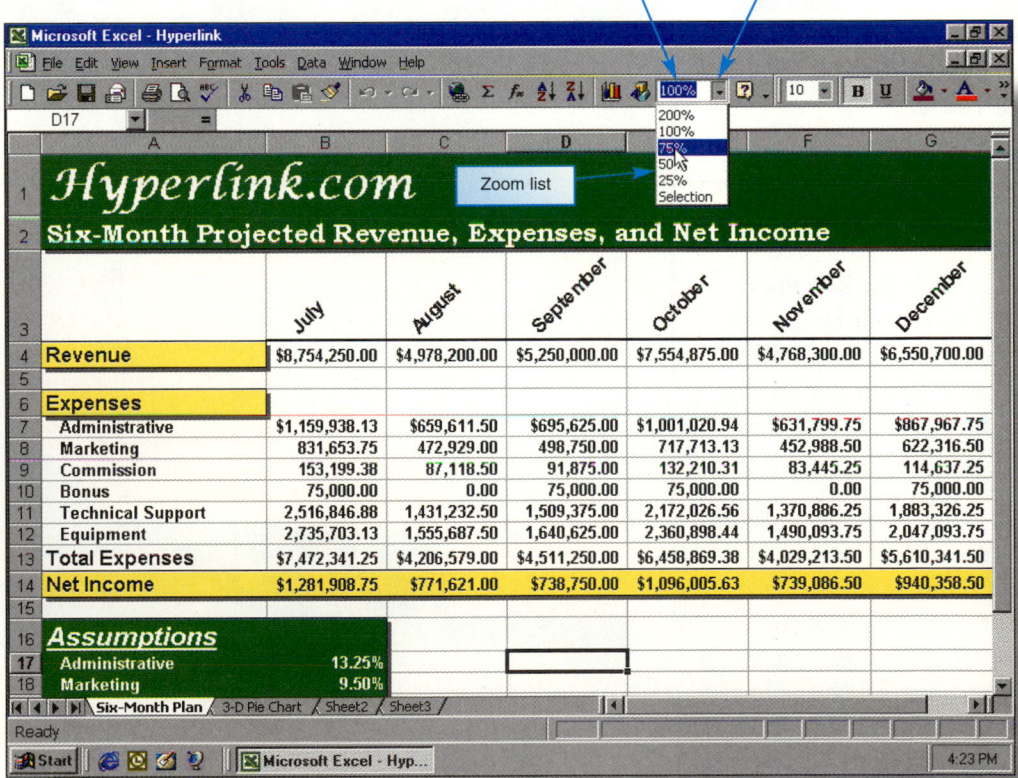

FIGURE 3-72

2 **Click 75%.**

Excel shrinks the display of the worksheet to 75% of its normal display (Figure 3-73). With the worksheet zoomed out to 75%, you can see more rows and columns than you did at 100% magnification. Many of the numbers, however, display as a series of number signs (#) because the columns are not wide enough to display the formatted numbers.

FIGURE 3-73

3 **Click the Zoom box arrow on the Standard toolbar and then click 100%.**

Excel returns to the default display of 100%.

4 **Click the 3-D Pie Chart tab at the bottom of the screen. Click the Zoom box arrow on the Standard toolbar and then click 100%.**

Excel changes the magnification of the chart from 72% (see Figure 3-69 on page E 3.56) to 100% (Figure 3-74). The chart displays at the same size as the printout of the chart.

FIGURE 3-74

5 **Enter** 72 **in the Zoom box to return the chart to its original magnification.**

Other Ways

1. On View menu click Zoom, click desired magnification, click OK button

2. Type desired percent magnification in Zoom box on Standard toolbar

Excel normally displays a chart at approximately 75% magnification at 800 x 600 resolution so that the entire chart displays on the screen. By changing the magnification to 100%, you can see only a part of the chart, but at a magnification that corresponds with the chart's size on a printout. Excel allows you to enter a percent magnification in the Zoom box between 10 and 400 for worksheets and chart sheets.

Splitting the Window into Panes

Previously in this project, you used the Freeze Panes command to freeze worksheet titles on a large worksheet so they always would display on the screen. When working with a large worksheet, you also can split the window into two or four window panes to view different parts of the worksheet at the same time. To split the window into four panes, select the cell where you want the four panes to intersect. Next, click the **Split command** on the Window menu. Follow the steps below to split the window into four panes.

 Steps **To Split a Window into Four Panes**

1 **Click the Six-Month Plan tab. Click cell D5, the intersection of the four proposed panes. Click Window on the menu bar and then point to Split.**

The Window menu displays (Figure 3-75).

FIGURE 3-75

2 **Click Split. Use the scroll arrows to display the four corners of the worksheet.**

Excel divides the window into four panes, and the four corners of the worksheet display (Figure 3-76).

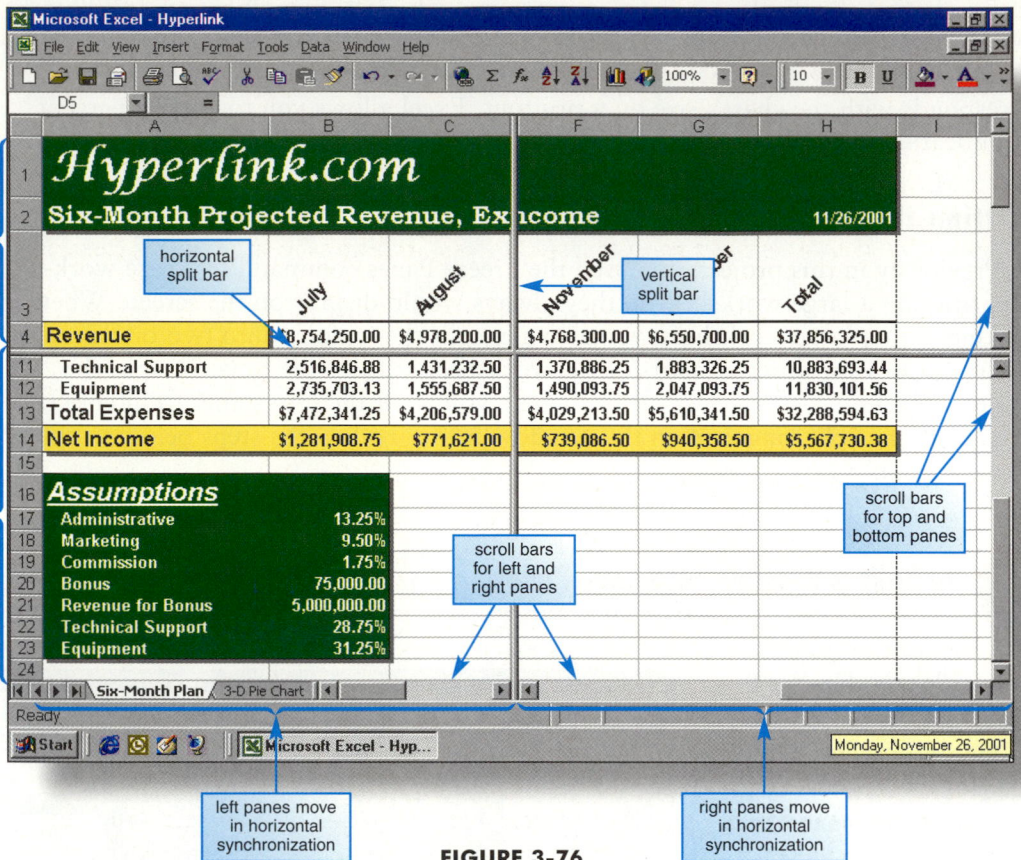

FIGURE 3-76

Other Ways

1. Drag horizontal split box and vertical split box to desired locations

More About

Splitting a Window

If you want to split the window into two panes, rather than four, drag the vertical split box or horizontal split box (Figure 3-75) to the desired location.

The four panes in Figure 3-76 are used to display the following: (1) the upper-left pane displays the range A1:C4; (2) the upper-right pane displays the range F1:I4; (3) the lower-left pane displays the range A11:C24; and (4) the lower-right pane displays the range F11:I24.

The vertical bar going up and down the middle of the window is called the **vertical split bar**. The horizontal bar going across the middle of the window is called the **horizontal split bar**. If you use the scroll bars below the window and to the right of the window to scroll the window, you will see that the panes split by the horizontal split bar scroll together vertically. The panes split by the vertical split bar scroll together horizontally. To resize the panes, drag either split bar to the desired location in the window.

You can change the values of cells in any of the four panes. Any change you make in one pane also takes effect in the other panes. To remove one of the split bars from the window, drag the split box to the edge of the window or double-click the split bar. Follow these steps to remove both split bars.

TO REMOVE THE FOUR PANES FROM THE WINDOW

1 Position the mouse pointer at the intersection of the horizontal and vertical split bars.

2 Double-click the split four-headed arrow.

Excel removes the four panes from the window.

What-If Analysis

The automatic recalculation feature of Excel is a powerful tool that can be used to analyze worksheet data. Recall from the Case Perspective on page E 3.4 the problem Frances Collins had when members of the board of directors suggested she change her assumptions to generate new projections. Because she had to calculate these values manually, it took her several minutes. The recalculations then rendered her chart useless.

Using Excel to scrutinize the impact of changing values in cells that are referenced by a formula in another cell is called **what-if analysis** or **sensitivity analysis**. Excel not only recalculates all formulas in a worksheet when new data is entered, but also redraws any associated charts.

In Project 3, the projected monthly expenses and net incomes in the range B7:G14 are dependent on the assumptions in the range B17:B23. Thus, if you change any of the assumption values, Excel immediately recalculates the projected monthly expenses in rows 7 through 13 and the projected monthly net incomes in row 14. Finally, because the projected monthly net incomes in row 14 change, Excel redraws the 3-D Pie chart, which is based on these numbers.

A what-if question for the worksheet in Project 3 might be, what if the first two and the fourth assumptions in the Assumptions table are changed as follows: Administrative 13.25% to 11.50%; Marketing 9.50% to 8.00%; and Bonus $75,000.00 to $50,000.00 — how would these changes affect the projected six-month net income in cell H14? To answer a question like this, you need to change only the first two and fourth values in the Assumptions table. Excel instantaneously recalculates the worksheet and redraws the 3-D Pie chart to answer the question regarding the projected six-month net income in cell H14.

The steps on the next page change the three assumptions as indicated in the previous paragraph and determine the new projected six-month net income in cell H14. To ensure that the Assumptions table and the projected six-month net income in cell H14 display on the screen at the same time, the steps on the next page also divide the window into two vertical panes.

More About

What-If Analysis

Besides manually changing assumptions in a worksheet, Excel has additional methods for answering what-if questions, including Goal Seeking, Solver, Pivot Tables, Scenario Manager, and the Analysis ToolPak.

Steps

To Analyze Data in a Worksheet by Changing Values

1 Use the vertical scroll bar to move the window so cell A4 is in the upper-left corner of the screen.

2 Drag the vertical split box (see Figure 3-75 on page E 3.61) from the lower-right corner of the screen to the left so that the vertical split bar is positioned in the middle of column F. Use the right scroll arrow to display the totals in column H in the right pane. Click cell B17.

Excel divides the window into two vertical panes and shows the totals in column H in the pane on the right side of the window (Figure 3-77).

FIGURE 3-77

3 Enter 11.5 in cell B17, 8 in cell B18, and 50000 in cell B20.

Excel immediately recalculates all the formulas in the worksheet, including the projected six-month net income in cell H13 (Figure 3-78).

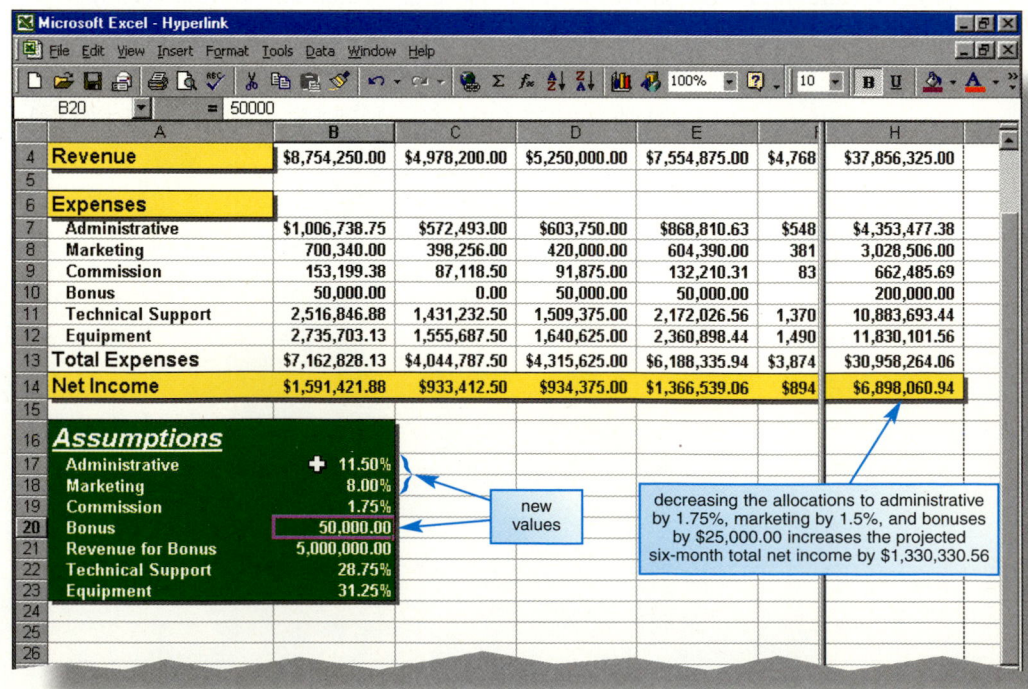

FIGURE 3-78

Each time you enter a new assumption, Excel recalculates the worksheet and redraws the 3-D Pie chart. This process usually takes less than one second, depending on how many calculations must be performed and the speed of your computer. Compare the projected six-month net incomes in Figures 3-77 and 3-78. By changing the values of the three assumptions (Figure 3-78), the projected six-month net income in cell H14 increases from $5,567,730.38 to $6,898,060.94. This translates into an increase of $1,330,330.56 for the projected six-month net income.

More About

Undo

The Undo button is ideal for returning the worksheet to its original state after you have changed the value of a cell to answer a what-if question.

Goal Seeking

If you know the result you want a formula to produce, you can use **goal seeking** to determine the value of a cell on which the formula depends. The following example closes and reopens the Hyperlink workbook and uses the **Goal Seek command** on the Tools menu to determine what projected marketing percentage in cell B18 will yield a projected six-month net income of $7,000,000.00 in cell H14, rather than $5,567,730.38.

 Steps   ## To Goal Seek

1 **Close the Hyperlink workbook without saving changes. Click the Open button on the Standard toolbar and then reopen Hyperlink.**

2 **Drag the vertical split box to the middle of column F. Scroll down so row 4 is at the top of the screen. Display column H in the right pane. Click cell H14, the cell that contains the projected six-month net income. Click Tools on the menu bar and then point to Goal Seek.**

The vertical split bar displays in the middle of column F, and the Tools menu displays (Figure 3-79).

FIGURE 3-79

3 **Click Goal Seek.**

The Goal Seek dialog box displays. The Set cell box is assigned the cell reference of the active cell in the worksheet (cell H14) automatically.

4 **Click the To value text box. Type 7,000,000 and then click the By changing cell box. Click cell B18 on the worksheet.**

The Goal Seek dialog box displays as shown in Figure 3-80. A marquee displays around cell B18.

FIGURE 3-80

5 **Click the OK button. When the Goal Seek Status dialog box displays, click the OK button.**

Excel immediately changes cell H14 from $5,567,730.38 to the desired value of $7,000,000.00. More importantly, Excel changes the marketing assumption in cell B18 from 9.50% to 5.72% (Figure 3-81).

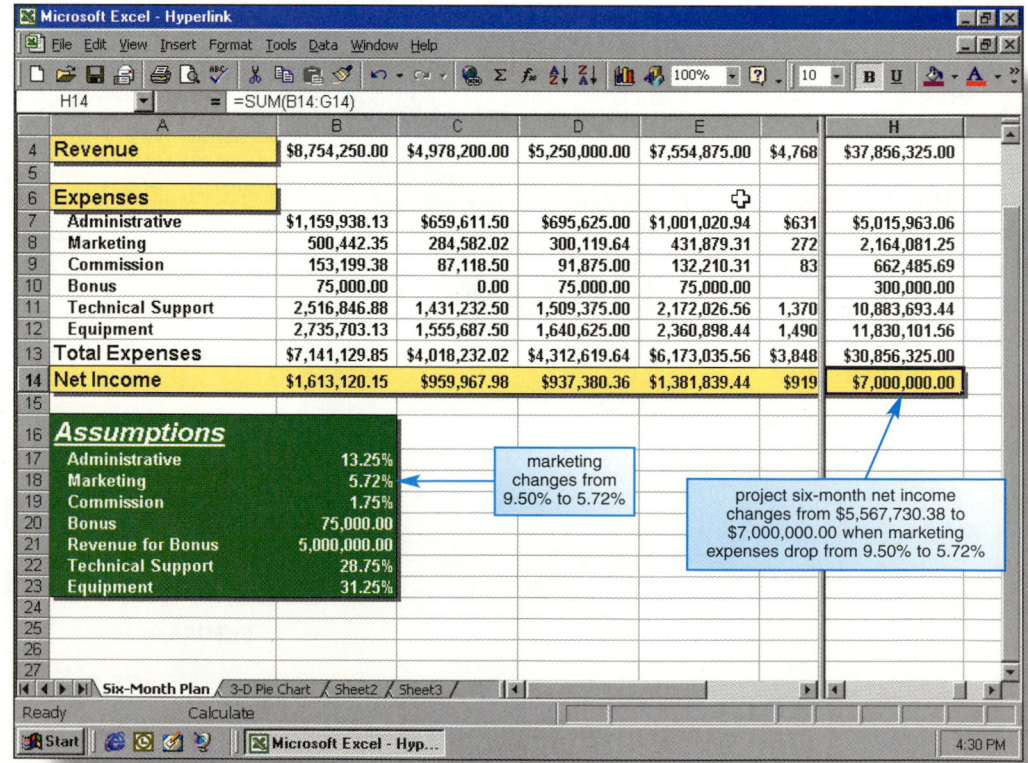

FIGURE 3-81

Goal seeking assumes you can change the value of only one cell referenced directly or indirectly. In this example, to change the projected six-month net income in cell H14 to $7,000,000.00, the marketing percentage in cell B18 must decrease by 3.78% from 9.50% to 5.72%.

You can see from this goal seeking example that the cell to change (cell B18) does not have to be referenced directly in the formula or function. For example, the projected six-month net income in cell H14 is calculated by the function =SUM(B14:G14). Cell B18 the marketing, is not referenced in the function. Instead, cell B18 is referenced in the formulas in rows 7 through 12, on which the projected monthly net incomes in row 13 are based. Excel is capable of goal seeking on the projected six-month net income by varying the marketing assumption.

Quitting Excel

To quit Excel, complete the following steps.

TO QUIT EXCEL

1. Click the Close button on the title bar.

2. If the Microsoft Excel dialog box displays, click the No button.

More About 2000

Goal Seeking

Goal seeking is a methodology in which you know what answer you want a formula in a cell to be, but you do not know the value to place in a cell that is involved in the formula. You can goal seek by changing the value in a cell that is indirectly used in the formula as illustrated in Figures 3-80 and 3-81.

CASE PERSPECTIVE SUMMARY

With the worksheet and chart developed in this project, the CEO of Hyperlink.com, Frances Collins, easily can respond to any what-if questions the board members ask the next time she presents her six-month plan. Questions that took several minutes to answer with paper and pencil now can be answered in a few seconds. Furthermore, computational errors are less likely to occur.

Project Summary

In creating the Hyperlink.com workbook, you learned how to work with large worksheets that extend beyond the window and how to use the fill handle to create a series. You learned to display hidden toolbars, dock a toolbar at the bottom of the screen, and hide an active toolbar. You learned about the difference between absolute cell references and relative cell references and how to use the IF function. You also learned how to rotate text in a cell, generate a series, freeze titles, change the magnification of the worksheet, display different parts of the worksheet through panes, and improve the appearance of a chart. Finally, this project introduced you to using Excel to do what-if analyzes by changing values in cells and goal seeking.

Quick Reference

For a table that lists how to complete the tasks covered in this book using the mouse, menu, shortcut menu, and keyboard, visit the Office 2000 Web page (www.scsite.com/office 2000/qr.htm), and then click Microsoft Excel 2000.

What You Should Know

Having completed this project, you now should be able to perform the following tasks:

▸ Add a Drop Shadow *(E 3.39)*

▸ Add Leader Lines to the Data Labels *(E 3.55)*

▸ Analyze Data in a Worksheet by Changing Values *(E 3.64)*

▸ Assign Formats to the Projected Revenue, Expenses, and Net Income *(E 3.34)*

▸ Bold the Font of the Entire Worksheet *(E 3.7)*

▸ Change Font Size, Add Background Colors, and Add Drop Shadows to Nonadjacent Selections *(E 3.41)*

▸ Change the Colors of the Pie Slices *(E 3.51)*

▸ Check Spelling in Multiple Sheets *(E 3.57)*

▸ Copy a Cell's Format Using the Format Painter Button *(E 3.11)*

▸ Copy a Range of Cells to a Nonadjacent Paste Area *(E 3.14)*

▸ Copy the Projected July Expenses and Net Income Using the Fill Handle *(E 3.30)*

▸ Determine the Projected Expenses by Category and Net Income *(E 3.31)*

▸ Display the Drawing Toolbar *(E 3.38)*

▸ Dock a Toolbar at the Bottom of the Screen *(E 3.39)*

▸ Draw a 3-D Pie Chart on a Separate Chart Sheet *(E 3.45)*

▸ Enter a Number with a Format Symbol *(E 3.19)*

▸ Enter an IF Function *(E 3.28)*

▸ Enter and Format the System Date *(E 3.22)*

▸ Enter Formulas Containing Absolute Cell References *(E 3.26)*

▸ Enter the Projected Revenue *(E 3.21)*

▸ Enter the Remaining Projected Expense and Net Income Formulas *(E 3.29)*

▸ Enter the Worksheet Titles *(E 3.7)*

▸ Explode the 3-D Pie Chart *(E 3.52)*

▸ Format the Assumptions Table *(E 3.42)*

▸ Format the Chart Title and Labels *(E 3.49)*

▸ Format the Worksheet Titles *(E 3.36)*

▸ Freeze Column and Row Titles *(E 3.20)*

▸ Goal Seek *(E 3.65)*

▸ Increase Column Widths and Enter Row Titles *(E 3.12)*

▸ Insert Rows *(E 3.16)*

▸ Preview and Print the Workbook in Landscape Orientation *(E 3.58)*

▸ Quit Excel *(E 3.67)*

▸ Remove the Four Panes from the Window *(E 3.62)*

▸ Rename the Sheets and Rearrange the Order of the Sheets *(E 3.56)*

▸ Rotate and Tilt the 3-D Pie Chart *(E 3.53)*

▸ Rotate Text and Use the Fill Handle to Create a Series of Month Names *(E 3.8)*

▸ Shrink and Magnify the View of a Worksheet or Chart *(E 3.59)*

▸ Split a Window into Four Panes *(E 3.61)*

▸ Start Excel and Reset Toolbars and Menus *(E 3.7)*

▸ Unfreeze the Worksheet Titles and Save the Workbook *(E 3.32)*

More About 2000

Microsoft Certification

The Microsoft Office User Specialist (MOUS) Certification program provides an opportunity for you to obtain a valuable industry credential - proof that you have the Excel 2000 skills required by employers. For more information, see Appendix D or visit the Shelly Cashman Series MOUS Web page at www.scsite.com/off2000/cert.htm.

Apply Your Knowledge

Project Reinforcement at www.scsite.com/off2000/reinforce.htm

1 Understanding the IF Function and Absolute Referencing

Instructions: Fill in the correct answers.

1. Determine the truth value (true or false) of the following logical tests, given the following cell values.
   A5 = 40; B6 = 29; C3 = 110; D7 = 10; and F4 = 125. Enter true or false.

   a. B6 < A5   Truth value: _____

   b. F4 = C3   Truth value: _____

   c. A5 + 15 * D7 / 5 <> C3   Truth value: _____

   d. C3 / D7 > A5 – B6   Truth value: _____

   e. F4 < (A5 + B6) * 2 -12   Truth value: _____

   f. C3 + 300 <= A5 * D7 + 10   Truth value: _____

   g. F4 + C3 > 2 * (F4 + 25)   Truth value: _____

   h. A5 + D7 <> 2 * (F4 / 5)   Truth value: _____

2. Write an IF function for cell C3 that assigns the value of cell D5 to cell C3 if the value in cell F2 is greater than the value in cell F3; otherwise the IF function assigns zero (0) to cell C3.
   Function: _____

3. Write an IF function for cell H5 that assigns the text "Eligible" if the value in cell H12 is three times greater than the value in cell H13; otherwise the IF function assigns the text "Not Eligible".
   Function: _____

4. A nested IF function is an IF function that contains another IF function in the value_if_true or value_if_false arguments. For example, =IF(D1 = "IN","Region 1", IF(D1 = "OH", "Region 2", "Not Applicable")) is a valid nested IF function. Start Excel and enter this IF function in cell C1 and then use the fill handle to copy the function down through cell C7. Enter the following data in the cells in the range D1:D7 and then write down the results that display in cells C1 through C7 for each set. Set 1: D1 = IL; D2 = IN; D3 = OH; D4 = MI; D5 = OH; D6 = IN; D7 = OH. Set 2: D1= WI; D2 = KY; D3 = IN; D4 = IL; D5 = IN; D6 = IN; D7 = OH.
   Function: _____

5. Write cell K5 as a relative reference, absolute reference, mixed reference with the row varying, and mixed reference with the column varying.
   _____   _____   _____   _____

6. Write the formula for cell B3 that divides cell F2 by the sum of cells A4 through A7. Write the formula so that when it is copied to cells C3 and D3, cell F2 remains absolute.
   Formula: _____

7. Write the formula for cell H5 that multiplies cell L8 times the sum of cells C4, D4, and E4. Write the formula so that when it is copied to cells H6, H7, and H8, cell L8 remains absolute.
   Formula: _____

8. Write the formula for cell J1 that multiplies cell P2 times the sum of cells Q10 through Q13. Write the formula so that when it is copied to cells K1 and L1, Excel adjusts all the cell references according to the new location.
   Formula: _____

In the Lab

1 R&R Hotel Indirect Expense Allocation

Problem: You are a work-study student at the local five-star R&R Hotel. Your work-study advisor at school and your supervisor at R&R Hotel have agreed on a challenging Excel project for you to do. They want you to create an indirect expense allocation worksheet (Figure 3-82) that will help the hotel administration better evaluate the profit centers described in Table 3-6.

R&R Hotel

INDIRECT EXPENSE ALLOCATION   11/26/2001

	Dining Room	Banquet Room	Lounge	Fitness Center	Business Center	Conference Rooms	Snack Shop	Arcade	Total
Revenue	$625,900.00	$478,350.00	$392,775.00	$53,230.00	$133,125.00	$78,450.00	$85,350.00	$17,435.00	$1,864,615.00
Cost of Sales	213,450.00	123,900.00	105,630.00	34,945.00	12,600.00	42,500.00	34,000.00	8,550.00	575,575.00
Direct Costs	145,750.00	62,000.00	48,460.00	12,500.00	6,345.00	18,750.00	30,200.00	6,200.00	330,205.00
Indirect Expenses									
Administrative	$26,182.46	$20,010.19	$16,430.44	$2,226.70	$5,568.84	$3,281.70	$3,570.33	$729.34	$78,000.00
Marketing	18,797.66	14,366.29	11,796.22	1,598.66	3,998.14	2,356.09	2,563.32	523.63	56,000.00
Energy	11,748.54	8,978.93	7,372.63	999.16	2,498.84	1,472.56	1,602.07	327.27	35,000.00
Maintenance	2,727.27	9,090.91	2,181.82	3,272.73	545.45	4,181.82	909.09	1,090.91	24,000.00
Depreciation	7,613.64	25,378.79	6,090.91	9,136.36	1,522.73	11,674.24	2,537.88	3,045.45	67,000.00
Insurance	1,136.36	3,787.88	909.09	1,363.64	227.27	1,742.42	378.79	454.55	10,000.00
Total Indirect Expenses	**$68,205.93**	**$81,612.99**	**$44,781.11**	**$18,597.25**	**$14,361.28**	**$24,708.83**	**$11,561.48**	**$6,171.14**	**$270,000.00**
Net Income	**$198,494.07**	**$210,837.01**	**$193,903.89**	**($12,812.25)**	**$99,818.72**	**($7,508.83)**	**$9,588.52**	**($3,486.14)**	**$688,835.00**
Square Footage	1,500	5,000	1,200	1,800	300	2,300	500	600	13,200
Planned Indirect Expenses									
Administrative	$78,000.00								
Marketing	$56,000.00								
Energy	$35,000.00								
Maintenance	$24,000.00								
Depreciation	$67,000.00								
Insurance	$10,000.00								

FIGURE 3-82

Table 3-6 R&R Hotel Worksheet Data								
	DINING ROOM	BANQUET ROOM	LOUNGE	FITNESS CENTER	BUSINESS CENTER	CONFERENCE ROOMS	SNACK SHOP	ARCADE
Revenue	625900	478350	392775	53230	133125	78450	85350	17435
Cost of Sales	213450	123900	105630	34945	12600	42500	34000	8550
Direct Costs	145750	62000	48460	12500	6345	18750	30200	6200
Square Footage	1500	5000	1200	1800	300	2300	500	600

In the Lab

Instructions Part 1: Do the following to create the worksheet shown in Figure 3-82.

1. Use the Select All button and Bold button to bold the entire worksheet. Enter the worksheet titles R&R Hotel in cell A1 and Indirect Expense Allocation in cell A2. Enter the system date in cell J2 using the NOW function. Format the date to the 3/4/1998 format style.

2. Enter the first four rows of data in Table 3-6 in rows 3 through 6. In row 3, use ALT+ENTER to display the column titles on two lines in a cell. Select the range J4:J6 and click the AutoSum button. Add a thick bottom border to the range B3:J3.

3. Enter the Square Footage row in Table 3-6 in row 16. Select cell J16 and use the AutoSum button to determine the sum of the values in the range B16:I16.

4. Change the following column widths: A = 26.00; B through I = 12.00, and J = 13.00. Change the height of row 16 to 39.00.

5. Enter the remaining row titles in the range A7:A17 as shown in Figure 3-82. Use the Indent button on the Formatting toolbar to indent the row titles in the range A8:A13.

6. Copy the range A8:A13 to the range A18:A23. Enter the numbers shown in the range B18:B23 of Figure 3-82 with format symbols.

7. The planned indirect expenses in the range B18:B23 are to be prorated across the profit center as follows: Administrative (row 8), Marketing (row 9), and Energy (row 10) on the basis of revenue volume; Maintenance (row 11), Depreciation (row 12), and Insurance (row 13) on the basis of square feet. Complete the following entries:

   a. Dining Room Administrative (cell B8) = Administrative Expenses * Dining Room Revenue / Total Revenue or =$B$18 * B4 / $J$4

   b. Marketing Administrative (cell B9) = Marketing Expenses * Dining Room Revenue / Total Revenue or =$B$19 * B4 / $J$4

   c. Energy Administrative (cell B10) = Energy Expenses * Dining Room Revenue / Total Revenue or =$B$20 * B4 / $J$4

   d. Maintenance Administrative (cell B11) = Maintenance Expenses * Dining Room Square Feet / Total Square Feet or =$B$21 * B16 / $J$16

   e. Depreciation Administrative (cell B12) = Depreciation Expenses * Dining Room Square Feet / Total Square Feet or =$B$22 * B16 / $J$16

   f. Insurance Administrative (cell B13) = Insurance Expenses * Dining Room Square Feet / Total Square Feet or =$B$23 * B16 / $J$16

   g. Total Indirect Expenses (cell B14) = SUM(B8:B13)

   h. Net Income (cell B15) = Revenue – (Cost of Sales + Direct Costs + Indirect Expenses) or =B4 – (B5 + B6 + B14)

   i. Use the fill handle to copy the range B8:B15 to the range C8:I15.

   j. Select the range J8:J15 and click the Auto Sum button on the Standard toolbar.

   k. Add a thick bottom border to the range B13:J13.

8. Use the Format Cells dialog box to format to Currency style with two decimal places and display negative numbers in parentheses to the following ranges: B4:J4; B8:J8; and B14:J15. Format to Comma style with two decimal places and display negative numbers in parentheses to the following ranges: B5:J6; B9:J13; and B16:J16.

(continued)

In the Lab

R&R Hotel Indirect Expense Allocation *(continued)*

9. Change the font in cell A1 to 48-point Brush Script MT (or a similar font). Change the font in cell A2 to 26-point Algerian (or a similar font). Change the font in cell A17 to 14-point italic and underlined.

10. Use the background color Blue-Gray (column 7, row 2) on the Fill Color palette, the foreground color White (column 8, row 5) on the Font Color palette, and a drop shadow (Shadow Type 6) for the following ranges: A1:J2; A7; A15:J15; and A17:B23. The Shadow button is on the Drawing toolbar.

11. Enter your name, course, laboratory assignment (Lab 3-1), date, and instructor name in the range A27:A31. Save the workbook using the file name, R&R Hotel.

12. Preview and print the worksheet. Preview and print the formulas version (CTRL+LEFT QUOTATION MARK) of the worksheet in landscape orientation using the Fit to option button in the Page Setup dialog box. After printing the formulas version, reset the print scaling to 100%. Press CTRL+LEFT QUOTATION MARK to display the values version of the worksheet. Save the workbook again.

Instructions Part 2: Draw a 3-D Pie chart (Figure 3-83) that shows the contribution of each category of indirect expense to the total indirect expenses. That is, chart the nonadjacent ranges A8:A13 (category names) and J8:J13 (data series). Show labels and percents. Do not show the legend. Do the following to the Pie chart:

1. Add the chart title and format it to 36-point Arial red, underlined font.
2. Explode the Administrative slice.
3. Select a slice and use the 3-D View command on the shortcut menu to change the elevation to 35° and the rotation to 80°.
4. Change the color of the slices as shown in Figure 3-83.
5. Drag the data labels away from the 3-D Pie chart so the leader lines from the data labels to the corresponding slices display.
6. Rename the sheets as follows: Chart1 to 3-D Pie Chart; Sheet1 to Planned Indirect Expenses. Rearrange the sheets so the Planned Indirect Expenses sheet is to the left of the 3-D Pie Chart sheet. Click the Planned Indirect Expenses tab.

FIGURE 3-83

In the Lab

7. Save the workbook using the file name R&R Hotel. Print both sheets.

Instructions Part 3: Using the numbers in Table 3-7, analyze the effect of changing the planned indirect expenses in the range B18:B23 on the net incomes for each profit center. Print the worksheet for each case. You should end with the following totals in cell J15: Case 1 = $639,335.00 and Case 2 = $745,335.00.

Table 3-7	What-If Data	
	CASE 1	CASE 2
Administrative	92,000.00	56,000.00
Marketing	65,000.00	47,000.00
Energy	42,000.00	32,000.00
Maintenance	36,000.00	20,000.00
Depreciation	72,000.00	51,000.00
Insurance	12,500.00	7,500.00

2 E-Book.com Seven-Year Projected Financial Statement

Problem: You were recently certified at the Expert level in Excel by the Microsoft Office User Specialist program. Following certification, you were promoted to spreadsheet specialist at E-Book.com, an e-commerce Web site on the Internet that sells books, videos, and CDs. Your manager has asked you to create a worksheet that will project the revenue, expenses, taxes, and income for the next seven years based on the assumptions in Table 3-8. The desired worksheet is shown in Figure 3-84.

Table 3-8	Data for Assumptions
ASSUMPTIONS	
Units Sold in Year 2000	8,492,016
Unit Cost	9.27
Annual Sales Growth	7.00%
Annual Price Decrease	5.00%
Margin	40.00%

	A	B	C	D	E	F	G	H
1	**E-Book.com**							
2	**Seven-Year Projected Financial Statement**							11/26/2001
3		2001	2002	2003	2004	2005	2006	2007
4	Revenue	131,201,647	133,366,474	135,567,021	137,803,877	140,077,641	142,388,922	144,738,339
5	Cost of Goods Sold	78,720,988	80,019,885	81,340,213	82,682,326	84,046,585	85,433,353	86,843,004
6	Gross Margin	52,480,659	53,346,590	54,226,808	55,121,551	56,031,056	56,955,569	57,895,336
7	**Expenses**							
8	Advertising	19,681,247	20,005,971	20,336,053	20,671,582	21,012,646	21,359,338	21,711,751
9	Rent	1,800,000	1,980,000	2,178,000	2,395,800	2,635,380	2,898,918	3,188,810
10	Salaries	23,616,296	24,005,965	24,402,064	24,804,698	25,213,975	25,630,006	26,052,901
11	Supplies	1,968,025	2,000,497	2,033,505	2,067,058	2,101,165	2,135,834	2,171,075
12	Maintenance	2,100,000	5,450,000	3,900,000	5,350,000	2,750,000	2,950,000	3,100,000
13	**Total Expenses**	49,165,568	53,442,434	52,849,622	55,289,138	53,713,166	54,974,096	56,224,537
14								
15	**Income Before Taxes**	3,315,091	(95,844)	1,377,186	(167,587)	2,317,890	1,981,473	1,670,799
16	Income Taxes	1,326,036	0	550,874	0	927,156	792,589	668,320
17	**Net Income**	1,989,054	(95,844)	826,312	(167,587)	1,390,734	1,188,884	1,002,479
18								
19	**Assumptions**							
20	Units Sold in Year 2000	8,492,016						
21	Unit Cost	9.27						
22	Annual Sales Growth	7.00%						
23	Annual Price Decrease	5.00%						
24	Margin	40.00%						
25								

FIGURE 3-84

(continued)

In the Lab

E-Book.com Seven-Year Projected Financial Statement *(continued)*

Instructions Part 1: Do the following to create the worksheet shown in Figure 3-84.

1. Use the Select All button and Bold button to bold the entire worksheet. Enter the worksheet titles in cells A1 and A2. Enter the system date in cell H2 using the NOW function. Format the date to the 3/14/1998 style.

2. Enter the seven column titles 2001 through 2007 in the range B3:H3. Begin each year with an apostrophe so that the years are entered as text. Text headings are required for the charting in Part 2. Center and italicize cell B3. Rotate its contents 45°. Use the Format Painter button to copy the format assigned to cell B3 to the range C3:H3.

3. Enter the row titles in the range A4:A24. Change the font size in cells A7, A13, A15, and A17 to 12 point. Change the font size in cell A19 to 14 point and underline the characters in the cell. Add a heavy bottom border to the range A3:H3.

4. Change the following column widths: A = 23.43; B through H = 11.00. Change the heights of rows 7, 13, 15, 16, and 17 to 24.00.

5. Enter the assumptions values in Table 3-8 in the range B20:B24. Use format symbols.

6. Assign the Comma style format with no decimal places to the range B4:H17.

7. Complete the following entries:
   a. 2001 Revenue (cell B4) = Units Sold 2000 * (Unit Cost / (1 − Margin)) or =B20 * (B21 / (1 − B24))
   b. 2002 Revenue (cell C4) = 2001 Revenue * (1 + Annual Sales Growth) * (1 − Annual Price Decrease) or =B4 * (1 + $B$22) * (1 − $B$23)
   c. Copy cell C4 to the range D4:H4.
   d. 2001 Cost of Goods Sold (cell B5) = 2001 Revenue − (2001 Revenue * Margin) or =B4 * (1 − $B$24)
   e. Copy cell B5 to the range C5:H5.
   f. 2001 Gross Margin (cell B6) = 2001 Revenue − 2001 Cost of Goods Sold or =B4 − B5
   g. Copy cell B6 to the range C6:H6.
   h. 2001 Advertising (cell B8) = 1000 + 15% * 2001 Revenue or =1000 + 15% * B4
   i. Copy cell B8 to the range C8:H8.
   j. 2001 Rent (cell B9) = 1,800,000
   k. 2002 Rent (cell C9) = 2001 Rent + 10% * 2001 Rent or =B9 + (10% * B9)
   l. Copy cell C9 to the range D9:H9.
   m. 2001 Salaries (cell B10) = 18% * 2001 Revenue or =18% * B4
   n. Copy cell B10 to the range C10:H10.
   o. 2001 Supplies (cell B11) = 1.5% * 2001 Revenue or =1.5% * B4
   p. Copy cell B11 to the range C11:H11.
   q. Maintenance: 2001 = 2,100,000; 2002 = 5,450,000; 2003 = 3,900,000; 2004 = 5,350,000; 2005 = 2,750,000; 2006 = 2,950,000; 2007 = 3,100,000
   r. 2001 Total Expenses (cell B13) = SUM(B8:B12)
   s. Copy cell B13 to the range C13:H13.
   t. 2001 Income Before Taxes (cell B15) = 2001 Gross Margin − 2001 Total Expenses or =B6 − B13
   u. Copy cell B15 to the range C15:H15.

In the Lab

v. 2001 Income Taxes (cell B16): If 2001 Income Before Taxes is less than zero, then 2001 Income Taxes equal zero; otherwise 2001 Income Taxes equal 40% * 2001 Income Before Taxes or =IF(B15 < 0, 0, 40% * B15)

w. Copy cell B16 to the range C16:H16.

x. 2001 Net Income (cell B17) = 2001 Income Before Taxes – 2001 Income Taxes or =B15 – B16

y. Copy cell B17 to the range C17:H17.

8. Change the font in cell A1 to 26-point Book Antiqua (or a similar font). Change the font in cell A2 to 16-point Book Antiqua (or a similar font). Change the font in cell H2 to 10-point Century Gothic (or a similar font). Change the background and font colors and add drop shadows as shown in Figure 3-84.

9. Enter your name, course, laboratory assignment (Lab 3-1), date, and instructor name in the range A27:A31. Save the workbook using the file name, e-book.

10. Preview and print the worksheet. Preview and print the formulas version (CTRL+LEFT QUOTATION MARK) of the worksheet in landscape orientation using the Fit to option button in the Page Setup dialog box. After printing the formulas version, reset the print scaling to 100%. Press CTRL+LEFT QUOTATION MARK to display the values version of the worksheet. Save the workbook again.

Instructions Part 2: Draw a 3-D Column chart (Figure 3-85) that compares the projected net incomes for the years 2001 through 2007. Use the nonadjacent ranges B3:H3 and B17:H17. Add the chart title and format it as shown in Figure 3-85. Rename and rearrange the sheets as shown in Figure 3-85. Save the workbook using the same file name (e-book) as defined in Part 1. Print both sheets.

Instructions Part 3:

If the 3-D Column chart is on the screen, click the Seven-Year Plan tab to display the worksheet. Divide the window into two panes by dragging the horizontal split bar between rows 6 and 7. Use the scroll bars to display both the top and bottom of the worksheet.

FIGURE 3-85

(continued)

In the Lab

E-Book.com Seven-Year Projected Financial Statement (*continued*)

Using the numbers in columns 2 and 3 of Table 3-9, analyze the effect of changing the annual sales growth (cell B22) and annual price decrease (cell B23) on the annual net incomes in row 17. The resulting answers are in column 4 of Table 3-9. Print both the worksheet and chart for each case.

Close the workbook without saving it, and then reopen it. Use the Goal Seek command to determine a margin (cell B24) that would result in a net income in 2007 of $5,000,000 (cell H17). You should end up with a margin of 43.94% in cell B24. After you complete the goal seeking, print only the worksheet. Do not save the workbook with the latest changes.

Table 3-9 Data to Analyze and Results			
CASE	ANNUAL SALES GROWTH	ANNUAL PRICE DECREASE	2007 RESULTING NETINCOME
1	12.55%	2.15%	$3,950,985
2	15.25%	-5.50	$10,215,981
3	25.50%	9.35%	$5,613,019

3 Modifying the Stars and Stripes Automotive Weekly Payroll Worksheet

Problem: Your supervisor in the Payroll department has asked you to modify the payroll workbook developed in Exercise 1 of the Project 2 In the Lab section on page E 2.68, so that it displays as shown in Figure 3-86. If you did not complete Exercise 1 in Project 2, ask your instructor for a copy of the Stars and Stripes Automotive workbook or complete that exercise before you begin this one.

	A	B	C	D	E	F	G	H	I	J	K
1	Stars and Stripes Automotive										
2	Weekly Payroll Report for	1/5/2002									
3	Employee	Rate	Hours	Dep.	YTD Soc. Sec.	Gross Pay	Soc. Sec.	Medicare	Fed. Tax	State Tax	Net Pay
4	Breeze, Linus	27.50	40.25	4	4,974.00	1,110.31	68.84	16.10	191.29	35.53	798.55
5	Santiago, Juan	18.75	56.00	1	5,540.20	1,200.00	13.70	17.40	232.31	38.40	898.19
6	Webb, Trevor	28.35	38.00	3	4,254.00	1,077.30	66.79	15.62	192.38	34.47	768.03
7	Sabol, Kylie	21.50	46.50	6	5,553.90	1,069.63	0.00	15.51	167.77	34.23	852.11
8	Ali, Abdul	19.35	15.00	9	3,447.60	290.25	18.00	4.21	0.00	9.29	258.76
9	Chung, Lee	17.05	28.00	5	4,825.50	477.40	29.60	6.92	57.02	15.28	368.58
10	Fritz, Albert	28.35	38.75	3	5,553.90	1,098.56	0.00	15.93	196.64	35.15	850.84
11	Totals		262.50		34,149.10	6,323.45	196.93	91.69	1,037.42	202.35	4,795.07
12											
13	Social Security Tax	6.20%									
14	Medicare Tax	1.45%									
15	Maximum Social Security	$5,553.90									

FIGURE 3-86

In the Lab

The major modifications requested by your supervisor include: (1) reformatting the worksheet; (2) adding computations of time and a half for hours worked greater than 40; (3) removing the conditional formatting assigned to the range E3:E8; (4) charging no federal tax in certain situations; (5) adding Social Security and Medicare deductions; (6) adding and deleting employees; and (7) changing employee information. The Stars and Stripes Automotive workbook, as created in Project 2, is shown in Figure 2-85 on page E 2.68.

Instructions Part 1: Open the workbook, Stars and Stripes Automotive, created in Project 2. Perform the following tasks.

1. Use the Select All button and the Clear command on the Edit menu to clear all formats.
2. Bold the entire worksheet. Delete rows 10 through 12. Insert a row above row 2. Modify the wording in the worksheet title in cell A1 and change its point size to 14 so it appears as shown in Figure 3-86. Enter the worksheet subtitle, Weekly Payroll Report for, in cell A2. Assign the NOW function to cell B2 and format it to the 3/14/1998 style.
3. Insert a new column between columns D and E by right-clicking the column E heading and inserting a column. Enter the new column E title, YTD Soc. Sec, in cell E3. Insert two new columns between columns F and G. Enter the new column G title, Soc. Sec., in cell G3. Enter the new column H title, Medicare, in cell H3. Freeze the panes (titles) in column A and rows 1 through 3.
4. Change the column widths and row heights as follows: A = 25.00; B = 9.43; C = 6.43; D = 6.00; E = 13.14; F through K = 9.71; and row 3 = 18.00. Right-align the column titles in the range B3:K3.
5. Delete row 9 (Goldstein, Kevin). Change Abdul Ali's hours worked to 15 and number of dependents to 9.
6. In column E, enter the YTD Social Security values listed in Table 3-10.
7. Insert two new rows immediately above the Totals row. Add the new employee data as listed in Table 3-11.
8. Use the Format Cells dialog box to assign a Comma style and two decimal places to the ranges B4:C11 and E4:K11. Center the range D4:D10.
9. Enter the Social Security and Medicare tax information headings in the range A13:A15. Enter the values in the range B13:B15. Use format symbols to format the numbers as shown in Figure 3-86.
10. Change the formulas to determine the gross pay in column F and the federal tax in column I.
    a. In cell F4, enter an IF function that applies the following logic:
       If Hours <= 40, then Gross Pay = Rate * Hours, otherwise Gross Pay = Rate * Hours + 0.5 * Rate * (Hours – 40)
    b. Copy the IF function in cell F4 to the range F5:F10.
    c. In cell I4, enter the IF function that applies the following logic:
       If (Gross Pay – Dependents * 38.46) > 0, then Federal Tax = 20% * (Gross Pay – Dependents * 38.46), otherwise Federal Tax = 0
    d. Copy the IF function in cell I4 to the range I5:I10.

Table 3-10	YTD Social Security Values
NAME	YTD SOC. SEC.
Breeze, Linus	4,974.00
Santiago, Juan	5,540.20
Webb, Trevor	4,254.00
Sabol, Kylie	5,553.90
Ali, Abdul	3,447.60

Table 3-11	New Employee Data			
EMPLOYEE	RATE	HOURS	DEPENDENTS	YTD SOC.SEC.
Chung, Lee	17.05	28	5	4,825.50
Fritz, Albert	28.35	38.75	3	5,553.90

(continued)

In the Lab

Modifying the Stars and Stripes Automotive Weekly Payroll Worksheet *(continued)*

11. An employee pays Social Security tax only if his or her YTD Social Security is less than the maximum Social Security in column E. Use the following logic to determine the Social Security tax for Linus Breeze in cell G4:

    If Soc. Sec. Tax * Gross Pay + YTD Soc. Sec. > Maximum Soc. Sec., then Maximum Soc. Sec. – YTD Soc. Sec., otherwise Soc. Sec. Tax * Gross Pay

12. Make sure references to the values in the social security tax table (B13:B15) are absolute, and then copy the IF function to the range G5:G10.

13. In cell H4, enter the following formula and then copy it to the range H5:H10:

    Medicare = Medicare Tax * Gross Pay

14. Copy the state tax in cell J4 to the range J5:J10.

15. In cell K4, enter the following formula and copy it to the range K5:K10:

    = Gross Pay – (Soc. Sec. + Medicare + Fed. Tax + State Tax)

16. Determine any new totals as shown in row 11 of Figure 3-86.

17. Enter your name, course, laboratory assignment (Lab 3-2), date, and instructor name in the range A18:A22.

18. Unfreeze the panes (titles). Save the workbook using the file name, Stars and Stripes Automotive 2.

19. Use the Zoom box on the Standard toolbar to change the view of the worksheet. One by one, select all the percents in the Zoom list. When you are done, return the worksheet to 100% magnification.

20. Preview the worksheet. If number signs display in place of numbers in any columns, adjust the column widths. Print the worksheet in landscape orientation. Save the worksheet using the same file name.

21. Preview and print the formulas version (CTRL+LEFT QUOTATION MARK) in landscape orientation using the Fit to option button in the Page Setup dialog box. Close the worksheet without saving the latest changes.

Instructions Part 2: Using the numbers in Table 3-12, analyze the effect of changing the Social Security tax in cell B13 and the Medicare tax in cell B14. Print the worksheet for each case. The first case should result in a total Social Security tax in cell G11 of $250.12. The second case should result in a total Social Security tax of $324.00.

Table 3-12 Social Security and Medicare Taxes		
CASE	SOCIAL SECURITY TAX	MEDICARE TAX
1	8%	2.75%
2	10.5%	2.25%

Cases and Places

The difficulty of these case studies varies:
▶ are the least difficult; ▶▶ are more difficult; and ▶▶▶ are the most difficult.

1 ▶ You are a managing editor for Swain Publishers, a company that produces paperback books sold worldwide. One of your responsibilities is to submit income projections to your publisher for the books you plan to sign. The projected first year net sales for the books you plan to do are shown in Table 3-13. Also included in the table are the percent of net sales for payment of royalties and manufacturing costs. Use the concepts and techniques presented in this project to create and format a worksheet that shows the projected royalties, projected manufacturing cost, net income for each book, and totals for the four numeric columns in Table 3-13. The net income for a book is equal to the net sales less the royalty and manufacturing costs.

Your publisher reviewed your plan and returned it, requesting printouts of the worksheet for the following set of values: Set 1 – Royalty 13.5%; Manufacturing Costs 31%; Set 2 – Royalty 14%; Manufacturing Costs 29%.

Table 3-13	Projected 1st Year Net Sales			
BOOK TITLE	NET SALES	ROYALTY	MANU. COSTS	NET INCOME
1	975,270.50	----	----	----
2	597,825.25	----	----	----
3	752,913.37	----	----	----
TOTAL	----	----	----	----
ASSUMPTIONS				
ROYALTIES	15.5%			
MANU. COSTS	21.5%			

2 ▶ Lite Power Company is a large utility company in the Southwest. The company earns revenues from the sale of natural gas and electricity. A fixed percentage of this revenue is spent on marketing, payroll, equipment, production costs, and administrative expenses. Lite Power's president has summarized the company's receipts and expenditures over the past year on a quarterly basis as shown in Table 3-14.

Table 3-14	Quarterly Company Receipts and Expenditures			
REVENUES	QUARTER 1	QUARTER 2	QUARTER 3	QUARTER 4
NATURAL GAS	52,349,812	67,213,943	55,329,781	51,690,655
ELECTRICITY	42,812,562	55,392,887	52,932,856	50,278,541
EXPENDITURES				
MARKETING	12.75%			
PAYROLL	32.65%			
EQUIPMENT	14.30%			
PRODUCTION	19.50%			
ADMINISTRATIVE	4.5%			

With this data, you have been asked to prepare a worksheet similar to Figure 3-1a on page E 3.5 for the next shareholders' meeting. The worksheet should show total revenues, total expenditures, and net income for each quarterly period. Include a chart that illustrates quarterly net income. Use the concepts and techniques presented in this project to create and format the worksheet and chart. During the meeting, one shareholder lobbied to reduce marketing expenditures by 2% and payroll costs by 6%. Perform a what-if analysis reflecting the proposed changes in expenditures.

Cases and Places

3 ▶ Candie's sweet shop is open year round, but most of the shop's production revolves around four holidays: Valentine's Day (6,125 lbs.), Easter (4,250 lbs.), Halloween (8,825 lbs.), and Christmas (5,975 lbs.). On these days 31% of the store's output is fudge, 13% is caramel, 43% is boxed chocolate, and the remaining 13% is holiday-specific candy (such as chocolate hearts or candy canes). The fudge sells for $6.55 per pound, the caramel for $4.95 per pound, the boxed chocolate for $7.25 per pound, and holiday-specific candy for $3.75 per pound. Candie's management is considering revising its production figures. They have asked you to create a worksheet they can use in making this decision. The worksheet should show the amount of each candy produced for each holiday, potential sales for each type of candy, total potential sales for each holiday, total candy produced for the four holidays, and total potential sales from each type of candy. Include an appropriate chart illustrating total potential sales for each candy type. Use the concepts and techniques presented in this project to create and format the worksheet.

4 ▶▶ Your uncle, Dollar Bill, wants to save enough money to send his little girl to a private school. He has job orders at his custom drapery shop for the next six months: $800 in January, $750 in February, $550 in March, $665 in April, $388 in May, and $767 in June. Each month, Uncle Dollar Bill spends 40.25% of the orders on material, 3.5% on patterns, 3.25% on his retirement account, and 44% on food and clothing. The remaining profits (orders – expenses) will be put aside for the girl's education. Aunt Penny has agreed to provide an additional $25 whenever Uncle Dollar Bill's monthly profit exceeds $50. Your uncle has asked you to create a worksheet that shows orders, expenses, profits, and savings for the next six months, and totals for each category. Uncle Dollar Bill would like you to (a) goal seek to determine what percentage of profits to spend on food and clothing if $800 is needed for the school, and (b) perform a what-if analysis to determine the effect of reducing the percentage spent on material to 25%. Use the concepts and techniques presented in this project to create and format the worksheet.

5 ▶▶▶ Balancing a budget is a significant challenge for many students attending college. Whether you work part-time or simply draw on a sum of money while going to school, you must equalize income and expenditures to maintain your budget. Use the concepts and techniques presented in this project to create and format a worksheet that reflects your monthly budget throughout the school year. Indicate the amount of money you have available each month. Hypothesize percentages for monthly expenditures (tuition, books, entertainment, and so on). On the basis of these assumptions, determine expenditures for each month. Include a row for occasional miscellaneous expenses (such as travel). Ascertain the amount of money remaining at the end of each month; this amount will become part or all of the money available for the subsequent month. Perform at least one what-if analysis to examine the effect of changing one or more of the values in the worksheet, and goal-seek to determine how an expenditure must be modified to have $500 more available at the end of the school year.

Microsoft **Excel 2000**

Microsoft Excel 2000

Creating Static and Dynamic Web Pages Using Excel

CASE PERSPECTIVE

Ryan Thomas is a project manager for Awesome Intranets, a computer company that specializes in the installation of intranets. Ryan has a workbook that he and his group use to project annual company sales by sales office (Figure 1a). The projections are based on historical sales patterns and sales for the first quarter. In the past, Ryan printed the worksheet and chart, sent it out to duplicate it, and mailed it to his distribution list. He also made his computer available to members of his workgroup who did not have Excel, so they could analyze sales using the workbook.

Awesome Intranets recently upgraded to Office 2000 because of its Web and collaboration capabilities. After attending an Office 2000 training session, Ryan had a great idea and called you for help. He would like to save the Excel workbook (Figure 1a) on the company's intranet as a Web page (Figure 1b) so members on the distribution list could display it using their browser. He also suggested publishing the same workbook on the company's intranet as a dynamic (interactive) Web page (Figure 1c) so his workgroup could use its browser to manipulate the formulas and Pie chart without requiring Excel 2000.

Introduction

Excel 2000 provides fast and easy methods for saving workbooks as Web pages that can be stored on the World Wide Web, a company's intranet, or a local hard drive. A user then can display the workbook using a browser, rather than Excel.

You can save a workbook, or a portion of a workbook, as a static Web page or a dynamic Web page. A **static (noninteractive) Web page** is a snapshot of the workbook. It is similar to a printed report in that you can view it through your browser, but you cannot modify it. A **dynamic (interactive) Web page** includes the interactivity and functionality of the workbook, such as formulas, charting, and the recalculation features of Excel.

As shown in Figure 1 on the next page, in this Web Feature you will save a workbook (Figure 1a) as a static Web page (Figure 1b) and view it using your browser. Then you will take the same workbook and save it as a dynamic Web page (Figure 1c) and view it using your browser. After displaying the dynamic Web page in your browser, you will change certain values to test the Web page's interactivity and functionality.

The Save as Web Page command on the File menu allows you to **publish** workbooks, which is the process of making them available to others; for example, on the World Wide Web or on a company's intranet. If you have access to a Web server, you can publish Web pages by saving them to a Web folder or to an FTP location. The procedures for publishing Web pages to a Web folder or FTP location using Microsoft Office applications are discussed in Appendix B.

In this Web Feature, for instructional purposes, you will create and save the Web pages and associated folders on a floppy disk.

(a) **Workbook Viewed in Excel**

FIGURE 1

browser is active

Awesome Intranets
Projected Quarterly Sales

	Quarter 1	Quarter 2	Quarter 3	Quarter 4	Total
San Jose	$155,321	$163,087	$164,640	$153,768	$636,816
Orlando	175,923	184,719	186,478	174,164	721,284
St. Louis	125,220	131,481	132,733	123,968	513,402
Redmond	192,134	201,741	203,662	190,213	787,749
Total	$648,598	$681,028	$687,514	$642,112	$2,659,252

(b) Static Web Page Viewed in Browser

save Pie chart and worksheet as dynamic Web page

browser is active

Web page maintains interactivity and functionality of worksheet formulas and Pie chart

Projected Quarterly Sales

■ San Jose
■ Orlando
■ St. Louis
■ Redmond

	A	B	C	D	E	F
1	San Jose	$155,321	$163,087	$164,640	$153,768	$636,816
2	Orlando	175,923	184,719	186,478	174,164	721,284
3	St. Louis	125,220	131,481	132,733	123,968	513,402
4	Redmond	192,134	201,741	203,662	190,213	787,749

(c) Dynamic Web Page Viewed in Browser

Saving an Excel Workbook as a Static Web Page

Once you have created an Excel workbook, you can save it as a static Web page so it can be published and then viewed using a Web browser, such as Internet Explorer. The file format that Excel saves the workbook in is called **HTML (hypertext markup language)**, which is a language browsers can interpret. Perform the following steps to save the workbook as a static Web page.

 To Save an Excel Workbook as a Static Web Page

1 Insert the Data Disk in drive A. If you do not have a copy of the Data Disk, see the inside back cover of this book. Start Excel and then open the workbook, Awesome Intranets, on drive A. Reset your toolbars as described in Appendix C. Click File on the menu bar and then point to Save as Web Page.

The File menu displays (Figure 2).

FIGURE 2

2 **Click Save as Web Page. When the Save As dialog box displays, type** Awesome Intranets Static Web Page **in the File name text box and then, if necessary, click the Save in box arrow and select 3½ Floppy (A:). Point to the Save button in the Save As dialog box.**

The Save As dialog box displays (Figure 3).

3 **Click the Save button. Click the Close button on the right side of the title bar to close Excel.**

Excel saves the workbook in HTML format on drive A using the file name, Awesome Intranets Static Web page.htm (see Figure 4 on the next page). Excel shuts down.

FIGURE 3

If you want to see how the workbook will display as a static Web page before you save it, you can click the **Web Page Preview command** on the File menu (Figure 2). This command will start your browser and display the static Web page. The Web Page Preview command is similar to the Print Preview command, which previews a printout of a workbook.

The Save As dialog box that displays when you use the Save as Web Page command is slightly different from the Save As dialog box that displays when you use the Save As command. When you use the Save as Web Page command, a **Save area** displays in the dialog box. Within the Save area are two option buttons, a check box, and a Publish button (Figure 3). You can select only one of the option buttons. The **Entire Workbook option button** is selected by default. This indicates Excel will save all the active sheets (Quarterly Sales and 3-D Pie Chart) in the workbook as a static Web page if you click the Save button. The alternative is the **Selection Sheet option button.** If you select this option, Excel will save only the active sheet (the one that is displaying in the Excel window) in the workbook. If you add a check mark to the **Add interactivity check box**, then Excel saves the sheet as a dynamic Web page. If you leave the Add interactivity check box unchecked, Excel saves the active sheet as a static Web page.

Publishing Web Pages

For more information on publishing Web pages using Excel, visit the Excel 2000 More About Web page (www.scsite.com/ex2000/more.htm) and click Publishing Web Pages Using Excel.

Viewing the Source Code

To view the HTML source code for the static Web page created in Excel, display the Web page in your browser, click View on the menu bar, and then click Source. If you are familiar with HTML, you will notice embedded XML (Extensible Markup Language) code. The XML code is used to hold the Excel formats so you can round-trip or open the HTML file in Excel.

The **Publish button** in the Save As dialog box is an alternative to the Save button. It allows you to customize the Web page further. In the previous set of steps, the Save button was used to complete the save. Later in this feature, the Publish button will be used to explain further how you can customize a Web page.

If you have access to a Web server and it allows you to save files to a Web folder, then you can save the Web page directly to the Web server by clicking the **Web Folders button** in the lower left corner of the Save As dialog box (Figure 3). If you have access to a Web server that allows you to save to an FTP, then you can select the FTP site under **FTP locations** in the Save in box just as you select any folder to save a file to. To save a workbook to a Web server, see Appendix B.

After Excel saves the workbook in Step 3 on the previous page, the HTML file displays in the Excel window as if it were saved as a Microsoft Excel workbook (.xls extension). Excel can continue to display the workbook in HTML format because within the HTML file that it created, it also saved the Excel formats that allow it to display the HTML file in Excel. This is referred to as **round tripping** the HTML file back to the application in which it was created.

When you save a static Web page, Excel also creates a folder on drive A. The folder contains the graphics required to display the Web page.

Viewing the Static Web Page Using Your Browser

With the static Web page saved on drive A, the next step is to view it using your browser as shown in the following steps.

 ## To View the Static Web Page Using Your Browser

1 **Click the Start button on the taskbar, point to Programs, and then click Internet Explorer.**

2 **When the Internet Explorer window displays, type** a:\awesome intranets static web page.htm **in the Address bar and then press the ENTER key.**

The Web page, Awesome Intranets Static Web Page.htm, displays with the Quarterly Sales sheet active (Figure 4).

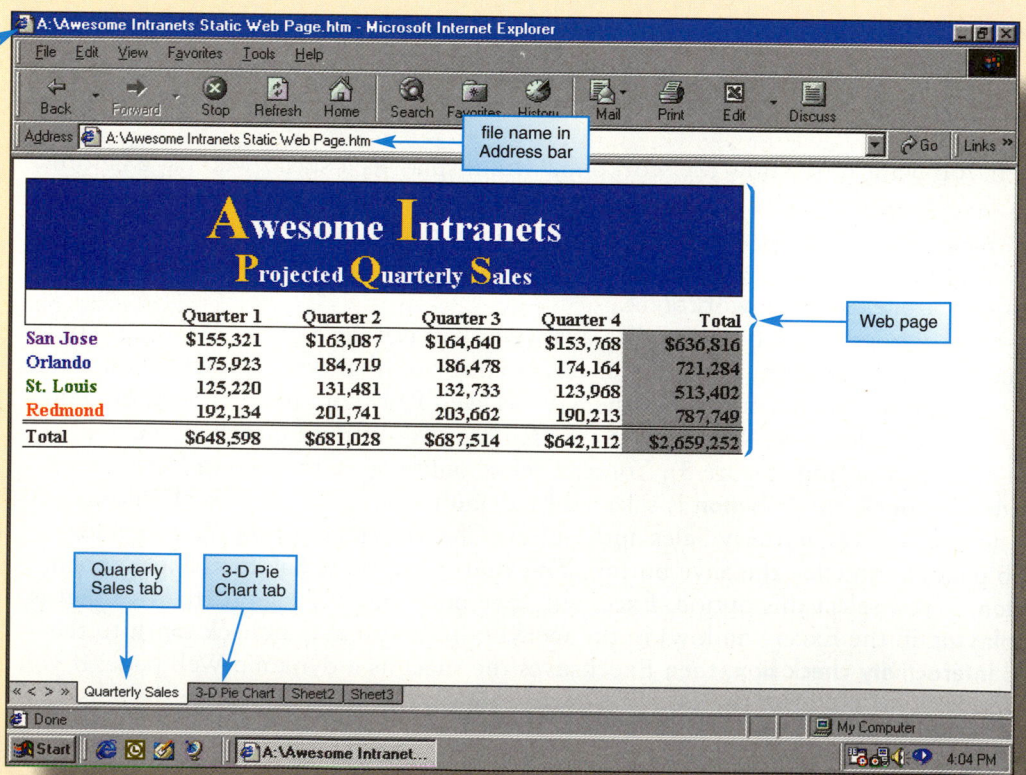

FIGURE 4

3 Click the 3-D Pie Chart tab at the bottom of the window. Use the scroll arrows to display the legend.

The 3-D Pie chart displays as shown in Figure 5.

4 Click the Close button at the right side of the Internet Explorer title bar.

The Internet Explorer window closes.

FIGURE 5

You can see from Figures 4 and 5 that the static Web page is an ideal media for distributing information to a large group of people. For example, the static Web page could be published to a Web server connected to the Internet and made available to anyone with a computer, browser, and the address of the Web page. Thus, publishing a static Web page of a workbook is an alternative to distributing printed copies of the workbook.

Figures 4 and 5 show that when you instruct Excel to save the entire workbook (see Figure 3 on page EW 1.5), it creates a Web page with tabs for each sheet in the workbook. Clicking a tab displays the corresponding sheet. If you want, you can use the Print command on the File menu in your browser to print the sheets one at a time.

Saving an Excel Chart as a Dynamic Web Page

This section publishes a dynamic Web page that includes Excel functionality and interactivity. The objective is to publish the 3-D Pie chart that is on the chart sheet in the Awesome Intranets workbook. The following steps use the Publish button in the Save As dialog box, rather than the Save button, to illustrate the additional publishing capabilities of Excel.

Steps To Save an Excel Chart as a Dynamic Web Page

1 **Insert the Data Disk in drive A. Start Excel and then open the workbook, Awesome Intranets, on drive A. Click File on the menu bar and then point to Save as Web Page.**

The File menu displays (Figure 6).

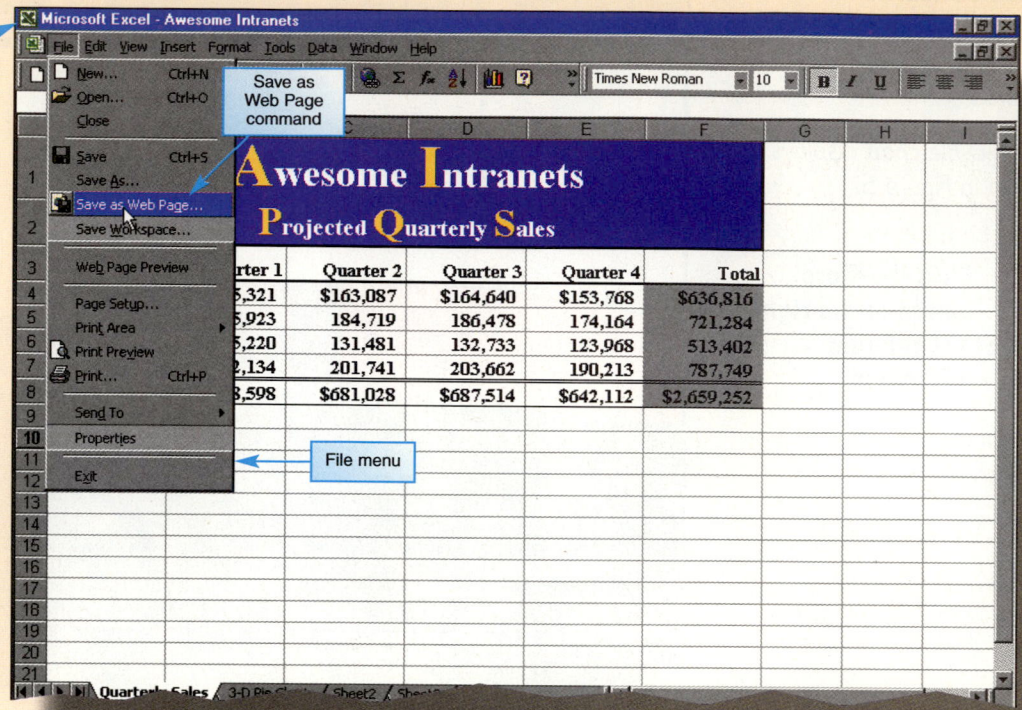

FIGURE 6

2 **Click Save as Web Page. When the Save As dialog box displays, type** Awesome Intranets Dynamic Web Page **in the File name text box and then, if necessary, click the Save in box arrow and select 3½ Floppy (A:). Point to the Publish button.**

The Save As dialog box displays (Figure 7). When you use the Publish button, you do not have to concern yourself with the option buttons and check box in the Save area.

FIGURE 7

3 Click the Publish button. When the Publish as Web Page dialog box displays, click the Choose box arrow and then click Items on 3-D Pie Chart. Click Add interactivity with in the Viewing options area. If necessary, select Chart functionality in the list box in the Viewing options area. Point to the Publish button.

The Publish as Web page dialog box displays (Figure 8). When you select Items on 3-D Pie Chart, Excel immediately displays the 3-D Pie Chart sheet in the Excel window.

FIGURE 8

4 Click the Publish button. Click the Close button on the right side of the Excel toolbar to close Excel.

Excel saves the dynamic Web page on the Data Disk in drive A using the file name, Awesome Intranets Dynamic Web Page.htm. Excel shuts down.

Excel allows you to save an entire workbook, a sheet in the workbook, or a range on a sheet as a Web page. In Figure 7, you have the option in the Save area to save the entire workbook or a sheet. These option buttons are used with the Save button. If you want to be more selective in what you save, then you can disregard the option buttons in the Save area in Figure 7 and click the Publish button as described in Step 3. The **Choose box** in the **Publish as Web Page dialog box** in Figure 8 allows you more options in what to include on the Web page. You also may save the Web page as a dynamic Web page (interactive) or a static Web page (noninteractive). The check box at the bottom of the dialog box gives you the opportunity to start your browser automatically and display the newly created Web page after you click the Publish button.

How Excel Saves Web Pages

A saved static (noninteractive) Web page includes an htm file and an additional folder to hold the graphics that display as part of the Web page. All the components of a dynamic (interactive) Web page are saved in a single HTML file.

Viewing and Manipulating the Dynamic Web Page Using Your Browser

With the dynamic Web page saved on drive A, the next step is to view it and manipulate it using your browser as shown in the following steps.

 Steps **To View and Manipulate the Static Web Page Using Your Browser**

1 **Click the Start button on the taskbar, point to Programs, and then click Internet Explorer.**

2 **When the Internet Explorer window displays, type** a:\awesome intranets dynamic web page.htm **in the Address bar and then press the ENTER key.**

The Web page, Awesome Intranets Dynamic Web Page.htm, displays as shown in Figure 9. This Web page contains the information from the Awesome Intranets workbook. The 3-D Pie chart displays as a 2-D Pie chart with the rows and columns of the worksheet that determine the Pie chart immediately below it.

FIGURE 9

3 **Click cell B4 and then enter 450000.**

The formulas in the work-sheet portion are recalculated and the size of the slices in the 2-D Pie chart change to agree with the new totals in column F (Figure 10).

4 **Click the Close button at the right side of the Internet Explorer title bar.**

The Internet Explorer window closes.

FIGURE 10

Figure 9 shows the result of saving the 3-D Pie chart as a dynamic Web page. Excel automatically changes the 3-D Pie chart to a 2-D Pie chart and adds the columns and rows from the worksheet below the chart. As shown in Figure 10, you can change the numbers in the worksheet that determine the size of the slices in the 2-D Pie chart and the Web page instantaneously recalculates all formulas and redraws the 2-D Pie chart. When cell B4 is changed from 192,134 to 450,000, the Web page recalculates the formulas in cells C4, D4, E4, and F4. The red slice in the 2-D Pie chart represents the value in cell F4. Thus, when the number in cell F4 changes from 787,749 to 1,845,000, the red slice in the 2-D Pie chart changes to a much larger slice of the pie. This interactivity and functionality allow you to share a workbook's formulas and charts with others who may not have access to Excel, but do have access to a browser.

More About Dynamic Web Pages

When you change a value in a dynamic Web page, it does not affect the saved workbook or the saved HTML file. If you save a modified Web page using the Save As command on the browser's File menu, it will save the original version and not the modified one you see on the screen.

Modifying the Worksheet on a Dynamic Web Page

Immediately above the rows and columns in the worksheet in Figure 10 is the **Spreadsheet toolbar**. The toolbar allows you to invoke the most commonly used worksheet commands. For example, you can select a cell immediately below a column of numbers and click the AutoSum button to sum the numbers in the column. Cut, copy, and paste capabilities also are available. The functions of the buttons on the Spreadsheet toolbar in Figure 10 are summarized in Table 1 on the next page.

Table 1	Spreadsheet Toolbar Buttons	
BUTTON	**NAME OF BUTTON**	**FUNCTION**
	Office Logo	Displays information about the Microsoft Office Web Component, including the version number you have installed
	Undo	Reverses the last command or actions, or deletes the last entry you typed
	Cut	Removes the selection and places it on the Clipboard
	Copy	Copies the selection to the Clipboard
	Paste	Inserts the contents of the Clipboard
	AutoSum	Adds a column or row of numbers automatically
	Sort Ascending	Sorts the selected items in ascending sequence
	Sort Descending	Sorts the selected items in descending sequence
	AutoFilter	Selects specific items you want to display in a list
	Export to Excel	Opens the Web page as a workbook in Excel
	Property Toolbox	Displays the Spreadsheet Property Toolbox so you can modify the worksheet
	Help	Displays Microsoft Spreadsheet Help

More *About* **2000**

Creating Links

You can add hyperlinks to an Excel workbook before you save it as a Web page. You can add hyperlinks that link to a Web page, a location in a Web page, or to an e-mail address that automatically starts the viewer's e-mail program.

In general, you can add formulas, format, sort, and export the Web page to Excel. Many additional Excel capabilities are available through the **Spreadsheet Property Toolbox** (Figure 11). You display the Spreadsheet Property Toolbox by clicking the Property Toolbox button on the Spreadsheet toolbar. When the Spreadsheet Property Toolbox displays, click the Format section bar. You can see in Figure 11, that many of the common formats, such as bold, italic, underline, font color, font style, and font size, are available through your browser for the purpose of formatting cells in the worksheet below the 2-D Pie chart on the Web page.

FIGURE 11

Modifying the dynamic Web page does not change the makeup of the original workbook or the Web page stored on disk, even if you use the Save As command on the browser's File menu. If you do use the Save As command in your browser, it will save the original htm file without any changes you made. You can, however, use the Export to Excel button on the toolbar to create a workbook that will include any changes you made in your browser. The Export to Excel button only saves the worksheet and not the 3-D Pie chart.

Quick Reference

For a table that lists how to complete the tasks covered in this book using the mouse, menu, shortcut menu, and keyboard, visit the Office 2000 Web page (www.scsite.com/office 2000/qr.htm), and then click Microsoft Excel 2000.

Microsoft Certification

The Microsoft Office User Specialist (MOUS) Certification program provides an opportunity for you to obtain a valuable industry credential - proof that you have the Excel 2000 skills required by employers. For more information, see Appendix D or visit the Shelly Cashman Series MOUS Web page at www.scsite.com/off2000/cert.htm.

CASE PERSPECTIVE SUMMARY

Ryan is pleased with the two Web pages you created. By publishing the static Web page on the company s intranet, he no longer has to mail printouts of the workbook to his distribution list. Furthermore, because he can make the worksheet and chart available as a dynamic Web page, members of his group no longer need to use his computer.

Web Feature Summary

This Web Feature introduced you to publishing two types of Web pages: static and dynamic. Whereas the static Web page is a snapshot of the workbook, a dynamic Web page adds functionality and interactivity to the Web page. Besides changing the data and generating new results with a dynamic Web page, you also can add formulas and change the formats in your browser to improve the appearance of the Web page.

What You Should Know

Having completed this project, you now should be able to perform the following tasks:

▶ Save an Excel Chart as a Dynamic Web Page *(EW 1.8)*
▶ Save an Excel Workbook as a Static Web Page *(EW 1.4)*
▶ View and Manipulate the Static Web Page Using Your Browser *(EW 1.10)*
▶ View the Static Web Page Using Your Browser *(EW 1.6)*

In the Lab

1 Shocking Sound International Web Page

Problem: You are employed as a spreadsheet analyst by Shocking Sound International. Your supervisor has asked you to create a static Web page and dynamic Web page from the company's annual sales workbook.

Instructions Part 1: Start Excel and open the Shocking Sound International workbook from the Data Disk. If you do not have a copy of the Data Disk, see the inside back cover of this book. Do the following:

1. Review the worksheet and chart so you have an idea of what the workbook contains.
2. Save the workbook as a Web page on drive A using the file name, Shocking Sound International Static Web Page. Make sure you select Entire Workbook in the Save area before you click the Save button. Close Excel.
3. Start your browser. Type `a:\shocking sound international static web page.htm` in the Address bar. When the Web page displays, click the tabs at the bottom of the window to view the sheets. As you view each sheet, print it in landscape orientation. Quit your browser.

Instructions Part 2: Start Excel and open the Shocking Sound International workbook from the Data Disk. Do the following:

1. Click File on the menu bar and then click Save as Web Page. Use the Publish button to save the workbook as a Web page on drive A using the file name, Shocking Sound International Dynamic Web Page. In the Publish as Web Page dialog box, select Items on Bar Chart in the Choose box, click the Add Interactivity with check box and add chart functionality. Click the Publish button. Close Excel.
2. Start your browser. Type `a:\shocking sound international dynamic web page.htm` in the Address bar. When the Web page displays, click cell B6 and then click the AutoSum button on the Spreadsheet toolbar twice. Cell B6 should equal $2,806,007. Print the Web page.
3. Enter the following gross sales: Asia = 235,000; Canada = 542,500; Europe = 300,500; Latin America = 200,000; and United States = 1,500,000. Cell B6 should equal $2,778,000. Print the Web page. Quit your browser.

2 Microprocessor Plus Web Page

Problem: You are a Web consultant for Microprocessor Plus. You have been asked to create a static Web page and dynamic Web page from the workbook that the company uses to project sales and payroll expenses.

Instructions Part 1: Start Excel and open the Microprocessor workbook from the Data Disk. If you do not have a copy of the Data Disk, see the inside back cover of this book. Do the following:

1. Display the 3-D Pie Chart sheet. Redisplay the Projected Budget sheet.
2. Save the workbook as a Web page on drive A using the file name, Microprocessor Plus Static Web Page. Make sure you select Entire Workbook in the Save area before you click the Save button. Close Excel.
3. Start your browser. Type `a:\microprocessor plus static web page.htm` in the Address bar. When the Web page displays, click the tabs at the bottom of the window to view the sheets. Print each sheet in landscape orientation. Quit your browser.

(continued)

In the Lab

Microprocessor Plus Web Page *(continued)*

Instructions Part 2: Start Excel and open the Microprocessor workbook from the Data Disk. Do the following:

1. Click File on the menu bar and then click Save as Web Page. Use the Publish button to save the workbook as a Web page on drive A using the file name, Microprocessor Plus Dynamic Web Page. In the Publish as Web Page dialog box, select Items on 3-D Pie Chart in the Choose box, click the Add Interactivity with check box with chart functionality. Click the Publish button. Close Excel.

2. Start your browser. Type `a:\microprocessor plus dynamic web page.htm` in the Address bar. When the Web page displays, print it in landscape.

3. Scroll down and change the values of the following cells: cell B15 = 15%; cell B16 = 5%; cell B17 = 25,000; cell B19 = 20.75%; and cell B20 = 6.75%. Cell H12 should equal $1,008,561.47. The 3-D Pie chart should change to display the new contributions to the projected payroll expenses. Print the Web page. Quit your browser.

Microsoft Excel 2000

Financial Functions, Data Tables, Amortization Schedules, and Hyperlinks

You will have mastered the material in this project when you can:

- Control the colors and thickness of outlines and borders
- Assign a name to a cell and refer to the cell in a formula by using the assigned name
- Determine the monthly payment of a loan using the financial function PMT
- Enter a series of percents using the fill handle
- Create a data table to analyze data in a worksheet
- Add a pointer to a data table using conditional formatting
- Determine a present value of a loan using the PV function
- Create an amortization schedule
- Analyze worksheet data by changing values
- Add a hyperlink to a workbook
- Protect and unprotect cells
- Analyze worksheet data by goal seeking

Making Your Home Where the Living is Best

Worksheets Help Buyers Attain the Goal

After college, many graduates begin their professions; a few travel or defer their careers for other interests, and some marry, buy homes, and start families. Owning a home is part of the American Dream, the ideal of a happy and successful life to which all may aspire. With the current trend continuing, however, in corporate downsizing, fluctuating interest rates, job insecurity, and wage freezes, this dream often remains to some just a desire that seems unattainable.

Creative lending institutions, however, work with customers' purse strings to explore various mortgage options. They often use worksheets such as the WeSavU National Bank Loan Analysis that you will create in this Excel project. The loan analysis in this project evaluates data by applying financial functions and an amortization schedule, and using an additional what-if tool, the data table, to guide consumers and help determine their ability to purchase a home. Another feature of Excel, allows you to add hyperlinks to a worksheet, making it possible to click a link in the worksheet to launch your Web browser application and display an associated Web page.

Citibank uses the Client Affordability and CitiShowcase worksheets, online loan forms and question and answer Web pages to help potential borrowers determine a maximum loan amount based on annual income, and establish down payments required to qualify for various mortgage options.

Home shoppers, particularly first-time buyers, often do not know whether they have a sufficient down payment and adequate income to purchase a home. Then they need to know maximum sales prices of homes they can afford. To provide this information, a Citibank loan officer retrieves the Client Affordability Analysis form on a notebook computer and interviews the clients. The officer asks the amount of annual income, monthly debt, and down payment and simultaneously inputs the figures in unprotected worksheet cells. Then the officer inputs current interest rates for particular loans, such as 8.75 percent on a 30-year fixed rate.

At this point, the worksheet program uses financial functions to determine the maximum loan amounts and monthly payments based on the clients' data.

If this client has an approximate sales price in mind, the worksheet will use this figure to determine if the property is affordable. For example, if the home is priced at $150,000, the worksheet computes that this price, coupled with other property expenses, amounts to 35.73 percent of the total gross income.

These figures then are examined using a data table that automates data analysis. Using the $150,000 home, the worksheet computes the annual income required to obtain 30-year fixed, 15-year fixed, and adjustable-rate mortgages with down payments of 25, 20, 10, and 5 percent. For example, the client needs an annual income of $40,365 and a 25 percent down payment of $37,500 to obtain a 30-year fixed mortgage with an interest rate of 8.75 percent and monthly payments of $1,111. Additional analysis indicates that the client needs to earn $57,525 with a 10-percent down payment of $15,000 to obtain a 15-year fixed mortgage at 8.25 percent with monthly payments of $1,583.

Citibank, like most lenders, uses these work-sheets as a starting point to help potential borrowers explore mortgage options. In an attempt to qualify the client for the mortgage, the loan officer considers compensating factors, such as a clean credit history, verifiable job offers, and length of time since graduation, particularly for first-time buyers. A strong financial picture can help make the dream attainable.

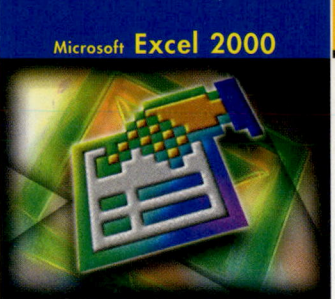

Microsoft Excel 2000

Financial Functions, Data Tables, Amortization Schedules, and Hyperlinks

P R O J E C T

4

CASE PERSPECTIVE

Leslie Alex recently was promoted to manager of financial services for WeSavU National Bank. His immediate challenge is to modernize the archaic procedures the board of directors believes are responsible for the recent slippage in personal loans. His first step is to computerize the procedures in the loan department. Leslie's intent is to have the loan officers generate the monthly payment, total interest, total cost, a table of varying interest rates, and an amortization schedule of a proposed loan when the customer comes in for an interview. The customer then can take home a printed copy of the information to review. He also wants the bank's Statement of Condition available via a hyperlink in case a customer questions the bank's worthiness.

Leslie recently took a one-day course on Microsoft Excel at the local community college. He learned that Excel has many financial functions, what-if tools, and Web capabilities. As Leslie's spreadsheet specialist, he has asked you to create a workbook that will generate the desired loan information, while ensuring that the loan officers will not render the worksheet useless by entering data into the wrong cells.

Introduction

Two of the more powerful aspects of Excel are its wide array of functions and its capability to organize answers to what-if questions. In earlier projects, you were introduced to several functions such as AVERAGE, MAX, SUM, IF, and MIN. In this project, you will learn about financial functions such as the PMT function that allows you to determine a monthly payment for a loan (upper-left side of Figure 4-1a). The upper-left side of Figure 4-1a is called the loan analysis section.

You also learned how to analyze data by using Excel's recalculation feature and goal seeking. This project revisits these two methods of analyzing data and describes an additional what-if tool called data tables. You use a data table to automate your data analyses and organize the answers returned by Excel. The data table section on the lower-left in Figure 4-1a answers 11 different what-if questions. The questions pertain to the effect the 11 different interest rates in column B have on the monthly payment, total interest, and total cost of a loan.

Another important loan analysis tool is the Amortization Schedule section (right side of Figure 4-1a). An amortization schedule shows the beginning and ending balances and the amount of payment that applies to the principal and interest over a period of time.

Another key feature of Excel is its capability to add hyperlinks to a worksheet. Hyperlinks are built-in links (file path names or URLs) to other Office documents or HTML files (Web pages). A hyperlink can be assigned to text in a cell or to an object, such as the stack of dollar bills graphic at the bottom of Figure 4-1a. When you click the stack of dollar bills graphic, Excel starts your browser and displays an HTML file (Figure 4-1b).

Finally, this project introduces you to cell protection. Cell protection ensures that users do not inadvertently change values that are critical to the worksheet.

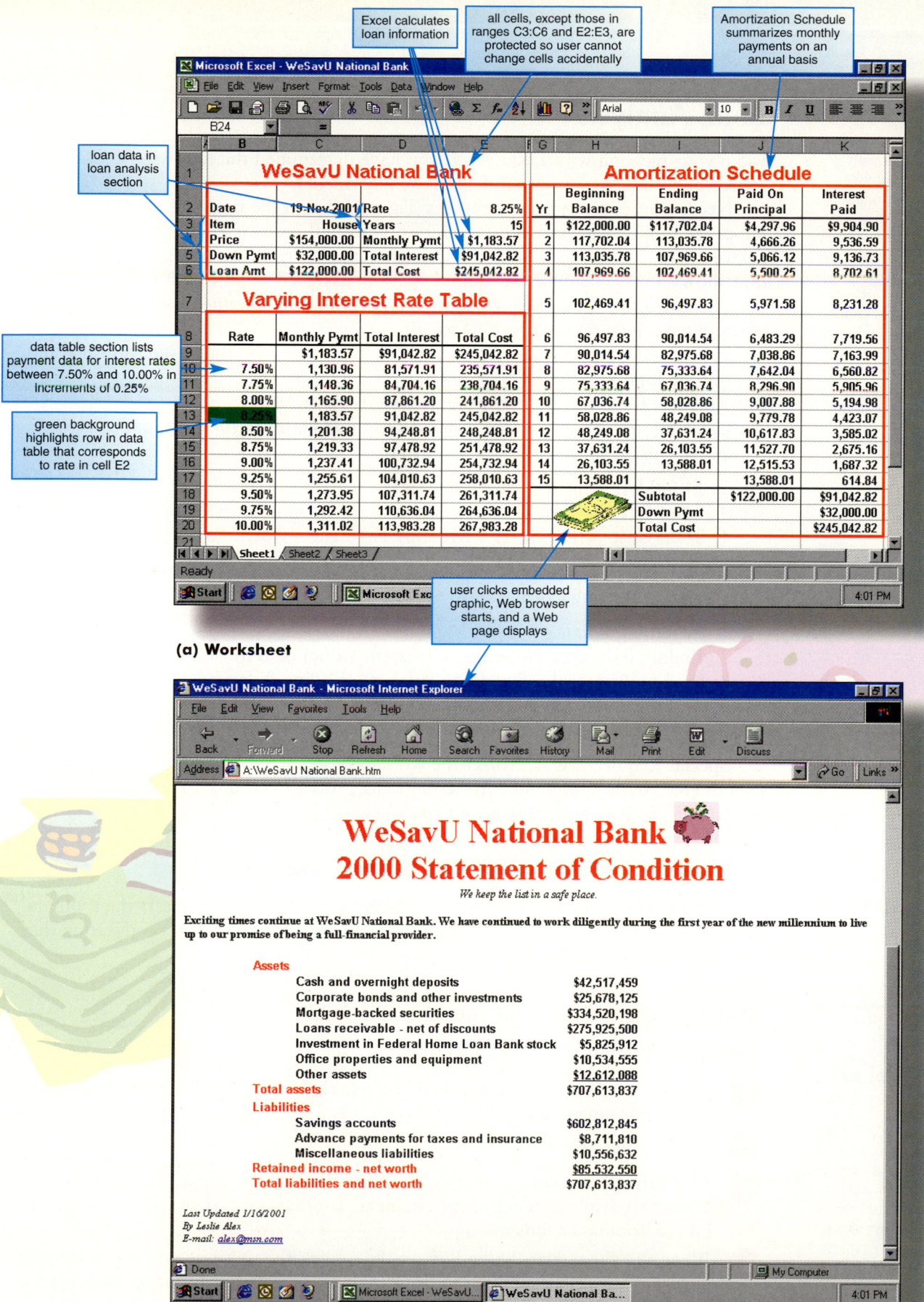

Excel calculates loan information

all cells, except those in ranges C3:C6 and E2:E3, are protected so user cannot change cells accidentally

Amortization Schedule summarizes monthly payments on an annual basis

loan data in loan analysis section

data table section lists payment data for interest rates between 7.50% and 10.00% in increments of 0.25%

green background highlights row in data table that corresponds to rate in cell E2

user clicks embedded graphic, Web browser starts, and a Web page displays

(a) Worksheet

(b) Web Page

FIGURE 4-1

E 4.5

Project Four — WeSavU National Bank Loan Analysis

From your meeting with Leslie Alex, you have determined the following needs, source of data, calculations, and special requirements.

Needs: An easy-to-read worksheet (Figure 4-1a on the previous page) that determines the monthly payment, total interest, and total cost for a loan; a data table that answers what-if questions based on changing interest rates; an amortization schedule that shows annual summaries; and a hyperlink assigned to an object so that when you click the object, the WeSavU National Bank's 2000 Statement of Condition displays (Figure 4-1b on the previous page) .

Source of Data: The data (item, price of item, down payment, interest rate, and term of the loan in years) is determined by the loan officer and customer when they initially meet for the loan.

Calculations: The following calculations must be made for each loan:

1. Loan Amount = Price – Down Payment
2. Monthly Payment = PMT function
3. Total Interest = 12 x Years x Monthly Payment – Loan Amount
4. Total Cost = 12 x Years x Monthly Payment + Down Payment

Use the Table command to create the data table. The Amortization Schedule involves the following calculations:

1. Beginning Balance = Loan Amount
2. Ending Balance = PV function (present value) or zero
3. Paid on Principal = Beginning Balance – Ending Balance
4. Interest Paid = 12 x Monthly Payment – Paid on Principal or zero
5. Column Totals = SUM function

Special Requirements: Protect the worksheet in such a way that the loan officers cannot enter data mistakenly into wrong cells. Add a hyperlink to an HTML file containing the bank's Statement of Condition.

Starting Excel and Resetting the Toolbars and Menus

Perform the following steps to start Excel. Steps 4 through 6 resets the toolbars and menus to their installation settings. For additional information on resetting the toolbars and menus, see Appendix B.

TO START EXCEL AND RESET THE TOOLBARS AND MENUS

1 Click the Start button on the taskbar.

2 Click New Office Document. If necessary, click the General tab in the New Office Document dialog box.

3 Double-click the Blank Workbook icon.

4 When the blank worksheet displays, click View on the menu bar, click the arrows to display the full menu, point to Toolbars, and then click Customize on the Toolbars submenu.

5 When the Customize dialog box displays, click the Options tab, make sure the top three check boxes have check marks, click the Reset my usage data button, and then click the Yes button.

6 Click the Toolbars tab. Click Standard, click the Reset button, and then click the OK button. Click Formatting, click the Reset button, and then click the OK button. Click the Close button.

The Standard and Formatting toolbars display as shown in Figure 4-1a on page E 4.5.

An alternative to Steps 1 through 3 is to click the Start button, point to Programs, and then click Microsoft Excel on the Programs submenu.

Changing the Font Style of the Entire Worksheet

The first step in this project is to change the font style of the entire worksheet to bold to ensure that the characters in the worksheet stand out.

TO CHANGE THE FONT STYLE OF THE ENTIRE WORKSHEET

1 Double-click the move handle on the Formatting toolbar (see Figure 4-2 on the next page).

2 Click the Select All button immediately above row heading 1 and to the left of column heading A.

3 Click the Bold button on the Formatting toolbar.

As you enter text and numbers onto the worksheet, they will display in bold.

Entering the Section Title, Row Titles, and System Date

The next step is to enter the loan analysis section title, row titles, and system date. To make the worksheet easier to read, the width of column A will be decreased to 0.5 points and used as a separator between the loan analysis section and the row headings on the left. Using a column as a separator between sections on a worksheet is a common technique used by spreadsheet specialists. The width of columns B through E will be increased so the intended values fit. The heights of rows 1 and 2, which contain the titles, will be increased so they stand out. The worksheet title also will be changed from 10-point to 16-point red font.

TO ENTER THE SECTION TITLE, ROW TITLES, AND SYSTEM DATE

1 Click cell B1. Type `WeSavU National Bank` as the section title and then press the ENTER key. Select the range B1:E1. Click the Merge and Center button on the Formatting toolbar.

2 With cell B1 active, click the Font Size box arrow on the Formatting toolbar and then click 16. Click the Font Color button on the Formatting toolbar to change the color of the font to red.

3 Drag through row headings 1 and 2 and then position the mouse pointer on the bottom boundary of row heading 2. Drag down until the ScreenTip, Height: 27.00 (36.00 pixels), displays.

4 Click cell B2, type `Date` and then press the ENTER key.

5 Click cell C2. Type `=now()` and then press the ENTER key.

Global Formatting

To assign formats to all the cells in all the worksheets in a workbook, click the Select All button, then right-click a tab and click Select All Sheets on the shortcut menu. Next, assign the formats. To deselect the sheets, hold down the SHIFT key and then click the Sheet1 tab. You also can select a cell or a range of cells and then select all sheets to assign formats to a cell or a range of cells on all the sheets in a workbook.

Unmerging

The Merge and Center button merges the selected cells and centers the text located in the leftmost cell. To unmerge a cell, you can click the Undo button on the Standard toolbar if the action still is available in the Undo list. If the action is not available in the Undo list, then right-click the merged cell, click Format Cells on the shortcut menu, click the Alignment tab, click the Merge cells check box, click the Horizontal arrow, click General in the list, and click the OK button.

6 Right-click cell C2 and then click Format Cells on the shortcut menu. When the Format Cells dialog box displays, click the Number tab, click Date in the Category list, scroll down in the Type list and click 14-Mar-1998. Click the OK button.

7 Enter the following row titles:

CELL	ENTRY	CELL	ENTRY	CELL	ENTRY
B3	Item	B6	Loan Amt	D4	Monthly Pymt
B4	Price	D2	Rate	D5	Total Interest
B5	Down Pymt	D3	Years	D6	Total Cost

Point with Care

Excel requires that you point to the object (cell, range, or toolbar) on the screen when you right-click to display the corresponding shortcut menu. For example, if you select the range A1:D5, and right-click cell F10, then the shortcut menu pertains to cell F10, and not the selected range A1:D5.

8 Position the mouse pointer on the right boundary of column heading A and then drag to the left until the ScreenTip, Width: .50 (6 pixels) displays.

9 Position the mouse pointer on the right boundary of column heading B and then drag to the right until the ScreenTip, Width: 10.14 (76 pixels) displays.

10 Click the column C heading to select it and then drag through column headings D through E. Position the mouse pointer on the right boundary of column heading C and then drag until the ScreenTip, Width: 12.29 (91 pixels), displays.

11 Click cell C2 to deselect the columns. Click the Save button on the Standard toolbar. Save the workbook on drive A using the file name WeSavU National Bank.

The loan analysis section title, row titles, and system date display as shown in Figure 4-2.

FIGURE 4-2

Left-Handed Mouse Users

Are you a lefty? You can change the functions of the left and right mouse buttons. Double-click the My Computer icon on the desktop, double-click the Control Panel icon, double-click the Mouse icon in Control Panel, depending on your Mouse software, click the Basics tab or Buttons tab, click the appropriate option button, and then click the OK button.

Outlining and Adding Borders

In previous projects, you were introduced to outlining using the Borders button on the Formatting toolbar. To control the color and thickness of the outline and borders, use the Border tab in the Format Cells dialog box. The following steps add an outline to the loan analysis section. To further subdivide the row titles and numbers, light borders also are added within the outline as shown in Figure 4-1a on page E 4.5.

Steps To Add an Outline and Borders to the Loan Analysis Section

1 Select the range B2:E6. Right-click the selected range and then point to Format Cells on the shortcut menu (Figure 4-3).

FIGURE 4-3

2 Click Format Cells. When the Format Cells dialog box displays, click the Border tab. Click the Color box arrow. Click the color red (column 1, row 3) on the palette. Click the heavy border in the Style box (column 2, row 6). Click the Outline button in the Presets area.

Excel previews the outline in the Border area (Figure 4-4).

FIGURE 4-4

3 Click the Color box arrow. Click Automatic (row 1) on the palette. Click the light border in the Style box (column 1, row 7). Click the vertical line button in the Border area.

Excel previews the vertical border in the Border area (Figure 4-5).

FIGURE 4-5

4 Click the OK button. Select cell B8 to deselect the range B2:E6.

Excel adds a red outline with vertical borders to the right side of each column in the range B2:E6 (Figure 4-6).

FIGURE 4-6

As shown in Figure 4-5, you can add a variety of outlines and borders with color to a cell or range of cells to improve its appearance. It is important that you select border characteristics in the order specified in the steps; that is, (1) choose the color; (2) choose the border line style; and (3) choose the border type. If you attempt to do these steps in any other order, you will not end up with the desired borders.

Formatting Cells Before Entering Values

While usually you format cells after you enter the values, Excel also allows you to format cells before you enter the values. The following steps assign the Currency style format with a floating dollar sign to the ranges C4:C6 and E4:E6 before the values are entered.

TO FORMAT CELLS BEFORE ENTERING VALUES

1 Select the range C4:C6. While holding down the CTRL key, select the nonadjacent range E4:E6. Right-click one of the selected ranges.

2 Click Format Cells on the shortcut menu. When the Format Cells dialog box displays, click the Number tab.

3 Click Currency in the Category list box and then click the fourth format, ($1,234.10), in the Negative numbers list box.

4 Click the OK button.

The ranges C4:C6 and E4:E6 are assigned the Currency style format with a floating dollar sign.

As you enter numbers into these cells, the numbers will display using the Currency style format. You also could have selected the range B4:E6 rather than the nonadjacent ranges and assigned the Currency style format to this range, which includes text. The Currency style format has no impact on text.

Entering the Loan Data

As shown in Figure 4-1a on page E 4.5, five items make up the loan data in the worksheet: the item to be purchased, the price of the item, the down payment, the interest rate, and the number of years until the loan is paid back (also called the term of the loan). These items are entered into cells C3 through C5 and cells E2 and E3. The following steps describe how to enter the following loan data: Item - House; Price - $154,000.00; Down Payment - $32,000.00; Interest Rate - 8.25%; and Years - 15.

TO ENTER THE LOAN DATA

1 Click cell C3. Enter House as the item. With cell C3 still active, click the Align Right button on the Formatting toolbar. Click cell C4 and enter 154000 for the price of the house. Click cell C5 and enter 32000 for the down payment.

2 Click cell E2. Enter 8.25% for the interest rate. Click cell E3 and enter 15 for the number of years.

The loan data displays in the worksheet as shown in Figure 4-7.

When to Format

Excel lets you format (1) empty cells before you enter data; (2) when you enter data (through the use of format symbols); (3) incrementally after entering sections of data; and, (4) after you enter all the data. Spreadsheet specialists usually format a worksheet in increments as they build the worksheet, but occasions do exist when it makes sense to format before you enter any data.

Percents

When entering a percent value, remember to append the percent sign (%) or Excel will use a number 100 times greater than the number you thought you entered. An alternative to using the percent sign is to enter the number with the decimal point moved two places to the left.

FIGURE 4-7

The values in cells C4 and C5 display using the Currency style with two decimal places, because this format was assigned to the cells prior to entering the values. Excel also automatically formats the interest rate to the Percent style with two decimal places, because the percent sign (%) was appended to 8.25 when it was entered into cell E2.

Calculating the four remaining entries in the loan analysis section of the worksheet - loan amount (cell C6), monthly payment (cell E4), total interest (cell E5), and total cost (cell E6) - require that you enter formulas that reference cells C4, C5, C6, E2, and E3. The formulas will be entered referencing names assigned to cells, such as Price, rather than cell references, such as C4, because names are easier to remember than cell references.

More About 2000

Names

Are you tired of writing formulas that make no sense when you read them because of cell references? Then the Name command is for you. This command allows you to assign names to cells. You then can use the names, such as Price, rather than the cell reference, such as B4, in the formulas you create.

Creating Cell Names Based on Row Titles

Worksheets often have column titles at the top of each column and row titles to the left of each row that describe the data within the worksheet. You can use these titles within formulas when you want to refer to the related data by **name**. Names are created through the use of the **Name command** on the Insert menu. You also can use the same command to define descriptive names that are not column titles or row titles to represent cells, ranges of cells, formulas, or constants.

Naming a cell that you plan to reference in a formula helps make the formula easier to read and remember. For example, the loan amount in cell C6 is equal to the price in cell C4 less the down payment in cell C5. Therefore, according to what you learned in the earlier projects, you can write the loan amount formula in cell C6 as =C4 – C5. By assigning the corresponding row titles in column B as the names of cells C4 and C5, however, you can write the loan amount formula as =Price – Down_Pymt, which is clearer and easier to understand than =C4 – C5.

To name cells, you select the range that encompasses the row titles that include the names and the cells to be named (range B4:C6) and then use the Name command on the Insert menu. This project does not use the names Date and Item to reference cells C2 and C3.

The following steps assign each row title in cells B4 through B6 to their adjacent cell in column C and also assigns each row title in cells D2 through D6 to their adjacent cell in column E.

To Create Names Based on Row Titles

1 **Select the range B4:C6. Click Insert on the menu bar. Point to Name and then point to Create on the Name submenu.**

Excel highlights the range B4:C6. The Insert menu and Name submenu display (Figure 4-8).

FIGURE 4-8

2 Click Create. When the Create Names dialog box displays, point to the OK button.

The Create Names dialog box displays (Figure 4-9). The Left column check box is selected automatically in the Create names in area because the direction of the cells containing text selected in Step 1 is downward.

3 Click the OK button. Select the range D2:E6. Click Insert on the menu bar, point to Name, and then click Create on the Name submenu. Click the OK button in the Create Names dialog box. Click cell B8 to deselect the range D2:E6

FIGURE 4-9

You now can use the names in the range B4:B6 and D2:D6 in formulas to reference the adjacent cells on the left. Excel is not case-sensitive with respect to names of cells. Hence, you can enter the names of cells in formulas in uppercase or lowercase. Some names, such as Down Pymt in cell B5, include a space because they are made up of two or more words. To use a name in a formula that is made up of two or more words, you replace any space with the **underscore character** (_). For example, Down Pymt is written as down_pymt when you want to reference the adjacent cell C5.

Consider these additional points regarding the assignment of names to cells:
1. A name can be a minimum of one character to a maximum of 255 characters.
2. If you want to assign a name that is not a text item in an adjacent cell, use the **Define command** on the Name submenu (Figure 4-8) or select the cell or range and type the name in the Name box in the formula bar.
3. Names are absolute cell references. This is important to remember if you plan to use the Copy command with formulas that contain names, rather than cell references.
4. The names display in alphabetical order in the Name box when you click the Name box arrow (Figure 4-10 on the next page).
5. Names are **global** to the workbook. That is, a name assigned on one worksheet in a workbook can be used on other sheets in the same workbook to reference the associated cell or range of cells.

Other Ways

1. Select range, press CTRL+SHIFT+F3
2. Select each cell individually, type name in Name box
3. On Insert menu point to Names, click Define, enter name

More About 2000

Names

You can create row and column names at the same time if you have a worksheet with column titles and row titles. Simply select the column titles and row titles along with the cells to name, and then on the Insert menu, click Name and on the Name submenu, click Create. In the Create Name dialog box, click both Top row and Left column, and then click the OK button. As a result, you can use the column title and row title separated by a space to refer to the intersecting cell.

FIGURE 4-10

Functions

Functions operate on data, called arguments, which are inserted between parentheses. Functions return to a cell a value, similarly to the way a formula returns a value.

Spreadsheet specialists often assign names to a cell or range of cells so they can select them quickly. If you want to select a cell that has been assigned a name, you can click the Name box arrow (Figure 4-10) and then click the name of the cell you want to select. This method is similar to using the Go To command on the Edit menu or the F5 key to select a cell, but it is much quicker.

Determining the Loan Amount

To determine the loan amount in cell C6, subtract the down payment in cell C5 from the price in cell C4. As indicated earlier, you could do this by entering the formula =C4 – C5 or you can enter the formula = price – down_pymt as shown in the following steps.

 To Enter the Loan Amount Formula Using Names

1   **Click cell C6. Type**
`=price – down_pymt.`

The formula displays in cell C6 and in the formula bar (Figure 4-11).

FIGURE 4-11

2 **Press the ENTER key.**

Excel assigns the formula =price – down_pymt to cell C6. The result of the formula ($122,000.00) displays in cell C6 using the Currency style format assigned earlier (Figure 4-12).

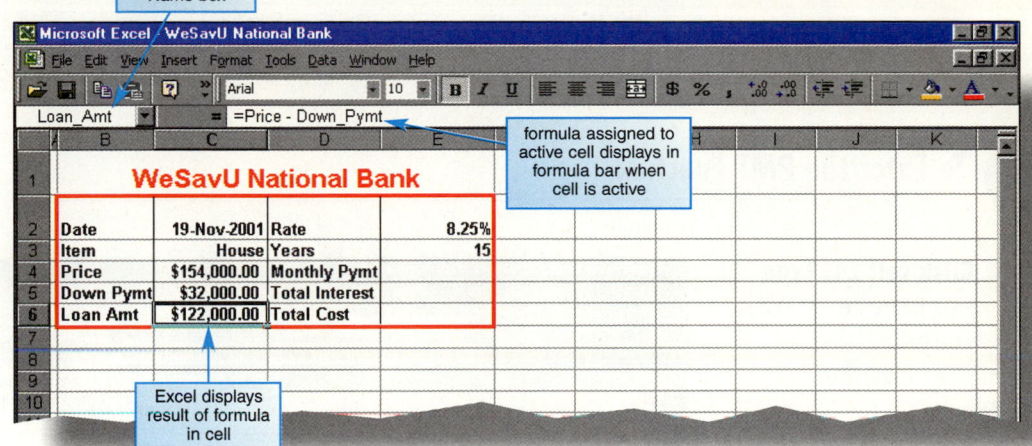

FIGURE 4-12

An alternative to creating names is to use labels. A **label** is a row title or column title, similar to the adjacent names created earlier. Any row title or column title can be used in formulas to reference corresponding cells. It is not necessary to enter commands to assign label names.

The major drawback to using labels in some applications is that they are **relative**, which means the label may very well reference a cell that is nonadjacent to the label. It also is important to note that Excel does not recognize labels in formulas unless you activate label usage. To activate **label usage**, click Tools on the menu bar, click Options, click the Calculation tab, and select Accept labels in formulas. Any row title or column title then can be used in formulas to reference corresponding cells.

Labels are different from names in the following ways: (1) labels are not absolute; (2) they cannot be used on other worksheets in the workbook; (3) they do not show up in the Names box (see Figure 4-10); and (4) you can use them without entering underscores in place of spaces.

Determining the Monthly Payment

The next step is to determine the monthly payment for the loan. You can use Excel's **PMT function** to determine the monthly payment in cell E4. The PMT function has three arguments – rate, payment, and loan amount. Its general form is

=PMT(rate, payment, loan amount)

where rate is the interest rate per payment period, payment is the number of payments, and loan amount is the amount of the loan.

In the worksheet shown in Figure 4-12, cell E2 displays the annual interest rate. Loan institutions, however, calculate interest on a monthly basis. The rate value in the PMT function, thus, is rate / 12 (cell E2 divided by 12), rather than just rate (cell E2). The number of payments (or periods) in the PMT function is 12 * years (12 times cell E3) because there are 12 months, or 12 payments, per year.

Excel considers the value returned by the PMT function to be a debit, and therefore, returns a negative number as the monthly payment. To display the monthly payment as a positive number, you can enter a negative sign before the loan amount. Thus, the loan amount is equal to –loan_amt. The PMT function for cell E4 is

=PMT(rate / 12, 12 * years, – loan_amt)

monthly interest rate   number of payments   loan amount

More About

The PMT Function

An alternative to requiring the user to enter an interest rate in percent form, such as 7.75%, is to allow the user to enter the interest rate as a number without an appended percent sign (7.75) and then divide the interest rate by 1200, rather than 12.

The following steps use the PMT function to determine the monthly payment in cell E4.

To Enter the PMT Function

 1 **Click cell E4. Type** `=pmt(rate / 12, 12 * years, -loan_amt)` **as the function.**

The PMT function displays in cell E4 and in the formula bar (Figure 4-13).

FIGURE 4-13

 2 **Press the ENTER key.**

Excel displays the monthly payment $1,183.57 in cell E4, based on a loan amount of $122,000.00 (cell C6) with an annual interest rate of 8.25% (cell E2) for a term of 15 years (cell E3).

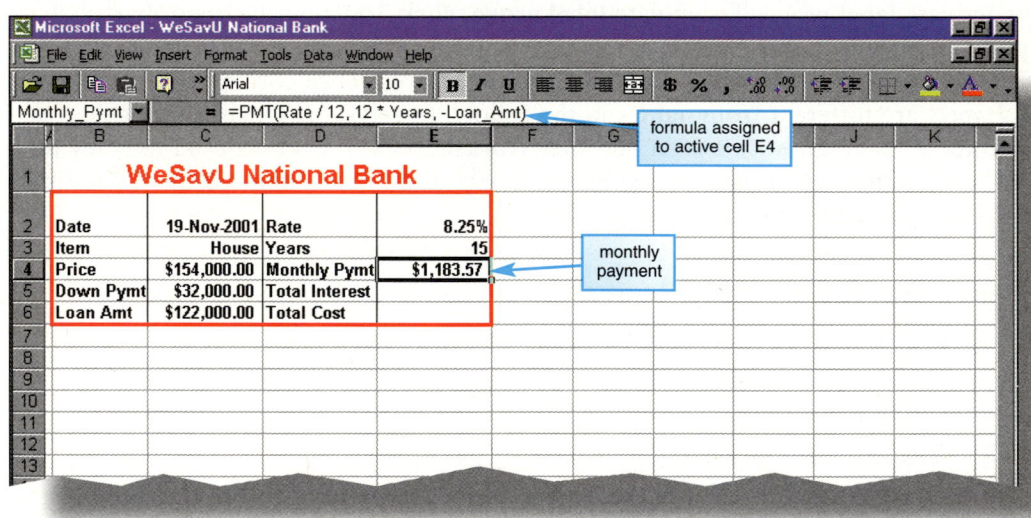

FIGURE 4-14

Other Ways

1. Click Paste Function button on Standard toolbar, click Financial in Function category box, click PMT in Function box
2. Click Edit Formula button in formula bar, click Function box arrow in formula bar, click PMT function

You could have entered the PMT function by clicking the Paste Function button on the Standard toolbar. When the Paste Function dialog box displays, click Financial in the Function category list box and then click PMT in the Function name list box. In addition to the PMT function, Excel provides more than 50 additional financial functions to help you solve the most complex finance problems. These functions save you from entering long, complicated formulas to obtain needed results. Table 4-1 summarizes three of the more often used financial functions.

Table 4-1 Financial Functions

FUNCTION	DESCRIPTION
FV(rate, periods, payment)	Returns the future value of an investment based on periodic, constant payments and a constant interest rate.
PMT(rate, periods, loan amount)	Returns the payments for a loan based on periodic, constant payments and a constant interest rate.
PV(rate, periods, payment)	Returns the present value of an investment; that is, the total amount that a series of payments is worth now.

Determining the Total Interest and Total Cost

The next step is to determine the total interest (WeSavU National Bank's gross profit for the loan) and the borrower's total cost of the item being purchased. The total interest (cell E5) is equal to the number of payments times the monthly payment, less the loan amount:

=12 * years * monthly_pymt – loan_amt

The total cost of the item to be purchased (cell E6) is equal to the number of payments times the monthly payment plus the down payment:

=12 * years * monthly_pymt + down_pymt

To enter the total interest and total cost formulas, perform the following steps.

TO DETERMINE THE TOTAL INTEREST AND TOTAL COST

1. Click cell E5. Enter the formula =12 * years * monthly_pymt – loan_amt to determine the total interest.

2. Click cell E6. Enter the formula =12 * years * monthly_pymt + down_pymt to determine the total cost.

3. Click cell B8 to deselect cell E6. Click the Save button on the Standard toolbar to save the workbook using the file name WeSavU National Bank.

Excel displays a total interest (bank's gross profit) of $91,042.82 in cell E5 and a total cost to the borrower of $245,042.82 in cell E6 for the house (Figure 4-15).

More About

Range Finder

Do not forget to check all formulas carefully. You can double-click a cell with a formula and Excel will highlight the cells that provide data to the formula.

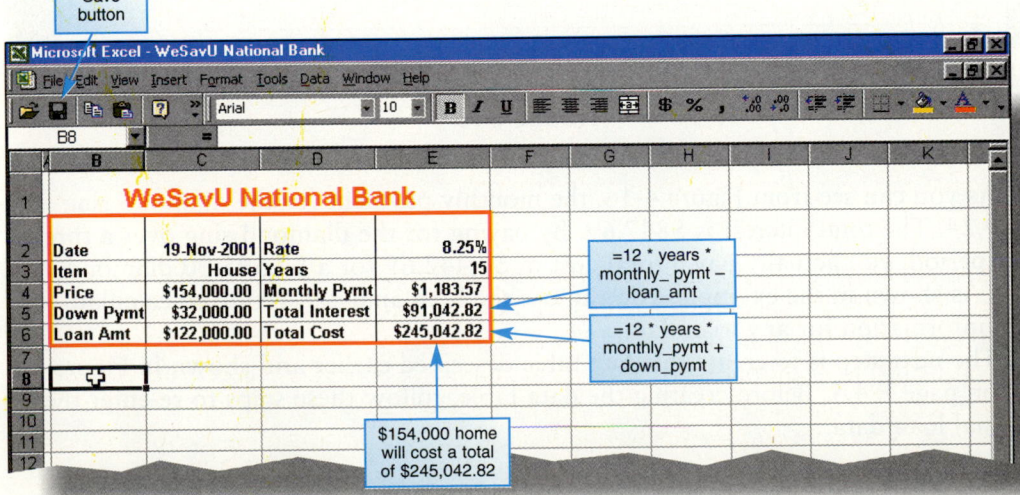

FIGURE 4-15

With the loan analysis section of the worksheet complete, you can use it to determine the monthly payment, total interest, and total cost for any loan data.

Entering New Loan Data

Assume you want to purchase a diamond ring for $7,595.00. You have $2,350.00 for a down payment and you want the loan for a term of 3 years. WeSavU National Bank currently is charging 10% interest for a three-year loan. The following steps show how to enter the new loan data.

TO ENTER NEW LOAN DATA

1 Click cell C3. Type Diamond Ring and then press the DOWN ARROW key.

2 In cell C4, type 7595 and then press the DOWN ARROW key.

3 In cell C5, type 2350 and then click cell E2.

4 In cell E2, type 10 and then press the DOWN ARROW key.

5 In cell E3, type 3 and then click cell B8.

Excel instantaneously recalculates the loan information in cells C6, E4, E5, and E6 (Figure 4-16).

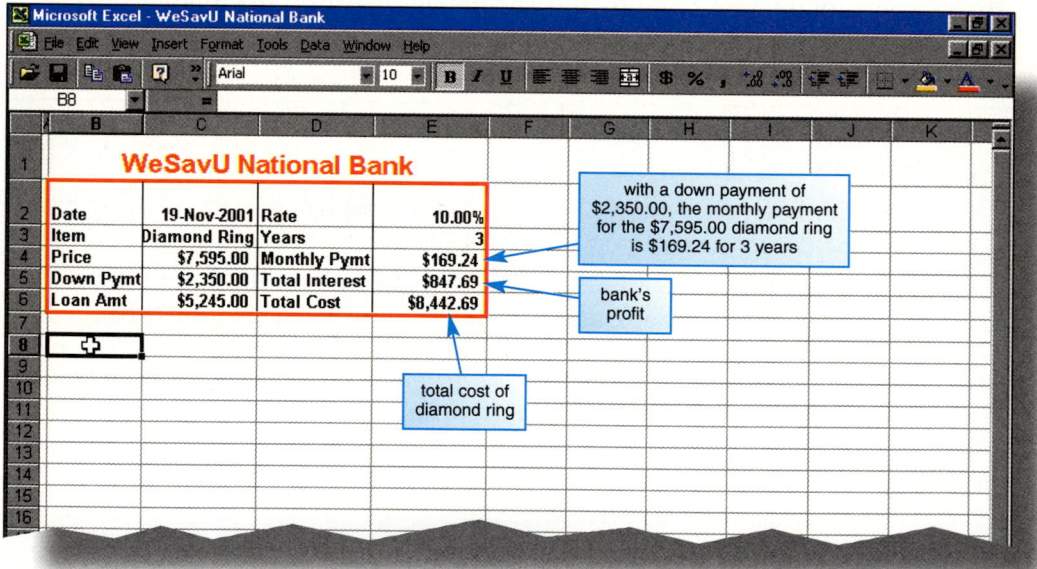

FIGURE 4-16

As you can see from Figure 4-16, the monthly payment for the diamond ring is $169.24. The total interest is $847.69. By paying for the diamond ring over a three-year period, you actually pay a total cost of $8,442.69 for a $7,595.00 diamond ring. As shown in the example, you can use the loan analysis section to calculate the loan information for any loan data.

The next step is to create the data table described earlier and shown in Figure 4-1 on page E 4.5. Before creating the data table, follow these steps to re-enter the original loan data.

TO ENTER THE ORIGINAL LOAN DATA

1 Click cell C3. Type House and then press the DOWN ARROW key.

2 In cell C4, type 154000 and then press the DOWN ARROW key.

3 In cell C5, type 32000 and then click cell E2.

4 In cell E2, type 8.25 and then press the DOWN ARROW key.

5 In cell E3, type 15 and then click cell B8.

Excel instantaneously recalculates all formulas in the worksheet each time you enter a value. The original loan information displays as shown earlier in Figure 4-15 on page E 4.17.

Using a Data Table to Analyze Worksheet Data

You already have seen that if you change a value in a cell, Excel immediately recalculates and displays the new results of any formulas that reference the cell directly or indirectly. But what if you want to compare the results of the formula for several different values? Writing down or trying to remember all the answers to the what-if questions would be unwieldy. If you use a data table, however, Excel will organize the answers in the worksheet for you automatically.

A **data table** is a range of cells that shows the answers generated by formulas in which different values have been substituted. The data table shown below the loan analysis section in Figure 4-17, for example, will display the resulting monthly payment, total interest, and total cost values based on different interest rates in column **B**.

More About

The Purpose of Data Tables

Data tables have one purpose, and that is to organize the answers to what-if questions. You can create two kinds of data tables. The first type involves changing one input value to see the resulting effect on one or more formulas. The second type involves changing two input values to see the resulting effect on one formula.

FIGURE 4-17

Data tables are built in an unused area of the worksheet (in this case, the range B7:E20). Within the table, you can vary one or two values and Excel will display the results of the specified formulas in table form. Figure 4-17 on the previous page illustrates the makeup of a one-input data table. With a **one-input data table**, you vary the value in one cell (in this worksheet, cell E2, the interest rate). Excel then calculates the results of one or more formulas and fills the table with the results. A **two-input data table** allows you to vary the values in two cells, but you can apply it to only one formula.

The interest rates that will be used to analyze the loan formulas in this project range from 7.50% to 10.00%, increasing in increments of 0.25%. The one-input data table shown in Figure 4-18 illustrates the impact of varying the interest rate on three formulas: the monthly payment (cell E4), total interest paid (cell E5), and the total cost of the item to be purchased (cell E6). The series of interest rates in column B are called **input values**.

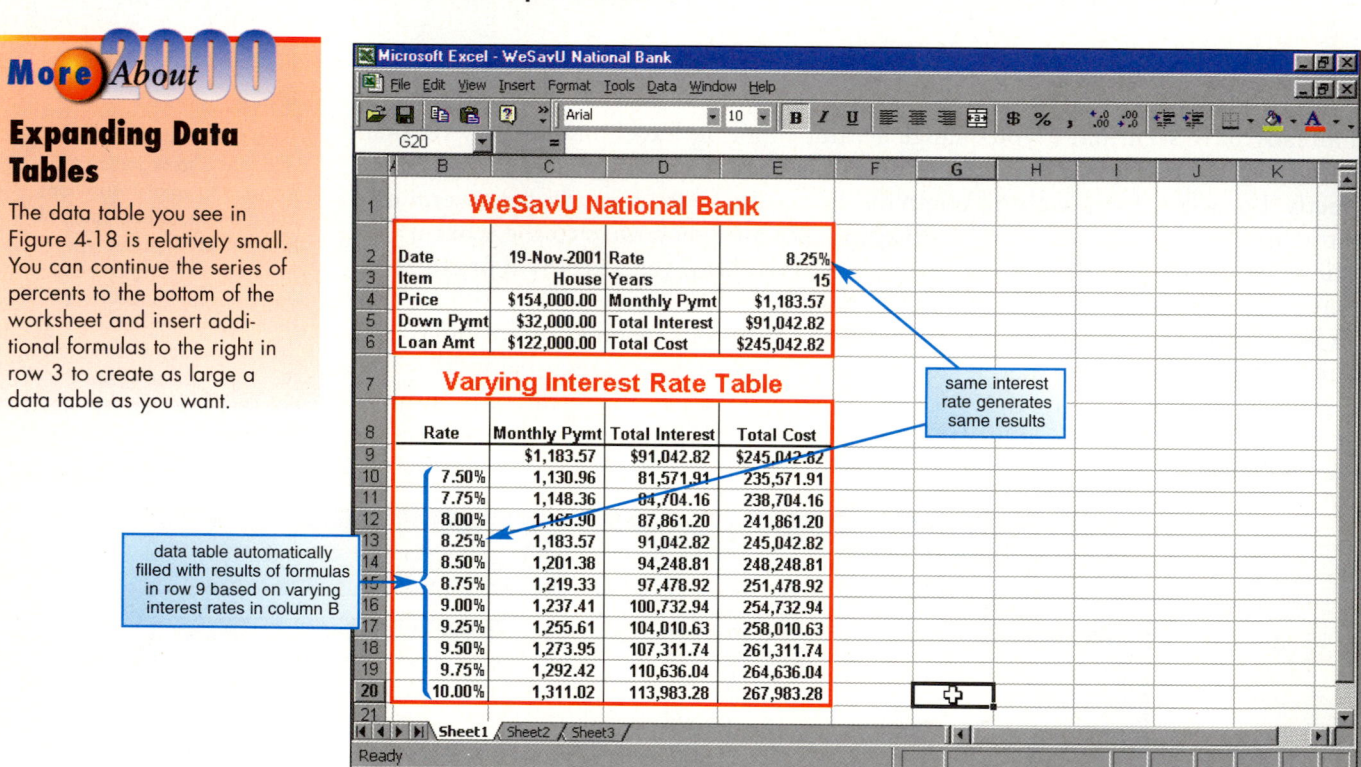

More About

Expanding Data Tables

The data table you see in Figure 4-18 is relatively small. You can continue the series of percents to the bottom of the worksheet and insert additional formulas to the right in row 3 to create as large a data table as you want.

FIGURE 4-18

To construct the data table shown in Figure 4-18, complete the following steps: (1) enter the data table section title and column titles in the range B7:E8; (2) adjust the heights of rows 7 and 8; (3) use the fill handle to enter the series of varying interest rates in column B; (4) enter the formulas in the range C9:E9 for which you want the data table to determine answers; (5) use the **Table command** on the **Data menu** to define the range B9:E20 as a data table and then identify the interest rate in cell B7 as the **input cell**, the one you want to vary; and (6) outline the data table so it has a professional appearance.

TO ENTER THE DATA TABLE TITLE AND COLUMN TITLES

1 Click cell B7. Type `Varying Interest Rate Table` as the data table section title. Press the ENTER key.

2 Click the Font Size box arrow on the Formatting toolbar and then click 16. Click the Font Color button on the Formatting toolbar to change the font color to red. Select the range B7:E7 and click the Merge and Center button on the Formatting toolbar.

3 Enter the column titles from the table on the right in the range B8:E8 as shown in Figure 4-19.

4 Select the range B8:E8 and then click the Center button on the Formatting toolbar to center the column titles.

5 Drag through row headings 7 and 8 and position the mouse pointer on the bottom boundary of row heading 8. Drag down until the ScreenTip, Height: 27.00 (36.00 pixels), displays. Click cell B10 to deselect rows 7 and 8.

CELL	ENTRY
B8	Rate
C8	Monthly Pymt
D8	Total Interest
E8	Total Cost

The data table title and column headings display as shown in Figure 4-19.

FIGURE 4-19

Data Table Errors

The most common error made by beginning Excel users when creating a one-input data table is to start the input values in the upper-left cell in the data table (see Figure 4-17 on page E 4.19).

Creating a Percent Series Using the Fill Handle

The next step is to create the percent series in column B using the fill handle. These percents will serve as the input data for the data table.

To Create a Percent Series Using the Fill Handle

1 Click cell B10 and enter 7.50% as the first number in the series. Select cell B11 and enter 7.75% as the second number in the series.

Excel shades the border of the copy and paste area (Figure 4-20). The ScreenTip, 10.00%, displays below the fill handle indicating the last value in the series. This value will display in cell B20.

2 Select the range B10:B11 and then point to the fill handle. Drag the fill handle through cell B20 and hold.

FIGURE 4-20

3 Release the mouse button. Click cell C9 to deselect the range B10:B20.

Excel generates the series of numbers from 7.50% to 10.00% in the range B10:B20 (Figure 4-21). The series increases in increments of 0.25%.

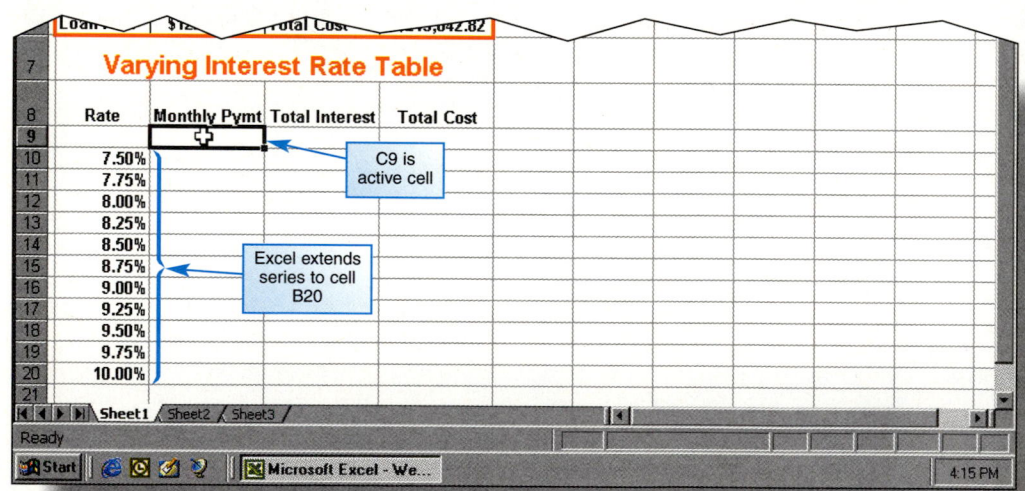

FIGURE 4-21

Excel will use the percents in column B to calculate the formulas to be evaluated and entered at the top of the data table in row 3. This series begins in cell B10, not cell B9, because the cell immediately to the left of the formulas in a one-input data table cannot include an input value.

Entering the Formulas in the Data Table

The next step in creating the data table is to enter the three formulas in cells C9, D9, and E9. The three formulas are the same as the monthly payment formula in cell E4, the total interest formula in cell E5, and the total cost formula in cell E6. The number of formulas you place at the top of a one-input data table depends on the application. Some one-input data tables will have only one formula, while others might have several. In this case, three formulas are affected when the interest rate changes.

Excel provides four ways to enter these formulas in the data table: (1) retype the formulas in cells C9, D9, and E9; (2) copy cells E4, E5, and E6 to cells C9, D9, and E9, respectively; (3) enter the formulas =monthly_pymt in cell C9, =total_interest in cell D9, and =total_cost in cell E9; or (4) enter the formulas =e4 in cell C9, =e5 in cell D9, and =e6 in cell E9.

The best alternative is the fourth one. That is, use the cell references preceded by an equal sign to define the formulas in the data table. This is the best method because: (1) it is easier to enter the cell references; and (2) if you change any of the formulas in the range E4:E6, the formulas at the top of the data table are updated automatically. Using the names of the cells in formulas is nearly as good an alternative. The reason why cell references are preferred over cell names is because if you use cell references, Excel assigns the format of the cell reference (Currency style format) to the cell. If you use cell names, Excel will not assign the format to the cell.

TO ENTER THE FORMULAS IN THE DATA TABLE

1 With cell C9 active, type =e4 and then press the RIGHT ARROW key.

2 Type =e5 in cell D9 and then press the RIGHT ARROW key.

3 Type =e6 in cell E9 and then click the Enter box or press the ENTER key.

The results of the formulas display in the range C9:E9 (Figure 4-22). Excel automatically assigns the Currency style format to cells C9 through E9 based on the formats assigned to cells E4 through E6.

FIGURE 4-22

It is important to understand that the entries in the top row of the data table (row 9) refer to the formulas that the loan department wants to evaluate using the series of percents in column B.

Defining the Data Table

After creating the percent interest rates series in column B and entering the formulas in row 9, the next step is to define the range B9:E20 as a data table.

Steps To Define a Range as a Data Table

1 **Select the range B9:E20. Click Data on the menu bar and then point to Table.**

The Data menu displays (Figure 4-23). The range to be defined as the data table begins with the formulas in row 9. The section title and column headings in the range B7:E8 are not part of the data table, even though they identify the data table and columns in the table.

FIGURE 4-23

Step 2

Click Table. When the Table dialog box displays, click the Column input cell text box. Click cell E2 in the loan analysis section as the input cell and then point to the OK button.

A marquee surrounds the selected cell E2, indicating it will be the input cell in which values from column B in the data table are substituted in the formula. $E$2 displays in the Column input cell text box in the Table dialog box (Figure 4-24).

FIGURE 4-24

Step 3

Click the OK button.

Excel calculates the results of the three formulas in row 9 for each interest rate in column B and immediately fills columns C, D, and E of the data table (Figure 4-25). The resulting values for each interest rate are displayed in the corresponding rows.

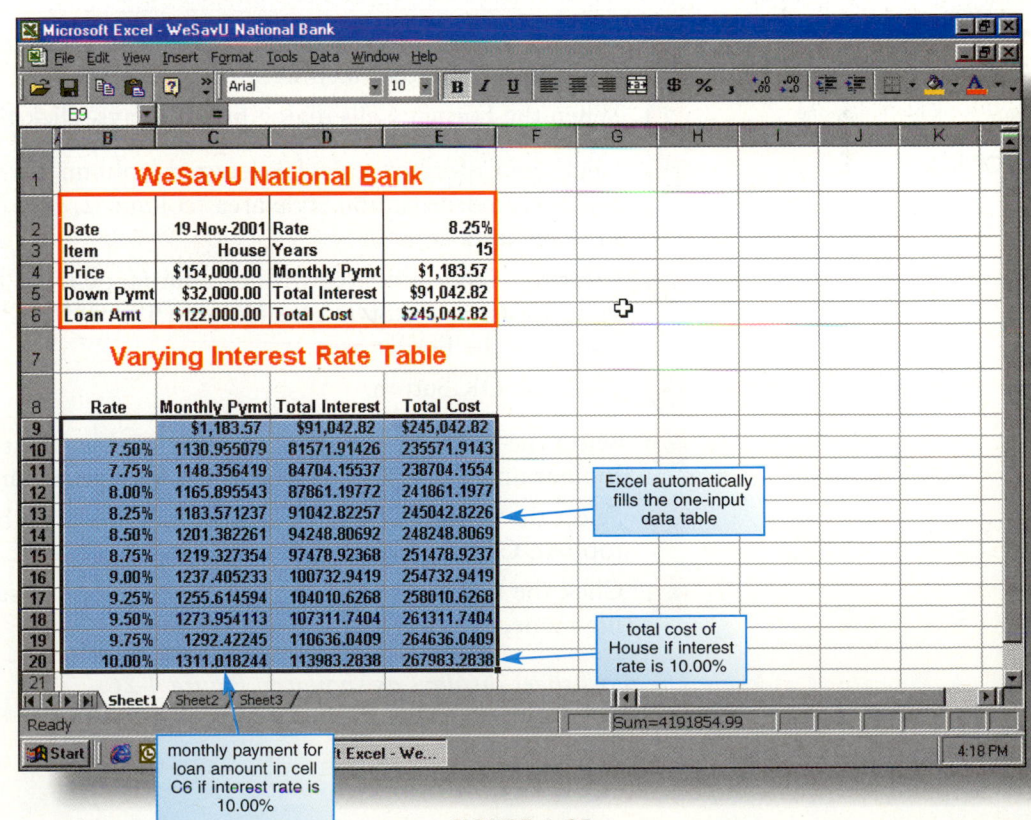

FIGURE 4-25

In Figure 4-25 on the previous page, the data table displays the monthly payment, total interest, and total cost for the interest rates in column B. For example, if the interest rate is 8.25% (cell E2), the monthly payment is $1,183.57 (cell E4). If, however, the interest rate is 9.75% (cell B19), the monthly payment is $1,292.42 rounded to the nearest cent (cell C19). If the interest rate is 7.50% (cell B10), then the total cost of the house is $235,571.91 rounded to the nearest cent (cell E10), rather than $245,042.82 (cell E6). Thus, a 0.75% decrease in the interest rate results in a $9,470.91 decrease in the total cost of the house. The results in the data table in Figure 4-25 will be formatted to the Comma style shortly.

The following list details important points you should know about data tables:

1. The formula(s) you are analyzing must have a cell reference to the input cell.
2. You can have as many active data tables in a worksheet as you want.
3. While only one value can vary in a one-input data table, the data table can analyze as many formulas as you want.
4. To add additional formulas to a one-input data table, enter them in adjacent cells in the same row as the current formulas (row 9 in Figure 4-25) and then define the entire new range as a data table by using the Table command on the Data menu.
5. You delete a data table as you would delete any other item on a worksheet. That is, select the data table and press the DELETE key.

Undoing Formats

If you started to assign formats to a range and then realize you made a mistake and want to start over, select the range, click Style on the Format menu, click Normal in the Style name list box, and click the OK button.

Formatting the Data Table

The next step is to format the data table to improve its readability.

TO OUTLINE AND FORMAT THE DATA TABLE

1 Select the range B8:E20. Right-click the selected range and then click Format Cells on the shortcut menu.

2 When the Format Cells dialog box displays, click the Border tab.

3 Click the Color box arrow. Select red (column 1, row 3) on the palette. Click the heavy border in the Style area (column 2, row 6). Click the Outline button in the Presets area.

4 Click the Color box arrow. Click Automatic (row 1) on the palette. Click the light border in the Style area (column 1, row 7). Click the vertical border button in the Border area.

5 Click the OK button.

6 Select the range B8:E8. Click the Borders button arrow on the Formatting toolbar and then click the Thick Bottom Border button (column 2, row 2).

7 Select the range C10:E20. Click the Comma Style button on the Formatting toolbar. Click cell G20 to deselect the range C10:E20.

8 Click the Save button on the Standard toolbar to save the workbook using the file name, WeSavU National Bank.

The worksheet displays as shown in Figure 4-26.

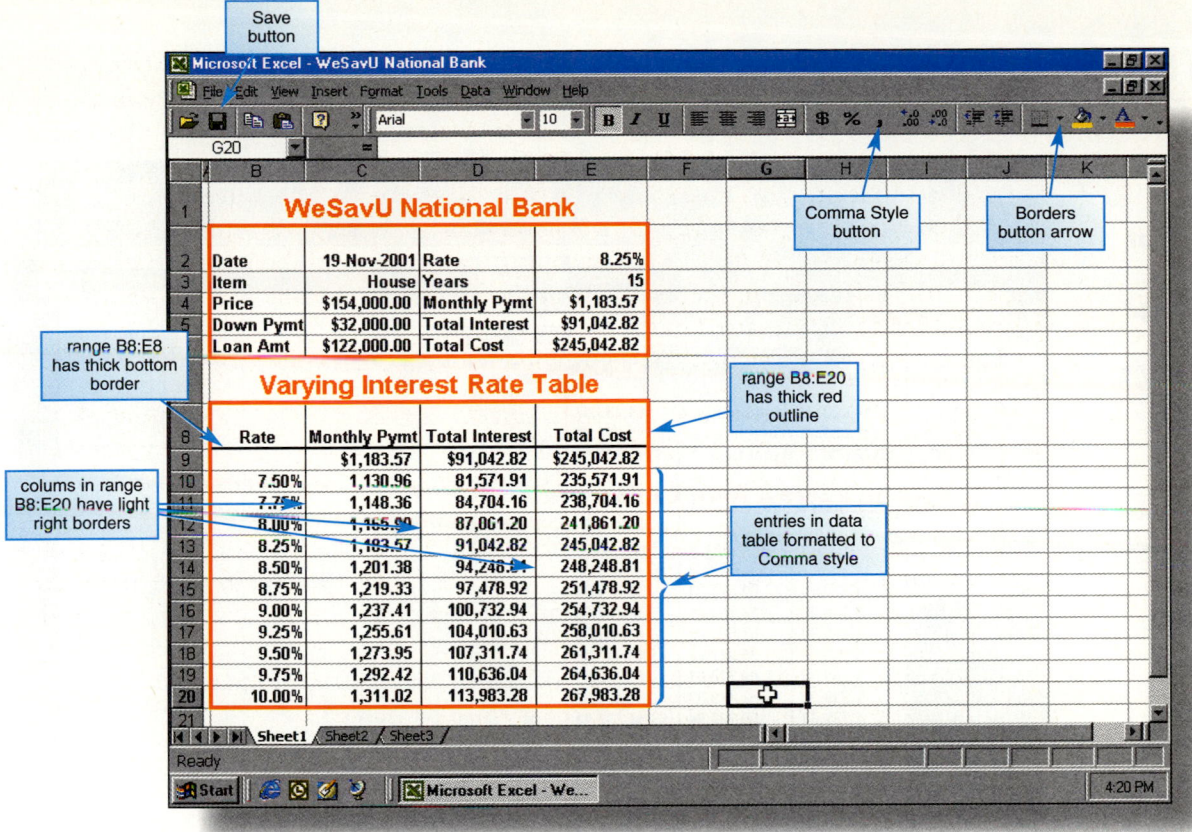

FIGURE 4-26

The data table is complete. Each time you enter new data into the loan analysis section, Excel recalculates all formulas, including the data table.

Adding an Input Value Pointer to the Data Table Using Conditional Formatting

If the interest rate in cell E2 is between 7.50% and 10.00% and its decimal portion is a multiple of 0.25 (such as 8.25%), then one of the rows in the data table agrees exactly with the monthly payment, interest paid, and total cost in the range E4:E6. For example, in Figure 4-26, row 13 (8.25%) in the data table agrees with the results in the range E4:E6, because the interest rate in cell B13 is the same as the interest rate in cell E2. Analysts often look for the row in the data table that agrees with the input cell results. To make this row stand out, you can use **conditional formatting** to color the background of the cell in column B that agrees with the input cell (cell E2) as shown in the steps on the next page.

Conditional Formatting

You can add up to three different conditions to a cell or range of cells. To include additional conditions, click the Add button in the Conditional Formatting dialog box. If more than one condition is true for a cell, then Excel applies the format of the first condition that is true.

To Add an Input Cell Pointer to the Data Table

1 Select the range B10:B20. Click Format on the menu bar and then point to Conditional Formatting.

The Format menu displays (Figure 4-27).

FIGURE 4-27

2 Click Conditional Formatting. When the Conditional Formatting dialog box displays, click equal to in the middle box of the Condition 1 area. Click the box on the right in the Condition 1 area (also called value 2 box) and then click cell E2 in the loan analysis section. Click the Format button, click the Patterns tab, and click the color green (column 4, row 2) on the color palette. Click the OK button in the Format Cells dialog box.

The Conditional Formatting dialog box displays as shown in Figure 4-28.

FIGURE 4-28

3 Click the OK button in the Conditional Formatting dialog box. Click cell G20 to deselect the range B10:B20.

Cell B13 in the data table, which contains 8.25%, displays with a green background because 8.25% is the same as the rate in cell E2 (Figure 4-29).

FIGURE 4-29

4 Enter 9.25 in cell E2.

Excel immediately displays cell B17 with a green background and cell B13 displays with a white background (Figure 4-30). Thus, the green background serves as a pointer in the data table to indicate the row that agrees with the input cell (cell E2).

5 Enter 8.25 in cell E2 to return the loan analysis section and data table section to their original states as shown in Figure 4-28.

FIGURE 4-30

Recalculation

Enter a value in a worksheet and Excel automatically recalculates all formulas and data tables. You can instruct Excel not to recalculate data tables, unless you press function key F9. To change recalculation, click Options on the Tools menu, click the Calculation tab, click Automatic except tables in the Calculation area, and then click the OK button.

When the loan officer using this worksheet enters a different percent in cell E2, the pointer will move or disappear. It will disappear whenever the interest rate in cell E2 is outside the range of the data table or its decimal portion is not a multiple of 0.25.

Creating an Amortization Schedule

The next step in this project is to create the Amortization Schedule shown on the right side of Figure 4-31. An **amortization schedule** shows the beginning and ending balances and the amount of payment that applies to the principal and interest for each year over the life of the loan. For example, if a customer wanted to pay off the loan after two years, the Amortization Schedule tells the loan officer what the payoff would be (cell I4 in Figure 4-31). The Amortization Schedule shown in Figure 4-31 will work only for loans of up to 15 years. You could, however, extend the table to any number of years. The Amortization Schedule also contains summaries in rows 18, 19, and 20. These summaries should agree exactly with the amounts in the loan analysis section in the range B1:E6.

Amortization Schedules

Hundreds of Web sites offer amortization schedules. Use a search engine with your browser to find several sites. Search for amortization schedule. For an example of a Web site that determines an amortization schedule, visit the Excel 2000 More About Web page (www.scsite.com/ex2000/more.htm) and click Amortization Schedule.

FIGURE 4-31

To construct the Amortization Schedule shown in Figure 4-31, complete the following steps: (1) adjust the column widths and enter the titles in the range G1:K2; (2) use the fill handle to create a series of integers in column G that represent the years 1 through 15; (3) enter the formulas in the range H3:K3 and then copy them to the range H4:K17; (4) enter the total formulas; (5) format the numbers; and (6) outline the Amortization Schedule to highlight it.

Changing Column Widths and Entering the Titles

The first step in creating the Amortization Schedule is to adjust the column widths and enter the Amortization Schedule section title and column titles.

TO CHANGE COLUMN WIDTHS AND ENTER TITLES

1 Position the mouse pointer on the right boundary of column heading F and then drag to the left until the ScreenTip, Width: .50 (6 pixels) displays.

2 Position the mouse pointer on the right boundary of column heading G and then drag to the left until the ScreenTip, Width: 3.00 (26 pixels), displays.

3 Drag through column headings H through K to select them. Position the mouse pointer on the right boundary of column heading K and then drag to the right until the ScreenTip, Width: 12.29 (91 pixels) displays.

4 Click cell G1. Type Amortization Schedule as the section title. Press the ENTER key

5 With cell G1 selected, click the Font Size box arrow on the Formatting toolbar and then click 16. Click the Font Color button on the Formatting toolbar to change the font color to red. Select the range G1:K1 and then click the Merge and Center button on the Formatting toolbar.

6 Enter the column titles from the table on the right in the range G2:K2. Where appropriate, press ALT+ENTER to enter the titles on two lines.

7 Select the range G2:K2 and then click the Center button on the Formatting toolbar. Click cell G3.

CELL	ENTRY
G2	Yr
H2	Beginning Balance
I2	Ending Balance
J2	Paid On Principal
K2	Interest Paid

The section title and column headings display as shown in Figure 4-32.

FIGURE 4-32

Column Borders

In this project, columns A and F are used as column borders to divide sections of the worksheet from one another as well as from the row headings. A column border is an unused column with a significantly reduced width. You also can use row borders to separate sections of a worksheet.

Creating a Series of Integers Using the Fill Handle

The next step is to create a series of numbers, using the fill handle, that represent the years during the life of the loan. The series begins with 1 (year 1) and ends with 15 (year 15).

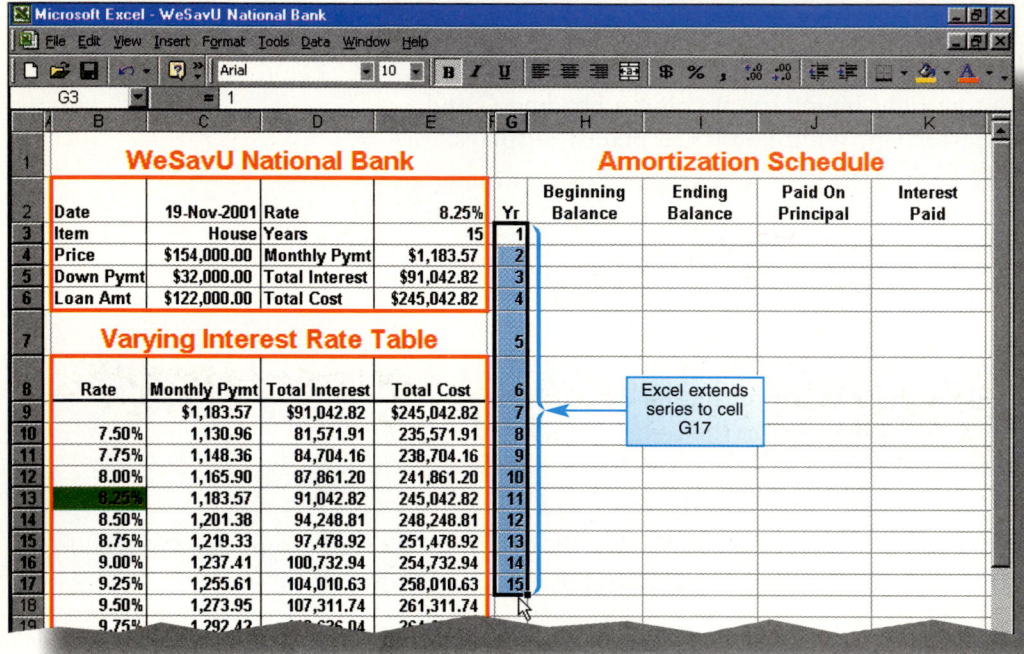

FIGURE 4-33

TO CREATE A SERIES OF INTEGERS USING THE FILL HANDLE

1 With cell G3 active, enter 1 as the initial year. Click cell G4 and enter 2 to represent the next year.

2 Select the range G3:G4 and point to the fill handle. Drag the fill handle through cell G17.

Excel creates the series of integers 1 though 15 in the range G3:G17 (Figure 4-33).

As you will see shortly, the series of integers in the range G3:G17 will play an important role in determining the ending balance and interest paid in the amortization schedule.

Entering the Formulas in the Amortization Schedule

The next step is to enter the four formulas in row 3 that form the basis of the amortization schedule. Later, these formulas will be copied through row 17. The formulas are summarized in Table 4-2.

Table 4-2	Formulas for the Amortization Schedule		
CELL	**DESCRIPTION**	**FORMULA**	**COMMENT**
H3	Beginning Balance	=C6	The beginning balance is the initial loan amount in cell C6.
I3	Ending Balance	=PV($E$2 /12, 12 * ($E$3 – G3), -$E$4)	The balance at the end of a year is equal to the present value of the monthly payments paid over the remaining life of the loan.
J3	Paid on Principal	=H3 – I3	The amount paid on the principal is equal to the beginning balance (cell H3) less the ending balance (cell I3).
K3	Interest Paid	=12 * $E$4 – J3	The interest paid during the year is equal to 12 times the monthly payment (cell E4) less the amount paid on the principal (cell J3).

Of the four formulas in Table 4-2, the most difficult to understand is the PV function that will be assigned to cell I3. The **PV function** returns the present value of an annuity. An **annuity** is a series of fixed payments (such as the monthly payment in cell E4) made at the end of a fixed number of terms (months) at a fixed interest rate. You can use the PV function to determine how much the borrower of the loan still owes at the end of each year.

The PV function can determine the ending balance after the first year (cell I3) by using a term equal to the number of months the borrower must still make payments. For example, if the loan is for 15 years (180 months), then the borrower still owes 168 payments after the first year. The number of payments outstanding can be determined from the formula 12 * (E3 – G3) or 12 * (15 – 1), which equals 168. Recall that column G contains integers that represent the years into the loan. After the second year, the number of payments remaining is 156, and so on.

If you assign the PV function to cell I3 as shown in Table 4-2, and you copy it down to the range I4:I17, the ending balances for each year will display properly. If, however, the loan is for less than 15 years, then the ending balances displayed for the years beyond the time the loan is due are invalid. For example, if a loan is taken out for 5 years, then the rows representing years 6 through 15 in the Amortization Schedule should be zero. The PV function, however, will display negative numbers even though the loan has already been paid off.

What is needed here is a way to assign the PV function to the range I3:I17 as long as the corresponding year in column G is less than or equal to the number of years in cell E3. If the corresponding year in column G is greater than the number of years in cell E3, then the ending balance for that year and the remaining years should be zero. As you know from previous projects, the IF function can handle this type of situation. The following IF function displays the value of the PV function or zero in cell I3 depending on whether the corresponding value in column G is less than or equal to the number of years in cell E3. Recall that the dollar signs within the cell references indicate the cell reference is absolute and, therefore, will not change as you copy the function downward.

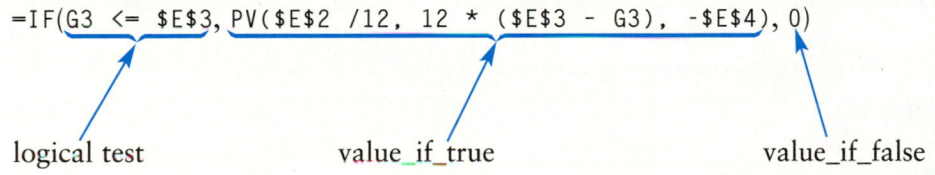

```
=IF(G3 <= $E$3, PV($E$2 /12, 12 * ($E$3 - G3), -$E$4), 0)
```

| logical test | value_if_true | value_if_false |

In the above formula, the logical test determines if the year in column G is less than or equal to the term of the loan in cell E3. If the logical test is true, then the IF function assigns the PV function to the cell. If the logical test is false, then the IF function assigns zero (0) to the cell.

The PV function in the IF function includes absolute cell references (cell references with dollar signs) to ensure that these cell references in column E do not change when the If function is later copied down the column. The steps on the next page enter the four formulas shown in Table 4-2 into row 3. Row 3 represents year 1 of the loan.

To Enter the Formulas in the Amortization Schedule

1 Select cell H3. Type =C6 **and then press the** RIGHT ARROW **key to enter the beginning balance of the loan. Type** =if(g3 <= e3, pv(e2 / 12, 12 * (e3 – g3), -e4), 0) **as the entry for cell I3.**

The loan amount displays in cell H3 as the first year's beginning balance using the same format as in cell C6. The IF function displays in cell I3 and in the formula bar (Figure 4-34).

FIGURE 4-34

2 Press the ENTER key.

Excel evaluates the IF function in cell I3 and displays the result of the PV function (117702.0408) because the value in cell G3 (1) is less than or equal to the term of the loan in cell E3 (15). With cell I3 active, the formula displays in the formula bar (Figure 4-35). If the borrower wanted to pay off the loan after one year, the cost would be $117,702.04.

FIGURE 4-35

3 **Click cell J3. Type** =h3 − i3 **and then press the RIGHT ARROW key. Type** =if(h3 > 0, 12 * e4 − j3, 0) **in cell K3.**

The amount paid on the principal after one year displays in cell J3 using the same format as in cell H3. The IF function displays in cell K3 and in the formula bar (Figure 4-36).

FIGURE 4-36

4 **Press the ENTER key.**

The interest paid after one year displays in cell K3 (Figure 4-37).

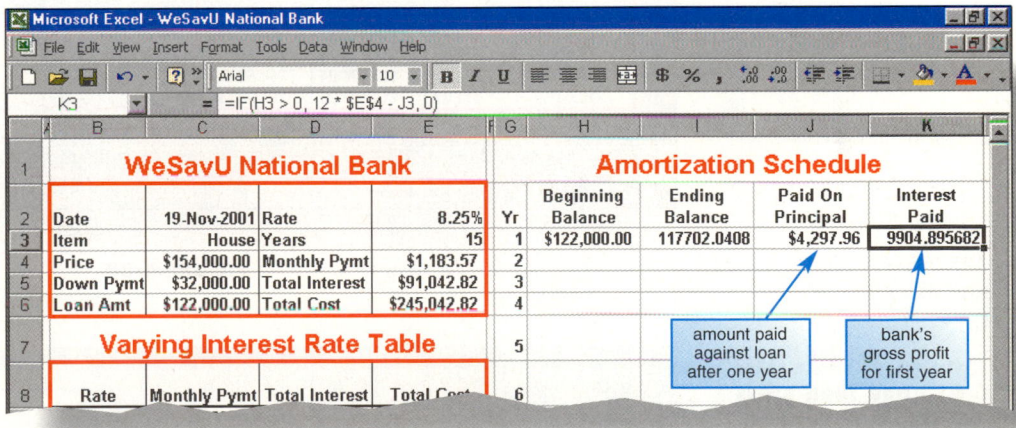

FIGURE 4-37

When you enter a formula in a cell, Excel assigns the cell the same format as the first cell reference in the formula. For example, when you enter =c6 in cell H3, Excel assigns the format in cell C6 to H3. The same applies to cell J3. Excel assigns the Currency style format to J3 because cell reference H3 is the first cell reference in the formula (=H3 − I3) assigned to cell J3 and cell H3 has a Currency style format. Although this method of formatting also works for most functions, it does not work for the IF function. Thus, the results of the IF functions in cells I3 and K3 display using the General format, which is the format of all cells when you open a new workbook.

With the formulas entered into the first row, the next step is to copy them to the remaining rows in the Amortization Schedule. The required copying is straight-forward except for the beginning balance column. To obtain the next year's beginning balance (cell H4), you have to use last year's ending balance (I3). Once cell I3 is copied to cell H4, then H4 can be copied to the range H5:H17.

To Copy the Formulas to Fill the Amortization Schedule

1 **Select the range I3:K3 and then point to the fill handle. Drag the fill handle down through row 17.**

The formulas in cells I3, J3, and K3 are copied to the range I4:K17 (Figure 4-38). Many of the numbers displayed are incorrect because most of the cells in column H do not contain beginning balances.

FIGURE 4-38

2 **Select cell H4. Type =I3 and then press the ENTER key.**

The ending balance for year 1 in cell I3 also displays as the beginning balance for year 2 in cell H4 (Figure 4-39).

FIGURE 4-39

3 With cell H4 active, point to the fill handle. Drag the fill handle down through row 17.

The formula in cell H4 (=I3) is copied to the range H5:H17 (Figure 4-40). Because the cell reference I3 in the formula in cell H4 is relative, Excel adjusts the row portion of the cell reference as it is copied downward. Thus, each new beginning balance in column H is equal to the ending balance of the previous year.

4 Click the Save button on the Standard toolbar to save the workbook using the file name, WeSavU National Bank.

FIGURE 4-40

The numbers that display in the Amortization Schedule in Figure 4-40 are now correct, although they need to be formatted to make them easier to read. Cell I17 shows that at the end of the 15th year, the ending balance is zero, which is what it should be for a 15-year loan.

Entering the Total Formulas in the Amortization Schedule

The next step is to determine the amortization schedule totals in rows 18 through 20. These totals should agree with the totals in the loan analysis section (range B1:E6).

Steps To Enter the Total Formulas in the Amortization Schedule

1 Click cell I18. Enter `Subtotal` as the row title. Select the range J18:K18. Double-click the move handle on the Standard toolbar. Click the AutoSum button on the Standard toolbar.

The total amount paid on the principal and the total interest paid display in cells J18 and K18, respectively (Figure 4-41)

FIGURE 4-41

2 Click cell I19. Enter `Down Pymt` as the row title. Click cell K19 and enter `=c5` as the down payment. Click cell I20. Enter `Total Cost` as the row title. Click K20 and enter `=j18 + k18 + k19` as the total cost.

The amortization schedule totals display as shown in Figure 4-42.

FIGURE 4-42

The formula assigned to cell K20 sums the amounts paid on the principal (cell J18), the total interest paid (cell K18), and the down payment (cell K19).

Here again, Excel assigns the same format to cell J18 as in cell J3, because cell J3 is the first cell reference in =SUM(J3:J17). Furthermore, cell J18 was selected first when the range J18:K18 was selected to determine the sum. Thus, Excel assigned cell K18 the same format as was assigned to cell J18. Finally, cell K19 was assigned the Currency style format, because cell K19 was assigned the formula =C5 and cell C5 has a Currency style format. For the same reason, the value in cell K20 displays in Currency style format.

Formatting New Loan Data

The final step in creating the amortization schedule is to format it so it is easier to read. The formatting is divided into two parts (1) format the numbers; and (2) add an outline and borders.

When the beginning balance formula (=C6) was entered earlier into cell H3, Excel automatically copied the Currency style format along with the value from cell C6 to cell H3. The following steps use the Format Painter button to copy the Currency style format from cell H3 to the range I3:K3. Finally, the Comma Style button on the Formatting toolbar will be used to assign the Comma style format to the range H4:K17.

TO FORMAT THE NUMBERS IN THE AMORTIZATION SCHEDULE

1 Click cell H3. Click the Format Painter button on the Standard toolbar. Drag through the range I3:K3 to assign the Currency style format to the numbers.

2 Double click the move handle on the Formatting toolbar. Select the range H4:K17. Click the Comma Style button on the Formatting toolbar. Select cell H19 to deselect the range H4:K17.

The numbers in the amortization schedule display as shown in Figure 4-43.

FIGURE 4-43

The Comma Style button on the Formatting toolbar was used purposely to format the body of amortization schedule because it uses the dash to represent zero (see cell I17). If the term of a loan is for less than 15 years, the amortization schedule will include zeros in cells. The dash has a more professional appearance than columns of zeros.

The following steps add the outline and borders to the amortization schedule.

TO ADD AN OUTLINE AND BORDERS TO THE AMORTIZATION SCHEDULE

1 Select the range G2:K20. Right-click the selected range and then click Format Cells on the shortcut menu.

2 When the Format Cells dialog box displays, click the Border tab.

3 Click the Color box arrow. Click red (column 1, row 3) on the palette. Click the heavy border in the Style area (column 2, row 6). Click the Outline button in the Presets area.

4 Click the Color box arrow. Click Automatic (row 1) on the palette. Click the light border in the Style area (column 1, row 7). Click the vertical line button in the Border area.

5 Click the OK button.

6 Select the range G2:K2. Click the Borders button arrow on the Formatting toolbar and then click Thick Bottom Border (column 2, row 2).

7 Select the range G17:K17 and click the Borders button arrow to assign it a thick bottom border.

8 Double-click the move handle on the Standard toolbar. Click the Save button on the Standard toolbar to save the workbook using the file name, WeSavU National Bank.

The worksheet displays as shown in Figure 4-44.

FIGURE 4-44

Entering New Loan Data

With the loan analysis, data table, and Amortization Schedule sections of the worksheet complete, you can use them to generate new loan information. For example, assume you want to purchase a 2002 Camaro for $28,500.00. You have $5,500.00 for a down payment and want the loan for 5 years. WeSavU National Bank currently is charging 9.50% interest for a 5-year automobile loan. The following steps show how to enter the new loan data.

TO ENTER NEW LOAN DATA

1 Click cell C3. Type 2002 Camaro and then press the DOWN ARROW key.

2 In cell C4, type 28500 and then press the DOWN ARROW key.

3 In cell C5, type 5500 and then press the ENTER key.

4 Click cell E2, type 9.50 and then press the DOWN ARROW key.

5 In cell E3, type 5 and then press the DOWN ARROW key. Click cell H19.

Excel automatically recalculates the loan information in cells C6, E4, E5, E6, the data table in the range B7:E20, and the Amortization Schedule in the range G3:K20 (Figure 4-45).

FIGURE 4-45

As you can see from Figure 4-45 on the previous page, the monthly payment for the 2002 Camaro is $483.04 (cell E4). The total interest is $5,982.57 (cell E5). The total cost of the $28,500.00 Camaro is $34,482.57 (cell E6). Because the term of the loan is for five years, rows 6 through 15 in the amortization schedule display a dash (-), which represents zero (0).

The following steps enter the original loan data.

TO ENTER THE ORIGINAL LOAN DATA

1 Click cell C3. Type House and then press the DOWN ARROW key.

2 In cell C4, type 154000 and then press the DOWN ARROW key.

3 In cell C5, type 32000 and then press the ENTER key.

4 Click cell E2, type 8.25 and then press the DOWN ARROW key.

5 In cell E3, type 15 and then click the Enter box or press the ENTER key. Click cell H20.

Excel automatically recalculates the loan information, the data table, and the amortization schedule as shown previously in Figure 4-44 on page E 4.40.

Adding a Hyperlink to the Worksheet

A **hyperlink** points to the location of a computer on which a destination file is stored. With Excel, you easily can create hyperlinks (Figure 4-46) to other files on your personal computer, your intranet, or the World Wide Web. The destination file (or hyperlinked file) can be any Office document or HTML file (Web page). Two primary worksheet elements exist to which you can assign a hyperlink:

1. **Text** – Enter text in a cell and make the text a hyperlink; text hyperlinks display in the color blue and are underlined.
2. **Embedded graphic** – Draw or insert a graphic, such as clip art, and then make the graphic a hyperlink.

You use the **Hyperlink command** on the shortcut menu to assign the hyperlink to the worksheet element.

More About

Hyperlinks

You can embed hyperlinks into an Excel worksheet that easily connect to important information on your local disk, on your company's intranet, or on the Internet. The information can be a Web page or another Office 2000 document, such as an Excel workbook.

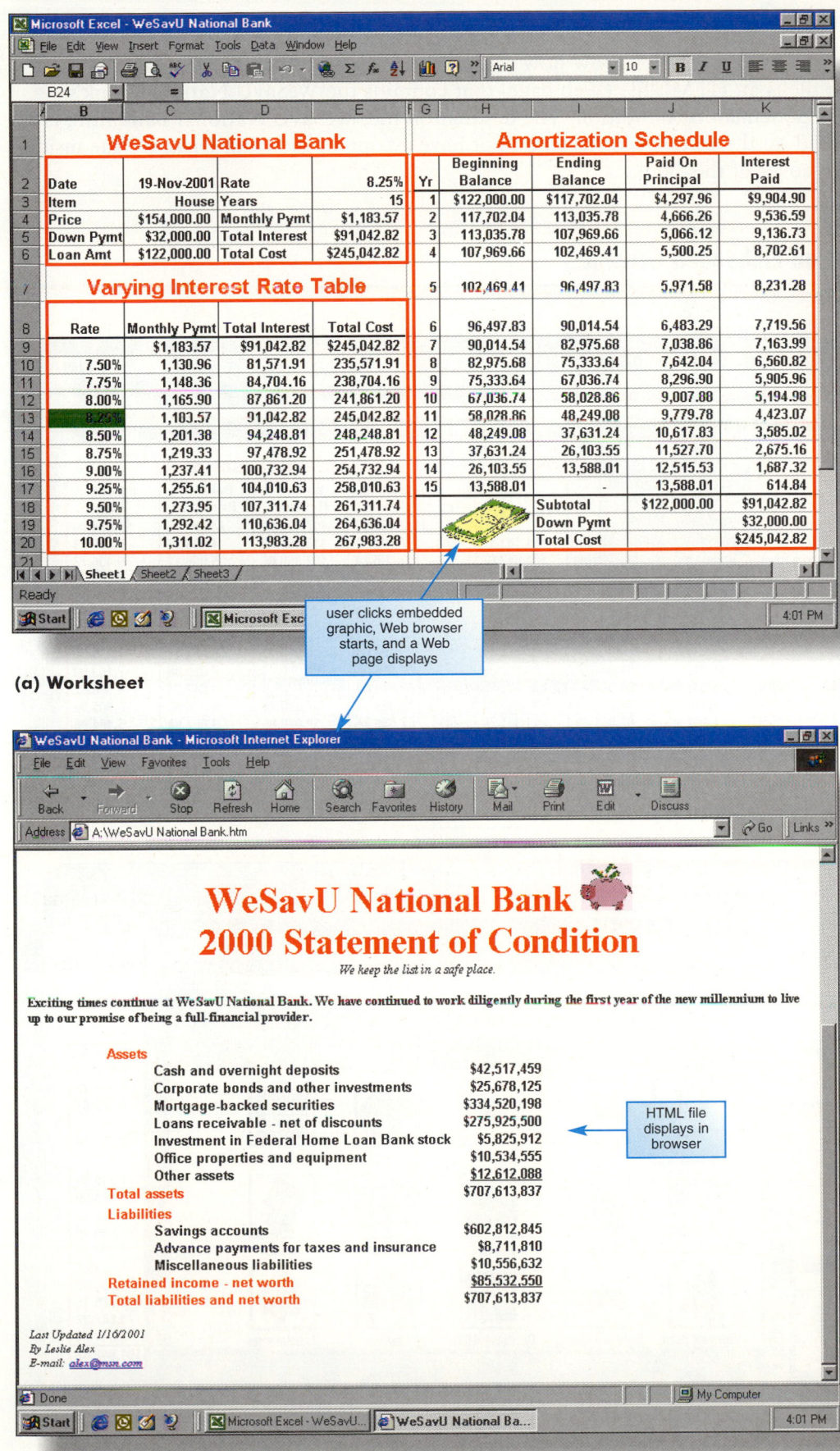

(a) Worksheet

user clicks embedded graphic, Web browser starts, and a Web page displays

HTML file displays in browser

(b) Web Page   **FIGURE 4-46**

Assigning a Hyperlink to an Embedded Graphic

The following steps show how to assign a hyperlink to a graphic. The destination file is an HTML file (Web page) that contains the WeSavU National Bank's 2000 Statement of Condition. The destination file, WeSavU National Bank.htm, is located on the Data Disk. If you do not have a copy of the Data Disk, see the inside back cover of this book.

 Steps ## To Assign a Hyperlink to an Embedded Graphic

1 **Click Insert on the menu bar. Point to Picture and then point to Clip Art on the Picture submenu.**

The Insert menu and Picture submenu display (Figure 4-47).

FIGURE 4-47

2 **Click Clip Art. When the Insert ClipArt window displays, point to the Business icon (column 3, row 2) in the Categories list box.**

The Insert ClipArt window displays (Figure 4-48). Each icon in the Categories list box represents a category of clip art.

FIGURE 4-48

3 Click the Business icon. If necessary, scroll down until the stack of dollar bills graphic displays. If the stack of dollar bills graphic is not available, select another one. Right-click the stack of dollar bills graphic and then point to Insert on the shortcut menu.

The shortcut menu displays (Figure 4-49).

FIGURE 4-49

4 Click Insert. Click the Close button in the Insert ClipArt window. Scroll down in the worksheet so the stack of dollar bills graphic is in full view.

Excel embeds the stack of dollar bills graphic below the data in the worksheet (Figure 4-50).

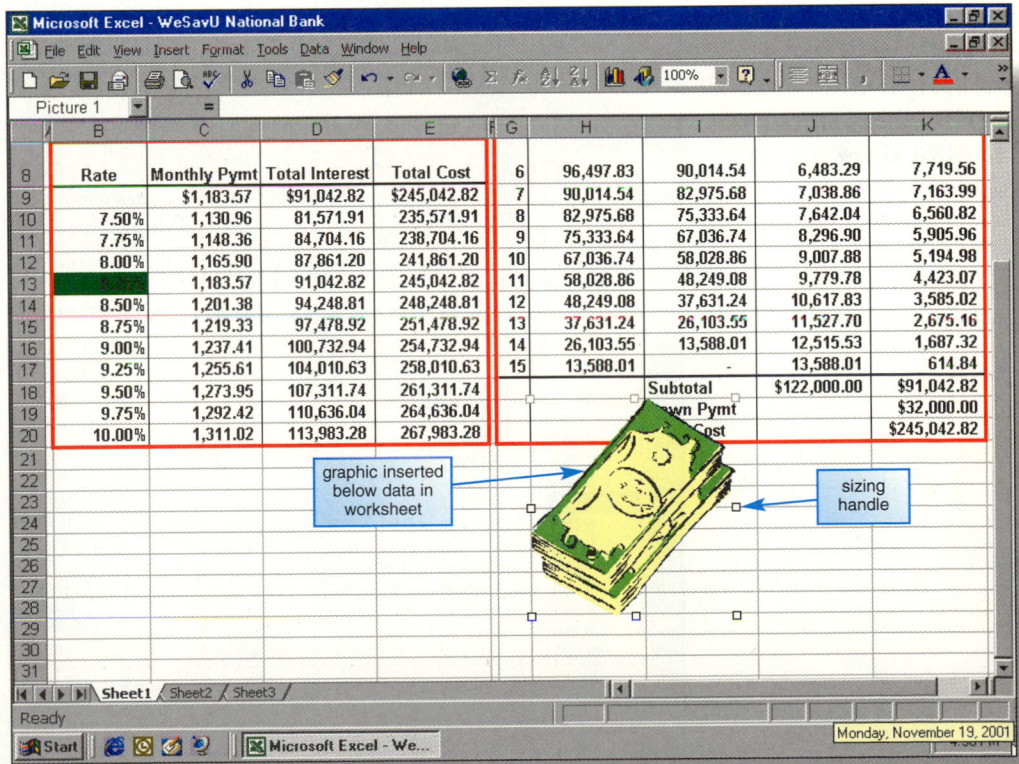

FIGURE 4-50

5 Drag the sizing handles to resize the graphic and then drag it so it displays in the range H18:H20.

The stack of dollar bills graphic displays (Figure 4-51).

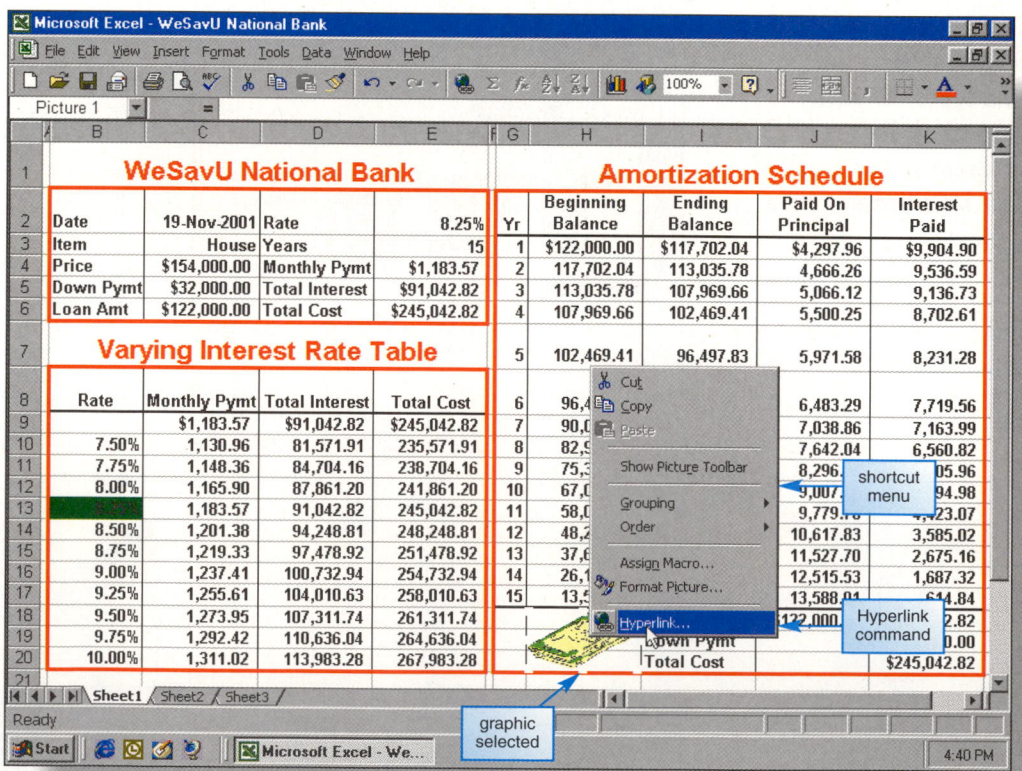

FIGURE 4-51

6 With the stack of dollar bills graphic selected, right-click it and then point to Hyperlink on the shortcut menu (Figure 4-52).

FIGURE 4-52

7 **Click Hyperlink. When the Insert Hyperlink dialog box displays, type** a:\wesavu national bank.htm **in the Type the file or Web page name text box. Point to the OK button.**

The Insert Hyperlink dialog box displays (Figure 4-53).

8 **Click the OK button. Click cell J19 to deselect the graphic. Click the Save button on the Standard toolbar to save the workbook using the file name, WeSavU National Bank.**

Excel assigns the hyperlink, a:\WeSavU National Bank.htm, to the stack of dollar bills graphic. Excel saves the workbook using the file name, WeSavU National Bank.

FIGURE 4-53

To edit the hyperlink, right-click the stack of dollar bills graphic to select it, point to Hyperlink on the shortcut menu, and then click Edit Hyperlink or click the Insert Hyperlink button on the Standard toolbar.

Displaying a Hyperlinked File

The next step is to display the hyperlinked file by clicking the stack of dollar bills graphic on the worksheet. Once you assign a hyperlink to an element in your worksheet, you can position the mouse pointer on the element to display the hyperlink as a ScreenTip. Clicking the stack of dollar bills graphic will display the hyperlinked file, as shown in the steps on the next page.

Other Ways

1. Click Insert Hyperlink button on Standard toolbar
2. On Insert menu click Hyperlink

Steps **To Display a Hyperlinked File**

1 With the Data Disk in drive A, point to the stack of dollar bills graphic.

The hyperlink displays as a ScreenTip (Figure 4-54).

		81,571.91	235,571.91	8	2,975.68	75,333.64	7,642.04	6,560.82
11	7.75%	1,148.36	84,704.16	238,704.16	9	75,333.64	67,036.74	8,296.90	5,905.96
12	8.00%	1,165.90	87,861.20	241,861.20	10	67,036.74	58,028.86	9,007.88	5,194.98
13	8.25%	1,183.57	91,042.82	245,042.82	11	58,028.86	48,249.08	9,779.78	4,423.07
14	8.50%	1,201.38	94,248.81	248,248.81	12	48,249.08	37,631.24	10,617.83	3,585.02
15	8.75%	1,219.33	97,478.92	251,478.92	13	37,631.24	26,103.55	11,527.70	2,675.16
16	9.00%	1,237.41	100,732.94	254,732.94	14	26,103.55	13,588.01	12,515.53	1,687.32
17	9.25%	1,255.61	104,010.63	258,010.63	15	13,588.01		13,588.01	614.84
18	9.50%	1,273.95	107,311.74	261,311.74			Subtotal	$122,000.00	$91,042.82
19	9.75%	1,292.42	110,636.04	264,636.04			Down Pymt		$32,000.00
20	10.00%	1,311.02	113,983.28	267,983.28			Total Cost		$245,042.82

a:\wesavu national bank.htm

mouse pointer changes to hand when moved on hyperlink

ScreenTip indicates file path

FIGURE 4-54

2 Click the stack of dollar bills graphic.

Excel starts your browser and displays the HTML file (Web page) as shown in Figure 4-55. The Web page contains the WeSavU National Bank 2000 Statement of Condition. Both the Excel button and browser button display on the taskbar.

3 When you are finished viewing the Web page, click the Back button to return to Excel.

The browser closes and the loan analysis worksheet displays in the active window.

browser activated

Back button

WeSavU National Bank - Microsoft Internet Explorer

File   Edit   View   Favorites   Tools   Help

Back   Forward   Stop   Refresh   Home   Search   Favorites   History   Mail   Print   Edit   Discuss

Address A:\WeSavU National Bank.htm

file path automatically displays in Address bar

WeSavU National Bank
2000 Statement of Condition
We keep the list in a safe place.

Exciting times continue at WeSavU National Bank. We have continued to work diligently during the first year of the new millennium to live up to our promise of being a full-financial provider.

Assets

Cash and overnight deposits	$42,517,459
Corporate bonds and other investments	$25,678,125
Mortgage-backed securities	$334,520,198
Loans receivable - net of discounts	$275,925,500
Investment in Federal Home Loan Bank stock	$5,825,912
Office properties and equipment	$10,534,555
Other assets	$12,612,088
Total assets	$707,613,837

HTML page displays

Liabilities

Savings accounts	$602,812,845
Advance payments for taxes and insurance	$8,711,810
Miscellaneous liabilities	$10,556,632
Retained income - net worth	$85,532,550
Total liabilities and net worth	$707,613,837

Excel button on taskbar indicates Excel is inactive

recessed browser button on taskbar indicates browser is active

Last Updated 1/16/2001
By Leslie Alex
E-mail: alex@msn.com

Done

Start   Microsoft Excel - WeSavU...   WeSavU National Ba...

FIGURE 4-55

If the hyperlink does not connect you to the destination file, make sure you typed the correct hyperlink in the Type the file or Web page name text box in the Insert Hyperlink dialog box (Figure 4-53 on the previous page). If you entered the hyperlink correctly and it still does not work, check to be sure the file exists on the Data Disk.

Protecting the Worksheet

When building a worksheet for novice users, you should protect the cells in the worksheet that you do not want changed, such as cells that contain text and formulas.

When you create a new worksheet, all the cells are assigned a locked status, but the lock is not engaged, leaving them unprotected. **Unprotected cells** are cells whose values you can change at any time. **Protected cells** are cells that you cannot change. If a cell is protected and the user attempts to change its value, Excel displays a dialog box with a message indicating the cells are protected.

You should protect cells only after the worksheet has been tested fully and displays the correct results. Protecting a worksheet is a two-step process:

1. Select the cells you want to leave unprotected and change their cell protection settings to an unlocked status.
2. Protect the entire worksheet.

At first glance, these steps may appear to be backwards. Once you protect the entire worksheet, however, you cannot change anything, including the locked status of individual cells.

In the loan analysis worksheet (Figure 4-56), the user should make changes to only five cells: the item in cell C3; the price in cell C4; the down payment in cell C5; the interest rate in cell E2; and the years in cell E3. These cells thus must remain unprotected. The remaining cells and the embedded stack of dollar bills graphic in the worksheet should be protected so they cannot be changed by the user.

The following steps show how to protect the loan analysis worksheet.

More About 2000

Protecting Worksheets

You can move from one unprotected cell to another unprotected cell in a worksheet by using the TAB and SHIFT+TAB keys.

 ## To Protect a Worksheet

1 Select the range C3:C5. Hold down the CTRL key and then select the nonadjacent range E2:E3. Right-click one of the selected ranges and then point to Format Cells on the shortcut menu.

The shortcut menu displays (Figure 4-56).

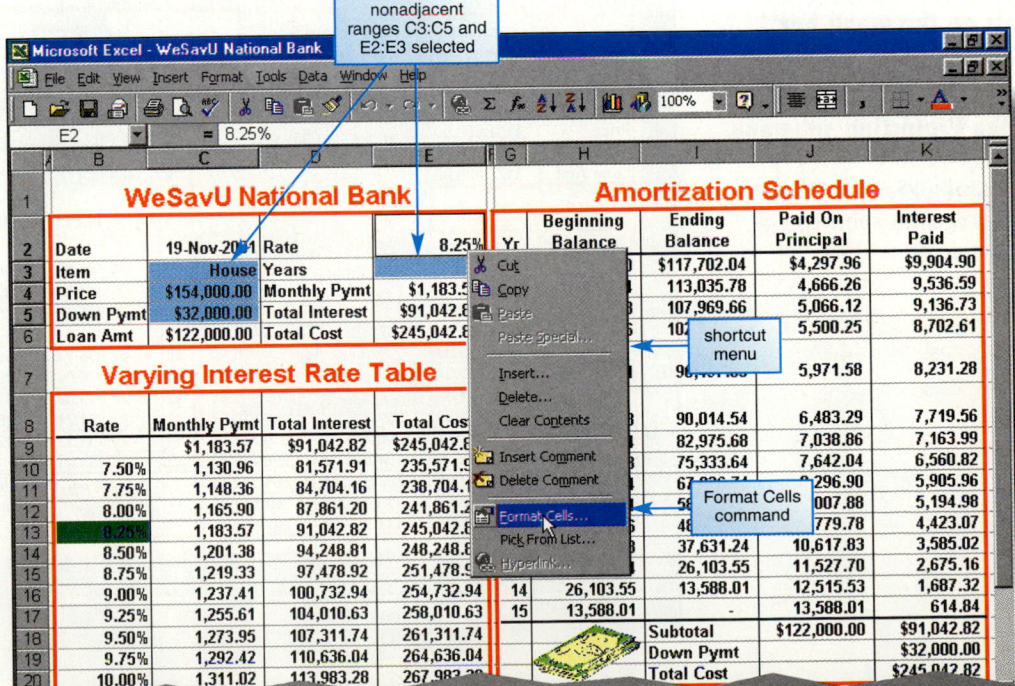

FIGURE 4-56

2 **Click Format Cells. When the Format Cells dialog box displays, click the Protection tab. Click the Locked check box to deselect it.**

The Protection sheet in the Format Cells dialog box displays with the check mark removed from the Locked check box. This means the selected cells will not be protected (Figure 4-57).

FIGURE 4-57

3 **Click the OK button. Click cell J19 to deselect the ranges C3:C5 and E2:E3. Click Tools on the menu bar. Point to Protection and then point to Protect Sheet on the Protection submenu.**

Excel displays the Tools menu and Protection submenu (Figure 4-58).

FIGURE 4-58

4 **Click Protect Sheet.**

The Protect Sheet dialog box displays (Figure 4-59). All three check boxes are selected, thus protecting the worksheet from changes to contents (except the cells left unlocked), objects, and scenarios.

5 **Click the OK button. Click the Save button on the Standard toolbar to save the protected workbook.**

FIGURE 4-59

All the cells in the worksheet are protected, except for the ranges C3:C5 and E2:E3.

The **Protect Sheet dialog box** in Figure 4-58 lets you enter a password. You should create a **password** when you want to keep others from changing the worksheet from protected to unprotected.

If you want to protect more than one sheet, select each one before you begin the protection process or click **Protect Workbook** on the **Protection submenu** that displays (Figure 4-57) when you point to **Protection** on the Tools menu.

Now when this workbook is turned over to the loan officers, they will be able to enter data in only the unprotected cells. If they try to change any protected cell, such as the monthly payment in cell E4, Excel displays a dialog box with a diagnostic message as shown in Figure 4-60.

To change any cells in the worksheet such as titles or formulas, unprotect the document by pointing to Protection on the Tools menu and then clicking **Unprotect Sheet.**

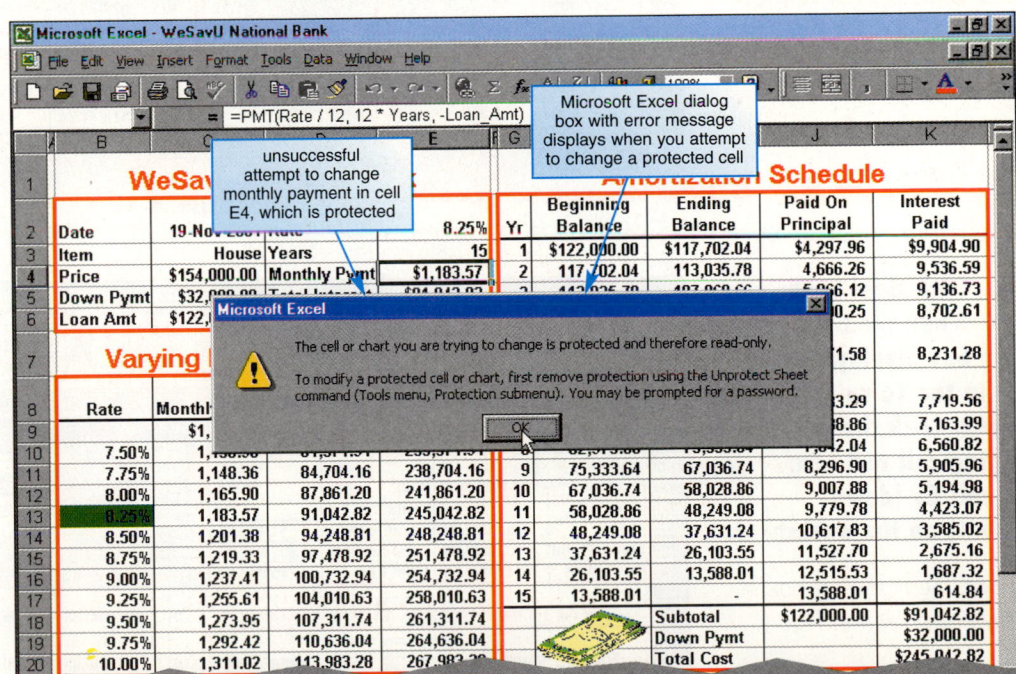

FIGURE 4-60

Goal Seeking to Determine the Down Payment for a Specific Monthly Payment

If you know the result you want a formula to generate, you can use goal seeking to determine what value is needed in a particular cell to produce that result. For example, you can use the **Goal Seek command** to determine what down payment is required to make the monthly payment for the House exactly $1,000.00, rather than the current $1,183.37.

To Determine the Down Payment for a Specific Monthly Payment Using the Goal Seek Command

1 Click cell E4, the cell with the monthly payment amount. Click Tools on the menu bar and then point to Goal Seek.

The Tools menu displays (Figure 4-61).

FIGURE 4-61

2 Click Goal Seek. When the Goal Seek dialog box displays, type 1000 in the To value text box. Click the By changing cell text box. Click cell C5 (down payment) on the worksheet.

The Goal Seek dialog box displays as shown in Figure 4-62

FIGURE 4-62

3 **Click the OK button.**

Excel displays the Goal Seek Status dialog box indicating it has found an answer. Excel also changes the monthly payment in cell E4 to the goal ($1,000.00) and changes the down payment in cell C5 to $50,922.13 (Figure 4-63).

4 **Click the Cancel button in the Goal Seek Status dialog box to undo the changes to the worksheet.**

FIGURE 4-63

As shown in Figure 4-63, if you want to pay exactly $1,000.00 a month and the House costs $154,000.00, the interest rate is 8.25%, and the term is 15 years, then you must pay a down payment of $50,922.13, or $18,922.13 more than the original $32,000.00 down payment.

In this goal seeking example, you do not have to reference directly the cell to vary in the formula or function. For example, the monthly payment formula in cell E4 is =PMT(Interest Rate / 12, 12 * Years, – Loan Amount). This formula does not include a direct reference to the down payment in cell C5. Because the loan amount, which is referenced in the PMT function, is based on the down payment, however, Excel is able to goal seek on the monthly payment by varying the down payment.

If you had clicked the OK button instead of the Cancel button in Step 4, then Excel would have made the changes to the worksheet based on the goal seek activity. If you do click the OK button, you can reset the worksheet to the values displayed prior to goal seeking by clicking the Undo button on the Standard toolbar.

Quitting Excel

To quit Excel, follow the steps below.

TO QUIT EXCEL

1 Click the Close button on the right side of the title bar.

2 If the Microsoft Excel dialog box displays, click the No button.

More About

Microsoft Certification

The Microsoft Office User Specialist (MOUS) Certification program provides an opportunity for you to obtain a valuable industry credential - proof that you have the Excel 2000 skills required by employers. For more information, see Appendix D or visit the Shelly Cashman Series MOUS Web page at www.scsite.com/off2000/cert.htm.

More About

Closing Files

If you have multiple workbooks opened, you can close them all at the same time by holding down the SHIFT key when you click the File menu. The Close command changes to Close All. Click Close All and Excel will close all open workbooks.

CASE PERSPECTIVE SUMMARY

The workbook you developed in this project will handle all of Leslie Alex's requirements for the loan department at WeSavU National Bank. The loan information, data table, and Amortization Schedule are easy to read in the protected worksheet, which will help with customer relations. The hyperlink associated with the stack of dollar bills graphic gives the loan officer quick access to the bank's 2000 Statement of Condition to answer customer questions.

Project Summary

In this project you learned how to use names, rather than cell references to enter formulas. You also learned how to use financial functions, such as the PMT and PV functions. You learned how to analyze data by creating a data table and amortization schedule. This project also explained how to add a hyperlink to a worksheet. Finally, you learned how to protect a document so a user can change only the contents of unprotected cells.

What You Should Know

Having completed this project, you now should be able to perform the following tasks:

- Add an Input Cell Pointer to the Data Table (E 4.28)
- Add an Outline and Borders to the Amortization Schedule (E 4.40)
- Add an Outline and Borders to the Loan Analysis Section (E 4.9)
- Assign a Hyperlink to an Embedded Graphic (E 4.44)
- Change Column Widths and Enter Titles (E 4.31)
- Change the Font Style of the Entire Worksheet (E 4.7)
- Copy the Formulas to Fill the Amortization Schedule (E 4.36)
- Create a Percent Series Using the Fill Handle (E 4.22)
- Create a Series of Integers Using the Fill Handle (E 4.32)
- Create Names Based on Row Titles (E 4.12)
- Define a Range as a Data Table (E 4.24)
- Determine the Down Payment for a Specific Monthly Payment Using the Goal Seek Command (E 4.52)
- Determine the Total Interest and Total Cost (E 4.17)
- Display a Hyperlinked File (E 4.48)

- Enter New Loan Data (E 4.18, E 4.41)
- Enter the Data Table Title and Column Titles (E 4.21)
- Enter the Formulas in the Amortization Schedule (E 4.34)
- Enter the Formulas in the Data Table (E 4.23)
- Enter the Loan Amount Formula Using Names (E 4.14)
- Enter the Loan Data (E 4.11)
- Enter the Original Loan Data (E 4.19, E 4.42)
- Enter the PMT Function (E 4.16)
- Enter the Section Title, Row Titles, and System Date (E 4.7)
- Enter the Total Formulas in the Amortization Schedule (E 4.38)
- Format Cells before Entering Values (E 4.11)
- Format Numbers in the Amortization Schedule (E 4.39)
- Outline and Format the Data Table (E 4.26)
- Protect a Worksheet (E 4.49)
- Quit Excel (E 4.53)
- Start Excel and Reset the Toolbars and Menus (E 4.6)

Apply Your Knowledge

✚ Project Reinforcement at www.scsite.com/off2000/reinforce.htm

1 What-If Analysis

Instructions: Start Excel and perform the following tasks.

1. Open the workbook Monthly Loan Payment on the Data Disk. See the inside back cover for instructions for downloading the Data Disk or see your instructor for information on accessing the files required for this book.
2. Use the Name command on the Insert menu to create names for cells in the range B3:B9 using the row titles in the range A3:A9.
3. Determine the loan amount in cell B8 by entering the formula: =Price – Down_Payment.
4. Determine the monthly payment in cell B9 by entering the function =PMT(Interest_Rate/12, 12 * Years, – Loan_Amount).
5. In the data table, assign the formulas in the table on the right to cells E4, F4, and G4.
6. Use the Table command on the Data menu to define the range D4:G11 as a one-input data table. Use cell B6 (interest rate) as the column input cell. The results should display as shown in Figure 4-64.

CELL	FORMULA
E4	=B9
F4	=12 * B7 * B9 + B5
G4	=F4 – B4

7. Add your name, course, computer laboratory assignment number (Apply Your Knowledge 4-1), date, and instructor name in column A beginning in cell A14.
8. Unlock the range B3:B7. Protect the worksheet.
9. Print the worksheet. Press CTRL+LEFT QUOTATION MARK and print the formulas version in landscape using the Fit to print option. Press CTRL+LEFT QUOTATION MARK to display the values version.
10. Save the workbook using the file name, Monthly Loan Payment 2.
11. Determine the monthly payment and print the worksheet for each data set: (a) Item = Summer Home; Price = $124,000.00; Down Payment = $32,000.00; Interest Rate = 8.75%; Years = 15 (b) Item = 25' Sailboat; Price = $32,000.00; Down Payment = $0.00; Interest Rate = 11.50%; Years = 7. You should get the following monthly payment results: (a) $919.49; (b) $556.37.

FIGURE 4-64

In the Lab

1 Linkup.com 401(k) Investment Model

Problem: You are a work study student for Linkup.com, a small start-up e-commerce company that hit it big when the company's investors took the company public. With the number of employees expected to reach 750 by the end of the year and the tight job market, the chief financial officer (CFO) has developed several employee benefit plans to keep current employees and attract new employees. One of the new employee benefits is a 401(k) plan. The CFO has asked you to develop a 401(k) investment model worksheet that will allow each current and prospective employee to see the effect (dollar accumulation) of investing a percent of his or her monthly salary over a period of years (Figure 4-65). The plan calls for the company to match the employee's investment dollar for dollar up to 3%. Thus, if an employee invests 5% of his or her annual salary, then the company matches the first 3%. If an employee invests only 2% of his or her annual salary, then the company matches the entire 2%. The CFO wants a data table to show the future value of the investment for different periods of time.

FIGURE 4-65

Instructions: With a blank worksheet on the screen, perform the following tasks.

1. Change the font of the entire worksheet to bold. Change the column widths to the following: A and D = 0.50; B = 20.00; C, F, and G = 13.00. Change the row heights to the following: 1 and 2 = 36.00; 3 = 4.50; and 4 = 27.00.

In the Lab

2. Enter the following worksheet titles: B1 = Linkup.com; B2 = 401(k) Investment Model. Change their font size to 26 point. One at a time, merge and center cells B1 and B2 across columns B through G. Change the background color of cells B1 and B2 to green (column 4, row 2 on the Fill Color palette). Change the font color to white (column 8, row 5 on the Font Color palette). Draw a thick black outline around cells B1 and B2.

3. Enter the row titles in column B, beginning in cell B4 as shown in Figure 4-65. Add the data in Table 4-3 to column C (also see Figure 4-65). Use the dollar and percent symbols to format the numbers in the range C4:C9.

Table 4-3	Employee Data
TITLE	ITEM
Employee Name	John Stokes
Annual Salary	$55,000.00
Percent Invested	5.00%
Company Match	3.00%
Annual Return	9.00%
Years	10

4. Use the Create command on the Name submenu (Insert menu) to assign the row titles in column B (range B4:B14) to the adjacent cells in column C. Use these names to enter the following formulas in the range C11:C14. Step 4e formats the displayed results of the formulas.
   a. Employee Monthly Contribution (cell C11) = Annual_Salary * Percent_Invested / 12
   b. Employer Monthly Contribution (cell C12) = IF(Percent_Invested < Company_Match, Percent_Invested * Annual_Salary / 12, Company_Match * Annual_Salary / 12)
   c. Total Monthly Contribution (cell C13) = SUM(C11:C12)
   d. Future Value (cell C14) = FV(Annual_Return/12, 12 * Years, -Total)
   e. If necessary, use the Format Painter button on the Standard toolbar to assign the Currency style format in cell C5 to the range C11:C14.

   The **Future Value function** in Step 4d returns to the cell the future value of the investment. The **future value** of an investment is its value at some point in the future based on a series of payments of equal amounts made over a number of periods earning a constant rate of return.

5. Add the green outline and black borders to the range B4:C14 as shown in Figure 4-65.

6. Use the concepts and techniques developed in this project to add the data table to the range E4:G15 as follows.
   a. Enter and format the table column titles in row 4.
   b. Use the fill handle to create the series of years beginning with 5 and ending with 50 in increments of 5 in column E, beginning in cell E6.
   c. In cells F5 and G5, use cell references to enter the formulas so Excel will copy the formats. That is, in cell F5, enter the formula =C14. In cell G5, enter the formula: =12 * C11 * C9.
   d. Use the Table command on the Data menu to define the range E5:G15 as a one-input data table. Use cell C9 as the column input cell.
   e. Format the numbers in the range F6:G15 to the Comma style format.
   f. Add the outline and borders as shown in Figure 4-65. Column F in the data table shows the future value of the investment for years 5 through 50 in multiples of 5. Column G shows the amount the employee invests for the specified years.

7. Add an orange pointer to the data table in the Years column that shows the row that equals the results in column C as shown in Figure 4-65.

8. Add your name, course, computer laboratory assignment number (Lab 4-1), date, and instructor name in column B beginning in cell B17.

(continued)

In the Lab

Linkup.com 401(k) Investment Model *(continued)*

9. Spell check the worksheet. Unlock the cells in the range C4:C9. Protect the worksheet.

10. Print the worksheet. Press CTRL+LEFT QUOTATION MARK and print the formulas version in landscape using the Fit to print option. Press CTRL+LEFT QUOTATION MARK to display the values version. Click the Save button on the Standard toolbar to save the workbook using the file name, Linkup.

11. Determine the future value for the data in Table 4-4. Print the worksheet for each data set.

12. You should get the following Future Value results in cell C14: Data Set 1 = $312,917.10; Data Set 2 = $1,105,118.72; and Data Set 3 = $582,511.04.

Table 4-4	Future Value Data		
	DATA SET 1	DATA SET 2	DATA SET 3
Employee Name	Fred Triples	Al Waiter	Sue Birts
Annual Salary	$75,000.00	$62,500.00	$78,000.00
Percent Invested	6%	8%	2.5%
Company Match	2.5%	3%	2%
Annual Return	8%	9.25%	6%
Years	20	30	40

2 Doug's LA Denim Ltd. Quarterly Income Statement and Break-Even Analysis

Problem: You are a consultant to Doug's LA Denim Ltd. Your area of expertise is cost-volume-profit (CVP) (also called break-even analysis), which investigates the relationship among a product's expenses (cost), its volume (units sold), and the operating income (gross profit). Any money a company earns above the break-even point is called operating income, or gross profit (row 10 in the Break-Even Analysis table in Figure 4-66). You have been asked to prepare a quarterly income statement and a data table that shows revenue, expenses, and income for units sold between 400,000 and 800,000 in increments of 25,000.

Microsoft Excel - Doug's LA Denim Ltd

File Edit View Insert Format Tools Data Window Help

	A	B	C		E	F	G	H
1	**Doug's LA Denim Ltd.**				**Break-Even**			
2	**Quarterly Income Statement**				**Analysis**			
3	Revenue				Units	Revenue	Expenses	Income
4		Units Sold	639,150			$14,700,450	$13,558,950	$1,141,500
5		Price per Unit	$23		400,000	9,200,000	10,450,000	(1,250,000)
6		Total Revenue	$14,700,450		425,000	9,775,000	10,775,000	(1,000,000)
7	Fixed Expenses				450,000	10,350,000	11,100,000	(750,000)
8		Administrative	$1,250,000		475,000	10,925,000	11,425,000	(500,000)
9		Leasing	1,300,000		500,000	11,500,000	11,750,000	(250,000)
10		Marketing	1,500,000		525,000	12,075,000	12,075,000	0
11		Salary and Benefits	1,200,000		550,000	12,650,000	12,400,000	250,000
12		Total Fixed Expenses	$5,250,000		575,000	13,225,000	12,725,000	500,000
13	Variable Expenses				600,000	13,800,000	13,050,000	750,000
14		Material Cost per Unit	$5		625,000	14,375,000	13,375,000	1,000,000
15		Total Material Cost	$3,195,750		650,000	14,950,000	13,700,000	1,250,000
16		Manufacturing Cost per Unit	$8		675,000	15,525,000	14,025,000	1,500,000
17		Total Manufacturing Cost	$5,113,200		700,000	16,100,000	14,350,000	1,750,000
18		Total Variable Expenses	$8,308,950		725,000	16,675,000	14,675,000	2,000,000
19	Summary				750,000	17,250,000	15,000,000	2,250,000
20		Total Expenses	$13,558,950		775,000	17,825,000	15,325,000	2,500,000
21		Operating Income	$1,141,500		800,000	18,400,000	15,650,000	2,750,000

FIGURE 4-66

In the Lab

Instructions: With a blank worksheet on the screen, perform the following tasks.

1. Change the font of the entire worksheet to bold. Change the column widths to the following: A = 21.00; B = 26.00; C = 13.71; D = 0.50; E = 7.14; and F through H = 11.14. Change the heights of rows 1 and 2 to 33.00.

2. Enter the following worksheet titles: A1 = Doug's LA Denim Ltd.; A2 = Quarterly Income Statement. Increase the font size in cell A1 and A2 to 20 points. One at a time, merge and center cells A1 and A2 across columns A through C. Change the background color of cells A1 and A2 to orange (column 2, row 2 on the Fill Color palette). Change the font color to white (column 8, row 5 on the Font Color palette). Add a thick black outline to the range A1:A2.

3. Enter the row titles in columns A and B as shown in Figure 4-66. Change the row titles in column A to 12 point. Add the data shown in Table 4-5 in column C. Use the dollar sign ($) and comma symbol to format the numbers in column C as you enter them.

4. Use the Create command on the Name submenu to assign the row titles in column B to the adjacent cells in column C. Use these names to enter the following formulas in column C:
   a. Total Revenue (cell C6) = Units_Sold * Price_per_Unit or =C4 * C5
   b. Total Fixed Expenses (cell C12) = SUM(C8:C11)
   c. Total Material Cost (cell C15) = Units_Sold * Material_Cost_per_Unit or =C4 * C14
   d. Total Manufacturing Cost (cell C17) = Units_Sold * Manufacturing_Cost_per_Unit or =C4 * C16
   e. Total Variable Expenses (cell C18) = Total_Material_Cost + Total_Manufacturing_Cost or =C15 + C17
   f. Total Expenses (cell C20) = Total_Fixed_Expenses + Total_Variable_Expenses or =C12 + C18
   g. Operating Income (cell C21) = Total_Revenue – Total_Expenses or =C6 – C20

5. If necessary, use the Format Painter button on the Standard toolbar to assign the Currency style format in cell C8 to the unformatted dollar amounts in column C.

6. Add a thick bottom border to the ranges B5:C5, B11:C11, and B17:C17 as shown in Figure 4-66.

7. Use the concepts and techniques developed in this project to add the data table to the range E1:H21 as follows:
   a. Add the data table titles Break-Even in cell E1 and Analysis in cell E2. Merge and center cells E1 and E2 across columns E through H. Increase the font size in cells E1 and E2 to 20 point. Format the background and font colors the same as the titles in cells A1 and A2. Enter the column titles in the range E3:H3 (see Figure 4-66).
   b. Use the fill handle to create the series of units sold in column E from 400,000 to 800,000 in increments of 25,000, beginning in cell E5.
   c. In cells F4, G4, and H4, use cell references to enter the formulas so Excel will copy the formats. That is, in cell F4, enter the formula =C6. In cell G4, enter the formula =C20. In cell H4, enter the formula =C21.

Table 4-5	Quarterly Income Data	
TITLE	**CELL**	**ITEM**
Units Sold	C4	639,150
Price per Unit	C5	$23
Administrative	C8	$1,250,000
Leasing	C9	$1,300,000
Marketing	C10	$1,500,000
Salary and Benefits	C11	$1,200,000
Material Cost per Unit	C14	$5
Manufacturing Cost per Unit	C16	$8

(continued)

In the Lab

Doug's LA Denim Ltd. Quarterly Income Statement and Break-Even Analysis *(continued)*

   d. Use the Table command on the Data menu to define the range E4:H21 as a one-input data table. Use cell C4 (units sold) as the column input cell.

   e. Use the Format Cells command on the shortcut menu to format the range F5:H21 to the Comma style format with no decimal places and negative numbers in red with parentheses. Add the borders shown in Figure 4-66 on page E 4.58.

8. Spell check the worksheet. Add your name, course, computer laboratory assignment number (Lab 4-2), date, and instructor name in column A beginning in cell A24.

9. Unlock the following cells: C4, C5, C14, and C16. Protect the worksheet.

10. Print the worksheet. Press CTRL+LEFT QUOTATION MARK and print the formulas version in landscape using the Fit to print option. Press CTRL+LEFT QUOTATION MARK to display the values version.

11. Save the workbook using the file name, Doug's LA Denim Ltd.

12. Determine the operating income for the data in Table 4-6. Print the worksheet for each data set.

Table 4-6 Operating Income Data				
TITLE	CELL	DATA SET 1	DATA SET 2	DATA SET 3
Units Sold	C4	775,000	425,000	650,000
Price per Unit	C5	$24	$26	$20
Material Cost per Unit	C14	$5	$12	$10
Manufacturing Cost per Unit	C16	$10	$6	$3

13. You should get the following Operating Income results in cell C21: Data Set 1 = $1,725,000; Data Set 2 = ($1,850,000); and Data Set 3 = ($700,000).

3 Confide In Us Loan Analysis and Amortization Schedule

Problem: Each student in your Office 2000 Applications course is assigned a real-world project that involves working with a local company. For your project, you are working with the Confide In Us Loan Company, a subsidiary of WeSavU National Bank. The manager of Confide In Us has asked you to create the loan information worksheet shown in Figure 4-67. She also wants a hyperlink added to the worksheet that displays the WeSavU National Bank 2000 Statement of Condition. Finally, she wants you to demonstrate the goal seeking capabilities of Excel.

In the Lab

```
Microsoft Excel - Confide In Us Loan Company                          _ |б|X
File  Edit  View  Insert  Format  Tools  Data  Window  Help           _ |б|X
[toolbar]  Arial          10    B  I  U
A42          =
```

	A	B	C	D	E	F
1	**Confide In Us Loan Company**					
2	**A Subsidiary of WeSavU National Bank**					
3	Price	$161,000.00		Rate	8.75%	
4	Down Pymt	$22,500.00		Years	30	
5	Loan Amount	$138,500.00		Monthly Pymt	$1,089.58	
6	Year	Beginning Balance	Ending Balance	Paid On Principal	Interest Paid	
7	1	$138,500.00	$137,504.49	$995.51	$12,079.45	
8	2	137,504.49	136,418.30	1,086.19	11,988.77	
9	3	136,418.30	135,233.16	1,185.14	11,889.82	
10	4	135,233.16	133,940.06	1,293.10	11,781.86	
11	5	133,940.06	132,529.16	1,410.90	11,664.06	
12	6	132,529.16	130,989.74	1,539.42	11,535.54	
13	7	130,989.74	129,310.08	1,679.66	11,395.30	
14	8	129,310.08	127,477.41	1,832.67	11,242.29	
15	9	127,477.41	125,477.79	1,999.62	11,075.34	
16	10	125,477.79	123,296.01	2,181.78	10,893.19	
17	11	123,296.01	120,915.49	2,380.53	10,694.43	
18	12	120,915.49	118,318.10	2,597.38	10,477.58	
19	13	118,318.10	115,484.11	2,833.99	10,240.97	
20	14	115,484.11	112,391.95	3,092.16	9,982.80	
21	15	112,391.95	109,018.11	3,373.84	9,701.12	
22	16	109,018.11	105,336.93	3,681.18	9,393.78	
23	17	105,336.93	101,320.41	4,016.52	9,058.44	
24	18	101,320.41	96,937.99	4,382.41	8,692.55	
25	19	96,937.99	92,156.36	4,781.63	8,293.33	
26	20	92,156.36	86,939.15	5,217.22	7,857.74	
27	21	86,939.15	81,246.66	5,692.48	7,382.48	
28	22	81,246.66	75,035.61	6,211.05	6,863.91	
29	23	75,035.61	68,258.77	6,776.85	6,298.11	
30	24	68,258.77	60,864.58	7,394.19	5,680.77	
31	25	60,864.58	52,796.81	8,067.77	5,007.19	
32	26	52,796.81	43,994.10	8,802.71	4,272.25	
33	27	43,994.10	34,389.50	9,604.60	3,470.36	
34	28	34,389.50	23,909.97	10,479.54	2,595.42	
35	29	23,909.97	12,475.79	11,434.18	1,640.78	
36	30	12,475.79	-	12,475.79	599.10	
37			Subtotal	$138,500.00	$253,748.82	
38			Down Pymt		$22,500.00	
39			Total Cost		$414,748.82	
40						

```
Sheet1 / Sheet2 / Sheet3 /
Ready
Start    Microsoft Excel - Con...                        5:02 PM
```

FIGURE 4-67

Instructions: With a blank worksheet on the screen, perform the following tasks to create the worksheet.

1. Bold the entire worksheet. Enter the worksheet title in cell A1 and change its font to 20-point Franklin Gothic Heavy red (or a similar font style). Enter the worksheet subtitle in cell A2 and change its font to 12-point red Franklin Gothic Medium (or a similar font style). One at a time, merge and center cells A1 and A2 across columns A through E.

(continued)

In the Lab

Confide In Us Loan Analysis and Amortization Schedule *(continued)*

2. Enter the text in the ranges A3:A5 and D3:D5.

3. Enter 161000 (price) in cell B3, 22500 (down payment) in cell B4, 8.75 (interest rate) in cell E3, and 30 (years) in cell E4 (Figure 4-67 on the previous page). Determine the loan amount in cell B5 by using the formula =B3 – B4. Determine the monthly payment in cell E5 by entering the PMT function =PMT(E3 / 12, 12 * E4, – B5)

4. Increase the widths of columns A through E to 15.00. In the range A3:E5, color the background red, the font white, and add a heavy outline to the range.

5. Enter the column titles for the amortization schedule in the range A6:E6. Center the right four column titles. Use the fill handle to generate the series of years in the range A7:A36.

6. Assign the formulas and functions to the cells indicated in Table 4-7.

7. Enter the total titles in the range C37:C39 as shown in Figure 4-67.

8. Copy cell B8 to the range B9:B36. Copy the range C7:E7 to the range C8:E36. Assign the Currency style format to the range B7:E7. Assign the Comma style format to the range B8:E36. Draw the borders shown in Figure 4-67.

9. Add your name, course, laboratory assignment number (Lab 4-3), date, and instructor name in column A beginning in cell A40.

10. Spell check the worksheet. Save the workbook using the file name, Confide In Us Loan Company. Print the worksheet with the loan data and loan information in Figure 4-67. Press CTRL+LEFT QUOTATION MARK and print the formulas version of the worksheet using the Fit to option.

Table 4-7	Cell Assignments
CELL	**FORMULA OR FUNCTION**
B7	=B5
C7	=IF(A7 <= $E$4, PV($E$3 / 12, 12 * ($E$4 – A7), -$E$5),0)
D7	=B7 – C7
E7	=IF(B7 > 0, 12 * $E$5 – D7, 0)
B8	=C7
D37	=SUM(D7:D36)
E37	=SUM(E7:E36)
E38	=B4
E39	=D37 + E37 + E38

11. Insert the clip art graphic shown in the range C3:C5. The clip art file name is famous people.wmf. When the Insert ClipArt window displays, search for the file using its file name. Assign the hyperlink a:\wesavu national bank.htm to the clip art graphic. Display and print the HTML file (Web page). You must have the Data Disk in drive A to display the HTML file.

12. Unlock the ranges B3:B5 and E3:E4. Protect the worksheet. Save the worksheet.

13. Use Excel's goal seeking capabilities to determine the down payment required for the loan data in Figure 4-67 if the monthly payment is set to $800.00. The down payment that results for a monthly payment of $800.00 is $59,309.45. Print the worksheet with the new monthly payment of $800.00. Close the workbook without saving changes.

Cases and Places

The difficulty of these case studies varies:
▶ are the least difficult; ▶▶ are more difficult; and ▶▶▶ are the most difficult.

1 ▶ After visiting several automobile showrooms, Stephanie Rogers has decided she wants to buy a new Honda Prelude. She will pay for the car by making monthly payments over a period of five years. Before she buys the car, Stephanie wants to know her monthly payment and how much she actually will pay for the car with all the interest. Create a worksheet based on the information provided by Stephanie. The cost of the car is $25,500.00; the interest is 10.75% for 5 years. She plans to put $2,500.00 down.

2 ▶ You can calculate the break-even point (number of units you must sell) if you know the fixed expenses, the price per unit, and the expense (cost) per unit. You are employed as a spreadsheet analyst for CD Music Emporium, the leader in CD sales. You have been asked to create a data table that analyzes the break-even point for prices between $5.00 and $10.00 in increments of $0.20. The following formula determines the break-even point:

Break-Even Point = Fixed Expenses / (Price per Unit – Expense per Unit)

Assume Fixed Expenses = $10,000,000; Price per Unit = $5.69; and Expense per Unit = $2.45.

Enter the data and formula into a worksheet and then create the data table. Use the Price per Unit as the input cell and the break-even value as the result. For a unit cost of $8.40, the data table should show a break-even point of 1,680,672.

3 ▶▶ Your aunt Myrna and uncle Frank have decided to save for the down payment on a house, after living for years in a tiny apartment. Frank's buddy, Jeb, who works for the city's Streets and Sanitation department, promises them he can get the pair an annual interest rate of 10% through a special city annuity program. Frank would like you to create a worksheet that determines how much their monthly payment must be so that in four years the value of the account is $25,000. *Hint*: Use the FV function with a monthly savings of $100. Then use the Goal Seek command to determine the monthly payment. Myrna realizes Frank is full of grand schemes that often go awry, so in case Frank's plans change, she has asked you also to compute the monthly payments to accumulate $25,000.00 for years 5 through 10 using the Goal Seek command. Enter the results below the worksheet.

4 ▶▶ Julio Quatorze, owner of Shrub and Trees Landscape Inc., recently purchased a new truck. Julio wants a worksheet that uses a financial function (SLN) to show the truck's straight-line depreciation and a formula to determine the annual rate of depreciation. Straight-line depreciation is based on an asset's initial cost, how long it can be used (called useful life), and the price at which it eventually can be sold (called salvage value). Julio has supplied the following information: Cost = $42,821; Salvage = $12,500; Life = 5 years; and Annual Rate of Depreciation = SLN / Cost.

Julio is not sure how much he will be able to sell the truck for. Create a data table that shows straight-line depreciation and annual rate of depreciation for salvage from $7,000 to $16,000 in $500 increments. Use Help to learn more about the SLN function.

Cases and Places

5 ▶▶ Ukari and Amin's dream for their daughter is that one day she will attend their alma mater, Chelios College. For the next ten years, they plan to make monthly payment deposits to a long-term savings account at a local bank. The account pays 7.25% annual interest, compounded monthly. Create a worksheet for the parents that uses a financial function to show the future value (FV) of their investment and a formula to determine the percentage of the college's tuition saved. Ukari and Amin have supplied the following information: Tuition = $120,000; Rate (per month) = 7.25% / 12; Nper (number of monthly payments) = 10 * 12; Pmt (payment per period) = $300; and percentage of Tuition Saved = FV / Tuition.

Ukari and Amin are not sure how much they will be able to save each month. Create a data table that shows the future value and percentage of tuition saved for monthly payments from $250 to $600, in $50 increments. Insert a clip art file and assign it a hyperlink to the HTML file, WeSavU National Bank.htm, on the Data Disk.

6 ▶▶ Dexter University is offering its faculty a generous retirement package. Professor Michael Holsum has accepted the proposal, but before moving to a warmer climate, he wants to settle his account with the school credit union. Professor Holsum has four years remaining on a five-year car loan, with an interest rate of 9.25% and a monthly payment of $383.00. The credit union is willing to accept the present value (PV) of the loan as a payoff. Develop an amortization schedule that shows how much Professor Holsum must pay at the end of each of the five years. Include the beginning and ending balance, the amount paid on the principal and the interest paid for years two through five. Because he has already paid for the first year, determine only the ending balance (present value) for year one.

7 ▶▶▶ Buying a car not only means finding one you like, but finding one you can afford as well. Many dealerships offer financing plans to prospective buyers. Visit an automobile dealership and pick out your favorite car. Talk to a salesperson about the cost, down payment, amount that must be borrowed, annual loan interest rate, and length of time for which the loan runs. With this information, develop a worksheet to calculate your monthly payment (PMT), total cost, and total interest. Add a data table that shows the effect on the monthly payment for varying interest rates three percentage points on either side of the annual loan interest rate given to you by the salesperson in increments of 0.25%. Also add an amortization schedule similar to the one developed in this project.

Microsoft Excel 2000

P R O J E C T

5

Creating, Sorting, and Querying a Worksheet Database

O B J E C T I V E S

You will have mastered the material in this project when you can:

- Create a worksheet database
- Add computational fields to a database
- Use the VLOOKUP function to look up a value in a table
- Change the range assigned to a Name
- Use a data form to display records, add records, delete records, and change field values in a worksheet database
- Sort a worksheet database on one field or multiple fields
- Display automatic subtotals
- Use a data form to find records that meet comparison criteria
- Filter data to display records that meet comparison criteria
- Use the advanced filtering features to display records that meet comparison criteria
- Apply database functions to generate information about a worksheet database

Security for the Millennium

Be Prepared

From the time you start your first job until the day of your retirement, you will be faced with the age-old concern about your economic security. Corporate America and the world economy continue to change. What was once loyalty to a company, with solid job status and opportunity for advancement, is now the constant threat of downsizing, cutbacks, mergers, and unemployment. The job no longer yields the tenure or relationships it has in the past. Workers fear losing their incomes due to injury or layoffs or company closures. Having sufficient funds for retirement is worrisome, especially when lifetimes may exceed 90 years in the near future. Only 30 percent of Americans, however, are set for retirement at age 55.

The Social Security program was created during the Great Depression to address economic security fears. Today, 95 percent of Americans are protected by the program, and nearly one in five receives Social Security benefits. More than 90 percent of senior citizens receive these funds. In addition, 15 million Americans of all ages receive Social Security disability and survivors benefits as compensation for losing a source of family income when severe injury or death strikes.

Social Security works by using pooled resources, much like an insurance program does. Workers contribute money that is invested in a trust fund. Since the inception of the program, more than $4.5 trillion has been paid into the system, and more than $4.1 trillion has been dispersed. Benefits generally are based on the amount a worker has contributed to the program during his or her career.

The Social Security Administration maintains a database that has a record for every person with a Social Security number. Similar to the SkateJam Sales Representative Database you will create in this Excel project, the SSA database has records that contain fields to store such data as Social Security number, last name, first name, gender, birth date, length of time the worker contributed Social Security funds, wages, date of death, date of disability, and birth date of widow or widower.

The data in these fields can be analyzed in computations, just as you will learn to do in this Excel project. For example, the SSA determines the total number of people who have received or are receiving various benefits and the average amount they receive. Also, the agency uses the data to manage its trust fund by predicting demands for benefits. By sorting records based on birth date, it can determine people who will reach retirement age each year and the amount of benefits they will draw. Using these figures, the SSA realizes that without taking any action, in 2019 the interest and tax revenues generated from the trust funds will be insufficient to meet these retirees' financial demands. If the agency then begins drawing on the trust fund principal, which is expected to grow to $3.3 trillion in 2019, that principal will be exhausted during the next ten years.

Anyone with a Social Security number can call the SSA 800 number to use this database to compute a Personal Earnings and Benefit Estimate Statement that shows Social Security earnings history and estimates how much has been paid in Social Security taxes. It also estimates future benefits and tells how to qualify for them. In addition, the SSA distributes a comparable interactive PC-compatible program, ANYPIA, that allows users to compute these estimates themselves. For details, visit Social Security Online at www.ssa.gov.

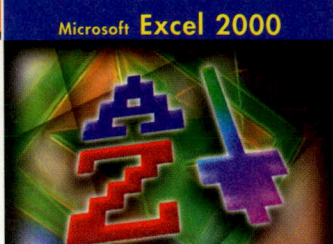

Creating, Sorting, and Querying a Worksheet Database

PROJECT

5

C A S E   P E R S P E C T I V E

SkateJam, Inc. pioneered the sport of in-line skating in the late 1970s as an off-season training tool for hockey players. The sport quickly caught on with general fitness enthusiasts and the population in general. Today, there are nearly 40 million in-line skaters.

Rosa Blade, who is the national sales manager for SkateJam, oversees one dozen sales representatives spread equally among six states: Arizona, California, Florida, New York, Pennsylvania, and Texas.

Rosa plans to use Excel 2000 to create, maintain, and query a worksheet database containing data about the SkateJam sales representatives. She has learned through the Excel Help system that a database can hold both data and formulas. Furthermore, she learned that Excel 2000 has a lookup function that can be used to grade the performance of sales reps based on the percentage of quota met.

Rosa has assigned you the challenge of creating the database. Besides creating the database, she wants you to demonstrate how to sort and query the database using Excel 2000's database capabilities.

Introduction

A **worksheet database**, also called a **database** or **list**, is an organized collection of data. For example, a list of club members, a list of students attending a college, an instructor's grade book, and a list of company sales representatives are databases. In these cases, the data related to a person is called a **record**, and the data items that make up a record are called **fields**. In a database of sales representatives, each one would have a separate record; some of the fields in the records might be name, hire date, age, and gender. A database record also can include formulas and functions. A field in a database that contains formulas or functions is called a **computational field**. A computational field displays results based on other fields in the database.

A worksheet's row-and-column structure can be used to organize and store a database (Figure 5-1). Each row of a worksheet can be used to store a record and each column to store a field. Additionally, a row of column titles at the top of the worksheet can be used as **field names** that identify each field.

Once you enter a database into a worksheet, you can use Excel to:

- Add and delete records
- Change the values of fields in records
- Sort the records so they display in a different order
- Determine subtotals for numeric fields
- Display records that meet comparison criteria
- Analyze data using database functions

This project illustrates all six of these database capabilities.

Gender is one of twelve
fields in the SkateJam
Sales Representative
Database

one field
displays in
each column

field names
(range A8:L8)

database

one record
displays in
each row

value in field
determined
from formula

value in field
determined
from function

FIGURE 5-1

Project Five — SkateJam Sales Representative Database

From your meeting with Rosa Blade, you have determined the following needs, source of data, and calculations.

Needs: Create a sales representative database (Figure 5-1). The field names, columns, types of data, and column widths are described in Table 5-1 on the next page. Because Rosa will use the database online as she travels among the offices, it is important that it be readable and that the database is visible on the screen. Therefore, some of the column widths listed in Table 5-1 on the next page are determined from the field names and not the maximum length of the data. The last two fields (located in columns K and L) use a formula and function based on data within each sales representative record.

Worksheet Databases

Although Excel is not a true database management system such as Access, FoxPro, or Oracle, it does give you many of the same capabilities as these dedicated systems. For example, in Excel you can create a database; add, change, and delete data in the database; sort data in the database; query the database; and create forms and reports.

Table 5-1   Database Column Information

COLUMN TITLES (FIELD NAMES)	COLUMN	TYPE OF DATA	COLUMN WIDTH
Lname	A	Text	9.00
Fname	B	Text	7.00
Gender	C	Text	7.00
Age	D	Numeric	5.00
Educ	E	Text	5.00
Hire Date	F	Date	10.00
St	G	Text	5.00
Sales Area	H	Text	10.00
Quota	I	Numeric	11.00
YTD Sales	J	Numeric	11.00
% of Quota	K	YTD Sales / Quota	11.00
Grade	L	VLOOKUP Function	7.00

Once the database is entered into the worksheet, it will be sorted and manipulated to illustrate how quickly information can be generated from a database.

Source of Data: Rosa will supply the sales representative data required for the database.

Calculations: The last two fields in the database in columns K and L are determined as follows:

1. % of Quota in column K = YTD Sales / Quota
2. Grade in column L = VLOOKUP function

The VLOOKUP function will be used to display the grades in column L based on the table in columns N and O in Figure 5-2. The DAVERAGE function will be used to find the average age of males and females in the database (range Q5:T6 in Figure 5-2). Finally, the DCOUNT function will be used to count the number of sales representatives who have a grade of A (range Q7:T7 in Figure 5-2). These two functions require that you set set up a criteria area (range Q1:S3) to tell Excel what items to average and count.

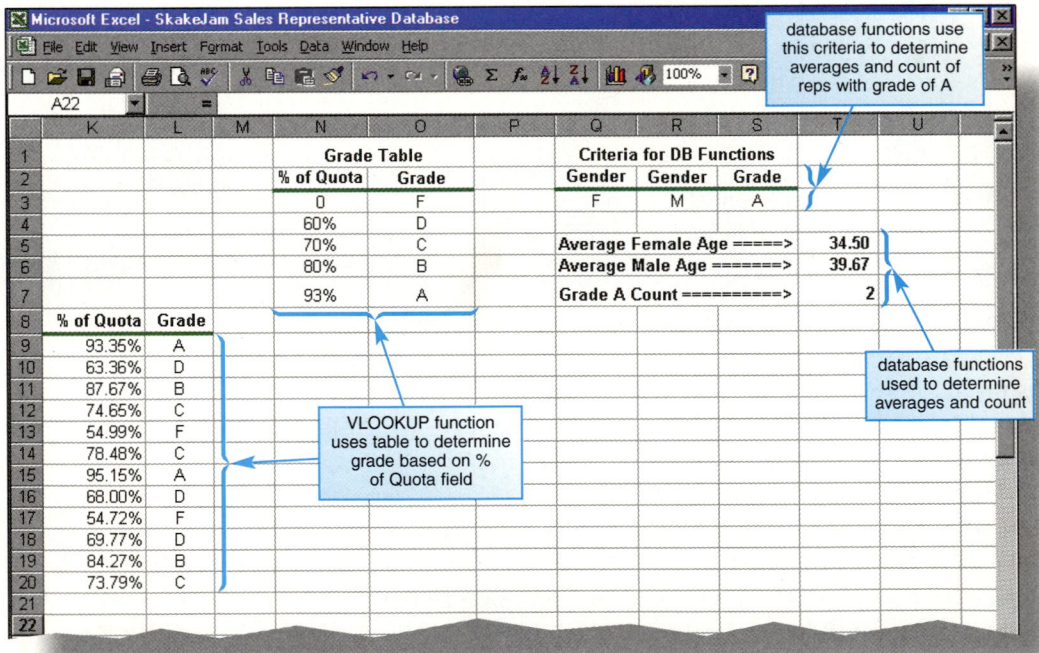

FIGURE 5-2

Starting Excel and Resetting the Toolbars and Menus

Perform the following steps to start Excel. Steps 4 through 6 reset the toolbars and menus to their installation settings. For additional information on resetting the toolbars and menus, see Appendix C.

TO START EXCEL AND RESET THE TOOLBARS AND MENUS

1 Click the Start button on the taskbar.

2 Click New Office Document. If necessary, click the General tab in the New Office Document dialog box.

3 Double-click the Blank Workbook icon.

4 When the blank worksheet displays, click View on the menu bar, point to Toolbars, and then click Customize on the Toolbars submenu.

5 When the Customize dialog box displays, click the Options tab, make sure the top three check boxes have check marks, click the Reset my usage data button, and then click the Yes button.

6 Click the Toolbars tab. Click Standard, click the Reset button, and then click the OK button. Click Formatting, click the Reset button, and then click the OK button. Click the Close button.

The Standard and Formatting toolbars display as shown in Figure 5-1 on page E 5.5.

Creating a Database

The three steps to creating a database in Excel are:

1. Set up the database
2. Assign a name to the range containing the database
3. Enter the data into the database

These steps are similar to what you would do with a traditional database package, such as Access 2000. The following pages illustrate these three steps for creating the SkateJam Sales Representative database.

Setting Up a Database

Setting up the database involves entering field names in a row in the worksheet and changing the column widths so the data will fit in the columns. Follow these steps to change the column widths to those specified in Table 5-1, to change the height of row 7 to 18 points and row 8 to 15 points to emphasize these rows, and to enter and format the database title and column titles (field names).

Although Excel does not require a database title to be entered, it is a good practice to include one on the worksheet to show where the database begins. With Excel, you usually enter the database several rows below the top. These blank rows will be used later to query the database. The following steps also change the name of Sheet1 to Sales Rep Database and save the workbook using the file name SkateJam Sales Representative Database.

TO SET UP A DATABASE

1 Use the mouse to change the column widths as follows: A = 9.00, B = 7.00, C = 7.00, D = 5.00, E = 5.00, F = 10.00, G = 5.00, H = 10.00, I = 11.00, J = 11.00, K = 11.00, and L = 7.00.

2 Click cell A7 and then enter SkateJam Sales Representative Database as the worksheet database title.

More About

Location of the Database

Always leave several rows empty above the database on the worksheet to set up a criteria area for querying the database. Some experienced Excel users also leave several columns to the left empty, beginning with column A, for additional worksheet activities. A range of blank rows or columns on the side of a database is called a moat of cells.

3 Double-click the move handle on the Formatting toolbar so it displays in its entirety. With cell A7 active, click the Font Size arrow on the Formatting toolbar and then click 14 in the Font list. Click the Bold button on the Formatting toolbar. Click the Font Color arrow on the Formatting toolbar and then click Green (column 4, row 2) on the color palette. Change the height of row 7 to 18.00.

4 Enter the column titles in row 8 as shown in Figure 5-3. Change the height of row 8 to 15.00.

5 Select the range A8:J8. Click the Bold button on the Formatting toolbar. Right-click the selected range and then click Format Cells on the shortcut menu. Click the Border tab. Click the Color box arrow in the Line area and then click Green (column 4, row 2) on the color palette. Click the heavy border in the Style box (column 2, row 6). Click the Underline button on the left side of the Border area. Click the OK button.

6 Click column heading C to select the entire column. Hold down the CTRL key and click column headings D, E, G, and L. Click the Center button on the Formatting toolbar so that all future entries in columns C, D, E, G, and L will be centered.

7 Right-click column heading F. Click Format Cells on the shortcut menu. When the Format cells dialog box displays, click the Number tab, click Date in the Category list box, scroll down in the Type box box and then click 3/14/1998 to display the future date entries with four-digit years. Click the OK button.

8 Click column heading I. Drag through column heading J to select both columns. Click the Comma Style button on the Formatting toolbar. Click the Decrease Decimal button on the Formatting toolbar twice so that all future numeric entries in columns I and J will display using the Comma style with zero decimal places. Click cell A10 to deselect columns I and J.

9 Double-click the Sheet1 tab at the bottom of the screen. Type `Sales Rep Database` as the sheet name. Press the ENTER key.

10 Click the Save button on the Standard toolbar. When the Save As dialog box displays, type `SkateJam Sales Representative Database` in the File name text box. Click 3½ Floppy (A:) in the Save in box and then click the Save button in the Save As dialog box.

More About

Toolbars

Are you tired of double-clicking the move handle to display a toolbar in its entirety? If so, you can display the Standard toolbar and Formatting toolbar on separate rows, one below the other. To display both toolbars on separate rows, right-click a toolbar, click Customize on the shortcut menu, click the Options tab in the Customize dialog box, click Standard and Formatting toolbars share one row to deselect it, and click the Close button.

The worksheet displays as shown in Figure 5-3.

FIGURE 5-3

Compare the column titles in row 8 in Figure 5-1 on page E 5.5 with Figure 5-3. In Figure 5-3, the two computational fields, % of Quota and Grade, are not included in columns K and L. These two fields will be added after the data is entered for the twelve sales representatives. In Excel, computational fields that depend on data in the database usually are entered after the data has been entered.

Naming a Database

Although Excel usually can identify a **database range** when you invoke a database-type command, assigning the name Database to the range eliminates any confusion when commands are entered to manipulate the database. Thus, as you create the SkateJam Sales Representative database shown in Figure 5-1, you first assign the range A8:J9 to the name Database by selecting the range and typing Database in the Name box on the left side of the formula bar. The range assigned to the name Database includes the column titles (row 8) and one blank row (row 9) below the column titles. The blank row is for expansion of the database. As records are added using a data form, Excel automatically expands the named range Database to include the last record. Later, when the database is expanded to include the two computational fields, % of Quota and Grade, the name Database will be redefined to encompass the new fields in columns K and L.

TO NAME THE DATABASE

1 Select the range A8:J9. Click the Name box in the formula bar and then type Database as the name for the selected range.

2 Press the ENTER key.

The worksheet displays as shown in Figure 5-4.

Using the Name box in the formula bar to name a range is a useful tool for many worksheet tasks. For example, if you name a cell or range of cells that you select often, you then can select the cell or range of cells by clicking the name in the Name box list.

FIGURE 5-4

Entering Records into the Database Using a Data Form

The next step is to use a data form to enter the sales representative records. A **data form** is an Excel dialog box that lists the field names in the database and provides corresponding boxes in which you enter the field values. The steps on the next page add the sales representative records to the database as shown in Figure 5-1. As indicated earlier, the computational fields in columns K and L will be added after the data is in the database.

Steps **To Enter Records into a Database Using a Data Form**

1 Click cell A9 to deselect the range A8:J9. Click Data on the menu bar and then point to Form.

The Data menu displays (Figure 5-5).

FIGURE 5-5

2 Click Form.

Excel displays the data form (Figure 5-6) with the sheet name Sales Rep Database on the title bar. The data form automatically includes the field names and corresponding text boxes for entering the field values. Excel selects the field names in the range A8:J8 because they are at the top of the range named Database.

FIGURE 5-6

3 Enter the first sales representative record into the data form as shown in Figure 5-7. Use the mouse or the TAB key to move the insertion point down to the next box. If you make a mistake, use the mouse or the SHIFT+TAB keys to move the insertion point to the previous text box in the data form to edit the entry. Point to the New button.

The first record displays in the data form (Figure 5-7).

FIGURE 5-7

4 Click the New button. Type the second sales representative record into the data form as shown in Figure 5-8. Point to the New button.

Excel adds the first sales representative record to row 9 in the database range on the worksheet. The second record displays in the data form (Figure 5-8).

FIGURE 5-8

5 **Click the New button to enter the second sales representative record. Use the data form to enter the next nine sales representative records in rows 11 through 19, as shown in Figure 5-1 on page E 5.5. Type the last sales representative record into the data form as shown in Figure 5-9. Point to the Close button.**

Excel enters the sales representative records into the database range as shown in Figure 5-9. The last record displays in the data form.

FIGURE 5-9

6 **Click the Close button to complete the record entry. Click the Save button on the Standard toolbar to save the workbook using the file name SkateJam Sales Representative Database.**

The data form closes and Excel enters the last sales representative record in row 20 of the database. The SkateJam Sales Representative Database displays as shown in Figure 5-10.

FIGURE 5-10

You also could create the database by entering the records in columns and rows as you would enter data into any worksheet and then assign the name Database to the range (A8:J20). The data form was illustrated here because it is considered to be a more accurate and reliable method of data entry, which automatically extends the range of the name Database to include any new records.

Moving from Field to Field in a Data Form

As described earlier in Step 3 in the previous section on page E 5.11, you can move from field to field in a data form using the TAB key, or you can hold down the ALT key and press the key that corresponds to the underlined letter in the name of the field to which you want to move. An underlined letter in a field name is called an **access key**. Thus, to select the field titled Fname in Figure 5-9, you would hold down the ALT key and press the M key (ALT+M), because M is the access key for the field name Fname.

Adding Computational Fields to the Database

The next step is to add the computational fields % of Quota in column K and Grade in column L. Then the name Database must be changed from the range A8:J20 to A8:L20 so it includes the two new fields.

Adding New Field Names and Determining the % of Quota

The first step in adding the two new fields is to enter and format the two field names in cells K8 and L8, and then enter the first % of Quota formula in cell K9. The formula for the % of Quota in cell K9 is YTD Sales / Quota or =J9 / I9.

More About

Big Brother

Excel is always watching what you are doing. If you enter the data into the database as you entered worksheets in past projects, you will notice Excel entering data automatically for you, based on the data entered into the column. For example, in the St column in Figure 5-11, if you type the letter P in cell G21, Excel will enter PA into the cell. You also can right-click an empty cell under a list of items in a column and click the Pick From List command. Excel will display a list of items in the column from which you can pick to assign to cell G21.

 To Enter New Field Names and the % of Quota Formula

1 Select cell K8. **Enter** % of Quota **as the new field name. Select cell L8. Enter** Grade **as the new field name. Double-click the move handle on the Standard toolbar to display it in its entirety. Click cell J8. Click the Format Painter button on the Standard toolbar. Drag through cells K8:L8. Select cell K9. Enter** =J9 / I9 **as the formula.**

The new field names display in cells K8 and L8, and the result of the % of Quota formula displays in cell K9 (Figure 5-11).

FIGURE 5-11

2 Double-click the move handle on the Formatting toolbar to display it in its entirety. With cell K9 selected, click the Percent Style button on the Formatting toolbar. Click the Increase Decimal button on the Formatting toolbar twice.

The % of Quota in cell K9 displays using the Percent style format with two decimal places (Figure 5-12).

3 With cell K9 selected, drag the fill handle down through cell K20.

The % of Quota displays for each sales representative (Figure 5-13).

FIGURE 5-12

FIGURE 5-13

The entries in the % of Quota column give the user an immediate evaluation of how well each sales representative's YTD Sales are in relation to their annual quota. Many people, however, dislike numbers as an evaluation tool. Most prefer simple letter grades, which when used properly can group the sales representatives in the same way an instructor groups students by letter grades. Excel has functions that allow you to assign letter grades based on a table as explained in the next section.

Using Excel's VLOOKUP Function to Determine Letter Grades

Excel has two lookup functions that are useful for looking up values in tables, such as tax tables, discount tables, parts tables, and grade scale tables. Both functions look up a value in a table and return a corresponding value from the table to the cell assigned the function. The **HLOOKUP function** is used when the table direction is horizontal or across the worksheet. The **VLOOKUP function** is used when a table direction is vertical or down the worksheet. The VLOOKUP function is by far the most often used, because most tables are vertical as is the table in this project.

The grading scale in this project (Table 5-2) is similar to one that your instructor uses to determine your letter grade. In Table 5-2, any score greater than or equal to 93% equates to a letter grade of A. Scores of 80 and less than 93 are assigned a letter grade of B, and so on.

The VLOOKUP function requires that the table only indicate the lowest score for a letter grade. Furthermore, the table entries must be in sequence from lowest score to highest scores. Thus, the entries in Table 5-2 must be resequenced for use with the VLOOKUP function so it appears as in Table 5-3.

The general form of the VLOOKUP function is:

=VLOOKUP(search argument, table range, column number)

The VLOOKUP function searches the leftmost column of a table (called the **table arguments**). In Table 5-3, the table arguments are the percents. The VLOOKUP function uses the % of Quota value (called the **search argument**) in the record of a sales representative to search the leftmost column for a particular value and then returns the corresponding value from the specified column (called the **table values**). In this example, the table values are the grades in the second or rightmost column.

For the VLOOKUP function to work correctly, the table arguments must be in ascending sequence, because the VLOOKUP function will return a table value based on the search argument being less than or equal to the table arguments. Thus, if the % of Quota value is 74.65% (fourth record in database), then the VLOOKUP function returns a grade of C because 74.65% is greater than or equal to 70% and less than 80%.

The steps on the next page show how to enter the table elements in Table 5-3 onto the worksheet and use the VLOOKUP function to determine the letter grade for each sales representative based on his or her % of Quota value.

Table 5-2 Typical Grade Table	
% OF QUOTA	GRADE
>=93%	A
80% to < 93%	B
70% to < 80%	C
60% to < 70%	D
0 to < 60%	F

Table 5-3 Typical Grade Table Modified for VLOOKUP Function	
% OF QUOTA	GRADE
0	F
60%	D
70%	C
80%	B
93%	A

To Create a Lookup Table and Use the VLOOKUP Function to Determine Letter Grades

1 Click cell N1 and then enter Grade Table as the table title. Click the Bold button on the Formatting toolbar. Drag through cell O1 and then click the Merge and Center button on the Formatting toolbar. Click cell N2. Enter the column titles and table entries in Table 5-3 on page E 5.15 in the range N2:O7. Select columns N and O and increase their width to 10.00. Click cell L8. Click the Format Painter button on the Standard toolbar. Drag through the range N2:O2. Click cell L9 to deselect the range N2:O2.

The table displays as shown in Figure 5-14.

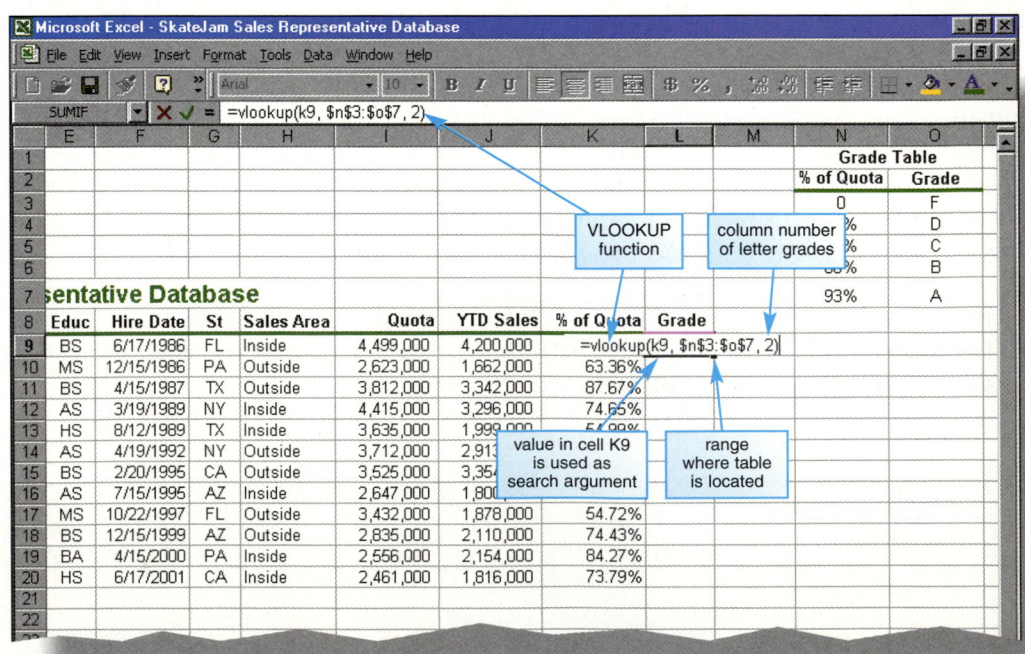

FIGURE 5-14

2 Type =vlookup (k9, n3:o7, 2) in cell L9.

The VLOOKUP function displays in the cell and in the formula bar (Figure 5-15). In this case, cell K9 is the search argument; n3:o7 is the table range; and 2 is the column number in the table range.

FIGURE 5-15

3   **Press the ENTER key.**

The VLOOKUP function returns to cell L9 a grade of A for a % of Quota value in cell K9 of 93.35% (Figure 5-16).

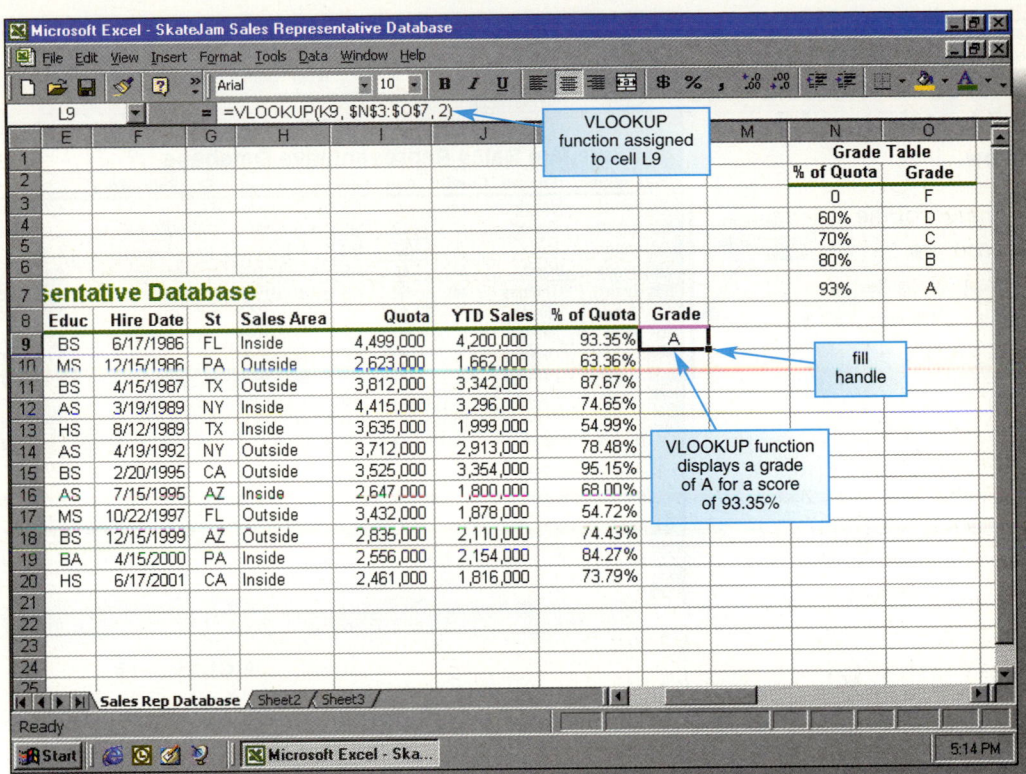

FIGURE 5-16

4   **With cell L9 selected, drag the fill handle through cell L20 to copy the function to the range L10:L20.**

The VLOOKUP function returns the grades shown in column L from the table of grades in columns N and O for the corresponding % of Quota values in column K (Figure 5-17).

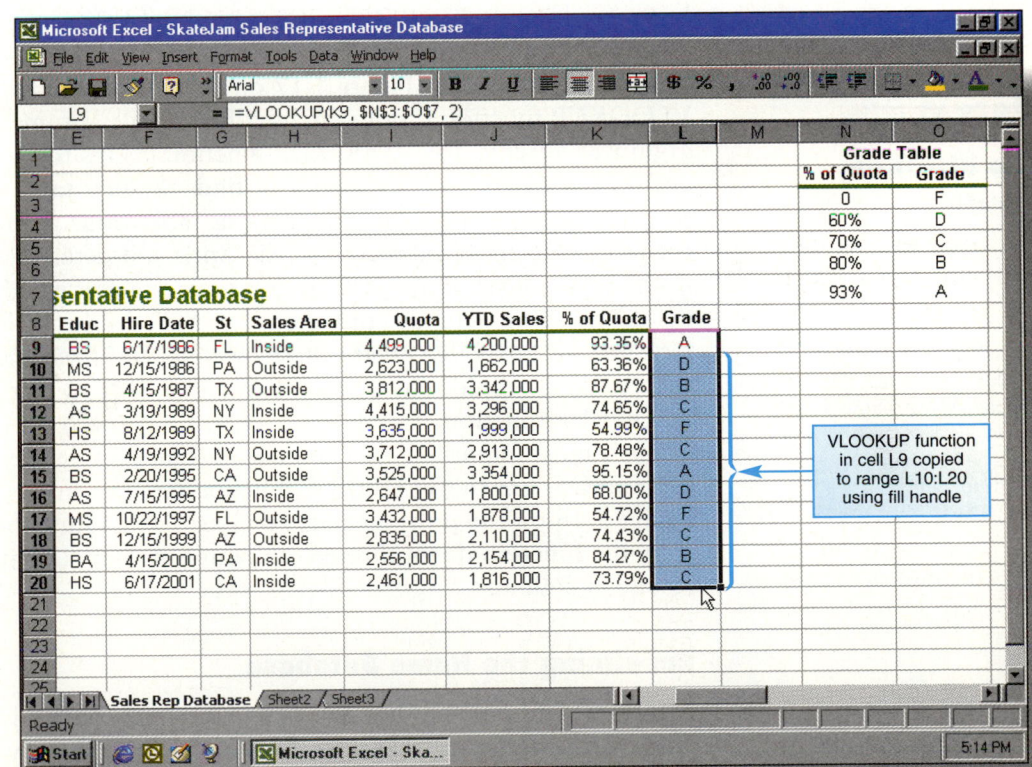

FIGURE 5-17

5 Select cell A22 to deselect the range L9:L20. Scroll down until row 7 is at the top of the window.

The entries for the database are complete (Figure 5-18).

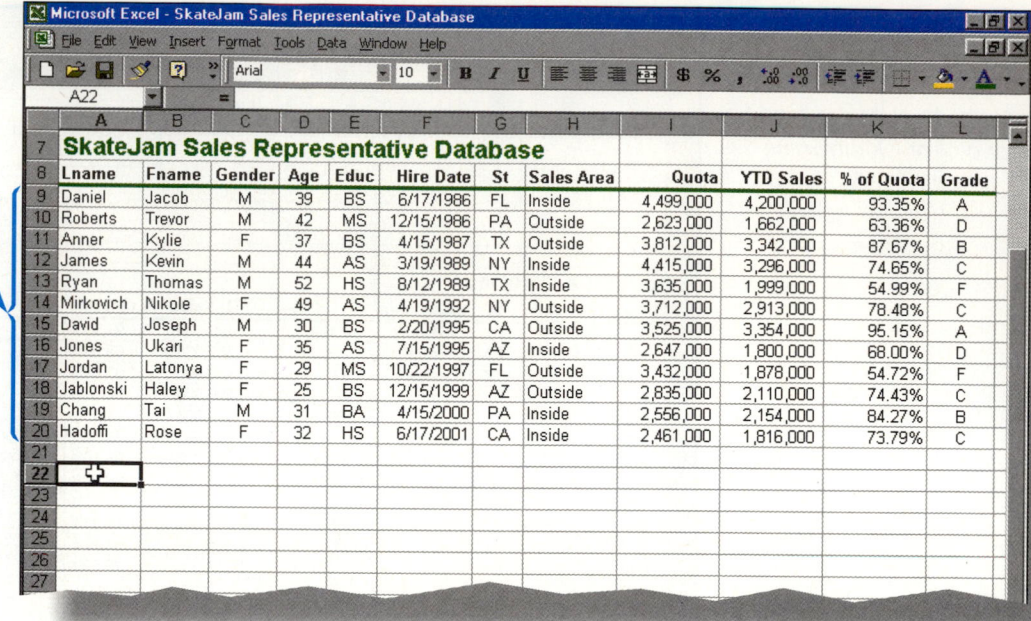

FIGURE 5-18

As shown in Figure 5-18, any % of Quota value below 60 returns a grade of F. Thus, the fifth record (Thomas Ryan) receives a grade of F because his % of Quota value is 54.98%. A percent of 60 is required to move up to the next letter grade. The last record (Rose Hadoffi) receives a grade of C because her % of Quota value is 73.79%, which is equal to or greater than 70% and less than 80%.

From column L in Figure 5-17 on the previous page, you can see that the VLOOKUP function is not searching for a table argument that matches the search argument exactly. The VLOOKUP function begins the search at the top of the table and works downward. As soon as it finds the first table argument greater than the search argument, it returns the previous table value. For example, when it searches the table with the third record (Kylie Anner), it determines the score is less than 93% in the first column in the table and returns the grade of B from the second column in the table, which actually corresponds to 80% in the table. The letter grade of F is returned for any value greater than or equal to 0 (zero) and less than 60. A score less than 0 (zero) would return an error message (#N/A) to the cell assigned the VLOOKUP function.

It is most important that you use absolute cell references for the table range ($N$3:$O$7) in the VLOOKUP function (see the entry in the formula bar shown in Figure 5-16 on the previous page) or Excel will adjust the cell references when you copy the function down through column L in Step 4. This will cause unexpected results in column L.

Redefining the Name Database

The final step in adding the two computational fields to the database is to redefine the name Database. Recall that it was originally defined as the range A8:J9 and it expanded automatically to the range A8:J20 by adding records through the use of the data form. To tie the two new fields to the database, the name Database must be redefined as the range A8:L20. The following steps show how to redefine the range assigned to a name.

The VLOOKUP Function

A score that is outside the range of the table causes the VLOOKUP function to return an error message (#N/A) to the cell. For example, any % of Quota score less than zero in column K of Figure 5-18 would result in the error message being assigned to the corresponding cell.

Steps ## To Redefine the Name Database

1 **Click Insert on the menu bar. Point to Name and then point to Define on the Name submenu.**

The Insert menu and Name submenu display (Figure 5-19).

FIGURE 5-19

2 **Click Define. When the Define Name dialog box displays, click Database in the Names in workbook list.**

The Define Name dialog box displays with the name Database selected (Figure 5-20). The Refers to box at the bottom of the dialog box indicates the range assigned to the name Database.

FIGURE 5-20

3 **Drag through the letter J in the range in the Refers to box.**

Excel displays a marquee around the original range assigned to the name Database (Figure 5-21).

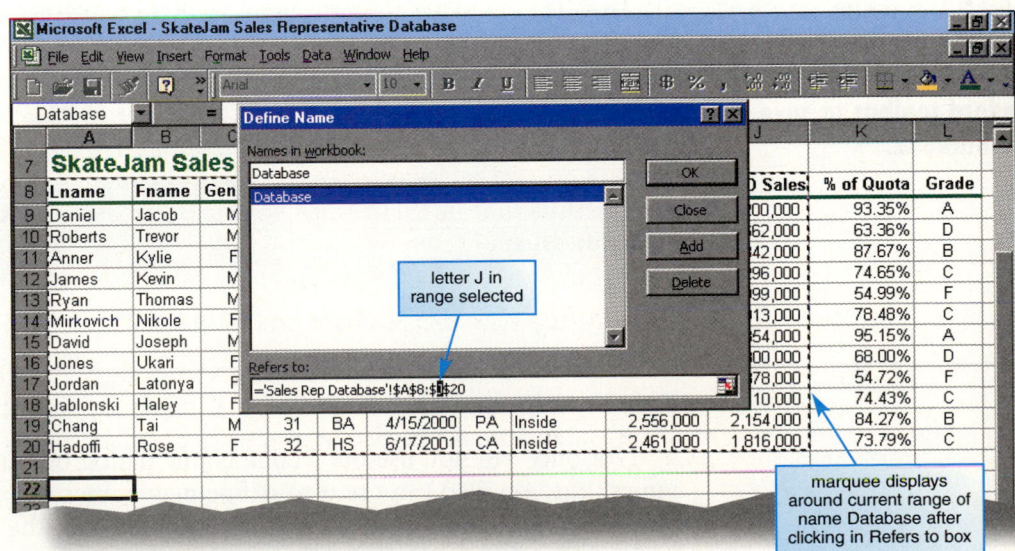

FIGURE 5-21

4 Type the letter L to replace the letter J in the Refers to box.

The new range in the Refers to box encompasses the two new fields in column K and L (Figure 5-22).

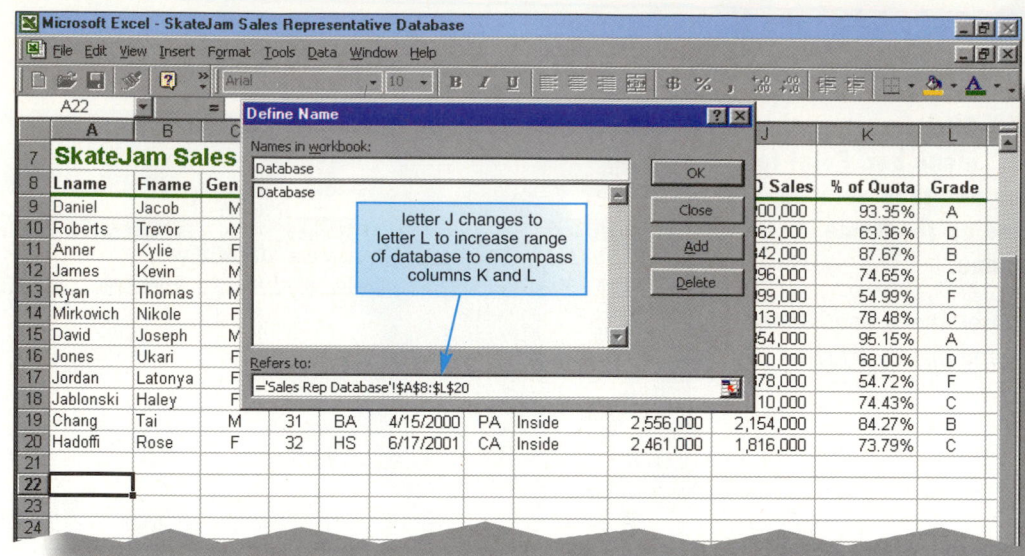

FIGURE 5-22

5 Click the OK button. Click the Name box arrow on the left side of the formula bar and then click the name Database.

Excel highlights the new range (A8:L20) assigned to the name Database (Figure 5-23).

6 Select cell A21 to deselect the range A8:L20. Click the Save button on the Standard toolbar to save the workbook.

FIGURE 5-23

Not only can you use the Define Name dialog box in Figure 5-22 to redefine names, but you also can use it to define new names through the use of the **Add button,** and you can delete names through the use of the **Delete button.** As shown in Figure 5-23, names are useful in a workbook to select ranges quickly for purposes of copying, printing, and formatting.

Guidelines to Follow When Creating a Database

When you create a database in Excel, you should follow some basic guidelines, as listed in Table 5-4.

Table 5-4   Guidelines for Creating a Database
DATABASE SIZE AND WORKBOOK LOCATION
1. Do not enter more than one database per worksheet.
2. Maintain at least one blank row between a database and other worksheet entries.
3. Do not store other worksheet entries in the same rows as your database.
4. Define the name Database as the database range.
5. A database can have a maximum of 256 fields and 65,536 records on a worksheet.
COLUMN TITLES (FIELD NAMES)
1. Place column titles (field names) in the first row of the database.
2. Do not use blank rows or rows with dashes to separate the column titles (field names) from the data.
3. Apply a different format to the column titles and the data. For example, bold the column titles and display the data below the column titles using a regular style.
4. Column titles (field names) can be up to 32,767 characters in length. The column titles should be meaningful.
CONTENTS OF DATABASE
1. Each column should have similar data. For example, employee hire date should be in the same column for all employees.
2. Format the data to improve readability, but do not vary the format of the data in a column.

Using a Data Form to View Records and Change Data

At any time while the worksheet is active, you can use the **Form command** on the Data menu to display records, add new records, delete records, and change the data in records. When a data form is opened initially, Excel displays the first record in the database. To display the ninth record as shown in Figure 5-24, click the Find Next button until the ninth record displays. Each time you click the **Find Next button**, Excel advances to the next record in the database. If necessary, you can use the **Find Prev button** to go back to a previous record. You also can use the vertical scroll bar in the middle of the data form to move between records.

FIGURE 5-24

To change data in a record, you first display it on a data form. Next, you select the fields to change. Finally, you use the DOWN ARROW key or the ENTER key to confirm or enter the field changes. If you change field values on a data form and then select the Find Next button to move to the next record without entering the field changes, these changes will not be made.

To add a new record, click the **New button** on the data form. Excel automatically adds the new record to the bottom of the database and increases the range assigned to the name Database. To delete a record, you first display it on a data form and then click the **Delete button**. Excel automatically moves all records below the deleted record up one row and appropriately redefines the range of the name Database.

Printing a Database

To print the database, follow the same procedures you followed in earlier projects. If the worksheet includes data that is not part of the database you want to print, then follow these steps to print only the database.

TO PRINT A DATABASE

1 Click File on the menu bar and then click Page Setup.

2 Click the Sheet tab in the Page Setup dialog box. Type `Database` in the Print Area text box.

3 Click the OK button.

4 Ready the printer and then click the Print button on the Standard toolbar.

Later, if you want to print the entire worksheet, delete the database range in the Print area text box in the Sheet tab of the Page Setup dialog box.

Sorting a Database

The data in a database is easier to work with and more meaningful if the records are arranged sequentially based on one or more fields. Arranging records in a specific sequence is called **sorting**. Data is in **ascending sequence** if it is in order from lowest to highest, earliest to most recent, or alphabetically from A to Z. For example, the records in the SkateJam Sales Representative Database were entered in order from the earliest hire date to the most recent hire date. Thus, the database shown in Figure 5-25 is sorted in ascending sequence by hire date. Data is in **descending sequence** if it is sorted from highest to lowest, most recent to earliest, or alphabetically from Z to A.

You can sort data by clicking the **Sort Ascending button** or **Sort Descending button** on the Standard toolbar or by clicking the **Sort command** on the Data menu. If you are sorting on a single field (column), use one of the Sort buttons on the Standard toolbar. If you are sorting on multiple fields, use the Sort command on the Data menu. If you use a button to sort, make sure you select a cell in the field on which to sort before you click the button. The field or fields you select to sort the records are called **sort keys**. The first sort example reorders the records by last name in ascending sequence.

Sorting the Database in Ascending Sequence by Last Name

Follow these steps to sort the records in ascending sequence by last name.

More About

Printing

An alternative to using the Sheet tab to print the database is to select the desired range and click Selection in the Print What area in the Print dialog box. You can also select the database and point to Print Area on the File menu. Next, click Set Print Area on the Print Area submenu. With the latter, the print area is set permanently until you click the Clear Print Area command on the Print Area submenu.

More About

Sorting

If a column you are sorting on contains numbers, text, and blanks, then Excel uses the following order of priority: numbers from smallest to largest positive; text; and blanks.

Steps **To Sort a Database in Ascending Sequence by Last Name**

1 Double-click the move handle on the Standard toolbar to display it in its entirety. Click cell A9 and then point to the Sort Ascending button on the Standard toolbar (Figure 5-25).

FIGURE 5-25

2 Click the Sort Ascending button.

Excel sorts the sales representative database in ascending sequence by last name (Figure 5-26).

FIGURE 5-26

Sorting a Database in Descending Sequence by Last Name

Follow the steps on the next page to sort the records in descending sequence by last name.

More About

Manipulating the Database

After naming the database range Database, you still can select a subset of the database, such as the last ten records, before completing an activity such as a sort operation. Excel will manipulate only the data in the selected range.

TO SORT A DATABASE IN DESCENDING SEQUENCE BY LAST NAME

1 If necessary, click cell A9 to make it active.

2 Click the Sort Descending button on the Standard toolbar.

Excel sorts the sales representative database in descending sequence by last name (Figure 5-27).

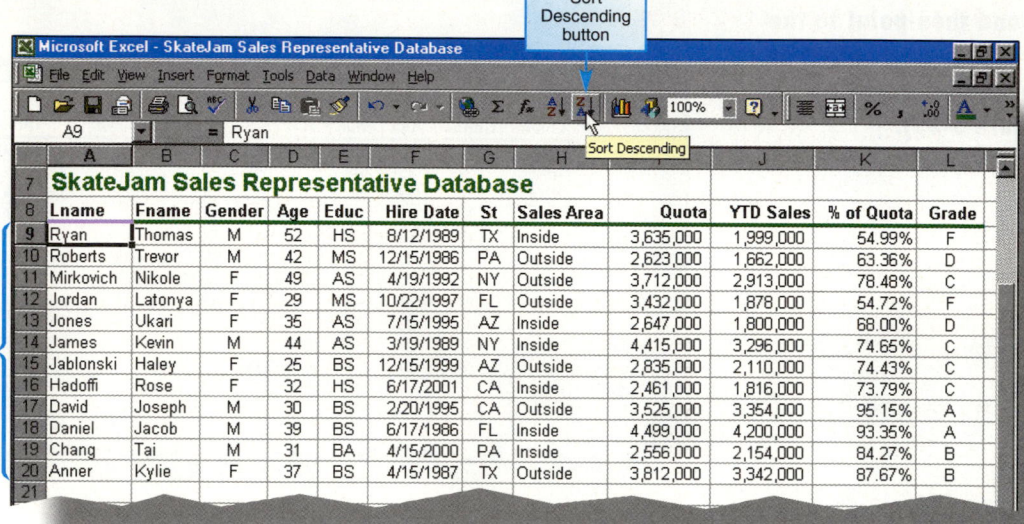

FIGURE 5-27

More About

Sorting

Some Excel users use the fill handle to create a series in an additional field in the database that is used only to reorder the records into their original sequence.

Returning a Database to Its Original Order

When you design a database, it is good practice to include a field that allows you to return the database to its original order. In the case of the SkateJam Sales Representative database, the records were entered in sequence by hire date. Follow these steps to return the records back to their original order in ascending sequence by hire date.

TO RETURN A DATABASE TO ITS ORIGINAL ORDER

1 Click cell F9.

2 Click the Sort Ascending button on the Standard toolbar.

Excel sorts the sales representative database in ascending sequence by hire date. The database displays in its original order (Figure 5-28).

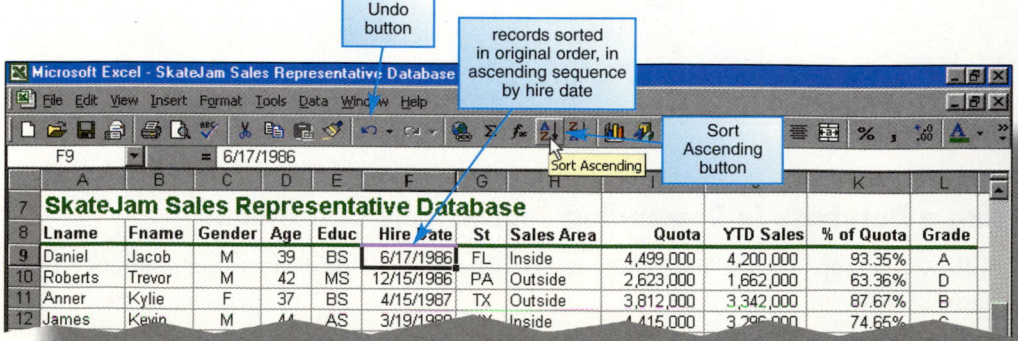

FIGURE 5-28

You also can undo a sort operation by performing one of the following actions:

1. Click the Undo button on the Standard toolbar.
2. Click the Undo Sort command on the Edit menu.

If you have sorted the database more than once, you can click the Undo button multiple times to undo the previous sorts.

Sorting a Database on Multiple Fields

Excel allows you to sort on a maximum of three fields in a single sort operation. For instance, the sort example that follows uses the Sort command on the Data menu to sort the SkateJam Sales Representative database by quota (column I) within education (column E) within gender (column C). The Gender and Educ fields will be sorted in ascending sequence; the Quota field will be sorted in descending sequence.

The phrase, sort by quota within education within gender, means that the records first are arranged in ascending sequence by gender code. Within gender, the records are arranged in ascending sequence by education code. Within education, the records are arranged in descending sequence by the quota.

In this case, gender is the **major sort key** (Sort by field), education is the **intermediate sort key** (first Then by field), and quota is the **minor sort key** (second Then by field).

To Sort a Database on Multiple Fields

1 **With a cell in the database active, click Data on the menu bar and then point to Sort.**

The Data menu displays (Figure 5-29).

FIGURE 5-29

2 **Click Sort. When the Sort dialog box displays, click the Sort by box arrow and then point to Gender in the list.**

Excel selects the database and the Sort dialog box displays. The Sort by list includes the field names in the database (Figure 5-30).

FIGURE 5-30

3 **Click Gender. Click the first Then by box arrow and then click Educ. Click the second Then by box arrow and then click Quota. Click Descending in the second Then by area. Point to the OK button.**

The Sort dialog box displays (Figure 5-31). The database will be sorted by quota within education within gender.

FIGURE 5-31

4 **Click the OK button. Excel sorts the SkateJam Sales Representative database by quota within education within gender as shown in Figure 5-32.**

records sorted in ascending sequence by gender

within each gender, records sorted in ascending sequence by education

within each education level, records sorted in descending sequence by quota

FIGURE 5-32

As shown in Figure 5-32, Excel sorts the records in ascending sequence by the gender codes (F or M) in column C. Within each gender code, the records are in ascending sequence by the education codes (AS, BA, BS, HS, and MS) in column E. Finally, within the education codes, the records are sorted in descending sequence by the quotas in column I. Remember, if you make a mistake in a sort operation, you can return the records to their original order by clicking the Undo button on the Standard toolbar.

Because Excel sorts the database using the current order of the records, the previous example could have been completed by sorting on one field at a time using the Sort buttons on the Standard toolbar, beginning with the minor sort key.

Sorting a Database on More than Three Fields

To sort on more than three fields, you must sort the database two or more times. The most recent sort takes precedence. Hence, if you plan to sort on four fields, you sort on the three least important keys first and then sort on the major key. For example, if you want to sort on last name (Lname) within job category (Sales Area) within state (St) within gender (Gender), you first sort on Lname (second Then by column) within Sales Area (first Then by column) within St (Sort by column). After the first sort operation is complete, you sort on the Gender field by clicking one of the cells in the Gender column and then clicking the Sort Ascending button or Sort Descending button on the Standard toolbar.

Displaying Automatic Subtotals in a Database

Displaying **automatic subtotals** is a powerful tool for summarizing data in a database. Excel requires that you sort the database only on the field on which you want subtotals to be based, and then use the **Subtotals command** on the Data menu. When the Subtotal dialog box displays, you select the subtotal function you want to use.

Sort Options

You can sort left to right across rows by clicking the Options button (Figure 5-31 on page E 5.26) and then clicking Sort left to right in the Orientation area. You also can click the Case sensitive check box, which would sort lowercase letters ahead of the same capital letters for an ascending sort.

More *About* **2000**

Sort Algorithms

Numerous sort algorithms are used with computers, such as the Bubble sort, Shaker sort, and Shell sort. For additional information on sorting, visit the Excel 2000 More About Web page (www.scsite.com/ex2000/more.htm) and click Sort Algorithms.

The field on which you sort prior to invoking the Subtotals command is called the **control field**. When the control field changes, Excel displays a subtotal for the numeric fields you select in the Subtotal dialog box. For example, if you sort on the St field and request subtotals for the Quota and YTD Sales fields, then Excel recalculates the subtotal and grand total each time the St field changes to a new state. The most common subtotal used with the Subtotals command is the SUM function, which displays a sum each time the control field changes.

In addition to displaying subtotals, Excel also creates an outline for the database. The following steps shows you how to display subtotals for the Quota field and YTD Sales field by state. Because the insertion of subtotals increases the number of rows, the Zoom box on the Standard toolbar is used to display the entire database.

Steps **To Display Subtotals in a Database**

① **Select cell G9. Click the Sort Ascending button on the Standard toolbar.**

The SkateJam Sales Representative database displays in ascending sequence by state (Figure 5-33).

FIGURE 5-33

② **Click Data on the menu bar and then point to Subtotals (Figure 5-34).**

FIGURE 5-34

3 Click **Subtotals**. When the Subtotal dialog box displays, click the At each change in box arrow and then click St. If necessary, select Sum in the Use function list. Click the Quota and YTD Sales check boxes in the Add subtotal to list. Point to the OK button.

The Subtotal dialog box displays (Figure 5-35). The At each change in box contains the St field. The Use function box contains Sum. In the Add subtotal to box, both Quota and YTD Sales are selected.

FIGURE 5-35

4 Click the OK button.

Excel inserts seven new rows in the SkateJam Sales Representative database. Six of the new rows contain Quota and YTD Sales subtotals for each state (Figure 5-36). The seventh new row displays grand totals for the Quota and YTD Sales fields. Excel also outlines the database, which causes the rightmost column to be outside the window.

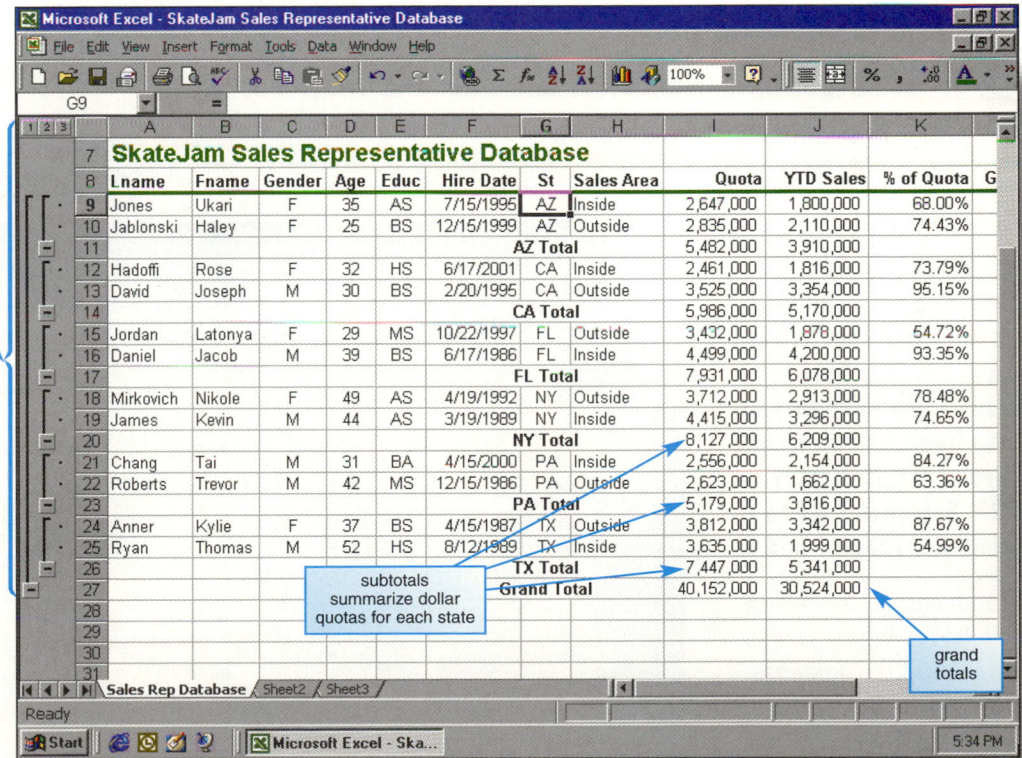

FIGURE 5-36

As shown in Figure 5-36 on the previous page, Excel has added six subtotal rows and one grand total row to the database. The names for each subtotal row are derived from the state names. Thus, in cell G11 of row 11 the text AZ Total names the Quota and YTD Sales totals for Arizona.

In Figure 5-35 on the previous page, the Use function box contains Sum, which instructs Excel to sum the fields selected in the Add subtotal to list. Additional functions are available by clicking the Use function box arrow. The frequently used subtotal functions are listed in Table 5-5.

Table 5-5 Frequently Used Subtotal Functions	
SUBTOTAL FUNCTION	DESCRIPTION
Sum	Sums a column
Count	Counts the number of entries in a column
Average	Determines the average of numbers in a column
Max	Determines the maximum value in a column
Min	Determines the minimum value in a column

Zooming Out on a Worksheet and Hiding and Showing Detail Data in a Subtotaled Database

The following steps show how to use the Zoom box on the Standard toolbar to reduce the magnification of the worksheet so that all fields display. The steps also illustrate how to use the outline features of Excel to display only the total rows.

Steps ## To Zoom Out on a Worksheet and Hide and Show Detail Data in a Subtotaled Database

1 **Click the Zoom box on the Standard toolbar. Type** 90 **and then press the ENTER key. Select columns I and J. Double-click the right boundary of column heading J to ensure the grand totals display in row 27. Select cell G9 to deselect the range I and J.**

Excel reduces the magnification of the worksheet so that all columns in the database display (Figure 5-37).

FIGURE 5-37

2 **Click the row level 2 symbol on the left side of the screen.**

Excel hides all detail rows and displays only the subtotal and grand total rows (Figure 5-38).

3 **Click the row level 3 symbol on the left side of the screen to display hidden detail rows. Click the Zoom box arrow on the Standard toolbar and then click 100% in the list.**

Excel displays the worksheet in normal size (Figure 5-36 on page E 5.29).

4 **Change the width of columns I and J back to 11.00.**

(Figure callouts: row level symbols; Zoom box arrow; shows only grand totals; hides all detail rows; shows all records; row level bar; show detail symbol; hide detail symbol; only total rows show)

	Lname	Fname	Gender	Age	Educ	Hire Date	St	Sales Area	Quota	YTD Sales	% of Quota	Grade
11								AZ Total	5,482,000	3,910,000		
14								CA Total	5,986,000	5,170,000		
17								FL Total	7,931,000	6,078,000		
20								NY Total	8,127,000	6,209,000		
23								PA Total	5,179,000	3,816,000		
26								TX Total	7,447,000	5,341,000		
27								Grand Total	40,152,000	30,524,000		

FIGURE 5-38

By utilizing the **outlining features** of Excel, you quickly can hide and show detail data. As described in Step 2, you can click the **row level symbols** to expand or collapse the worksheet. Row level symbol 1 hides all rows except the Grand Total row. Row level symbol 2 hides the detail records so the subtotal and grand total rows display as shown in Figure 5-38. Row level symbol 3 displays all rows.

The minus and plus symbols to the left on the row level bar in Figure 5-38 are called the show detail symbol (+) and hide detail symbol (-). If you click the **show detail symbol** (+), Excel displays the hidden detail records. If you click the **hide detail symbol** (-), Excel hides the detail records within the row level bar. The **row level bar** indicates which detail records will be hidden if you click the corresponding hide detail symbol.

You can outline any worksheet by using the **Group and Outline command** on the Data menu.

Removing Subtotals from the Database

You can remove subtotals and the accompanying outline from a database in two ways: you can click the Undo button on the Standard toolbar, or you can click the **Remove All button** in the Subtotal dialog box. The steps on the next page show how to use the Remove All button to remove subtotals from a database.

More About

Outlining

When you hide data using the outline features, you can chart the resulting rows and columns as if they were adjacent to one another. Thus, in Figure 5-38, you can chart the quotas by state as an adjacent range even though they are not in adjacent rows when the worksheet displays in normal form.

To Remove Subtotals from a Database

1 **Click Data on the menu bar and then click Subtotals.**

Excel selects the database and the Subtotal dialog box displays (Figure 5-39).

2 **Click the Remove All button.**

Excel removes all subtotal and total rows and the outline from the database so it displays as shown previously in Figure 5-33 on page E 5.28.

FIGURE 5-39

Outlining

Use of the Group and Outline command on the Data menu is especially useful with large worksheets where the user can get lost in the sea of numbers. Outlining allows the user to hide the detail records to reduce the complexity of the worksheet.

As shown in the previous sections, Excel makes it easy to add and remove subtotals from a database. Thus, you can generate quickly the type of information that database users need to help them make decisions about products or a company's direction.

Before moving on to the next section, complete the following steps to sort the SkateJam Sales Representative database into its original order in ascending sequence by hire date.

TO SORT THE DATABASE BY HIRE DATE

1 Click cell F9.

2 Click the Sort Ascending button on the Standard toolbar.

The records in the SkateJam Sales Representative database are sorted in ascending sequence by hire date.

Finding Records Using a Data Form

Once you have created the database, you might want to view records that meet only certain conditions, or comparison criteria. **Comparison criteria** are one or more conditions that include the field names and entries in the corresponding boxes in a data form. Displaying records that pass a test is called **querying the database**. For example, you can instruct Excel to find and display only those records that pass the test:

Gender = M **AND** Age >= 42 **AND** Sales Area = Inside **AND** Quota > 2,600,000

You use the same relational operators (=, <, >, >=, <=, and <>) to enter comparison criteria on a data form that you used to formulate conditions in IF functions. For a record to display in the data form, it has to pass **all** four parts of the test. Finding records that pass a test is useful for viewing specific records, as well as maintaining the database. When a record that passes the test displays in the data form, you can change the field values or delete it from the database.

To find records in the database that pass a test made up of comparison criteria, you can use the Find Prev and Find Next buttons together with the **Criteria button** in the data form. The following steps illustrate how to use a data form to find records that pass the test described at the bottom of page E 5.32.

More *About*

Databases

Have you ever wondered how a company got your name in its database? A company's customer or contacts database constitutes a major portion of its assets. Many companies sell their databases to non-competing companies, sometimes for millions of dollars. If one company has your name in its database, then chances are several other companies do too.

Steps **To Find Records Using a Data Form**

1 **Click Data on the menu bar and then click Form.**

The first record in the SkateJam Sales Representative Database displays in the data form (Figure 5-40).

FIGURE 5-40

2 **Click the Criteria button in the data form.**

Excel clears the field values in the data form and displays a data form with blank text boxes.

3 **Enter** M **in the Gender text box,** >=42 **in the Age text box,** Inside **in the Sales Area text box, and** >2,600,000 **in the Quota text box. Point to the Find Next button.**

The data form displays with the comparison criteria entered as shown in Figure 5-41.

FIGURE 5-41

4 **Click the Find Next button.**

Excel immediately displays the fourth record in the database because it is the first record that meets the comparison criteria (Figure 5-42). Kevin James is a 44-year old male who works as an Inside sales rep whose Quota is $4,415,000. The first three records in the sales representative database failed to meet one or more of the four criteria.

5 **Use the Find Next and Find Prev buttons to display the other record in the database that passes the test (Thomas Ryan). When you are finished displaying the record, click the Close button in the data form.**

FIGURE 5-42

Two records in the database pass the test: record 4 (Kevin James) and record 5 (Thomas Ryan). Each time you click the **Find Next button**, Excel displays the next record that passes the test. You also can use the **Find Prev button** to display the previous record that passed the test. If you click the Find Next button and the record displaying does not change, then there are no more records downward in the database that meet the criteria.

In Figure 5-41 on the previous page, no blank characters appear between the relational operators and the values. As you enter comparison criteria, remember that leading or trailing blank characters have a significant impact on text comparisons.

You also should note that Excel is not **case sensitive**. That is, Excel considers uppercase and lowercase characters in a comparison criterion to be the same. For example, the lowercase letter m is the same as uppercase letter M.

Using Wildcard Characters in Comparison Criteria

If you are querying on text fields, you can use **wildcard characters** to find records that have certain characters in a field. Excel has two wildcard characters, the question mark (?) and the asterisk (*). The **question mark (?)** represents any single character in the same position as the question mark. For example, if the comparison criteria for Lname (last name) is =Ry?n, then any last name must have the following to pass the test: Ry as the first two characters, any third character, and the letter n as the fourth character. In this database, only Ryan (record 5 in row 13) passes the test.

More About 2000

Comparison Criteria

An alternative to using the * at the end of a letter or phrase is to use the >= relational operator. For example, A* is the same as >=A.

An **asterisk** (*) can be used in a comparison criteria to represent any number of characters in the same position as the asterisk. Jo*, *i, Ch*g, are examples of valid text entries with the asterisk wildcard character. Querying the Lname field with Jo* means all text that begins with the letters Jo. Jones (record 8 in row 16) and Jordan (record 9 in row 17) pass the test. Querying the Lname field with *i, means all text that ends with the letter i pass the test. Jablonski (record 10 in row 18) and Hodaffi (record 12 in row 20) pass the test. Querying the Lname field with Ch*g, means all text that begins with the letters Ch and ends with the letter g pass the test. Only Chang (record 12 in row 20) passes the test.

Using Computed Criteria

Using **computed criteria** to query a database involves using a formula in comparison criteria. For example, using the computed criterion > Quota / 100000 in the Age field in a data form finds all records whose Age field is greater than the corresponding Quota field divided by 100000.

Filtering a Database Using AutoFilter

An alternative to using a data form to find records that meet comparison criteria is to use AutoFilter. Whereas the data form displays only one record at a time, **AutoFilter** displays all records that meet the criteria as a subset of the database. AutoFilter hides records that do not pass the test, thus displaying only those that pass the test.

To apply AutoFilter to a database, use the **Filter command** on the Data menu and the **AutoFilter command** on the **Filter submenu**. Excel responds by adding **AutoFilter arrows** that are arrows added directly to the cells containing the field names at the top of the database (row 8). Clicking an arrow displays a list of all the items in the field (column). If you select an item from the list, Excel immediately hides records that do not contain the item. The item you select from the list is called the **filter criterion**. If you then select a filter criterion from a second field, Excel displays a subset of the first subset.

The following steps show how to use AutoFilter to display those records in the SkateJam Sales Representative Database that pass the following test:

Gender = F **AND** St = AZ

Steps To Apply AutoFilter to a Database

1 Select any cell in the database. Click Data on the menu bar. Point to Filter on the Data menu and then point to AutoFilter on the Filter submenu (Figure 5-43).

FIGURE 5-43

2 **Click AutoFilter.**

AutoFilter arrows display to the right of each field name in row 8 (Figure 5-44).

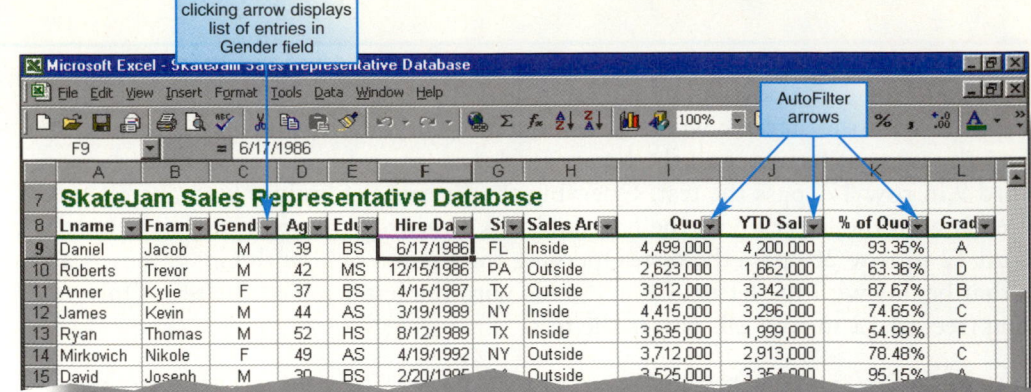

FIGURE 5-44

3 **Click the Gender arrow and then point to F in the Gender list.**

A list of the entries in the Gender field displays (Figure 5-45). The entries (All), (Top 10…), and (Custom…) are found in every AutoFilter list. When you first click AutoFilter on the Filter submenu, the filter criteria for each field in the database is set to All. Thus, all records display.

FIGURE 5-45

4 **Click F. Click the St arrow and then point to AZ in the list.**

Excel hides all records representing males, so that only records representing females display (Figure 5-46). The St list displays.

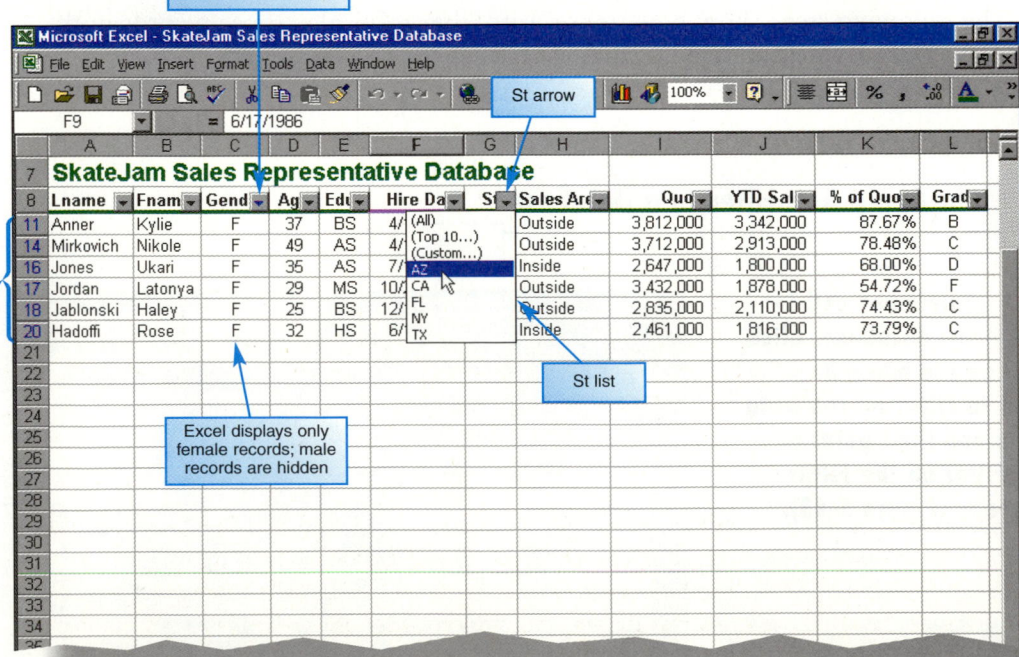

FIGURE 5-46

5 Click AZ in the St list.

Excel hides all records repre-
senting females who do not
live in Arizona. As shown in
Figure 5-47, only two records
pass the filter criteria Gender
= F AND St = AZ.

FIGURE 5-47

When you select a second filter criterion, Excel adds it to the first. Hence, in the case of the previous steps, each record must pass two tests to display as part of the final subset of the database. Other important points regarding AutoFilter include the following:

1. When AutoFilter is active, Excel displays the AutoFilter arrows used to establish the filter and the row headings of the selected records in blue.
2. If you have multiple lists (other columns of data) on the worksheet, make sure to select a cell within the database prior to invoking AutoFilter.
3. If a single cell is selected prior to applying AutoFilter, Excel assigns arrows to all field names in the database. If you select certain field names, Excel assigns arrows to only the selected field names.
4. To remove a filter criteria for a single field, select the All option from the list for that field.
5. If you plan to have Excel determine automatic subtotals for a filtered database, apply AutoFilter first and then apply Subtotals because Excel does not recalculate after selecting the filter criteria.

Removing AutoFilter

AutoFilter is like a **toggle switch**. That is, if you click it once, Excel adds the AutoFilter arrows to the field names in the database. If you click it again, Excel removes the arrows from the field names and displays all records in the database. If you want to keep the arrows but display all the records, click the **Show All command** on the Filter submenu.

The steps on the next page show how to display all records and remove the AutoFilter arrows from the field names by clicking AutoFilter on the Filter submenu.

AutoFilter

The AutoFilter command is unavailable if the worksheet is protected.

Steps ## To Remove AutoFilter

1 **Select a cell in the database below one of the field names. Click Data on the menu bar. Point to Filter and then point to AutoFilter on the Filter submenu.**

The Data menu and Filter submenu display (Figure 5-48).

2 **Click AutoFilter.**

All the records in the SkateJam Sales Representative Database display. The arrows to the right of the field names in row 8 disappear.

FIGURE 5-48

Entering Custom Criteria with AutoFilter

One of the options available in all of the AutoFilter lists is (Custom...). The (**Custom...**) option allows you to select custom criteria, such as multiple options or ranges of numbers. The following steps show how to enter custom criteria to display records in the SkateJam Sales Representative Database that represent employees whose ages are in the range 38 to 52 inclusive ($38 \leq Age \leq 52$).

Steps ## To Enter Custom Criteria

1 **Select cell A9. Click Data on the menu bar. Point to Filter and then click AutoFilter on the Filter submenu. Click the Age arrow and then point to (Custom...) in the Age list.**

The Age list displays (Figure 5-49).

FIGURE 5-49

2 Click (Custom...). When the Custom AutoFilter dialog box displays, click the top-left box arrow and then click is greater than or equal to. Type 38 in the top-right box. Click is less than or equal to in the bottom-left list. Type 52 in the bottom-right box. Point to the OK button.

The Custom AutoFilter dialog box displays (Figure 5-50). The And option button is selected indicating that both conditions must be true.

FIGURE 5-50

3 Click the OK button.

The records in the database that represent SkateJam sales representatives whose ages are between 38 and 52 inclusive display (Figure 5-51). Records that represent employees whose ages are not between 38 and 52 inclusive are hidden.

4 After viewing the records that meet the custom criteria, point to Filter on the Data menu, and then click AutoFilter to display all the records in the database.

FIGURE 5-51

In Figure 5-50, you can click the And option button or the Or option button to select the AND or the OR operator. The **AND operator** indicates that both parts of the criteria must be true; the **OR operator** indicates that only one of the two must be true. Use the AND operator when the custom criteria is continuous over a range of values, such as Age between 38 **AND** 52 inclusive ($38 \leq Age \leq 52$). Use the OR operator when the custom criteria is not continuous, such as Age less than or equal to 40 **OR** greater than or equal to 50 ($40 \geq Age \geq 50$).

As indicated at the bottom of the Custom AutoFilter dialog box in Figure 5-50, you can use wildcard characters to build custom criteria just as you can with data forms.

Using a Criteria Range on the Worksheet

Rather than using a data form or AutoFilter to establish criteria, you can set up a **criteria range** on the worksheet and use it to manipulate records that pass the comparison criteria. Using a criteria range on the worksheet involves two steps:

1. Create the criteria range and name it Criteria.
2. Use the Advanced Filter command on the Filter submenu (Figure 5-48).

Creating a Criteria Range on the Worksheet

To set up a criteria range, you first copy the database field names to another area of the worksheet. If possible, copy the field names above the database, in case the database is expanded downward or to the right in the future. Next, you enter the comparison criteria in the row immediately below the field names you just copied to the criteria range. You then use the Name box in the formula bar to name the criteria range Criteria. The following steps show how to set up a criteria range in the range A2:L3 to find records that pass the test:

Gender = F **AND** Age > 34 **AND** Grade > B

A grade greater than the letter B means that sales representatives with grades of C, D, and F pass the test.

More *About* **2000**

Logical Operators

AND means each and every one of the comparison criteria must be true. OR means only one of the comparison criteria must be true.

Steps *To Set Up a Criteria Range on the Worksheet*

1 **Select the range A7:L8. Click the Copy button on the Standard toolbar. Select cell A1. Press the ENTER key to copy the contents on the Office Clipboard to the paste area A1:L2. Change the title in cell A1 to** Criteria Area. **Enter** F **in cell C3. Enter** >34 **in cell D3. Enter** >B **in cell L3.**

The worksheet displays (Figure 5-52).

FIGURE 5-52

2 **Select the range A2:L3. Click the Name box in the formula bar and then type** Criteria **as the range name. Press the ENTER key. Select cell A9 to deselect the range A2:L3.**

Excel defines the name Criteria to be the range A2:L3.

As you set up a criteria range, remember the following important points:

1. To ensure the field names in the criteria range are spelled exactly the same as in the database, use the Copy button on the Standard toolbar or the Copy command on the Edit menu to copy the database field names to the criteria range as shown in the previous set of steps.
2. The criteria range is independent of the criteria set up in a data form.
3. If you include a blank row in the criteria range (for example, rows 2 and 3 and the blank row 4) all records will pass the test.
4. You can print the criteria range by entering the name Criteria in the Print Area box on the Sheet tab in the Page Setup dialog box, just as you printed the database range (see page E 5.22).

Filtering a Database Using the Advanced Filter Command

The **Advanced Filter command** is similar to the AutoFilter command, except that it does not filter records based on comparison criteria you select from a list. The Advanced Filter command instead uses the comparison criteria set up in a criteria range (A2:L3) on the worksheet. Follow these steps to apply an Advanced Filter to display the records in the SkateJam Sales Representative Database that pass the test established in Figure 5-52 (Gender = F **AND** Age >34 **AND** Grade >B).

More *About* **2000**

Criteria

You can use wildcard characters (?, *) to build the criteria. If the criteria calls for searching for a question mark (?) or asterisk (*), precede either one with a tilde (~). For example, to search for the text What?, enter What~? in the criteria area.

 Steps   **To Apply an Advanced Filter to a Database**

1 If necessary, click cell A9 to select a cell in the Database range. Click Data on the menu bar. Point to Filter and then point to Advanced Filter on the Filter submenu.

The Data menu and Filter submenu display (Figure 5-53).

FIGURE 5-53

2 Click Advanced Filter. When the Advanced Filter dialog box displays, point to the OK button.

The Advanced Filter dialog box displays (Figure 5-54). In the Action area, the Filter the list, in-place option button is selected automatically. Excel automatically selects the database (range A8:L20) in the List range box, because the active cell (cell A9) is within the database range. Excel also selects the criteria range (A2:L3) in the Criteria range box, because earlier you assigned the name Criteria to the range A2:L3.

FIGURE 5-54

3 Click the OK button.

Excel hides all records that do not meet the comparison criteria, leaving only two records on the worksheet (Figure 5-55). Nikole Mirkovich and Ukari Jones are the only two sales representatives that are female, older than 34, and have a grade of C, D, or F.

FIGURE 5-55

Like the AutoFilter command, the Advanced Filter command displays a subset of the database. The primary difference between the two is that the Advanced Filter command allows you to create more complex comparison criteria, because the criteria range can be as many rows long as necessary, allowing for many sets of comparison criteria.

To display all the records in the SkateJam Sales Representative database, complete the following steps:

TO DISPLAY ALL RECORDS IN THE DATABASE

 Click Data on the menu bar and then point to Filter.

2 Click Show All on the Filter submenu.

All the records in the SkateJam Sales Representative Database display.

Extracting Records

If you select the **Copy to another location option button** in the Action area of the Advanced Filter dialog box, Excel copies the records that meet the comparison criteria to another part of the worksheet, rather than displaying them as a subset of the database. The location where the records are copied is called the **extract range**. The extract range is set up much like the criteria range was set up earlier. Once the records that meet the comparison criteria in the criteria range are **extracted** (copied to the extract range), you can manipulate and print them as a group.

Creating an Extract Range and Extracting Records

To create an extract range, copy the field names of the database to an area on the worksheet, preferably well below the database range. Next, name this range Extract by using the Name box in the formula bar. Finally, use the Advanced Filter command to extract the records. The steps on the next page show how to set up an extract range below the SkateJam Sales Representative Database and extract records that meet the following criteria, as entered in the Criteria area:

Gender = F **AND** Age > 34 **AND** Grade > B

Microsoft **Excel 2000**

 Steps **To Create an Extract Range on the Worksheet and Extract Records**

1 Select range A7:L8. Click the Copy button on the Standard toolbar. Select cell A24. Press the ENTER key to copy the contents on the Office Clipboard to the paste area A24:L25. Change the title in cell A24 to Extract Area. Select the range A25:L25. Type the name Extract in the Name box and then press the ENTER key. Click cell A20 to make a cell in the database active. Click Data on the menu bar. Click Filter and then point to Advanced Filter.

The worksheet displays (Figure 5-56). The name Extract is assigned to only the field names in row 25. When the records are extracted, Excel automatically will copy the records to the rows below the range named Extract.

FIGURE 5-56

2 Click Advanced Filter. When the Advanced Filter dialog box displays, click Copy to another location in the Action area. Point to the OK button.

The Advanced Filter dialog box displays (Figure 5-57). Excel automatically assigns the range A8:L20 to the List range box because the active cell (A20) is within the range of the database. Excel also automatically assigns the range named Criteria (A2:L3) to the Criteria range box and the range named Extract (A25:L25) to the Copy to box.

FIGURE 5-57

Click the OK button.

Excel copies any records that meet the comparison criteria in the criteria range (see Figure 5-55 on page E 5.42) from the SkateJam Sales Representative Database to the extract range (Figure 5-58).

Microsoft Excel - SkateJam Sales Representative Database

File Edit View Insert Format Tools Data Window Help

A20 = Hadoffi

SkateJam Sales Representative Database

Lname	Fname	Gender	Age	Educ	Hire Date	St	Sales Area	Quota	YTD Sales	% of Quota	Grade
Daniel	Jacob	M	39	BS	6/17/1986	FL	Inside	4,499,000	4,200,000	93.35%	A
Roberts	Trevor	M	42	MS	12/15/1986	PA	Outside	2,623,000	1,662,000	63.36%	D
Anner	Kylie	F	37	BS	4/15/1987	TX	Outside	3,812,000	3,342,000	87.67%	B
James	Kevin	M	44	AS	3/19/1989	NY	Inside	4,415,000	3,296,000	74.65%	C
Ryan	Thomas	M	52	HS	0/12/1989	TX	Inside	3,635,000	1,999,000	54.99%	F
Mirkovich	Nikole	F	49	AS	4/19/1992	NY	Outside	3,712,000	2,913,000	78.48%	C
David	Joseph	M	30	BS	2/20/1995	CA	Outside	3,525,000	3,354,000	95.15%	A
Jones	Ukari	F	35	AS	7/15/1995	AZ	Inside	2,647,000	1,800,000	68.00%	D
Jordan	Latonya	F	29	MS	10/22/1997	FL	Outside	3,432,000	1,878,000	54.72%	F
Jablonski	Haley	F	25	BS	12/15/1999	AZ	Outside	2,835,000	2,110,000	74.43%	C
Chang	Tai	M	31	BA	4/15/2000	PA	Inside	2,556,000	2,154,000	84.27%	B
Hadoffi	Rose	F	32	HS	6/17/2001	CA	Inside	2,461,000	1,816,000	73.79%	C

gender = F   age > 34   grade > B

Extract Area

Lname	Fname	Gender	Age	Educ	Hire Date	St	Sales Area	Quota	YTD Sales	% of Quota	Grade
Mirkovich	Nikole	F	49	AS	4/19/1992	NY	Outside	3,712,000	2,913,000	78.48%	C
Jones	Ukari	F	35	AS	7/15/1995	AZ	Inside	2,647,000	1,800,000	68.00%	D

records that meet criteria age > 34, gender = F, and grade > B

Sales Rep Database / Sheet2 / Sheet3 /

Ready

Start   Microsoft Excel - Ska...   5:58 PM

FIGURE 5-58

When you set up the extract range, you do not have to copy all of the field names in the database to the proposed extract range. Instead, you can copy only those field names you want and they can be in any order. You also can type the field names rather than copy them, although this method is not recommended.

When you invoke the Advanced Filter command and select the Copy to another location option button, Excel clears all the cells below the field names in the extract range. Hence, if you change the comparison criteria in the criteria range and invoke the Extract command a second time, Excel clears the previously extracted records before it copies a new set of records that pass the new test.

In the previous example, the extract range was defined as a single row containing the field names (range A25:L25). When you define the extract range as just one row, any number of records can be extracted from the database; Excel will expand the extract range to include all rows below the first row (row 25) to the bottom of the worksheet, if needed. The alternative is to define an extract range with a fixed number of rows. If you define a fixed-size extract range, however, and if more records are extracted than there are rows available, Excel displays a dialog box with a diagnostic message indicating the extract range is full.

More About Comparison Criteria

The way you set up the comparison criteria in the criteria range determines the records that will pass the test when you use the AutoFilter command. The sections on the next page describe examples of different comparison criteria.

A Blank Row in the Criteria Range

If the criteria range contains a blank row, it means that no comparison criteria have been defined. Thus, all records in the database pass the test. For example, the blank row in the criteria range shown in Figure 5-59 means that all records will pass the test.

FIGURE 5-59

Using Multiple Comparison Criteria with the Same Field

If the criteria range contains two or more entries under the same field name, then records that pass either comparison criterion pass the test. For example, based on the criteria range shown in Figure 5-60, all records that represent sales representatives that work in FL **OR** TX will pass the test.

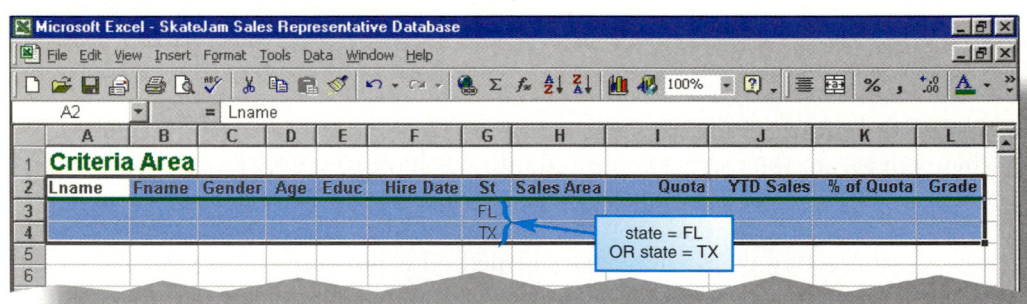

FIGURE 5-60

If an **AND** operator applies to the same field name (Age > 50 **AND** Age < 55), then you must duplicate the field name (Age) in the criteria range. That is, add the field name Age to the right of Grade (cell M2), delete the name Criteria by using the Name command on the Insert menu, and then redefine the name Criteria to include the second Age field using the Name box in the formula bar.

Comparison Criteria in Different Rows and Under Different Fields

When the comparison criteria under different field names are in the same row, then records pass the test only if they pass all the comparison criteria. If the comparison criteria for the field names are in different rows, then the records must pass only one of the tests. For example, in the criteria range shown in Figure 5-61, sales representatives who are male (M) **OR** Inside sales representatives pass the test.

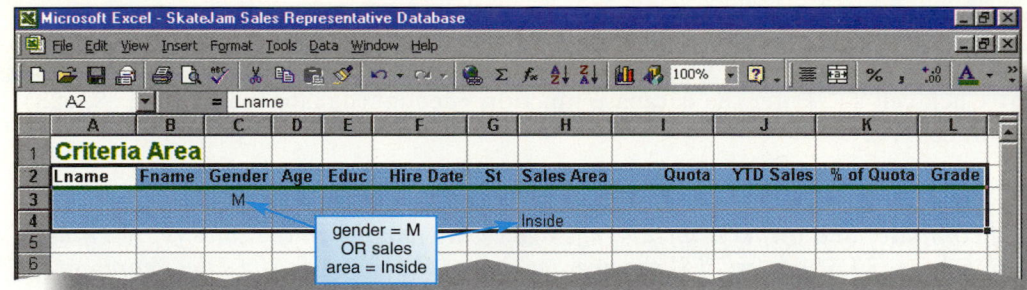

FIGURE 5-61

Using Database Functions

Excel has 13 database functions that you can use to evaluate numeric data in a database. One of the functions is called the DAVERAGE function. As the name implies, you use the **DAVERAGE function** to find the average of numbers in a database field that pass a test. This function serves as an alternative to finding an average using the Subtotals command on the Data menu. The general form of the DAVERAGE function is:

=DAVERAGE(database, "field name", criteria range)

where database is the name of the database, field name is the name of the field in the database, and criteria range is the comparison criteria or test to pass.

Another often used database function is the DCOUNT function. The **DCOUNT function** will count the number of numeric entries in a database field that pass a test. The general form of the DCOUNT function is:

=DCOUNT(database, "field name", criteria range)

where database is the name of the database, field name is the name of the field in the database, and criteria range is the comparison criteria or test to pass.

In the following steps the DAVERAGE function is used to find the average age of the female sales representatives and the average age of the male sales representatives in the database. The DCOUNT function is used to count the number of sales representative records that have a grade of A. The first step sets up the criteria areas that are required by these two functions.

Database Functions

Database functions are useful when working with lists of data, such as the one in this project. Remembering the function arguments and their order within parentheses is not easy. Thus, it is recommended that you use the Function Wizard button on the Standard toolbar to assign a database function to your worksheet.

TO USE THE DAVERAGE AND DCOUNT DATABASE FUNCTIONS

1 Click cell Q1 and enter Criteria for DB Functions as the criteria area title. Double-click the move handle on the Formatting toolbar to display it in its entirety. Select the range Q1:S1 and click the Merge and Center button on the Formatting toolbar. Click the Bold button on the Formatting toolbar.

2 Select cell Q2 and enter Gender as the field name. Select cell R2 and enter Gender as the field name. Select cell S2 and enter Grade as the field name. Double-click the move handle on the Standard toolbar to display it in its entirety. Select cell L8. Click the Format Painter button on the Standard toolbar. Drag through the range Q2:S2. Enter F in cell Q3 as the code for females. Enter M in cell R3 as the code for males. Enter A in cell S3 as the grade.

3 Enter Average Female Age = = = = => in cell Q5. Enter Average Male Age = = = = = = => in cell Q6. Enter Grade A Count = = = = = = = = = > in cell Q7.

4 Click cell T5. Enter the database function =daverage(database, "Age", Q2:Q3) in cell T5.

5 Click cell T6. Enter the database function =daverage(database, "Age", R2:R3) in cell T6.

6 Click cell T7. Enter the database function =dcount(database, "Age", S2:S3) in cell T7.

7 Click the Save button on the Standard toolbar to save the workbook.

Excel computes and displays the average age of the females in the sales representative database (34.50) in cell T5, the average age of the males in the sales representative database (39.67) in cell T6, and a count of the sales representatives who have a grade of A in cell T7 (Figure 5-62).

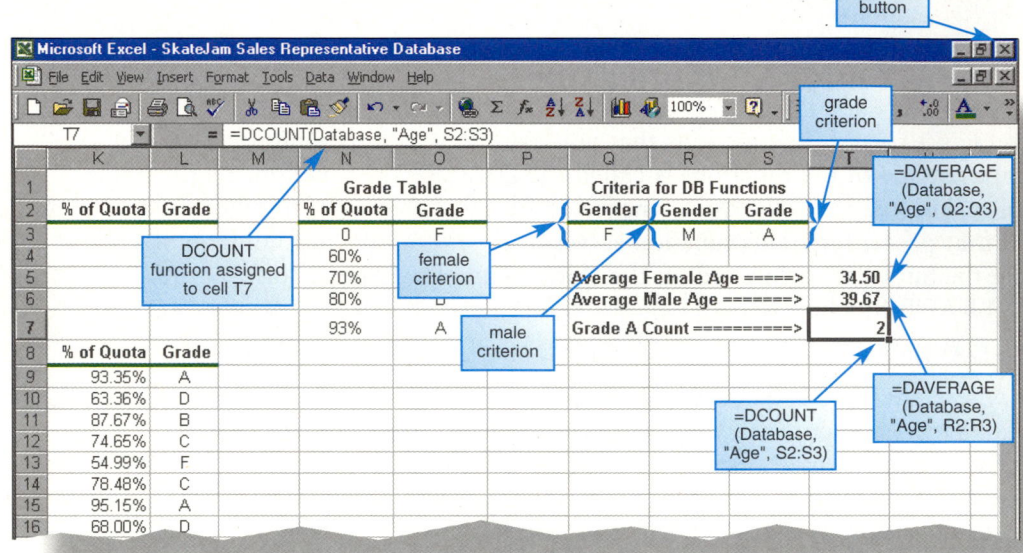

FIGURE 5-62

In Figure 5-62, the first value in the DCOUNT function, database, refers to the sales representative database defined earlier in this project (range A8:L20). The second value "Age" identifies the field on which to compute the average. The third value, S2:S3, is the criteria range for the grade count. In the case of the DCOUNT function, it is required that you select a numeric field to count. Excel requires that you surround the field name Age with quotation marks unless the field has been assigned a name through the Name Box in the formula bar.

Other database functions that are similar to the functions described in previous projects include the DMAX, DMIN, and DSUM functions. For a complete list of the database functions, click the Paste Function button on the Standard toolbar. When the Paste Function dialog box displays, select Database in the Function category list. The database functions display in the Function name box. If you select a database function in the Function name list, Excel displays a description of the function above the OK button in the dialog box.

Quitting Excel

The project is complete. To quit Excel, follow the steps below.

TO QUIT EXCEL

1 Click the Close button on the right side of the title bar.

2 If the Microsoft Excel dialog box displays, click the No button.

CASE PERSPECTIVE SUMMARY

The SkateJam Sales Representative Database created in this project will allow Rosa Blade, the national sales manager, to generate information that will help her make decisions regarding the sales force. She can sort the database to get different views, use a data form to display and change records, generate subtotals, and query the database using a data form, the Filter command, or AutoFilter command. She also can use the database functions to generate additional information about the sales force.

Project Summary

In this project, you learned how to create, sort, and filter a database. Creating a database involves naming a range in the worksheet Database. You then can add, change, and delete records in the database through a data form. Sorting a database can be achieved using the Sort Ascending and Sort Descending buttons on the Standard toolbar or by using the Sort command on the Data menu.

Once a database is sorted, you can use the Subtotals command on the Data menu to generate subtotals that display within the database range. Filtering a database involves displaying a subset of the database or copying (extracting) records that pass a test. Finally, this project showed you how to use database functions and lookup functions.

What You Should Know

Having completed this project, you now should be able to perform the following tasks:

▶ Apply an Advanced Filter to a Database *(E 5.41)*

▶ Apply AutoFilter to a Database *(E 5.35)*

▶ Create a Lookup Table and Use the VLOOKUP Function to Determine Letter Grades *(E 5.16)*

▶ Create an Extract Range on the Worksheet and Extract Records *(E 5.44)*

▶ Display All Records in the Database *(E 5.43)*

▶ Display Subtotals in a Database *(E 5.28)*

▶ Enter Custom Criteria *(E 5.38)*

▶ Enter New Field Names and the % of Quota Formula *(E 5.13)*

▶ Enter Records into a Database Using a Data Form *(E 5.10)*

▶ Find Records Using a Data Form *(E 5.33)*

▶ Name the Database *(E 5.9)*

▶ Print a Database *(E 5.22)*

▶ Quit Excel *(E 5.48)*

▶ Redefine the Name Database *(E 5.19)*

▶ Remove AutoFilter *(E 5.38)*

▶ Remove Subtotals from a Database *(E 5.32)*

▶ Return a Database to Its Original Order *(E 5.24)*

▶ Set Up a Criteria Range on the Worksheet *(E 5.40)*

▶ Set Up a Database *(E 5.7)*

▶ Sort the Database by Hire Date *(E 5.32)*

▶ Sort a Database in Ascending Sequence by Last Name *(E 5.23)*

▶ Sort a Database in Descending Sequence by Last Name *(E 5.24)*

▶ Sort a Database on Multiple Fields *(E 5.25)*

▶ Start Excel and Reset the Toolbars and Menus *(E 5.7)*

▶ Use the DAVERAGE and DCOUNT Database Functions *(E 5.47)*

▶ Zoom Out on a Worksheet and Hide and Show Detail Data in a Subtotaled Database *(E 5.30)*

Apply Your Knowledge

➕ **Project Reinforcement at www.scsite.com/off2000/reinforce.htm**

1 Querying the Affiliated Union Database

Instructions: Assume that the figures that accompany each of the following six problems make up the criteria range for the Affiliated Union Database shown in Figure 5-63. Fill in the comparison criteria to select records from the database according to these problems. So that you understand better what is required for this assignment, the answer is given for the first problem. You can open the Affiliated Union Database workbook from the Data Disk and use the Filter command to verify your answers.

12	**Affiliated Union Database**					
13	**Employee**	**Gender**	**Age**	**Dept**	**Trade**	**Seniority**
14	Jordon, Jesse	M	48	1	Operator	7
15	Peat, Jeffrey	M	32	3	Machinist	5
16	Hill, Judith	F	36	2	Operator	12
17	Jenings, Carl	M	35	1	Oiler	15
18	Lyndowe, Jodi	F	32	3	Oiler	13
19	Jean, Marcell	F	23	1	Operator	4
20	Pylerski, Alex	M	45	2	Operator	23
21	Sanchez, Juan	M	25	3	Machinist	7
22	Snow, Ali	M	48	1	Oiler	0
23	Beet, Sharon	F	22	2	Operator	0
24	Chun, Li	M	35	3	Oiler	15

◀ ◀ ▶ ▶ \ Union / Sheet2 / Sheet3 /

Ready

🏁Start | 🌐 💠 🎨 📝 | ☒ Microsoft Excel - Affil...

FIGURE 5-63

1. Select records that represent females younger than 30 years old.

EMPLOYEE	GENDER	AGE	DEPT	TRADE	SENIORITY
	F	<30			

2. Select records that represent an Operator or Oiler

EMPLOYEE	GENDER	AGE	DEPT	TRADE	SENIORITY

3. Select records that represent male members whose last names begin with the letter J and who work in department 1.

EMPLOYEE	GENDER	AGE	DEPT	TRADE	SENIORITY

4. Select records that represent female members who are at least 32 years old and have at least 10 years of seniority.

EMPLOYEE	GENDER	AGE	DEPT	TRADE	SENIORITY

5. Select records that represent male members or members who have no more than 12 years of seniority.

EMPLOYEE	GENDER	AGE	DEPT	TRADE	SENIORITY

6. Select records that represent a Machinist or Operator who is at least 40 years old.

EMPLOYEE	GENDER	AGE	DEPT	TRADE	SENIORITY

1 Filtering and Sorting the Special Guys Apparel Database

Problem: The company you consult for, Special Guys Apparel, supplies men's apparel to retail stores throughout the United States. The national sales force is divided into districts within divisions within regions. The three regions are the Eastern region (1), Midwest region (2), and Western region (3). The management has hired you to create a sales force database (Figure 5-64), run queries against the database, generate various sorted reports, and generate subtotal information.

![Microsoft Excel - Special Guys Apparel screenshot]

Special Guys Apparel

Region	Division	District	Number	Lname	Fname	Hire Date	Age	Gender	Educ	Sales
3	B	2	299	Green	Rosy	8/11/1998	48	F	BS	2,893,219.75
1	A	1	313	Dragovich	Max	12/21/1998	34	M	BS	9,300,845.00
3	A	3	210	Andrews	Zoe	9/14/1999	45	F	MS	2,465,942.50
1	A	2	108	Harpers	Gerald	9/24/1999	25	F	MS	4,544,023.30
2	B	2	298	Christian	Jenny	10/12/1999	24	F	BS	2,109,583.75
1	B	2	207	March	Jeanne	11/13/1999	44	F	HS	3,718,292.35
1	B	3	99	Janssen	Susan	10/10/2000	33	F	BS	2,167,301.56
1	B	2	208	Sharp	Joe	12/11/2000	27	M	MS	989,483.28
2	A	1	406	Sushee	Lee	5/17/2001	38	M	BS	6,921,032.60
1	B	1	212	Brandon	Karen	7/19/2001	31	F	HS	5,560,345.43
2	A	1	432	Groetl	Mike	6/14/2002	32	M	MS	1,034,054.75
2	A	3	312	Waters	Rene	6/15/2002	54	F	BS	2,210,459.47
2	B	2	120	Rodriquez	Rolando	7/18/2002	31	M	HS	4,893,014.45

FIGURE 5-64

Instructions Part 1: Start Excel. Create the database shown in Figure 5-64 using the techniques learned in this project. In particular, enter and format the database title and field names in rows 6 and 7. Name the range A7:K8 Database. Use a data form to enter the data in rows 8 through 20. Enter your name, course number, laboratory assignment (Lab 5-1), date, and instructor name in the range A40:A44. Save the workbook using the file name Special Guys Apparel.

(continued)

In the Lab

Filtering and Sorting the Special Guys Apparel Database *(continued)*

Instructions Part 2: Step through each filter exercise in Table 5-6 and print the results for each in portrait orientation using the Fit to option on the Page Setup dialog box.

To complete a filter exercise, select the appropriate drop-down arrow(s) and option(s) in the lists. Use the (Custom...) option for field names that do not contain appropriate selections. After printing each filtered solution, point to Filter on the Data menu and click Show All on the Filter submenu. After the last filter exercise, remove the drop-down arrows by clicking AutoFilter on the Filter submenu. You should end up with the following number of records for Filters 1 through 12: 1 = 4; 2 = 2; 3 = 2; 4 = 5; 5 = 4; 6 = 7; 7 = 3; 8 = 7; 9 = 4; 10 = 0; 11 = 4; and 12 = 13.

Table 5-6	Special Guys Apparel Filter Criteria									
FILTER	**REGION**	**DIVISION**	**DISTRICT**	**LNAME**	**FNAME**	**HIRE DATE**	**AGE**	**GENDER**	**EDUC**	**SALES**
1	1	B								
2	2	A	1							
3				Begins with S						
4								M		
5							>27 and < 45		BS or MS	
6						After 1/1/2000				
7					Begins with J					
8										>2,500,000
9							>30	M		
10					Ends with E		>50	F	HS	
11							<35	F		
12	All	All	All	All	All	All	All	All	All	All

Instructions Part 3: Sort the database according to the following six sort problems. Print the database for each sort problem in portrait orientation using the Fit to option in the Page Setup dialog box. Begin problems 2 through 6 by sorting on the Hire Date field to put the database back in its original order.

1. Sort the database in ascending sequence by region.
2. Sort the database by district within division within region. All three sort keys are to be in ascending sequence.
3. Sort the database by division within region. Both sort keys are to be in descending sequence.
4. Sort the database by salesperson number within district within division within region. All four sort keys are to be in ascending sequence.

In the Lab

5. Sort the database in descending sequence by sales.

6. Sort the database by district within division within region. All three sort keys are to be in descending sequence.

7. Hide columns J and K by selecting them and pressing CTRL+0 (zero). Print the database. Select columns I and L. Press CTRL+SHIFT+RIGHT PARENTHESIS to display the hidden columns. Close the Special Guys Apparel database without saving changes.

Instructions Part 4: Open the Special Guys Apparel database. Sort the database by district within division within region. Select ascending sequence for all three sort keys. Use the Subtotals command on the Data menu to generate subtotals for sales by region (Figure 5-65). Change column A to best fit. Print the worksheet. Click row level symbol 1 and print the worksheet. Click row level symbol 2 and print the worksheet. Click row level symbol 3. Remove all subtotals. Close the database without saving changes.

FIGURE 5-65

Microsoft **Excel 2000**

In the Lab

2 Filtering and Sorting a Database of Office 2000 Specialists

Problem: Office Temps, Inc. specializes in supplying consultants to companies in need of Office 2000 expertise. The president of the company, Juanita Jeffries, developed a database (Figure 5-66) that shows the expertise of each employee the company sends out as a consultant. She has asked you to sort, query, and determine some averages from the database. Carefully label each required printout by using the part number and step. If there are multiple printouts in a step, label them a, b, c, and so on.

FIGURE 5-66

Instructions Part 1: Perform the following tasks.

1. Start Excel and open the database Office 2000 Specialist Database from the Data Disk. If you do not have a copy of the Data Disk, see the inside back cover of this book for instructions for downloading it.

2. Complete the following tasks.

   a. Sort the records in the database into ascending sequence by name. John Biagi should display first in the database. Arnold Zingo should display last. Print the sorted version in portrait orientation using the Fit to option in the Page Setup dialog box.

   b. Sort the records in the database by age within gender. Select ascending sequence for the gender code and descending sequence for the age. Julie Kay should be the first record. Print the sorted version as indicated in Step 2a.

In the Lab

c. Sort the database by PowerPoint within Access within Excel within Word. Use the Sort Descending button on the Standard toolbar on all fields. Sort first on PowerPoint, then Access, then Excel, and finally Word. Those who are experts in all four applications should rise to the top of the database. Print the sorted version as indicated in Step 2a. Close the workbook without saving it.

Instructions Part 2: If necessary, open the workbook Office 2000 Specialist Database (Figure 5 67). Select a cell within the database range. Use the Form command on the Data menu to display a data form. Use the Criteria button in the data form to enter the comparison criteria for the tasks below Figure 5-67. Use the Find Next and Find Prev buttons in the data form to find the records that pass the comparison criteria. Write down and submit the names of the employees who pass the comparison criteria for items a through d. Close the data form after each query and then reopen it by clicking the Form command on the Data menu. You should end up with the following number of records for items a through d: a = 2; b = 3; c = 5; and d = 2.

FIGURE 5-67

a. Find all records that represent specialists who are female and are experts in Word and Outlook.

b. Find all records that represent specialists with more than 5 years' experience (Yrs) and who are experts in Word, PhotoDraw, and FrontPage.

c. Find all records that represent male specialists who are at least 26 years old and are experts in Excel.

d. Find all records that represent specialists who have at least 10 years' experience (Yrs) and who are experts in Excel, Access, and PhotoDraw.

(continued)

In the Lab

Filtering and Sorting a Database of Office 2000 Specialists *(continued)*

e. Close and then re-open the data form. All specialists who did not know Publisher were sent to a seminar on the application. Use the Find Next button in the data form to locate the records of these employees and change the Publisher field entry in the data form from the letter N to the letter Y. Make sure you press the ENTER key or press the DOWN ARROW key after changing the letter. Print the worksheet as indicated in Step 2a of Part 1. Close the database without saving the changes.

Instructions Part 3: Open the workbook Office 2000 Specialist Database. Click a cell within the database range. Click Data on the menu bar and then point to Filter. Use the AutoFilter command on the Filter submenu and redo Part 2 a, b, c, and d. Use the Show All command on the Filter submenu before starting items b, c, and d. Print the worksheet as indicated in Step 2a of Part 1 for each problem. Click AutoFilter on the Filter submenu to remove the Auto-Filter arrows. Close the workbook without saving the changes.

Instructions Part 4: Open the workbook Office 2000 Specialist Database. Add a criteria range by copying the database title and field names (range A9:M10) to range A1:M2 (Figure 5-67). Change cell A1 to `Criteria Area`. Use the Name box in the formula bar to name the criteria range (A2:M3) Criteria. Add an extract range by copying the database title and field names (range A9:M10) to range A37:M38. Change cell A37 to `Extract Area`. Use the Name box in the formula bar to name the extract range (range A38:M38) Extract. The top of your worksheet should look similar to the top of the screen shown in Figure 5-68.

FIGURE 5-68

1. With a cell active in the database range, use the Advanced Filter command on the Filter submenu to extract records that pass the tests in the following items a through e. Print the entire worksheet after each extraction as indicated in Step 2a of Part 1.

    a. Extract the records that represent specialists who are female and older than 25 (Figure 5-68). You should extract six records.

    b. Extract the records that represent male specialists who are experts in Access, but not in PhotoDraw. You should extract three records.

In the Lab

c. Extract the records that represent female specialists who are at least 30 years old and have a count of 8. The field Count in column M uses the **COUNTIF function** to count the number of Ys in a record. A count of 8 means the record represents a specialist with expertise in all areas. You should extract one record.

d. Extract the records that represent specialists whose last name begins with the letter S. You should extract three records.

e. Extract the records that represent specialists who are experts in three applications or less. You should extract four records. Save the workbook using the file name Office 2000 Specialist Database Final. Close the workbook.

Instructions Part 5: Open the workbook Office 2000 Specialist Database Final created in Part 4. If you did not do Part 4, then open the Office 2000 Specialist Database from the Data Disk.

Scroll to the right to display cell O1 in the upper left corner of the window. Enter the criteria in the range O1:Q3 as shown in Figure 5-69. Enter the row titles in cells O5:O7 as shown in Figure 5-69.

Use the database function DAVERAGE and the appropriate criteria in the range O1:Q3 to determine the average age of the males and females in the range. Use the database function DCOUNT and the appropriate criteria in the range O1:Q3 to determine the record count of those who have expertise in Excel. The DCOUNT function requires that you choose a numeric field in the database to count. Print the range O1:R7. Save the workbook using the file name Office 2000 Specialist Database Final.

FIGURE 5-69

In the Lab

3 Creating and Manipulating the Eta Chi Rho Social Club Database

Problem: You are a member of Eta Chi Rho, a social club for adult learners returning to school. The president has asked for a volunteer to create a database made up of the club's members (Figure 5-70). You decide it is a great opportunity to show your Excel skills. Besides including a member's GPA in the database, the president also would like a GPA letter grade assigned to each member.

Eta Chi Rho Social Club

Student ID	Lname	Fname	Gender	Age	Major	GPA	Grade
310356	Calloway	Kim	F	24	Computer Science	3.31	B
315823	Ruiz	Santiago	M	28	Law Enforcement	2.70	C
321893	Washington	Fred	M	21	Political Science	4.00	A
323451	Smith	Kate	F	27	Anthropology	1.90	D+
339156	Franks	Rebecca	F	32	Pre-medicine	3.56	B+
321761	Cline	Joan	F	26	Nursing	4.25	A+
332013	Edwards	Fred	M	23	Engineering	2.85	C+
333821	Hawn	Linus	M	22	Education	3.10	B-
334132	Julio	Jim	M	21	Accounting	1.75	D+
340326	Waters	Kathy	F	25	History	0.90	F

Grade Table	
GPA	Grade
0.00	F
1.00	D-
1.25	D
1.75	D+
2.00	C-
2.25	C
2.75	C+
3.00	B-
3.25	B
3.50	B+
3.90	A-
4.00	A
4.25	A+

FIGURE 5-70

Instructions Part 1: Use the concepts and techniques developed in this project to create the database shown in the range A6:H17 in Figure 5-70.

1. Enter the database title in cell A6 and the column titles in row 7. Define the range A7:G8 as Database. Format the titles as shown in Figure 5-70.
2. Use the Form command on the Data menu to enter the data shown in the range A8:G17.

In the Lab

3. Enter the Grade table in the range A19:B33. In cell H8, enter the function =vlookup(G8, $A$21:$B$33, 2) to determine the letter grade that corresponds to the GPA in cell G8. Copy the function in cell H8 to the range H9:H17.

4. Redefine the name Database as the range A7:H17.

5. Enter your name, course number, laboratory assignment (Lab 5-3), date, and instructor name in the range F20:F24.

6. Save the workbook using the file name Eta Chi Rho. Print the worksheet. At the bottom of the printout, explain why the dollar signs ($) are necessary in the VLOOKUP function in step 3.

Instructions Part 2: Use a data form to change the following GPAs: 310356 = 2.80; 339156 = 3.4; 340326 = 1.35. Close the data form. The three member's grades should display as C+, B, and D, respectively. Print the worksheet. Close the workbook without saving changes.

Instructions Part 3: Open the workbook Eta Chi Rho. Use the Criteria button and the Find Next and Find Prev buttons in the data form to display records that meet the following criteria:

1. Gender = F; GPA > 3 (Three records pass the test.)
2. Age > 27 (Two records pass the test.)
3. Gender = M; Age < 25 (Four records pass the test.)

   Print the worksheet and write down the Student IDs of the records that pass the tests. Close the workbook without saving the changes.

Instructions Part 4: Open the workbook Eta Chi Rho. Sort the database as follows. Print the database after each sort.

1. Sort the database in ascending sequence by last name.
2. Sort the database by Age within Gender. Use descending sequence for both fields.
3. Sort the database by letter grade within Gender. Use ascending sequence for both fields.
   Close the workbook without saving the changes.

Instructions Part 5: Open the workbook Eta Chi Rho. Use the concepts and techniques presented in this project to set up a Criteria area above the database, set up an Extract area below the Grade table, and complete the following extractions. For each extraction, it is important that you select a cell in the database before using the Advanced Filter command. Extract the records that meet the three criteria sets in Part 3 above. Print the worksheet for each criteria set. Extract the records that meet the following criteria: 25 < Age < 30. It is necessary that you add a second field called Age to the immediate right of the Criteria range and redefine the Criteria area to include the new field. Three records pass the final test. Save the workbook with the last criteria set using the file name Eta Chi Rho 2.

Cases and Places

The difficulty of these case studies varies:
◗ are the least difficult; ◗◗ are more difficult; and ◗◗◗ are the most difficult.

1 ◗ Academic classes, like individuals, may have distinct personalities and characteristics. A database can help reveal a class's idiosyncrasies. Create a Student database from the student data in Table 5-7. Begin the database title (Student Database) in row 7. Use the column headings as the field names in the database. Print the worksheet. Save the workbook. Print the worksheet after each of the following sorts: (1) sort the database in ascending sequence by last name; (2) sort by major within age within gender (all in descending sequence); and (3) sort the database by class in ascending sequence. With the database sorted by class, display subtotals for the number of credit hours. Print the worksheet. Use a data form to find all male students who have earned more than 75 credit hours towards graduation. Write the number who pass the test at the bottom of the Subtotals printout.

Table 5-7	Student Database						
LNAME	**FNAME**	**AGE**	**GENDER**	**STATE**	**CLASS**	**MAJOR**	**CREDIT HRS**
Berlin	Fredrick	21	M	IN	Senior	CIS	110
James	John	18	M	IL	Freshman	ENG	16
Manous	Nick	23	M	MI	Junior	CS	76
Franker	Holly	19	F	IN	Sophomore	CS	33
Steppes	Amos	20	M	IN	Junior	NS	59
Francisco	Julio	19	M	TN	Sophomore	MET	35
Deeks	George	24	M	KY	Senior	EET	112
Kurtz	Len	36	M	KY	Freshman	CS	18
Kelly	Joan	28	F	IL	Junior	EET	72
Winder	Heidi	23	F	MI	Senior	EET	115

Cases and Places

2 ▸ You work for Abdul's Sports Incorporated. Abdul's Sports sells sporting equipment to high schools and colleges in the Midwest. You have been asked to create an inventory database from the data in Table 5-8. Use the column headings in the table as the field names in the database. Enter the database title Abdul's Sports Inventory Database in cell A8 and enter the database immediately below it. The Amount and Priority fields are computational fields. Amount equals Inventory times Price. The Priority field ranks the items 1 through 5 based on their inventory. The higher the number, the stronger the possibility that the company should put the item on sale or market it better. Create a Priority table in the range J1:K7 from the data shown Table 5-9. Use the VLOOKUP function to determine the rank. Print the worksheet. Save the workbook.

Table 5-8	Abdul's Sports Inventory Database						
ORDER NO	ORDER DATE	PART NO	DESCRIPTION	INVENTORY	PRICE	AMOUNT	PRIORITY
116712	11/2/2001	FD13	Soccer Ball	130	14.75		
128185	11/3/2001	DF13	Racquet	225	24.30		
128185	11/3/2001	SD45	Tennis Ball	375	0.50		
128186	11/4/2001	QW23	Football	22	32.45		
128187	11/4/2001	UT67	Trunks	78	6.50		
128187	11/4/2001	QG56	Hip Pads	25	50.45		
128187	11/4/2001	DE34	Shoulder Pads	115	75.25		
128188	11/4/2001	AD34	Helmet	645	90.50		
128189	11/5/2001	AG19	Jersey	250	15.23		
128189	11/5/2001	WR45	Wristband	195	2.25		
142191	11/5/2001	QH78	Go Cart	140	125.65		

Table 5-9	Priority Categories
INVENTORY	PRIORITY
0	1
50	2
100	3
200	4
300	5

Cases and Places

3 ▶ Open the database created in Cases and Places Exercise 2. Print the database for each of the following: (1) sort the database in ascending sequence by inventory; (2) sort the database by amount (descending) within priority (ascending); and (3) sort the database in ascending sequence by order number. With the database sorted by order number, use the Subtotals command to determine amount subtotals for each order number. Print the worksheet with the subtotals. Use row level symbol 2 to display only subtotals. Print the worksheet.

4 ▶ Open the database created in Cases and Places Exercise 2. Use the concepts and techniques described in this project to filter (query) the database using the AutoFilter and Show All commands on the Filter submenu. Print the worksheet for each of the following independent queries: (1) priority equal to 1; (2) inventory greater than 175; (3) order number equals 128187 and part number equals DE34; and (4) price greater than 50 and amount greater than 15,000. The number of records that display are: (1) 2; (2) 5; (3) 1; and (4) 2.

5 ▶▶ Open the database created in Cases and Places Exercise 1. Use the concepts and techniques presented in this project to create a Criteria area and an Extract area. Use the Advanced AutoFilter command to extract records. Print the Extract area for each of the following: (1) males; (2) females; (3) males older than 21; (4) CS majors with less than 40 credit hours; (5) males less than 21 years old from the state of Indiana (6) female seniors; and (7) students between the ages of 19 and 21, inclusive. The number of records that display are: (1) 7; (2) 3; (3) 3; (4) 2; (5) 1; (6) 1; and (7) 4.

6 ▶▶ Open the database created in Cases and Places Exercise 1. Use the concepts and techniques presented in this project to determine the average age of males; the average age of females; the average number of credit hours accumulated by students from IN. Count the number of students that are seniors.

7 ▶▶▶ You work for the classified ads section of your local newspaper. Your editors have decided to introduce a new service in which readers can call the office and inquire if a particular car is being advertised. The editors have assigned this task to you. Begin by creating a database with fields for car manufacturer, model, year, price, mileage, and engine size. Then enter 20 ads in today's newspaper. If any information is missing, enter NA (not available). Test the project by performing queries to find records of cars from each of the past five years.

Microsoft Excel 2000

Creating Templates and Working with Multiple Worksheets and Workbooks

You will have mastered the material in this project when you can:

- Create and use a template
- Use the ROUND function
- Utilize custom format codes
- Define, apply, and remove a style
- Copy data among worksheets in a workbook
- Drill an entry through worksheets
- Add a worksheet to a workbook
- Create formulas that use 3-D references to cells in different sheets in a workbook
- Summarize data using consolidation
- Draw a 3-D Cone chart
- Use WordArt to create a title
- Create and modify lines and objects
- Add comments to cells
- Add a header or footer to a workbook
- Change the page margins
- Set print titles and options
- Insert a page break
- Use the Find and Replace commands
- Consolidate data by linking workbooks

Financial Diagnosis:

A Healthy Outlook?

According to some financial planners, only two percent of Americans have healthy financial outlooks. Most are on the road to financial diaster with debt incurred for student, automobile, and personal loans; credit card charges; home mortgages; and other expenses. If a family tragedy should strike, such as the death of a spouse, it is unlikely that the surviving spouse would be prepared to pay the bills and maintain the present style of living.

How much money actually is needed to face these emergencies? One way to determine monetary status is by summarizing immediate and monthly cash needs, which are contained in the reports generated by the Financial EKG Plus program used by Country Companies® Insurance Group financial planners. The Country Companies started business in 1925 primarily to insure the property of farms. Today they are credited with protecting the lives, health, and assets of hundreds of thousands of families. They do it backed by caring agents and solid financial strength using the Financial EKG.

This worksheet analysis gives a detailed review of the current financial situation, projects the amount needed to meet the family's needs, and then uses these figures in other worksheets to determine how much should be invested each month in various life insurance options to secure the added financial protection.

As in the multiple worksheets in the Home Entertainment Systems profit potential workbook you will create in this Excel project, the Financial EKG uses headers and footers to standardize the worksheet design. On each page, the forms use the company name, Country Companies Financial EKG Plus, and the current date as the header and the text, This proposal was prepared by:, and the insurance agent's name as the footer.

The agent uses the first worksheet to determine the family's immediate cash needs, which is the difference between total cash needed and total cash available. To compute cash needed, the agent enters data for the following fields in the worksheet form: last expenses (medical bills, burial expenses), debt liquidation (loans, credit cards), contingency fund (home-care, child-care), mortgage/rent payment fund (10 years' rent or the mortgage balance), and the educational/vocational fund (four-year undergraduate education). The total cash available is the sum of Social Security death benefits, total liquid assets, and existing life insurance. Normally a cash shortage exists.

The agent then enters data used to compute the surviving spouse's income needs through retirement. He or she estimates how much cash the surviving spouse and child need to maintain their current style of living, the spouse's earnings, and Social Security benefits. The worksheet uses an average four-percent rate of growth on money and computes the total amount of cash the family will need while the child is a minor, during the blackout period between the time the child is 16 and the spouse retires, and during retirement.

When this income need is added to the cash shortage, the total represents the amount that should be invested to cover this family's financial future in time of tragedy.

The Financial EKG then uses another worksheet that references the cell containing this total cash needed. Three life insurance options are reported: term with increasing premiums, whole life with increasing premiums, and whole life with fixed premiums. For each option, the worksheet computes total premiums paid, cash value and dividends, insurance policy value, and monthly income at age 65. For a better understanding of insurance terminology, the Country Companies Web site offers an insurance terms glossary (www.countrycos.com).

These reports help a family prepare for an unexpected loss of income. Thus, by using Financial EKG today, they can be on the road to a healthy financial outlook.

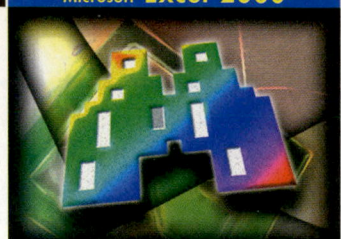

Microsoft Excel 2000

Creating Templates and Working with Multiple Worksheets and Workbooks

P R O J E C T

6

C A S E   P E R S P E C T I V E

A creative marketing campaign and unique sales model have helped a recent start-up company, Home Entertainment Systems (HES), grow to become one of the premier small companies in the United States. The company, which sells a variety of home entertainment systems over the World Wide Web, maintains its inventory at its three former stores in Pittsburgh, Indianapolis, and Phoenix. The company's sales model is unique in that customers sign up on the Web to purchase a home entertainment system over a two-week period. The price continues to decrease as more customers buy the system. At the end of two-weeks, a final price is determined.

Even more exciting is that a major competitor recently sent HES's president, Santiago Biagi, a letter of intent to purchase the company. As part of due diligence, the competitor has requested that Santigo supply a report that shows the total gross profit potential based on the month-end inventory.

Santiago has asked you to consolidate the inventory data from the three stores onto one worksheet and to create a chart that compares the gross profit potentials of the systems (Figure 6-1).

Introduction

Many business-type applications, such as the one described in the Case Perspective, require data from several worksheets in a workbook to be summarized on one worksheet. Suppose, for example, your firm maintains data for three different units within the company on three separate worksheets in a workbook. You can click the tabs at the bottom of the Excel window to move from worksheet to worksheet. You can enter formulas on one worksheet that reference cells found on the other worksheets, which allows you to summarize worksheet data. The process of summarizing data found on multiple worksheets on one worksheet is called **consolidation**.

Another important concept is the use of a template. A **template** is a special workbook or worksheet you can create and then use as a pattern to create new, similar workbooks or worksheets. A template usually consists of a general format (worksheet title, column and row titles, and numeric format) and formulas that are common to all the worksheets. For example, in the Home Entertainment Systems workbook, the worksheets for each of the three store locations and the company worksheet are identical (Figure 6-1), except for the data. One way to create the workbook is to first create a template, save it, and then copy it as many times as necessary to a workbook.

Several other techniques are introduced in this project, including rounding, custom format codes, creating a format style, adding comments to a cell, headers and footers, using WordArt to create a title, using the Find and Replace commands, various print options, and linking workbooks.

(a) Pittsburgh Worksheet

(b) Indianapolis Worksheet

(c) Phoenix Worksheet

(d) Company Worksheet

(e) 3-D Cone Chart

FIGURE 6-1

Project Six — Home Entertainment Systems Profit Potential

From your meetings with Santiago Biagi, you have accumulated the following workbook specifications:

Needs: The workbook Santiago has in mind will require five worksheets — one for each of the three store locations, a summary worksheet for the company, and a chart on a separate sheet that compares the profit potential of the different systems (Figure 6-1 on the previous page).

Because the three stores have the same seven categories of systems, the inventory worksheets are identical, except for the units on hand. You thus can create a template (Figure 6-2) and then copy it to worksheets in the same workbook.

Source of Data: The units on hand for each system category will be collected from the business managers of the respective stores. The average unit cost of each system category is available from the main office.

Calculations: The following calculations are required for the template (Figure 6-2):

1. Total Cost in column D = Units On Hand * Average Unit Cost
2. Average Unit Price in column E = Average Unit Cost / (1 − .65)
3. Total Value in column F = Units On Hand * Average Unit Price
4. Profit Potential in column G = Total Value − Total Cost
5. Use the SUM function in columns B, D, F, and G to total each column.

After using the template to create the multiple-worksheet workbook, use the SUM function to determine the units on hand totals in column B of the Company sheet (Figure 6-1d).

Graph Requirements: Include a 3-D Cone chart on a separate chart sheet that compares the profit potential for each system category on the Company sheet.

Starting Excel

To start Excel, follow the steps summarized below.

TO START EXCEL

1. Click the Start button on the taskbar.

2. Click New Office Document. If necessary, click the General tab in the New Office Document dialog box.

3. Double-click the Blank Workbook icon.

4. When the blank worksheet displays, click View on the menu bar, point to Toolbars, and then click Customize on the Toolbars submenu.

5. When the Customize dialog box displays, click the Options tab, make sure the top three check boxes have check marks, click the Reset my usage data button, and then click the Yes button.

6. Click the Toolbars tab. Click Standard, click the Reset button, and then click the OK button. Click Formatting, click the Reset button, and then click the OK button. Click the Close button.

The Standard and Formatting toolbars display as shown in Figure 6-2.

More *About*

Templates

Templates are most helpful when you need to create several similar or identical workbooks. They help reduce work and ensure consistency. Templates can contain: (1) text and graphics, such as a company name and logo; (2) formats and page layouts, such as styles and custom headers and footers; and (3) formulas or macros.

FIGURE 6-2

Creating the Template

Learning how to use templates is important, especially if you plan to use a similar worksheet design or layout for several worksheets or workbooks. In Project 6, for instance, the four worksheets in the inventory workbook (Figure 6-1) are nearly identical. Thus, the first step in building the Home Entertainment Systems workbook is to create and save a template that contains the labels, formulas, and formats used on each of the sheets. Once the template is saved on disk, you can use it every time you begin developing a similar workbook. Because templates help speed and simplify their work, many Excel users create a template for each application on which they work. Templates can be simple — possibly using a special font or worksheet title — or more complex — perhaps utilizing specific formulas and format styles, such as the template for Project 6.

To create a template, you follow the same basic steps used to create a workbook. The only difference between developing a workbook and a template is the way you save the file.

Bolding the Font and Changing the Column Widths of the Template

The first step in this project is to change the font style of the entire template to bold and adjust the column widths as follows: columns A, and C through G = 13.00; and column B = 8.14. Perform the steps on the next page to apply this formatting.

More About 2000

Built-In Templates

A set of templates is available with Excel that provides solutions to common business problems. To view the templates, click New on the File menu, and then click the Spreadsheet Solutions tab. Many more templates that solve a wide range of problems are available at the Microsoft Office Update Site. To download templates, visit the Excel 2000 More About Web page (www.scsite.com/ex2000/more.htm) and click More Excel Add-Ins and Templates.

TO BOLD THE FONT AND CHANGE THE COLUMN WIDTHS IN THE TEMPLATE

1 Click the Select All button immediately above row heading 1 and to the left of column heading A.

2 Click the Bold button on the Formatting toolbar. Click column heading A.

3 Drag the right boundary of column heading A right until the ScreenTip, Width: 13.00 (97 pixels), displays.

4 Click column heading B. Drag the right boundary of column heading B to the left until the ScreenTip, Width: 8.14 (62 pixels), displays.

5 Click column heading C. Drag through to column heading G. Drag the right boundary of column heading G right until the ScreenTip, Width: 13.00 (97 pixels), displays. Click cell A14 to deselect columns C through G.

Excel assigns the Bold font style to all cells in the worksheet. Columns A and C through G have a width of 13.00. Column B has a width of 8.14.

Entering the Template Title and Row Titles

The following steps enter the worksheet titles in cells A1 and A2 and the row titles in column A.

TO ENTER THE TEMPLATE TITLE AND ROW TITLES

1 Click cell A1. Type Home Entertainment Systems and then press the DOWN ARROW key. Type Store Profit Potential and then press the DOWN ARROW key twice to make cell A4 active.

2 Type System and then press ALT+ENTER. Type Category and then press the DOWN ARROW key.

3 With cell A5 active, enter the remaining row titles in column A as shown in Figure 6-3.

The template title and row titles display in column A as shown in Figure 6-3. Because the entry in cell A4 requires two lines, Excel automatically increases the height of row 4.

Entering Column Titles and the System Date

The next step is to enter the column titles in row 4 and the system date in cell G3.

More *About*

Dummy Numbers

As you develop more sophisticated workbooks, it will become increasingly important that you create good test data to ensure your workbooks are error free. The more you test a workbook, the more confident you will be in the results generated. Select test data that tests the limits of the formulas.

TO ENTER COLUMN TITLES AND THE SYSTEM DATE IN THE TEMPLATE

1 Click cell B4. Type Units and then press ALT+ENTER. Type On Hand and then press the RIGHT ARROW key.

2 Type Average and then press ALT+ENTER. Type Unit Cost and then press the RIGHT ARROW key.

3 With cell D4 active, enter the remaining column titles in row 4 as shown in Figure 6-3.

4 Click cell G3. Type =now() and then press the ENTER key. Select cell A14 to deselect cell G3.

The column titles and system date display as shown in Figure 6-3.

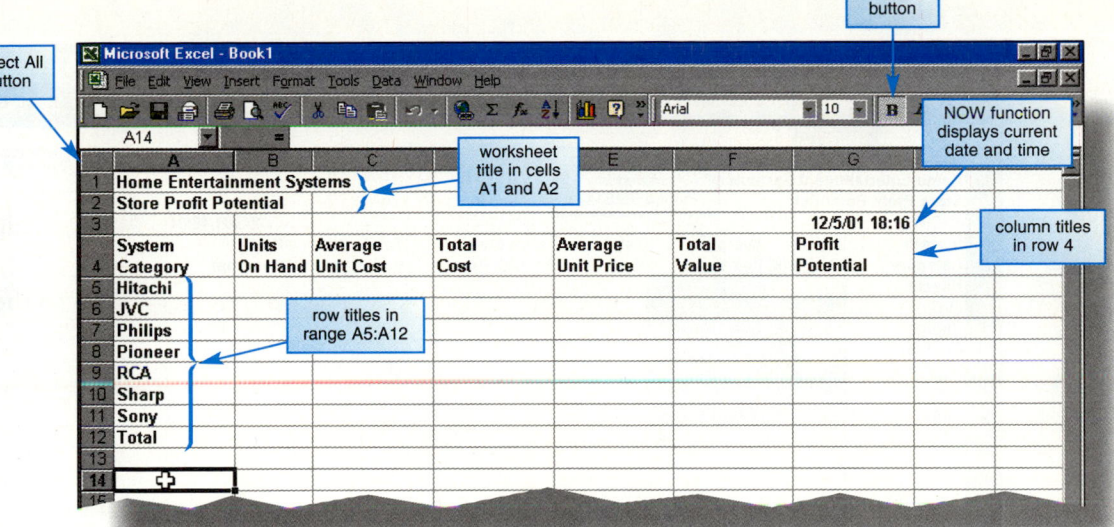

FIGURE 6-3

Entering Dummy Data in the Template

When you create a template, you should use **dummy data** in place of actual data to verify the formulas in the template. Selecting simple numbers such as 1, 2, and 3 allows you to check quickly to see if the formulas are generating the proper results. While creating the Home Entertainment Systems Template in Project 6, dummy data is used for the Units On Hand in the range B5:B11 and the Average Unit Costs in the range C5:C11.

The dummy data is entered by using the fill handle to create a series of numbers in columns B and C. The series in column B begins with 1 and increments by 1; the series in column C begins with 2 and increments by 2. Recall, to create a series you enter the first two numbers so Excel can determine the increment amount. If the cell to the right of the start value is empty and you want to increment by 1, however, you can create a series by entering only one number. Perform the following to create the two series of numbers.

 Steps **To Enter Dummy Data in the Template Using the Fill Handle**

1 Type 1 in cell B5 and then press the ENTER key. Select the range B5:C5. Drag the fill handle through cells B11 and C11.

Excel surrounds the range B5:C11 with a gray border (Figure 6-4). A ScreenTip displays showing the final value in the series that will be assigned to cell B11.

FIGURE 6-4

Release the mouse button.

Excel creates the series 1 through 7 in increments of 1 in the range B5:B11 (Figure 6-5).

FIGURE 6-5

 Click cell C5. Type 2 and then press the DOWN ARROW key. Type 4 and then press the ENTER key. Select the range C5:C6. Drag the fill handle through cell C11 and then release the mouse button.

Excel creates the series 2 through 14 in increments of 2 in the range C5:C11 (Figure 6-6).

FIGURE 6-6

Other Ways

1. Enter first number, while holding down CTRL key drag through range
2. Enter start value, select range, on Edit menu point to Fill, click Series, enter parameters, click OK button

---

It is important to remember, if you create a linear series by selecting the cell to the right of the start value, then that selected cell must be empty.

The more common types of series used in Excel are a **date/time series** (Jan, Feb, Mar, etc.), an **AutoFill series** (1, 1, 1, etc.), and a **linear series** (1, 2, 3, etc.). A fourth type of series is a growth series. A **growth series** multiplies values by a constant factor. You can create a growth series by pointing to Fill on the Edit menu and then clicking Series. When the Series dialog box displays, click the Growth option button and then click the OK button. For example, if you enter 2 in cell D5 and 4 in cell D6, select the range D5:D15, and create a growth series, Excel will create the series 2, 4, 8, 16, 32, 64, 128, 256, 512, 1024, 2048 in the range D5:D15.

The ROUND Function and Entering the Formulas in the Template

The next step is to enter the four formulas for the first system category (Hitachi) in the range D5:G5. When you multiply or divide decimal numbers that result in an answer with more decimal places than the format allows, you run the risk of the column totals being a penny or so off. For example, in this project, the Currency and Comma style formats display two decimal places. And yet the formulas result in several additional decimal places that Excel maintains for computation purposes. For this reason, it is recommended that you use the **ROUND function** on formulas that potentially can result in more decimal places than the format displays. The general form of the ROUND function is

=ROUND (number, number of digits)

where the number argument can be a number, a cell reference that contains a number, or a formula that results in a number; and the number of digits argument, which can be any positive or negative number, determines how many places will be rounded. The following is true about the ROUND function:

1. If the number of digits argument is greater than 0 (zero), then the number is rounded to the specified number of digits.
2. If the number of digits argument is equal to 0 (zero), then the number is rounded to the nearest integer.
3. If the number of digits argument is less than 0 (zero), then the number is rounded to the left of the decimal point.

The four formulas to enter are shown in Table 6-1. To illustrate the ROUND function, it is applied to the formula assigned to cell E5.

Table 6-1	Formulas Used to Determine Profit Potential		
CELL	**DESCRIPTION**	**FORMULA**	**ENTRY**
D5	Total Cost	Units On Hand x Average Unit Cost	=B5 * C5
E5	Average Unit Price	ROUND(Average Unit Cost / (1−.65), 2)	=ROUND(C5 / (1−.65), 2)
F5	Total Value	Units on Hand x Average Unit Price	=B5 * E5
G5	Profit Potential	Total Value − Total Cost	=F5 − D5

The most difficult formula to understand in Table 6-1 is the one that determines the average unit price, which also is called the average selling price. To make a net profit, companies must sell their merchandise for more than the unit cost of the merchandise plus the company's operating expenses (taxes, warehouse rent, upkeep, and so forth). To determine what selling price to set for an item, companies often first establish a desired margin.

Most companies look for a margin of 60% to 75%. Home Entertainment Systems, for example, tries to make a margin of 65% on its products. The formula for the average unit price in Table 6-1 helps the company determine the price at which to sell an item so that it ends up with a 65% margin. For example, if an item costs Home Entertainment Systems $1.00, the company must sell it for $2.86 [$1.00 / (1−.65)] to make a 65% margin. Of this $2.86, $1.00 goes to pay the cost of the item; the other $1.86 is the gross profit potential (65% x $2.86 = $1.86).

The steps on the next page use Point mode to enter the four formulas in Table 6-1 in the range D5:G5. After the formulas are entered for the Hitachi system category in row 5, the formulas will be copied for the remaining six system categories.

The Magical Fill Handle

Using the fill handle, you can create different types of series. To select the type of series to create, right-drag the fill handle. When you release the right mouse button, a shortcut menu displays from which you can select the type of series to create.

Fractions

The forward slash (/) has multiple uses. For example, dates often are entered using the slash. In formulas, the slash represents division. What about fractions? To enter a fraction, such as ½, type .5 or 0 1/2 (i.e., type zero, followed by a space, followed by the number 1, followed by a slash, followed by the number 2). If you type 1/2, Excel will store the value in the cell as the date January 2.

To Enter the Formulas Using Point Mode and Determine Totals in the Template

1 **Click cell D5. Type = to start the formula. Click cell B5. Type * (asterisk) and then click cell C5. Click the Enter box in the formula bar.**

The formula =B5*C5 displays in the formula bar and the value 2 (1 x 2) displays as the total cost in cell D5 (Figure 6-7).

FIGURE 6-7

2 **Click cell E5. Type =round(c5/ (1-.65), 2) and then click the Enter box in the formula bar.**

The value 5.71 (5.7142857 rounded to two decimal places) displays as the average unit price in cell E5 and the formula =ROUND(C5/(1-0.65), 2) displays in the formula bar (Figure 6-8).

FIGURE 6-8

3 **Click cell F5. Type = to start the formula. Click cell B5. Type * (asterisk) and then click cell E5. Click the Enter box in the formula bar.**

The value 5.71 (1 x 5.71) displays as the total value in cell F5 and the formula =B5*E5 displays in the formula bar (Figure 6-9).

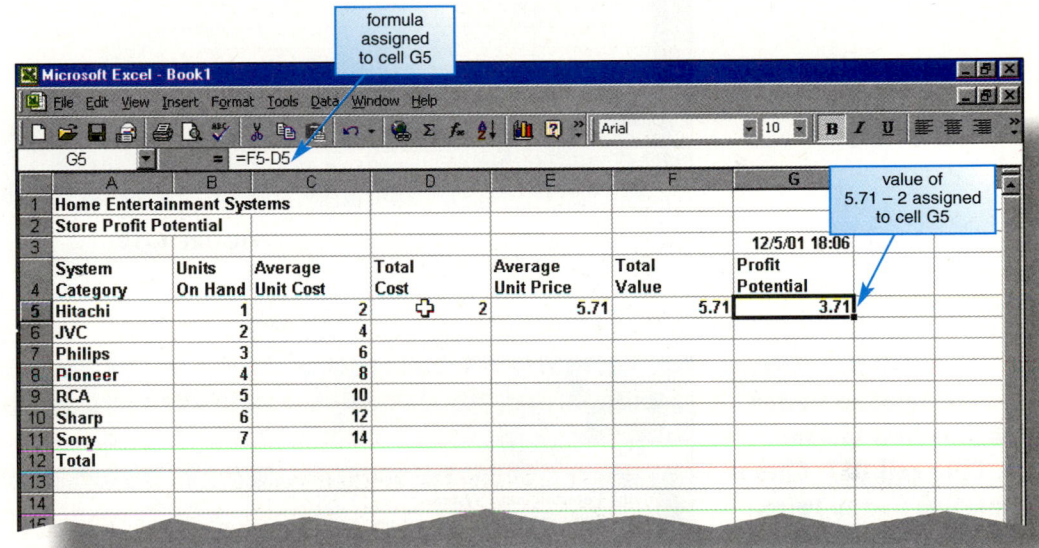

FIGURE 6-9

4 **Click cell G5. Type = to start the formula. Click cell F5. Type – (minus sign) and then click cell D5. Click the Enter box in the formula bar.**

The value 3.71 (5.71 – 2) displays as the profit potential in cell G5 and the formula =F5 – 5 displays in the formula bar (Figure 6-10).

FIGURE 6-10

5 **Select the range D5:G5 and then point to the fill handle.**

The range D5:G5 is selected and the mouse pointer changes to a cross hair when positioned on the fill handle (Figure 6-11).

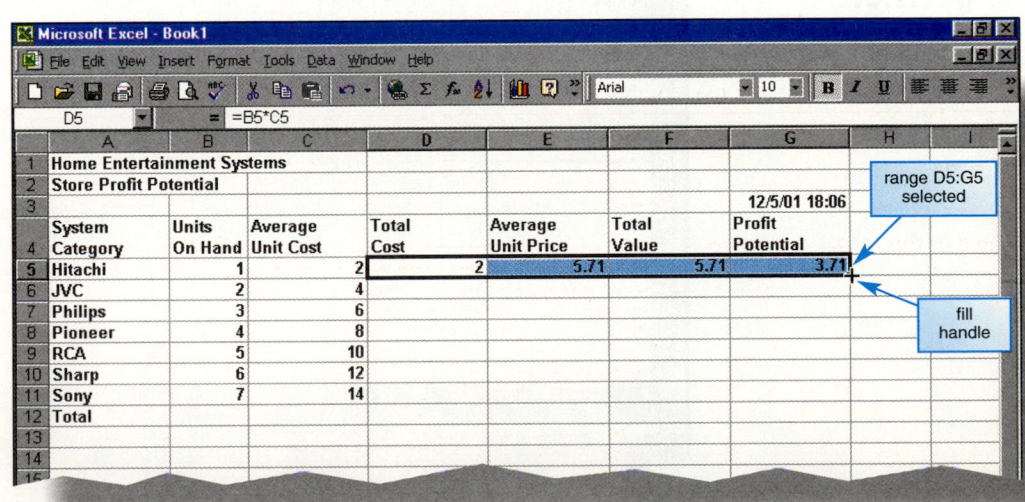

FIGURE 6-11

6 **Drag down through the range D6:G11.**

Excel copies the formulas in the range D5:G5 to the range D6:G11. Excel automatically adjusts the cell references so each formula references the data in the row to which it is copied (Figure 6-12).

FIGURE 6-12

7 **Click cell B12. Click the AutoSum button on the Standard toolbar twice. Click cell D12. Click the AutoSum button twice. Select the range F12:G12. Click the AutoSum button. Select cell A14 to deselect the range F12:G12.**

The totals for columns B, D, F, and G display in row 12 (Figure 6-13).

FIGURE 6-13

The values Excel generates from the formulas are based on the dummy data entered in columns B and C. After you save and format the template, you will use it to create the Home Entertainment Systems workbook. You then will enter the actual data for the different system categories.

Saving the Template

Saving a template is just like saving a workbook, except that you select Template in the Save as type box in the Save As dialog box. The following steps save the template on drive A using the file name Home Entertainment Systems Template.

 To Save a Template

1 **Click the Save button on the Standard toolbar. When the Save As dialog box displays, type** Home Entertainment Systems Template **in the File name text box. Click the Save as type box arrow and then click Template in the list. Click the Save in box arrow and then click 3½ Floppy (A:). Point to the Save button in the Save As dialog box.**

The Save As dialog box displays (Figure 6-14).

2 **Click the Save button in the Save As dialog box.**

Excel saves the template Home Entertainment Systems on the floppy disk in drive A. The file name Home Entertainment Systems Template displays on the title bar as shown in Figure 6-15 on the next page.

FIGURE 6-14

Formatting the Template

The next step is to format the template so it displays as shown in Figure 6-15. As you format the template, keep in mind that each of the sheets for which the template is used contains the same formats. The following list summarizes the steps required to format the template.

1. Change the font of the template title in cells A1 and A2. Center cells A1 and A2 across columns A through G. Change the background color, change the font color, and add a heavy outline border to the range A1:A2.
2. Format the column titles and add borders.
3. Assign the Currency style format with a floating dollar sign to the non-adjacent ranges C5:G5 and D12:G12.
4. Assign a Custom style format to the range C6:G11.
5. Assign a Comma style format to the range B5:B12.
6. Assign borders to rows 4 and 12.
7. Create a format style and assign it to the date in cell G3.

FIGURE 6-15

Formatting the Template Title

The steps used to format the template title include changing cell A1 to 36-point Britannic Bold font (or a similar font); changing cell A2 to 16-point Arial font; centering both titles across columns A through G; changing the title background color to red and the title font to white; and drawing a thick box border around the title area. Perform the following steps to format the template title.

TO FORMAT THE TEMPLATE TITLE

1 Double-click the move handle on the Formatting toolbar.

2 Click cell A1. Click the Font box arrow on the Formatting toolbar and then click Britannic Bold (or a similar font) in the list. Click the Font Size box arrow on the Formatting toolbar and then click 36 in the list. Select the range A1:G1. Click the Merge and Center button on the Formatting toolbar.

3 Click cell A2. Click the Font Size box arrow on the Formatting toolbar and then click 16 in the list. Select the range A2:G2. Click the Merge and Center button on the Formatting toolbar.

4 Select the range A1:A2. Click the Fill Color button arrow on the Formatting toolbar and then click Red (column 1, row 3) on the Fill Color palette.

5 Click the Font Color button arrow on the Formatting toolbar and then click White (column 8, row 5) on the Font Color palette.

6 Click the Borders button arrow on the Formatting toolbar and then click Thick Box Border (column 4, row 3) on the Borders palette.

The template title area displays as shown in Figure 6-16.

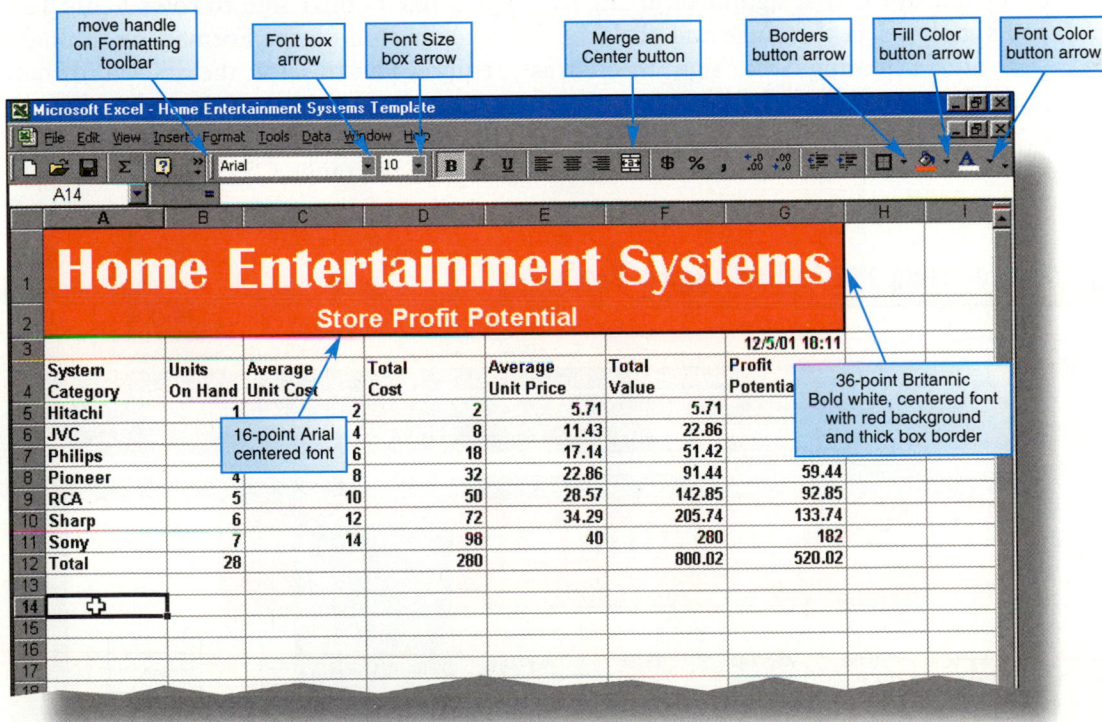

FIGURE 6-16

When you increase the font size, Excel automatically increases the heights of rows 1 and 2 so the tallest letter will display properly in the cells.

Formatting the Column Titles and Total Line

Next, center and underline the column titles and draw a top and double bottom border on the totals in row 12. Perform the steps on the next page to apply this formatting.

TO FORMAT THE COLUMN TITLES AND TOTAL LINE

1 Select the range A4:G4. Click the Center button on the Formatting toolbar. Click the Borders button arrow on the Formatting toolbar and then click Bottom Border (column 2, row 1) on the Borders palette.

2 Point to the boundary below row 4. Drag down until the ScreenTip, Height: 39.00 (52 pixels), displays.

3 Select the range A12:G12. Click the Borders button arrow on the Formatting toolbar and then click Top and Double Bottom Border (column 4, row 2) on the Borders palette.

The column titles in row 4 and the totals in row 12 display as shown in Figure 6-17.

Special Formatting

Excel has formats for ZIP codes, telephone numbers, and Social Security numbers. Click Special in the Category list box in the Format Cells dialog box. The formats will display in the Type list box. These formats automatically will add dashes in the appropriate positions. All you have to do is enter the digits.

Applying Number Formats Using the Format Dialog Box

As shown in Figure 6-15 on page E 6.16, the template for this project follows the standard accounting format for a table of numbers; that is, it displays floating dollar signs in the first row of numbers (row 5) and the totals row (row 12). Recall that while a fixed dollar sign always displays in the same position in a cell (regardless of the number of significant digits), a floating dollar sign always displays immediately to the left of the first significant digit. To assign a fixed dollar sign to rows 5 and 12, you simply select the range and click the Currency button on the Formatting toolbar. Assigning a floating dollar sign, by contrast, requires you to select the desired format in the Format Cells dialog box.

The following steps use the Format Cells dialog box to assign a Currency style with a floating dollar sign and two decimal places to the range C5:G5 and D12:G12.

Steps To Assign a Currency Style Using the Format Dialog Box

1 Select the range C5:G5. While holding down the CTRL key, select the nonadjacent range D12:G12. Right-click one of the selected ranges.

The shortcut menu displays (Figure 6-17).

FIGURE 6-17

2 Click Format Cells on the shortcut menu. When the Format Cells dialog box displays, click the Number tab. Click Currency in the Category list box. Click the fourth item ($1,234.10) in the Negative numbers list box and then point to the OK button.

The Format Cells dialog box displays as shown in Figure 6-18. The selected format will apply a Currency style with a floating dollar sign and two decimal places to the selected ranges.

FIGURE 6-18

3 Click the OK button. Select cell A14 to deselect the nonadjacent ranges.

Excel assigns the Currency style with a floating dollar sign and two decimal places to the selected ranges (Figure 6-19).

FIGURE 6-19

Other Ways

1. On Format menu click Cells, click Number tab, select format, click OK button

2. Press CTRL+1, click Number tab, select format, click OK button

More About 2000

Creating Customized Formats

Each format symbol within the format code has special meaning. Table 6-2 summarizes the frequently used format symbols and their meanings. For additional information on creating format codes, use the Office Assistant or Answer Wizard and search for, create a custom number format.

Creating a Customized Format Code

Every format style listed in the Category list box in the Number sheet of the Format Cells dialog box shown in Figure 6-18 on the previous page has a format code assigned to it. A **format code** is a series of format symbols (Table 6-2) that define how a format displays. To view the entire list of format codes that come with Excel, select Custom in the Category list box. Before you begin to create your own format codes or modify a customized format code, you should understand their makeup. As shown below, a format code can have up to four sections: positive numbers, negative numbers, zeros, and text. Each section is divided by a semicolon.

$*#,##0.00 ; [Blue]#,##0.00; 0.00; "The answer is "@

for positive numbers   for negative numbers   for zero numbers   for text

A format code need not have all four sections. For most applications, a format code will have only a positive section and possibly a negative section.

Table 6-2	Format Symbols in Format Codes	
FORMAT SYMBOL	**EXAMPLE OF SYMBOL**	**DESCRIPTION**
# (number sign)	###.##	Serves as a digit placeholder. If more digits are to the right of the decimal point than are number signs, Excel rounds the number. Extra digits to the left of the decimal point are displayed.
0 (zero)	0.00	Functions like a number sign (#), except that if the number is less than 1, Excel displays a zero in the ones place.
. (period)	#0.00	Ensures a decimal point will display in the number. The placement of symbols determines how many digits display to the left and right of the decimal point.
% (percent)	0.00%	Displays numbers as percentages of 100. Excel multiplies the value of the cell by 100 and displays a percent sign after the number.
, (comma)	#,##0.00	Displays comma as a thousands separator.
( )	#0.00;(#0.00)	Displays parentheses around negative numbers.
$ or + or −	$#,##0.00;($#,##0.00)	Displays a floating sign ($, +, or −).
* (asterisk)	$*##0.00	Displays a fixed sign ($, +, or −) to the left in the cell followed by spaces until the first significant digit.
[color]	#.##;[Red]#.##	Displays the characters in the cell in the designated color. In the example, positive numbers display in the default color and negative numbers display in red.
" " (quotation marks)	$0.00 "Surplus";$-0.00 "Shortage"	Displays text along with numbers entered in a cell.
_ (underscore)	#,##0.00_)	Skips the width of the character that follows the underline.

The next step is to assign a customized Comma style to the range C6:G11. To assign a customized Comma style, you select the Custom category in the Format Cells dialog box, select a format code close to the desired one, and then modify or customize it. Perform the following steps to assign a customized format code to the range C6:G11. The last step uses buttons on the Formatting toolbar to assign a Comma style with no decimal places to column B.

Format Codes

Excel has the same format code capabilities as any programming language, such as COBOL.

 Steps **To Create a Custom Format Code**

1 Select the range C6:G11 and then right-click it. Click Format Cells on the shortcut menu. When the Format Cells dialog box displays, click Custom in the Category list box. Scroll down and click #,##0.00_);[Red](#,##0.00) in the Type list box. In the Type text box, change the word Red to Blue. Point to the OK button.

The Format Cells dialog box displays as shown in Figure 6-20. The Custom format has been modified to display negative numbers in blue. Excel displays a sample of the first number in the selected range in the Sample area.

FIGURE 6-20

2 **Click the OK button. Select the range B5:B12. Click the Comma Style button on the Formatting toolbar. Click the Decrease Decimal button on the Formatting toolbar twice. Select cell A14.**

The numbers in the template display as shown in Figure 6-21. When numbers with more than three whole number digits are entered in the range B5:B12, the Comma style format will show in the range.

Save button

Comma Style button

Decrease Decimal button

Comma style format with no decimal places

custom format #,## 0.00_);[Blue] (#,##0.00) applied to range C6:G11

FIGURE 6-21

Other Ways

1. On Format menu click Cells, click Number tab, select format, click OK button
2. Press CTRL+1, click Number tab, select format, click OK button

When you create a new custom format code, Excel adds it to the bottom of the Type list box in the Numbers sheet in the Format Cells dialog box to make it available for future use.

Creating and Applying a Style

A **style** is a group of format specifications that are assigned to a style name. Excel includes several styles as described in Table 6-3. Excel assigns the Normal style to all cells when you open a new workbook.

Using the Style command on the Format menu, you can assign a style to a cell, a range of cells, a worksheet, or a workbook in the same way you assign a format using the buttons on the Formatting toolbar. In fact, the Currency Style button, Comma Style button, and Percent Style button assign the Currency, Comma, and Percent styles in Table 6-3, respectively.

Table 6-3	Styles Available with All Workbooks
STYLE NAME	DESCRIPTION
Normal	Number = General; Alignment = General, Bottom Aligned; Font = Arial 10; Border = No Borders; Patterns = No Shading; Protection = Locked
Comma	Number = (*#,##0.00);_(*(#,##0.00);_(*"-"_);_(@_)
Comma(0)	Number = (*#,##0_);_(*(#,##0);_(*"-"_);_(@_)
Currency	Number = ($#,##0.00_);_($*(#,##0.00);_($*"-"??_);_(@_)
Currency(0)	Number = ($#,##0_);_($*(#,##0);_($*"-"_);_(@_)
Percent	Number = 0%

With the Style command, you also can add new styles, modify styles, delete styles, and merge styles from other workbooks. You add a new style to a workbook or merge styles when you plan to use a group of format specifications over and over.

The following steps create a new style called Four-Digit Year by modifying the existing Normal style. The new Four-Digit Year style will include the following formats: Number = d-mmm-yyyy; Alignment = Horizontal Center, Bottom Aligned; and Font = Arial 10, Bold.

More About

Normal Style

The Normal style is the format style that Excel initially assigns all cells in a workbook. If you change the Normal style, Excel formats all cells not assigned another style the new format specifications.

 To Create a New Style

1 **Click Format on the menu bar and then point to Style.**

The Format menu displays as shown in Figure 6-22.

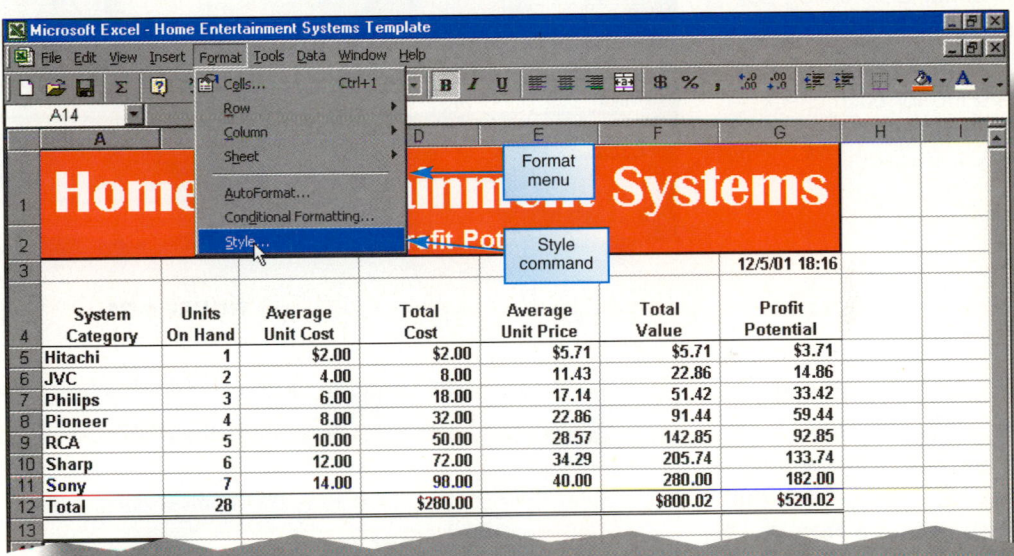

FIGURE 6-22

2 **Click Style. When the Style dialog box displays, drag through Normal in the Style name text box and then type** Four-Digit Year **as the new style name. Point to the Modify button.**

The Style dialog box displays with the new style name Four-Digit Year (Figure 6-23).

FIGURE 6-23

3 Click the Modify button. When the Format Cells dialog box displays, if necessary, click the Number tab, click Date in the Category list, and then click 14-Mar-1998 in the Type list. Point to the Alignment tab.

The Format Cells dialog box displays (Figure 6-24). The Format Cells dialog box contains a tab for each check box in the Style dialog box.

FIGURE 6-24

4 Click the Alignment tab. Click the Horizontal box arrow and then click Center. Click the OK button in the Format Cells dialog box. Click Font, Borders, Patterns, and Protection to deselect the check boxes in the Style Includes area. Point to the Add button.

The Style dialog box displays the formats assigned to the Four-Digit Year (Figure 6-25).

5 Click the Add button to add the new style to the style list available with this template. Click the OK button.

The new style Four-Digit Year becomes part of the list of styles available with this template.

FIGURE 6-25

Other Ways

1. Press ALT+O, press S

Applying a Style

In earlier steps, cell G3 was assigned the NOW function. This project calls for centering the date and displaying it with a four-digit year. To accomplish this task, the following steps assign the Four-Digit Year style to cell G3.

 To Apply a Style

1 Click cell G3. Click Format on the menu bar and then click Style. Click the Style name box arrow and then click Four-Digit Year in the list. Point to the OK button.

The Style dialog box displays (Figure 6-26).

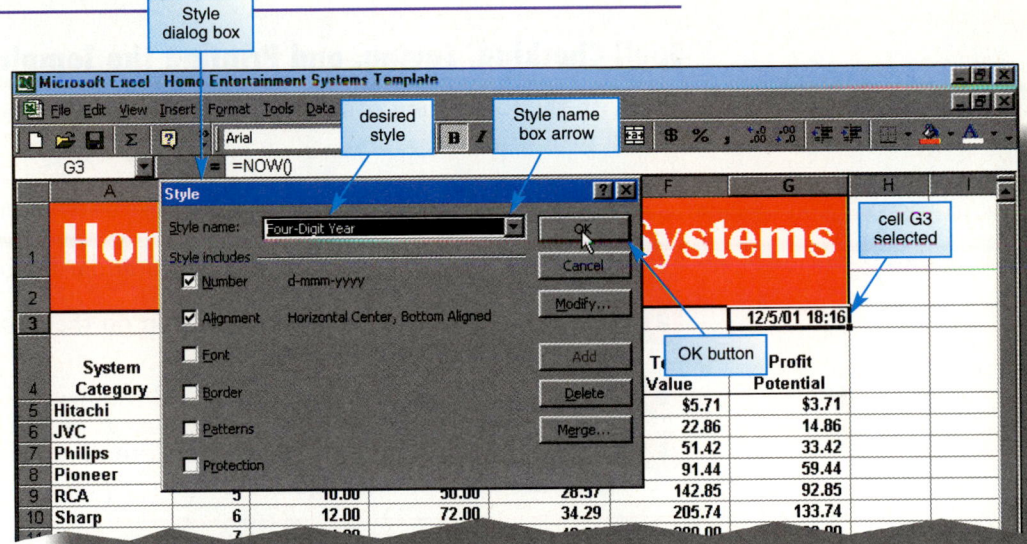

FIGURE 6-26

2 Click the OK button.

Excel assigns the Four-Digit Year style to cell G3 (Figure 6-27).

FIGURE 6-27

Other Ways

1. Press ALT+O, press S

Keep in mind the following additional points concerning styles:

1. If you assign two styles to a range of cells, Excel adds the second style to the first rather than replacing it.

2. Do not delete the default styles that come with Excel because some of the buttons on the toolbars are dependent on them.
3. You can merge styles from another workbook into the active workbook through the use of the Merge button in the Style dialog box. You must, however, open the workbook that contains the desired styles before you use the Merge button.
4. The six check boxes in the Style dialog box are identical to the six tabs in the Format Cells dialog box.

Spell Checking, Saving, and Printing the Template

With the formatting complete, the next step is to spell check the template, save it, and then print it.

TO SPELL CHECK, SAVE, AND PRINT THE TEMPLATE

1 Double-click the move handle on the Standard toolbar.

2 Click cell A1. Click the Spelling button on the Standard toolbar. Change any misspelled words.

3 Click the Save button on the Standard toolbar.

4 Click the Print button on the Standard toolbar. Click the Close button on the template title bar (see Figure 6-27 on the previous page).

Excel saves the template using the file name Home Entertainment Systems Template, prints the template, and finally closes the template.

Alternative Uses of Templates

Before continuing on and using the template to create the Home Entertainment Systems workbook, you should be aware of some additional uses of templates. As you have seen when you begin a new Office document, Excel includes a default Blank Workbook template, which you double-click to open a new workbook. This blank workbook acts like a template in that it contains the defaults that you see whenever you start Excel.

You can save a template to the folder: c:\windows\application data\microsoft\templates. Once a template is saved in this folder, you can select it by clicking the New command on the File menu. For example, if you save the Home Entertainment Systems Template file to this folder, you then can open it by clicking the New command on the File menu.

If you save a formatted template in the folder: c:\microsoft office\office\xlstart using the file name Book, Excel uses it as the default Blank Workbook template every time you begin or insert a blank workbook.

Creating a Workbook from a Template

Once you have saved the template on disk, you can begin the second phase of this project: using the template to create the Home Entertainment Systems workbook shown in Figure 6-1 on page E 6.5. As shown by the three tabs at the bottom of Figure 6-28, Excel's default Blank Workbook template includes three worksheets. The Home Entertainment Systems workbook, however, requires four sheets — one for each of the three store locations and one for the company totals. Thus, a worksheet must be added to the workbook. Perform the following steps to add a worksheet to the workbook.

More *About* **2000**

Opening a Workbook at Startup

You can instruct Windows to open a workbook (or template) automatically when you turn on your computer by adding the workbook (or template) to the Startup folder. Use Explorer to copy the file to the Startup folder. The Startup folder is in the Programs folder and the Programs folder is in the Start Menu folder.

To Open a Template and Add a Worksheet

1 **Click the Open button on the Standard toolbar. When the Open dialog box displays, click the Files of type box arrow and click Templates. Click the Look in box arrow and click 3½ Floppy (A:). Double-click Home Entertainment Systems Template.**

Excel opens the file, Home Entertainment Systems Template, as shown earlier in Figure 6-27.

2 **Click the Sheet2 tab at the bottom of the screen. Click Insert on the menu bar and then point to Worksheet.**

The Insert menu displays (Figure 6-28).

FIGURE 6-28

3 **Click Worksheet.**

Excel adds a fourth worksheet between Sheet1 and Sheet2. Recall that Sheet1 contains the template. As shown on the sheet tab, Sheet4 is the name of the new worksheet (Figure 6-29).

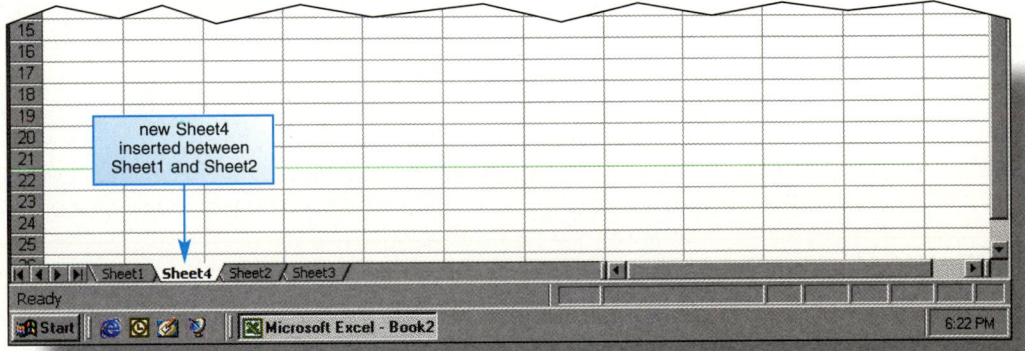

FIGURE 6-29

Other Ways

1. Right-click sheet tab, click Insert, double-click Worksheet icon
2. Right-click sheet tab, click Move or Copy, click Create a copy, click OK button

You can add up to a total of 255 worksheets. An alternative to adding worksheets is to change the default number of worksheets before you open a new workbook. To change the default number of worksheets in a blank workbook, click Options on the Tools menu, click the General tab, and change the number in the Sheets in new workbook box. You also can delete a worksheet by right-clicking the tab of the worksheet you want to delete and then clicking Delete on the shortcut menu.

With four worksheets, you now can copy the template on the Sheet1 worksheet to the three blank worksheets in the workbook.

 Steps **To Create a Workbook from a Template**

1 **Click the Sheet1 tab to display the template. Click the Select All button and then click the Copy button on the Standard toolbar.**

The template is selected as shown in Figure 6-30. The template, including all data and formats, is copied to the Office Clipboard.

FIGURE 6-30

2 Click the Sheet4 tab. While holding down the SHIFT key, click the Sheet3 tab so all three blank worksheets are selected. Click the Paste button on the Standard toolbar.

The template is copied to Sheet4, Sheet2, and Sheet3. Because multiple sheets are selected, the term [Group] follows the template name on the title bar (Figure 6-31).

[Group] indicates multiple worksheets are selected

Paste button

contents of Sheet4 after copy and paste operation

Sheet4, Sheet2, and Sheet3 selected

FIGURE 6-31

3 Click the Sheet1 tab. Press the ESC key to remove the marquee surrounding the selection. Hold down the SHIFT key and click the Sheet3 tab. Click cell A14 to deselect the worksheet on each sheet. Hold down the SHIFT key and click the Sheet1 tab. Click Save As on the File menu. Type Home Entertainment Systems in the File name text box. Click Microsoft Excel Workbook in the Save as type list. If necessary, click 3½ Floppy (A:) in the Save in list. Click the Save button in the Save As dialog box.

Excel saves the workbook on drive A using the file name Home Entertainment Systems. Sheet1 is the active worksheet.

Drilling an Entry Down through Worksheets

The next step is to enter the average unit cost for each system category (Table 6-4) in the range C5:C11. The average unit costs for each category are identical on all four sheets. For example, the average unit cost for the Hitachi category in cell C5 is $3,212.37 on all four sheets. To speed data entry, Excel allows you to enter a number once and drill it through worksheets so it displays in the same cell on all the selected worksheets. This technique is referred to as **drilling an entry**. The steps on the next page drill the seven average unit cost entries in Table 6-4 through all four worksheets.

Table 6-4	Average Unit Cost Entries
SYSTEM CATEGORY	**AVERAGE UNIT COST**
Hitachi	3212.37
JVC	224.13
Philips	995.21
Pioneer	4123.82
RCA	1175.47
Sharp	1023.85
Sony	109.80

To Drill an Entry Through Worksheets

1 With Sheet1 active, hold down the SHIFT key and then click the Sheet3 tab. Click cell C5. Type 3212.37 and then press the DOWN ARROW key. Enter the six remaining average unit costs in Table 6-4 on the previous page in the range C6:C11.

All four tabs at the bottom of the screen are selected. The word Sheet1 on the first tab is bold, indicating it is the active sheet. The average unit cost entries display as shown in Figure 6-32.

	System Category	Units On Hand	Average Unit Cost	Total Cost	Average Unit Price	Total Value	Profit Potential
							5-Dec-2001
5	Hitachi	1	$3,212.37	$3,212.37	$9,178.20	$9,178.20	$5,965.83
6	JVC	2	224.13	448.26	640.37	1,280.74	832.48
7	Philips	3	995.21	2,985.63	2,843.46	8,530.38	5,544.75
8	Pioneer	4	4,123.82	16,495.28	11,782.34	47,129.36	30,634.08
9	RCA	5	1,175.47	5,877.35	3,358.49	16,792.45	10,915.10
10	Sharp	6	1,023.85	6,143.10	2,925.29	17,551.74	11,408.64
11	Sony	7	109.80	768.60	313.71	2,195.97	1,427.37
12	Total	28		$35,930.59		$102,658.84	$66,728.25

Home Entertainment Systems — Store Profit Potential

all four sheets selected

average unit costs entered on Sheet1 also are assigned to the same cells on Sheet4, Sheet2, and Sheet3

FIGURE 6-32

2 Hold down the SHIFT key and then click the Sheet1 tab to deselect Sheet4, Sheet2, and Sheet3. One at a time, click the Sheet4 tab, the Sheet2 tab, and the Sheet3 tab.

The four sheets are identical (Figure 6-33). Each is made up of the data and formats assigned earlier to the template.

average unit costs display on all four sheets

Sheet1 Sheet4 Sheet2 Sheet3

FIGURE 6-33

In the previous set of steps, seven new numbers were entered on one worksheet. As shown in Figure 6-33, by drilling the entries through the four other worksheets, twenty-eight new numbers now display, seven on each of the four worksheets. This capability of drilling data through worksheets is an efficient way to enter data that is common among worksheets.

Modifying the Pittsburgh Sheet

With the skeleton of the Home Entertainment Systems workbook created, the next step is to modify the individual sheets. The following steps modify the Pittsburgh sheet by changing the sheet name and worksheet subtitle, changing the color of the title area, and entering the units on hand in column B.

TO MODIFY THE PITTSBURGH SHEET

1 Double-click the Sheet4 tab and then type `Pittsburgh` as the sheet name.

2 Double-click cell A2, drag through the word Store, and type `Pittsburgh` to change the worksheet subtitle.

3 Double-click the move handle on the Formatting toolbar to display it in its entirety. Select the range A1:A2. Click the Fill Color button arrow on the Formatting toolbar. Click Blue (column 6, row 2) on the Fill Color palette.

4 Enter the data listed in Table 6-5 in the range B5:B11.

5 Click the Save button on the Standard toolbar.

The Pittsburgh sheet displays as shown in Figure 6-34.

More About

Drilling an Entry

Besides drilling a number down through a workbook, you can drill a format, a function, or a formula down through a workbook.

Table 6-5	Pittsburgh Units on Hand
CELL	UNITS ON HAND
B5	5
B6	234
B7	45
B8	12
B9	28
B10	30
B11	1015

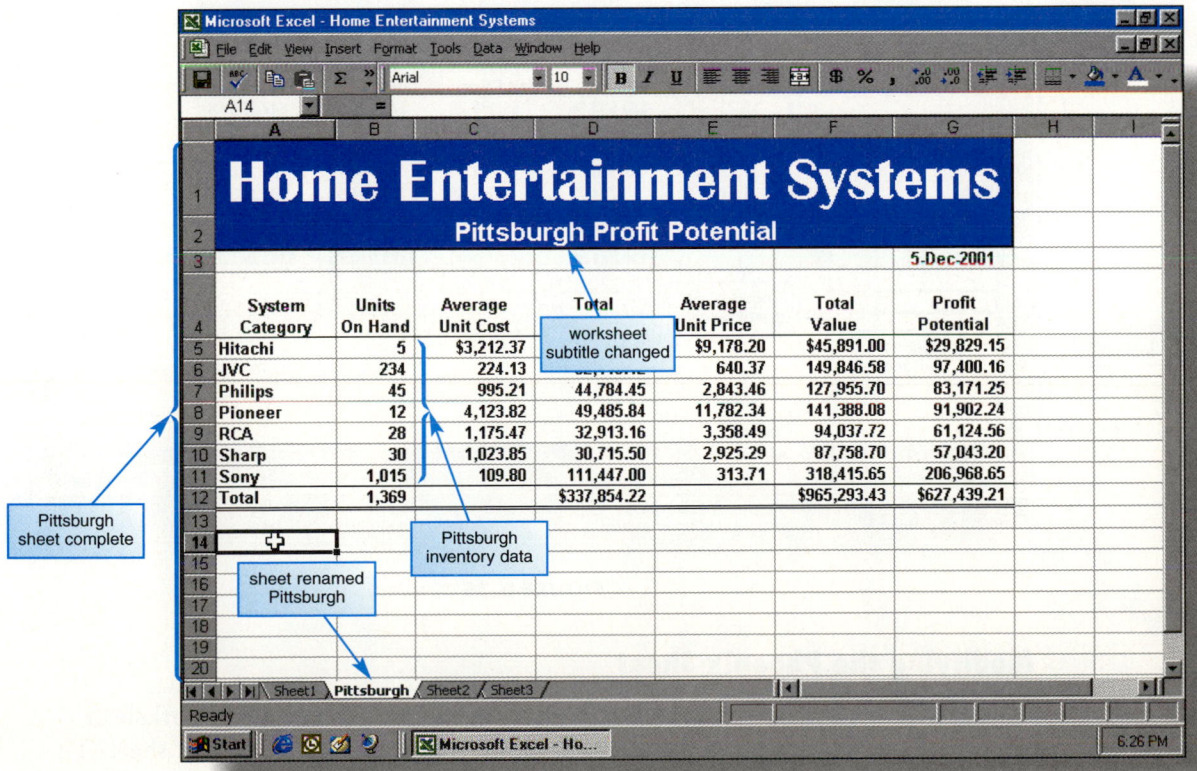

FIGURE 6-34

As you enter the new data, Excel immediately recalculates the formulas on all four worksheets.

Modifying the Indianapolis Sheet

The following steps modify the Indianapolis sheet.

Table 6-6	Indianapolis Units on Hand
CELL	**UNITS ON HAND**
B5	8
B6	75
B7	13
B8	8
B9	10
B10	29
B11	9

TO MODIFY THE INDIANAPOLIS SHEET

1 Double-click the Sheet2 tab and then type Indianapolis as the sheet name.

2 Double-click cell A2, drag through the word Store, and type Indianapolis as the worksheet subtitle.

3 Select the range A1:A2. Click the Fill Color button arrow on the Formatting toolbar. Click Green (column 4, row 2) on the Fill Color palette.

4 Enter the data in Table 6-6 in the range B5:B11.

5 Click the Save button on the Standard toolbar.

The Indianapolis sheet displays as shown in Figure 6-35.

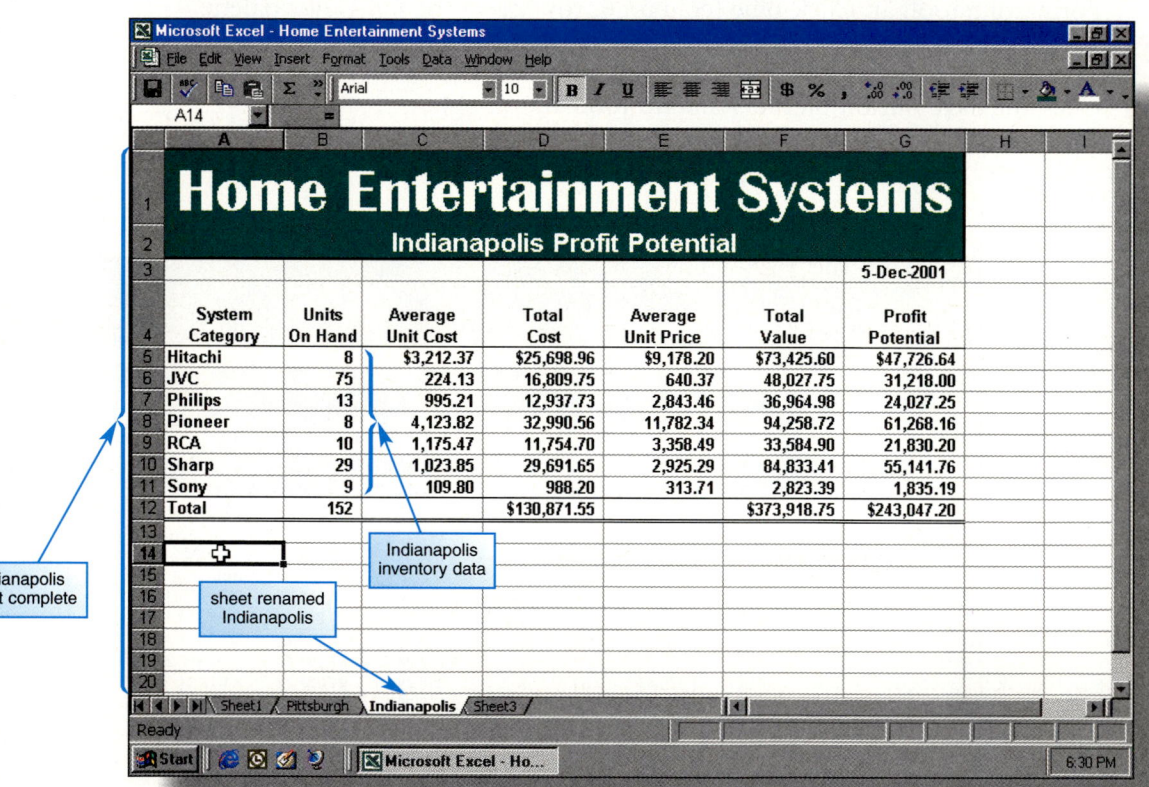

FIGURE 6-35

Modifying the Phoenix Sheet

As with the Pittsburgh and Indianapolis sheets, the sheet name, worksheet subtitle, data, and background colors must be changed on the Phoenix sheet. The following steps modify the Phoenix sheet.

TO MODIFY THE PHOENIX SHEET

1 Double click the Sheet3 tab and then type Phoenix as the sheet name.

2 Double click cell A2, drag through the word store and type Phoenix to change the worksheet subtitle.

3 Select the range A1:A2. Click the Fill Color button arrow on the Formatting toolbar. Click Violet (column 7, row 3) on the Fill Color palette.

4 Enter the data in Table 6-7 in the range B5:B11.

5 Click the Save button on the Standard toolbar.

The Phoenix sheet displays as shown in Figure 6-36.

Table 6-7	Phoenix Units on Hand
CELL	**UNITS ON HAND**
B5	5
B6	82
B7	16
B8	3
B9	13
B10	82
B11	2

FIGURE 6-36

With the three store sheets complete, the next step is to modify Sheet1, which will serve as the consolidation worksheet containing totals of the data on the Pittsburgh, Indianapolis, and Phoenix sheets. Because this sheet contains totals of the data, you need to understand how to reference cells in other sheets in a workbook before modifying Sheet1.

Referencing Cells in Other Sheets in a Workbook

To reference cells in other sheets in a workbook, you use the sheet name, which serves as the **sheet reference**, and the cell reference. For example, you refer to cell B5 on the Pittsburgh sheet as shown below.

=Pittsburgh!B5

More About

Importing Data

Unit costs often are maintained in another workbook, a file, or a database. If the unit costs are maintained elsewhere, ways exist to link to a workbook or import data from a file or database into a workbook. For information on importing data, see the Get External Data command on the Data menu.

More About

Sheet Tabs

If you right-click a tab, a short-cut menu displays with several commands to modify the workbook. Commands include Insert, Delete, Rename, Move, or Copy. All these commands relate to manipulating sheets in a workbook. For example, you can use this menu to insert a new sheet, delete the active sheet, rename the active sheet, or move or copy the active sheet.

Using this method, you can sum cell B5 on the three store sheets by selecting cell B5 on the Sheet1 sheet and then entering:

= Pittsburgh!B5 + Indianapolis!B5 + Phoenix!B5

A much quicker way to total this is to use the SUM function as follows:

=SUM(Pittsburgh:Phoenix!B5)

The SUM argument (Pittsburgh:Phoenix!B5) instructs Excel to sum cell B5 on each of the three sheets (Pittsburgh, Indianapolis, and Phoenix). The colon (:) between the first sheet and the last sheet means to include these sheets and all sheets in between, just as it does with a range of cells on a sheet. A range that spans two or more sheets in a workbook, such as Pittsburgh:Phoenix!B5, is called a **3-D range**. The reference to this range is a **3-D reference**.

A sheet reference, such as Phoenix!, always is absolute. Thus, the sheet reference remains constant when you copy formulas.

Entering a Sheet Reference

You can enter a sheet reference in a cell by typing it or by clicking the appropriate sheet tab while in Point mode. When you click the sheet tab, Excel activates the sheet and automatically adds the sheet name and an exclamation point after the insertion point in the formula bar. Next, click or drag through the cells you want to reference on the sheet.

If the range of cells to be referenced is located on several worksheets (as when selecting a 3-D range), click the first sheet tab and then click the cell or drag through the range of cells. Next, while holding down the SHIFT key, click the sheet tab of the last sheet you want to reference. Excel will include the cell(s) on the end sheets and all the sheets in between.

Modifying the Company Sheet

This section modifies the Company sheet by changing the sheet name, subtitle, and entering the SUM function in each cell in the range B5:B11. The SUM functions will determine the total units on hand by system category for the three stores. Cell B5 on the Company sheet, for instance, will equal the sum of the Hitachi category units on hand in cells Pittsburgh!B5, Indianapolis!B5, and Phoenix!B5. Before determining the totals, perform the following steps to change the sheet name from Sheet1 to Company and the worksheet subtitle to Company Profit Potential.

More About

3-D References

If you are adding numbers on noncontiguous sheets, hold down the CTRL key rather than the SHIFT key when selecting the sheets.

TO RENAME A SHEET AND MODIFY THE WORKSHEET TITLE

1. Double-click the Sheet1 sheet tab.

2. Type Company and then press the ENTER key.

3. Double-click cell A2, drag through the word Store, and type Company as the worksheet subtitle. Press the ENTER key

Excel changes the name of Sheet1 to Company and the worksheet subtitle to Company Profit Potential.

The following steps enter the 3-D references used to determine the total units on hand for each of the seven system categories.

Steps To Enter and Copy 3-D References

1 **Double-click the move handle on the Standard toolbar to show it in its entirety. Click cell B5 and then click the AutoSum button on the Standard toolbar.**

The SUM function displays without a selected range (Figure 6-37).

FIGURE 6-37

2 **Click the Pittsburgh tab and then click cell B5. While holding down the SHIFT key, click the Phoenix tab.**

A marquee surrounds cell Pittsburgh!B5 (Figure 6-38). All four sheet tabs are selected; the Pittsburgh tab displays in bold because it is the active sheet. The SUM function displays in the formula bar.

FIGURE 6-38

3 **Click the Enter box in the formula bar.**

The SUM function is entered in cell Company!B5 and the Company sheet becomes the active sheet. The sum of the cells Pittsburgh!B5, Indianapolis!B5, and Phoenix!B5 displays in cell B5 of the Company sheet. The SUM function assigned to cell B5 displays in the formula bar (Figure 6-39).

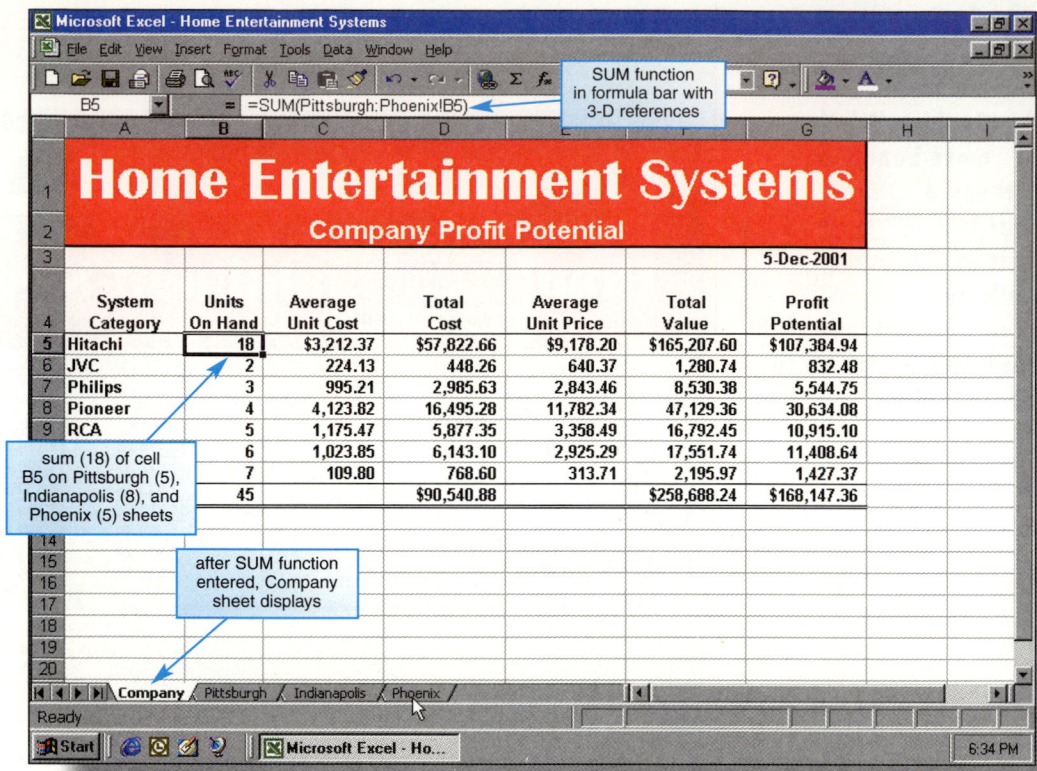

FIGURE 6-39

4 **With cell B5 active, point to the fill handle.**

The mouse pointer changes to a cross hair on the fill handle (Figure 6-40).

FIGURE 6-40

5 **Drag the fill handle through cell B11.**

Excel copies the SUM function in cell B5 to the range B6:B11 (Figure 6-41). Excel automatically adjusts the cell references in the SUM function to reference the corresponding cells on the other three sheets in the workbook. The total units on hand for each system category displays.

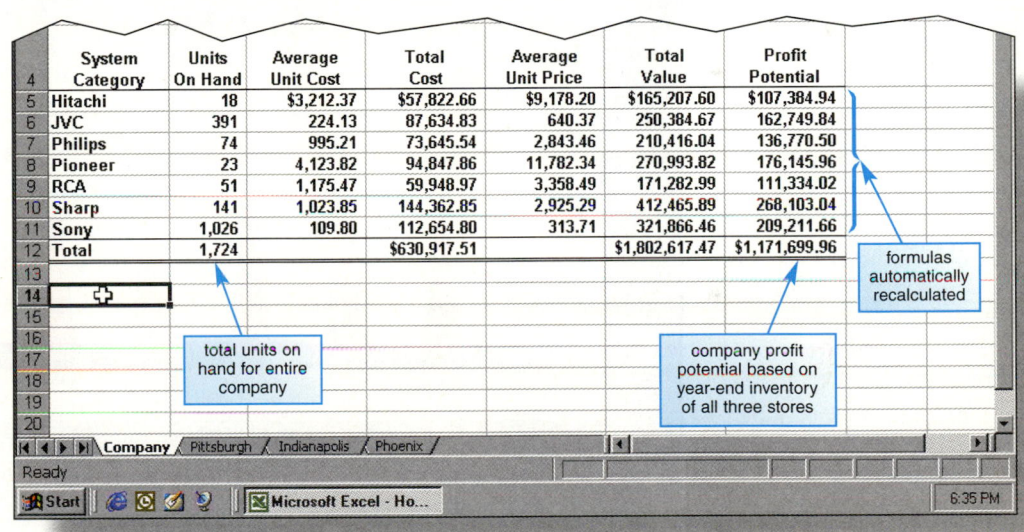

B5 = =SUM(Pittsburgh:Phoenix!B5)

Home Entertainment Systems
Company Profit Potential

5-Dec-2001

System Category	Units On Hand	SUM function in cell B5 copied to range B6:B11	Total Cost	Average Unit Price	Total Value	Profit Potential
Hitachi	18		57,822.60	$9,178.20	$165,207.60	$107,384.94
JVC	391	224.13	87,634.83	640.37	250,384.67	162,749.84
Philips	74	995.21	73,645.54	2,843.46	210,416.04	136,770.50
Pioneer	23	4,123.82	94,847.86	11,782.34	270,993.82	176,145.96
RCA	51	1,175.47	59,948.97	3,358.49	171,282.99	111,334.02
Sharp	141	1,023.85	144,362.85	2,925.29	412,465.89	268,103.04
Sony	1,026	109.80	112,654.80	313.71	321,866.46	209,211.66
Total	1,724		$630,917.51		$1,802,617.47	$1,171,699.96

FIGURE 6-41

6 **Click cell A14 to deselect the range B6:B11. Click the Save button on the Standard toolbar to save the Home Entertainment Systems workbook.**

All the formulas on the Company sheet are recalculated based on the total units on hand for each system category. The Company sheet is complete (Figure 6-42).

System Category	Units On Hand	Average Unit Cost	Total Cost	Average Unit Price	Total Value	Profit Potential
Hitachi	18	$3,212.37	$57,822.66	$9,178.20	$165,207.60	$107,384.94
JVC	391	224.13	87,634.83	640.37	250,384.67	162,749.84
Philips	74	995.21	73,645.54	2,843.46	210,416.04	136,770.50
Pioneer	23	4,123.82	94,847.86	11,782.34	270,993.82	176,145.96
RCA	51	1,175.47	59,948.97	3,358.49	171,282.99	111,334.02
Sharp	141	1,023.85	144,362.85	2,925.29	412,465.89	268,103.04
Sony	1,026	109.80	112,654.80	313.71	321,866.46	209,211.66
Total	1,724		$630,917.51		$1,802,617.47	$1,171,699.96

formulas automatically recalculated

total units on hand for entire company

company profit potential based on year-end inventory of all three stores

Company / Pittsburgh / Indianapolis / Phoenix /

Ready

Start | Microsoft Excel - Ho... | 6:35 PM

FIGURE 6-42

As shown in cell G12 in Figure 6-42, Home Entertainment Systems has a month-end profit potential of $1,171,699.96, based on the inventory data submitted by the three stores. If a store calls in a correction to the units on hand for any system category, Santiago Biagi, simply has to select the sheet that represents the store and enter the correction. All formulas, including those on the Company sheet, will be recalculated immediately, and Santiago quickly can see the most up-to-date profit potential.

Other Ways

1. Click Paste Function button, click Math & Trig in Function Category list box, click SUM in Function name list box, click OK button, enter parameters, click OK button

2. On Insert menu click Function, click Math & Trig in Function Category list box, click SUM in Function name list box, click OK button, enter parameters, click OK button

3. Click Edit Formula box in formula bar, click Sum in Function list box, enter parameters, click OK button

With the four worksheets in the Home Entertainment Systems workbook complete, the next step is to draw a 3-D Cone chart.

Drawing the 3-D Cone Chart

The 3-D Cone chart is similar to a 3-D Bar chart in that it can be used to show trends or illustrate comparisons among items. The 3-D Cone chart in Figure 6-43, for example, compares the profit potential of each of the seven system categories. WordArt is used to draw the curved chart title Profit Potential. A text box and arrow are used to highlight the system category with the greatest profit potential.

FIGURE 6-43

The following steps create the 3-D Cone chart.

To Draw a 3-D Cone Chart

1 **With the Company sheet active, select the range A5:A11. While holding down the CTRL key, select the range G5:G11. Click the Chart Wizard button on the Standard toolbar. When the Chart Wizard – Step 1 of 4 – Chart Type dialog box displays, click Cone in the Chart type list box. If necessary, click Column with a conical shape (column 1, row 1) in the Chart sub-type area. Point to the Next button.**

The Chart Wizard – Step 1 of 4 – Chart Type dialog box displays as shown in Figure 6-44. The nonadjacent range selection displays behind the dialog box.

FIGURE 6-44

2 **Click the Next button.**

The Chart Wizard – Step 2 of 4 – Chart Source Data dialog box displays with a sample of the 3-D Cone chart and the nonadjacent data range selection (Figure 6-45). Because nonadjacent ranges are selected down the sheet, Excel automatically determines series are in columns.

FIGURE 6-45

3 Click the Next button. When the Chart Wizard – Step 3 of 4 – Chart Options dialog box displays, click the Legend tab. Click Show Legend to deselect it so the legend does not display with the chart.

The Chart Wizard – Step 3 of 4 – Chart Options dialog box displays (Figure 6-46).

FIGURE 6-46

4 Click the Next button. When the Chart Wizard – Step 4 of 4 – Chart Location dialog box displays, click As new sheet.

The Chart Wizard – Step 4 of 4 – Chart Location dialog box displays (Figure 6-47). Because the As new sheet option button is selected, the chart will be drawn on a separate chart sheet.

FIGURE 6-47

5 **Click the Finish button.**

Excel draws the 3-D Cone chart. The chart sheet, which is named Chart1, is inserted as the first sheet in the work-book (Figure 6-48).

6 **Click the wall behind the cones. Click the Fill Color button arrow on the Formatting toolbar. Click Light Yellow (column 3, row 5). Click one of the cones to select all the cones. Click the Fill Color button arrow on the Formatting toolbar. Click Red (column 1, row 3).**

The 3-D Cone chart displays as shown earlier in Figure 6-43 on page E 6.38.

FIGURE 6-48

7 **Double-click the Chart1 tab and then type** `3-D Cone Chart` **as the sheet name. Press the ENTER key. Drag the 3-D Cone Chart sheet tab to the right of the Phoenix sheet tab.**

Other Ways

1. Select chart range, press F11

The 3-D Cone chart compares the profit potential of the seven system categories. You can see from the chart that the Sharp category has the greatest profit potential and that the Hitachi category has the least profit potential.

Adding a Chart Title Using the WordArt Tool

In earlier projects, you added a chart title by using the Chart Wizard and then for-matted it using the Formatting toolbar. This section shows you how to add a chart title and create special text formatting effects using the WordArt tool. The **WordArt tool** allows you to create shadowed, skewed, rotated, and stretched text on a chart sheet or worksheet. The WordArt design is called an **object**. You start the WordArt tool by clicking the WordArt button on the Drawing toolbar. Perform the steps on the next page to add a Chart title using the WordArt tool.

Steps

To Add a Chart Title Using the WordArt Tool

1 With the chart sheet displaying on the screen, click the Drawing button on the Standard toolbar. When the Drawing toolbar displays, dock it at the bottom of the screen by dragging it below the tabs.

The Drawing toolbar displays at the bottom of the screen (Figure 6-49).

FIGURE 6-49

2 Click the Insert WordArt button on the Drawing toolbar. When the WordArt Gallery dialog box displays, click the design in column 5, row 1 in the Select a WordArt style area. Point to the OK button.

The WordArt Gallery dialog box displays (Figure 6-50).

FIGURE 6-50

3 Click the OK button. When the Edit WordArt Text dialog box displays, type Profit Potential as the title of the 3-D Cone chart. Point to the OK button.

The Edit WordArt Text dialog box displays (Figure 6-51). Profit Potential will be the chart title.

FIGURE 6-51

4 Click the OK button.

The WordArt object (Profit Potential) displays in the middle of the chart sheet (Figure 6-52). The WordArt toolbar displays.

FIGURE 6-52

5 Point to the center of the WordArt object and drag it above the cones in the chart and then drag the sizing handles to resize it as shown in Figure 6-53.

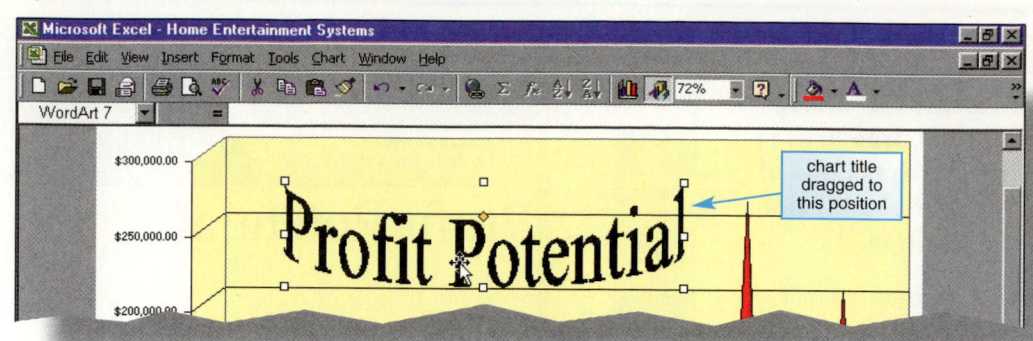

FIGURE 6-53

6 With the WordArt object selected, click the Fill Color button arrow on the Formatting toolbar to change the color to red.

The color of the WordArt object changes to red (Figure 6-54). Even though the title appears to be made up of text, the chart title is an object. Thus, you use the Fill Color button, rather than the Font Color button, to change the color of the object.

FIGURE 6-54

7 Click outside the chart area.

Excel hides the WordArt toolbar. The chart title is finished (Figure 6-55).

1. On Insert menu point to Picture, click WordArt on Picture submenu
2. Right-click toolbar, click WordArt, click Insert WordArt button

FIGURE 6-55

Once you add a WordArt object to your workbook, you can use the WordArt toolbar to edit it. The buttons on the WordArt toolbar and their functions are described in Table 6-8. Like the other Excel toolbars, you can display or hide the WordArt toolbar by right-clicking any toolbar and then clicking WordArt on the shortcut menu.

Adding a Text Box and Arrow to the Chart

A text box and arrow can be used to **annotate** (callout or highlight) other objects or elements in a worksheet or chart. For example, in a worksheet, you may want to annotate a particular cell or group of cells by adding a text box and arrow. In a chart, you may want to emphasize a column or slice of a Pie chart.

A **text box** is a rectangular area of variable size in which you can add text. You use the sizing handles to resize a text box in the same manner you resize an embedded chart. If the text box has the same color as the background, then the text appears as if it was written freehand because the box itself does not show. An **arrow** allows you to connect an object, such as a text box, to an item that you want to annotate.

To draw a text box, click the **Text Box button** on the Drawing toolbar. Move the cross hair to one corner of the desired location and drag to the diagonally opposite corner. Once the mouse pointer changes to a cross hair, you also can click the upper-left corner of the desired location and Excel will draw a box that you can resize later. To enter text within the box, click the box and begin typing.

To draw an arrow, click the **Arrow button** on the Drawing toolbar. Move the cross hair pointer to one end of the line you want to draw. Drag the mouse pointer to draw the line. The arrowhead appears at the end of the line where you released the mouse button.

The steps on the next page add the text box and arrow shown earlier in Figure 6-43 on page E 6.38.

Table 6-8	Buttons on the WordArt Toolbar	
BUTTON	**NAME**	**FUNCTION**
	Insert WordArt	Starts the WordArt tool
	Edit Text	Edits text
	WordArt Gallery	Displays the WordArt Gallery dialog box
	Format Object	Formats an object
	WordArt Shape	Changes the shape of an object
	Free Rotate	Rotates an object
	WordArt Same Letter Heights	Switches between the same and different letter height in an object
	WordArt Vertical Text	Changes the design from horizontal to vertical
	WordArt Alignment	Changes the alignment of an object
	WordArt Character Spacing	Changes the character spacing in an object

Drawing Objects

To draw multiple objects, such as text boxes and arrows, double-click the corresponding button. The button will stay recessed, allowing you to draw more objects, until you click the corresponding button. If you need a series of identical objects, create one object, then use the Copy and Paste buttons.

Steps **To Add a Text Box and Arrow**

1 **Click the Text Box button on the Drawing toolbar. Point to the upper-left corner of the planned text box location (Figure 6-56) and then drag the cross hair to the lower-right corner. Type** Greatest Profit Potential **as the text. Drag through the text. Right-click the text and then click Format Text Box. When the Format Text Box dialog box displays, change the font to 12-point red, bold. Click the OK button. If necessary, use the sizing handles to resize the text box.**

The text box displays as shown in Figure 6-56.

FIGURE 6-56

2 **Click the Arrow button on the Drawing toolbar. Point immediately to the left of the letter P in Profit in the text box. Drag to the cone representing Sharp. Release the mouse button.**

The arrow points to the cone representing Sharp (Figure 6-57).

FIGURE 6-57

3 **Click the Drawing button on the Standard toolbar to hide the Drawing toolbar.**

The 3-D Cone chart is complete (Figure 6-58).

FIGURE 6-58

Besides text boxes, you can use the **AutoShapes button** on the Drawing toolbar to draw more eloquent callouts, such as flowchart symbols, stars and banners, and balloons that are similar to what is used to display words in a comic book.

Adding Comments to a Workbook

Comments, or **notes,** in a workbook are used to describe the function of a cell, a range of cells, a sheet, or the entire workbook. Comments are used to identify entries that might otherwise be difficult to understand.

In Excel, you can assign comments to any cell in the worksheet using the **Comment command** on the Insert menu or the **Insert Comment command** on the shortcut menu. Once a comment is assigned, you can read the comment by pointing to the cell. Excel will display the comment in a **comment box**. In general, overall workbook comments should include the following:

1. Worksheet title
2. Author's name
3. Date created
4. Date last modified (use N/A if it has not been modified)
5. Template(s) used, if any
6. A short description of the purpose of the worksheet

The steps on the next page assign a workbook comment to cell A14 on the Company sheet.

To Assign a Comment to a Cell

1 **Click the Company tab to display the Company sheet. Right-click cell A14. Point to Insert Comment on the shortcut menu.**

The shortcut menu displays (Figure 6-59).

FIGURE 6-59

2 **Click Insert Comment. When the comment box displays, drag the lower-right handle to resize the comment box as shown in Figure 6-60.**

Excel adds a small red triangle, called a comment indicator, to cell A14. A small black arrow attached to the comment box points to the comment indicator (Figure 6-60).

3 **Enter the comment shown in Figure 6-60 in the comment box.**

FIGURE 6-60

4 **Click cell A17 and then point to cell A14.**

The comment box displays (Figure 6-61).

5 **Click the Save button on the Standard toolbar to save the workbook.**

FIGURE 6-61

The **comment indicator** in the upper-right corner of cell A14 indicates the cell has a comment associated with it. To read the comment, point to the cell and the note will display on the worksheet. To edit the comment, right-click the cell and then click **Edit Comment** on the shortcut menu, or click the cell and then press SHIFT+F2. To delete the comment, right-click the cell and then click **Delete Comment** on the shortcut menu.

When working with comments, you have three options regarding their display on the worksheet:

1. **None** – do not display the comment indicator or comment
2. **Comment indicator only** – display the comment indicator, but not the comment unless you point to it
3. **Comment & indicator** – display both the comment indicator and comment at all times

You select one of the three by clicking Options on the Tools menu and making your selection in the Comments area in the View sheet. If you choose None, then the comment will not display when you point to the cell with the comment. Thus, it becomes a hidden comment.

Other Ways

1. On Insert menu click Comment
2. Press SHIFT+F2

More About

Printing Comments

You can print comments assigned to cells as follows: click File on the menu bar, click Page Setup, in the Page Setup dialog box, click the Sheet tab, click the Comments box arrow, and then click where you want the comments printed in relation to the worksheet printout.

Adding a Header and Changing the Margins

A **header** is printed at the top of every page in a printout. A **footer** is printed at the bottom of every page in a printout. By default, both the header and footer are blank. You can change either so information, such as the workbook author, date, page number, or tab name, prints at the top or bottom of each page.

More About 2000

Selecting Cells

If you double-click the top of the heavy border surrounding the active cell, Excel will make the first empty cell below any non-blank cell in the column the active cell. If you double-click the left side of the heavy border surrounding the active cell, Excel will make the first empty cell to the right of any non-blank cell in the row the active cell.

Sometimes you will want to change the margins to increase or decrease the white space surrounding the printed worksheet or chart. The default **margins** in Excel are set to the following: Top = 1"; Bottom = 1"; Left = .75"; Right = .75". The header and footer are set at .5" from the top and bottom, respectively. You also can center a printout horizontally and vertically.

Changing the header and footer and changing the margins are all part of the **page setup**, which defines the appearance and format of a page. To change page setup characteristics, select the desired sheet(s) and click the **Page Setup command** on the File menu. Remember to select all the sheets you want to modify before you change the headers, footers, or margins, because the page setup characteristics will change only for selected sheets.

As you modify the page setup, remember that Excel does not copy page setup characteristics when one sheet is copied to another. Thus, even if you assigned page setup characteristics to the template before copying it to the Home Entertainment Systems workbook, the page setup characteristics would not copy to the new sheet. The following steps use the Page Setup dialog box to change the headers and margins and center the printout horizontally.

 Steps To Change the Header and Margins and Center the Printout Horizontally

1 If necessary, click the Company tab to make it active. While holding down the SHIFT key, click the 3-D Cone Chart tab. Click File on the menu bar and then point to Page Setup.

Excel displays the File menu (Figure 6-62). The five sheet tabs at the bottom of the window are selected.

FIGURE 6-62

2 **Click Page Setup. When the Page Setup dialog box displays, click the Header/Footer tab. Point to the Custom Header button.**

Samples of the default header and footer display (Figure 6-63). The entry (none) indicates that the headers and footers are blank.

FIGURE 6-63

3 **Click the Custom Header button. When the Header dialog box displays, click the Left section text box. Type** Nikole Rai **and then press the ENTER key. Type** Profit Potential **and then click the Center section text box. Click the Sheet Name button. Click the Right section text box. Type** Page **followed by a space and then click the Page Number button. Type a space and then type** of **followed by a space. Click the Total Pages button. Point to the OK button in the Header dialog box.**

The Header dialog box displays with the new header (Figure 6-64).

FIGURE 6-64

4 **Click the OK button.**

The Header/Footer sheet in the Page Setup dialog box displays as shown in Figure 6-65.

FIGURE 6-65

5 **Click the Margins tab. Click Horizontally in the Center on page area to center the worksheet on the page. Click the Top box and then type** 1.5 **to change the top margin to 1.5". Point to the Print Preview button.**

The Margins sheet in the Page Setup dialog box displays as shown in Figure 6-66.

FIGURE 6-66

6 **Click the Print Preview button in the Page Setup dialog box to preview the workbook.**

The Company sheet displays as shown in Figure 6-67. Although difficult to read, the header displays at the top of the page. While the mouse pointer is a magnifying glass, you can click the page to get a better view.

7 **After previewing the printout, click the Close button on the Print Preview toolbar. Click the Save button on the Standard toolbar to save the workbook with the new page setup characteristics.**

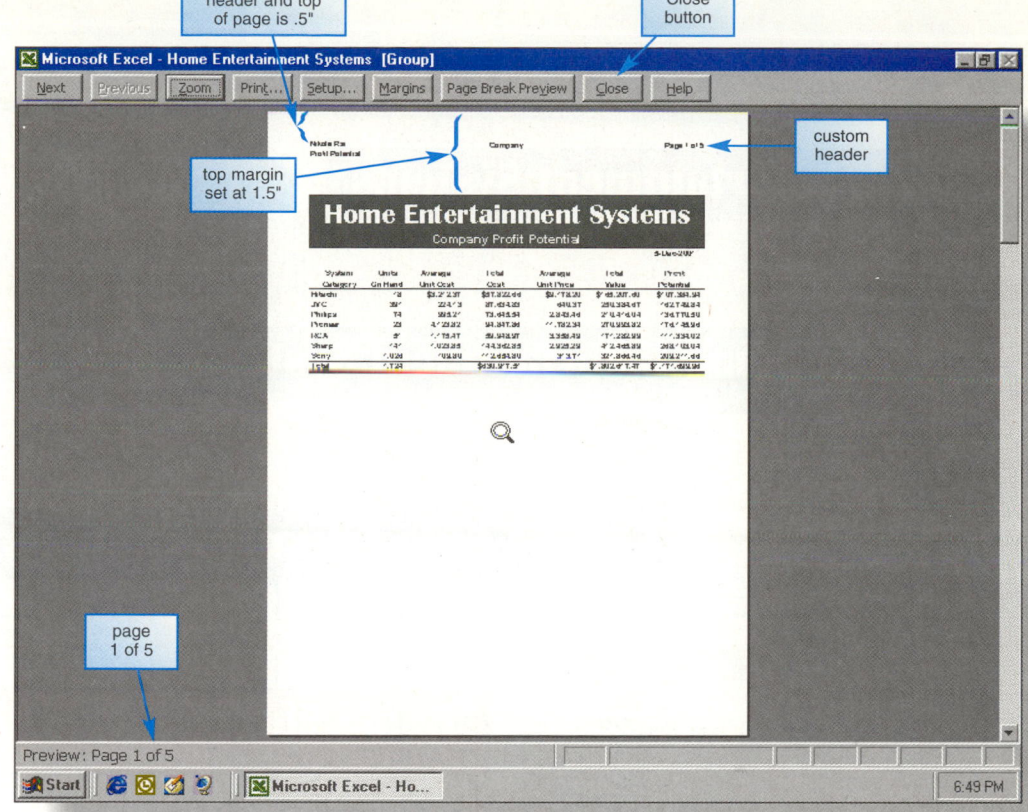

FIGURE 6-67

When you click a button in the Header dialog box (Figure 6-64 on page E 6.51), Excel enters a code (similar to a format code) into the active header section. A code such as &[Page] instructs Excel to insert the page number. Table 6-9 summarizes the buttons, their codes, and their functions in the Header or Footer dialog box.

1. Press ALT+F, press U

Printing the Workbook and Print Options

This section describes how to print the five-page workbook and then describes additional print options available in Excel. The following steps print the workbook.

TO PRINT THE WORKBOOK

1 Ready the printer.

2 If the five sheets in the workbook are not selected, click the Company tab and then, while holding down the SHIFT key, click the 3-D Cone tab.

3 Click the Print button on the Standard toolbar.

4 Hold down the SHIFT key and click the Company tab.

The workbook prints as shown in Figures 6-68a and 6-68b on the next page.

Table 6-9	Buttons in the Header Dialog Box	
BUTTON	**CODE**	**FUNCTION**
A		Displays the Font dialog box
#	&[Page]	Inserts a page number
	&[Pages]	Inserts a total number of pages
	&[Date]	Inserts the system date
	&[Time]	Inserts the system time
	&[File]	Inserts the file name of the workbook
	&[Tab]	Inserts the tab name

(a) Worksheets

(b) Chart

FIGURE 6-68

Changing Sheet Settings

Up to this point you have been introduced to several different print options, such as changing the orientation, fit to option, changing the margin, adding a header and footer, and centering a worksheet on a page. This section describes additional print options available in the Sheet tab in the Page Setup dialog box (Figure 6-69). These print options pertain to the way the worksheet will appear in the printed copy.

FIGURE 6-69

Table 6-10 summarizes the print options available on the Sheet tab.

Table 6-10	Print Options Available Using the Sheet Tab
PRINT OPTION	**DESCRIPTION**
Print area text box	Excel prints from cell A1 to the last occupied cell in a worksheet unless you instruct it to print a selected area. You can select a range to print with the mouse or you can enter a range in the Print area text box. The range can be a name. Noncontiguous ranges will print on a separate page.
Print titles area	This area is used to print row titles and column titles on each page of a worksheet that exceeds a page. You must specify a range, even if you are designating one column (i.e., 1:4 means the first four rows).
Gridlines check box	This check box determines whether gridlines will print.
Black and white check box	A check mark in this check box speeds up printing and saves ink if you have colors in a worksheet and are not printing on a color printer.
Draft quality check box	A check mark in this check box speeds up printing by ignoring formatting and not printing most graphics.
Row and column headings check box	A check mark in this check box instructs Excel to include the column headings (A, B, C, etc.) a and row headings (1, 2, 3, etc.) in the printout.
Page order area	Determines the order in which multipage worksheets will print.

Templates

Applying page setup characteristics to a template will not work because they are not part of the pasted worksheets. Thus, the page setup characteristics assigned to a template apply only to the first sheet in a workbook created by copying the template to multiple worksheets in the workbook.

Headers and Footers

You can turn off headers and footers for a printout by selecting (none) in the Header box and in the Footer box in the Header/Footer sheet in the Page Setup dialog box. This is true especially when printing charts for slides. If the 3-D Cone Chart (Figure 6-68) prints without the header, then you must select the 3-D Cone Chart sheet individually and add the header.

Printing

To speed up printing and save ink of worksheets with background colors, select the Black and White option in the Sheet tab in the Page Setup dialog box.

Page Breaks

If the dotted line representing a page break does not display, click Tools on the menu bar, click Options, click the View tab, and click Page breaks in the Windows option area.

Page Breaks

You can insert page breaks in a worksheet at the top of any row to control how much of a worksheet prints on a page. This is especially useful if you have a worksheet that is several pages long and you want certain parts of the worksheet to print on separate pages. For example, if you had a worksheet comprised of ten departments in sequence and each department had many rows of information, and you wanted each department to begin on a new page, then inserting page breaks would satisfy the requirement.

To insert a page break, you select a cell in the row that you want to print on the next page and then you invoke the **Page Break command** on the Insert menu. Excel displays a dotted line to indicate the beginning of a new page. To remove a page break, you select a cell in the row immediately below the dotted line that indicates the page break you want to remove, and then you invoke the **Remove Page Break command** on the Insert menu.

The following steps show how to insert a page break between rows 11 and 12 and then remove the same page break.

 To Insert and Remove a Page Break

---

1 Click cell A12. Click Insert on the menu bar and then point to Page break.

The Insert menu displays (Figure 6-70).

FIGURE 6-70

2 Click Page Break.

Excel draws a dotted line above row 12 indicating a page break (Figure 6-71).

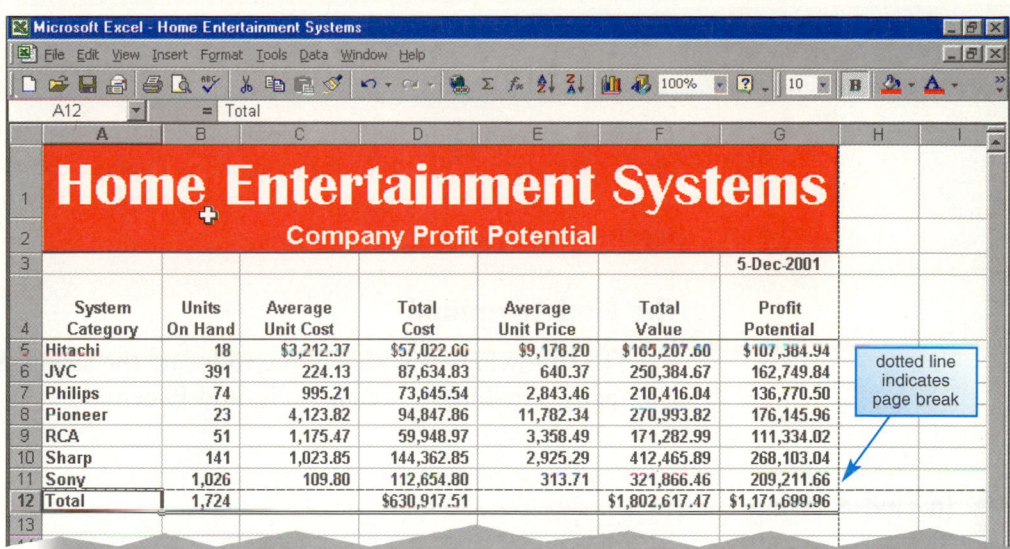

FIGURE 6-71

3 If necessary, click cell A12. Click Insert on the menu bar and then point to Remove Page break.

The Insert menu displays (Figure 6-72).

4 Click Remove Page Break to remove the page break.

FIGURE 6-72

Other Ways

1. Press ALT+I, press B

You can select any cell in the row immediately below where you want a page break or where you want to remove a page break. You also can select the row heading. The Page Break command on the Insert menu changes to Remove Page Break when you select a cell immediately below a page break symbol.

An alternative to using the Page Break command on the Insert menu to insert page breaks is to click the Print Preview button on the Standard toolbar and then click the **Page Break Preview button**. Once the Page Break preview displays, you can drag the blue boundaries, which represent page breaks, to new locations.

The Find and Replace Commands

The **Find command** on the Edit menu is used to locate a string. A **string** can be a single character, a word, or a phrase. The **Replace command** on the Edit menu is used to locate and replace a string with another string. The Find and Replace commands are not available for a chart sheet.

The Find Command

The following steps show how to locate the string, Sony, in the four worksheets: Company, Pittsburgh, Indianapolis, and Phoenix.

Steps To Find a String

1 **With the Company sheet active, hold down the SHIFT key and then click the Phoenix tab. Click Edit on the menu bar and then point to Find.**

The Edit menu displays (Figure 6-73).

FIGURE 6-73

2 When the Find dialog box displays, type Sony in the Find what text box. Click the Look in box arrow and then select Formulas. Click the Find Next button.

Excel makes cell A11 the active cell (Figure 6-74). It is the first cell with the string, Sony, that Excel came across searching from the top by rows.

3 Continue clicking the Find Next button to find the string, Sony, on the four selected sheets. Click the Close button to terminate the Find command. Hold down the SHIFT key and then click the Company tab to deselect the other worksheets.

FIGURE 6-74

The **Look in box** in the Find dialog box allows you to select Values, Formulas, or Comments. If you select **Values**, Excel will look only in cells that do not have formulas. If you select Formulas, Excel will look in all cells. If you select **Comments**, then it will look only in comments. If you place a check mark in the **Match case check box**, then Excel will stop only on cells that have the string in the same case. For example, sony is not the same as Sony. If you place a check mark in the Find entire cells only check box, then Excel will stop only on cells that have only the string and no other characters.

If the Find command does not find the string you are searching for, then it displays a dialog box indicating it has searched the selected worksheets without success.

The Replace Command

The **Replace command** is similar to the Find command, except that the search string is replaced by a new string. The steps on the next page show how to replace Sony with Sony ET.

More *About*

The Find Command

You can use the Look in box, Match case check box, and Find entire cells only check box in the Find dialog box to speed up searches, especially in a large worksheet.

Steps

To Replace a String with Another String

1 **With the Company sheet active, hold down the SHIFT key and then click the Phoenix tab. Click Edit on the menu bar and then click Replace.**

2 **When the Replace dialog box displays, type** Sony **in the Find what text box and** Sony ET **in the Replace with text box. Click the Find Next button. Point to the Replace button.**

Excel makes cell A11 the active cell (Figure 6-75). It is the first cell with the string, Sony, that Excel came across searching from the top by rows.

FIGURE 6-75

3 **Click the Replace button.**

Excel replaces the string, Sony, in cell A11 with Sony ET (Figure 6-76).

4 **Continue to click the Find Next button and Replace button to replace the string, Sony, with Sony ET in other cells in the selected worksheets. Click the Close button to terminate the Find command. Hold down the SHIFT key and then click the Company tab to deselect the other worksheets.**

FIGURE 6-76

Other **Ways**

1. Press CTRL+H

The Replace dialog box also has a Replace All button. If you click the **Replace All button**, Excel immediately replaces all occurrences of Sony with Sony ET throughout the selected worksheets.

Closing the Workbook

The following steps close the Home Entertainment Systems workbook without saving changes.

TO CLOSE THE WORKBOOK

1 Click the Close button on the right side of the workbook title bar (Figure 6-76).

2 When the Microsoft Excel dialog box displays, click the No button.

Excel closes the workbook without saving changes. Excel remains active.

Consolidating Data by Linking Workbooks

Earlier in this project, the data from three worksheets were consolidated onto another worksheet in the same workbook using 3-D references. An alternative to this method is to consolidate data from worksheets in other workbooks. Consolidating data from other workbooks also is referred to as **linking**. A **link** is a reference to a cell or range of cells in another workbook. In this case, the 3-D reference also includes a workbook name. For example, the following 3-D reference pertains to cell B5 on the Pittsburgh sheet in the workbook HES Pittsburgh PP located on drive A.

'A:\[hes pittsburgh pp.xls]Pittsburgh'!B5

location   workbook name   sheet name   cell reference

The single quotation marks surrounding the location, workbook name, and sheet name are required if any spaces are in any of the three names. If the workbook you are referring to is in the same folder as the active workbook, then the location (A:\) is not needed. The brackets surrounding the workbook name are required.

To illustrate linking cells between workbooks, the Company, Pittsburgh, Indianapolis, and Phoenix worksheets from the workbook created earlier in this project are on the Data Disk in separate workbooks as described in Table 6-11. In the workbook names in Table 6-11, the HES stands for Home Entertainment Systems and the PP stands for Profit Potential.

The steps on the next page show how to consolidate in the workbook HES Company PP the data in the Units on Hand column (column B) in the three store workbooks.

More About

Consolidation

Consolidate data across different workbooks using the Consolidate command on the Data menu. For more information, use the Office Assistant or Answer Wizard or click the Microsoft Excel Help button on the Standard toolbar, click the Index tab, and obtain information on the consolidating data topic.

Table 6-11 Workbook Names	
WORKSHEET IN HOME ENTERTAINMENT SYSTEMS	**SAVED USING THE WORKBOOK NAME**
Company	HES Company PP
Pittsburgh	HES Pittsburgh PP
Indianapolis	HES Indianapolis PP
Phoenix	HES Phoenix PP

More About 2000

Using a Workspace File

If you use a group of Workbooks together, such as in this section, you can save time opening them by creating a workspace file. A workspace file contains the workbook names and folder locations, their positions on the screen, and window sizes. Before you invoke the Save Workspace command on the File menu, open the workbooks you want in the workspace and activate the workbook you want active. Later, when you open the workspace file, it opens all the workbooks in the workspace and displays the one that was active when you created the workspace file.

TO CONSOLIDATE DATA BY LINKING WORKBOOKS

1 Open the workbooks HES Company PP, HES Pittsburgh PP, HES Indianapolis PP, and HES Phoenix PP.

2 Click Window on the menu bar and then click HES Company PP. Click cell B5. Click the AutoSum button on the Standard toolbar.

3 Click Window on the menu bar and then click HES Pittsburgh PP. Click cell B5. Delete the dollar signs ($) in the reference to cell B5 in the formula bar. Click immediately after B5 in the formula bar and then type , (comma).

4 Click Window on the menu bar and then click HES Indianapolis PP. Click cell B5. Delete the dollar signs ($) in the reference to cell B5 in the formula bar. Click immediately after B5 in the formula bar and then type , (comma).

5 Click Window on the menu bar, and then click HES Phoenix PP. Click cell B5. Delete the dollar signs ($) in the reference to cell B5 in the formula bar. Press the ENTER key.

6 With cell B5 active on the Company sheet in the HES Company PP workbook, drag the fill handle down to cell B11.

7 Click the Save button on the Standard toolbar. Click the Print button on the Standard toolbar.

The total units on hand at the three stores for each system category display in the range B5:B11 on the Company sheet in the HES Company PP workbook (Figure 6-77).

Quick Reference

For a table that lists how to complete the tasks covered in this book using the mouse, menu, shortcut menu, and keyboard, visit the Office 2000 Web page (www.scsite.com/office 2000/qr.htm), and then click Microsoft Excel 2000.

FIGURE 6-77

An alternative to opening all four workbooks and using Point mode, is to open the workbook HES Company PP and use the keyboard to enter the SUM function in cell B5 as shown in the formula bar in Figure 6-77.

It is necessary that you remember these two important points about this SUM function. First, as you build the SUM function for cell B5, the cell reference inserted by Excel each time you click a cell in a workbook is an absolute cell reference ($B$5). You must go into the formula and change these to relative cell references because the SUM function later is copied to the range B6:B11 in Step 6. If the cell references are left as absolute, then the copied function always would refer to cell B5 in the three workbooks no matter where you copy the SUM function. Second, because the three cells being summed in this example are not adjacent to one another, the cell references must be separated by commas in the SUM function.

Updating Links

Later, when you open the HES Company PP workbook, also called the **dependent workbook**, Excel will ask you whether you want to update the links. The linked workbooks are called the **source workbooks**. If the three source workbooks also are open, then Excel will update the links (recalculate) automatically in the HES Company PP workbook when a value is changed in any one of the source workbooks. If the source workbooks are not open, then Excel will display a dialog box that will give you the option to update the links. In the latter case, Excel reads the data in the source workbooks on disk and recalculates formulas in the dependent workbook, but it does not open the source workbooks.

You also can use the Links command on the Edit menu to update the links at any time. For example, with the dependent workbook HES Company PP open, you can invoke the **Links command** on the Edit menu to recalculate, open a source workbook, or change the source workbook. The Links dialog box also displays the names of all the linked workbooks (Figure 6-78).

Microsoft Certification

The Microsoft Office User Specialist (MOUS) Certification program provides an opportunity for you to obtain a valuable industry credential - proof that you have the Excel 2000 skills required by employers. For more information, see Appendix D or visit the Shelly Cashman Series MOUS Web page at www.scsite.com/off2000/cert.htm.

FIGURE 6-78

Quitting Excel

To quit Excel, complete the steps on the next page.

TO QUIT EXCEL

1. Click the Close button on the right side of the title bar.

2. If the Microsoft Excel dialog box displays, click the No button.

CASE PERSPECTIVE SUMMARY

Santiago Biagi, president and CEO of Home Entertainment Systems, is sure to be pleased with many aspects of the workbook developed in this project. The use of multiple sheets, for example, allows for better organization of the data, while the 3-D Cone chart makes it easy to pinpoint the system category with the greatest profit potential. This workbook should answer any due diligence questions put forth by the buyout candidate. Perhaps the best aspect of the way the workbook is used, however, is the use of the template: even if the buyout does not work out, Santiago can use the template in the future to add additional stores to the existing workbook or create new, similar workbooks.

Project Summary

This project introduced you to creating and using a template, customizing formats, creating styles, changing chart types, drawing and enhancing a 3-D Cone chart using WordArt, and annotating using text boxes and arrows. You also learned how to reference cells in other sheets and add comments to a cell. To enhance a printout, you learned how to add a header and footer and to change margins. Finally, you learned how to customize a printout, add and remove page breaks, use the Find and Replace commands, and link cell entries from external workbooks.

What You Should Know

Having completed this project, you now should be able to perform the following tasks:

- Add a Chart Title Using the WordArt Tool *(E 6.40)*
- Add a Text Box and Arrow *(E 6.46)*
- Apply a Style *(E 6.25)*
- Assign a Comment to a Cell *(E 6.48)*
- Assign a Currency Style Using the Format Dialog Box *(E 6.18)*
- Bold the Font and Change the Column Widths in the Template *(E 6.8)*
- Change the Header and Margins and Center the Printout Horizontally *(E 6.50)*
- Close the Workbook *(E 6.61)*
- Consolidate Data by Linking Workbooks *(E 6.62)*
- Create a Custom Format Code *(E 6.21)*
- Create a New Style *(E 6.23)*
- Create a Workbook from a Template *(E 6.28)*
- Draw a 3-D Cone Chart *(E 6.39)*
- Drill an Entry through Worksheets *(E 6.30)*
- Enter Column Titles and the System Date in the Template *(E 6.8)*
- Enter Dummy Data in the Template Using the Fill Handle *(E 6.9)*
- Enter the Formulas Using Point Mode and Determine Totals in the Template *(E 6.12)*
- Enter the Template Title and Row Titles *(E 6.8)*
- Find a String *(E 6.58)*
- Format the Column Titles and Total Line *(E 6.18)*
- Format the Template Title *(E 6.17)*
- Insert and Remove a Page Break *(E 6.56)*
- Modify the Indianapolis Sheet *(E 6.32)*
- Modify the Phoenix Sheet *(E 6.33)*
- Modify the Pittsburgh Sheet *(E 6.31)*
- Open a Template and Add a Worksheet *(E 6.27)*
- Print the Workbook *(E 6.53)*
- Quit Excel *(E 6.64)*
- Rename a Sheet and Modify the Worksheet Title *(E 6.34)*
- Replace a String with Another String *(E 6.60)*
- Save a Template *(E 6.15)*
- Spell Check, Save, and Print the Template *(E 6.26)*
- Start Excel *(E 6.6)*
- Enter and Copy 3-D References *(E 6.35)*

1 Consolidating Data in a Workbook

Instructions Part 1: Follow the steps below to consolidate the four quarterly sheets on the Annual Totals sheet in the workbook Annual Payroll. The Annual Totals sheet should display as shown in the lower screen in Figure 6-79.

1. Open the workbook Annual Payroll from the Data Disk. If you do not have a copy of the Data Disk, see the inside back cover of this book.

2. One by one, click the first four tabs and review the quarterly totals. Click the Annual Totals tab.

3. Determine the annual totals by using the SUM function and 3-D references to sum the hours worked and gross pay for each employee. If necessary, use the Format Painter button to copy the format of cell C23 to cell B23 to redisplay the underline in cell B23.

4. Save the workbook using the file name Annual Totals 1.

5. Add a header that includes your name and course number in the Left section, the computer laboratory exercise number (Apply 6-1) in the Center section, and the system date and your instructor's name in the Right section. Add the page number and total number of pages to the footer.

6. Select all five sheets. Use the Page Setup command to center all worksheets on the page and print gridlines. Preview and print the five worksheets. Hold down the SHIFT key and then click the Annual Totals tab to select the sheet. Save the workbook with the new page setup using the same file name as in Step 4.

Quarter One Totals

Employee	Rate of Pay	Hours Worked	Gross Pay
A104F	9.35	611.75	5,719.86
C213K	6.50	523.25	3,401.13
W137J	15.65	498.60	7,803.09
Y129T	18.55	525.50	9,748.03
Total		2,159.10	26,672.10

Quarter Two Totals

Employee	Rate of Pay	Hours Worked	Gross Pay
A104F	9.35	563.00	5,264.05
C213K	6.50	398.45	2,589.93
W137J	15.65	567.30	8,878.25
Y129T	18.55	512.90	9,514.30
Total		2,041.65	26,246.52

Quarter Three Totals

Employee	Rate of Pay	Hours Worked	Gross Pay
A104F	9.35	227.50	2,127.13
C213K	6.50	734.50	4,774.25
W137J	15.65	520.00	8,138.00
Y129T	18.55	487.50	9,043.13
Total		1,969.50	24,082.50

Quarter Four Totals

Employee	Rate of Pay	Hours Worked	Gross Pay
A104F	9.35	612.00	5,722.20
C213K	6.50	397.00	2,580.50
W137J	15.65	672.35	10,522.28
Y129T	18.55	549.85	10,199.72
Total		2,231.20	29,024.70

Annual Payroll Totals

Employee	Hours Worked	Gross Pay
A104F	2,014.25	18,833.24
C213K	2,053.20	13,345.80
W137J	2,258.25	35,341.61
Y129T	2,075.75	38,505.16
Total	8,401.45	106,025.81

FIGURE 6-79

Instructions Part 2: Open the workbook Annual Payroll from the Data Disk. Save each of the five sheets as separate workbooks using the tab names as the file names. Close all workbooks. Open the Annual Totals workbook. Use 3-D references from the four quarterly workbooks to determine totals on the Annual Totals workbook. Print the Annual Totals workbook.

In the Lab

1 Designing a Template for Swing Productions

Problem: For the first month of your work-study program, you have been answering the telephone at the main office of Swing Productions. Your immediate supervisor knows your real specialty is designing workbooks and wants to utilize your Excel skills. She has asked you to create a template for the management to use when they create new Excel workbooks (Figure 6-80).

Instructions: Start Excel and perform the following steps to create a template.

1. Change the font of all cells to 12-point Arial bold. Increase all row heights to 18.00. (*Hint:* Click the Select All button to make these changes.)

2. Use the Style command on the Format menu to create the format style called Comma (4) as shown in Figure 6-80. Display the Comma style, change the name in the Style name box from Comma to Comma (4), and use the Modify button to change the decimal places to 4 and the font to Arial 12, Bold.

FIGURE 6-80

3. Add a comment to cell F1 to identify the template and its purpose, as shown in Figure 6-80. Include your name as the author.

4. Use WordArt to create the title shown in the range A1:F5. Use the style in column 4, row 1 of the WordArt Gallery dialog box. Change the color of the title to red. Draw a thick red bottom border across the range A5:F5. Add the subtitle in cell D6. Change its font style to Britannic Bold.

5. Enter your name, course, computer laboratory assignment (Lab 6-1), date, time, and instructor's name as the header. Add a page number as the footer.

6. Use the Save As command to save the template, selecting Template in the Save as type list. Save the template using the file name Swing Productions Template.

In the Lab

7. Print the template and comment. To print the comment, click the Sheet tab in the Page Setup dialog box. Click the Comments box arrow and then click At end of sheet. The comment will print on a separate sheet. After the comment prints, deselect printing the comment by clicking the Comment box arrow in the Sheet tab in the Page Setup dialog box and then clicking (None).

8. Close the template and then reopen it. Save the template as a regular workbook using the file name Swing Productions. Close the workbook.

2 Using a Template to Create a Multiple-Sheet Workbook

Problem: Custom Fragrances is a mail-order company that specializes in unique bath oils and perfumes. The company has outlets in three cities — Baltimore, Columbus, and Portland — and a corporate office in Houston. All of the outlets sell their products via the Web, telephone, mail, and walk-in. Every year, the corporate officers in Houston use a template to create a year-end sales analysis workbook. The workbook contains four sheets, one for each of the three outlets and one for the company totals. The Company Totals sheet displays as shown in Figure 6-81.

The template is on the Data Disk. Mr. Malone, the company's chief financial officer (CFO), has asked you to use the template to create the year-end sales analysis workbook.

Instructions Part 1: Perform the following tasks.

1. Open the template, Custom Fragrances Template, from the Data Disk. Add a worksheet to the workbook and then paste the template to the three empty sheets. Save the workbook using the file name Custom Fragrances. Make sure Microsoft Excel Workbook is selected in the Save as type list.

FIGURE 6-81

(continued)

In the Lab

Using a Template to Create a Multiple-Sheet Workbook *(continued)*

2. From left to right, rename the sheet tabs Company, Baltimore, Columbus, and Portland. Enter the data in Table 6-12 onto the three city sheets. On each sheet, change the subtitle in cell A2 to reflect the city. Choose a different background color for each sheet.

3. On the Company sheet, use the SUM function, 3-D references, and the fill handle to total the corresponding cells on the three city sheets. First, compute the sum in cell B4 and then compute the sum in cell B5. Copy the range B4:B5 to the range C4:E5. The Company sheet should resemble the top of Figure 6-81. Save the workbook.

Table 6-12	Custom Fragrances Sales Data			
		BALTIMORE	**COLUMBUS**	**PORTLAND**
Web	Sales	2,546,120	3,189,732	1,929,843
	Returns	396,362	572,001	212,600
Phone	Sales	1,732,918	2,381,900	829,000
	Returns	356,821	195,610	101,785
Mail	Sales	987,502	1,328,712	564,912
	Returns	200,675	396,897	111,715
Walk-in	Sales	356,810	578,420	296,500
	Returns	48,349	76,198	72,210

4. Create an embedded Clustered bar chart with a 3-D visual effect in the range A8:F27 on the Company sheet. Chart the range A3:E5 on the Company sheet. Do not include a chart title. If necessary, reduce the font size of the labels on both axes to 8 point. Use the chart colors shown in Figure 6-81. Use the WordArt button on the Drawing toolbar to add the chart title. Add the text box and arrow as shown in Figure 6-81. Save the workbook.

5. Select all four sheets. Change the header to include your name, course, computer laboratory exercise (Lab 6-2), date, and instructor's name. Change the footer to include the page number and total pages. Add the comment shown in cell A30. Preview and then print the entire workbook, including the comment. Save the workbook with the new page setup characteristics.

Instructions Part 2: The following corrections were sent in: (a) Baltimore Walk-in Sales 425,190; (b) Columbus Web Returns 225,115; (c) Portland Mail Sales 725,300. Enter these corrections. The Company Total Net Sales should equal $14,556,800. Print all the worksheets. Do not print the comment.

Instructions Part 3: Select all the worksheets in the Custom Fragrances workbook and do the following:

1. Select cell A1 on the Company sheet. Use the Find command to locate all occurrences of the word Sales. You should find 12 occurrences of the word Sales.

2. Click Find entire cells only in the Find dialog box. Use the Find command to find all occurrences of the word Sales. You should find three occurrences.

3. Use the Replace command to replace the word Web with the acronym WWW on all four sheets. Print all four sheets. Do not save the workbook.

In the Lab

3 Returning Real-Time Stock Quotes to the High-Tech Stock Portfolio Worksheet

Problem: You have been investing in the stock market for the past few years and you maintain a summary of your stock market investments in an Excel workbook (Figure 6-82a). Each day you go through the Business section of the newspaper and manually update the current prices in column G to determine the value of your equities. You recently heard about the Web query capabilities of Excel and have decided to use them to update your stock portfolio automatically.

Instructions: Perform the steps on the next page to have Web queries automatically update the current price in column G and the major indices in the range B12:B15 of Figure 6-82a.

(a) High-Tech Stock Portfolio Worksheet

(b) Enter Parameter Value Dialog Box

(d) Major Indices

(c) Real-Time Stock Quotes

FIGURE 6-82

(continued)

In the Lab

Returning Real-Time Stock Quotes to the High-Tech Stock Portfolio Worksheet *(continued)*

1. Start Excel and open the workbook High-Tech Stock Portfolio on the Data Disk. If you do not have a copy of the Data Disk, see the inside back cover of this book. After reviewing the High-Tech Stock Portfolio worksheet on your screen, you should notice that it lacks current prices in column G and the major indices in the range B12:B15.

2. Click Sheet2 and then click cell A1. Click Data on the menu bar, point to Get External Data, and then click Run Saved Query on the Get External Data submenu. When the Run Query dialog box displays, double-click Microsoft Investor Stock Quotes. When the Returning External Data to Microsoft Excel dialog box displays, click the OK button. When the Enter Parameter Value dialog box displays, click the Investment Analysis tab at the bottom of the screen and drag through the range B3:B10. Click Use this value/reference for future refreshes. The Enter Parameter Value dialog box should display as shown in Figure 6-82b on the previous page. Click the OK button. The Web query should return a worksheet with real-time stock quotes to the Stock Quotes sheet similar to the one shown in Figure 6-82c on the previous page. Rename the Sheet2 tab Stock Quotes.

3. Click the Investment Analysis tab. Click cell G3. Type = (equal sign). Click the Stock Quotes tab. Click cell D4 (the last price for Cisco Systems). Press the ENTER key. Use the fill handle to copy cell G3 to the range G4:G10. You now should have current prices for the stock portfolio that are the same as the last prices on the Stock Quotes sheet in column D. Click cell A17 and save the workbook using the file name High-Tech Stock Portfolio Final.

4. Click Sheet3 and then click cell A1. Click Data on the menu bar, point to Get External Data, and then click Run Saved Query on the Get External Data submenu. When the Run Query dialog box displays, double-click Microsoft Investor Major Indices. When the Returning External Data to Microsoft Excel dialog box displays, click the OK button. Rename the Sheet3 tab Major Indices. A worksheet similar to the one shown in Figure 6-82d should display.

5. Click the Investment Analysis tab. Click cell B12. Type = (equal sign). Click the Major Indices tab. Click cell D4 (the last Dow Jones Industrial Index). Press the ENTER key. Click cell B13. Type = (equal sign). Click the Major Indices tab. Click cell D5 (the last Nasdaq Combined Composite Index). Press the ENTER key. Click cell B14. Type = (equal sign). Click the Major Indices tab. Click cell D10 (the last Russell 2000 Stock Index). Press the ENTER key. Click cell B15. Type = (equal sign). Click the Major Indices tab. Click cell D9 (the last Dow Jones Transportation Index). Press the ENTER key. Click cell A17 and then save the workbook using the file name High-Tech Stock Portfolio Final.

6. With the Investment Analysis sheet active, click View on the menu bar, point to Toolbars, and then click External Data. If necessary, drag the External Data toolbar to the lower-right corner as shown in Figure 6-82a.

7. Select all three worksheets. Use the Page Setup command on the File menu to enter your name, course, computer laboratory assignment (Lab 6-3), date, and instructor name as the header. Add a page number as the footer. Change the top margin to 1.5".

8. Print the three worksheets in landscape orientation. Use the Fit to option in the Page sheet on the Page Setup dialog box to print the sheets on one page.

9. Click the Refresh All button on the External Data toolbar (Figure 6-82a). Print the three worksheets.

10. Click the Stock Quotes tab. Use the Zoom box on the Standard toolbar to shrink the view of the worksheet to 65% so it displays in its entirety.

Cases and Places

The difficulty of these case studies varies:
▶ are the least difficult; ▶▶ are more difficult; and ▶▶▶ are the most difficult.

1 ▶ Holly Volley, assistant tennis coach, has jotted down notes on three players (Table 6-13) based on a recent match. Make a template that Coach Volley can use to evaluate her players. Include each statistic, the percentage of winners (winner/total shots), the percentage of errors (errors/total shots), and what Coach Volley calls the "success rate" (percentage of winners – percentage of errors). Use the template to develop a worksheet for each player. Summarize the results on a Team worksheet. Compute the percents on the Team worksheet in a manner similar to the player's worksheets.

Table 6-13 Summary Notes on Players			
ROB RALLY	TOTAL SHOTS	WINNERS	ERRORS
Forehand	192	42	25
Backhand	192	34	26
Volley	15	0	8
Service	98	17	5
Service Return	118	29	17
LORI LOVE	TOTAL SHOTS	WINNERS	ERRORS
Forehand	238	74	62
Backhand	156	65	23
Volley	36	18	3
Service	114	21	0
Service Return	108	60	9
FREDDIE FOREHAND	TOTAL SHOTS	WINNERS	ERRORS
Forehand	198	37	13
Backhand	168	24	39
Volley	102	84	3
Service	72	33	6
Service Return	108	40	46

2 ▶ Stylish Weddings, Inc. has been a successful full-service wedding planning company for 25 years in Chicago, Illinois. After launching its Web site three years ago, the company has attracted so many clients from Europe that the owners opened a shop in Paris. The Chicago and Paris shops' assets last year, respectively, were: cash $317,325 and $132,650; accounts receivable $107,125 and $74,975; marketable securities $196,425 and $76,250; inventory $350,395 and $175,750; and equipment $25,000 and $17,500. The liabilities for each store were: notes payable $28,300 and $26,000; accounts payable $78,450 and $80,125; and income tax payable $62,000 and $20,000. The stockholders' equity was: common stock $731,170 and $268,375 and retained earnings $96,350 and $82,625. Design a template as a balance sheet to reflect the figures above. Include totals for current assets, total assets, current liabilities, total liabilities, total stockholders' equity, and liabilities and stockholders' equity. Use the template to create a balance sheet for each store and consolidated balance sheet for the corporation.

Cases and Places

3 ▶ Progressive Programs sells computer software and supplies. Merchandise is divided into six categories based on profit margin: individual application packages (22%), integrated application packages (9%), entertainment software (16%), system software (25%), learning aids (18%), and supplies (10%). Last year's sales data has been collected for the Harlem Street Store and Zapata Avenue Store as shown in Table 6-14.

Table 6-14	Last Year's Sales for Harlem Street and Zapata Avenue Stores	
	HARLEM STREET STORE	**ZAPATA AVENUE STORE**
Individual applications	$48,812	$42, 864
Integrated applications	40,135	63, 182
Entertainment software	52, 912	52, 345
System software	12, 769	15, 278
Learning aids	8, 562	11, 397
Supplies	34, 215	24, 921

Develop a template that can be used to determine marketing strategies for next year. Include sales, profit margins, profits (sales x profit margin), total sales, total profits, and functions to determine the most and least sales, profit margins, and profits. Use the template to create a worksheet for each store, a consolidated worksheet for the entire company, and a chart on a separate sheet reflecting the company's profits by category.

4 ▶▶ Gifts for Any Occasion has noticed a sharp increase in business since it started a Web site that allows people to order gifts over the Internet. The Company also started a free gift information service on the Web that has contributed to an additional increase in sales. The owner of Gifts for Any Occasion needs a worksheet representation of the business increases based on the data in Table 6-15. Create a

Table 6-15		Gifts for Any Occasion Sales		
	QTR	**CONSUMABLE**	**NON-CONSUMABLE**	**OUT OF STATE**
2001	1	82,345.25	56,924.65	0
	2	108,540.00	78,213.50	1
	3	113,956.20	82,130.75	0
	4	203,725.80	98,320.60	2
2002	1	412,500.45	303,750.40	27
	2	435,210.75	268,921.50	96
	3	508,383.70	315,245.90	224
	4	723,912.20	375,835.70	309

worksheet for each year and one for the totals, adding a column for quarter totals and a row for item totals. Include the percentage of annual growth (2002 – 2001) / 2001 on the Company Totals worksheet. Add an embedded 3-D Pie chart to the Company Totals worksheet that shows the sales contribution of each quarter to the two-year sales total.

Microsoft **Excel 2000**

Microsoft Excel 2000

Linking an Excel Worksheet to a Word Document

C A S E   P E R S P E C T I V E

Each month, the director of sales for Home Networks, Inc., LaShondra West, sends out a memorandum to all the regional sales managers in the organization showing the previous month's sales by office. She currently uses Word to produce the memorandum that includes a table of the monthly sales. The wording in the memorandum remains constant month to month. The data in the table changes each month.

LaShondra recently heard of the Object Linking and Embedding (OLE) capabilities of Microsoft Office 2000 and wants to use them to create the basic memorandum (Figure 1a on the next page) using Word and maintain the monthly sales on an Excel worksheet (Figure 1b). Each month, she envisions sending out the Word document with the updated worksheet (Figure 1c). Once the link is established, she can update the worksheet each month, modify the date in the memorandum, and then print and distribute the memorandum to the regional sales managers.

As LaShondra's technical assistant, she has asked you to handle the details of linking the Excel worksheet to the memorandum.

Introduction

With Microsoft 2000, you can incorporate parts of documents or entire documents, called **objects**, from one application into another application. For example, you can copy a worksheet created in Excel into a document created in Word. In this case, the worksheet in Excel is called the **source document** (copied from) and the document in Word is called the **destination document** (copied to). Copying objects between applications can be accomplished in three ways: (1) copy and paste; (2) copy and embed; and (3) copy and link.

All of the Microsoft Office applications allow you to use these three methods to copy objects between applications. The first method uses the Copy and Paste buttons. The latter two use the Paste Special command on the Edit menu and are referred to as **Object Linking and Embedding**, or **OLE**. Table 1 on page EI 1.3 summarizes the differences among the three methods.

You would use copy and link over the other two methods when an object is likely to change and you want to make sure the object reflects the changes in the source document or if the object is large, such as a video clip or sound clip. Thus, if you link a portion or all of a worksheet to a memorandum, and update the worksheet monthly in Excel, any time you open the memorandum in Word, the latest updates of the worksheet will display as part of the memorandum (Figure 1 on the next page).

(a) Word

(b) Excel

(c) Word Document and Linked Excel Worksheet

FIGURE 1

Table 1	Three Methods of Copying Objects Between Applications
METHOD	CHARACTERISTICS
Copy and paste	Source document becomes part of the destination document. Object may be edited, but the editing features are limited to those in the destination application. An Excel worksheet becomes a Word table. If changes are made to values in the Word table, any original Excel formulas are not recalculated.
Copy and embed	Source document becomes part of the destination document. Object may be edited in the destination application using source editing features. Excel worksheet remains a worksheet in Word. If changes are made to values in the worksheet with Word active, Excel formulas will be recalculated, but the changes are not updated in the Excel worksheet in the workbook on disk. If you use Excel to change values in the worksheet, the changes will not show in the Word document the next time you open it.
Copy and link	Source document does not become part of the destination document even though it appears to be part of it. Rather, a link is established between the two documents so that when you open the Word document, the worksheet displays as part of it. When you attempt to edit a linked worksheet in Word, the system activates Excel. If you change the worksheet in Excel, the changes will show in the Word document the next time you open it.

Opening a Word Document and an Excel Workbook

Both the Word document (Monthly Sales Memorandum.doc) and the Excel workbook (Monthly Sales Summary.xls) are on the Data Disk. If you do not have a copy of the Data Disk, see the inside back cover of this book. The first step in linking the Excel worksheet to the Word document is to open both the document in Word and the workbook in Excel as shown in the following steps.

Steps To Open a Word Document and an Excel Workbook

 Insert the Data Disk in drive A. Click the Start button on the taskbar and then click Open Office document on the Start menu. When the Open Office Document dialog displays, click 3½ Floppy (A:) in the Look in box. Select the Excel folder. Double-click the Word file name, Monthly Sales Memorandum.

Word becomes active and the Monthly Sales Memorandum displays in Normal View (Figure 2).

FIGURE 2

2 **Click the Start button on the taskbar and then click Open Office document on the Start menu. When the Open Office Document dialog displays, click 3½ Floppy (A:) in the Look in box. Double-click the Excel file name, Monthly Sales Summary.**

Excel becomes active and the Monthly Sales Summary workbook displays (Figure 3). At this point, Word is inactive. Excel is the active window as shown on the taskbar.

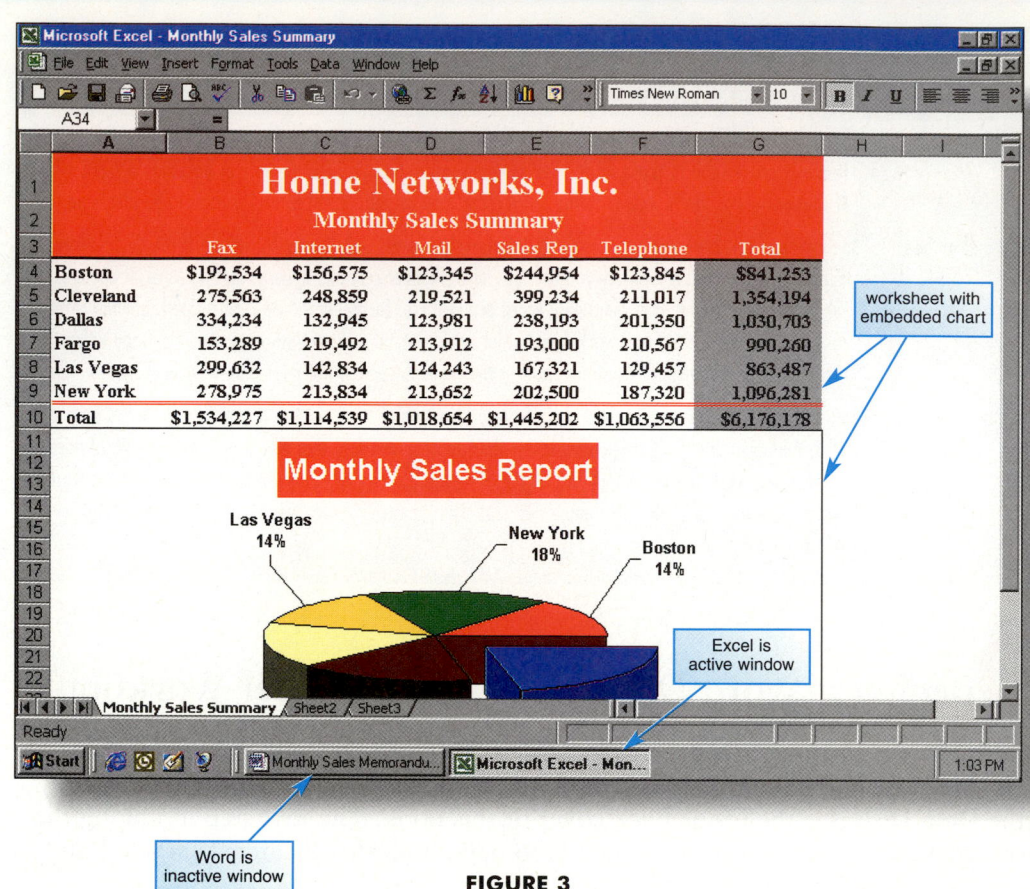

FIGURE 3

With both Word and Excel open, you can switch between the applications by clicking the appropriate button on the taskbar.

Linking an Excel Worksheet to a Word Document

With both applications running, the next step is to link the Excel worksheet to the Word document as shown in the following steps.

Scrap

You can store objects to embed on the desktop, rather than using the Office Clipboard. When you use this technique, the objects are called **scrap**. To accomplish this task, part of the desktop must be visible behind the window of the source application. Next, point to a border of the object and then right-drag it from the source application onto the desktop. Once on the desktop, Windows displays the object as an icon. When the shortcut menu displays, click Create Scrap Here. Next, activate the destination document and then drag the scrap from the desktop onto the destination document and drop it where you want it inserted. To delete a scrap from the desktop, right-click it and then click Delete on the shortcut menu.

Steps To Link an Excel Worksheet to a Word Document

1 With the Excel window active, select the range A1:G28. Click the Copy button to place the selected range on the Office Clipboard.

Excel displays a marquee around the range A1:G28 (Figure 4).

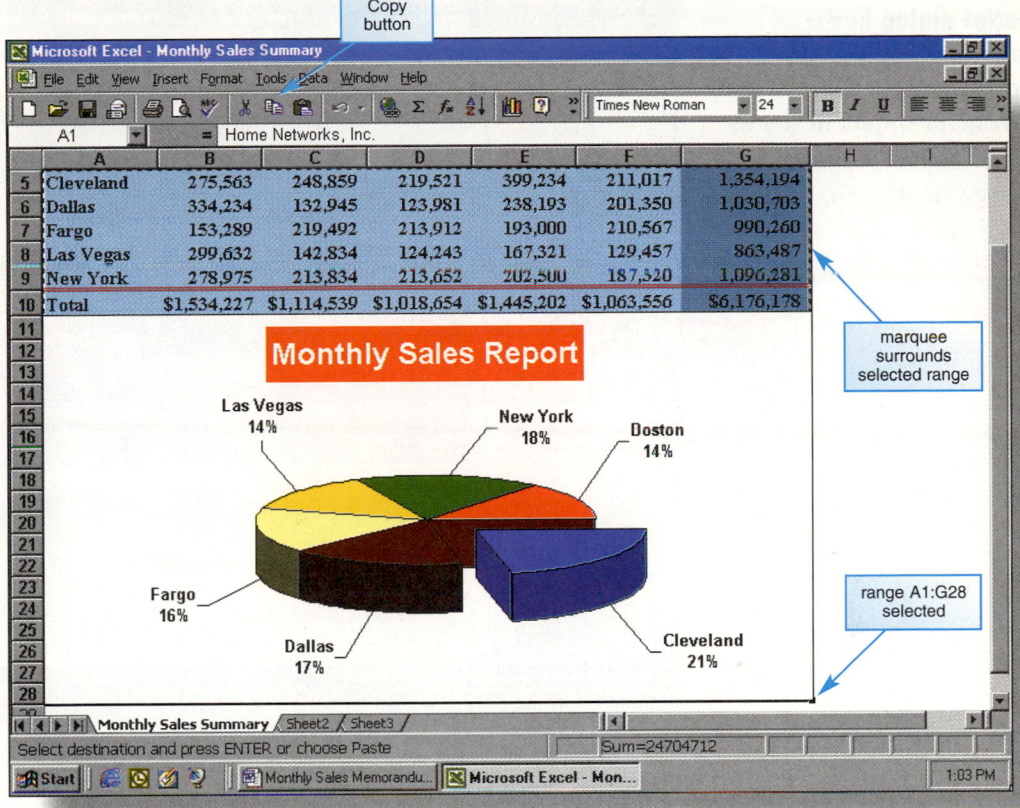

FIGURE 4

2 Click the Monthly Sales Memorandum button on the taskbar to activate the Word window. Click below the last line of text to position the insertion point where the worksheet will display in the document. Click Edit on the menu bar and then point to Paste Special.

The Monthly Sales Memorandum document and the Edit menu display on the screen. The insertion point blinks at the bottom of the document (Figure 5).

FIGURE 5

3 Click Paste Special. When the Paste Special dialog box displays, click Paste link, click Microsoft Excel Worksheet Object in the As list box. Point to the OK button.

The Paste Special dialog box displays (Figure 6).

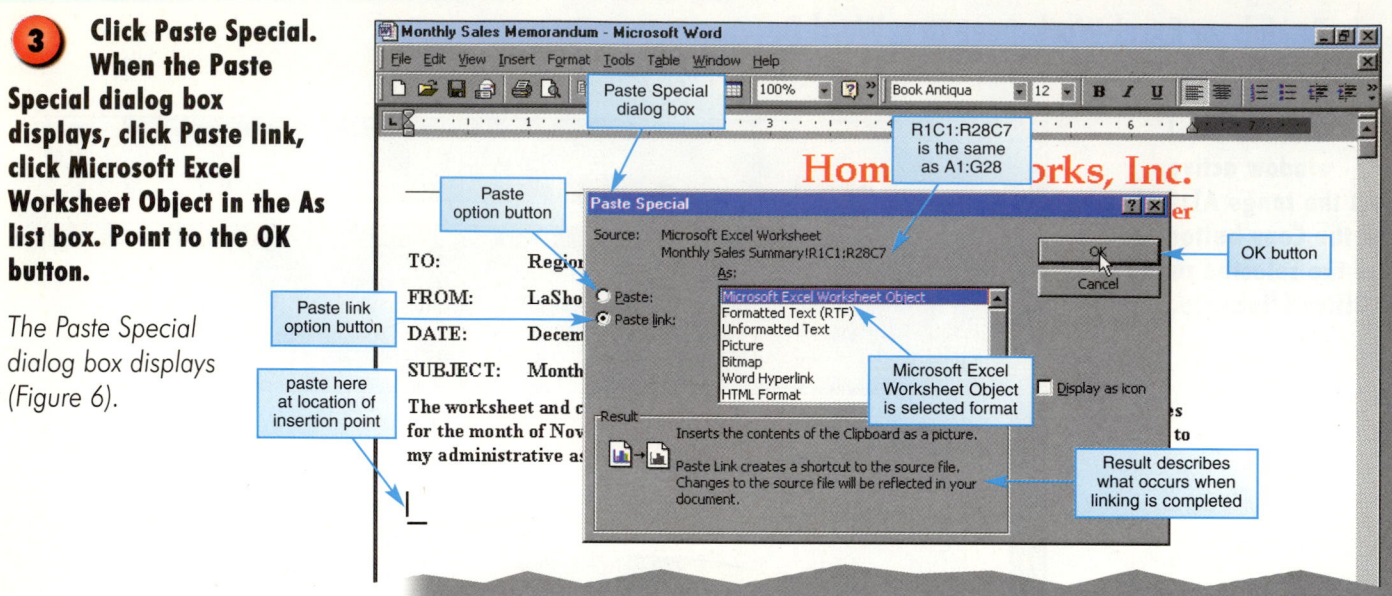

FIGURE 6

4 Click the OK button.

Word switches to Print Layout View. The range A1:G28 of the worksheet displays in the Word document beginning at the location of the insertion point (Figure 7).

FIGURE 7

The Excel worksheet now is linked to the Word document. If you save the Word document and reopen it, the worksheet will display just as it does in Figure 7. If you want to delete the worksheet, select it and then press the DELETE key. The next section shows how to print and save the memo with the linked worksheet.

Printing and Saving the Word Document with the Linked Worksheet

The following steps print and then save the Word document with the linked worksheet.

 Steps **To Print and Save the Memo with the Linked Worksheet**

1 **With the Word window active, click the Print button on the Standard toolbar.**

The memo and the worksheet print as one document (Figure 8).

2 **Click File on the menu bar and then click Save As. Type** `Monthly Sales Memorandum 11-2001` **in the File name text box. Click the OK button.**

Excel saves the Word document on your floppy disk using the file name Monthly Sales Memorandum 11-2001.doc.

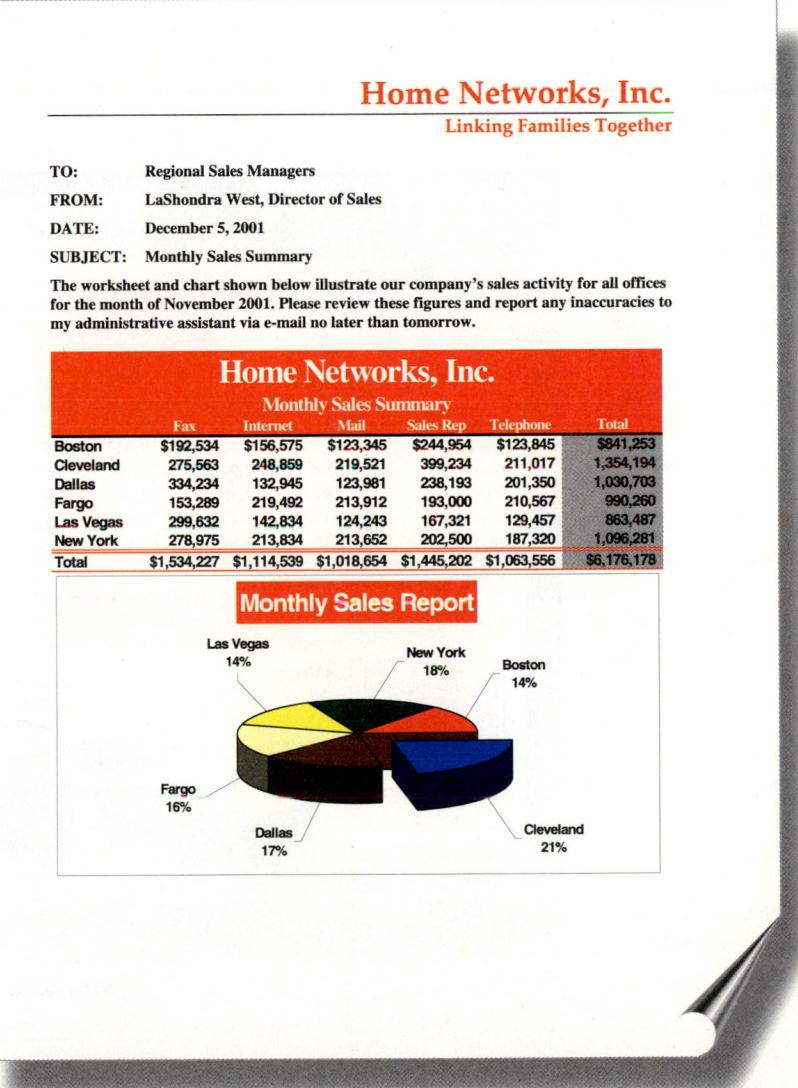

Home Networks, Inc.
Linking Families Together

TO: Regional Sales Managers

FROM: LaShondra West, Director of Sales

DATE: December 5, 2001

SUBJECT: Monthly Sales Summary

The worksheet and chart shown below illustrate our company's sales activity for all offices for the month of November 2001. Please review these figures and report any inaccuracies to my administrative assistant via e-mail no later than tomorrow.

Home Networks, Inc.
Monthly Sales Summary

	Fax	Internet	Mail	Sales Rep	Telephone	Total
Boston	$192,534	$156,575	$123,345	$244,954	$123,845	$841,253
Cleveland	275,563	248,859	219,521	399,234	211,017	1,354,194
Dallas	334,234	132,945	123,981	238,193	201,350	1,030,703
Fargo	153,289	219,492	213,912	193,000	210,567	990,260
Las Vegas	299,632	142,834	124,243	167,321	129,457	863,487
New York	278,975	213,834	213,652	202,500	187,320	1,096,281
Total	$1,534,227	$1,114,539	$1,018,654	$1,445,202	$1,063,556	$6,176,178

Monthly Sales Report

Las Vegas 14%
New York 18%
Boston 14%
Cleveland 21%
Dallas 17%
Fargo 16%

FIGURE 8

If you quit both applications and reopen Monthly Sales Memorandum 11-2001, the worksheet will display in the document even though Excel is not running. Because Word supports object linking and embedding (OLE), it is capable of displaying the linked portion of the Excel workbook without Excel running.

The next section describes what happens when you attempt to edit the linked worksheet while Word is active.

Editing the Linked Worksheet

You can edit any of the cells in the worksheet while it displays as part of the Word document. To edit the worksheet, double-click it. If Excel is running, the system will switch to it and display the linked workbook. If Excel is not running, the system will start it automatically and display the linked workbook. The following steps show how to change the amount sold by the sales rep in Las Vegas (cell E8) from $167,321 to $300,000.

 Steps | **To Edit the Linked Worksheet**

 1 **With the Word window active and the Monthly Sales Memorandum 11-2001 document active, double-click the worksheet. When the Excel window becomes active, double-click the title bar to maximize the window.**

Windows switches from Word to Excel and displays the original workbook Monthly Sales Summary.

 2 **Click cell E8 and then enter** 300000 **as the new value for the sales rep in Las Vegas.**

Excel recalculates all formulas in the workbook and redraws the 3-D Pie chart (Figure 9).

FIGURE 9

③ Click the Monthly Sales Memorandum button on the taskbar.

The Word window becomes active. The monthly sales amount for the sales rep in Las Vegas, which was 167,321 now is 300,000. New totals display for the sales reps column, the Las Vegas total, and the company total (Figure 10).

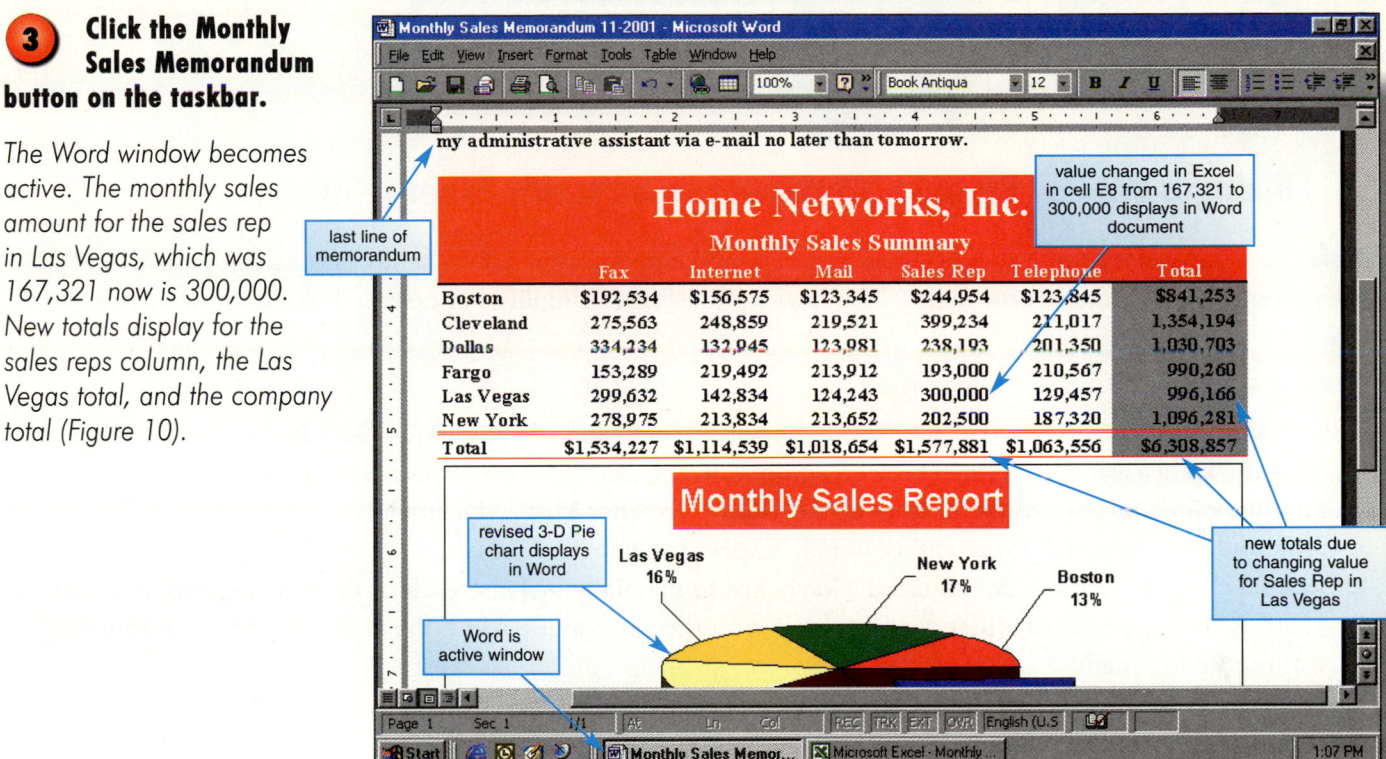

FIGURE 10

As you can see from the previous steps, you double-click a linked object when you want to edit it. Windows will activate the application and display the workbook or document from which the object came. You can then edit the object and return to the destination application. Any changes made to the object will display in the destination document.

If you want the edited changes to the linked workbook to be permanent, you must save the Monthly Sales Summary workbook before quitting Excel.

CASE PERSPECTIVE SUMMARY

As the sales for the previous month are sent in from the various offices to LaShondra, she updates the Excel workbook. She then opens the Word memorandum from the previous month and modifies the date. After saving the Word document, she prints it and distributes the updated version to the regional sales managers.

Integration Feature Summary

This Integration Feature introduced you to Object Linking and Embedding (OLE). OLE allows you to bring together data and information that has been created in different applications. When you link an object to a document and save it, only a link to the object is saved with the document. You edit a linked object by double-clicking it. The system activates the application and opens the file in which the object was created. If you change any part of the object and then return to the destination document, the updated object will display.

In the Lab

1 Linking a Weekly Expense Worksheet to a Weekly Expense Memo

Problem: Your supervisor, Radjika James, at N-Dash Communications, Inc., sends out a weekly memo with expense figures to the district managers. You have been asked to simplify her task by linking the weekly expense worksheet to a memo.

Instructions: Perform the following tasks.

1. One at a time, open the document Weekly Expense Memo and the workbook Weekly Expense Summary from the Data Disk.
2. Link the range A1:E17 to the bottom of the Weekly Expense Memo document.
3. Print and then save the document as Weekly Expense Memo 12-17-01.
4. Double-click the worksheet and use the keyboard to manually increase each of the nine expense amounts by $200. Activate the Word window and print it with the new values. Close the document and workbook without saving them.

2 Linking a Weekly Expense Memo to a Weekly Expense Workbook

Problem: Your supervisor, Radjika James, at N-Dash Communications, Inc., has asked you to link the Word document to the Excel workbook, rather than the Excel workbook to the Word document the way it was done in exercise 1.

Instructions: Complete the following tasks.

1. One at a time, open the document Weekly Expense Memo and the workbook Weekly Expense Summary from the Data Disk.
2. With the Excel window active, insert 18 rows above row 1 and then select cell A1. Activate the Word document and copy the entire document. Embed the Word document at the top of the Weekly Office Expenses worksheet. To embed, click the Paste link option button in the Paste Special dialog box and then select Microsoft Word Document Object in the As list box.
3. Print the Weekly Office Expenses sheet and then save the workbook as Weekly Expense with Memo 12-17-01.
4. With the Excel window active, double-click the embedded document and then delete the first sentence in the paragraph. Activate the Excel window and then print the worksheet with the modified memo. Close the workbook and document without saving them.

Microsoft Excel 2000

PROJECT

7

Using Visual Basic for Applications (VBA) with Excel

OBJECTIVES

You will have mastered the material in this project when you can:

- Use the Undo button to undo multiple changes
- Use passwords to allow an authorized user to access the protection scheme
- Use the macro recorder to create a macro
- Execute a macro
- Customize a toolbar by adding a button
- Customize a menu by adding a command
- Understand Visual Basic for Applications code
- Add controls to a worksheet, such as command buttons, scroll bars, check boxes, and spin buttons
- Assign properties to controls
- Write a procedure to automate data entry into your worksheet
- Validate incoming data
- Explain event-driven programs

Start Planning Today
Turn Your Paycheck into a Nest Egg

How many years until you retire? 40? 25? 10? 5? Not a clue? Whenever you do receive that last paycheck, you need to be prepared for the financial and emotional impact of not commuting to work daily.

Some experts recommend starting retirement savings with the very first paycheck. But how can you save for retirement when you have tuition payments, a car loan, utility bills, and rent or mortgage payments? The answer is careful planning, starting right now.

Fewer than 50 percent of Americans are saving specifically for their retirement needs, although nearly 75 percent know they should be increasing retirement dollars. Financial planners previously estimated that retirees needed 70 percent of their preretirement income to live relatively comfortably during their golden years. Today, however, some planners have bumped up their estimates to 100 percent.

Workers are retiring earlier and living longer than ever before. Considering that the average person spends 18 years in retirement, you need to plan for that time early in your career. During your retirement, you will be faced with buying new cars, replacing your appliances, putting a new roof on your home, and needing prescription drugs and hearing aids.

Inflation is a factor in the retirement picture, too. If you spend $25,000 on living expenses the year you retire, you will need $56,000 for these same expenses 20 years later if inflation rises four percent yearly.

You have no control over some retirement plans, such as Social Security or a company pension. You have absolute control, however, over other preretirement strategies, such as IRAs and company-sponsored savings plans. One of the most appealing investment options is a 401(k) plan. This strategy allows investors to shelter their money, meaning they do not pay taxes on the funds until they retire. Many employers contribute to their employees' 401(k) plan, sometimes as much as 50 percent of the employee's contribution.

In this Excel project, you will see just how advantageous 401(k) plans can be. You will use the Visual Basic for Applications programming language to build a planning worksheet for the Golden Years.com Internet company. You then will input current salary, employee investment, employer match, rate of return, and years of service. You will see that regular contributions to this 401(k) plan for 45 years could yield more than $4 million, even without receiving salary increases.

So where do you start planning for your retirement? The Internet abounds with sites brimming with financial calculators and investment strategies. Begin with the Social Security Administration's site (www.ssa.gov) and find a link to the Social Security Benefit Estimate Program that calculates your potential Social Security payments. Other sites, such as the Administration on Aging (www.aoa.dhhs.gov/retirement), the American Savings Education Council (www.asec.org), and SmartMoney (www.smartmoney.com), have a multitude of interactive tools and worksheets.

Whatever investment strategy you choose, the sooner you start saving, the more prepared you will be to crack your nest egg and live your golden years with financial security.

Microsoft **Excel 2000**

Microsoft Excel 2000

Using Visual Basic for Applications (VBA) with Excel

P R O J E C T

7

C A S E   P E R S P E C T I V E

Nelson Portugal is vice president of personnel for Golden Years.com, a senior multi-service Internet company. Nelson's main task is to convince potential and current employees that Golden Years.com offers excellent benefits.

Golden Years.com's most lucrative benefit is a 401(k) plan. A **401(k) plan** is a retirement savings program that allows employees to invest pretax dollars through payroll deductions.

Nelson has a planning workbook. Any change to the data causes the planning workbook to recalculate all formulas instantaneously, thus showing the results of investing in the company's 401(k) plan.

Nelson wants to put the workbook on the company's intranet so potential and current employees easily can determine the financial advantages of the 401(k) plan. The problem is that without an easy-to-use interface that steps the user through the entry of data, there is too much room for error. Nelson has asked you to use Visual Basic for Applications to create a user-friendly interface for entering data into the workbook in three phases.

Introduction

Before a computer can take an action and produce a desired result, it must have a step-by-step description of the task to be accomplished. The step-by-step description is a series of precise instructions called a **procedure**. A procedure also is called a **program** or **code**. The process of writing a procedure is called **computer programming**. Every Excel command on a menu and button on a toolbar has a corresponding procedure that executes when you click the command or button. **Execute** means that the computer carries out the step-by-step instructions. In a Windows environment, the instructions associated with a task are executed when an **event** takes place, such as clicking a button, clicking a command, dragging a scroll box, or right-clicking a cell.

Because a command or button in Excel does not exist for every possible worksheet task, Microsoft has included a powerful programming language called Visual Basic for Applications. The **Visual Basic for Applications (VBA)** programming language allows you to customize and extend the capabilities of Excel.

In this project, you will learn how to create macros using a code generator called a **macro recorder**. A **macro** is a procedure made up of VBA code. It is called a macro, rather than a procedure, because it is created using the macro recorder. You also will learn how to add buttons to toolbars and commands to menus and associate these with macros. Finally, you will learn the basics of VBA including creating the interface, setting the properties, and writing the code.

Project Seven — Golden Years.Com's 401(k) Planning Worksheet

From your meeting with Nelson, you have determined the following needs and source of data.

Needs: The easy-to-use interface for the 401(k) planning workbook will be implemented in three phases:

Phase 1 – Create a macro using the macro recorder that prints the worksheet in portrait orientation using the Fit to option. Assign the macro to a button on the Standard toolbar (Figure 7-1a) and to a command on the File menu so the user can execute the macro by clicking the button or the command.

Phase 2 – Create a button on the worksheet as shown in Figure 7-1a, assign the button properties, and write an associated procedure (Figure 7-1b) that steps the user through entering the required data in the range C5:C10.

Phase 3 – Create an area on the worksheet called an Adjustment Center (Figure 7-2 on the next page) that allows the user to enter his or her name and annual salary using a button and the remaining data using scroll bars, a check box, and spin buttons. Verify that the annual salary entered is positive.

Source of Data: The workbook shown in Figure 7-1a, without the button on the worksheet and the button on the toolbar, is available to you on the Data Disk under the file name Golden Years.

(a) Worksheet

(b) Visual Basic for Applications

FIGURE 7-1

FIGURE 7-2

Starting Excel and Opening a Workbook

Perform the following steps to start Excel, reset the toolbars, and open the workbook Golden Years from the Data Disk.

TO START EXCEL AND OPEN A WORKBOOK

1 Insert the Data Disk in drive A. See the inside back cover of this book for instructions for downloading the Data Disk.

2 Click the Start button on the taskbar and then click Open Office Document.

3 When the Open Office Document dialog box displays, click the Look in box arrow and then click 3½ Floppy (A:). Double-click Golden Years in the list.

4 When the Golden Years workbook displays, click Tools on the menu bar, and then click Customize.

5 When the Customize dialog box displays, click the Options tab, make sure the top three check boxes are selected, click the Reset my usage data button, and then click the Yes button.

6 Click the Toolbars tab. Click Standard, click the Reset button, and then click the OK button. Click Formatting, click the Reset button, and then click the OK button. Click Worksheet Menu Bar, click the Reset button, and then click the OK button. Click the Close button.

The Golden Years workbook displays in the Excel window (Figure 7-3).

The 401(k) Investment Model sheet in the Golden Years workbook is divided into two parts (Figure 7-3). The left side contains the data (range C5:C10) and the results (range C12:C15). The key cell is C15, which displays the future value of the investment.

The right side of the worksheet is a data table that varies the years of service in column E and organizes the results of four formulas in the range F7:I15 — future value (column F), employee investment (column G), employer match (column H), and return on investment (column I). In this worksheet, the return on investment is the future value less the sum of the employee and employer investment.

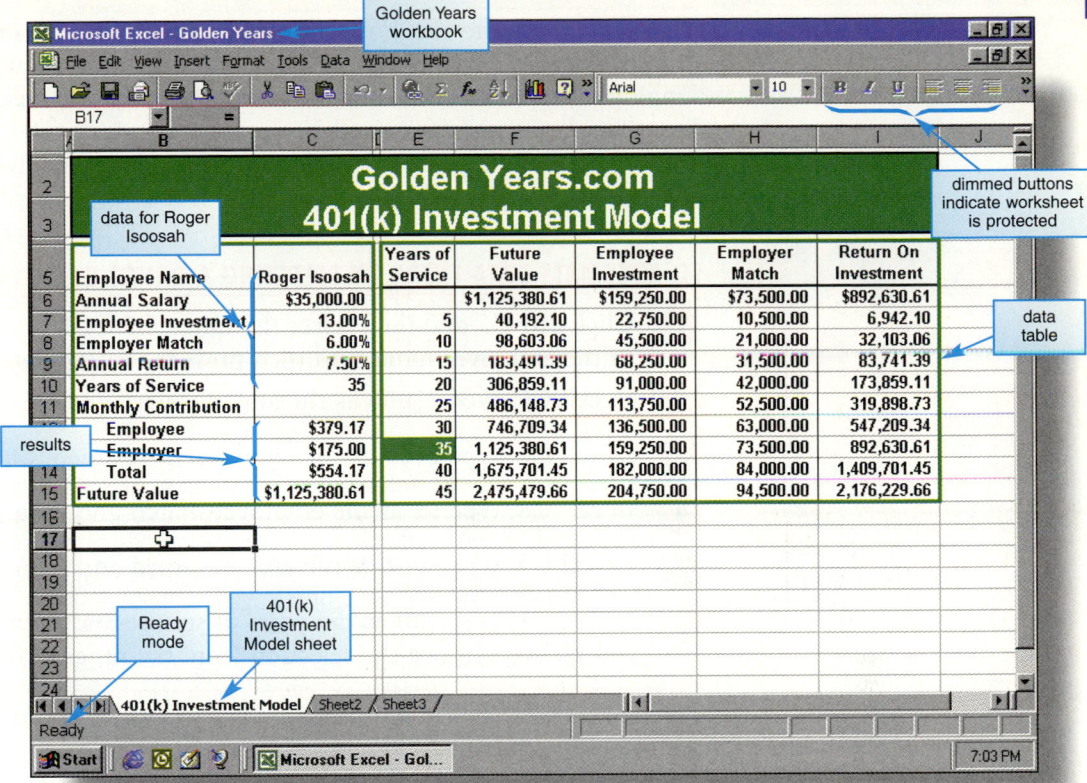

FIGURE 7-3

Many of the buttons on the toolbars are dimmed. When buttons are dimmed and Excel is in Ready mode, then the worksheet is protected. In this case, the cells in the range C5:C10 are unlocked so users can enter data, but the rest of the cells in the worksheet are protected, and therefore, cannot be changed. Later in this project, the worksheet will be unprotected so changes can be made to it.

Gaining Confidence in a Workbook Created by Someone Else

When you modify a workbook created by someone else, such as Golden Years, you should learn as much as you can about the workbook before you modify it. You can learn more about a workbook by doing the following:

1. Press CTRL+ LEFT QUOTATION MARK (`) to display the formulas version to gain an understanding of what formulas and functions are used in the workbook, and which cells are referenced by the formulas and functions.
2. Use Range Finder or the auditing commands to show which cells are referenced in formulas and functions. You double-click a cell with a formula or function to activate Range Finder.
3. Check which cells are locked and which cells are unlocked. Usually all cells in a workbook are locked, except for those in which you enter data. For example, on the 401(k) Investment Model worksheet in Golden Book, only the cells in the range C5:C10 are unlocked.
4. Enter sample data and verify the results.

More About 2000

Gaining Confidence in a Workbook

Additional ways exist to uncover details of workbooks created by someone else. For example, the File | Page Setup, File | Print Preview, Tools | Options, and Insert | Name | Define commands can tell you if the author used any peculiar settings. The Tools | Macro | Macros command will list the macros in the workbook.

To illustrate the entry of sample data, the following employee data will be used: Employee Name (cell C5) — Sarah Dakota; Annual Salary (cell C6) — $73,000.00; Employee Investment (cell C7) – 6.50%; Employer Match (cell C8) – 5.00%; Annual Return (cell C9) – 5.50%; and Years of Service (cell C10) – 30. Before entering the data, select the range C5:C10 so that Excel automatically makes the next cell in the range the active one when you complete a cell entry by pressing the ENTER key.

401(k) Plans

Most employers who contribute to 401(k) plans require an employee to be vested before the employer-matching contributions are assigned to the employee. Usually a company requires an employee to be employed continually for 3 to 5 years to be vested. 401(k) plans, however, can be transferred from one employer to another.

TO AUTOMATE DATA ENTRY BY SELECTING A RANGE OF CELLS

1 Click cell C5 and then select the range C5:C10. In cell C5, type Sarah Dakota as the employee name and then press the ENTER key.

2 In cell C6, type 73000 as the annual salary and then press the ENTER key.

3 In cell C7, type 6.5% as the employee investment and then press the ENTER key.

4 In cell C8, type 5% as the employer match and then press the ENTER key.

5 In cell C9, type 5.5% as the annual return and then press the ENTER key.

6 In cell C10, type 30 as the years of service and then press the ENTER key. Click cell B17 to remove the selection from the range C5:C10.

The worksheet displays with the updated results, including a new future value of $639,147.65 in cell C15 (Figure 7-4).

As shown in Figure 7-4, if Sarah Dakota earns $73,000 a year and invests 6.5% of her income a year in the 401(k) plan, then in 30 years her investment will be worth $639,147.65. If she works an additional ten years, then cell F14 shows Sarah's investment will be worth an astonishing $1,218,002.28. These future values assume the annual return on the investment will be a conservative 5.5%. They also assume that Sarah will never get a raise, which means the investment could be worth significantly more if she does get raises, because she is investing a percentage of her income, rather than a fixed amount.

Outside of winning the lotto or a large inheritance, a 401(k) plan is the easiest way for a person on a fixed income to legally become a millionaire at some point in his or her lifetime. Once you start drawing funds from a 401(k) plan, you are required to pay taxes on what you withdraw. If you withdraw any funds before you are 59½ years old, then you must pay a 10 percent penalty on withdrawals.

Undo button arrow

Microsoft Excel - Golden Years

File Edit View Insert Format Tools Data Window Help

Arial   10   B I U

B17

data for Sarah Dakota

data table shows results for different years

Golden Years.com
401(k) Investment Model

	B	C	E Years of Service	F Future Value	G Employee Investment	H Employer Match	I Return On Investment	J
5	Employee Name	Sarah Dakota						
6	Annual Salary	$73,000.00		$639,147.65	$142,350.00	$109,500.00	$387,297.65	
7	Employee Investment	6.50%	5	48,187.88	23,725.00	18,250.00	6,212.88	
8	Employer Match	5.00%	10	111,588.85	47,450.00	36,500.00	27,638.85	
9	Annual Return	5.50%	15	195,005.74	71,175.00	54,750.00	69,080.74	
10	Years of Service	30	20	304,757.67	94,900.00	73,000.00	136,857.67	
11	Monthly Contribution		25	449,158.69	118,625.00	91,250.00	239,283.69	
12	Employee	$395.42	30	639,147.65	142,350.00	109,500.00	387,297.65	
13	Employer	$304.17	35	889,116.85	166,075.00	127,750.00	595,291.85	
14	Total	$699.58	40	1,218,002.28	189,800.00	146,000.00	882,202.28	
15	Future Value	$639,147.65	45	1,650,718.06	213,525.00	164,250.00	1,272,943.06	

future value of Sarah Dakota's 401(k) investment

green background indicates year in data table that agrees with years of service in cell C10

FIGURE 7-4

As shown in the previous set of steps, when you select a range before entering data, Excel automatically advances one cell down when you press the ENTER key. If the worksheet consists of multiple columns and you enter the last value in a column, then Excel moves to the top of the next column.

Follow these steps to change the data in the range C5:C10 back to its original values.

TO UNDO A GROUP OF ENTRIES USING THE UNDO BUTTON

1 Click the Undo button arrow on the Standard toolbar (Figure 7-4).

2 When the Undo list displays, drag from the top down through Sarah Dakota and then release the left mouse button. Click cell B17.

Excel changes the range C5:C10 back to its original values and recalculates all formulas and the data table. The 401(k) Investment Model worksheet displays as shown earlier in Figure 7-3 on page E 7.7.

More About

The Undo Button

To undo recent actions one at a time, click the Undo button on the Standard toolbar. To undo several actions, click the Undo button arrow and select from the list. Excel will undo the selected action as well as all the actions above it.

Unprotecting a Password-Protected Worksheet

The 401(k) Investment Model worksheet in the Golden Years workbook is protected. When a worksheet is protected, users cannot change data in locked cells or modify the worksheet in any manner. Thus, before modifying the worksheet in the three phases, it must be unprotected. A **password** ensures that users will not unprotect the worksheet by using the Unprotect command. The 401(k) Investment Model worksheet password is fortune.

A password, such as fortune, can contain any combination of letters, numerals, spaces, and symbols, and it can be up to 15 characters long. Passwords are case-sensitive, so if you vary the capitalization when you assign the password, you must type the same capitalization later when you unprotect the worksheet.

The following steps show how to unprotect the password-protected worksheet.

Steps To Unprotect a Password-Protected Worksheet

1 **Click Tools on the menu bar, point to Protection, and then point to Unprotect Sheet on the Protection submenu.**

The Tools menu and Protection submenu display (Figure 7-5).

FIGURE 7-5

Click Unprotect Worksheet. When the Unprotect Sheet dialog box displays, type fortune **in the Password text box and then point to the OK button.**

The Unprotect Sheet dialog box displays (Figure 7-6). Excel displays asterisks in place of the password fortune so no one can look over your shoulder and copy the password.

 Click the OK button.

Excel unprotects the 401(k) Investment Model worksheet.

FIGURE 7-6

Other Ways

1. Press ALT+T, press P, press P

More About 2000

Password-Protection

Excel offers three basic levels of password-protection: (1) file level when you save it on disk; (2) workbook level so the window cannot be modified; and (3) worksheet level so locked cells cannot be changed. The first level is available through the Save As command. The second and third levels are available through the Protection command on the Tools menu.

With the worksheet unprotected, you can modify the contents of cells regardless of whether they are locked or unlocked. If you decide to password-protect a worksheet, make sure you write down the password and keep it in a secure place. If you lose the password, you cannot open or gain access to the password-protected worksheet.

The Protection submenu shown in Figure 7-5 on the previous page also has an **Unprotect Workbook command**. The workbook protection level protects the structure and windows of the workbook, but not individual worksheets. Protecting the structure of a workbook means that users cannot add, delete, move, hide, unhide, or rename sheets. Protecting a workbook's windows means users cannot move, resize, hide, unhide, or close them.

Although it is not necessary in this project to unprotect the workbook, you can do so by invoking the Unprotect Workbook command and using fortune as the password.

Phase 1 — Recording a Macro and Assigning It to a Toolbar Button and Menu Command

The first phase of this project creates a macro to automate printing the worksheet in portrait orientation using the Fit to option. Recall that the Fit to option ensures that the worksheet will fit on one page. The orientation for the printout was set to landscape in Golden Years. The planned macro will change the orientation from landscape to portrait and use the Fit to option to force it to fit on one page. It will then reset the print settings back to their original settings.

The purpose of this macro is to give users the option of printing the worksheet in landscape orientation by clicking the Print button on the Standard toolbar or executing the macro to print the worksheet in portrait orientation. Once the macro is created, it will be assigned to a button on the Standard toolbar and a command on the File menu.

Recording a Macro

Excel has a **macro recorder** that creates a macro automatically based on a series of actions you perform while it is recording. As with a tape recorder, the macro recorder records everything you do to a workbook over time. The macro recorder can be turned on, during which time it records your activities, and then turned off to stop the recording. Once the macro is recorded, it can be played back, or executed, as often as you want.

It is easy to create a macro. Simply turn on the macro recorder and carry out the steps to be recorded.

1. Switch from landscape orientation to portrait orientation and from 100% normal size printing to fit to one page.
2. Print the worksheet.
3. Switch from portrait orientation to landscape orientation and from fit to one page to 100% normal size printing.
4. Stop the macro recorder.

What is impressive about the macro recorder is that you actually step through the task as you create the macro. Therefore, you see exactly what the macro will do before you use it.

When you first create the macro, you have to name it. The name then is used later to reference the macro when you want to execute it. The macro name in this project is PrintPortrait. **Macro names** can be up to 255 characters long; they can contain numbers, letters, and underscores; they cannot contain spaces and other punctuation. Perform the following steps to record the macro.

The Macro Recorder

The macro recorder is unforgiving. Once it is turned on, Excel records every action you take. If you make a mistake, you must start over. For this reason, you need to plan carefully from start to finish what you intend to do before you turn the macro recorder on.

Steps: To Record a Macro to Print the Worksheet in Portrait Orientation Using the Fit to Option

1 **Click Tools on the menu bar. Point to Macro and then point to Record New Macro on the Macro submenu.**

The Tools menu and Macro submenu display (Figure 7-7).

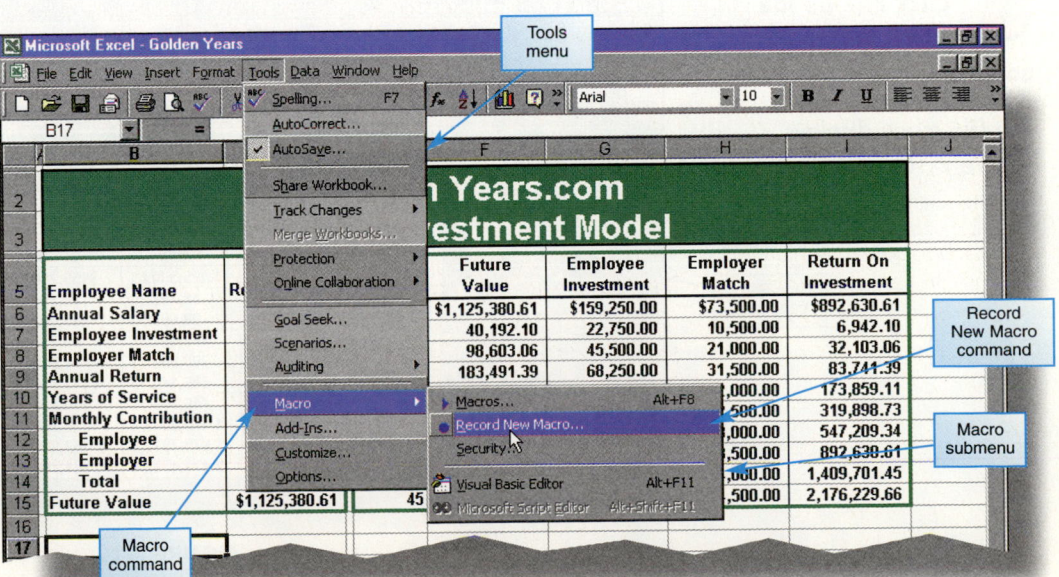

FIGURE 7-7

2 **Click Record New Macro. When the Record Macro dialog box displays, type** PrintPortrait **in the Macro name text box. Type** r **in the Shortcut key text box, and then type** Macro prints worksheet in portrait orientation on one page **in the Description text box. Make sure the Store macro in box displays This Workbook. Point to the OK button.**

The Record Macro dialog box displays as shown in Figure 7-8. The shortcut key for executing the macro is CTRL+R.

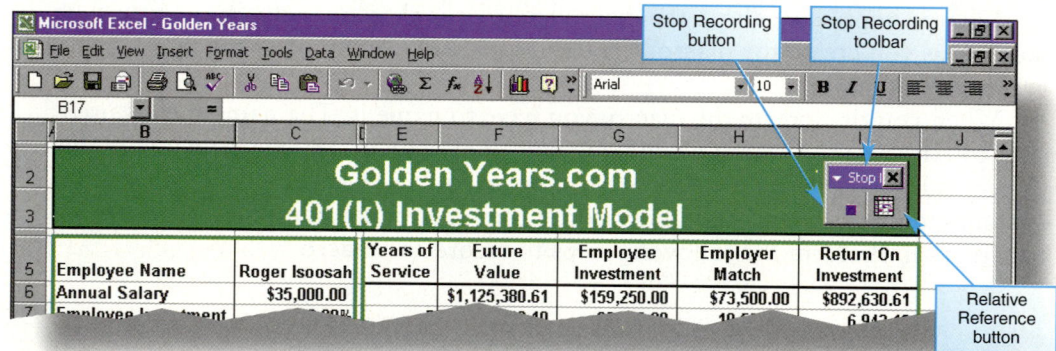

FIGURE 7-8

3 **Click the OK button.**

The Stop Recording toolbar displays. Any task you do will be part of the macro. When you are finished recording the macro, clicking the Stop Recording button on the Stop Recording toolbar ends the recording.

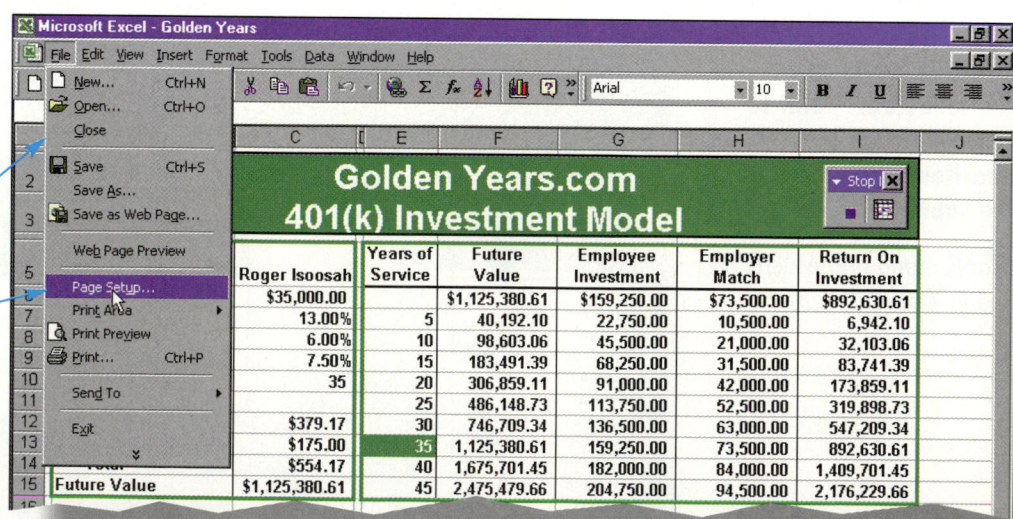

FIGURE 7-9

4 **Click File on the menu bar and then point to Page Setup.**

The File menu displays (Figure 7-10).

FIGURE 7-10

5 Click Page Setup. When the Page Setup dialog box displays, click the Page tab, click Portrait in the Orientation area, click Fit to in the Scaling area, and then point to the Print button.

The Page Setup dialog box displays as shown in Figure 7-11.

FIGURE 7-11

6 Click the Print button. When the Print dialog box displays, click the OK button. Click File on the menu bar and then click Page Setup. When the Page Setup dialog box displays, if necessary, click the Page tab, click Landscape in the Orientation area, click Adjust to in the Scaling area, type 100 in the % normal size box, and then point to the OK button.

After the worksheet prints in portrait orientation on one page, the Page Setup dialog box displays as shown in Figure 7-12.

FIGURE 7-12

7 Click the OK button. Point to the Stop Recording button on the Stop Recording toolbar (Figure 7-13).

8 Click the Stop Recording button.

Excel stops recording the worksheet activities and hides the Stop Recording toolbar.

Save button

Stop Recording button

workbook close button

Microsoft Excel - Golden Years

File Edit View Insert Format Tools Data Window Help

Arial 10 B I U

B17

Golden Years.com
401(k) Investment Model

Employee Name	Roger Isoosah	Years of Service	Future Value	Employee Investment	Employer Match	Ret. Investment
Annual Salary	$35,000.00		$1,125,380.61	$159,250.00	$73,500.00	$892,630.61
Employee Investment	13.00%	5	40,192.10	22,750.00	10,500.00	6,942.10
Employer Match	6.00%	10	98,603.06	45,500.00	21,000.00	32,103.06
Annual Return	7.50%	15	183,491.39	68,250.00	31,500.00	83,741.39
Years of Service	35	20	306,859.11	91,000.00	42,000.00	173,859.11
Monthly Contribution		25	486,148.73	113,750.00	52,500.00	319,898.73
Employee	$379.17	30	746,709.34	136,500.00	63,000.00	547,209.34
Employer	$175.00	35	1,125,380.61	159,250.00	73,500.00	892,630.61
Total	$554.17	40	1,675,701.45	182,000.00	84,000.00	1,409,701.45

Stop

Stop Recording

FIGURE 7-13

If you recorded the wrong actions, delete the macro and record it again. You delete a macro by clicking Tools on the menu bar, pointing to Macro on the Tools menu, and then clicking Macros on the Macro submenu. When the Macro dialog box displays, click the name of the macro (PrintPortrait) and then click the Delete button. Finally, record the macro again.

In the Record Macro dialog box (Figure 7-8 on page E 7.12), you select the location to store the macro in the Store macro in box. If you want a macro to be available whenever you use Microsoft Excel, select Personal Macro Workbook in the Store macro in list. This selection causes the macro to be stored in the **Personal Macro Workbook**, which is part of Excel. If you click New Workbook, then Excel stores the macro in a new workbook. Most macros created with the macro recorder are workbook-specific, and thus, are stored in the active workbook.

The following steps protect the 401(k) Investment Model worksheet, save the workbook using the file name Golden Years1, and then close the workbook.

TO PASSWORD-PROTECT THE WORKSHEET, SAVE THE WORKBOOK, AND CLOSE THE WORKBOOK

1 Click Tools on the menu bar, point to Protection, and then click Protect Sheet on the Protection submenu. When the Protect Sheet dialog box displays, type fortune in the Password text box and then click the OK button. When the Confirm Password dialog box displays, type fortune and then click the OK button.

2 Click File on the menu bar and then click Save As. When the Save As dialog box displays, type Golden Years1 in the File name text box. Make sure 3½ Floppy (A:) displays in the Save in box and then click the Save button.

3 Click the workbook's Close button on the right side of its menu bar to close the workbook and leave Excel active.

Excel protects the worksheet, saves the workbook on drive A, and then closes the Golden Years1 workbook.

Opening a Workbook with a Macro and Executing the Macro

A **computer virus** is a potentially damaging computer program designed to affect, or infect, your computer negatively by altering the way it works without your knowledge or permission. Currently, more than 13,000 known computer viruses exist and an estimated six new viruses are discovered each day. The increased use of the networks, the Internet, and e-mail has accelerated the spread of computer viruses.

To combat this evil, most computer users run antivirus programs that search for viruses and destroy them before they ever have a chance to infect the computer. Macros are a known carrier of viruses, because of the ease at which a person can add code to macros. For this reason, each time you open a workbook with a macro associated with it, Excel displays a Microsoft Excel dialog box warning that a macro is attached and that macros can contain viruses. Table 7-1 summarizes the buttons users can select from to continue the process of opening a workbook with macros.

More About

Macro Viruses

To guard against macro viruses in workbooks created by someone else, you should purchase antivirus software that is designed to detect and repair files infected with a virus. For more information on antivirus software, visit the Excel 2000 More About Web page (www.scsite.com/ex2000/more.htm) and click Antivirus Software.

Table 7-1	Buttons in the Microsoft Excel Dialog Box When Opening a Workbook with Macros
BUTTON	**DESCRIPTION**
Disable Macros	Macros are unavailable to the user
Enable Macros	Macros are available to the user to execute
More Info	Opens the Microsoft Excel Help window and displays information on viruses and workbook macros

If you are confident of the source (author) of the workbook and macros, click the Enable Macros button. If you are uncertain about the reliability of the source of the workbook and macros, then click the Disable Macros button. For more information on this topic, click the More Info button.

The following steps open the Golden Years1 workbook to illustrate the Microsoft Excel dialog box that displays when a workbook contains a macro. The steps then show how to execute the recorded macro PrintPortrait by using the short-cut key CTRL+R. Recall that the shortcut key was established in Step 2 of the previous set of steps.

More About

Antivirus Software

If your antivirus software is compatible with Office 2000, then you can select the lowest level of security in the Security dialog box. You display the Security dialog box by clicking Tools on the menu bar, Macro on the Tools menu, and Security on the Macro sub-menu. The antivirus software will scan all incoming workbooks for viruses, regardless of the level of security you choose.

Steps ## To Open a Workbook with a Macro and Execute the Macro

1 **With Excel active, click File on the menu bar and then click Open. When the Open dialog box displays, click the Look in box arrow, and then click 3 ½ Floppy (A:). Double-click the file name Golden Years1.**

The Microsoft Excel dialog displays (Figure 7-14).

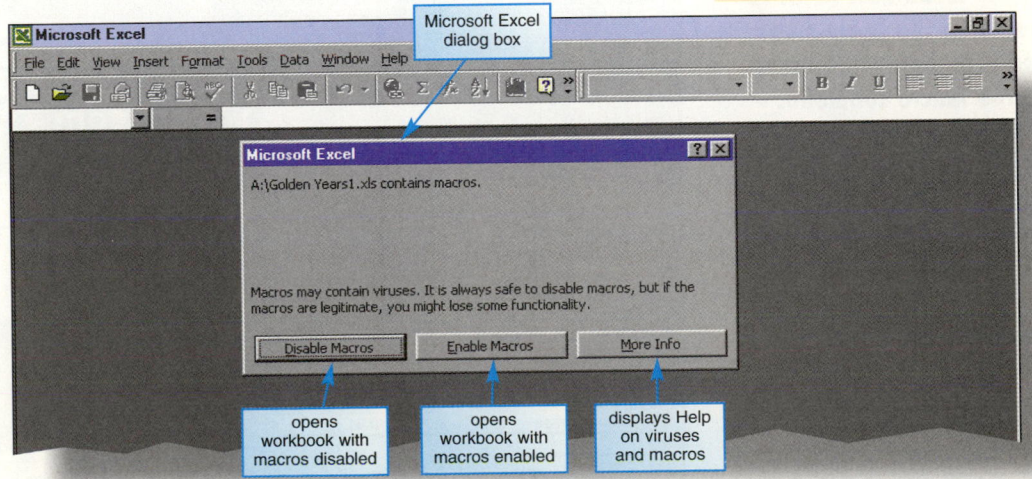

FIGURE 7-14

2 Click the Enable Macros button. When the 401(k) Investment Model worksheet in the Golden Years1 workbook displays, press CTRL+R.

Excel opens the workbook Golden Years1. The Excel window blinks for several seconds as the macro executes. The report prints as shown in Figure 7-15.

Golden Years.com
401(k) Investment Model

Employee Name	Roger Isoosah	Years of Service	Future Value	Employee Investment	Employer Match	Return On Investment
Annual Salary	$35,000.00		$1,125,380.61	$159,250.00	$73,500.00	$892,630.61
Employee Investment	13.00%	5	40,192.10	22,750.00	10,500.00	6,942.10
Employer Match	6.00%	10	98,603.06	45,500.00	21,000.00	32,103.06
Annual Return	7.50%	15	183,491.39	68,250.00	31,500.00	83,741.39
Years of Service	35	20	306,859.11	91,000.00	42,000.00	173,859.11
Monthly Contribution		25	486,148.73	113,750.00	52,500.00	319,898.73
Employee	$379.17	30	746,709.34	136,500.00	63,000.00	547,209.34
Employer	$175.00	35	1,125,380.61	159,250.00	73,500.00	892,630.61
Total	$554.17	40	1,675,701.45	182,000.00	84,000.00	1,409,701.45
Future Value	$1,125,380.61	45	2,475,479.66	204,750.00	94,500.00	2,176,229.66

worksheet printed in portrait orientation using Fit to option

FIGURE 7-15

Other Ways

1. On Tools menu point to Macro, click Macros, double-click macro name
2. Press ALT+F8, double-click macro name
3. Click Run Macro button on Visual Basic toolbar

If you are running antivirus software, you may want to turn off the security warning shown in Figure 7-14 on the previous page. You can turn off the security warning by clicking Tools on the menu bar, pointing to Macro, and then clicking **Security** on the Macros submenu. When the **Security dialog box** displays, click the **Low option button**. Then the next time you open a workbook with an attached macro, Excel will open the workbook immediately, rather than display the dialog box shown in Figure 7-14.

Viewing a Macro's VBA Code

As described earlier, a macro is comprised of VBA code, which is created automatically by the macro recorder. You can view the VBA code through the Visual Basic Editor. The **Visual Basic Editor** is used by all Office applications to enter, modify, and view VBA code. To view the macro's VBA code, complete the following steps.

Steps To View a Macro's VBA Code

1 Click Tools on the menu bar. Point to Macro on the Tools menu and then point to Macros on the Macro submenu.

The Tools menu and Macro submenu display (Figure 7-16).

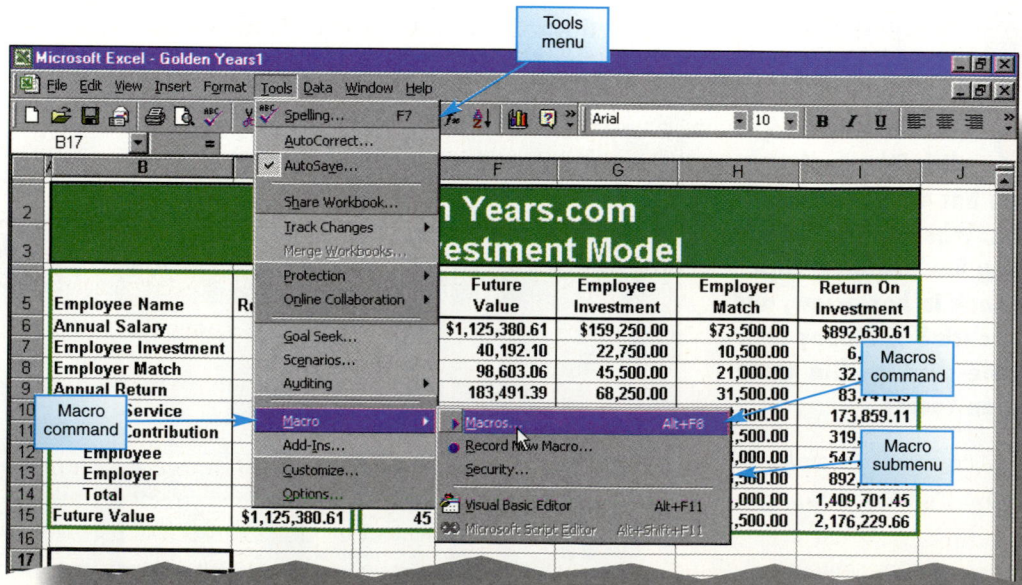

FIGURE 7-16

2 Click Macros. When the Macro dialog box displays, click PrintPortrait in the list, and then point to the Edit button.

The Macro dialog box displays as shown in Figure 7-17.

FIGURE 7-17

3 Click the Edit button.

The Visual Basic Editor starts and displays the VBA code in the macro PrintPortrait (Figure 7-18). Your screen may display differently depending on how it displayed the last time the Visual Basic Editor was activated.

4 Scroll through the VBA code. When you are finished, click the Visual Basic Editor Close button on the right side of the title bar.

FIGURE 7-18

It is this set of instructions, beginning with line 1 in Figure 7-18 and continuing sequentially to the last line, that is executed when you invoke the macro. By scrolling through the VBA code, you can see that the macro recorder generates a lot of instructions. In this case, 75 lines of code are generated to print the worksheet in portrait orientation using the Fit to option.

Other Ways

1. Click Visual Basic Editor button on Visual Basic toolbar

More About 2000

The Visual Basic Editor Window

If the window displaying the VBA code displays differently than the one shown in Figure 7-18, double-click the Code window's title bar to maximize the window. If the Project window or Properties window display on the left side of the Visual Basic Editor window, then click their Close buttons.

Customizing Toolbars and Menus

You can customize toolbars and menus by adding buttons and commands, deleting buttons and commands, and changing the function of buttons and commands. Once you add a button to a toolbar or a command to a menu, you can assign a macro to the button or command. You customize a toolbar or menu by invoking the **Customize command** on the Tools menu. The key to understanding how to customize a toolbar or menu is to recognize that when the Customize dialog box is open, Excel's toolbars and menus are in Edit mode. **Edit mode** allows you to modify the toolbars and menus.

CUSTOMIZING A TOOLBAR The following steps add a button to the Standard toolbar, change the button image, and assign the PrintPortrait macro to the button.

 Steps **To Add a Button to a Toolbar, Assign the Button a Macro, and Use the Button**

1 Click Tools on the menu bar and then point to Customize.

The Tools menu displays (Figure 7-19)

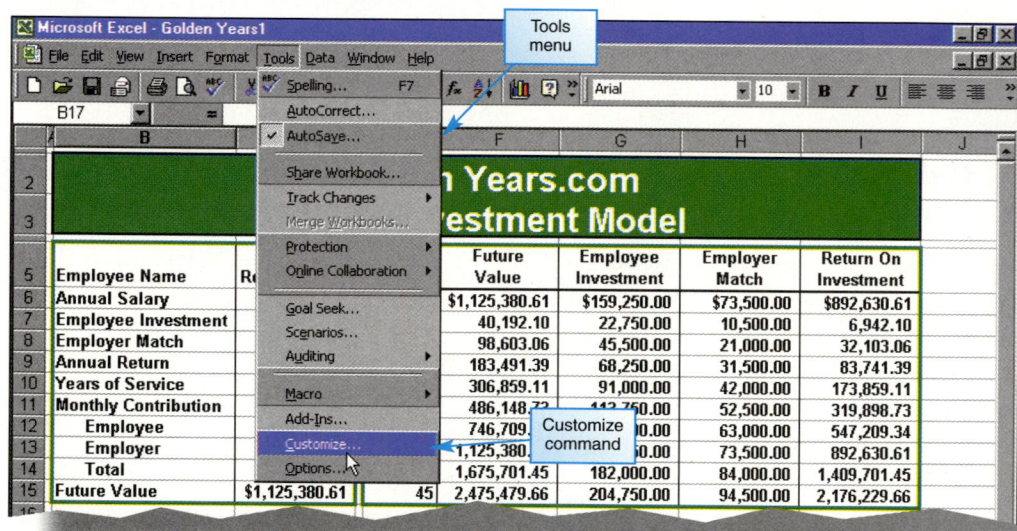

FIGURE 7-19

2 Click Customize. When the Customize dialog box opens, click the Commands tab. Scroll down in the Categories list and then click Macros.

The Customize dialog box displays as shown in Figure 7-20. The two items in the Commands list for the Macro category are Custom Menu Item and Custom Button.

FIGURE 7-20

3 Drag the button with the smiley face image in the Commands list to the right of the Microsoft Excel Help button on the Standard toolbar.

The button with the smilly face image displays next to the Microsoft Excel Help button on the Standard toolbar (Figure 7-21). A heavy border surrounds the button with the smiley face image indicating Excel is in Edit mode.

FIGURE 7-21

4 Right-click the button with the smiley face image on the Standard toolbar. When the shortcut menu displays, type `Print Portrait` in the Name text box. Point to Change Button Image on the shortcut menu. When the Change Button Image palette displays, point to the button with the eye image.

Excel displays a palette of button images to select from (Figure 7-22).

FIGURE 7-22

5 **Click the button with the eye image. Right-click the button with the eye image on the Standard toolbar and then point to Assign Macro on the shortcut menu.**

Excel replaces the button with the smiley face image on the Standard toolbar with the button with the eye image (Figure 7-23) and the shortcut menu displays.

FIGURE 7-23

6 **Click Assign Macro. When the Assign Macro dialog box displays, click PrintPortrait and then point to the OK button.**

The Assign Macro dialog box displays as shown in Figure 7-24.

FIGURE 7-24

7 Click the OK button. Click the Close button at the bottom of the Customize dialog box. Point to the Print Portrait button on the Standard toolbar.

Excel quits Edit mode. The Print Portrait button displays on the Standard toolbar with the ScreenTip Print Portrait (Figure 7-25).

8 Click the Print Portrait button on the Standard toolbar.

After a few seconds, the worksheet prints in portrait orientation as shown in Figure 7-15 on page E 7.16.

FIGURE 7-25

The previous steps illustrate how easy it is in Excel to add a button to a toolbar and assign the button a macro.

Excel includes a complete repertoire of commands for editing buttons on a toolbar as shown on the shortcut menu in Figure 7-23. Table 7-2 briefly describes each of the commands on the shortcut menu.

Other Ways

1. Right-click toolbar, click Customize on shortcut menu, click Commands tab

2. Click View, click Toolbars, click Customize, click Commands tab

3. Click Modify Selection button in Customize dialog box

Table 7-2 Summary of Commands on the Button Shortcut Menu

COMMAND	DESCRIPTION
Reset	Changes the icon on the selected button to the original icon and disassociates the macro with the button
Delete	Deletes the selected button
Name box	Changes the ScreenTip for a button and changes the command name for a command on a menu
Copy Button Image	Copies the button image to the Office Clipboard
Paste Button Image	Pastes the button image on the Office Clipboard to the selected button
Reset Button Image	Changes the button image back to the original image
Edit Button Image	Allows you to edit the button image
Change Button Image	Allows you to choose a new button image
Default Style; Text Only (Always); Text Only (in Menus); Image and Text	Allows you to choose one of the four styles to indicate how the button should look
Begin a Group	Groups buttons by drawing a vertical line (divider) on the toolbar (see the group dividing line in Figure 7-25)
Assign Hyperlink	Assigns a hyperlink to a Web page or Office document to the button
Assign Macro	Assigns a macro to the button

Creating Toolbars

You can create new toolbars and add buttons to them, rather than add buttons to current toolbars. To create a new toolbar, click the Toolbars tab in the Customize dialog box and then click the New button.

You can add as many buttons as you want to a toolbar. You also can change the image on any button or change a button's function. For example, when in Edit mode (the Customize dialog box is active) you can right-click the Save button on the Standard toolbar and assign it a macro or hyperlink. The next time you click the Save button, the macro will execute or Excel will launch the application associated with the hyperlink, rather than saving the workbook. You reset the toolbars to their installation default by clicking the Toolbars tab in the Customize dialog box, selecting the toolbar in the Toolbars box, and then clicking the Reset button. Because it is so easy to change the buttons on a toolbar, each project in this book begins by resetting the toolbars.

As you add buttons, other buttons on the toolbar will be demoted to the More Buttons box.

CUSTOMIZING A MENU Up to this point, you have been introduced to using a shortcut key and button to execute a macro. Excel also allows you to add commands to a menu. The following steps show how to add a command to the File menu to execute the PrintPortrait macro.

To Add a Command to a Menu, Assign the Command a Macro, and Invoke the Command

1 Click Tools on the menu bar and then click Customize. When the Customize dialog box displays, if necessary, click the Commands tab. Scroll down in the Categories box and then click Macros. Click File on the menu bar to display the File menu.

The Customize dialog box and File menu display as shown in Figure 7-26.

FIGURE 7-26

2 **Drag the Custom Menu Item entry from the Commands list in the Customize dialog box immediately below the Print command on the File menu.**

Excel adds Custom Menu Item to the File menu (Figure 7-27). A heavy border surrounds Custom Menu Item on the File menu indicating Excel is in the Edit mode.

FIGURE 7-27

3 **Right-click Custom Menu Item on the File menu and then click the Name text box on the shortcut menu. Type** Print Po&rtrait   Ctrl+R **as the new name of this entry on the File menu. Point to Assign Macro on the shortcut menu.**

The shortcut menu displays (Figure 7-28). The ampersand (&) preceding the letter r in Portrait instructs Excel to use the letter r as the access key. The **access key** *is the underlined letter that you can press to invoke the command when the menu displays.*

FIGURE 7-28

4 **Click Assign Macro on the shortcut menu. When the Assign Macro dialog box displays, double-click Print Portrait. Click the Close button at the bottom of the Customize dialog box. Click File on the menu bar and then point to Print Portrait.**

Excel quits the Edit mode. The File menu displays with the new command Print Portrait on the menu (Figure 7-29). The underlined letter r in Portrait is the access key.

5 **Click Print Portrait on the File menu.**

After several seconds, the worksheet prints in portrait orientation as shown in Figure 7-15 on page E 7.16.

FIGURE 7-29

6 **Click the Save button on the Standard toolbar to save the workbook using the file name Golden Years1.**

Other **Ways**

1. Right-click toolbar, click Customize on shortcut menu, click Commands tab
2. Click View, click Toolbars, click Customize, click Commands tab

You have the same customization capabilities with menus as you do with toolbars. All of the shortcut commands described in Table 7-2 on page E 7.21 apply to menus as well. Any command specific to buttons pertains to editing the button image on the left side of a command on a menu.

An alternative to adding a command to a menu is to add a new menu name to the menu bar and add commands to its menu. You can add a new menu name to the menu bar by selecting New Menu in the Categories list of the Customize dialog box (Figure 7-27 on the previous page) and dragging New Menu from the Commands list to the menu bar.

Phase 2 — Creating a Procedure to Automate the 401(k) Data Entry

Earlier on page E 7.8, the data for Sarah Dakota was entered to calculate new future value information. A novice user, however, might not know what cells to select or how much 401(k) data is required to obtain the desired results. To facilitate entering the 401(k) data, Phase 2 calls for creating a Command Button control (Figure 7-30a) and an associated procedure (Figure 7-30b) that steps the user through entering the data using dialog boxes.

(a) Worksheet with Button

Microsoft Excel - Golden Years2

File Edit View Insert Format Tools Data Window Help

Arial 10 B I U

A1 =

Print Portrait

	B	C	D	E	F	G	H	I	J
2					**Golden Years.com**				
3					**401(k) Investment Model**				
5	Employee Name	Roger Isoosah		Years of Service	Future Value	Employee Investment	Employer Match	Return On Investment	
6	Annual Salary	$35,000.00			$1,125,380.61	$159,250.00	$73,500.00	$892,630.61	
7	Employee Investment	13.00%		5	40,192.10	22,750.00	10,500.00	6,942.10	
8	Employer Match	6.00%		10	98,603.06	45,500.00	21,000.00	32,103.06	
9	Annual Return	7.50%		15	183,491.39	68,250.00	31,500.00	83,741.39	
10	Years of Service	35		20	306,859.11	91,000.00	42,000.00	173,859.11	
11	Monthly Contribution			25	486,148.73	113,750.00	52,500.00	319,898.73	
12	Employee	$379.17		30	746,709.34	136,500.00	63,000.00	547,209.34	
13	Employer	$175.00		35	1,125,380.61	159,250.00	73,500.00	892,630.61	
14	Total	$554.17		40	1,675,701.45	182,000.00	84,000.00	1,409,701.45	
15	Future Value	$1,125,380.61		45	2,475,479.66	204,750.00	94,500.00	2,176,229.66	
16									
17		New Data							
18									

Command Button control

Microsoft Visual Basic - Golden Years2.xls [design] - [Sheet1 (Code)]

File Edit View Insert Format Debug Run Tools Add-Ins Window Help

Ln 16, Col 63

CommandButton1   Click

```
' New Data Button Procedure            Author:   Thomas Ryan
' Date Created: 12/5/2001
' Run from:   401(k) Investment Model Sheet by clicking button labeled New Data
' Function:   When executed, this procedure accepts 401(k) investment data which
'             causes Excel to calculate a new future value and other investment
'             information.
'
Private Sub CommandButton1_Click()
    Range("C5:C10").ClearContents
    Range("A1").Select
    Range("C5").Value = InputBox("Employee Name?", "Enter")
    Range("C6").Value = InputBox("Annual Salary?", "Enter")
    Range("C7").Value = InputBox("Employee Investment in %?", "Enter")
    Range("C8").Value = InputBox("Employer Match in %?", "Enter")
    Range("C9").Value = InputBox("Annual Return in %?", "Enter")
    Range("C10").Value = InputBox("Years of Service?", "Enter")
End Sub
```

first executable statement

(b) Procedure   **FIGURE 7-30**

A **Command Button control** is different from a toolbar button in that it is an object you draw on the worksheet. Once you trigger the event by clicking the Command Button control, the instructions in the associated procedure guide the user through entering the required 401(k) data in the range C5:C10. The Command Button control also is the user interface. The **user interface** can be as simple as a button and as complex as a series of windows that accept data and display results. The user interface, together with the procedure, is called an **application**. Thus, the name Visual Basic for Applications.

If you step through the procedure (Figure 7-30b) beginning at the line just below Private Sub CommandButton1_Click(), you can see how a procedure methodically steps the user through entering the data in the range C5:C10:

1. The first line clears the range C5:C10.
2. The second line selects cell A1.
3. Lines three through eight accept data for the cells in the range C5:C10, one cell at a time.

Applications are built using the three-step process shown in Figure 7-31 on the next page: (1) create the user interface; (2) set the properties; and (3) write the VBA code. Before you can create the user interface, the 401(k) Investment Model worksheet in the Golden Years1 workbook must be unprotected. The steps on the next page unprotect the worksheet.

More About 2000

Visual Basic for Applications

All of the applications in Office 2000 (Word, Excel, Access, and PowerPoint) use Visual Basic for Applications. Thus, what you learn in this project applies to the other applications as well. Today, Visual Basic is the most widely used Windows applications programming language.

Step 1 - Create the User Interface

Step 2 - Set the Properties

(a) Worksheet with Button

Command Button control is user interface

properties of Command Button control

(b) Properties Window for Button

Step 3 - Write the VBA Code

VBA code entered using Visual Basic Editor

(c) VBA Code Associated with Button

FIGURE 7-31

TO UNPROTECT A PASSWORD-PROTECTED WORKSHEET

1. With the Golden Years1 workbook open, click Tools on the menu bar, point to Protection, and then click Unprotect Worksheet on the Protection submenu.

2. When the Protect dialog box displays, type fortune as the password and then click the OK button.

Step 1 – Create the User Interface

The most common way to execute a procedure in Excel is to create a Command Button control. To create the control, click the **Command Button button** on the **Control Toolbox toolbar.** You use the mouse to locate and size the control in the same way you locate and size an embedded chart. You then assign properties and the procedure to the control while Excel is in Design mode.

With respect to Visual Basic for Applications, Excel has two modes: Design mode and Run mode. **Design mode** allows you to resize controls, assign properties to controls, and enter VBA code. **Run mode** means that all controls are active. That is, if you click a control it triggers the event and Excel executes the procedure associated with the control. The following steps add a Command Button control to the worksheet.

Design Mode

If Excel is in Run mode and you click any control button on the Control Toolbox toolbar, Excel immediately switches to Design mode.

 To Add a Command Button Control to the Worksheet

1 Right-click a toolbar at the top of the screen. When the shortcut menu displays, click Control Toolbox.

The Control Toolbox toolbar displays.

2 Click the Command Button button on the Control Toolbox toolbar. Move the mouse pointer (a cross hair) to the upper-left corner of cell B17. Drag the mouse pointer so the rectangle defining the button area appears as shown in Figure 7-32 and hold.

A light border surrounds the proposed button area in the worksheet (Figure 7-32). When you click the Command Button button, Excel automatically switches to Design mode.

FIGURE 7-32

3 Release the left mouse button.

Excel displays the button with the default caption CommandButton1 (Figure 7-33). Because Excel is in design mode and the button is selected, the button is surrounded by sizing handles.

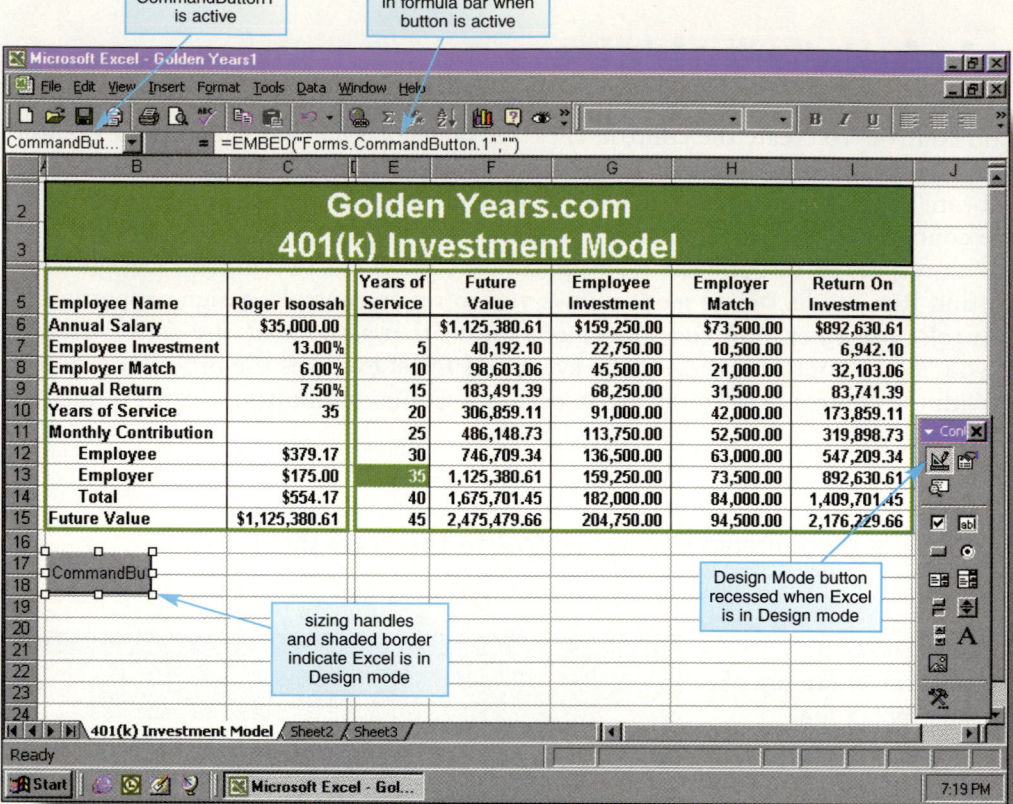

CommandButton1 is active

button code displays in formula bar when button is active

sizing handles and shaded border indicate Excel is in Design mode

Design Mode button recessed when Excel is in Design mode

FIGURE 7-33

Other Ways

1. Click Design Mode button on Visual Basic toolbar

The Control Toolbox toolbar buttons are summarized in Table 7-3. Many of the buttons allow you to add controls that you have worked with previously in Excel to the worksheet, such as check boxes, list boxes, and scroll bars.

Another toolbar that may be helpful as you use Visual Basic for Applications is the **Visual Basic toolbar**. The Visual Basic toolbar is shown in Figure 7-34. You can display the Visual Basic toolbar by right-clicking a toolbar and then clicking Visual Basic on the shortcut menu.

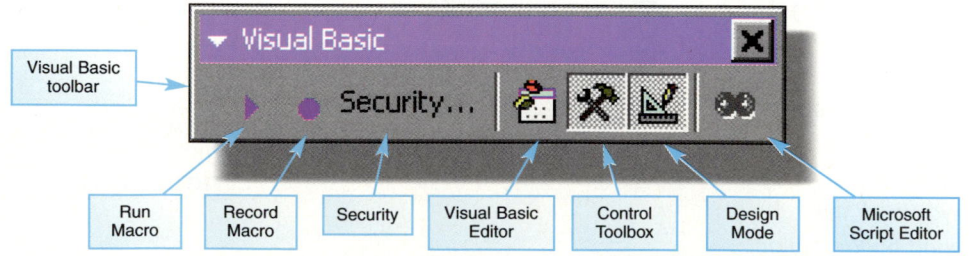

Visual Basic toolbar

Run Macro   Record Macro   Security   Visual Basic Editor   Control Toolbox   Design Mode   Microsoft Script Editor

FIGURE 7-34

Table 7-3	Summary of Buttons on the Control Toolbox Toolbar	
BUTTON	NAME	FUNCTION
	Design Mode	Changes to design mode; Design Mode button changes to Exit Design Mode button when in design mode
	Properties	Displays Properties window
	View Code	Displays VBA code in Visual Basic Editor
	Check Box	Adds a Check Box control
	Text Box	Adds a Text Box control
	Command Button	Adds a Command Button control
	Option Button	Adds an Option Button control
	List Box	Adds a List Box control
	Combo Box	Adds a Combo Box control
	Toggle Button	Adds a Toggle Button control
	Spin Button	Adds a Spin Button control
	Scroll Bar	Adds a Scroll Bar control
	Label	Adds a Label control
	Image	Adds an Image control
	More Controls	Displays a list of additional controls

Step 2 – Set the Properties

A Command Button control has 25 different **properties** (Figure 7-31b on page E 7.26), such as caption (the words on the face of the button), background color, foreground color, height, width, font, and so on. Once you add a Command Button control to a worksheet, you can change any one of the 25 properties to improve its appearance and modify how it works. The steps on the next page change the button's caption, the font size of the caption, and the color of the caption.

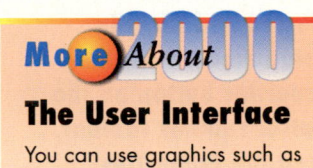

More About 2000

The User Interface

You can use graphics such as clip art instead of a Command Button button to serve as the control that you click to trigger the event.

More About 2000

More Controls

The last button described in Table 7-3 is the More Controls button. If you click the More Controls button, nearly 200 additional controls display, similar to those in Table 7-3, that are available to incorporate in a user interface.

Steps: To Set the Command Button Control Properties

1 With the Command Button control selected and Excel in design mode, click the Properties button on the Control Toolbox toolbar. When the Properties window displays, if necessary, click the Alphabetic tab, click Caption, and then type New Data as the caption. Click ForeColor, click the ForeColor arrow, click the Palette tab, and then point to the color green (column 5, row 5).

Excel displays the Properties window for the Command Button control (Figure 7-35). The Caption property is New Data and the ForeColor Palette sheet displays.

FIGURE 7-35

2 Click the color green. Click Font in the Properties window and then click the Font button. When the Font dialog box displays, click Bold in the Font style list and 12 in the Size list. Point to the OK button.

The Properties window and Font dialog box display as shown in Figure 7-36.

FIGURE 7-36

3 **Click the OK button.**

The Command Button control and its Properties window display as shown in Figure 7-37.

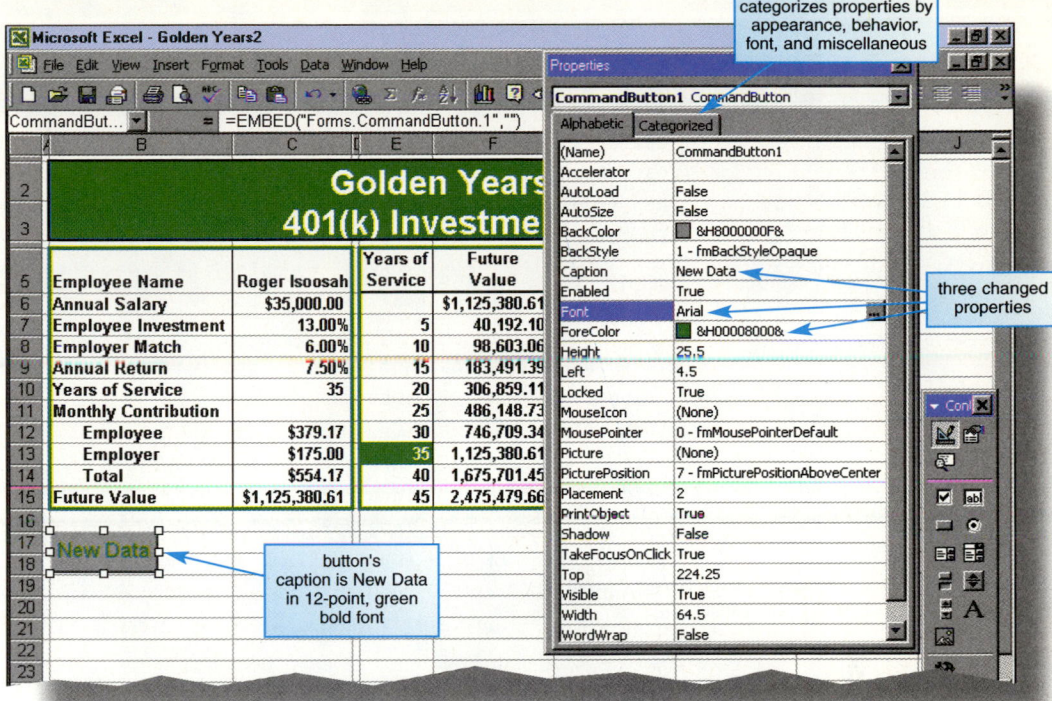

FIGURE 7-37

Other Ways

1. In Design mode, right-click control, click Properties on shortcut menu
2. Click Properties Window button on toolbar when Visual Basic Editor is active

The Properties window (Figure 7-37) has two tabs, Alphabetic and Categorized. The **Alphabetic list** displays the properties in alphabetical order. The **Categorized list** displays the properties in categories, such as appearance, behavior, font, and miscellaneous.

Depending on the application, you can modify any one of the Command Button control properties shown in Figure 7-35 on page E 7.30, much like you changed the Caption and Font properties in the previous steps.

Step 3 – Write the VBA Code

The next step is to write and then enter the procedure that will execute when you click the New Data button.

PLANNING A PROCEDURE When you trigger the event that executes a procedure, Excel steps through the Visual Basic statements one at a time, beginning at the top of the procedure. Thus, when you plan a procedure, remember that the order in which you place the statements in the procedure is important because the order determines the sequence of execution.

Once you know what you want the procedure to do, write the VBA code on paper similar to Table 7-4 on the next page. Then, before entering the procedure into the computer, test it by putting yourself in the position of Excel and stepping through the instructions one at a time. As you do so, think about how it affects the worksheet. Testing a procedure before entering it is called **desk checking** and is an important part of the development process.

Adding comments before a procedure will help you remember its purpose at a later date. In Table 7-4, the first seven lines are comments. **Comments** begin with the word Rem or an apostrophe ('). These comments contain overall documentation and are placed before the procedure, above the Sub statement. Comments have no effect on the execution of a procedure; they simply provide information about the procedure, such as name, creation date, and function.

More About

Improving Productivity

Looking for ways to improve your productivity? If you find yourself entering the same Excel steps repeatedly, you can use the macro recorder or VBA to complete the steps automatically. This can improve your productivity by eliminating routine tasks and simplifying complex tasks.

LINE	VBA CODE
	Table 7-4 New Data Button Procedure
1	' New Data Button Procedure Author: Thomas Ryan
2	' Date Created: 12/5/2001
3	' Run from: 401(k) Investment Model Sheet by clicking button labeled New Data
4	' Function: When executed, this procedure accepts 401 (k) investment data which
5	' causes Excel to calculate a new future value and other investment
6	' information.
7	'
8	Private Sub CommandButton1_Click()
9	Range("C5:C10").ClearContents
10	Range("A1").Select
11	Range("C5").Value = InputBox("Employee Name?", "Enter")
12	Range("C6").Value = InputBox("Annual Salary?", "Enter")
13	Range("C7").Value = InputBox("Employee Investment in %?", "Enter")
14	Range("C8").Value = InputBox("Employer Match in %?", "Enter")
15	Range("C9").Value = InputBox("Annual Return in %?", "Enter")
16	Range("C10").Value = InputBox("Years of Service?", "Enter")
17	End Sub

A procedure begins with a **Sub statement** and ends with an **End Sub statement** (lines 8 and 17 in Table 7-4). The Sub statement includes the keyword Private or Public followed by the name of the procedure, which Excel determines from the name of the button (CommandButton1), and the event that causes the procedure to execute (Click). **Private** means that the procedure can be executed only from this workbook. **Public** means that it can be executed from other workbooks or programs. Thus, the name of the Command Button control procedure is CommandButton1_Click.

The parentheses following the keyword Click in the Sub statement in line 8 are required. They indicate that arguments can be passed from one procedure to another. Passing arguments is beyond the scope of this project, but the parentheses still are required. The End Sub statement signifies the end of the procedure and returns Excel to Ready mode.

The first executable statement in Table 7-4 is line 9, which clears the cells in the range C5:C10. Line 10 selects cell A1 to remove clutter from the screen. One at a time, lines 11 through 16 accept data from the user and assign the data to the cells in the range C5:C10. Each one of the six statements handles one cell each. To the right of the equal sign in lines 11 through 16 is the InputBox function. A **function** returns a value to the program. In this case, the InputBox function displays a dialog box and returns the value entered by the user. For example, in line 11 the InputBox function displays a dialog box with the message, "Employee Name?" When the user responds and enters a name, the InputBox function returns the value entered to the program and assigns it to cell C5.

To enter a procedure, you use the Visual Basic Editor. To activate the Visual Basic Editor, Excel must be in Design mode. With the control selected, you click the **View Code button** on the Control Toolbar toolbar.

The **Visual Basic Editor** is a full-screen editor, which allows you to enter a procedure by typing the lines of VBA code as if you were using word processing software. At the end of a line, you press the ENTER key or use the DOWN ARROW key to move to the next line. If you make a mistake in a statement, you can use the arrow keys and the DELETE or BACKSPACE key to correct it. You also can move the insertion point to previous lines to make corrections.

Entering VBA Comments

If a horizontal line displays between the comment and Sub statement, press the ENTER key after the last comment to begin a new line. Then, press the DELETE key to delete the horizontal line.

USING THE VISUAL BASIC EDITOR TO ENTER A PROCEDURE The following steps activate the Visual Basic Editor and create the procedure for the New Data button.

 Steps To Enter the New Data Button Procedure

1 With Excel in Design mode and the New Data button selected, point to the View Code button on the Control Toolbox toolbar.

The selected New Data button and Control Toolbox toolbar display as shown in Figure 7-38.

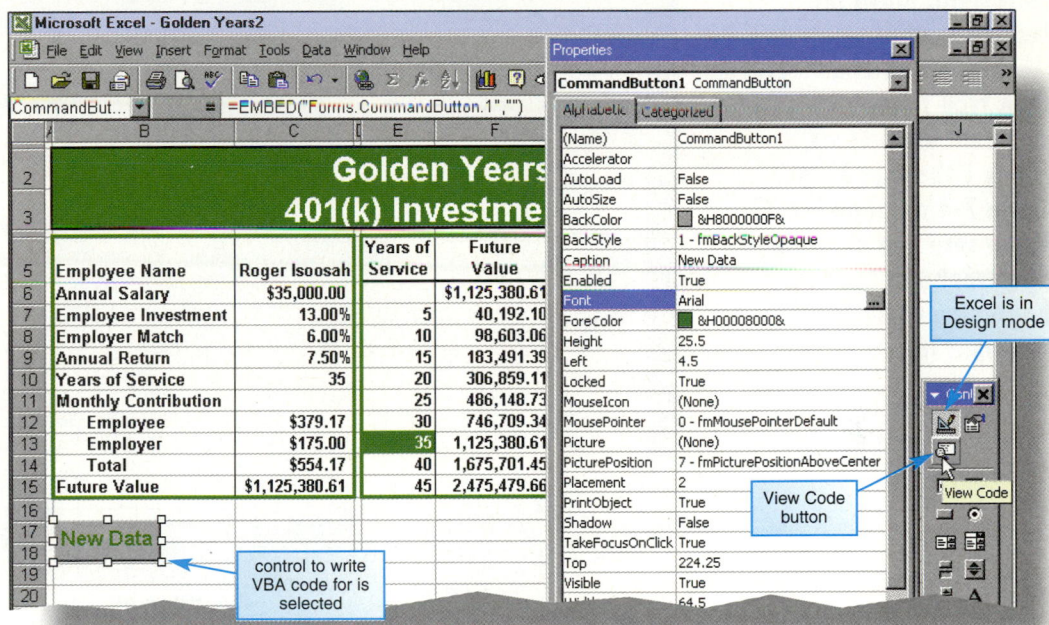

FIGURE 7-38

2 Click the View Code button. When the Visual Basic Editor displays, if the Project Explorer window displays on the left, click its Close button. Double-click the title bar to maximize the Code window on the right.

Excel starts the Visual Basic Editor and displays the Microsoft Visual Basic window (Figure 7-39). The Visual Basic Editor automatically inserts the Sub and End Sub statements and positions the insertion point between the two statements as shown.

FIGURE 7-39

3 **Click to the left of the letter P in the word Private on the first line and then press the ENTER key to add a blank line before the Sub statement. Move the insertion point to the blank line and then type the seven comment statements (lines 1 through 7) in Table 7-4 on page E 7.32. Make sure you enter an apostrophe at the beginning of each comment line.**

Excel automatically displays the comment lines in green (Figure 7-40).

FIGURE 7-40

4 **Position the insertion point on the blank line between the Sub and End Sub statements. Enter lines 9 through 16 in Table 7-4 on page E 7.32. For clarity, indent all lines between the Sub statement and End Sub statement by three spaces.**

The Command Button control procedure is complete (Figure 7-41).

FIGURE 7-41

5 **Click the Close button on the right side of the Microsoft Visual Basic title bar to return to the worksheet.**

The worksheet displays as shown in Figure 7-42.

6 **Click the Exit Design Mode button on the Control Toolbox toolbar. Click the Close button on the right side of the Control Toolbox toolbar title bar to hide it.**

Excel returns to Run mode, which means if you click the New Data button, Excel will execute the associated procedure.

FIGURE 7-42

Two ways exist to return control to the worksheet from the Visual Basic Editor. The Close button (Figure 7-41) closes the Visual Basic Editor and returns control to the worksheet. The **View Microsoft Excel button** on the Visual Basic toolbar (Figure 7-41), returns control to Excel, but only minimizes the Visual Basic Editor. If you plan to switch between Excel and the Visual Basic Editor, then use the View Microsoft Excel button, otherwise use the Close button.

More About Visual Basic for Applications

Visual Basic for Applications includes many more statements than those presented here. Even this simple procedure, however, should help you understand the basic makeup of a Visual Basic statement. For example, each of the statements within the procedure shown in Figure 7-41 includes a period. The entry on the left side of the period tells Excel which object you want to affect. An **object** can be a cell, a range, a chart, a worksheet, a workbook, a button, or any other control you create on a worksheet. The entry on the right side of the period tells Excel what you want to do to the object. You can place a method or property on the right side of the period. For example, the statement

```
Range("C5:C10").ClearContents
```

object   method

clears the range C5:C10. You use a **method**, such as ClearContents, to change an object's behavior. In this case, the method ClearContents is changing the behavior of the range by deleting its contents.

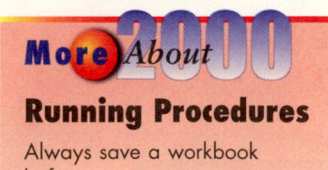

More About 2000

Running Procedures

Always save a workbook before you execute a procedure in case it does something unexpected. This is especially true when testing a procedure.

Earlier you were shown how to change an object's properties using the Properties window (Figure 7-35 on page E 7.30). The following example shows that you also can change an object's property during execution of a procedure. The object in this case is a Command Button control.

```
CommandButton1.Caption = "401(k) Data"
```

name of control   property

This statement changes the Caption property of the button to 401(k) Data during execution of the procedure.

The second statement in the procedure in Figure 7-41

```
Range("A1").Select
```

selects cell A1, which, in effect, hides the heavy border that surrounds the active cell. Several of the statements in the procedure also include equal signs. An **equal sign** instructs Excel to make an assignment to a cell. For example, when executed as part of the procedure

```
Range("C5").Value = InputBox("Employee Name?", "Enter")
```

instructs Excel to display a dialog box called Enter with the prompt message, Employee Name?, and then assigns cell C5 the value entered by the user in response to the dialog box. Thus, the first argument in the InputBox function is the message to the user and the second argument identifies the dialog box in its title bar.

Testing the 401(k) Data Entry Procedure

Perform the steps below to enter the following 401(k) data: Employee Name (cell C5) – Crystal Deal; Annual Salary (cell C6) - $72,500.00; Employee Investment (cell C7) – 8.50%; Employer Match (cell C8) – 3.00%; Annual Return (cell C9) – 9.50%; and Years of Service (cell C10) – 40. Before attempting to enter data using the New Data button, it is important that you exit Design mode and close the Control Toolbox toolbar as indicated in Step 6 of the previous set of steps.

 Steps ## To Enter 401(k) Data Using the New Data Button

1 **Click the New Data button. When Excel displays the first Enter dialog box with the prompt message, Employee Name?, type** Crystal Deal **as the employee name.**

Excel clears the range C5:C10 and then selects cell A1. Next, it displays the Enter dialog box shown in Figure 7-43.

FIGURE 7-43

2 Click the OK button in the Enter dialog box or press the ENTER key. When Excel displays the next Enter dialog box with the prompt message, Annual Salary?, type 72500 as the annual salary.

Excel assigns the text Crystal Deal to cell C5 and displays the second Enter dialog box as shown in Figure 7-44.

FIGURE 7-44

3 Click the OK button in the Enter dialog box. When Excel displays the next Enter dialog box with the prompt message, Employee Investment in %?, type 8.5% as the employee investment. (Remember to type the percent (%) sign.)

Excel assigns $72,500.00 to cell C6 and displays the third Enter dialog box as shown in Figure 7-45.

FIGURE 7-45

4 Click the OK button in the Enter dialog box. When Excel displays the next Enter dialog box with the prompt message, **Employer Match in %?**, type **3%** as the employer match.

Excel assigns the 8.50% to cell C7 and displays the fourth Enter dialog box as shown in Figure 7-46.

FIGURE 7-46

5 Click the OK button in the Enter dialog box. When Excel displays the next Enter dialog box with the prompt message, **Annual Return in %?**, type **9.5%** as the annual return.

Excel assigns 3.00% to cell C8 and displays the fifth Enter dialog box as shown in Figure 7-47.

FIGURE 7-47

6 **Click the OK button in the Enter dialog box. When Excel displays the next Enter dialog box with the prompt message, Years of Service?, type** 40 **as the years of service.**

Excel assigns 9.5% to cell C9 and displays the sixth Enter dialog box as shown in Figure 7-48.

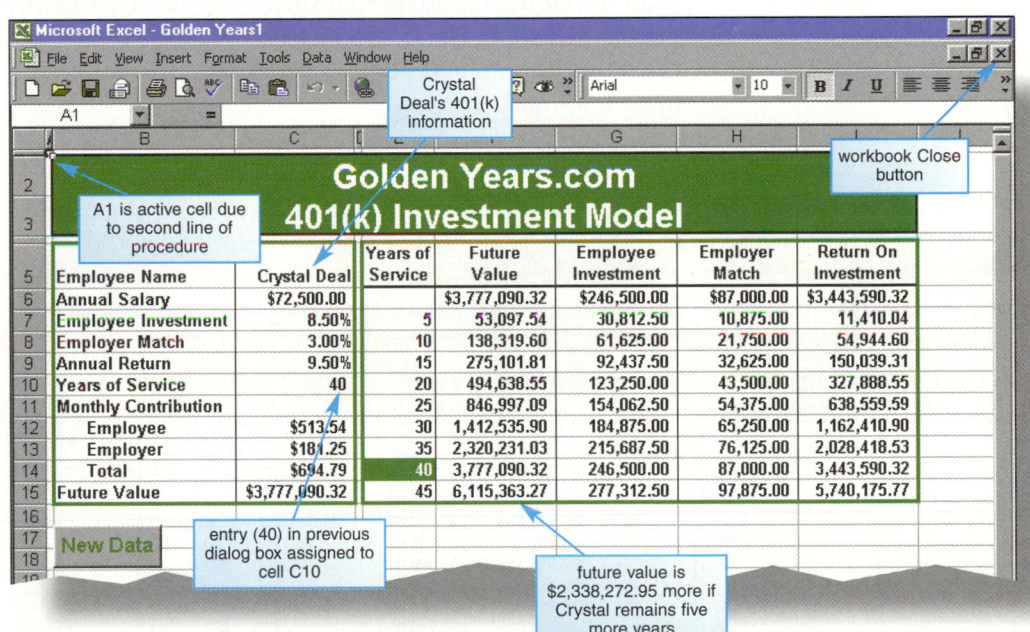

FIGURE 7-48

7 **Click the OK button in the Enter dialog box.**

Excel assigns 40 to cell C10 and displays the results for Crystal Deal in the range C12:C15 (Figure 7-49). Excel also recalculates the data table.

FIGURE 7-49

Figure 7-49 shows that the future value of Crystal Deal's investment of $513.54 a month (cell C12) for 40 years is an impressive $3,777,090.32 (cell F14). Crystal's total 401(k) investment is $246,500.00 (cell G14) and the total employer match is $87,000.00 (cell H14).

Based on this example, you can see the significance of using a VBA to automate the worksheet tasks, especially if the users know little about computers. In this worksheet, each time the user clicks the New Data button, the procedure guides him or her through entering the 401(k) data and placing it in the correct cells.

With Phase 2 of this project complete, the final step is to protect the worksheet and save the workbook.

Data Validation

The VBA code entered in Step 4 on page E 7.34 does not check the incoming data to be sure it is reasonable. For example, if a user enters a negative value for the Years of Service in Step 6 on the previous page, then Excel will calculate an incorrect Future Value. In the next phase of this project, you will learn how to write VBA code that will ensure that unreasonable numbers are rejected. See the VBA code in Figure 7-80 on page E 7.63 for an example.

TO PROTECT A WORKSHEET AND SAVE THE WORKBOOK

1 Click Tools on the menu bar, point to Protection, and then click Protect Worksheet on the Protection submenu.

2 When the Protect Sheet dialog box displays, type fortune in the Password text box and then click the OK button. When the Confirm Password dialog box displays, type fortune and then click the OK button.

3 Click File on the menu bar and then click Save As. When the Save As dialog box displays, type Golden Years2 in the File name text box. Make sure 3½ Floppy (A:) displays in the Save in box and then click the Save button.

4 Click the Golden Years2 Close button on the right side of its menu bar.

Phase 2 of this project is complete.

Phase 3 — Creating an Adjustment Center to Automate the 401(k) Data Entry

The final phase of this project requires that you add additional controls to the worksheet to automate the 401(k) data entry. In Phase 2, all of the data was entered using input dialog boxes that displayed one after the other when you triggered the event by clicking the New Data button. This phase uses input dialog boxes for only the name and annual salary. The remaining data (employee investment, employer match, annual return, and years of service) is entered using scroll bars, a check box, and spin buttons.

Consider the Adjustment Center in Figure 7-50. When you click the Name and Salary button, Excel displays input dialog boxes to accept the employee name for cell C5 and the annual salary for cell C6.

The Employee Investment scroll bar immediately below the Name and Salary button allows you to set the employee investment in cell C7. Recall that a scroll bar is made up of three separate areas you can click or drag – the **scroll arrows** on each side that you can click; the **scroll box** between the scroll buttons that you can drag; and the **scroll bar** that you can click that extends from one scroll arrow to the other.

FIGURE 7-50

The Employee Investment scroll bar has a minimum value of 0% and a maximum value of 13%. When you click one of its scroll arrows, the employee investment percent in cell C7 increases or decreases by 0.5%, depending on which scroll arrow you click. If you click the scroll bar on either side of the scroll box, the employee investment percent in cell C7 increases or decreases by 1%. Finally, you can drag the scroll box to the right or left to increase or decrease the employee investment percent in cell C7.

The Employer Match scroll bar (bottom center in Figure 7-50) works the same way, except that the change in the employer match is 0.25% when you click a scroll arrow, and the scroll bar runs from 0% to 6%.

The Employer Match check box in the middle of the Adjustment Center in Figure 7-50 indicates if the Employer Match scroll bar is enabled or disabled. If the check mark is present, then the scroll bar below the check box is enabled. If the check mark is removed, then cell C8 is set equal to 0% and the scroll bar is disabled.

The Annual Return spin button in the upper-right corner of the Adjustment Center increases or decreases the annual return in cell C9 by 0.25% each time you click a spin button arrow. A **spin button** has two buttons, one to increment and one to decrement the value in the cell with which it is associated. The Years of Service spin button in the lower-right corner of the Adjustment Center increases or decreases the years of service in cell C10 by one each time you click a spin button arrow.

The following steps open the workbook Golden Years1, save it using the file name Golden Years3, unprotect the 401(k) Investment Model worksheet, and display the Control Toolbox toolbar.

TO OPEN AND SAVE A WORKBOOK, UNPROTECT A WORKSHEET, AND DISPLAY THE CONTROL TOOLBOX TOOLBAR

1 Click the Open button on the Standard toolbar. When the Open dialog box displays, click the Look in box arrow and select 3½ Floppy (A:). Double-click Golden Years1.

2 Click File on the menu bar and then click Save As. When the Save As dialog box displays, type `Golden Years3` in the File name text box and then click the Save button in the Save As dialog box.

3 Click Tools on the menu bar, point to Protection, and then click Unprotect Sheet on the Protection submenu. When the Unprotect dialog box displays, type `fortune` in the Password text box and then click the OK button.

4 Double-click the move handle on the Formatting toolbar (see Figure 7-51). Right-click a toolbar and then click Control Toolbox. Drag the Control Toolbox toolbar to the lower-right corner of the window.

Excel opens the workbook Golden Years1, saves it using the file name Golden Years3, unprotects the 401(k) Investment Model worksheet, and displays the Control Toolbox toolbar.

Step 1 – Create the User Interface

The first step is to create the Adjustment Center user interface shown in Figure 7-50. After creating the gray background for the Adjustment Center in the range B17:I23, the following must be added to it:

1. A Command Button control
2. Two Scroll Bar controls
3. A Check Box control
4. Two Spin Button controls
5. Label controls to identify controls and display data

When you first create a user interface, you position the controls as close as you can to their final location on the screen, and then after setting the properties you finalize the locations of the controls. Therefore, the following steps make no attempt to position the controls exactly in the locations shown in Figure 7-50.

Steps **To Add Controls to a User Interface**

1 Select the range B17:I23. Click the Fill Color arrow on the Formatting toolbar and then click Gray – 25% (column 8, row 4) on the Fill Color palette. Click the Borders button arrow on the Formatting toolbar and then click Thick Box Border (column 4, row 3) on the Borders palette.

2 Click the Command Button button on the Control Toolbox toolbar and then drag the mouse pointer so the control displays as shown in Figure 7-51.

FIGURE 7-51

3 Click the Scroll Bar button on the Control Toolbox toolbar and then move the mouse pointer to approximately the center of cell B22. Drag the mouse pointer so the Scroll Bar control displays as shown in Figure 7-52.

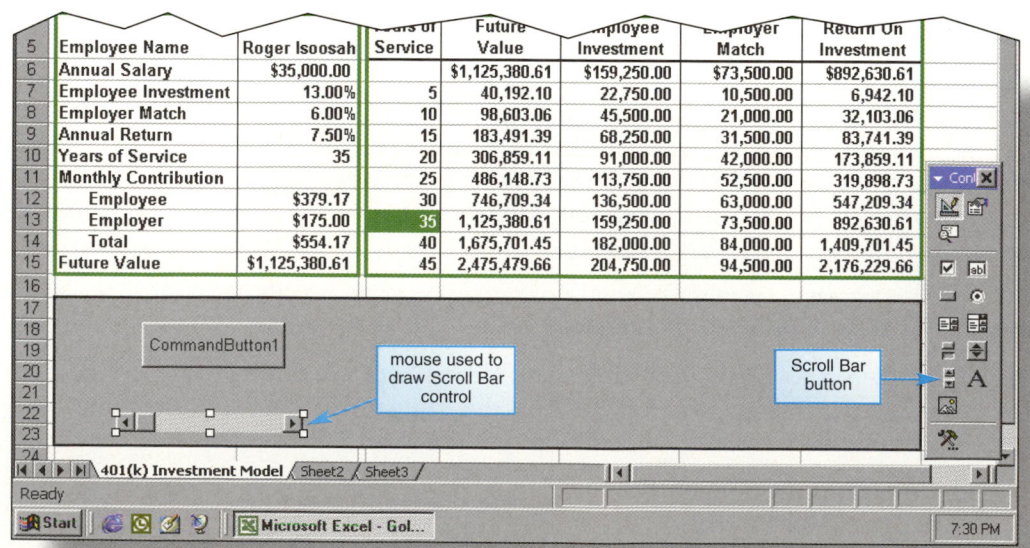

FIGURE 7-52

4 Point to the Scroll Bar control. Hold down the **CTRL** key and then drag a copy of the Scroll Bar control to the location shown in Figure 7-53. It is important that you release the left mouse button before you release the **CTRL** key.

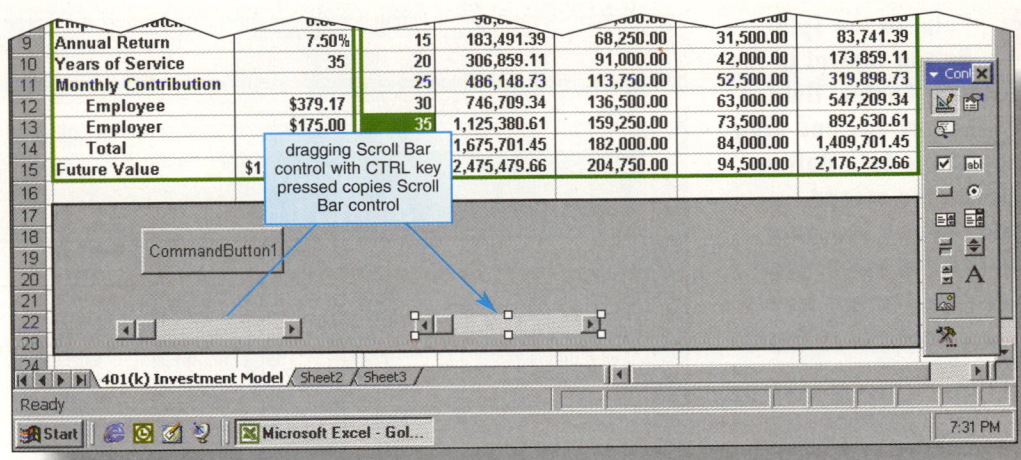

FIGURE 7-53

5 Click the Check Box button on the Control Toolbox toolbar and then move the mouse pointer to the upper-left corner of the location of the Check Box control shown in Figure 7-54. Drag the mouse pointer so the rectangle defining the Check Box control area displays with half of the word CheckBox1 showing.

The check box will be resized after its caption is changed later in this project.

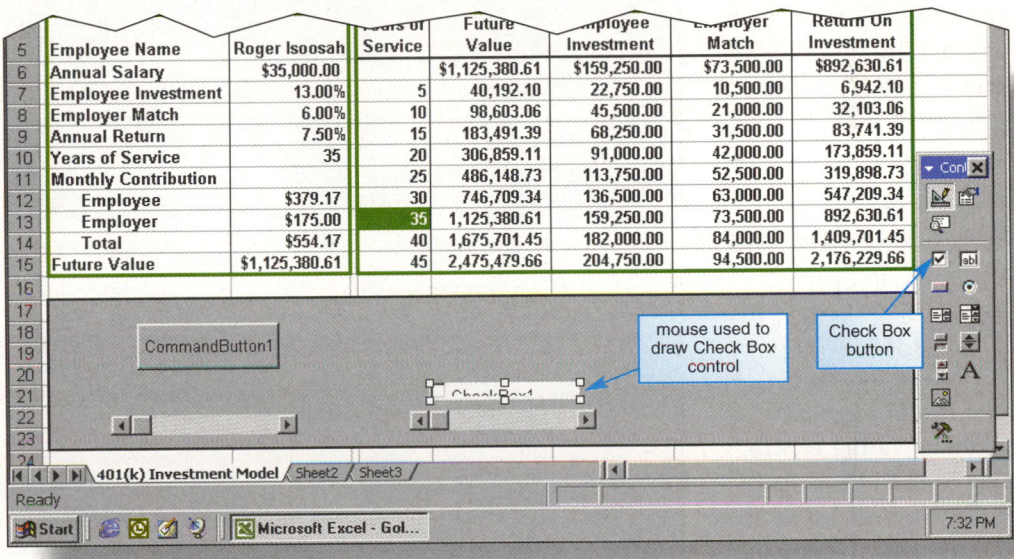

FIGURE 7-54

6 Click the Spin Button button on the Control Toolbox toolbar and then move the mouse pointer to the upper-left corner of the location of the Spin Button control shown in Figure 7-55. Drag the mouse pointer so the rectangle defining the Spin Button control area displays as shown in Figure 7-55.

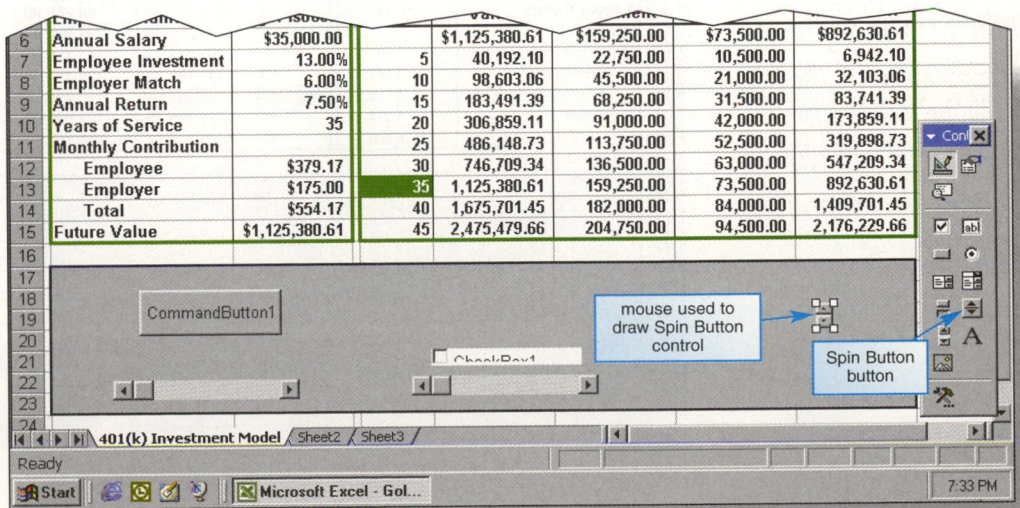

FIGURE 7-55

7 Point to the Spin Button control in the Adjustment Center. Hold down the CTRL key and drag a copy of the Spin Button control to the second location shown in Figure 7-56. It is important that you release the left mouse button before you release the CTRL key.

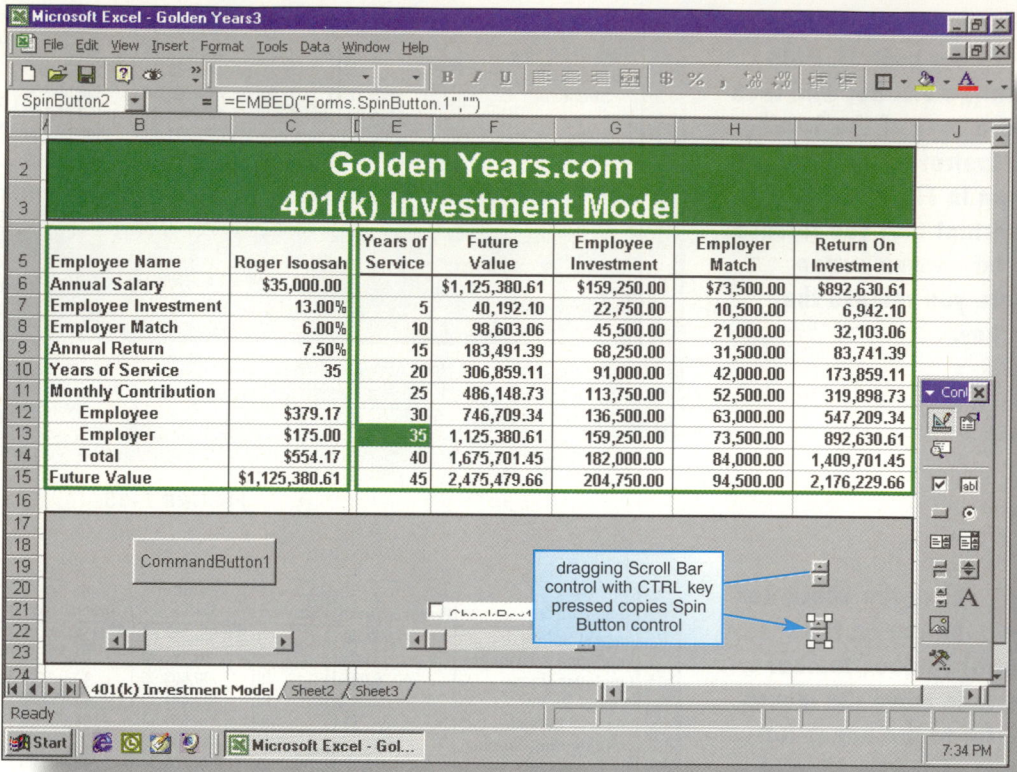

FIGURE 7-56

8 Click the Label button on the Control Toolbox toolbar and then move the mouse pointer to the left of the Scroll Bar control below the CommandButton1 button. Drag the mouse pointer so the rectangle defining the Label control displays as shown in Figure 7-57.

This Label control is used to indicate the lowest value (zero) on the scroll bar.

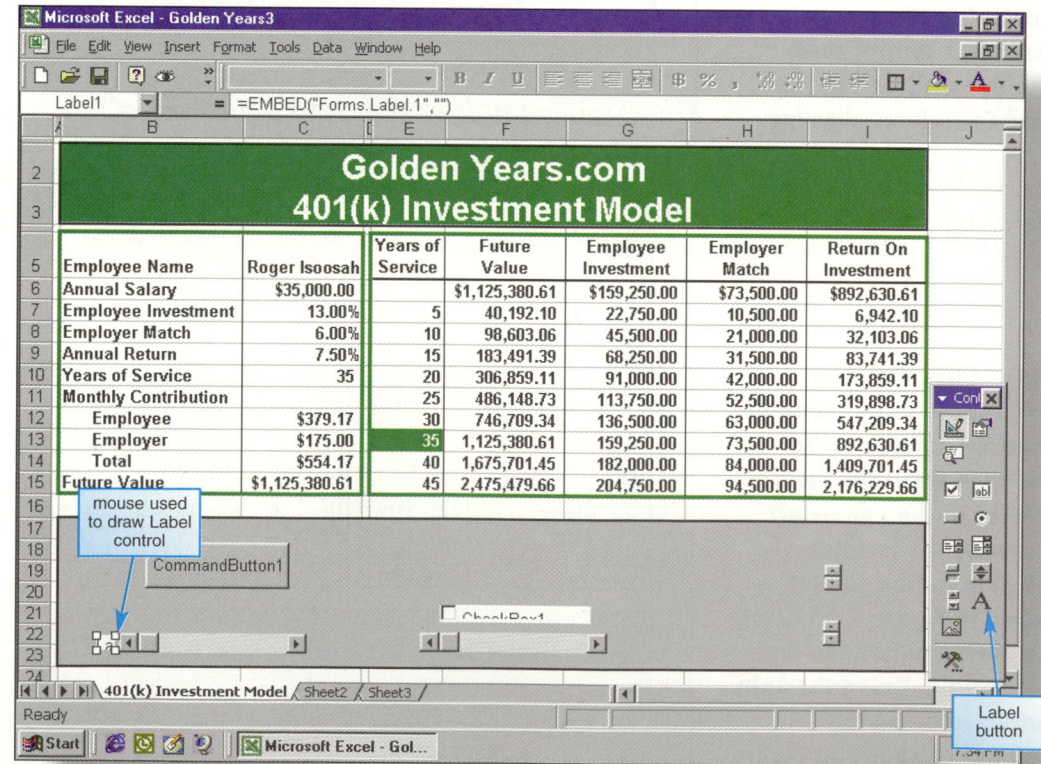

FIGURE 7-57

9 Point to the Label control. Hold down the CTRL key and then drag a copy of the Label control created in Step 8 immediately above the left Scroll Bar control. With the CTRL key held down, drag the newly copied Label control to the next location where a Label control is required. Continue in this fashion until you have a total of ten Label controls as shown in Figure 7-58.

All the controls needed for this application are in the Adjustment Center.

FIGURE 7-58

When you create a Label control, a caption is associated with it. The Caption property for the first Label control is Label1. For the next Label control you create, the Caption property is Label2, and so on. Because of the size of the Label controls in Figure 7-58, you can only see a portion of the caption, such as the La.

If you compare Figure 7-58 with Figure 7-50 on page 7.41, you will notice that except for captions and some minor repositioning of the controls, the Adjustment Center user interface is complete. If you want to delete a control, select it while in Design mode and press the DELETE key. If you want to resize a control, select it while in design mode and drag its sizing handles. If you want to reposition a control, select it and drag it to its new location.

Step 2 – Set the Properties

The next step is to set the properties for the sixteen controls that make up the user interface. The sixteen controls can best be seen by referring to Figure 7-50 on page E 7.41 counting the button, labels, scroll bars, check box, and spin buttons. The properties will be set as follows:

1. **Constant Label and Check Box** — Set the BackColor property of the Label controls that identify other controls and the Check Box control to Button Face gray so it agrees with the gray background of the user interface. Set the Font property to Bold. Set the Caption property and Text Align property for each Label control that identifies another control. Increase the font size of the Adjustment Center title to size 20.

2. **Command Button** – Change the Caption property to Name and Salary and resize the button so the entire caption shows.

3. **Employee Investment Scroll Bar** – Change the Name property to scrEmployeeInvest, the SmallChange property to 50 (0.5%), the LargeChange property to 100 (1%), the Min property to 0 (0%), and the Max property to 1300 (13%).

Other Ways

1. Select control, click CTRL+C to copy, click CTRL+V to paste

2. Select control, click Copy button on Standard toolbar; click Paste button on Standard toolbar

3. Right-click control, click Copy on shortcut menu, click Paste on shortcut menu

4. Select control, on Edit menu click Copy, on Edit menu click Paste

4. **Employer Match Scroll Bar** — Change the Name property to scrEmployerMatch, the SmallChange property to 25 (0.25%), the LargeChange property to 100 (1%), the Min property to 0 (0%), and the Max property to 600 (6%).

5. **Employer Match Check Box** – Change the Name property to chkEmployerMatch and the Caption property to Employer Match. Resize the check box so the new caption displays.

6. **Annual Return Spin Button** – Change the Name property to spnAnnualReturn, the SmallChange property to 25 (0.25%), the Min property to 0 (0%), and the Max property to 10000 (100%).

7. **Years of Service Spin Button** – Change the Name property to spnYearsofService, the SmallChange property to 1, the Min property to 1, and the Max property to 75.

8. **Annual Return Label** – Change the Name property to lblAnnualReturn, the Caption property to 5%, the Font property to Bold, the TextAlign property to align right, and the SpecialEffect property to sunken.

9. **Years of Service Label** – Change the Name property to lblYearsofService, the Caption property to 10, the Font property to Bold, the TextAlign property to align right, and the SpecialEffect property to sunken.

Excel automatically assigns the first Command Button control the name CommandButton1. If you create a second Command Button control, Excel will call it CommandButton2, and so on. In the controls just listed, some will have their Name property changed as indicated, while others will not. Usually, you do not change the Name property of Label controls that identify other controls in the user interface. On the other hand, controls that are referenced in the VBA code should be given names that help you recall the control. Table 7-5 summarizes the controls whose Name property will be changed because they will be referenced in the VBA code.

Table 7-5 Referenced Controls and Their Names	
CONTROL	NAME
Employee Investment Scroll Bar	scrEmployeeInvest
Employer Match Scroll Bar	scrEmployerMatch
Employer Match Check Box	chkEmployerMatch
Annual Return Spin Button	spnAnnualReturn
Years of Service Spin Button	spnYearsofService
Annual Return Label	lblAnnualReturn
Years of Service Label	lblYearsofService

The name of a control, such as scrEmployeeInvest, must begin with a letter, cannot exceed 255 characters, and cannot have a space, period, exclamation point, or the characters @, &, $, or #. You should develop a naming convention of your own and then use it consistently to name controls. In this book, the first three characters of the name identify the control. For example: scr stands for scroll bar; chk stands for check box; and spn stands for spin button. Following the three characters are words that identify what the control is controlling. In this case, scrEmployeeInvest is a scroll bar controlling the value in cell C7, the Employee Investment. You also must make sure that the names are unique in an application, because duplicate names are not allowed.

SETTING THE CONSTANT LABELS AND CHECK BOX PROPERTIES When you create a Label control, it has a white background. If the Label control identifies another control, the background color is changed so it becomes part of the user interface background. If the Label control is going to display a value that varies, the background is left white. The following steps use the SHIFT key to select all the Label controls that identify other controls and the Check Box control so that the BackColor property can be changed for all selected items at once. The Font property of the selected controls is also changed to bold. After the BackColor and Font are changed, then each Label control is selected and the properties are set.

To Set Properties of the Constant Label Controls and Check Box Control

1 **With Excel in Design mode, click the Label control in the lower-left corner of the user interface. Hold down the SHIFT key and then one at a time, click the Label controls that will remain constant and the Check Box control (bottom of Figure 7-59). Release the SHIFT key. Click the Properties button on the Control Toolbox toolbar. When the Properties window displays, click BackColor, click the BackColor arrow, if necessary, click the System tab, and then point to Button Face in the list.**

The selected Label controls, the Check Box control, and the Properties window display as shown in Figure 7-59.

FIGURE 7-59

2 **Click Button Face. Click Font in the Properties window and then click the Font button. When the Font dialog box displays, click Bold in the Font style list and then point to the OK button.**

The Properties window and Font dialog box display as shown in Figure 7-60. The selected Label controls and Check Box control have a gray background.

FIGURE 7-60

3 Click the OK button. Click the ESC key to deselect the Label controls and Check Box control. Click the Label control in the lower-left corner of the user interface. Click Caption in the Properties window and then type 0 as the caption. Click TextAlign in the Properties window, click the TextAlign arrow, and then click 2 - fmTextAlignCenter.

The Label control in the lower-left corner is selected and the Properties window displays its properties as shown in Figure 7-61. Only a portion of the zero (0) displays in the Label control in the Adjustment Center.

FIGURE 7-61

4 Click the Label control to the right of the Employee Investment scroll bar. Click Caption in the Properties window and then type 13 as the caption. Click TextAlign in the Properties window, click the TextAlign arrow, and then click 2 - fmTextAlignCenter. Resize the Label control so the caption 13 is visible.

The Properties window for the selected Label control displays as shown in Figure 7-62.

FIGURE 7-62

PROJECT 7

5 Click the Label control on the left side between the Command Button control and the Scroll Bar control. Click Caption in the Properties window and then type `Employee Investment` as the caption. Click TextAlign in the Properties window. Click the TextAlign arrow and then click 2 - fmTextAlignCenter. Resize the Label control so the caption Employee Investment is visible

The Properties window displays as shown in Figure 7-63.

FIGURE 7-63

6 Click the Label control to the left of the second Scroll Bar control. Click Caption in the Properties window and then type `0` as the caption. Click TextAlign in the Properties window, click the TextAlign arrow, and then click 2 - fmTextAlignCenter. Click the Label control on the right side of the second Scroll Bar control. Click Caption in the Properties window and then type `6` as the caption. Click TextAlign in the Properties window, click the TextAlign arrow, and then click 2 - fmTextAlignCenter.

The Properties window for the selected Label control displays as shown in Figure 7-64.

FIGURE 7-64

7 **Click the Label control above the Check Box control. Click Caption in the Properties window and then type** Adjustment Center **as the caption. Click TextAlign in the Properties window, click the TextAlign arrow, and then click 2 - fmTextAlignCenter. Click Font in the Properties window and then click the Font button. When the Font dialog box displays, click 20 in the Size list and then click the OK button. Resize the Label control so the caption displays in its entirety.**

The Properties window for the selected Label control displays as shown in Figure 7-65.

FIGURE 7-65

8 **Click the Label control in the upper-right corner of the user interface, above the top Spin Button control. Click Caption in the Properties window and then type** Annual Return **as the caption. Click TextAlign in the Properties window, click the TextAlign arrow, and then click 2 - fmTextAlignCenter. Resize the Label control so the caption Annual Return is visible.**

The Properties window for the selected Label control displays as shown in Figure 7-66.

FIGURE 7-66

9 **Click the Label control above the lower Spin Button control. Click Caption in the Properties window and then type** Years of Service **as the caption. Click TextAlign in the Properties window, click the TextAlign arrow, and then click 2 - fmTextAlignCenter. Resize the Label control so the caption Years of Service is visible.**

The Properties window for the selected Label control displays as shown in Figure 7-67.

FIGURE 7-67

Every control has its own set of properties. When you select multiple controls as in Step 1 on page E 7.47, then Excel displays only those properties that are common to the controls selected.

SETTING THE COMMAND BUTTON CONTROL PROPERTIES The next step is to change the caption on the Command Button control from CommandButton1 to Name and Salary, and resize it so the caption on the button displays in its entirety.

To Set the Command Button Control Properties

1 With Excel in Design mode, click the Command Button control in the Adjustment Center. Click Caption in the Properties window and then type Name and Salary **as the caption. Drag one of the sizing handles surrounding the Command Button control so that the caption displays in its entirety.**

The button and its properties display as shown in Figure 7-68.

FIGURE 7-68

As you can see from the Properties window shown in Figure 7-68, a Command Button control has many different properties. One that may interest you that is not being used in this project is the MousePointer property. If you click MousePointer in the Properties window and then click the MousePointer arrow, you will see several mouse pointers listed, many that you are familiar with from your experiences in Excel. If you change the MousePointer property, the mouse pointer will change when you point to the button. You can choose from the Hour Glass, I-beam, arrow, and cross.

SETTING THE EMPLOYEE INVESTMENT SCROLL BAR PROPERTIES The next step is to set the Employee Investment Scroll Bar properties. The function of this Scroll Bar control is to assign cell C7 a value. When you use a control, such as a scroll bar, you must set the Min and Max properties. The **Min property** is the least value the control can register. The **Max property** is the maximum value the control can register. You also have to set the SmallChange and LargeChange values. The **SmallChange property** is the value the control will change by each time you click the scroll arrow. The **LargeChange** property is the value the control will change by each time you click the scroll bar.

You only can assign whole numbers for these four properties. This increases the complexity of the VBA code because the cell in question must be assigned a decimal number. Thus, to assign the cell the maximum value 0.13 (13%), you must actually set the Maximum property to 1300, and then later in the VBA code divide by 10000 to assign the cell a value of 0.13.

Steps To Set the Employee Investment Scroll Bar Properties

1 **With Excel in Design mode, click the Employee Investment scroll bar. Click Name in the Properties window and then type** `scrEmployeeInvest` **as the name. Change the LargeChange property to 100, the Max property to 1300, the Min property to 0, and the SmallChange property to 50.**

The Employee Investment scroll bar Properties window displays as shown in Figure 7-69

FIGURE 7-69

Excel automatically will determine how far to move the scroll button on the scroll bar when you click the scroll button (small change) and when you click the scroll boxes (large change) from the four numeric values entered in Step 1.

SETTING THE EMPLOYER MATCH SCROLL BAR PROPERTIES The step on the next page sets the Employer Match Scroll Bar properties. The property settings are similar to those assigned to the Employee Investment scroll bar. Once the VBA code is written, this scroll bar will assign a value to cell C8.

Steps **To Set the Employer Match Scroll Bar Properties**

1 **With Excel in Design mode, click the Employer Match scroll bar. Click Name in the Properties window and then type** scrEmployerMatch **as the name. Change the LargeChange property to** 100**, the Max property to** 600**, the Min property to** 0**, and the SmallChange property to** 25**.**

The Employer Match scroll bar Properties window displays as shown in Figure 7-70

FIGURE 7-70

 More About

The Max Property

One of the more difficult concepts to understand about scroll bars is why the Max property is set to such a large number (600 in Figure 7-70), when the maximum value of the scroll bar is only 6% (.06). The two reasons are (1) the Max property can be set equal to only a whole number; and (2) the large number allows you to assign reasonable increments to the SmallChange and LargeChange properties of the scroll bar.

SETTING THE EMPLOYER MATCH CHECK BOX PROPERTIES The Employer Match check box enables or disables the Employer Match Scroll Bar control. If the Employer Match check box contains a check mark, then the Employer Match scroll bar is enabled and it can be used to change the value in cell C8. If the check box is empty, then the Employer Match scroll bar control is disabled. The VBA code will enable or disable the scroll bar based on the check box status. The following step sets the Employer Match Check Box properties.

To Set the Employer Match Check Box Properties

1 **With Excel in Design mode, click the Employer Match check box. Click Name in the Properties window and then type** `chkEmployerMatch` **as the name. Click Caption in the Properties window and then type** Employer Match **as the caption. Click Value in the Properties window and then type** True**. Resize the Check Box control so the caption Employer Match is visible.**

The Employer Match check box Properties window displays as shown in Figure 7-71.

FIGURE 7-71

Setting the Value property to True inserts a check mark in the Employer Match check box. Because the insertion point is still active in the Value property, the check mark does not show in Figure 7-71. The check mark does show up in Figure 7-72 on the next page.

SETTING THE ANNUAL RETURN AND YEARS OF SERVICE SPIN BUTTON PROPERTIES The Annual Return spin button increments or decrements the value in cell C9 by 0.25%. The Years of Service spin button increments or decrements the value in cell C10 by one. With a spin button, the up arrow increases the value and the down arrow decreases the value. The Label controls to the left of the Spin Button controls (Figure 7-70) indicate the values assigned to the associated cells. The Min, Max, and SmallChange properties must be set. The SmallChange property indicates the change each time you click an arrow.

The steps on the next page set the properties for the Annual Return and Years of Service spin buttons.

Properties

Many properties, such as the Value property (Figure 7-71), can be only one of two states — True or False. If it is True, then the property is turned on. If it is False, then the property is turned off. For example, assigning the Value property the value True, means that the check mark will display in the Employee Match check box.

Steps

To Set Properties for the Annual Return Spin Button and Years of Service Spin Button

1 **With Excel in Design mode, click the Annual Return spin button. Drag the Properties window to the left side of the Excel window. Click Name in the Properties window and then type** spnAnnualReturn **as the name. Change the Max property to** 10000**, the Min property to** 0**, and the SmallChange property to** 25**.**

The Annual Return spin button Properties window displays as shown in Figure 7-72.

FIGURE 7-72

2 **Click the Years of Service spin button. Click Name in the Properties window and then type** spnYearsofService **as the name. Change the Max property to** 75**, the Min property to** 1**, and the SmallChange property to** 1**.**

The Years of Service spin button Properties window displays as shown in Figure 7-73

FIGURE 7-73

The least value the Annual Return spin button can be set to is 0 (0%). The greatest value is 10000 (100%). Once the VBA code is written, each time you click a button, the annual return in cell C9 will change by 0.25%. At this point in the project, no relationship exists between the Annual Return spin button and cell C9. This relationship will be established later in the VBA code. A similar relationship will be established between the Years of Service spin button and cell C10.

SETTING THE LABEL CONTROL PROPERTIES FOR THE ANNUAL RETURN AND YEARS OF SERVICE SPIN BUTTONS   The Label controls to the left of the two Spin Button controls will be used to display the values of their respective spin buttons. Thus, when you click one of the Annual Return spin buttons, the new value will display in the Label control next to the spin button as well as in cell C9. The following steps set the Name property, Caption property, SpecialEffect property, and TextAlign property for the two Label controls to the left of the Spin Button controls. The SpecialEffect property option will give the two Label controls a 3-D sunken appearance.

 Steps **To Set the Label Control Properties for the Annual Return and Years of Service Spin Button**

1 **With Excel in Design mode,** click the Label control to the left of the Annual Return spin button. Click Name in the Properties window and then type `lblAnnualReturn` as the name. Click Caption in the Properties window and then type 5% as the caption. Change the Font property to bold. Change the SpecialEffect property to 2 - fmSpecialEffectSunken and the TextAlign property to 3 - fmTextAlignRight. Resize the Label control as shown in Figure 7-74.

The Annual Return Spin Button label Properties window displays as shown in Figure 7-74.

FIGURE 7-74

2 Click the Label control to the left of the Years of Service Spin Button control. Click Name in the Properties window and then type `lblYearsofService` as the name. Change the Font property to bold. Click Caption in the Properties window and then type 10 as the caption. Change the SpecialEffect property to 2 - fmSpecialEffectSunken and the TextAlign property to 3 - fmTextAlignRight. Resize the Label control as shown in Figure 7-75.

The Years of Service Spin Button label Properties window displays as shown in Figure 7-75

FIGURE 7-75

3 Click the Properties window Close button on the right side of its title bar.

The Adjustment Center displays as shown in Figure 7-76.

FIGURE 7-76

Later in the VBA code, the Label controls will be set equal to the corresponding Spin Button controls through the use of the names. For example, the VBA statement

```
lblAnnualReturn = spnAnnualReturn.Value / 100 & "%"
```

assigns the value of the Annual Return Spin Button control divided by 100 to the its corresponding Label control. The & "%" appends a percent sign to the number that displays in the Label control.

FINE-TUNING THE USER INTERFACE After setting the properties for all the controls, you can fine-tune the size and location of the controls in the Adjustment Center. With Excel in Design mode, you have three ways to reposition a control:

1. Drag the control to its new location.
2. Select the control and use the arrow keys to reposition it.
3. Select the control and set the control's Top and Left properties in the Properties window.

To use the third technique, you need to know the distance the control is from the top of row 1 (column headings) and the far left of column A (row headings) in points. Recall, that a point is equal to 1/72 of an inch. Thus, if the Top property of a control is 216, then the control is 3 inches (216 / 72) from the top of the window.

You also can resize a control in two ways:

1. Drag the sizing handles.
2. Select the control and set the control's Height and Width properties in the Properties window.

As with the Top and Left properties, the Height and Width properties are measured in points. Table 7-6 lists the exact points for the Top, Left, Height, and Width properties of each of the controls in the Adjustment Center.

The Microsoft Script Editor

The Microsoft Script Editor allows you to develop complex Web pages that interact with your company's data, whether the data is in Excel or a database. The Script Editor generates what is known as Active Server Pages. These Web pages contain both HTML and program code. For more information, click Tools, point to Macro, and then click Microsoft Script Editor. When the Microsoft Script Editor displays, click Help on the menu bar, and then click Contents.

Table 7-6 Exact Locations of Controls in Adjustment Center				
CONTROL	TOP	LEFT	HEIGHT	WIDTH
Name and Salary Command Button	241.5	58.5	27	90.75
Employee Investment Label	276	51.75	13.5	102.75
Employee Investment Scroll Bar	293.25	40.5	12.75	124.5
Employee Investment 0 Label	294	32.25	13.5	6.75
Employee Investment 13 Label	294	168	13.5	12
Adjustment Center Label	234.75	168	22.5	200.25
Employer Match Check Box	272.25	226.5	16.5	99
Employer Match Scroll Bar	293.25	209.25	12.75	124.5
Employer Match 0 Label	294	200.25	13.5	6.75
Employer Match 6 Label	294	337.5	13.5	6.75
Annual Return Label	237	399	12	102
Annual Return Spin Button	252.75	462	17.25	13.5
Annual Return Label	252.75	432	17.25	30
Years of Service Label	273.75	401.25	12	102
Years of Service Spin Button	288	462	17.25	13.5
Years of Service Label	288	432	17.25	30

The following steps resize and reposition the controls in the Adjustment Center using the values in Table 7-6.

Steps **To Resize and Reposition the Controls in the Adjustment Center**

1 **Click the Properties button on the Control Toolbox toolbar. Drag the Properties window to the right side of the Excel window. Click the Name and Salary button. Change its Top, Left, Height, and Width properties to those listed in Table 7-6.**

The Name and Salary Command Button control Properties window displays as shown in Figure 7-77.

FIGURE 7-77

2 **One at a time, select the controls and change their Top, Left, Height, and Width properties to those listed in Table 7-6. Close the Properties window and then deselect the Years of Service label by clicking cell A1.**

The Adjustment Center displays as shown in Figure 7-78.

3 **Click the Save button on the Standard toolbar.**

Excel saves the workbook using the file name Golden Years3.

FIGURE 7-78

Step 3 – Write the Code

The next step is to write a procedure for each of the following six controls: (1) Name and Salary Button; (2) Employee Investment Scroll Bar; (3) Employer Match Check Box; (4) Employer Match Scroll Bar; (5) Annual Return Spin Button; and (6) Years of Service Spin Button.

NAME AND SALARY BUTTON PROCEDURE The function of the Name and Salary button is to accept the employee name and annual salary. It also assigns values to the names of the Scroll Bar controls and Spin Button controls, which in turn resets the values in the range C7:C10. The Name and Salary Button procedure is shown in Table 7-7.

Table 7-7	Name and Salary Button Procedure	
LINE	**VBA CODE**	
1	' Name and Salary Button Procedure	Author: Thomas Ryan
2	' Date Created: 12/5/2001	
3	' Run from: 401(k) Investment Model Sheet by clicking button labeled Name and	
4	' Salary	
5	' Function: This procedure initializes the scroll bars and spin buttons,	
6	' clears the range C5:C6, selects cell A1, accepts the employee	
7	' name (cell C5) and annual salary (cell C6), and validates the	
8	' annual salary before assigning it to cell C6.	
9	'	
10	Private Sub CommandButton1_Click()	
11	scrEmployeeInvest = 100	
12	scrEmployerMatch = 0	
13	spnAnnualReturn = 500	
14	spnYearsofService = 10	
15	Range("C5:C6").ClearContents	
16	Range("A1").Select	
17	Range("C5").Value = InputBox("Employee Name?", "Enter")	
18	AnnualSalary = InputBox("Annual Salary?", "Enter")	
19	Do While AnnualSalary <= 0	
20	AnnualSalary = InputBox("Annual salary must be >= to zero.", "Please Re-enter")	
21	Loop	
22	Range("C6").Value = AnnualSalary	
23	End Sub	

In Table 7-7, lines 1 through 9 are comments and have no bearing on the execution of this procedure. Comments help you remember the function of a procedure. Lines 10 and 23 identify the beginning and end of the procedure. Lines 11 through 14 initialize the Scroll Bar controls and Spin Buttons controls by assigning values to their names. Line 15 clears cells C5 and C6 in preparation to receive the employee name and annual salary. Line 16 selects cell A1 so the heavy border surrounding the active cell does not clutter the screen.

Line 17 accepts the employee name and assigns it to cell C5. Lines 18 through 22 accept and validate the annual salary to ensure it is greater than zero. The annual salary is accepted in line 18. Line 19 is called a **Do-While statement**. It tests to see if the annual salary accepted in line 18 is less than or equal to zero. If the annual salary is less than or equal to zero, line 20 displays an error message and requests that the user reenter the annual salary. The **Loop statement** in line 21 transfers control back to the corresponding Do-While statement in line 19, which tests the annual salary again.

More About

Looping

VBA has several statements that allow looping through a series of statements. They are Do-While or Do-Until, which loops while or until a condition is True; For-Next, which uses a counter to repeat statements a specified number of times; and For Each-Next, which repeats a group of statements for each object in a collection.

The VBA code in lines 19 through 21 is called a **loop**. If the variable AnnualSalary is greater than zero, then the Do-While statement in line 19 transfers control to line 22, which assigns the value of AnnualSalary to cell C6. Line 23 halts execution of the procedure and returns Excel to Ready mode.

The variable AnnualSalary first was used in line 18. A **variable** is a location in the computer's memory whose value can change as the program executes. You create variables in VBA code as you need them. In this case, a variable is needed to hold the value accepted from the user in lines 18 and 20. Variable names follow the same rules as control names (see page E 7.46).

The following steps enter the Name and Salary Button procedure shown in Table 7-7 on the previous page.

To Enter the Name and Salary Button Procedure

1 **With Excel in Design mode, click the View Code button on the Control Toolbox toolbar (see Figure 7-38 on page E 7.33). Click the Object box arrow at the top of the window and then click CommandButton1 in the alphabetical list.**

The Visual Basic Editor starts. When the CommandButton1 control is selected, the Visual Basic Editor displays the Sub and End Sub statements for the procedure and positions the insertion point between the two statements (Figure 7-79).

FIGURE 7-79

2 Click before the P in Private and then press the ENTER key. Enter the lines 1 through 9 in Table 7-7 on page E 7.61. Click the blank line between the Sub and End Sub statements. Enter lines 11 through 22 in Table 7-7.

The Name and Salary Button procedure displays as shown in Figure 7-80.

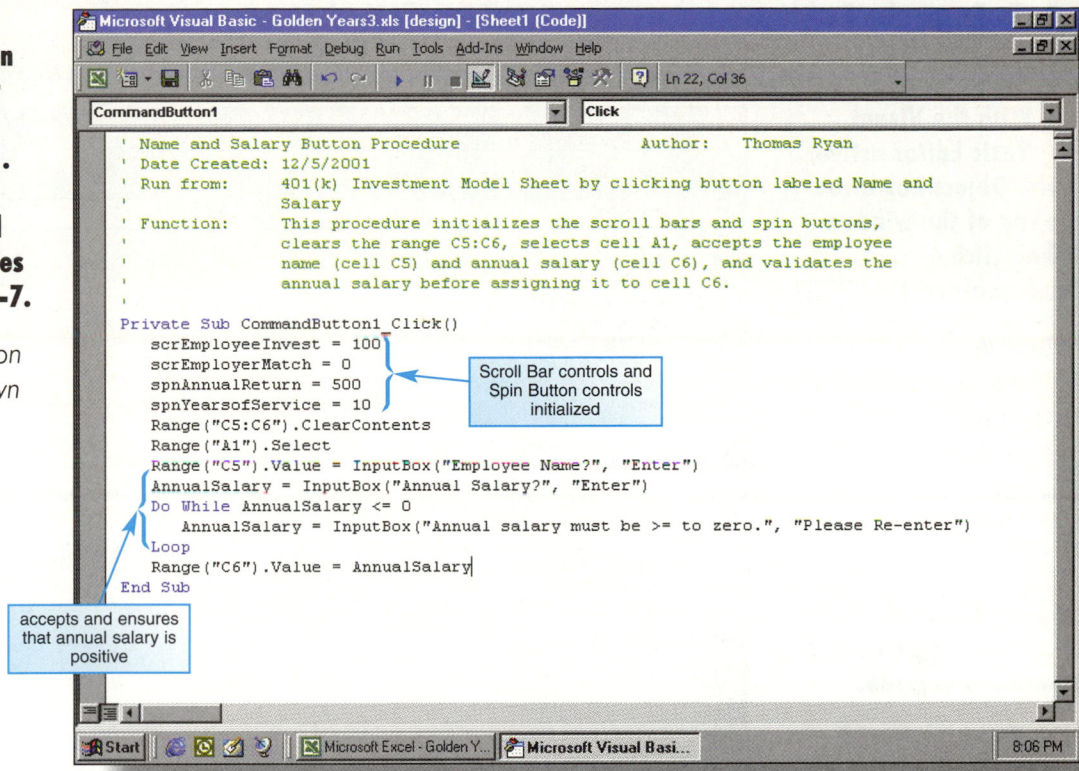

FIGURE 7-80

EMPLOYEE INVESTMENT SCROLL BAR PROCEDURE The Employee Investment Scroll Bar procedure assigns the value of the scroll bar to cell C7. The procedure is shown in Table 7-8.

Table 7-8	Employee Investment Scroll Bar Procedure
LINE	*STATEMENT*
1	' Employee Investment Scroll Bar Procedure Author: Thomas Ryan
2	' Date Created: 12/5/2001
3	' Run from: 401(k) Investment Model Sheet by clicking the scroll bar labeled
4	' Employee Investment
5	' Function: This procedure assigns the value of the Employee Investment scroll
6	' bar to cell C7.
7	'
8	Private Sub scrEmployeeInvest_Change()
9	Range("C7").Value = scrEmployeeInvest.Value / 10000
10	End Sub

In Table 7-8, the first seven lines are comments. Lines 8 and 10 define the beginning and end of the procedure. Line 9 assigns the value of the Scroll Bar control (scrEmployeeInvest) divided by 10000 to cell C7. Recall that the scroll bar was assigned a Max property of 1300, which is equivalent to 130,000%. Thus, the value of scrEmployeeInvest must be divided by 10000 to assign the correct percentage value to cell C7. The steps on the next page enter the Employee Investment Scroll bar procedure shown in Table 7-8.

To Enter the Employee Investment Scroll Bar Procedure

1 **With the Visual Basic Editor active,** click the Object box arrow at the top of the window and then click **scrEmployeeInvest.**

The Visual Basic Editor displays the Sub and End Sub statements for this procedure and positions the insertion point between the two statements.

2 **Enter the VBA code shown in Table 7-8 on the previous page.**

The Employee Investment Scroll Bar procedure displays as shown in Figure 7-81.

FIGURE 7-81

EMPLOYER MATCH CHECK BOX PROCEDURE As with the other procedures, the Employer Match Check Box procedure executes only when you click the check box. If the check box is checked, then the name of the check box (chkEmployerMatch) is equal to the logical value True. If the check box is unchecked, then the name of the check box is equal to the logical value False. Adding a check mark or removing a check mark triggers the event that executes the Employee Match Check Box procedure shown in Table 7-9.

LINE	STATEMENT
Table 7-9	**Employer Match Check Box Procedure**
1	' Employer Match Check Box Procedure Author: Thomas Ryan
2	' Date Created: 12/5/2001
3	' Run from: 401(k) Investment Model Sheet by clicking check box labeled
4	' Employer Match
5	' Function: This procedure assigns the value of the Employer Match scroll bar
6	' or 0 (zero) to cell C8.
7	'
8	Private Sub chkEmployerMatch_Click()
9	If chkEmployerMatch.Value = True Then
10	Range("C8").Value = scrEmployerMatch.Value / 10000
11	Else
12	scrEmployerMatch = 0
13	Range("C8").Value = 0
14	End If
15	End Sub

In Table 7-9, lines 1 through 7 are comments. Lines 8 and 15 define the beginning and end of the procedure. Lines 9 through 14 include an If-Then-Else statement. An **If-Then-Else statement** represents a two-way decision with action specified for each of the two alternatives. The computer never executes both the true and false alternatives. It selects one or the other.

If the logical test (chkEmployerMatch = True) is true in line 9 of Table 7-9, then line 10 is executed and cell C8 is set equal to scrEmployerMatch divided by 10000. If the logical test is false, then lines 12 and 13 are executed. Line 12 repositions the scroll box to zero percent (0%) and line 13 sets cell C8 equal to zero percent (0%). The following steps enter the code.

To Enter the Employer Match Check Box Procedure

1 **With the Visual Basic Editor active, click the Object box arrow at the top of the window and then click chkEmployerMatch.**

The Visual Basic Editor displays the Sub and End Sub statements for this procedure and positions the insertion point between the two statements.

2 **Enter the VBA code shown in Table 7-9.**

The Employer Match Check Box procedure displays as shown in Figure 7-82.

FIGURE 7-82

EMPLOYER MATCH SCROLL BAR PROCEDURE The Employer Match Scroll Bar procedure executes whenever you use the Scroll Bar control below the check box. The Scroll Bar control is active only when the Employer Match Check Box control is checked. The Scroll Bar control event assigns the value of scrEmployerMatch to cell C8. The Employer Match Scroll Bar procedure is shown in Table 7-10.

Table 7-10   Employer Match Scroll Bar Procedure

LINE	STATEMENT
1	' Employer Match Scroll Bar Procedure Author: Thomas Ryan
2	' Date Created: 12/5/2001
3	' Run from: 401(k) Investment Model Sheet by clicking the scroll bar labeled
4	' Employer Match
5	' Function: This procedure assigns the value of the Employer Match scroll bar
6	' to cell C8.
7	'
8	Private Sub scrEmployerMatch_Change()
9	If chkEmployerMatch.Value = True Then
10	Range("C8").Value = scrEmployerMatch.Value / 10000
11	End If
12	End Sub

In Table 7-10, line 10 in the If-Then statement assigns the value of the scroll bar (scrEmployerMatch) divided by 10000 to cell C8. This statement, however, is only executed if the logical test in line 9 (chkEmployerMatch =True) is true. Thus, the Employer Match Check Box control determines whether the Scroll Bar control is active. The following steps enter the code.

 Steps : **To Enter the Employer Match Scroll Bar Procedure**

1 **With the Visual Basic Editor active, click the Object box arrow at the top of the window and then click scrEmployerMatch.**

The Visual Basic Editor displays the Sub and End Sub statements for this procedure and positions the insertion point between the two statements.

2 **Enter the VBA code shown in Table 7-10.**

The Employer Match Scroll Bar procedure displays as shown in Figure 7-83.

FIGURE 7-83

ANNUAL RETURN SPIN BUTTON PROCEDURE   The Annual Return Spin Button procedure executes whenever you click one of it buttons. Its function is to set the percent value in cell C9 and in the corresponding Label control. Recall that you set the SmallChange property to 25, which when divided by 10000 equals 0.25%. The Annual Return Spin Button Control procedure is shown in Table 7-11.

Table 7-11   Annual Return Spin Button Procedure

LINE	STATEMENT
1	' Annual Return Spin Button Procedure Author: Thomas Ryan
2	' Date Created: 12/5/2001
3	' Run from: 401(k) Investment Model Sheet by clicking the spin button
4	' labeled Annual Return
5	' Function: This procedure assigns the value of the Annual Return spin button
6	' to cell C9.
7	'
8	Private Sub spnAnnualReturn_Change()
9	lblAnnualReturn = spnAnnualReturn.Value / 100 & "%"
10	Range("C9").Value = spnAnnualReturn.Value / 10000
11	End Sub

In Table 7-11, line 9 uses the names of the two controls to assign the value of the Spin Button control to the Label control. In this case, spnAnnualReturn is divided by 100 because a percent should display as a whole number percent in the Label control. The & "%" at the end of line 9 appends a percent sign to the value. Line 10 assigns the value of spnAnnualReturn divided by 10000 to cell C9. The following steps enter the code.

To Enter the Annual Return Spin Button Procedure

1 **With the Visual Basic Editor active, click the Object box arrow at the top of the window and then click spnAnnualReturn.**

The Visual Basic Editor displays the Sub and End Sub statements for this procedure and positions the insertion point between the two statements.

2 **Enter the VBA code shown in Table 7-11.**

The Annual Return Spin Button procedure displays as shown in Figure 7-84.

FIGURE 7-84

YEARS OF SERVICE SPIN BUTTON PROCEDURE The Years of Service Spin Button procedure determines the value assigned to cell C10 and in the corresponding Label control and is executed by Excel when the user clicks one of the buttons making up the Spin Button control. The procedure is shown in Table 7-12.

Table 7-12   Years of Service Spin Button Procedure

LINE	STATEMENT
1	' Years of Service Spin Button Procedure Author: Thomas Ryan
2	' Date Created: 12/5/2001
3	' Run from: 401(k) Investment Model Sheet by clicking the spin button
4	' labeled Years of Service
5	' Function: This procedure assigns the value of the Years of Service spin
6	' button to cell C10.
7	'
8	Private Sub spnYearsofService_Change()
9	lblYearsofService = spnYearsofService
10	Range("C10").Value = spnYearsofService
11	End Sub

In Table 7-12, line 9 assigns spnYearsofService (value of the Spin Button control) to the corresponding Label control. Line 10 assigns the value of spnYearsofService to cell C10. The following steps enter the code.

 To Enter the Years of Service Spin Button Procedure

1 **With the Visual Basic Editor active, click the Object box arrow at the top of the window and then click spnYearsofService.**

The Visual Basic Editor displays the Sub and End Sub statements for this procedure and positions the insertion point between the two statements.

2 **Enter the VBA code shown in Table 7-12.**

The Years of Service Spin Button procedure displays as shown in Figure 7-85.

FIGURE 7-85

The VBA code is complete. The following steps close the Visual Basic Editor, quit Design mode, protect the worksheet, and save the workbook. Before closing the Visual Basic Editor, you should verify your code by comparing it with Figures 7-80 through 7-85.

TO CLOSE THE VISUAL BASIC EDITOR, PROTECT THE WORKSHEET, AND SAVE THE WORKBOOK

1 Click the Close button on the right side of the Visual Basic Editor title bar.

2 When the Excel window displays, click the Exit Design Mode button on the Control Toolbox toolbar. Close the Control Toolbox toolbar.

3 Click Tools on the menu bar, point to Protection, and then click Protect Sheet. When the Protect dialog box displays, enter fortune in the Password text box. Verify the password when prompted.

4 Click the Save button on the Standard toolbar to save the workbook using the file name Golden Years3.

Testing the Controls

The final step is to test the controls in the Adjustment Center. Use the following data: Employee Name – Ukari Eiffel; Annual Salary (cell C6) — $56,000.00; Employee Investment (cell C7) – 10%; Employer Match (cell C8) – 5%; Annual Return (cell C9) – 8.25%; and Years of Service (cell C10) – 30.

TO TEST THE CONTROLS IN THE ADJUSTMENT CENTER USER INTERFACE

1 Click the Name and Salary button in the Adjustment Center.

2 When Excel displays the Enter dialog box with the prompt message, Employee Name?, type Ukari Eiffel as the employee name.

3 When Excel displays the Enter dialog box with the prompt message, Annual Salary? Type the negative number -56000 as the annual salary.

4 When Excel displays the Enter dialog box with the prompt message, Annual salary must be >= to zero. Type 56000 as the annual salary.

5 Use the Employee Investment scroll bar to change the value in cell C7 to 10%.

6 Click the Employer Match check box if it does not have a check mark.

7 Use the Employer Match scroll bar to change the value in cell C8 to 5%.

8 Click the Annual Return spin button arrows to change the value in cell C9 to 8.25%.

9 Click the Years of Service spin button arrows to change the value in cell C10 to 30.

The future value of Ukari Eiffel's 401(k) investment is $1,097,753.30 as shown in cell C15 of Figure 7-86 on the next page. If she changes her years of service to 45 years, the 401(k) investment is worth $4,015,614.71 (cell F15). Both future value amounts assume she will never get a raise.

More About

Debugging VBA Code

The Visual Basic Editor allows you to locate the source of errors in your code using the Debug menu. You can set breakpoints in your code that will cause Excel to stop executing your code at a certain point. At that time, Excel shows the current executing code in the Editor. You can point at variables in your code to make sure they are set correctly. Alternatively, you can step through your code line by line to make sure that the code is being executed in the order that you expect it to. Click Microsoft Visual Basic Help on the Help menu in the Visual Basic Editor for more information about debugging.

More About

The Visual Basic Editor

When you open the Visual Basic Editor, the same Visual Basic windows display that displayed when you closed it the last time.

Quick Reference

For a table that lists how to complete the tasks covered in this book using the mouse, menu, shortcut menu, and keyboard, see the Excel Quick Reference Summary at the back of this book or visit the Office 2000 Web page (www.scsite.com/office 2000/qr.htm), and then click Microsoft Excel 2000.

FIGURE 7-86

Microsoft Certification

The Microsoft Office User Specialist (MOUS) Certification program provides an opportunity for you to obtain a valuable industry credential – proof that you have the Excel 2000 skills required by employers. For more information, see Appendix D or visit the Shelly Cashman Series MOUS Web page at www.scsite.com/off2000/cert.htm.

If the controls in the Adjustment Center do not work as indicated here, then unprotect the worksheet, display the Control Toolbox toolbar, click the Design Mode button on the Control Toolbox toolbar, and check the controls' properties and VBA code.

Quitting Excel

The project is complete. To quit Excel, follow the steps below.

TO QUIT EXCEL

1 Click the Close button on the right side of the title bar.

2 If the Microsoft Excel dialog box displays, click the No button.

CASE PERSPECTIVE SUMMARY

With the three workbooks developed in this project, the vice president of personnel, Nelson Portugal, can post the new workbook to the intranet as you complete each phase. The final phase, Golden Years3, includes the easy-to-use Adjustment Center interface that allows the user to enter any reasonable 401(k) data with ease, and quickly determine the future value of the investment.

Project Summary

In this project, you learned how to unprotect and protect a worksheet and workbook using a password. In Phase 1, you learned how to record a macro and assign it to a button on a toolbar and to a command on a menu. In Phase 2, you learned how to create a Command Button control, assign it properties, and write VBA code that executes when you click the button. In Phase 3, you learned how to create a user interface made up of a Command Button control, Scroll Bar controls, a Check Box control, Label controls, and Spin Button controls. In this phase, you learned about many of the frequently used properties in Visual Basic for Applications. You also learned how to write VBA code that included looping and decision making.

What You Should Know

Having completed this project, you should be able to perform the following tasks:

▶ Add a Button to a Toolbar, Assign the Button a Macro, and Use the Button (E 7.18)

▶ Add a Command Button Control to the Worksheet (E 7.27)

▶ Add a Command to a Menu, Assign the Command a Macro, and Invoke the Command (E 7.22)

▶ Add Controls to a User Interface (E 7.42)

▶ Automate Data Entry by Selecting a Range of Cells (E 7.8)

▶ Close the Visual Basic Editor, Protect the Worksheet, and Save the Workbook (E 7.69)

▶ Enter 401(k) Data Using the New Data Button (E 7.36)

▶ Enter the Annual Return Spin Button Procedure (E 7.67)

▶ Enter the Employee Investment Scroll Bar Procedure (E 7.64)

▶ Enter the Employer Match Check Box Procedure (E 7.65)

▶ Enter the Employer Match Scroll Bar Procedure (E 7.66)

▶ Enter the Name and Salary Button Procedure (E 7.62)

▶ Enter the New Data Button Procedure (E 7.33)

▶ Enter the Years of Service Spin Button Procedure (E 7.68)

▶ Open a Workbook with a Macro and Execute the Macro (E 7.15)

▶ Open and Save a Workbook, Unprotect a Worksheet, and Display the Control Toolbox Toolbar (E 7.41)

▶ Protect a Worksheet and Save the Workbook (E 7.40)

▶ Password-Protect the Worksheet, Save the Workbook, and Close the Workbook (E 7.14)

▶ Quit Excel (E 7.70)

▶ Record a Macro to Print the Worksheet in Portrait Orientation Using the Fit to Option (E 7.11)

▶ Resize and Reposition the Controls in the Adjustment Center (E 7.60)

▶ Set Properties for the Annual Return Spin Button and Years of Service Spin Button (E 7.56)

▶ Set Properties of the Constant Label Controls and Check Box Control (E 7.47)

▶ Set the Command Button Control Properties (E 7.30, E 7.52)

▶ Set the Employee Investment Scroll Bar Properties (E 7.53)

▶ Set the Employer Match Check Box Properties (E 7.55)

▶ Set the Employer Match Scroll Bar Properties (E 7.54)

▶ Set the Label Control Properties for the Annual Return and Years of Service Spin Button (E 7.57)

▶ Start Excel and Open a Workbook (E 7.6)

▶ Test the Controls in the Adjustment Center User Interface (E 7.69)

▶ Undo a Group of Entries Using the Undo Button (E 7.9)

▶ Unprotect a Password-Protected Worksheet (E 7.9)

▶ View a Macro's VBA Code (E 7.16)

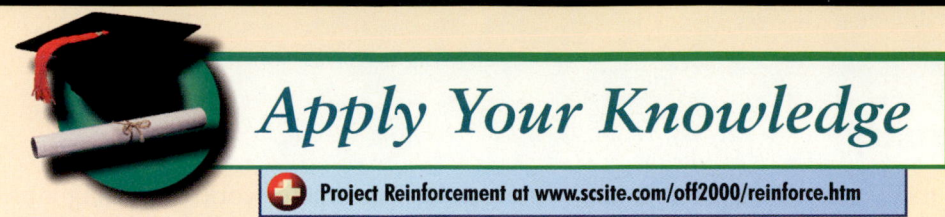

Apply Your Knowledge

✚ **Project Reinforcement at www.scsite.com/off2000/reinforce.htm**

1 Creating Macros and Customizing Menus and Toolbars

Instructions: Start Excel and perform the following tasks.

1. Open the Black Hat Cabinetry payroll workbook (Figure 7-87a) from the Data Disk. If you do not have a copy of the Data Disk, then see the inside back cover of this book.
2. Reset the toolbars to their installation settings (see Step 6 on page E 7.6).
3. Unprotect the worksheet. The password is black.
4. Enter your name, course, laboratory assignment number (Apply 7-1), date, and instructor name in the range A11:A15.
5. Use the Record New Macro command to create a macro that prints the range A2:B15. Call the macro PrintNameRate, use the shortcut CTRL+N, change the name of the author in the Description box to your name, and store the macro in this workbook. When the Stop Recording toolbar displays, do the following: (a) select the range A2:B15; (b) click File on the menu bar and then click Print; (c) click the Selection option in the Print what area of the Print dialog box; (d) click the OK button; and (e) click the Stop Recording button on the Stop Recording toolbar.
6. Press ALT+F8 to display the Macro dialog box. Run the PrintNameRate macro. Press ALT+F8 to display the Macro dialog box a second time. Select the PrintNameRate macro and then click the Edit button. When the Visual Basic Editor displays the macro, click File on the menu bar and then click Print. Hand in both printouts to your instructor.
7. Add a button to the Standard toolbar (Figure 7-87a) and a command to the File menu (Figure 7-87b). Assign the button and command the PrintNameRate macro.
8. Run the macro as follows: (a) click the button you added to the Standard toolbar; (b) on the File menu, click the Print Name and Rate command; and (c) press CTRL+N. Hand in the three printouts to your instructor.
9. Protect the worksheet. Use the first six characters of your last name as the password. Save the workbook using the file name Black Hat Cabinetry1.
10. Reset the toolbars to their installation settings (see Step 6 on page E 7.6).

FIGURE 7-87

In the Lab

1 Automating a Loan Analysis Worksheet

Problem: Your consulting firm specializes in Visual Basic for Applications. The president of Auto Loans +, Marcus Shehee, has contracted with you to automate the entry of loan data into a Loan Analysis worksheet.

Instructions Part 1: Start Excel and perform the following tasks.

1. Open the Auto Loans + workbook from the Data Disk. If you do not have a copy of the Data Disk, then see the inside back cover of this book.
2. Reset the toolbars to their installation settings (see Step 6 on page E 7.6).
3. Unprotect the Loan Analysis worksheet. The password is auto.
4. Display the Control Toolbox toolbar. Click the Command Button button on the Control Toolbox toolbar. Draw the button in the range D3:D5 as shown in Figure 7-88a on the next page.
5. With the Command Button control selected, click the Properties button on the Control Toolbox toolbar. Change the following properties: (a) Caption = Loan Data; (b) ForeColor = Purple (column 8, row 6 on the palette); and (c) PrintObject = False.
6. Click the View Code button on the Control Toolbox toolbar. Enter the procedure shown in Figure 7-88b on the next page. Check your code carefully. On the File menu, click Print to print the procedure.
7. Close the Microsoft Visual Basic Editor. Click the Exit Design Mode button on the Control Toolbox toolbar. Hide the Control Toolbox toolbar.
8. Enter your name, course, laboratory assignment number (Lab 7-1), date, and instructor name in the range B17:B21.
9. Use the newly created button to determine the monthly payment for the following loan data and print the worksheet for each data set: (a) Price = $46,500; Down Payment = $13,250; Interest Rate = 9.50%; and Years = 5; (b) Price = $29,750; Down Payment = $3,000; Interest Rate = 10.75%; and Years = 3. The Monthly Payment for (a) is $698.31 and for (b) is $872.60.
10. Protect the worksheet. Use the password auto. Save the workbook using the file name Auto Loans + Automated.

Instructions Part 2: With the workbook Auto Loans + Automated created in Part 1 open, do the following:

1. Unprotect the worksheet. The password is auto.
2. Use the Record New Macro command to create a macro that prints the formulas version of the worksheet. Call the macro PrintFormulas, use the shortcut CTRL+F, change the name of the author in the Description box to your name, and store the macro in this workbook.
3. With the Stop Recording toolbar on the screen, do the following: (a) press CTRL+SINGLE LEFT QUOTATION MARK; (b) on the File menu, click Page Setup, click Landscape option, click Fit to option, click the Print button in the Page Setup dialog box, and then click the OK button; (c) press CTRL+LEFT SINGLE QUOTATION MARK; (d) on the File menu, click Page Setup, click Portrait option, click Adjust to option, type 100 in the Adjust to box, and then click the OK button; and (e) click the Stop Recording button on the Stop Recording toolbar.
4. Press ALT+F8 to display the Macro dialog box. Run the PrintFormulas macro. Press ALT+F8 to display the Macro dialog box a second time. Select the PrintFormulas macro and then click the Edit button. When the Visual Basic Editor displays the macro, click File on the menu bar and then click Print. Hand in both printouts to your instructor.

(continued)

In the Lab

Automating a Loan Analysis Worksheet *(continued)*

5. Add a button to the Standard toolbar (Figure 7-88a) and a command to the File menu (Figure 7-88c). Assign the button and command the PrintFormulas macro.

6. Run the macro as follows: (a) click the button you added to the Standard toolbar; (b) on the File menu, click Print Formulas; and (c) press CTRL+F. Hand in the three printouts to your instructor. The button will not print as part of the worksheet because the PrintObject property was set to False earlier.

7. Do not protect the worksheet because the Print Formulas macro will not work with a protected worksheet. Save the workbook using the file name Auto Loans + Automated2.

(a) Worksheet

button added to Standard toolbar

(c) File Menu

command added to File menu

```
' Loan Data Button Procedure                 Author:    Jim Quasney
' Date Created: 12/12/2002
' Run from:    Loan Analysis Sheet by clicking button labeled Loan Data
' Function:    When executed, this procedure accepts loan data data which
'              causes Excel to calculate a new monthly payment.
'
Private Sub CommandButton1_Click()
    Range("C3:C4").ClearContents
    Range("F3:F4").ClearContents
    Range("A15").Select
    Range("C3").Value = InputBox("Price?", "Enter")
    Range("C4").Value = InputBox("Down Payment?", "Enter")
    Range("F3").Value = InputBox("Annual Interst Rate?", "Enter")
    Range("F4").Value = InputBox("Length of Loan in Years?", "Enter")
End Sub
```

(b) Visual Basic Code

FIGURE 7-88

In the Lab

2 Automating a Projected Income Statement

Problem: You are in charge of the Help Desk at KT Ltd. Your primary responsibility is to help users with their computer hardware and software problems. The chief financial officer (CFO) informed your manager that she needs a workbook (Figure 7-89) automated to make it easier for her accountants to use. Because you are taking an advanced Excel course in the evening that includes Visual Basic for Applications, she has asked you to automate the data entry in cells D4 (Units Sold); D5 (Price per Unit); D14 (Material Cost per Unit); and D16 (Manufacturing Cost per Unit). All other cells in the worksheet use formulas.

Instructions: Start Excel and complete the following tasks.

FIGURE 7-89

1. Open the KT Ltd workbook from the Data Disk. If you do not have a copy of the Data Disk, see the inside back cover of this book.
2. Reset the toolbars to their installation settings (see Step 6 on page E 7.6).
3. Unprotect the Projected Income Statement worksheet. The password is kt.
4. Color the background of the range F16:I21 gray (column 8, row 4 on the Fill Color palette). Draw a thick box border (column 4, row 3 on the Borders palette) around the range F16:I21.
5. Display the Control Toolbox toolbar. Use the concepts and techniques developed in this project to add the fourteen controls shown in the lower-right corner of Figure 7-89. The Units Sold scroll bar should assign a value to cell D4. The Price Per Unit spin button should assign a value to cell D5. The Material Cost Per Unit scroll button should assign a value to cell D14. The Mfg Cost Per Unit spin button should assign a value to cell D16.
6. Modify the properties of the fourteen controls as described in Table 7-13 on the next page.
7. Enter your name, course, laboratory assignment number (Lab 7-2), date, and instructor name in the range B23:B27. Save the workbook using the file name KT Ltd Automated.
8. The Reset Button procedure should set the Units Sold scroll bar (scrUnitsSold) to 50000; the Price Per Unit Spin Button (spnPrice) to 2000; the Material Cost Per Unit (spnMaterialCost) to 250; and the Mfg Cost Per Unit (spnMfgCost) to 250. It should also select cell A1.

(continued)

In the Lab

Automating a Projected Income Statement *(continued)*

Table 7-13 Controls and Their Properties

CONTROL	NAME	CAPTION	BACK COLOR	FONT	TEXT ALIGN	WORD WRAP	SPECIAL EFFECT	MAX	MIN	SMALL CHG	LARGE CHG
Reset Button	btnReset	Reset		8-point bold							
0 Label		0	Gray - 25%	8-point bold	Center						
Units Sold Label		Units Sold	Gray - 25%	8-point bold	Center						
100,000 Label		100,000	Gray - 25%	8-point bold	Center						
Units Sold Scroll Bar	scrUnitsSold							100000	0	100	1000
Price Per Unit Label		Price Per Unit	Gray - 25%	8-point bold	Center	True					
Price Per Unit Spin Button	spnPrice							9999	0	10	
Price Per Unit Spin Button Label		$20.00		10-point bold	Right		Sunken				
Material Cost Per Unit Label		Material Cost Per Unit	Gray - 25%	8-point bold	Center	True					
Material Cost Per Unit Spin Button	spnMaterialCost							9999	0	10	
Material Cost Per Unit Spin Button Label		$2.50		10-point bold	Right		Sunken				
Mfg Cost Per Unit Label		Mfg Cost Per Unit	Gray - 25%	8-point bold	Center	True					
Mfg Cost Per Unit Spin Button	spnMfgCost							9999	0	10	
Mfg Cost Per Unit Spin Button Label		$2.50		10-point bold	Right		Sunken				

9. The Units Sold Scroll Bar procedure should assign the value of the scroll bar (scrUnitsSold) to cell D4. For example,

```
Range("D4").Value = scrUnitsSold.Value
```

10. The Price Per Unit Spin Button procedure should assign the value of spnPrice / 100, formatted to the Currency style, to the Price Per Unit Spin Button Label control. It should also assign the value of spnPrice / 100 to cell D5. For example,

```
lblPrice = Format$(spnPrice.Value / 100, "currency")
Range("D5").Value = spnPrice.Value / 100
```

The Format$ function in the first line formats the result that will display in the Price Per Unit Spin Button Label control to include a floating dollar sign and two decimal positions to the right of the decimal. The value assigned to cell D5 will display in the same format because the cell was formatted to the Currency style as part of the normal worksheet formatting.

11. The Material Cost Per Unit Spin Button procedure should assign the value of spnMaterialCost / 100, formatted to the Currency style, to the Material Cost Per Unit Spin Button Label control. It should also assign the value of spnMaterialCost / 100 to cell D14. For example,

In the Lab

```
lblMaterialCost = Format$(spnMaterialCost.Value / 100, "currency")
Range("D14").Value = spnMaterialCost.Value / 100
```

12. The Mfg Cost Per Unit Spin Button procedure should assign the value of the spnMfgCost / 100, formatted to the Currency style, to the Mfg Cost Per Unit Spin Button Label control. It should also assign the value of spnMfgCost / 100 to cell D16. For example,

```
lblMfgCost = Format$(spnMfgCost.Value / 100, "currency")
Range("D16").Value = spnMfgCost.Value / 100
```

13. Click the Microsoft Excel button on the taskbar. Click the Exit Design Mode button on the Control Toolbox toolbar. Hide the Control Toolbox toolbar. Print the worksheet.

14. Use the newly designed user interface to determine the operating income for the following projections and print the worksheet for each data set: (a) Units Sold = 72,000; Price per Unit = $22.40; Material Cost per Unit = $3.50; and Manufacturing Cost per Unit = $2.90. (b) Units Sold = 47,000; Price per Unit = $5.50; Material Cost per Unit = $1.50; and Manufacturing Cost per Unit = $0.90. The Operating Income in cell D21 for (a) is $262,000 and for (b) is ($744,300).

15. Click the Visual Basic Editor button on the taskbar. On the File menu, click Print to print the VBA code. Close the Visual Basic Editor.

16. Protect the worksheet. Use the password kt. Click the Save button on the Standard toolbar to save the workbook using the file name KT Ltd Automated.

3 Automating a Five-Year Projected Financial Statement

Problem: As the spreadsheet specialist at BroadBand.com, you have been asked to use your Visual Basic for Applications skills to automate the Five-Year Projected Financial Statement worksheet shown in Figure 7-90 on the next page. The objective is to simplify data entry for the company's financial analysts. This worksheet projects financial information for a five-year period based on the previous year's sales and additional data. The user interface on the right side of the screen accepts the assumptions in the range B21:B25. The numbers in rows 5 through 18 are based on these assumptions.

The user interface has two buttons, one spin button, and three scroll bars. The Reset Assumptions button resets the assumptions as follows: (a) cell B21 = 50,000; (b) cell B22 = $5.00; (c) cell B23 = 10%; (d) cell B24 = 5%; and (e) cell B25 = 60%. The Units Sold in 2000 button accepts and ensures the units sold in 2000 is greater than zero and then assigns it to cell B21. The Unit Cost spin button changes the unit cost in cell B22. The Annual Sales Growth scroll bar changes the annual sales growth in cell B23. The Annual Price Decrease scroll bar changes the annual price decrease in cell B24. The Margin scroll bar changes the margin in cell B25.

Instructions: Start Excel and complete the following tasks.

1. Open the BroadBand workbook from the Data Disk. If you do not have a copy of the Data Disk, see the inside back cover of this book.

2. Reset the toolbars to their installation settings (see Step 6 on page E 7.6).

3. Unprotect the Financial Statement worksheet. The password is broadband.

4. Color the background of the range H2:J18 gray (column 8, row 4 on the Fill Color palette). Draw a thick box border (column 4, row 3 on the Borders palette) around the range H2:J18.

(continued)

In the Lab

Automating a Five-Year Projected Financial Statement *(continued)*

5. Display the Control Toolbox toolbar. Use the concepts and techniques developed in this project to add the seventeen controls shown on the right side of Figure 7-90.

6. Modify the properties of the seventeen controls as described in Table 7-14.

7. Enter your name, course, laboratory assignment number (Lab 7-3), date, and instructor name in the range H21:H25. Save the workbook using the file name BroadBand Automated.

FIGURE 7-90

8. The Reset Assumptions Button procedure resets the assumptions as follows:

```
Range("B21").Value = 50000
spnUnitCost = 500
scrAnnualSalesGrowth = 1000
scrAnnualPriceDecrease = 500
scrMargin = 6000
Range("J25").Select
```

9. The Units Sold in 2000 Button procedure accepts and validates the units sold in 2000 in cell B21 as follows:

```
UnitsSold = InputBox("Units Sold in 2000?", "Enter")
Do While UnitsSold <= 0
    UnitsSold = InputBox("Units Sold in 2000 must be > zero.", "Please Re-enter")
Loop
Range("B21").Value = UnitsSold
```

10. The Units Cost Spin Button procedure enters the unit cost in the Unit Cost Spin Button Label control and in cell B22 as follows:

```
lblUnitCost = Format$(spnUnitCost.Value / 100, "currency")
Range("B22").Value = spnUnitCost.Value / 100
```

The Format$ function in the first line formats the result that will display in the Unit Cost Spin Button Label control to include a floating dollar sign and two decimal positions to the right of the decimal.

In the Lab

Table 7-14 Controls and Their Properties

CONTROL	NAME	CAPTION	BACK COLOR	FONT	TEXT ALIGN	WORD WRAP	SPECIAL EFFECT	MAX	MIN	SMALL CHG	LARGE CHG
Reset Assumptions Button	btnReset	Reset Assumptions		8-point bold		True					
Units Sold in 2000 Button	btnUnitsSold	Units Sold in 2000		8-point bold							
Unit Cost Label		Unit Cost	Gray - 25%	8-point bold	Center						
Unit Cost Spin Button	spnUnitCost							10000	0	10	
Unit Cost Spin Button Label		$5.00		10-point bold	Right		Sunken				
All three 0 Labels		0	Gray - 25%	8-point bold	Center						
All three 100 Labels		100	Gray - 25%	8-point bold	Center						
Annual Sales Growth Label		Annual Sales Growth	Gray - 25%	8-point bold	Center						
Annual Sales Growth Scroll Bar	scrAnnualSales Growth							10000	0	25	100
Annual Price Decrease Label		Annual Price Decrease	Gray - 25%	8-point bold	Center						
Annual Price Decrease Scroll Bar	scrAnnualPrice Decrease							10000	0	25	100
Margin Label		Margin	Gray - 25%	8-point bold	Center						
Margin Scroll Bar	scrMargin							10000	0	25	100

The value assigned to cell B22 will display in the same format because the cell was formatted to the Currency style as part of the normal worksheet formatting.

11. The Annual Sales Growth Scroll Bar procedure changes the annual sales growth in cell B23 as follows:
    `Range("B23").Value = scrAnnualSalesGrowth.Value / 10000`

12. The Annual Price Decrease Scroll Bar procedure and the Margin Scroll Bar procedure work in a fashion similarly to the Annual Sales Growth scroll bar, except that they assign values to cells B24 and B25, respectively.

13. Click the Microsoft Excel button on the taskbar. Click the Exit Design Mode button on the Control Toolbox toolbar. Hide the Control Toolbox toolbar. Print the worksheet.

14. Use the newly designed interface to determine the five-year projections based on the following assumptions and print the worksheet for each data set: (a) Units Sold in 2000 = 78,000; Unit Cost = $6.70; Annual Sales Growth = 20%; Annual Price Decrease = 7.5%; and Margin = 62.5% and (b) Units Sold in 2000 = 97,000; Unit Cost = $12.50; Annual Sales Growth = 18.5%; Annual Price Decrease = 2.5%; and Margin = 66%. The Net Income for the year 2005 in cell F18 for (a) is $452,761 and for (b) is $1,580,253.

15. Click the Visual Basic Editor button on the taskbar. On the File menu, click Print to print the VBA code. Close the Visual Basic Editor.

16. Protect the worksheet. Use the password broadband. Click the Save button on the Standard toolbar to save the workbook using the file name BroadBand Automated.

Cases and Places

The difficulty of these case studies varies:
◗ are the least difficult; ◗◗ are more difficult; and ◗◗◗ are the most difficult.

1 ◗ Open the workbook Solar Works from the Data Disk. Print the Projections worksheet. Create a macro that prints the cell formulas version of the Projections worksheet in landscape orientation using the Fit to option. Make sure the macro resets the Page Setup options before terminating. Execute the macro. Print the macro. Save the workbook with the name Solar Works1. Hand in the three printouts to your instuctor.

2 ◗ Open the workbook Solar Works from the Data Disk. Create a Command Button control to the right of the Assumptions box. Change the button's caption to Assumptions. Write a procedure for the Command Button control that accepts data for each of the five assumptions in the range B21:B25. Print the Projections worksheet. Print the Command Button control procedure. Use the Assumptions button to enter the following data sets and then print the worksheet for each data set: (a) Manufacturing = 38%; R & D = 6%; Marketing = 15%; Corporate = 16%; Commissions = 5%. (b) Manufacturing = 43%; R & D = 9%; Marketing = 10%; Corporate = 18%; Commissions = 6%. The Total Net Income in cell E18 for (a) is $1,021,151.80 and for (b) is $714,806.26. Save the workbook with the name Solar Works2. Hand in the four printouts to your instructor.

3 ◗ Using a browser search engine, such as AltaVista, type the keywords `Visual Basic for Applications`. Visit three Web pages that show VBA code solving a problem. Print each Web page. Hand in the three printouts to your instructor.

4 ◗◗ Open the workbook Solar Works from the Data Disk. Create a well-balanced user interface made up of a Reset button and five scroll bars, one for each of the cells in the range B21:B25. Have the Reset button set the five assumptions to 50%, 10%, 15%, 15%, and 5%, respectively. The scroll bars should range from 0% to 100% and increment by 0.25% (scroll arrows) and 1% (scroll bars). Use the titles in the Assumptions box in the range A21:A25 for the names of the scroll bars. Print the worksheet. Use the interface to enter the data specified in Cases and Places Exercise 2 above. Save the workbook with the name Solar Works3. Hand in the three printouts to your instructor.

5 ◗◗◗ Open the workbook Dollar Bill's Bank Loan Analysis from the Data Disk. Modify the procedure associated with the New Loan button on the worksheet so that it validates the price, down payment, interest rate, and years as follows: (a) the price must be between $0.00 and $50,000.00 inclusive; (b) the down payment must be between $0.00 and $50,000.00 inclusive; (c) the interest rate must be between 5% and 30% inclusive; and (d) the years must be between 0.25 and 15 inclusive. Print the procedure. Create and enter two sets of valid data. Print the worksheet for each set. Hand in the three printouts to your instructor.

Microsoft **Excel 2000**

Microsoft Excel 2000

P R O J E C T

8

Auditing, Data Validation, and Solving Complex Problems

You will have mastered the material in this project when you can:

O B J E C T I V E S

- Use the Auditing toolbar to analyze a worksheet
- Add data validation rules to cells
- Use trial and error to solve a problem on a worksheet
- Use Excel's Solver to solve a complex problem
- Password protect a workbook file
- Use Excel's Scenario Manager to record and save different sets of what-if assumptions and the corresponding results
- Create a Scenario Summary of scenarios
- Create a Scenario PivotTable
- Set and change the properties of a worksheet

Food for Thought

Worksheets Help Serve the Community

Health-conscious Americans not only are looking for ways to maintain health and fitness, but also are concerned about the needs of less-fortunate citizens. At least one person in every ten in the United States relies on food pantries and soup kitchens to avoid going hungry. Interestingly, 60 percent of these people have graduated from high school and have attended college. One in five is a child.

Although difficult to comprehend, it is estimated that 30 million Americans are in danger of going hungry. In large part, these families and individuals are helped through the efforts of America's Second Harvest, the nation's largest hunger-relief charity network of food banks. Corporate donors, local businesses, and individuals provide surplus food to the food banks, which then is distributed to more than 50,000 local agencies. A network of 189 food banks serves all 50 states and Puerto Rico, and distributes more than one billion pounds of donated food and groceries each year.

Among Second Harvest's food banks is the Greater Chicago Food Depository. The Food Depository collects donated surplus food from wholesale food manufacturers; produce growers and distributors, food store chains, and restaurants. After gathering the food, Food Depository drivers deliver the provisions to warehouses where the products are distributed later to charitable food pantries, soup kitchens, and shelters throughout the Chicago area.

With the huge distribution of food each year, employees needed a more efficient method of keeping track of these goods than using manual methods. With the ease in which Excel can be used to facilitate auditing and analyzing data, the Food Depository developed Excel worksheets, similar to the worksheet developed in this project.

In Project 8, the Union Cafeteria has a need to audit, validate data, and solve complex problems related to providing healthy meals for various sports teams on campus.

The majority of the project concentrates on working with the cafeteria's menu planning worksheet to solve complex problems that involve changing values in cells to arrive at a solution while abiding by constraints imposed by changes.

The Food Depository uses Excel worksheets to organize, tabulate, and summarize hundreds of pallets and thousands of pounds of food shipped each week to its warehouses. The worksheets are useful particularly for analyzing the food quantities to ensure that packagers receive food deliveries just when they need it. Improved quality control at processing plants also is a result, eliminating food surpluses, excess shipments, and fewer mislabeled and slightly damaged packages.

Now when drivers deliver to the warehouses, employees keep track of inventory, are able to provide instant analysis, and project storage needs. One of their Excel worksheets contains a template to enter the quantity of salvage goods; a second worksheet records items that need repacking. Workers generate reports, study the worksheets to determine their needs, prepare for the amounts of foods expected to arrive the following day, and survey how much warehouse space is needed to ensure sufficient room for the products.

The Excel worksheets have been a tremendous help in providing the Food Depository with the tools they need to efficiently feed more than 300,000 Chicagoans annually. Food for thought.

Microsoft Excel 2000

Auditing, Data Validation, and Solving Complex Problems

P R O J E C T

8

C A S E   P E R S P E C T I V E

College sports are very competitive and teams are looking for any advantage they can find to boost their performance. Recently, the Union Cafeteria has been receiving requests from various campus sport teams for special meal requirements. Groups, such as the volleyball and track teams, would like to have meals prepared based on certain nutritional needs. As the assistant cafeteria manager, you have been asked to prepare a worksheet that will select the correct serving portions of various foods to meet the needs of the track team. You have been given the additional task of maximizing the cafeteria's profit on each meal.

Maxine Hill, your manager, has given you a list of foods, their serving size, and their nutritional value. You also have the cost per serving of each item and the price for which each serving can be sold. Each item must be dished out in a predetermined serving size and cannot be sold in partial servings. For example, a hamburger can consist of two servings of beef, but not one and a half. Both Maxine and the track team coach also have asked for documentation that shows the nutritional requirements have been satisfied.

Introduction

This project introduces you to auditing a worksheet, data validation, and solving complex problems. Auditing allows you to check both the cells being referenced in a formula and the formulas that reference a cell. Auditing a worksheet is especially helpful when you want to learn more about a workbook created by someone else or you want to verify the formulas in a newly created workbook.

Data validation allows you to define cells in such a way that only certain values are accepted. This feature also allows you to display a prompt message when the user selects the cell and an error message if the user attempts to enter a value outside of a valid range that you define.

The majority of this project introduces you to solving complex problems that involve changing values of cells to arrive at a solution, while abiding by constraints imposed on the changing values. The worksheet in Figure 8-1a on page E 8.6 shows the details of the special meal requirements for this project as described in the Case Perspective. Columns B, C, and D each refer to one of the three dishes that can make up a meal, Beef, Potatoes, and Mixed Vegetables. The row titles in rows 4 through 8 in column A refer to the characteristics of each serving, such as Serving Price, Serving Cost, Profit per Serving, Fat Content, and Carbohydrate Content. Row 9 is where you enter the number of servings of each food category. In this case, the number of servings must be between 1 and 4. Once you enter the number of servings of each food in cells B9, C9, and D9, Excel determines the results of the suggested meal in rows 11 through 15, Total Fat in Meal, Total Carbohydrate in Meal, Total Price, Total Cost, and Total Profit. The objective here is to keep the fat content low, keep carbohydrates high, and maximize the profit.

The only way to solve some problems is to keep trying different data, in this case varying the servings of the three different types of food, until you are satisfied with the solution. This process is called trial and error. Often, you can use trial and error to solve a problem on your own. Other times, so many possible solutions exist to a problem, that the best way to solve the problem is to use a computer. Excel gives you tools to solve such problems. One of these tools is Solver. Solver allows you to specify up to 200 different cells that can be adjusted to find a solution to a problem. Solver allows you to place constraints on the variables. A constraint is a limitation on the possible values that a cell can contain. Once you define the constraints and tell Solver what to look for, it will try many possible solutions until it finds the best one.

In Figure 8-1b on the next page, the values of cells B9, C9, and D9 have been modified by Solver to find the best combination of servings for a meal where beef is the main entrée. When Solver finishes solving a problem, you can instruct it to create an Answer Report. An Answer Report (Figures 8-1c and 8-1e on page E 8.7) shows the answer that Solver found, the values that were manipulated by Solver to find the answer, and the constraints that were used to solve the problem.

Excel's Scenario Manager is a what-if analysis tool that allows you to record and save different sets of what-if assumptions used to forecast the outcome of a worksheet model. You will use Scenario Manager to manage two different sets of Solver data. Figure 8-1d on the next page shows a scenario where chicken has substituted beef as the main entrée. Scenario Manager also allows you to create reports that summarize the scenarios on your worksheet. Figure 8-1f on page E 8.7 shows a Scenario Summary and Scenario PivotTable that concisely report the differences in the two scenarios in Figures 8-1b and 8-1d.

Project Eight — Union Cafeteria Menu Planning Worksheet

After your discussion with Maxine, you determine the following needs and source of data.

Needs: The track team would like the cafeteria to come up with a meal that has no more than 25 grams of fat, and at least 40 grams of carbohydrates. Maxine would like you to determine the best meal that includes servings of a chicken dish or a beef dish, a potato dish, and a mixed vegetables dish. The meal must consist of at least one serving of each dish, and no more than four servings of each dish. When determining the amounts of each dish to include in the meal, you must maximize the profit to the cafeteria while operating within the constraints that the track team has placed on you.

More About 2000

Constraints

The constraints of a problem are the rules that you must follow to solve a given problem. You even may add constraints to cells that are not referenced in the formulas you are solving. Solver will modify these types of cells to meet the constraints, but they will not affect the solution. For example, you can change row or column headers, or worksheet headers to explain better to the user the results of a Solver solution.

More About 2000

The Solver Add-In

If you do not have Solver installed on your computer, see your instructor about obtaining the Microsoft Office 2000 CD-ROMs. To load the Solver Add-In, use the Add-Ins command on the Tools menu and then check the Solver option box and follow the instructions.

E 8.5

Microsoft **Excel 2000**

(b) Solution with Beef as Main Entrée

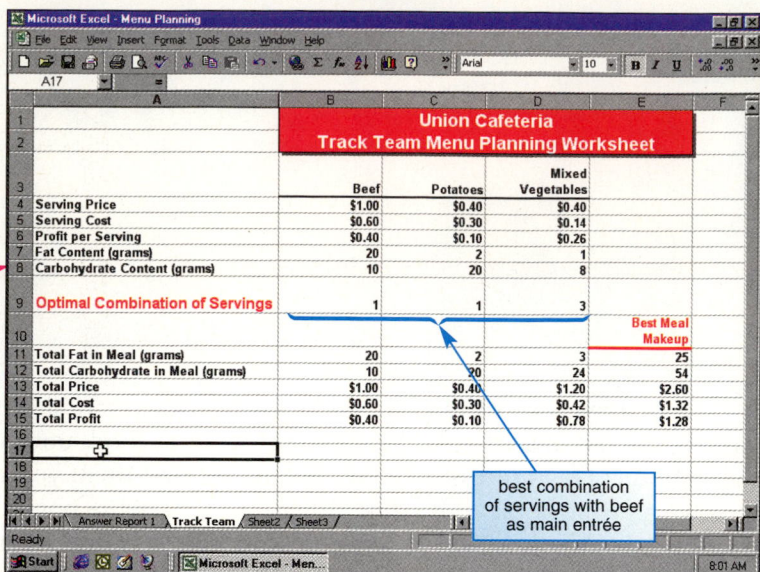

(a) Worksheet without a Solution

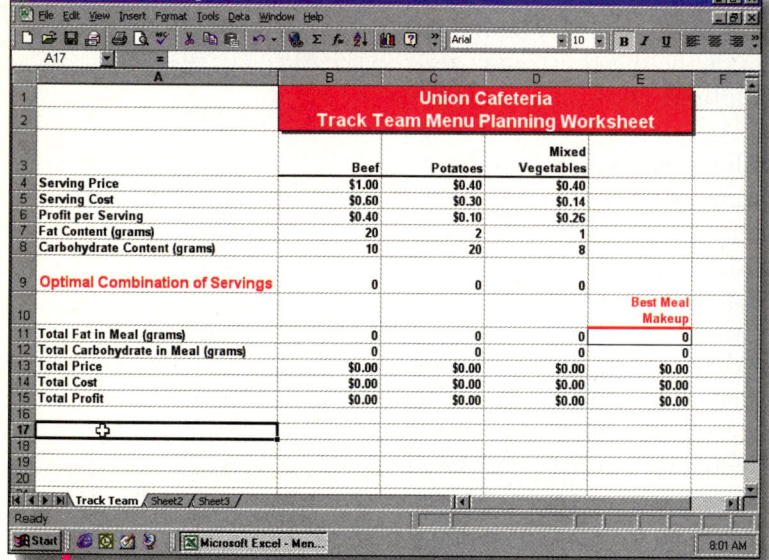

(d) Solution with Chicken as Main Entrée

FIGURE 8-1

(c) Answer Report with Beef as Main Entrée

summary of two possible meal scenarios

results proving problems' constraints are met

(e) Answer Report with Chicken as Main Entrée

(f) Scenario Summary and Scenario PivotTable of Solutions

Finally, reports need to be generated for the coach that indicate the nutritional needs have been met.

Source of Data: The workbook shown in Figure 8-1a on page E 8.6 is available on the Data Disk under the file name Menu Planning.

Starting Excel and Opening a Workbook

Perform the following steps to start Excel, reset the toolbars, and open the workbook Menu Planning from the Data Disk.

TO START EXCEL AND OPEN A WORKBOOK

1 Insert the Data Disk in drive A. See the inside back cover of this book for instructions for downloading the Data Disk.

2 Click the Start button on the taskbar and then click Open Office Document.

3 When the Open Office Document dialog box displays, click the Look in box arrow and then click 3½ Floppy (A:). Double-click Menu Planning in the list.

4 When the Menu Planning workbook displays, click Tools on the menu bar, and then click Customize.

5 When the Customize dialog box displays, click the Options tab, make sure the top three check boxes are selected, click the Reset my usage button, and then click the Yes button.

6 Click the Toolbars tab. Click Standard, click the Reset button, and then click the OK button. Click Formatting, click the Reset button, and then click the OK button. Click the Close button.

The Menu Planning workbook displays in the Excel window (Figure 8-2).

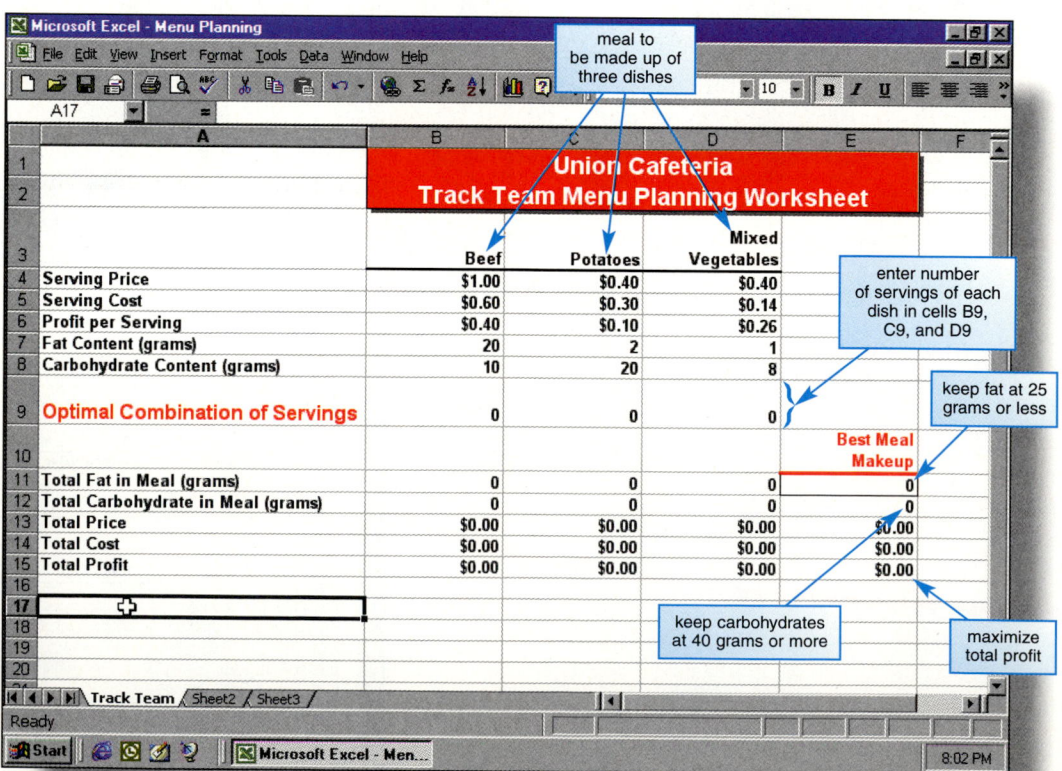

FIGURE 8-2

The Track Team sheet shown in Figure 8-2 consists of information for three types of dishes. Rows 4 through 8 show the information for one serving of each type of dish. Row 9 contains the optimal combination of servings, which is the information that needs to be determined in this project. Rows 11 through 15 show the totals for each dish based on the serving amounts entered in the range B9:D9. As cells B9, C9, and D9 change, the values in the range B11:D15 are updated. Finally, the grand totals for the entire meal are calculated in the range E11:E15. The goals are to keep the total fat in the meal (cell E11) less than or equal to 25, keep the total carbohydrates in the meal (cell E12) greater than or equal to 40, and maximize the total profit made on each meal (cell E15).

The current worksheet displays beef as one of the dishes. One of the requirements is to create meals within the constraints for both beef and chicken. Therefore, the information in column B needs to be modified later in the project to reflect the price, cost, and nutritional properties of the chicken dish.

Auditing

The term **auditing** refers to the practice of proving the correctness of a worksheet. The **Auditing toolbar** supplies several tools that you can use to analyze the formulas in a worksheet.

Auditing is useful both for analyzing a complex worksheet and for finding the source of errors that may occur in your worksheet. Excel provides visual auditing tools that display cues in the worksheet to help you understand the worksheet. These cues take the form of tracer arrows and circles around cells. **Tracer arrows** are blue arrows that point from cell to cell and let you know what cells are referenced in a formula in a particular cell. Tracer arrows become red when one of the cells referenced contains an error.

Displaying the Auditing Toolbar

When you want to audit a worksheet, you can display the Auditing toolbar. The Auditing toolbar contains buttons that allow you to trace the details of a formula or locate the source of errors in a worksheet. The Auditing toolbar is accessible only through the Tools menu. To view the Auditing toolbar, complete the steps on the next page.

More About

Auditing

Auditing is a very important job function in corporations and government. For more information about auditing, visit the Excel 2000 More About Web page (www.scite.com/ex2000/more.htm) and click Auditing.

Steps | To Display the Auditing Toolbar

1 **Click Tools on the menu bar, point to Auditing, and then point to Show Auditing Toolbar on the Auditing submenu.**

The Tools menu and Auditing submenu display (Figure 8-3).

FIGURE 8-3

2 **Click Show Auditing Toolbar.**

The Auditing toolbar displays (Figure 8-4). Excel displays the Auditing toolbar on the screen in the same location and with the same shape as it displayed the last time it was used.

FIGURE 8-4

 Ways

1. Press ALT+T, press U, press S

Tracing Precedents with the Auditing Toolbar

A formula that relies on other cells for a computation is said to have precedents. **Precedents** are cells that are referenced in a formula. For example, if you assign cell A5 the formula =A1+A2, then cells A1 and A2 are precedents of cell A5. Tracing precedent cells shows you how a particular cell is calculated. Often a precedent cell has precedents itself. For instance, in the previous example, if you assign cell A1 the formula =B1+B2, then cell A1, which is a precedent of cell A5, also has precedents. Excel allows you to trace the precedents of precedents as well. However, you can audit only one cell at a time. That is, Excel does not allow you to audit ranges. The following steps show the precedent cells for the total profit of the best meal makeup in cell E15.

 Steps **To Trace Precedents**

1 **Click cell E15 and then click the Trace Precedents button on the Auditing toolbar.**

Excel draws an arrow across the range B15:E15.

2 **Click the Trace Precedents button two more times.**

Excel draws arrows indicating the precedents of the cells in the range B15:D15 (Figure 8-5).

FIGURE 8-5

The arrows shown in Figure 8-5 have arrowheads on cells that are traced, and dots on cells that are direct precedents of the cells with arrowheads. For example, cell B15 is a precedent of cell E15, the total profit cell, and cell B15 has precedents above it in cells B4, B5, B9, B13, and B14. As you click the Trace Precedents button, you visually can follow the levels of precedents through the worksheet.

 Other Ways

1. On Tools menu point to Auditing, click Trace Precedents
2. Press ALT+T, press U, press T

Removing Precedent Arrows with the Auditing Toolbar

After understanding the precedents of a particular cell, you can remove the precedent arrows one level at a time.

 Steps **To Remove the Trace Precedent Arrows**

① **Click the Remove Precedent Arrows button on the Auditing toolbar.**

Excel removes the arrows across the range B4:D12, the last level of precedent arrows added.

② **Click the Remove Precedent Arrows button two more times on the Auditing toolbar.**

Excel removes the remaining precedent arrows (Figure 8-6).

FIGURE 8-6

 Other Ways

1. On Tools menu point to Auditing, click Remove All Arrows
2. Press ALT+T, press U, press A

More About 2000

Tracing Precedents and Dependents

When no more levels of precedents are available on the worksheet, Excel will beep if you try to trace another level. If you double-click a tracer arrow, the cell at the end of the arrow will be selected. This is useful on complex worksheets where the destination of an arrow may not be easy to follow.

By using the Trace Precedents and Remove Precedent Arrows buttons in combination, you slowly can begin to see the structure of the worksheet that is hidden in the formulas within the cells. By doing more analysis, you can assure yourself that you understand the worksheet and that no obvious errors are apparent to the casual viewer.

Tracing Dependents with the Auditing Toolbar

A cell is a **dependent** if it is referenced in a formula in another cell. Often, it is useful to find out where a cell is being used in a worksheet to perform subsequent calculations. In other words, which cells in the worksheet use the cell in question? The following steps trace the dependents of the optimal servings of beef in cell B9.

To Trace Dependents

① Click cell B9 and then click the Trace Dependents button on the Auditing toolbar.

Excel draws arrows to cells B11, B12, B13, and B14.

② Click the Trace Dependents button two more times.

Excel draws arrows indicating the remaining dependents of cell B9 (Figure 8-7).

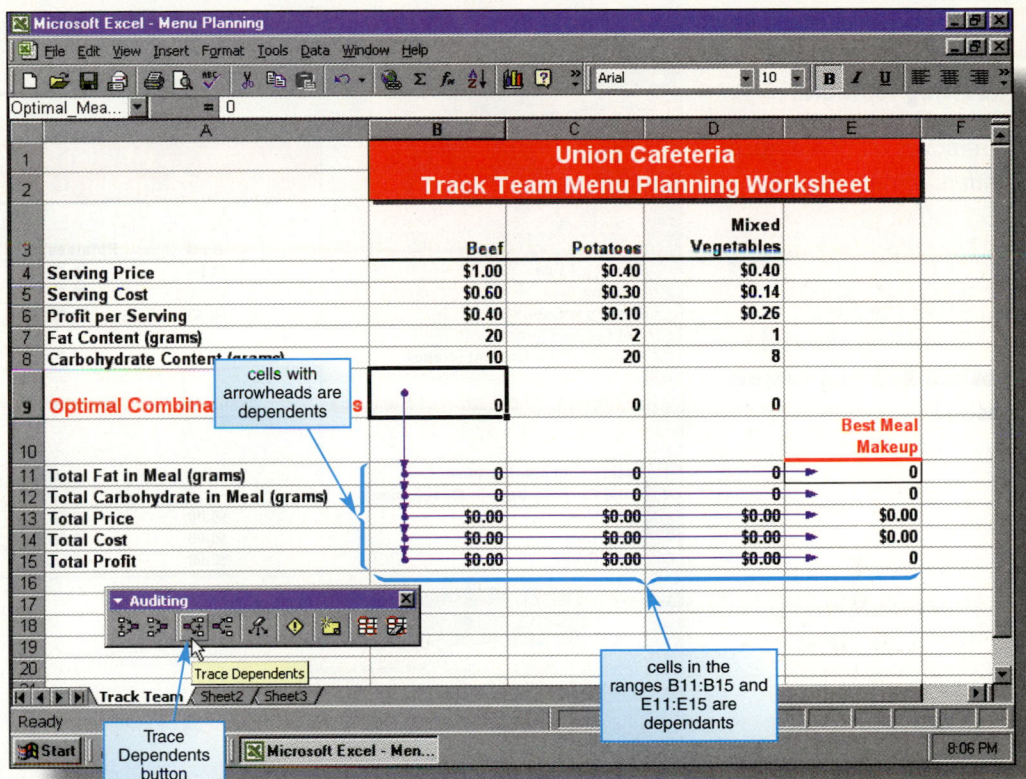

FIGURE 8-7

Figure 8-7 indicates that cells B11, B12, B13, and B14 depend on cell B9. Subsequently, cells B15 and the range E11:E15 depend on those cells. Clearly, before any results can be computed in cells B15 and the range E11:E15, cell B9 must have a value.

Removing All Arrows with the Auditing Toolbar

When you have finished auditing the worksheet with the Auditing toolbar, the easiest way to clear all of the trace arrows is to use the **Remove All Arrows button** on the Auditing toolbar.

Other Ways

1. On Tools menu point to Auditing, click Trace Dependents
2. Press ALT+T, press U, press D

To Remove the Trace Dependent Arrows

1 **Click the Remove All Arrows button on the Auditing toolbar.**

Excel removes all of the trace dependent arrows (Figure 8-8).

2 **Click the Close button on the right side of the Auditing toolbar to close it.**

FIGURE 8-8

Other Ways

1. On Tools menu point to Auditing, click Remove All Arrows
2. Press ALT+T, press U, press A

Sometimes, a cell has precedents or dependents on other worksheets or in other workbooks. In this case, Excel will draw a dashed arrow to an icon of a worksheet to indicate that the precedent or dependent is outside of the current worksheet. If you click the dashed arrow and the workbook that contains the precedent or dependent is open, Excel displays the Go To dialog box that allows you to navigate to that location.

Figure 8-9 shows the buttons on the Auditing toolbar. Table 8-1 summarizes the buttons on the Auditing toolbar.

FIGURE 8-9

Table 8-1 Summary of Buttons on the Auditing Toolbar		
BUTTON	**NAME**	**FUNCTION**
	Trace Precedents	Draws tracer arrows from the cells that affect the formula in the current cell.
	Remove Precedent Arrows	Removes tracer arrows from one level of precedents on the active worksheet.
	Trace Dependents	Draws tracer arrows to the cells that use the current cell in their formula.
	Remove Dependent Arrows	Removes tracer arrows from one level of dependents on the active worksheet.
	Remove All Arrows	Removes all tracer arrows drawn with the Trace Precedents and Trace Dependents buttons.
	Trace Error	If the active cell contains an error value, draws tracer arrows to the cells that may be causing the error value to appear.
	New Comment	Attaches a comment to the active cell.
	Circle Invalid Data	Draws circles around the cells that contain values outside of the limits defined by using the Validation command on the Data menu.
	Clear Validation Circles	Clears the circles drawn by the Circle Invalid Data button.

The **Trace Error button** is used when you see an error in a cell and want to trace the source of the error. If you see an error in a cell, including #DIV/0!, #NAME?, #NA, #NULL!, #NUM!, #REF!, and #VALUE!, the Trace Error button will display red tracer arrows to inform you of the precedents of the cell that contains the error. You then can inspect the precedent cells to see if you can determine the cause of the error and correct it.

The **New Comment button** allows you to place comments in cells so you can make notes to yourself or to others about questionable data in the worksheet. For example, if you are auditing someone else's worksheet and you believe that a cell should be the precedent of a particular cell, you can make a note that will display when the other user opens the worksheet. Comments are discussed further in Project 9.

The **Circle Invalid Data button** and the **Clear Validation Circles button** are used in combination with Excel's data validation capability discussed in the next section. If a cell contains data validation parameters and the current data in the cell is outside of those validation criteria, the Circle Invalid Data button draws a circle around the cell. The Clear Validation Circles button is used to clear these circles.

More About 2000

Validation Circles

Validation circles are red to indicate that these cells contain error values. Excel will display a maximum of 256 invalid data circles at a time.

Data Validation, Trial and Error, and Goal Seek

Often, it is necessary to limit the values that should be placed in a particular cell. Excel allows you to place limitations on the values of cells by using data validation. **Data validation** restricts the values that may be entered into a cell by the worksheet user. Excel allows you to determine the restrictions placed on data entered into a cell, set an input message that the user will see when selecting the cell, and set an error message that displays when a user violates the restrictions placed on the cell. By implementing these features, you limit the possibilities for error on a worksheet by giving the user as much information as possible about how to use the worksheet properly.

One important aspect of Excel's data validation is that the rules apply only when the user enters data into the cell manually. That is, if a cell is calculated by a formula or set in a way other than direct input by the user, Excel does not check the validation rules.

Adding Data Validation to Cells

Recall from the Needs section for this project on page E 8.5, serving sizes must be whole numbers and at least one of each type of serving must be included in a meal, but no more than four of each type per meal. By examining the worksheet, you can see that cells B9, C9, and D9 must have these restrictions. Data validation is added to cells by using the **Validation command** on the Data menu.

More About 2000

Data Validation

If you have the Office Assistant turned on, Data Validation input and error messages will be displayed as part of the Assistant. Input and error messages can be up to 255 characters in length.

Steps To Add Data Validation

1 **Select the range B9:D9. Click Data on the menu bar and then point to Validation.**

The Data menu displays (Figure 8-10).

FIGURE 8-10

2

2 **Click Validation. When the Data Validation dialog box displays, click the Allow box arrow and then select Whole number. Click the Data box arrow and then select between. Type** 1 **in the Minimum text box and type** 4 **in the Maximum text box. Point to the Input Message tab.**

The Data Validation dialog box displays (Figure 8-11).

FIGURE 8-11

3 **Click the Input Message tab and then type** Serving Size **in the Title text box. Type** Enter a serving size that is greater than zero and less than five. **in the Input message text box. Point to the Error Alert tab.**

The Input Message tab displays (Figure 8-12).

FIGURE 8-12

4 **Click the Error Alert tab and then type** Serving Size Error **in the Title text box. Type** You must enter a serving size that is greater than zero and less than five. **in the Error message text box and then point to the OK button.**

The Error Alert tab displays (Figure 8-13).

 5 **Click the OK button.**

FIGURE 8-13

When the user selects one of the cells in the range B9:D9, Excel displays the input message defined in Figure 8-12 on the previous page. When the user enters a value other than one through four in cells B9:D9, the error message defined in Figure 8-13 displays.

Excel allows several types of validation to be performed in the Validation criteria area shown in Figure 8-11 on the previous page. Table 8-2 shows the various criteria types available in the Validation criteria area.

 About

Validation Types

When using the Custom validation type, you can use a formula that evaluates to either true or false. If the value is false, then the user may not enter data in the cell. For example, if you have a cell that contains an employee's salary, you may want to disallow the user from entering a percentage in a cell that contains the employee's raise for this year if the salary is zero, indicating that the employee is no longer with the company.

Table 8-2	Types of Validation Criteria Allowed
ALLOW	**MEANING**
Any value	Allows the user to enter anything in the cell. Use if you simply want to display an input message.
Whole number	Allows whole numbers in a specific range. Use the Data box to specify how the validation takes place.
Decimal	Allows decimal numbers in a specific range. Use the Data box to specify how the validation takes place.
List	Specifies a range where a list of valid values can be found.
Date	Allows a range of dates.
Time	Allows a range of times.
Text length	Allows a certain length text string to be input. Use the Data box to specify how the validation takes place.
Custom	Allows user to specify a formula that will validate the data entered by the user.

The Ignore blank check box should be cleared if you want to require that the user enter something in the cell. By leaving the Ignore blank check box selected, Excel allows the user to select the cell, and then leave the cell with no data being entered.

Using Trial and Error to Solve a Complex Problem

Trial and error refers to the practice of adjusting cells in a worksheet manually to try to find a solution to a problem. In the Track Team worksheet, you could adjust cells B9, C9, and D9 until the criteria for fat content and carbohydrate content are met. While many combinations of possible values exist, you could try keeping one or two of the values constant while adjusting the others.

Trial and error is more than just guessing. Because you understand the constraints on the problem and the goals, you use logic to make subsequent trials better than the previous. For example, if you increase the servings of potatoes by two and it causes the total fat content of the meal to exceed 25, you may try to increase the serving by one to see if that keeps the totals within the constraints.

 To Use Trial and Error to Attempt to Solve a Complex Problem

1 **Click cell B9 and type 5 as the number of servings of beef and then press the ENTER key. Point to the Retry button.**

The Serving Size Error dialog box displays (Figure 8-14), because 5 is outside the limits of acceptable values for this cell. The Serving Size ScreenTip displays because cell B9 is selected.

FIGURE 8-14

2 Click the Retry button. Type 2 as the number of servings of beef in cell B9. Click cell C9 and then type 2 as the number of servings of potatoes. Click cell D9, type 2 as the number of servings of mixed vegetables, and then press the ENTER key.

The Serving Size ScreenTip displays because cell D9 is selected. Excel displays the new values and updates the totals in the range B11:E15 as shown in Figure 8-15. The value of 46 in cell E11 indicates that the maximum allowable fat content of 25 grams has been exceeded.

FIGURE 8-15

3 Click cell B9, type 1 as the number of servings of beef, and then press the ENTER key.

Excel displays the recalculated values for the worksheet (Figure 8-16). The value of 26 in cell E11 again indicates that the maximum allowable fat content of 25 grams has been exceeded.

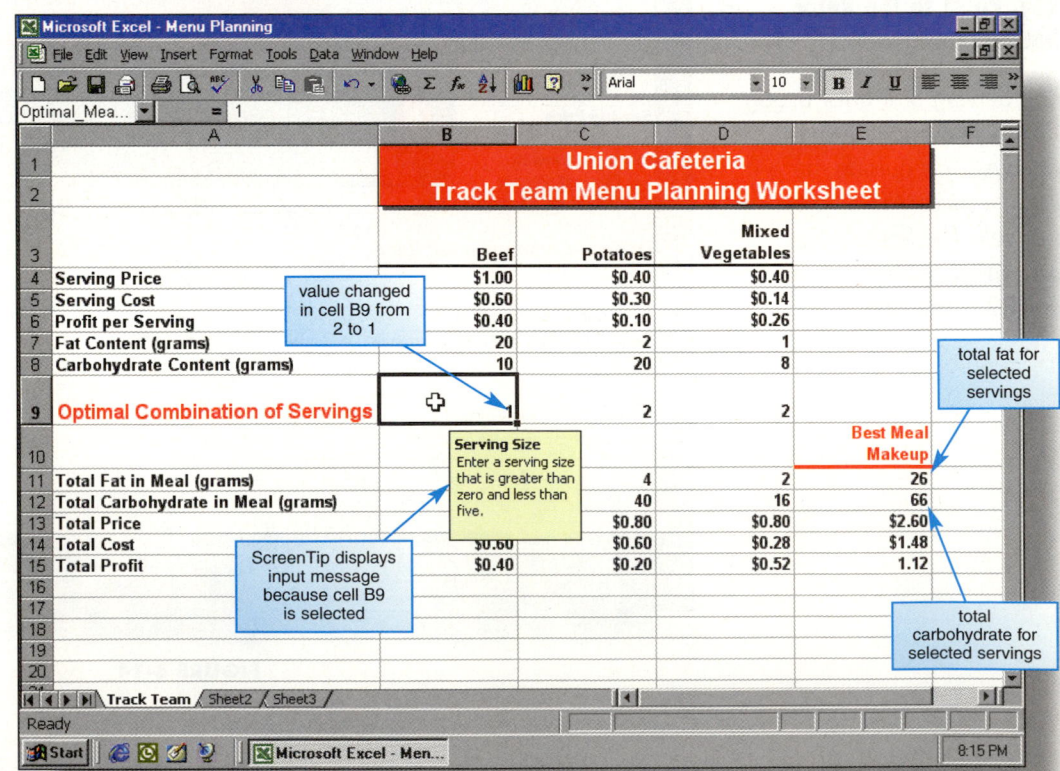

FIGURE 8-16

Trial and error can be used on simple problems in many cases. Many limitations exist to using trial and error, however. The Menu Planning worksheet has three cells (B9, C9, and D9) that can be adjusted to solve the problem. Because each cell can contain a value between 1 and 4, 64 different combinations are possible that you could try, many of which may give the proper fat and carbohydrate contents to the meal. The biggest drawback to using trial and error in this situation is that you must maximize the profit while meeting the other conditions. Rather than using trial and error to test all 64 possible meal combinations and see which one produces the most profit while meeting the nutritional constraints, Excel provides other tools to help solve problems where cells can contain a number of values.

Goal Seeking to Solve a Complex Problem

If you know the result you want a formula to produce, you can use **goal seeking** to determine the value of a cell on which a formula depends. In the Menu Planning worksheet, the total fat content for the meal is one result that can be sought by varying the number of servings of one of the meal items. Goal seeking takes trial and error one step further by automatically changing the value of a cell until a single criteria is met in another cell. In this case, suppose you suspect that by varying the number of mixed vegetable servings, you can achieve the goal of 25 grams of fat for the meal. In doing this, you hope that the other constraints of the problem also are satisfied.

The following steps show how goal seek can be used to alter the servings of mixed vegetables to keep the total fat content of the meal less than or equal to 25 grams.

Goal Seeking

Goal seeking is a methodology in which you know what answer you want a formula in a cell to be, but you do not know the value to place in a cell that is involved in the formula. You can goal seek by changing the value in a cell that is used indirectly in the formula.

 To Use the Goal Seek Command to Attempt to Solve a Complex Problem

1 Click cell E11, the cell that contains the total fat content in the meal. Click Tools on the menu bar and then point to Goal Seek.

The Tools menu displays (Figure 8-17).

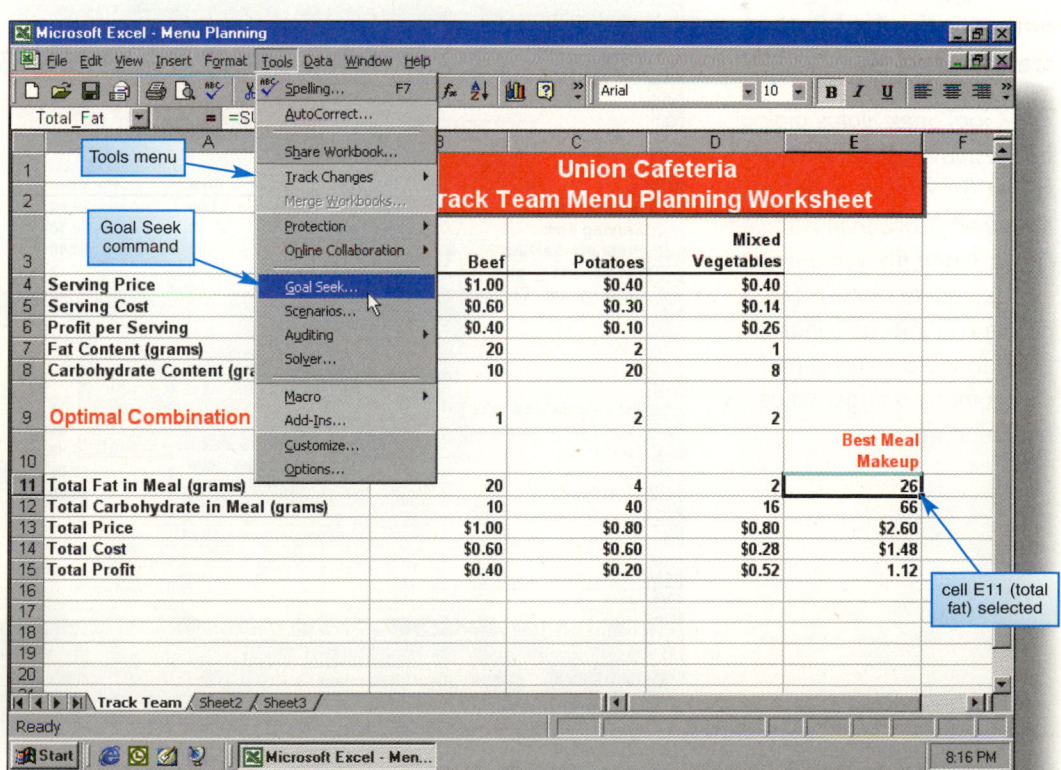

FIGURE 8-17

2 **Click Goal Seek.**

The *Goal Seek dialog box* displays. The Set cell box is assigned the cell reference of the active cell in the worksheet (cell E11) automatically.

3 **Click the To value text box. Type** 25 **and then click the By changing cell box. Click cell D9 on the worksheet. Point to the OK button.**

The Goal Seek dialog box displays as shown in Figure 8-18. A marquee displays around cell D9.

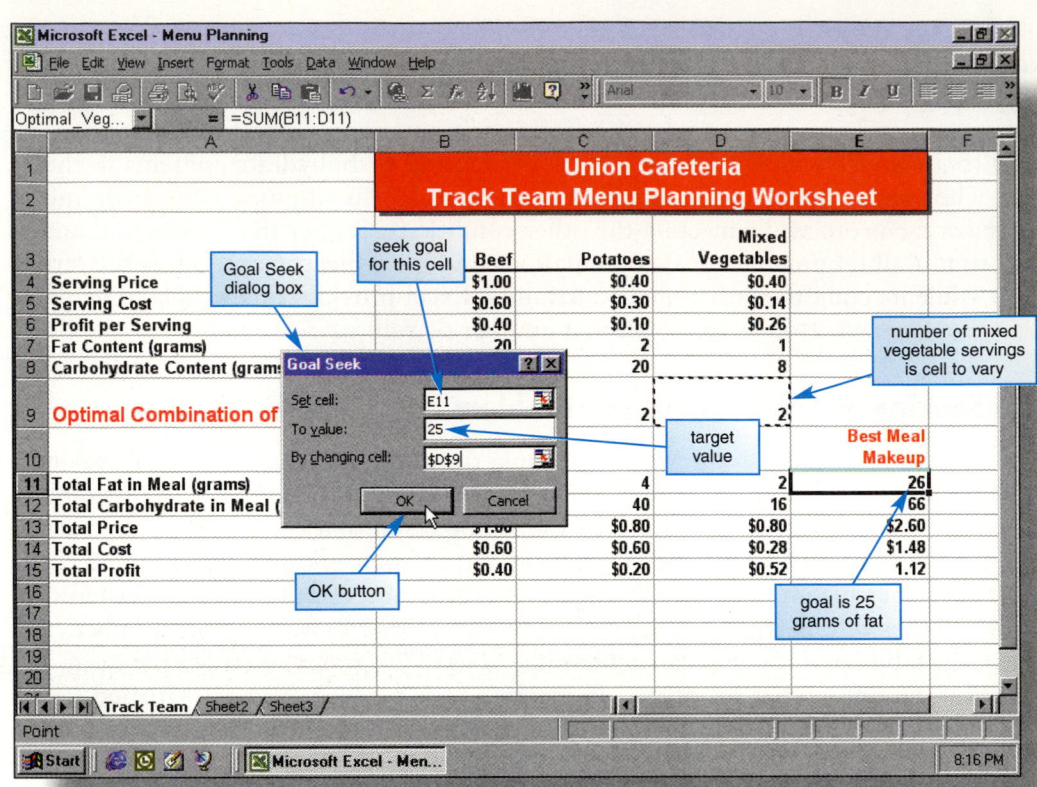

FIGURE 8-18

4 **Click the OK button. Point to the OK button in the Goal Seek Status dialog box.**

The *Goal Seek Status dialog box* displays as shown in Figure 8-19. Excel changes the number of servings in cell D9 to 1 and the value in cell E11 is updated to 25. The dialog box indicates that Excel found a solution and shows that the target value has been met.

FIGURE 8-19

The Goal Seek Status dialog box disappears and Excel displays the updated worksheet (Figure 8-20).

	Union Cafeteria Track Team Menu Planning Worksheet				
	Beef	**Potatoes**	**Mixed Vegetables**		
4 Serving Price	$1.00	$0.40	$0.40		
5 Serving Cost	$0.60	$0.30	$0.14		
6 Profit per Serving	$0.40	$0.10	$0.26		
7 Fat Content (grams)	20	2	1		
8 Carbohydrate Content (grams)	10	20	8		
9 **Optimal Combination of Servings**	1	2	1		
10				**Best Meal Makeup**	
11 Total Fat in Meal (grams)	20	4	1	25	
12 Total Carbohydrate in Meal (grams)	10	40	8	58	
13 Total Price	$1.00	$0.80	$0.40	$2.20	
14 Total Cost	$0.60	$0.60	$0.14	$1.34	
15 Total Profit	$0.40	$0.20	$0.26	$0.86	

servings are within acceptable range

fat content meets requirement

carbohydrate content meets requirement

total profit

FIGURE 8-20

Goal seeking assumes you can change the value of only one cell referenced directly or indirectly. In this example, to change the fat content to 25 grams per serving, the number of servings of mixed vegetables must change to 1. This assumes that no other serving sizes change.

As you learned previously, you do not have to reference directly the cell to vary in the formula or function. The total fat content is calculated as a sum of the cells in the range B11:D11. The formula does not include a direct reference to the mixed vegetable serving size in cell D9. Because the total fat in the mixed vegetable servings is dependent on the number of servings of mixed vegetables, however, Excel is able to goal seek on the total fat content by varying the number of servings of mixed vegetables.

The total fat content (cell E11) and the total carbohydrate content (cell E12) satisfy the nutritional needs of the meal. Still, you have no way of knowing whether the constraint of maximizing profit (cell E15) has been achieved. Your manager requires that total profit be maximized while satisfying the nutritional needs of the track team. Surely, other combinations of the three meal items satisfy the nutritional requirements and produce greater total profit than $0.86 per meal as shown in Figure 8-20.

Using Solver to Solve Complex Problems

Solver allows you to solve complex problems where a number of variables can be changed in a worksheet in order meet a goal in a particular cell. As just stated, goal seeking allows you to change only one cell, and trial and error requires too much uncertainty and time to solve complex problems adequately.

Solver uses a technique called linear programming to solve problems. **Linear programming** is a complex mathematical process used to solve problems that include multiple variables and the minimizing or maximizing of result values. Solver

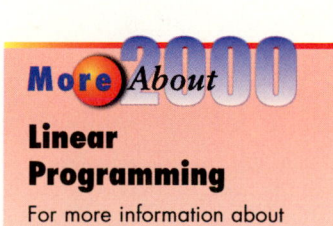

essentially tries as many possible combinations of solutions as it can. On each attempt to solve the problem, Solver checks to see if it has found a solution.

Figure 8-21a shows the results of using Solver on the Track Team worksheet. Cells B9, C9, and D9 are called the changing cells. **Changing cells** are those cells that will be modified by Solver to solve the problem. The total profit in cell E15 serves as the **target cell**, which means that Solver will attempt to meet some criteria (maximize profit) in this cell by varying the changing cells. **Constraints** are the requirements that have been placed on certain values in the problem. For example, the total fat in the meal must not exceed 25 grams, and the total carbohydrates in the meal must not be less than 40 grams.

Figure 8-21b shows a Solver Answer Report. An **Answer Report** is a worksheet that displays the results of a Solver calculation in a concise format. The report satisfies the requirement to document the results of the menu analysis.

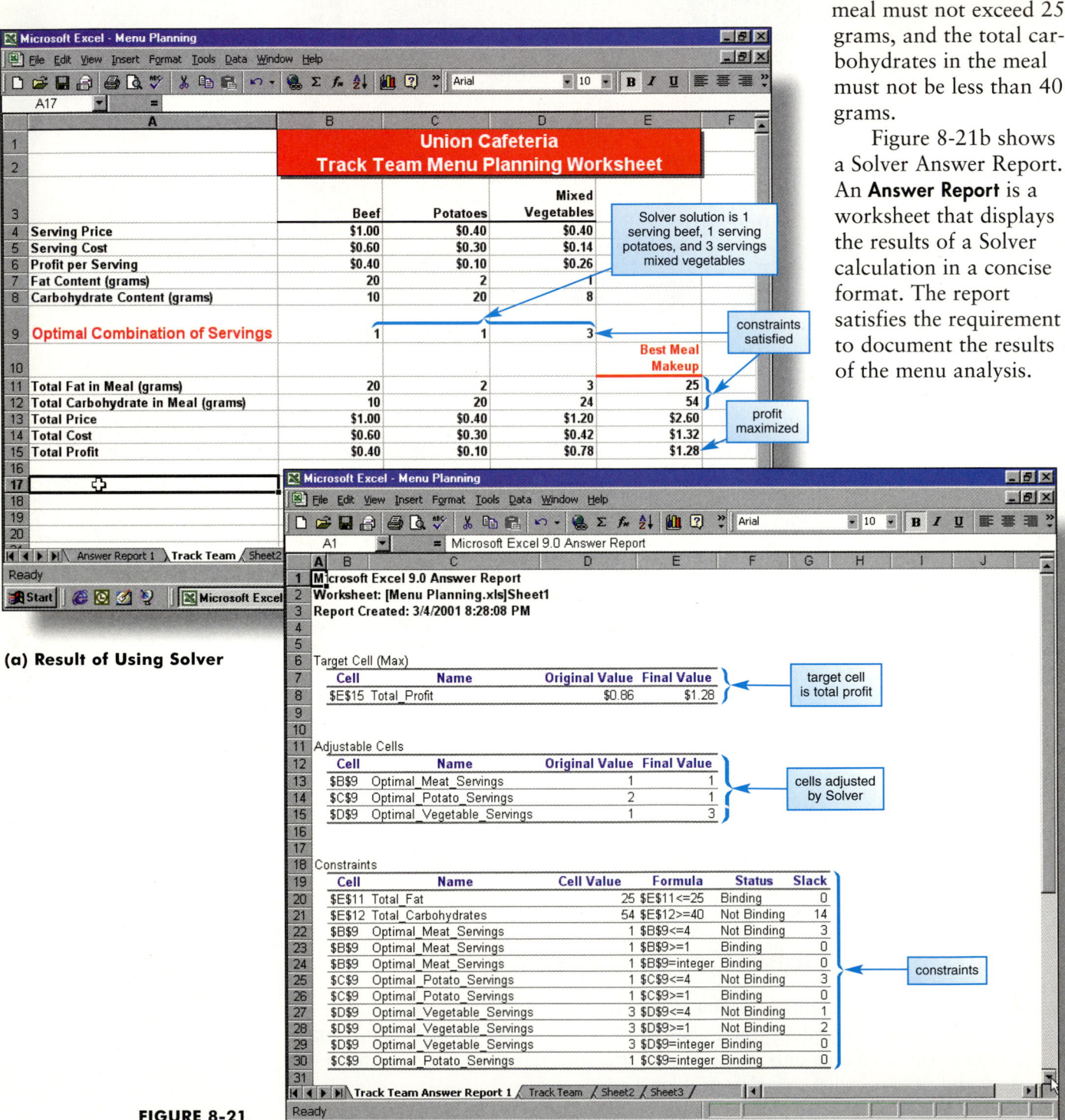

(a) Result of Using Solver

FIGURE 8-21

(b) Solver Answer Report

Using Solver to Find the Optimal Combination of Servings

The Tools menu contains the **Solver command**, which starts Solver. If the Solver command does not display on your Tools menu, then you must use the Add-Ins command on the Tools menu to add it. The cell that is the target for Solver is the total profit cell, E15. The goal is to maximize the value in that cell. The cells that can be changed by Solver to accomplish this goal are cells B9, C9, and D9, which contain the number of servings of each dish. The constraints are summarized in Table 8-3.

The following steps show how to use Solver to solve the Menu Planning worksheet within the given constraints.

Table 8-3	Additional Constraints for Solver	
CELL	OPERATOR	CONSTRAINT
B9	<=	4
B9	>=	1
B9	int	
C9	<=	4
C9	>=	1
C9	int	
D9	<=	4
D9	>=	1
D9	int	
E11	<=	25
E12	>=	40

 To Use Solver to Find the Optimal Combination

1 **Click Tools on the menu bar and then point to Solver.**

The Tools menu displays (Figure 8-22).

FIGURE 8-22

2 Click Solver. When the Solver Parameters dialog box displays, click cell E15 to set the target cell. Click the By Changing Cells box and then select the range B9:D9. Point to the Add button.

Excel displays the *Solver Parameters dialog box* as shown in Figure 8-23. The *Set Target Cell* displays as *Total_Profit* because *Total_Profit* is the cell name for cell E15 in the original worksheet.

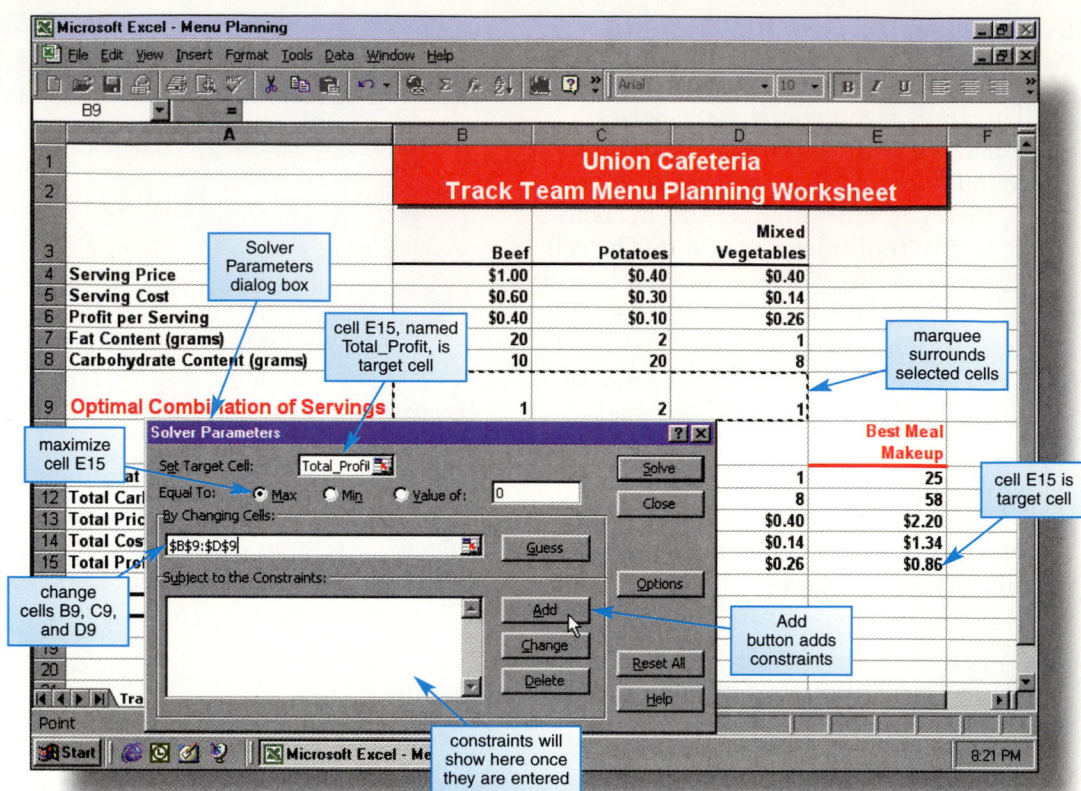

FIGURE 8-23

3 Click the Add button. Click cell B9 to set the value of the Cell Reference box. If necessary, click the middle box arrow and then select <= in the list. Type 4 in the Constraint text box and then point to the Add button.

The *Add Constraint dialog box* displays with the first constraint (Figure 8-24). This constraint means that cell B9 must be less than or equal to 4.

FIGURE 8-24

4 Click the Add button. Click cell B9 to set the value of the Cell Reference box. Click the middle box arrow and then select >= in the list. Type 1 in the Constraint text box and then point to the Add button.

The values for the second constraint display (Figure 8-25). This constraint means that cell B9 must be greater than or equal to 1.

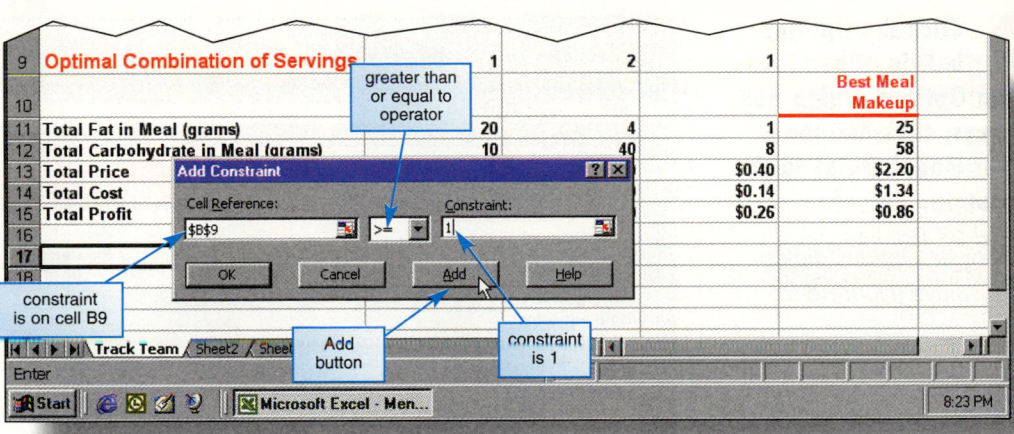

FIGURE 8-25

5 Click the Add button. Click cell B9 to set the value of the Cell Reference box. Click the middle box arrow and then select int in the list. Point to the Add button.

The values for the third constraint display (Figure 8-26). This constraint means that cell B9 must be assigned an integer.

FIGURE 8-26

6 Click the Add button. Enter the remaining constraints shown in Table 8-3 on page E 8.25, beginning with the contraints for cell C9. When finished with the final constraint, click the OK button. Point to the Options button.

Excel displays all of the constraints in the Subject to the Constraints list box (Figure 8-27).

FIGURE 8-27

7 Click the Options button. When the Solver Options dialog box displays, click Assume Linear Model. Point to the OK button.

The *Solver Options dialog box* displays (Figure 8-28).

FIGURE 8-28

8 Click the OK button. When the Solver Parameters dialog box displays again, click the Solve button.

The *Solver Results dialog box* displays. Excel indicates that it has found a solution to the problem (Figure 8-29).

FIGURE 8-29

9 Select Answer in the Reports list and then point to the OK button.

The Solver Results dialog box displays as shown in Figure 8-30.

FIGURE 8-30

10 Click the OK button.

Excel displays the values found by Solver and recalculates the totals (Figure 8-31). All of the constraints of the problem have been satisfied.

FIGURE 8-31

Figure 8-31 shows that all of the constraints in the problem have been satisfied. The profit is $1.28 per meal, which is much better than the result of $0.86 that was calculated using the Goal Seek command in Figure 8-20 on page E 8.23.

When adding constraints, as shown in Figure 8-24 on page E 8.26, Solver allows you to enter a cell reference followed by an operator. If the operator is <=, >= or =, you enter the constraint value in the **Constraint cell box**. The constraint can be a value or a cell reference. The other valid operators are **int**, for an integer value, or **bin**, for cells that contain only one of two values, such as yes/no or true/false.

Other Ways

1. Press ALT+T, press V

Solver Parameters

Sometimes Solver will give you a message telling you that the target cell values do not converge. This means that Solver can meet all of the constraints, but the target value, such as the Total Profit in cell E15 in Figure 8-31 on the previous page, can be increased or decreased indefinitely. Usually, this means that you have not specified enough constraints.

Solver Models

When you save a model, which is a collection of the data in the target cell, changing cells, and constraints, Excel does not save the solution as well. The solution can be saved separately by using the Save Scenario option in the Solver Results dialog box shown in Figure 8-29 on page E 8.28. When saving a model, the data is saved in an area you select in a worksheet. You should carefully note where you save models because Excel does not label or mark the model in any way.

Solver Scenarios

When you click the Save Scenario button in the Solver Results dialog box, Solver creates a record of the values of the changing cells that solved the problem. You can name this result and then be able to recall it in the future. It is important to note that the target cell value is not changed, just the changing cells' values.

Rather than selecting the range B9:D9 as the changing cells in Step 6, clicking the **Guess button** in the Solver Parameters dialog box (Figure 8-27 on page E 8.27) would have Solver try to determine which cells affect the target cell. The button works much the same way as the Trace Precedents button does on the Auditing toolbar. Solver searches the formula in the target cell to determine which cells are precedents of the target cell and then adds these cells to the **By Changing Cells box** for you. The Guess button is not always accurate, however, which would have required a change to the cells selected by Solver.

The **Change button** and **Delete button** in the Solver Parameters dialog box in Figure 8-27 allow you to edit the constraints that display in the Subject to the Constraints list box.

The Solver Options dialog box in Figure 8-28 on page E 8.28 contains several technical parameters that allow you to configure the inner workings of Solver. Many of the other parameters are beyond the scope of this discussion. Usually, you already have the information for a problem that lets you determine which parameters you need to vary. Table 8-4 shows the meaning of some of the parameters that you may use from time to time.

Table 8-4 Commonly Used Solver Parameters in the Solver Options Dialog Box	
PARAMETER	**MEANING**
Max Time	The total time that Solver should spend trying different solutions expressed in seconds.
Iterations	The number of different combinations of possible answer values that Solver should try.
Tolerance	Instructs Solver how close it must come to the target value to consider the problem to be solved. For example, if the target value is 100 and the Tolerance is 5%, then 95 is an acceptable answer.
Assume Linear Model	If selected, assumes that this problem is linear in nature. That is, the changing values have a proportional effect on the value of the target cell.
Assume Non-Negative	If selected, for all changing cells that do not have constraints on them, Solver should keep these numbers positive.

Excel saves the current Solver parameters automatically. Only the most recent parameters are saved. If you want to use new values in Solver and want to save the target cell, changing cell, and constraint values for Solver, the **Load Model button** and **Save Model button** in the Solver Options dialog box allow you to save the values and then re-use them in the future.

The **Save Scenario button** shown in Figure 8-29 on page E 8.28 allows you to save the results of Solver in a separate area in your workbook. Scenarios are discussed in detail later in this project.

When using Solver, two other issues must be kept in mind. First, some problems do not have solutions. The constraints may be constructed in such a way that an answer cannot be found that satisfies all of the constraints. Second, sometimes multiple answers solve the same problem. Solver does not indicate when this is the case, and you will have to use your own judgment to determine if this is the case. As long as you are confident that you have given Solver all of the constraints for a problem, however, all answers should be equally valid.

Viewing a Solver Answer Report

The **Solver Answer Report** summarizes the problem that you have presented to Solver. It shows the original and final values of the target cell along with the original and final values of the cells that Solver adjusted to find the answer. Additionally, it lists all of the constraints that you imposed on Solver.

The Answer Report documents that a particular problem has been solved correctly. Because it lists all of the relevant information in a concise format, you use the Answer Report to make certain that you have entered all of the constraints and allowed Solver to vary all the cells necessary to solve the problem. You also can use the report to reconstruct the Solver model in the future.

More *About*

Other Solver Reports

The Sensitivity Report shows how sensitive the Solver solution is to changes in the constraints and the target cell. The Limits Report shows the upper and lower values that the changing cells can have and still solve the problem given the constraints. Both of these reports are generated as separate worksheets in the current workbook, just as the Answer Report.

 Steps   To View the Answer Report

1 **Click the Answer Report 1 tab at the bottom of the window.**

The Solver Answer Report displays (Figure 8-32).

FIGURE 8-32

2 **Double-click the Answer Report 1 tab** and type Track Team Answer Report 1 **as the worksheet name. Use the scroll bar to scroll down to view the remaining cells of the Answer Report.**

The tab shows the new worksheet name and the remainder of the Answer Report displays (Figure 8-33).

FIGURE 8-33

Figure 8-33 displays additional information about the constraints that you placed on the problem and how the constraints were used to solve the problem. Column F, the **Status column**, indicates whether the constraint was binding or not. A constraint that is **binding** is one that limited the final solution in some way. For example, the total fat content of the meal is binding because the solution maximizes the amount of fat allowed by the track team. No more fat content is allowed in the meal. A constraint that is **not binding** is one that was not a limiting factor in the solution that Solver came up with. The total amount of carbohydrates in the meal is not binding because the solution could have included more or less carbohydrates if necessary to meet the other constraints.

Column G, the **Slack column**, shows the difference between the value in the cell in that row and the limit of the constraint. Cell G21 shows that the slack for the Total_Carbohydrates is 14. This means that the solution contains 14 more grams of carbohydrates than the minimum required in the constraints. Cells that are binding have zero slack.

Saving the Workbook with Passwords

Excel allows you to protect your data at the worksheet level, workbook level, and file level. At the worksheet level, you protect cells. At the workbook level, you protect the Excel window. Both of these levels of protection are available through the Protection command on the Tools menu as described in Project 7. The highest level of protection is file protection. **File protection** lets you assign a password to a workbook for users who are allowed to view the workbook and a separate password for users who are permitted to modify the workbook.

File protection is performed when Excel saves a workbook. Even though you are the workbook creator, you will be prompted for the passwords when you open the workbook later. The following steps save the workbook with passwords.

Steps To Save the Workbook with Passwords

① **Click the Track Team tab at the bottom of the window. Click File on the menu bar and then click Save As. Type** Menu Planning2 **in the File name text box and, if necessary, select 3½ Floppy (A:) in the Save in list. Click the Tools button on the Save As dialog box toolbar and then point to General Options.**

The Save As dialog box and Tools button menu display (Figure 8-34).

FIGURE 8-34

② **Click General Options. Type** cafeteria **in the Password to open text box. Type** cafeteria **in the Password to modify text box. Point to the OK button.**

The Save Options dialog box displays. Excel displays asterisks in the place of the password cafeteria in both text boxes so no one is able to see the password you typed (Figure 8-35).

FIGURE 8-35

3 **Click the OK button and then type** cafeteria **in the Reenter password to proceed text box. Point to the OK button.**

The Confirm Password dialog box displays. Again, Excel displays asterisks in the place of the password cafeteria (Figure 8-36).

FIGURE 8-36

4 **Click the OK button and type** cafeteria **in the Reenter password to modify text box. Point to the OK button.**

The Confirm Password dialog box displays for the password to modify the workbook (Figure 8-37).

FIGURE 8-37

5 **Click the OK button and then point to the Save button in the Save As dialog box.**

The Save As dialog box displays (Figure 8-38).

6 **Click the Save button.**

Excel saves the password protected file to drive A.

FIGURE 8-38

1. With Save As dialog box open, press ALT+L, press G

The workbook now is protected with a password and when a user opens the workbook, Excel will prompt for a password to view the workbook. If the user enters the correct password, Excel prompts for the password to modify the workbook. At this point, the user may choose to open the workbook as read-only, meaning that the user can only view the contents of the workbook and not modify the workbook. The **Read-only recommended check box** shown in Figure 8-35 on page E 8.33 allows you to notify users who open your workbook that it is best to open the workbook as read-only.

Using Scenario Manager to Analyze Data

Excel's **Scenario Manager** allows you to record and save different sets of what-if assumptions (data values) called scenarios. For example, each different main entrée (beef and chicken) can be considered a scenario. A meal containing beef and meeting the other constraints is the first scenario. The second scenario consists of a meal that contains chicken, which has different amounts of fat and carbohydrates and different costs. Each set of values in these examples represents a what-if assumption. The primary uses of Scenario Manager are to:

1. Create different scenarios with multiple sets of changing cells
2. Build summary worksheets that contain the different scenarios
3. View the results of each scenario on your worksheet

The remainder of this project shows how to use Scenario Manager for each of the three uses listed above. Once you create the scenarios, you can instruct Excel to build the summary worksheets, including a Scenario Summary and a Scenario PivotTable.

Saving the Current Data as a Scenario

The current data on the worksheet consists of the Beef scenario and contains the values that correctly solve one of the problems presented. These values can be saved as a scenario that can be accessed later or compared side by side with other scenarios. The steps on the next page create the Beef scenario using the **Scenarios command** on the Tools menu.

More About

Read-Only Workbooks

You can save a file and recommend read-only access to others who open the worksheet. This is not a guarantee, however, that the user will follow the recommendation. To ensure that the worksheet truly is read-only, you must use a file password and keep the password to yourself.

More About

Scenario Manager

Worksheets are used primarily for what-if analysis. You enter values into cells and instantaneously the results change in the dependent cells. As you continue to change values in the key cells, you lose the previous results. If you want to go back, you have to reenter the data. Scenario Manager allows you to store the different sets of values (called scenarios) so you can redisplay them easily with a few clicks of the mouse button. Each scenario can have up to 32 sets of changing cells.

Steps: To Save the Current Data as a Scenario

1 Click **Tools** on the menu bar and point to **Scenarios**.

The Tools menu displays (Figure 8-39).

FIGURE 8-39

2 Click **Scenarios**. When the **Scenario Manager** dialog box displays, point to the **Add** button.

The Scenario Manager dialog box displays indicating that no scenarios are defined (Figure 8-40). It also instructs you to choose Add to add scenarios.

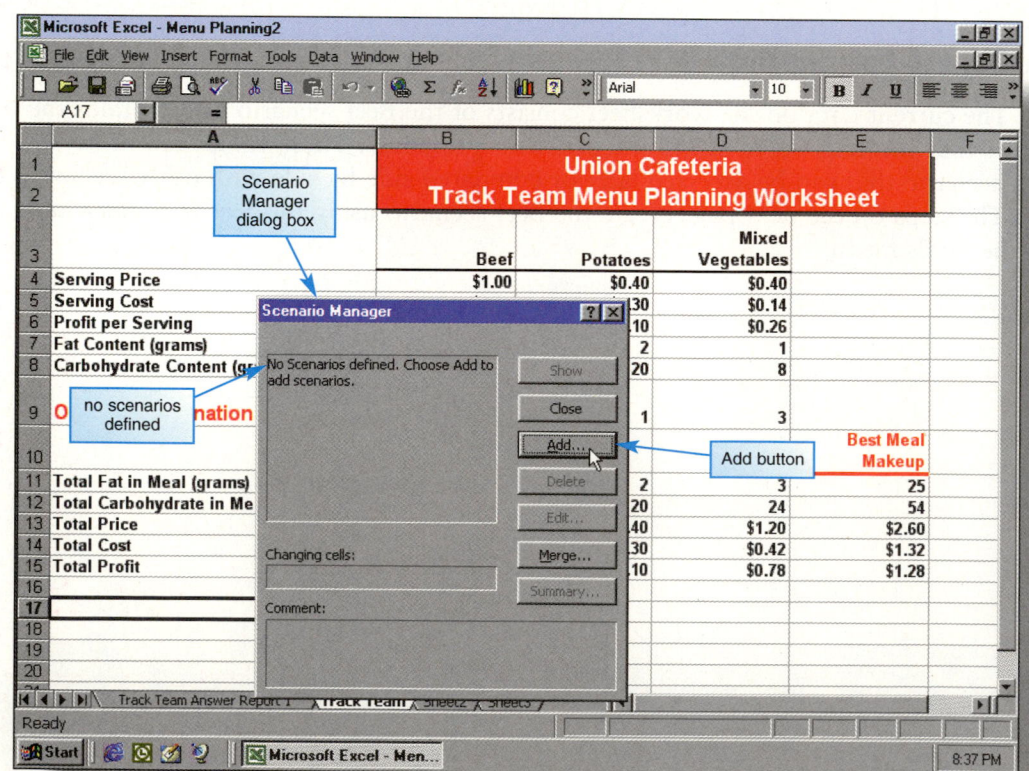

FIGURE 8-40

3 Click the Add button. When the Add Scenario dialog box displays, type Beef in the Scenario name text box. Point to the Collapse Dialog button.

The *Add Scenario dialog box displays (Figure 8-41).*

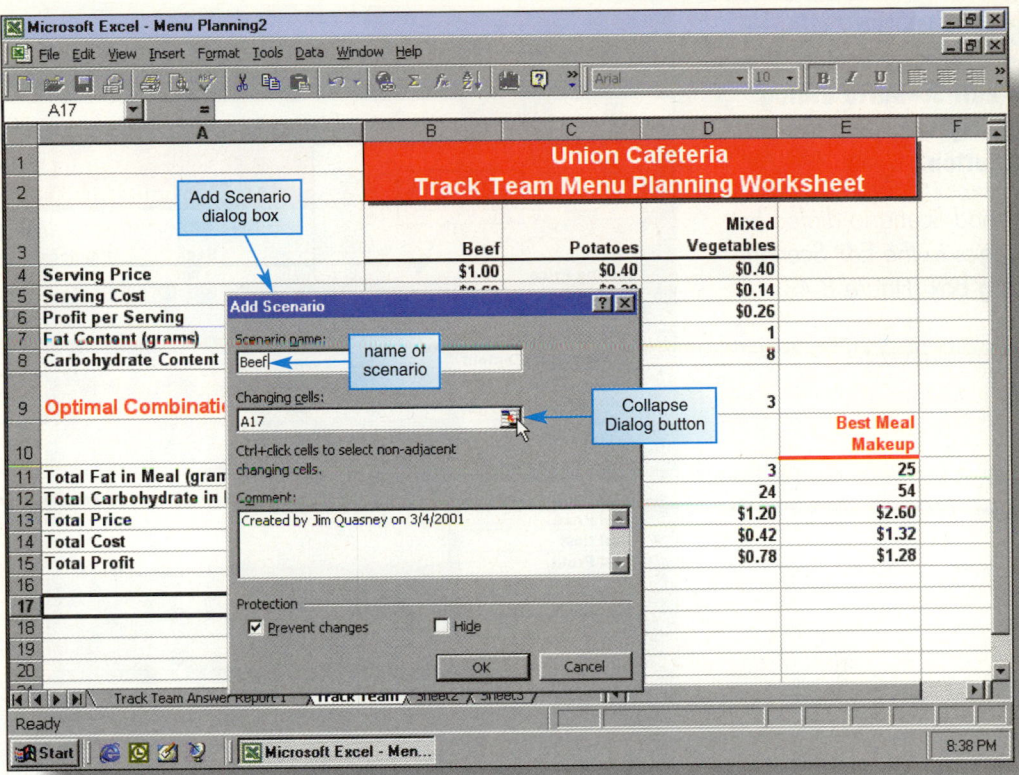

FIGURE 8-41

4 Click the Collapse Dialog button. When the Add Scenario – Changing cells dialog box displays, click cell B3, hold down the CTRL key, and then click cells B4, B5, B7, B8, B9, C9, and D9. Release the CTRL key. Point to the Collapse Dialog button in the Add Scenario - Changing cells dialog box.

A marquee displays around the selected cells. Excel assigns the cells to the Changing cells text box (Figure 8-42).

FIGURE 8-42

5 **Click the Collapse Dialog button. When the Edit Scenario dialog box displays, point to the OK button.**

The Add Scenario dialog box changes to the *Edit Scenario dialog box* (Figure 8-43).

FIGURE 8-43

6 **Click the OK button. When the Scenario Values dialog box displays, point to the OK button.**

The *Scenario Values dialog box* displays. The cell names selected display in a numbered list with their current values (Figure 8-44). Because names were assigned to these cells when the worksheet was created, the cell names, rather than cell references, display in the numbered list.

FIGURE 8-44

7 **Click the OK button. When the Scenario Manager dialog box displays, point to the Close button.**

The Beef scenario displays in the Scenario list (Figure 8-45). Excel displays the names of the Changing cells in the Changing cells box.

8 **Click the Close button in the Scenario Manager dialog box.**

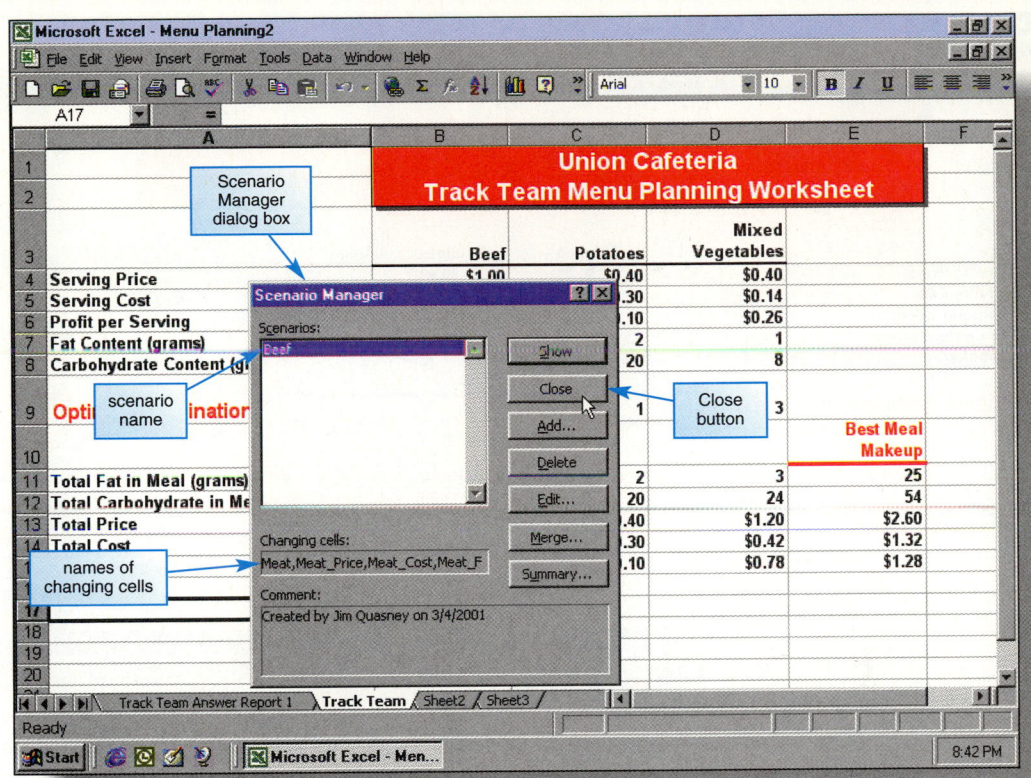

FIGURE 8-45

Once the scenario has been saved, you can recall it at any time using Scenario Manager. In Figure 8-44, the values of the cells in the Scenario Values dialog box are defaulted to the current changing cells in the worksheet. By changing the text boxes next to the cell names, you can save different values in the scenario from what is shown in the worksheet.

The next step is to change the values on the worksheet to show the data when using a chicken dish as the main entrée.

Creating a New Scenario

Because the Beef scenario is saved, you can enter the data for the Chicken scenario directly in the worksheet and then use Solver to solve the Chicken scenario (Figure 8-46a on the next page) in the same way that you solved the Beef scenario. The same constraints apply for both scenarios, so Solver does not require you to reenter all of the constraints. The Answer Report (Figure 8-46b on the next page) meets the requirement that you create supporting documentation for your answer. After solving the Chicken scenario, you save the scenario in the same manner that you saved the Beef scenario.

1. Press ALT+T, press E

More About 2000

New Scenarios

When beginning to create scenarios in a worksheet, the following guidelines help in organizing the data. First, create a base scenario that contains the original values of the worksheet. Second, name the cells that will be changing cells and result cells, as has been done in the worksheet in this project. Finally, if you plan to save different types of scenarios in a worksheet (that is different changing cells), use a naming convention for the scenarios that will help you remember which scenarios contain which set of changing cells.

(a) Result of Using Solver with Chicken as Main Entrée

(b) Solver Answer Report with Chicken as Main Entrée

FIGURE 8-46

The relevant information for the Chicken scenario (Figure 8-46a) is that the serving price is 80 cents per serving, the serving cost is 55 cents per serving, the fat content of one serving is 10 grams, and the carbohydrate content is 20 grams per serving. These values must be entered into the appropriate cells before you can use Solver.

Steps **To Add the Data for a New Scenario**

1 **Click cell B3 and type** Chicken **as the column heading. Click cell B4 and type** .80 **as the serving price. Click cell B5 and type** .55 **as the serving cost. Click cell B7 and type** 10 **as the fat content in grams. Click cell B8, type** 20 **as the carbohydrate content in grams, and then press the ENTER key.**

The menu planning worksheet displays with the chicken entrée replacing the beef entrée (Figure 8-47).

FIGURE 8-47

Next, Solver must be used to find the optimal combination of servings that satisfies the constraints and maximizes profit for the Union Cafeteria.

Using Solver to Find a New Solution

Just as with the Beef scenario, the Chicken scenario must be solved before saving it as a scenario. Figure 8-47 shows that the total fat and total carbohydrate content of the current solution satisfies the requirements of less than or equal to 25 grams of fat, and at least 40 grams of carbohydrates. It is unknown, however, whether the solution maximizes the total profit. Solver takes this requirement into consideration.

To Use Solver to Find a New Solution

1 Click Tools on the menu bar and then point to Solver (Figure 8-48).

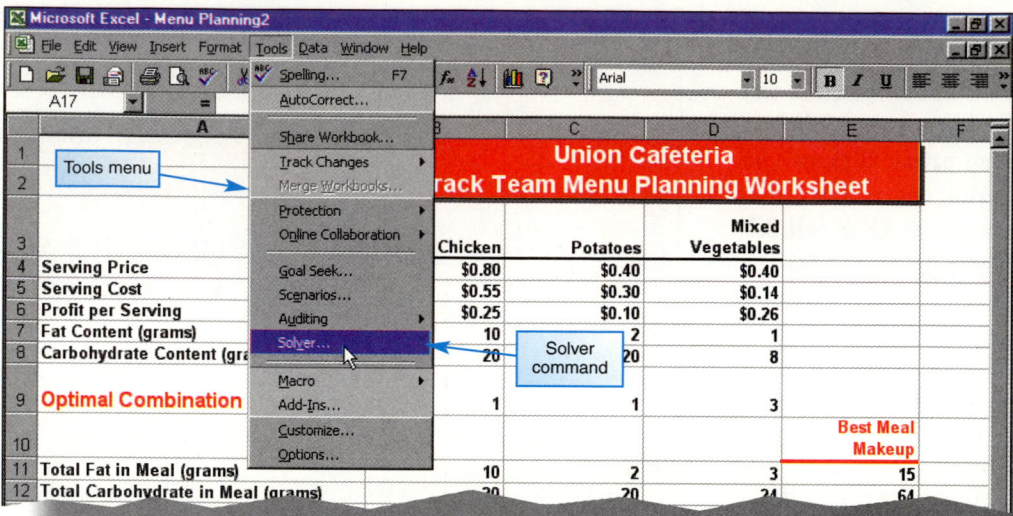

FIGURE 8-48

2 Click Solver. When the Solver Parameters dialog box displays, point to the Solve button.

The Solver Parameters dialog box displays with the previous target cell and constraints (Figure 8-49). Because the constraints remain the same for chicken as they were for beef, no additional entries are required in the Solver Parameters dialog box.

FIGURE 8-49

3 Click the Solve button. When the Solver Results dialog box displays, click Answer in the Reports list. Point to the OK button.

The Solver Results dialog box displays indicating that Solver found a solution to the problem (Figure 8-50).

FIGURE 8-50

④ Click the OK button.

The solution displays in the worksheet. The constraints have been satisfied (Figure 8-51).

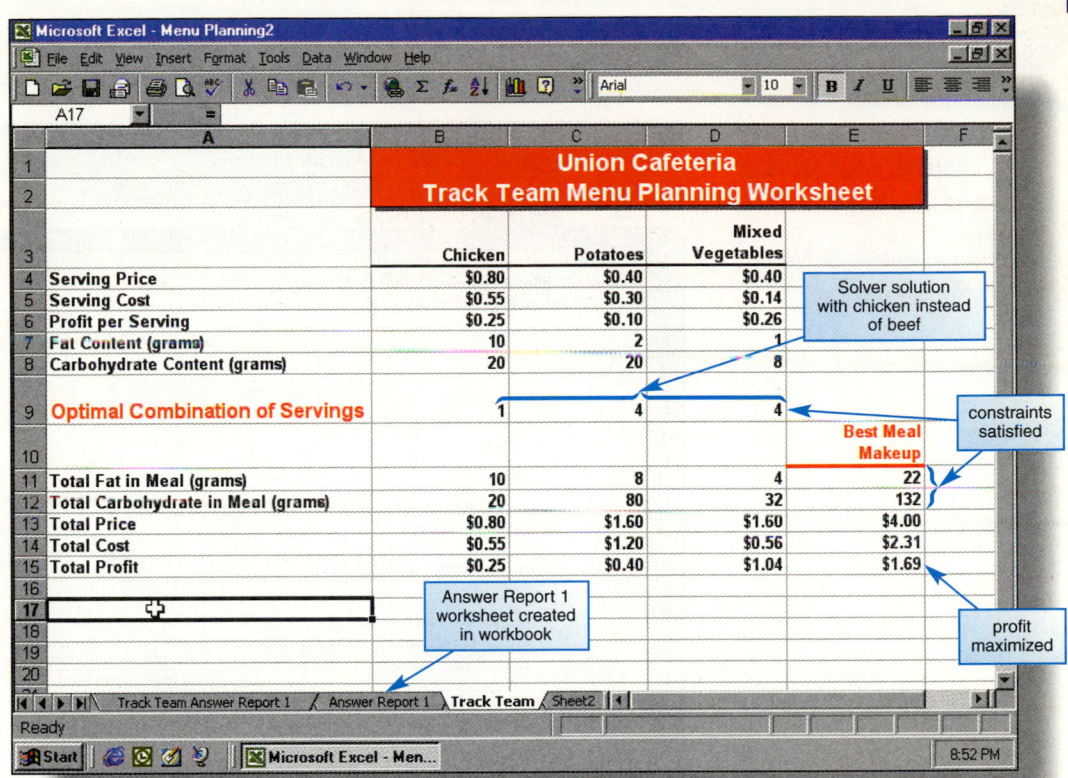

FIGURE 8-51

As shown in Figure 8-51, Solver found a solution that satisfies all of the constraints and maximizes profit. With the beef entrée, the servings breakdown was one serving of beef, one serving of potatoes, and three servings of mixed vegetables (Figure 8-31 on page E 8.29). With the chicken entrée, the servings breakdown is one serving of chicken, four servings of potatoes, and four servings of mixed vegetables (Figure 8-51). The profit for the beef entrée was $1.28. The profit for the chicken entrée is $1.69.

The next step is to view the Answer Report for the chicken entrée solution that will be presented to the track team coach.

Other Ways

1. Press ALT+T, press V
2. Press ALT+S

More About 2000

Quick Reference

For a table that lists how to complete the tasks covered in this book using the mouse, menu, shortcut menu, and keyboard, see the Excel Quick Reference Summary at the back of this book or visit the Office 2000 Web page (www.scsite.com/off2000/qr.htm), and then click Microsoft Excel 2000.

Steps: To View the Second Answer Report

1
Click the Answer Report 1 tab at the bottom of the window.

The chicken entrée Solver Answer Report displays (Figure 8-52).

FIGURE 8-52

2
Double-click the Answer Report 1 tab and then type Track Team Answer Report 2 **as the worksheet name. Use the scroll bar to scroll down to view the remaining cells of the chicken entrée Answer Report.**

The worksheet is renamed and the remainder of the Answer Report for the chicken entrée displays (Figure 8-53).

FIGURE 8-53

The Answer Report indicates that the meal has three fewer grams of fat than the maximum allowed, and 92 more grams of carbohydrates than the minimum allowed. The meal is low in fat and high in carbohydrates, which is what the track team coach wanted. Furthermore, the profit on the chicken meal is far better than that of the beef meal.

The next step is to save the chicken entrée solution as a scenario so that it can be referenced in the future.

Saving the Second Solver Solution as a Scenario

The power of Scenario Manager becomes evident when you begin adding additional scenarios to your worksheet. Multiple scenarios can be compared side by side. Using multiple scenarios on the same worksheet also saves time by recycling the work that you did to create the initial worksheet.

To Save the Second Solver Solution as a Scenario

1 **Click the Track Team tab at the bottom of the window. Click Tools on the menu bar and then point to Scenarios (Figure 8-54).**

FIGURE 8-54

2 **Click Scenarios. When the Scenario Manager dialog box displays, point to the Add button (Figure 8-55).**

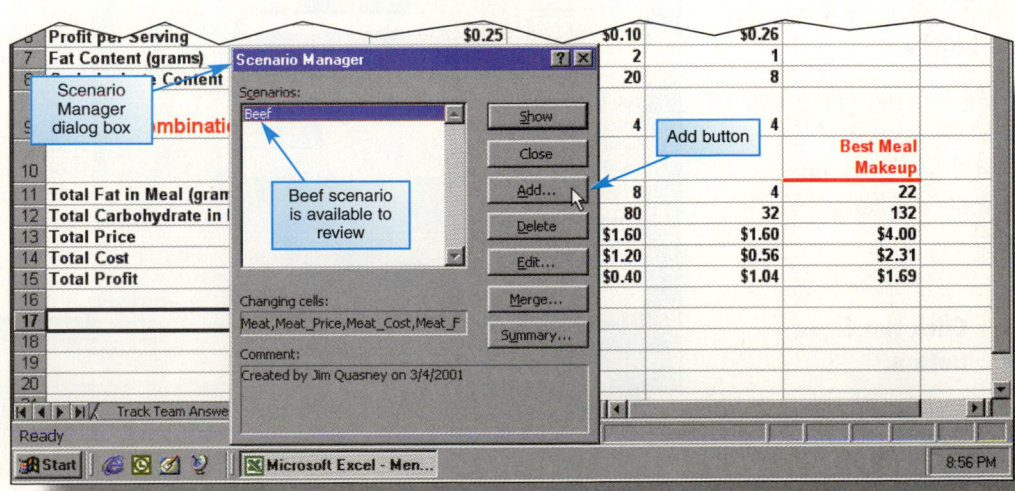

FIGURE 8-55

3 **Click the Add button. Type** Chicken **in the Scenario name text box and then point to the OK button.**

The Add Scenario dialog box displays. The Changing cells box defaults to the previous values used in the Beef scenario (Figure 8-56).

FIGURE 8-56

4 **Click the OK button. When the Scenario Values dialog box displays, point to the OK button.**

The Scenario Values dialog box displays with the values from the worksheet (Figure 8-57).

FIGURE 8-57

5 **Click the OK button. When the Scenario Manager dialog box displays, point to the Close button.**

Chicken displays along with Beef in the Scenarios list (Figure 8-58). Each name represents a different scenario.

6 **Click the Close button.**

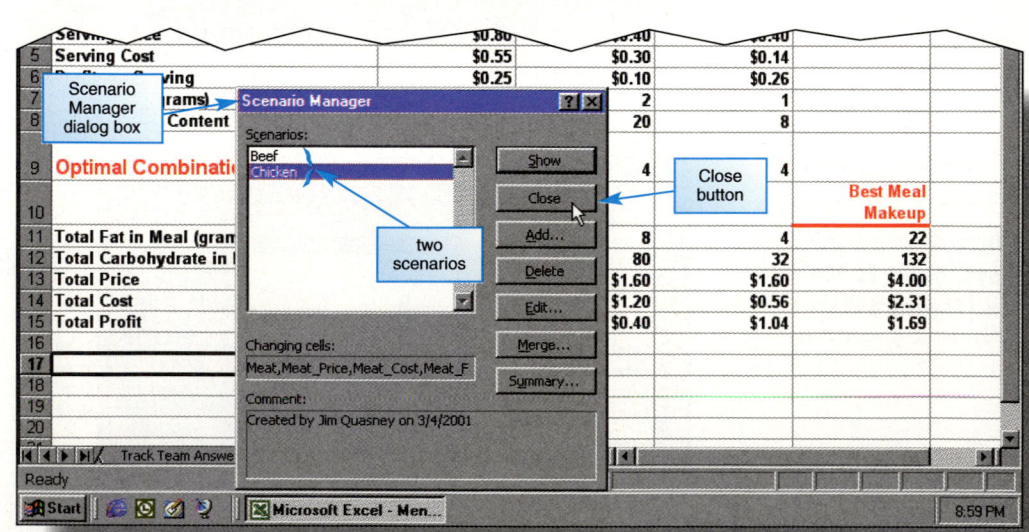

FIGURE 8-58

The Chicken scenario now can be recalled using Scenario Manager. Figure 8-57 shows the list of changing cells for the scenario. Instead of entering the data in the worksheet, you simply could enter values here for adding new scenarios. Because Solver is needed to find a solution to the scenario, however, the values were entered on the worksheet first.

The next step is to use Scenario Manager to show the Beef scenario in the worksheet.

Showing a Scenario

Once a scenario is saved, you use the **Show button** in the Scenario Manager dialog box to display the scenario. The following steps show you how to apply the Beef scenario created earlier directly to a worksheet.

More About

Showing Scenarios

You can add a list of scenarios to your toolbar by using the Customize command on the Toolbars submenu of the View menu. Click the Commands tab and select Tools. Drag the Scenario command with the drop-down arrow up to the toolbar. You then can quickly switch between scenarios on the worksheet.

 ## To Show a Saved Scenario

1 Click Tools on the menu bar and then point to Scenarios (Figure 8-59).

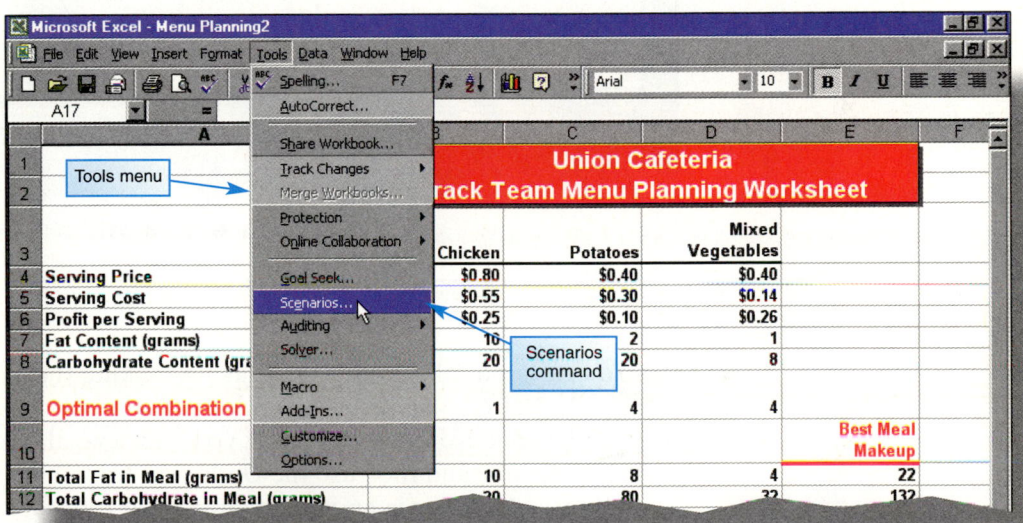

FIGURE 8-59

2 Click Scenarios. When the Scenario Manager dialog box displays, if necessary, select Beef in the Scenarios list and then point to the Show button (Figure 8-60).

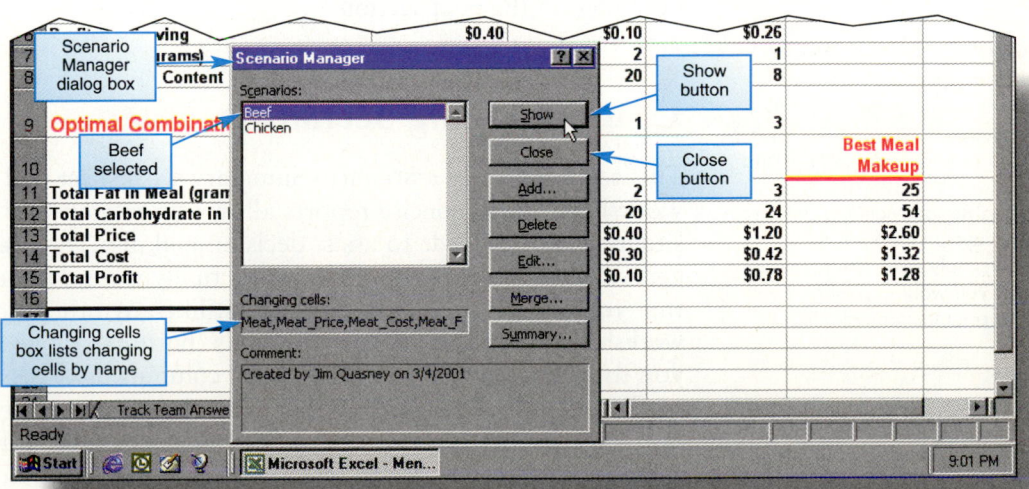

FIGURE 8-60

3 **Click the Show button and then click the Close button.**

Excel displays the data in the worksheet for the Beef scenario (Figure 8-61).

	A	B	C	D	E	F
			Union Cafeteria			
1			**Track Team Menu Planning Worksheet**			
2						
3		**Beef**	**Potatoes**	**Mixed Vegetables**		
4	**Serving Price**	$1.00	$0.40	$0.40		
5	**Serving Cost**	$0.60	$0.30	$0.14		
6	**Profit per Serving**	$0.40	$0.10	$0.26		
7	**Fat Content (grams)**	20	2	1		
8	**Carbohydrate Content (grams)**	10	20	8		
9	**Optimal Combination of Servings**	1	1	3		
10					**Best Meal Makeup**	
11	**Total Fat in Meal (grams)**	20	2	3	25	
12	**Total Carbohydrate in Meal (grams)**	10	20	24	54	
13	**Total Price**	$1.00	$0.40	$1.20	$2.60	
14	**Total Cost**	$0.60	$0.30	$0.42	$1.32	
15	**Total Profit**	$0.40	$0.10	$0.78	$1.28	

FIGURE 8-61

You can undo the scenario results by clicking the Undo button on the Standard toolbar. If desired, you then can click the Redo button on the Standard toolbar to display the scenario results again. If you had several saved scenarios, you could display each one and then use the Undo and Redo buttons to switch between them.

Scenario Manager is an important what-if tool for organizing assumptions. Using Scenario Manager, you can define different scenarios with up to 32 changing cells per scenario. Once you have entered the scenarios, you can show them one by one or you can create a Scenario Summary worksheet or a Scenario PivotTable worksheet as described in the next section.

Summarizing Scenarios

This section creates a Scenario Summary worksheet and a Scenario PivotTable worksheet. These concise reports allow you to view and manipulate several what-if situations side by side to assist decision making. The **Scenario Summary worksheet** generated by the Scenario Manager actually is an outlined worksheet (Figure 8-62a) that you can print and manipulate just like any other worksheet. An **outlined worksheet** is one that contains symbols (buttons) above and to the left, which allows you to collapse and expand rows and columns.

The **PivotTable worksheet** (Figure 8-62b) generated by the Scenario Manager also is a worksheet that you can print and manipulate like other worksheets. A **PivotTable** is a table that summarizes large amounts of information and can be manipulated to show the data from different points of view. The Scenario PivotTable compares the results of scenarios.

More *About* 2000

Report Manager

Report Manager is an Add-in that allows you to print several scenarios at once. Typically, you would need to use the Show button in the Scenario Manager dialog box for each scenario you want to print and then print the worksheet. By using Report Manager, which displays on the View menu, you simply select the scenarios that you want to print and you can print them all at once.

(b) Scenario PivotTable Worksheet

(a) Scenario Summary Worksheet

FIGURE 8-62

Creating a Scenario Summary Worksheet

The Scenario Summary worksheet in Figure 8-62a displays the total fat, total carbohydrates, total price, total cost, and total profit for the current worksheet values and the two scenarios. The optimal serving sizes calculated by Solver are shown for meals that include either beef or chicken as the main entrée.

Microsoft **Excel 2000**

To Create a Scenario Summary

1 Click Tools on the menu bar and then point to Scenarios (Figure 8-63).

FIGURE 8-63

2 Click Scenarios. When the Scenario Manager dialog box displays, point to the Summary button.

The Scenario Manager dialog box displays (Figure 8-64).

FIGURE 8-64

3 Click the Summary button. When the Scenario Summary dialog box displays, point to the OK button.

The Scenario Summary dialog box displays (Figure 8-65). The Scenario summary option button is selected in the Report type area. The dialog box offers the choice of creating a Scenario summary or a Scenario PivotTable.

FIGURE 8-65

4 **Click the OK button.
When the Scenario
Summary displays, double-
click the Scenario Summary
tab and then type** Track
Team Scenario Summary
as the worksheet name.

*The Scenario Summary work-
sheet displays as shown in
Figure 8-66.*

FIGURE 8-66

Column D in the Scenario Summary worksheet in Figure 8-66 shows the results
of the current values in the Menu Planning2 worksheet, which is the Beef scenario;
columns E and F show the results of the two scenarios. The Scenario Summary
worksheet makes it easier to compare the results of the scenarios. For example, in
the Beef scenario, even though fewer portions are served, the profit is less than the
Chicken scenario because the cost of one serving of beef is higher than that of
chicken. Subsequently, the Union Cafeteria stands to make a better profit if the track
team chooses more chicken meals than beef meals. Perhaps this indicates how the
Union Cafeteria should go about marketing its meals to the track team.

In the Chicken scenario, the cost of the meal is much higher than that of the Beef
scenario. Even though the price of a serving of chicken is less than that of beef, more
servings of chicken are required to meet the nutritional requirements.

Working with an Outlined Worksheet

Excel automatically outlines the Scenario Summary worksheet. The outline symbols display above and to the left of the worksheet (Figure 8-66). You click the outline symbols to expand or collapse the worksheet. For example, if you click the **show
detail symbol**, Excel displays additional rows or columns that are summarized on the
displayed row or column. If you click a **hide detail symbol**, Excel hides any detail
rows that extend through the length of the corresponding row level bar or column
level bar. You also can expand or collapse a worksheet by clicking the **row level
symbol** or **column level symbol** above and to the left of row title 1.

An outline is especially useful when working with large worksheets. To remove
an outline, point to Group and Outline on the Data Menu and then click Clear
Outline on the Group and Outline submenu.

More About 2000

Scenario PivotTables

A Scenario PivotTables is a powerful analysis tool for comparing the results of scenarios when the differences and causes of the differences among scenarios are not completely obvious. You can compare scenarios side by side, perform sorts and filters on the values of the result cells, and rotate rows and columns of the table to gain a different perspective on the results.

Creating a Scenario PivotTable

Excel also provides the Scenario PivotTable tool to help analyze and compare the results of multiple scenarios. A **Scenario PivotTable** gives you the ability to summarize the scenario data and then rotate the table's row and column titles to obtain different views of the summarized data. The PivotTable to be created in this project is shown in Figure 8-62b on page E 8.49. The table summarizes the Beef and Chicken scenarios and displays the result cells for the two scenarios for easy comparison.

PivotTables are powerful data analysis tools because they allow you to view the data in various ways by interchanging or pairing up the row and column fields by dragging the buttons located above cells A1, A4, and B3 in Figure 8-62b. The process of rotating the field values around the data fields will be discussed in the next project.

To create the PivotTable shown in Figure 8-62b, perform the following steps.

 Steps To Create a Scenario PivotTable

1 Click the Track Team tab at the bottom of the window. Click Tools on the menu bar and then click Scenarios. When the Scenario Manager dialog box displays, point to the Summary button.

The Scenario Manager dialog box displays (Figure 8-67).

FIGURE 8-67

2 Click the Summary button. When the Scenario Summary dialog box displays, click Scenario PivotTable. Point to the OK button.

The Scenario Summary dialog box displays as shown in Figure 8-68. The range E11:E15 displays in the Result cells box from the previous time this dialog box displayed.

FIGURE 8-68

3 **Click the OK button.**

The Scenario PivotTable worksheet displays with the cell names of the changing values in column A (Figure 8-69). At this point the report appears useless. **Note:** *Your worksheet may display differently. You may not have to resize the column width in Step 4.*

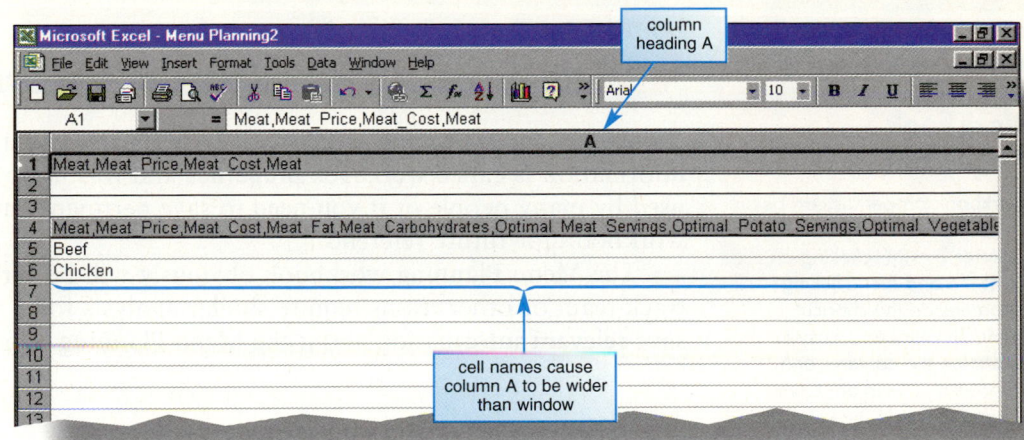

FIGURE 8-69

4 **Right-click column heading A. When the shortcut menu displays, click Column Width. When the Column Width dialog box displays, type 35 in the Column width text box. Click the OK button. Double-click the Scenario PivotTable tab and then type** Track Team Scenario PivotTable **as the worksheet name. Click cell A8.**

The Scenario PivotTable displays within the viewable area of the worksheet. The result cells of the two scenarios display in rows 5 and 6 as shown in Figure 8-70.

FIGURE 8-70

5 **Click the Save button on the Standard toolbar to save the workbook using the file name Menu Planning2.**

Once the PivotTable is created, you can treat it like any other worksheet. Thus, you can print or chart a PivotTable. If you update the data in one of the scenarios, click the **Refresh Data command** on the Data menu. If you show a scenario and change values on the scenario worksheet, that is not the same as changing the scenario. If you want to change the data in a scenario, you must use Scenario Manager.

Other Ways

1. Press ALT+T, press E

More *About*

Workbook Properties

Workbook properties can be viewed from Windows Explorer by right-clicking an Excel file and then clicking Properties on the shortcut menu. This makes it easy to determine the contents and purpose of a workbook without opening it. If the user has the View as Web Page option button selected in Windows Explorer, then the user can see a preview of the workbook if the Save preview picture option button is selected in the Summary sheet.

Changing the Properties on a Workbook

Excel allows you to store a variety of information about each workbook. This information is called **workbook properties** and it is useful when workbooks will be used by many people or if you need to save pertinent data about the purpose of the workbook for future reference.

The Menu Planning workbook obviously will be very useful in the future if the track team or other teams require similar analysis for a meal. The following steps save relevant information about the Menu Planning workbook for future reference.

Steps **To Change Workbook Properties**

1 **Click the Track Team tab at the bottom of the window. Click File on the menu bar and then point to Properties (Figure 8-71).**

FIGURE 8-71

2 **Click Properties. When the Menu Planning2 Properties dialog box displays, click the Summary tab. Type** Track Team Menu Planning **in the Title text box. Type** March 2001 Goals **in the Subject text box. Type** Maxine Hill **in the Manager text box. In the Comments text box, type** Planning meal for March 4, 2001. Goals met with chicken and beef. **Point to the OK button.**

The summary fields display in the Menu Planning2 Properties dialog box as shown in Figure 8-72.

FIGURE 8-72

3 **Click the OK button.**

4 **Click the Save button on the Standard toolbar to save the workbook using the file name Menu Planning2.**

The **Workbook Properties dialog box** contains other useful information about the workbook. Then **General tab** displays data about the workbook file, including the size of the file, creation date, date modified, and the date the file was last accessed. The **Save preview picture check box** selected on the **Summary tab** saves an image of the current worksheet that will be visible in the Open dialog box when the file is selected by the user. The **Statistics tab** displays some of the file data from the General tab in addition to a record of when the file was last opened and modified.

The **Contents tab** displays a list of all the worksheets and charts contained in the workbook. This feature allows you to search large workbooks quickly that contain many worksheets and charts when you are looking for a particular worksheet or chart.

The **Custom tab** allows you to create your own workbook properties. For example, you can add fields such as document number, editor, your telephone number, division, group, owner, or any other field you want to store with the workbook. For each item you define, you can set the data type for the value. Valid data types are Text, Date, Number, and Yes or No.

Other Ways

1. Press ALT+F, press I

More About

Custom Properties

You can set up custom properties that link to cells in your workbook in addition to using text fields. For example, you can have a property that contains the value in the total profit cell in the Track Team worksheet.

Quitting Excel

The project is complete. To quit Excel, follow the steps below.

TO QUIT EXCEL

1 Click the Close button on the right side of the title bar.

2 If the Microsoft Excel dialog box displays, click the No button.

CASE PERSPECTIVE SUMMARY

With the two solved scenarios developed in this project, Maxine Hill confidently can take the results to the track team to illustrate that nutritional requirements have been satisfied. She also has the confidence that the Union Cafeteria is maximizing its profit when delivering what the customer wants. The worksheet can be used in the future to develop meals for other teams.

Project Summary

In this project, you learned how to use a number of techniques to approach problem solving, including trial and error, goal seek, and Solver. You learned how to analyze a worksheet using the Auditing toolbar. You learned how to use data validation on cells and inform the user about the validation rules. Using Scenario Manager, you learned how to manage different problems on the same worksheet and then summarize the results of the scenarios with a Scenario Summary and a Scenario PivotTable. Finally, you learned how to save a workbook file with passwords and modify the properties of a workbook.

What You Should Know

Having completed this project, you now should be able to perform the following tasks:

▶ Add Data Validation *(E 8.16)*

▶ Add the Data for a New Scenario *(E 8.41)*

▶ Change Workbook Properties *(E 8.54)*

▶ Create a Scenario PivotTable *(E 8.52)*

▶ Create a Scenario Summary *(E 8.50)*

▶ Display the Auditing Toolbar *(E 8.10)*

▶ Quit Excel *(E 8.56)*

▶ Remove the Trace Dependent Arrows *(E 8.14)*

▶ Remove the Trace Precedent Arrows *(E 8.12)*

▶ Save the Second Solver Solution as a Scenario *(E 8.45)*

▶ Save the Current Data as a Scenario *(E 8.36)*

▶ Save the Workbook with Passwords *(E 8.33)*

▶ Show a Saved Scenario *(E 8.47)*

▶ Start Excel and Open a Workbook *(E 8.8)*

▶ Trace Dependents *(E 8.13)*

▶ Trace Precedents *(E 8.11)*

▶ Use Solver to Find the Optimal Combination *(E 8.25)*

▶ Use Solver to Find a New Solution *(E 8.42)*

▶ Use the Goal Seek Command to Attempt to Solve a Complex Problem *(E 8.21)*

▶ Use Trial and Error to Attempt to Solve a Complex Problem *(E 8.19)*

▶ View the Second Answer Report *(E 8.44)*

▶ View the Answer Report *(E 8.31)*

More About 2000

Microsoft Certification

The Microsoft Office User Specialist (MOUS) Certification program provides an opportunity for you to obtain a valuable industry credential - proof that you have the Excel 2000 skills required by employers. For more information, see Appendix D or visit the Shelly Cashman Series MOUS Web page at www. scsite.com/off2000/cert.htm.

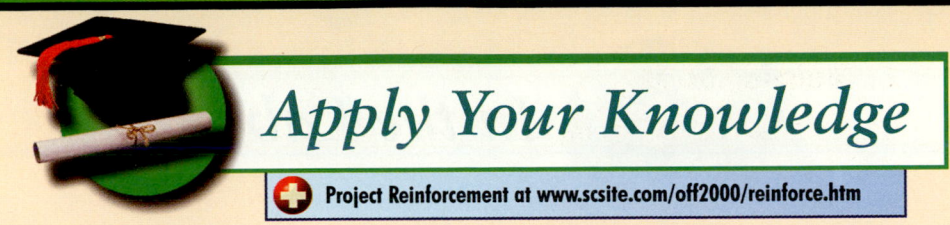

Apply Your Knowledge

✚ Project Reinforcement at www.scsite.com/off2000/reinforce.htm

1 Determining the Optimal Product Mix for a Truck Shipment

Instructions: Andreakis College Supply, Inc. ships truckloads of products to campuses for sale to local distributors. Follow the steps below to use trial and error, and then Solver to find the optimal product mix that should be shipped in a truck of 2,000 cubic feet based on the current product costs and prices. The products available for shipment include computers, stereos, and dorm-sized refrigerators. The company must ship at least 15 computers, 20 stereos, and 35 refrigerators with each shipment.

	Computers	Stereos	Dorm Sized Refrigerators	Shipment Totals
Andreakis College Supply Shipment Planning Worksheet				
Item Sales Price	1,000.00	350.00	200.00	
Item Cost	800.00	235.00	175.00	
Profit per Item	200.00	115.00	25.00	
Cubic Feet per Item	18	8	24	
Optimal Number of Items to Ship	16	109	35	
Total Cost	12,800.00	25,615.00	6,125.00	44,540.00
Total Profit	3,200.00	12,535.00	875.00	16,610.00
Total Cubic Feet	288	872	840	2000

FIGURE 8-73

1. Open the workbook Andreakis College Supply from the Data Disk. If you do not have a copy of the Data Disk, see the inside back cover of this book.
2. Enter your name, course, laboratory assignment number (Apply 8-1), date, and instructor name in the range A15:A19.
3. Using trial and error, enter values in cells B8, C8, and D8 to try to solve the problem.
4. Use Solver to find a solution to the problem so that the profit on the shipment is maximized. Allow Solver to change cells B8, C8, and D8. The total cubic feet of the items should not exceed 2,000 cubic feet. The results in B8, C8, and D8 should be integer values. Also, use the Assume Linear Model option in Solver.
5. Instruct Solver to create the Answer Report for your solution. Solver should find the answer as shown in Figure 8-73.
6. Go into the workbook properties and enter a title for the workbook of Andreakis College Supply Shipping Workbook. Enter your name in the Author field and your instructor's name in the Manager field.
7. Print the worksheet and the Answer Report 1 worksheet. Hand in the two printouts to your instructor.

In the Lab

1 Gaining Confidence in the Shocking Sound International Worksheet

Problem: You have been given the task of taking over the job of another employee who has retired. Your first task is to learn about some of the Excel workbooks for which you now are responsible.

Instructions: Start Excel and perform the following tasks.

1. Open the Shocking Sound International workbook from the Data Disk. If you do not have a copy of the Data Disk, then see the inside back cover of this book.

2. Display the Auditing toolbar. Trace two levels of precedents for cell E12. Trace one level of the precedents for cell D12. Trace one level of the dependents for cell B4. The worksheet should display as shown in Figure 8-74.

FIGURE 8-74

3. Enter your name, course, laboratory assignment number (Lab 8-1), date, and instructor's name in the range B15:B19. Print the worksheet.

4. Remove all trace arrows. Enter the value of zero in cell B6.

5. Use the Trace Error button on the Auditing toolbar to trace the error in cell E12. Use the Trace Error button to trace the error in cell E11. Print the worksheet.

6. Select the range B4:B8. Open the Data Validation dialog box. Create a validation rule that forces the user to enter a positive whole number in the cells in the selected range. Clear the Ignore blank check box.

7. Click the Error Alert tab and then create an error message with the title `Gross Sales` that contains the message `Enter a positive whole number for Gross Sales`. Click the OK button.

8. Reenter the value of zero in cell B6 and then press the ENTER key to view the error message. Select Retry and then enter 650,000 in cell B6. Print the worksheet. Hand in the three printouts to your instructor.

In the Lab

2 Finding the Optimal Advertising Mix

Problem: Dean and Karen's Pet Shop holds sales each month. The store's owners would like you to maximize the audience that advertisements reach in a variety of media. The owners have identified a local newspaper, a local radio station, and the local cable television station as advertising targets. Each type of media claims to be able to target a certain number of individuals in Dean and Karen's target audience with each advertisement. Each media type has a limit on how many advertisements can be placed each week and the prices vary from month to month (Figure 8-75).

(a) Answer Report

Scenario Summary

	Current Values:	October campaign	November campaign
Changing Cells:			
$B$6	75	75	75
$C$6	150	100	150
$D$6	150	200	150
Result Cells:			
$B$9	7	7	7
$C$9	20	20	20
$D$9	3	3	3
$E$9	30	30	30
$E$10	163500	163500	163500
$E$11	3975	3125	3975

Notes: Current Values column represents values of changing cells at

(b) Scenario Summary

Microsoft Excel 9.0 Answer Report
Worksheet: [Book1]Sheet1
Report Created: 3/18/2001 3:44:19 PM

Target Cell (Max)

Cell	Name	Original Value	Final Value
$E$10	Total people reached	0	155000

Adjustable Cells

Cell	Name	Original Value	Final Value
$B$9	Ads placed Newspaper	0	6
$C$9	Ads placed Radio	0	20
$D$9	Ads placed TV	0	0

Constraints

Cell	Name	Cell Value	Formula	Status	Slack
$E$11	Total Cost	2450	$E$11<=2500	Not Binding	50
$B$9	Ads placed Newspaper	6	$B$9<=7	Not Binding	1
$C$9	Ads placed Radio	20	$C$9<=20	Binding	0
$D$9	Ads placed TV	0	$D$9<=10	Not Binding	10
$B$9	Ads placed Newspaper	6	$B$9=integer	Binding	0
$C$9	Ads placed Radio	20	$C$9=integer	Binding	0
$D$9	Ads placed TV	0	$D$9=integer	Binding	0
$B$9	Ads placed Newspaper	6	$B$9>=0	Not Binding	6
$C$9	Ads placed Radio	20	$C$9>=0	Not Binding	20
$D$9	Ads placed TV	0	$D$9>=0	Binding	0

Answer Report 1 / Answer Report 2 / Scenario Summary / Monthly Sale

FIGURE 8-75

(continued)

In the Lab

Finding the Optimal Advertising Mix *(continued)*

Instructions: Start Excel and perform the following tasks.

1. Open the Dean and Karen workbook from the Data Disk.
2. Use Solver to determine the best mix of advertising for the sale in the first week of October. The advertising budget for October is $2,500. The newspaper allows a maximum of seven ads per week, the radio station allows a maximum of twenty advertisement spots per week, and the cable television station allows a maximum of ten advertisements per week. The costs for the month of October are already in the worksheet. Use the Assume Linear Model option in Solver. Instruct Solver to create an Answer Report if it can find a solution to the problem. Figure 8-75a shows the values that Solver should find for this situation.
3. Save the current worksheet as a scenario named `October campaign`. The Changing cells are in the range B6:D6.
4. Enter your name, course, laboratory assignment number (Lab 8-2), date, and instructor's name in the range B15:B19. Print the worksheet and Answer Report.
5. The sale in the week of November is much larger and is allocated a budget of $4,000. Radio advertisements will cost $150 each for that week and cable television advertisements will also cost $150 for that week. The cost of newspaper advertisements remains unchanged.
6. Use Solver to solve to the problem. Instruct Solver to create an Answer Report if it can find a solution to the problem. Solver should find that the optimal combination reaches 163,500 people, and includes seven newspaper advertisements, 20 radio advertisements, and three cable television advertisements.
7. Save the current worksheet as a scenario named `November campaign`. Print the worksheet and Answer Report (Figure 8-75a on the previous page).
8. Create a Scenario Summary (Figure 8-75b on the previous page) showing the two scenarios that you have saved in Scenario Manager. Save the workbook with the password, lab8-2, and with the file name, Dean and Karen2. Print the Scenario Summary.

3 **Finding the Best Production Mix**

Problem: Southern Manufacturing produces four types of file cabinets in its shop. Each type of file cabinet requires a different amount of labor input and a different amount of materials to produce a single cabinet. As the production assistant, it is your job to determine the best mix of file cabinet types to produce based on the amount of available labor and material for a given week (Figure 8-76). The company can produce no more than 15 Cabinet Type 1 and Cabinet Type 3 units in a week. Furthermore, the company must always produce at least 5 Cabinet Type 2 units each week.

Instructions: Start Excel and perform the following tasks.

1. Open the Southern Manufacturing workbook from the Data Disk. If you do not have a copy of the Data Disk, then see the inside back cover of this book.
2. Use Solver to determine the mix of products that maximizes the number of units produced in the week. The total amount of labor hours available in the first week of June is 800, and $3,000 worth of materials are available. Use the Assume Linear Model option in Solver. Instruct Solver to create an Answer Report if it can find a solution to the problem. Figure 8-76a shows the values that Solver should find. If necessary, change the assumptions for the Hours of Labor per Unit in cells B5:E5 to show the values of 17 for Cabinet Type 1, 25 for Cabinet Type 2, 9 for Cabinet Type 3, and 15 for Cabinet Type 4.

In the Lab

(a) Answer Report

(b) Scenario Summary

(b) Scenario Summary

Scenario Summary			
	Current Values:	June, Week 1	June, Week 2
Changing Cells:			
$B$5	17	17	25
$C$5	25	25	25
$D$5	9	9	20
$E$5	15	15	20
$B$6	75	75	75
$C$6	95	95	95
$D$6	45	45	45
$E$6	80	80	80
$B$8	14	14	0
$C$8	5	5	5
$D$8	15	15	15
$E$8	10	10	18
Result Cells:			
$F$8	44	44	38
$F$10	648	648	785
$F$11	3,000	3,000	2,590

(a) Answer Report

Microsoft Excel 9.0 Answer Report
Worksheet: [Southern Manufacturing.xls]Production Planning
Report Created: 3/21/2001 2:06:11 AM

Target Cell (Max)

Cell	Name	Original Value	Final Value
$F$8	Units to Manufacture Totals	0	44

Adjustable Cells

Cell	Name	Original Value	Final Value
$B$8	Units to Manufacture Cabinet Type 1	0	14
$C$8	Units to Manufacture Cabinet Type 2	0	5
$D$8	Units to Manufacture Cabinet Type 3	0	15
$E$8	Units to Manufacture Cabinet Type 4	0	10

Constraints

Cell	Name	Cell Value	Formula	Status	Slack
$F$11	Total Value of Material for the Week Totals	3,000	$F$11<=3000	Binding	0
$F$10	Total Hours for the Week Totals	648	$F$10<=800	Not Binding	152
$B$8	Units to Manufacture Cabinet Type 1	14	$B$8>=0	Not Binding	14
$C$8	Units to Manufacture Cabinet Type 2	5	$C$8>=0	Not Binding	5
$D$8	Units to Manufacture Cabinet Type 3	15	$D$8>=0	Not Binding	15
$E$8	Units to Manufacture Cabinet Type 4	10	$E$8>=0	Not Binding	10
$B$8	Units to Manufacture Cabinet Type 1	14	$B$8=integer	Binding	0
$C$8	Units to Manufacture Cabinet Type 2	5	$C$8=integer	Binding	0
$D$8	Units to Manufacture Cabinet Type 3	15	$D$8=integer	Binding	0
$E$8	Units to Manufacture Cabinet Type 4	10	$E$8=integer	Binding	0
$D$8	Units to Manufacture Cabinet Type 3	15	$D$8<=15	Binding	0
$B$8	Units to Manufacture Cabinet Type 1	14	$B$8<=15	Not Binding	1
$C$8	Units to Manufacture Cabinet Type 2	5	$C$8>=5	Binding	0

FIGURE 8-76

In the Lab

Finding the Best Production Mix *(continued)*

3. Save the current worksheet as a scenario named June, Week 1. The Changing cells are the ranges B5:E6 and B8:E8.

4. Enter your name, course, laboratory assignment number (Lab 8-3), date, and instructor's name in the range B13:B17. Print the worksheet.

5. The production manager feels that perhaps the assumptions about how many labor hours it takes to produce certain products are not correct. The new assumptions are that Cabinet Type 1 takes 25 labor hours to produce, Cabinet Type 2 still takes 25 hours to produce, Cabinet Type 3 takes 20 hours to produce, and Cabinet Type 4 takes 20 hours to produce. Enter these new values in the worksheet.

6. Use Solver to find a solution to the problem. Instruct Solver to create an Answer Report if it can find a solution to the problem. Solver should report that the optimal number of units of Cabinet Type 1 is none, of Cabinet Type 2 is 5, of Cabinet Type 3 is 15, and of Cabinet Type 4 is 18.

7. Save the current worksheet as a scenario named June, Week 2. Print the worksheet and the Answer Report (Figure 8-76a).

8. Create a Scenario Summary (Figure 8-76b) showing the two scenarios that you have saved in Scenario Manager.

9. Save the workbook with the password, lab8-3, and with the file name, Southern Manufacturing2. Print the Scenario Summary worksheet.

Cases and Places

The difficulty of these case studies varies:
▶ are the least difficult; ▶▶ are more difficult; and ▶▶▶ are the most difficult.

1 ▶ Open the workbook Microprocessor Plus on the Data Disk. Use the Auditing toolbar to learn about the worksheet. Trace three levels of precedents for cell H12, the Total Payroll Expense. Print the worksheet with the arrows and hand it in to your instructor. Use Data Validation to limit a user's input on cell B15, the Base Salary, to a decimal value between .15 and .45. Use Data Validation to limit a user's input on cell B17, the Bonus, to a whole number between 5,000 and 25,000. Use Data Validation to allow the worksheet user to select a commission from a list that ranges from 0% to 5% in increments of .5%. Add appropriate input and error messages for the data validation as well. Save the worksheet as Microprocessor Plus2.

2 ▶ Martha Short is planning a sale in her garden shop for a few items. The store has 90 square feet of space available for the items in the sale. Table 8-5 shows the items available for sale, how much they cost Martha to purchase, how much they will be sold for, and how much space each item takes up. The amount that Martha wants to spend on purchases is $375. Martha does not think that she can sell more than 40 gardening tool sets. Create a worksheet with the necessary information and use Solver to determine the most profitable combination of items to purchase for the sale and create an Answer Report. Print the worksheet and Answer Report and hand them in to your instructor.

Table 8-5 Sale Item Information

ITEM NAME	COST	SELLING PRICE	SQUARE FEET
Garden Hose Reel	$7	$15	3
Gardening Tool Set	$6	$12	2

3 ▶ Using a browser search engine, such as AltaVista, type the keywords Linear Programming. Visit three Web pages that discuss how Linear Programming is used in real-world situations to solve business problems. Print each Web page. Hand in the three printouts to your instructor.

(continued)

Cases and Places

4 ▶▶ Open the workbook Microprocessor Plus on the Data Disk. Create four scenarios based on the four different compensation plans outlined in Table 8-6. Create a Scenario Summary that summarizes the result cells of H4, H7, H8, H9, H10, H11, and H12. Print the Scenario Summary worksheet. Hand in the printout to your instructor.

Table 8-6

ASSUMPTION	SCENARIO 1	SCENARIO 2	SCENARIO 3	SCENARIO 4
Base Salary	30%	25%	30%	10%
Commissions	2.5%	3.0%	2.5%	4%
Bonus	$17,750.00	$17,750.00	$15,000.00	$25,000.00
Net Sales for Bonus	$500,000.00	$500,000.00	$450,000.00	$475,000.00
Benefits	23.75%	23.75%	20.00%	25.00%
Payroll Tax	10.25%	10.25%	10.25%	10.25%

5 ▶▶▶ Your Uncle Bucks has asked for some help in picking stocks to purchase. He rates the risk level of stocks on a scale from zero to one. He wants to keep the value of each stock in his portfolio below 15 percent of the total value of his portfolio. He would like to minimize the risk level with the $50,000 he has to invest now by investing at least $45,000 of the money in certain stocks. The stocks he wants to purchase, their current price, and risk levels are shown in Table 8-7. Create the necessary worksheet and use Solver to determine the lowest risk combination of stocks in which to invest his funds.

Table 8-7 Stocks to Consider in Portfolio

STOCK	CURRENT PRICE PER SHARE	RISK FACTOR
INTC	80	.3
MSFT	91	.6
COMS	31	.22
MOT	87	.33
AOL	118	.8
YHOO	156	.75
IBM	122	.34

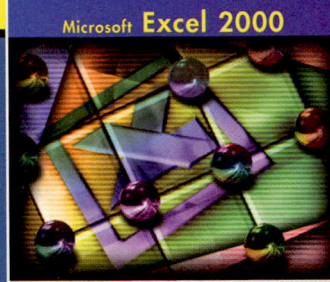

Microsoft **Excel 2000**

Microsoft Excel 2000

P R O J E C T

9

Importing External Data, Tracking and Routing Changes, and Creating Data Maps, PivotCharts, and PivotTables

You will have mastered the material in this project when you can:

O B J E C T I V E S

- Import data from a text file
- Import data from an Access database
- Import data from a Web page
- Insert, edit, and remove a comment
- Explain collaboration techniques
- Track changes and share a workbook
- Route a worksheet to other users
- Accept and reject tracked changes made to a workbook
- Create, edit, and format a data map
- Create a PivotChart and PivotTable
- Analyze a worksheet database using a PivotChart
- Analyze a worksheet database using a PivotTable
- Explain the concepts of sharing and merging workbooks

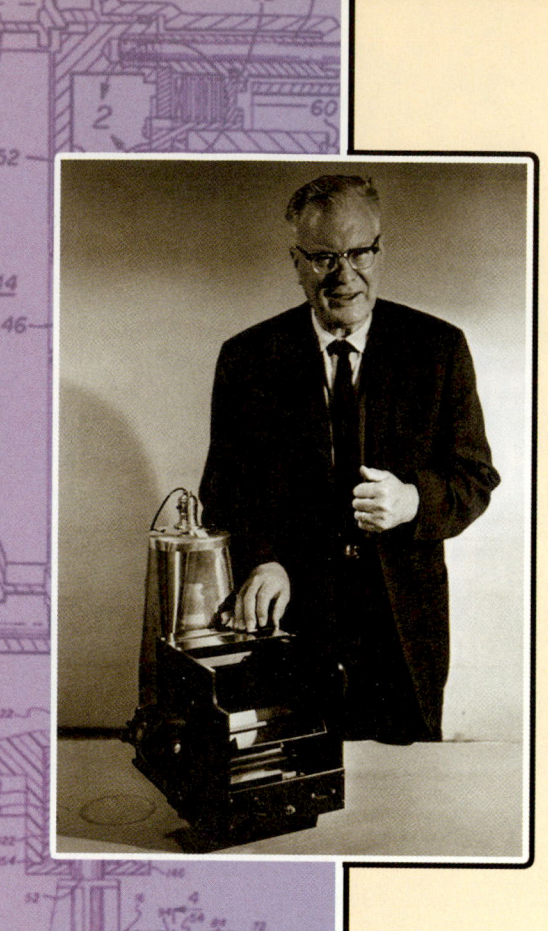

Necessity
The Mother of Invention

Necessity has been called The Mother of Invention. In an effort to find a more efficient or simplified way to perform a difficult task, many a creative project has resulted. That is how it all began for Chester Carlson, inventor of the photocopier.

In 1938, Carlson worked as a patent analyzer for an electrical component maker. In this capacity, he was required to spend numerous hours reviewing highly technical documents and drawings. Then he prepared the paperwork and applications submitted to the U.S. Patent and Trademark Office to register the company's inventions and ideas. It was during this time that Carlson developed his idea of an automated copying process. The patent office required multiple copies, which he had to duplicate manually, and redrawing the copies took hours. With his experience and technical expertise, Carlson went to work to find a better alternative.

His research led to the development of a technique based on photoconductivity, in which some materials change their electrical properties when exposed to light. He received a patent for his process, called electrophotography. In 1944, Carlson changed the name to xerography, a term derived from the Greek words for dry, and writing. He sold his right to a company that coined the word, Xerox, as the trademark for the new invention. The copier and the words, xerography (to describe the process) and Xerox (to identify the products), were introduced simultaneously in 1948. Today, Xerox, The Document Company, continues to be a major player in the document-imaging industry with innovative products.

The current light lens process when you set your original on the glass is a system of lamps, mirrors, and lenses that expose the image on a belt that has a positive electrical charge of static electricity. Digital copying uses scanner technology. To the casual observer, a digital copier looks just like the traditional light lens copier, but it provides significant advantages: not only is the image created using scanner technology, for a perfect copy, digital copiers can fully integrate with office systems for network printing, faxing, and scanning.

Most businesses utilize traditional or digital copier machines. The result of Carlson's original invention has spawned an expansive industry that markets, supplies, and services this document-imaging equipment. One such organization is Danka Office Imaging Company, Inc., providing product solutions, supplies, service, and support worldwide. The company maintains a computerized infrastructure that manages people, inventories, and marketing and product information in an extensive worksheet database from a variety of sources. Danka service field engineers are equipped with laptop computers that can access the latest data and product information on the Web for fast diagnostics and repair.

Similarly, in Project 9, you will gather information by importing data into an Excel workbook from a text file, an Access database, and a Web page. After ensuring the imported data is correct, you will analyze the data using a PivotChart and PivotTable. Excel gives you the ability to have an interactive view of worksheet data and summarize the information by rotating the table's rows and columns. Then, you will create a data map to display logistical data by geographic location.

In today's connected world, the ability to use and analyze data from a variety of sources is a necessity. As one necessity results in a related invention, the creative process continues as increasingly new demands generate better ways to perform tasks in a variety of ways.

Microsoft Excel 2000

Importing External Data, Tracking and Routing Changes, and Creating Data Maps, PivotCharts, and PivotTables

C A S E   P E R S P E C T I V E

José Velez is the marketing manager for the Burrito Land chain of fast food restaurants. The company owns restaurants in three states: New York, Texas, and Illinois. Restaurants are located on the street, in shopping malls, and in gas stations. José suspects that a shift in consumer habits has resulted in better performance for street-based restaurants.

José has requested the individual Burrito Land state offices send information regarding each store's sales along with other profile information. José has asked you, his assistant, to gather this information and produce some supporting documentation that will either confirm or reject his suspicions. José would like the data in a concise, easy-to-read format so he can present the findings to the board of directors. Each state has sent its information in different formats, because each state office operates independently of the corporate headquarters.

With your Excel background, you realize that PivotTables and PivotCharts would be helpful. Also, an Excel data map can be used to show variations in the data based on the state in which the restaurant is located.

Introduction

In today's connected world, the ability to use and analyze data from a wide variety of sources is a necessity. In this project, you will learn how to **import**, or bring, data from various external sources into an Excel worksheet and then analyze that data.

Suppose you routinely do business with a company that stores data in text format (Figure 9-1a on page E 9.6) rather than in a workbook. To make use of that data, you first input the data, and then format and manipulate it. Businesses also receive data in various database formats, such as Microsoft Access tables (Figure 9-1b), and from Web pages (Figure 9-1c).

Businesses routinely create charts to represent data visually. A **data map** (Figure 9-1f) is a type of chart that is a geographic map. It displays logistical data such as demographics, inventories, or marketing by state, region, or country. For example, Burrito Land owns restaurants in three states. To look at sales trends and current markets by geographic region, a data map can use color, symbols, and legends to represent the data and display the big picture.

Another visual way to analyze data is through the use of PivotCharts and PivotTables. A **PivotChart** (Figure 9-1g) is an interactive chart that provides the user with ways to graphically analyze data by varying the fields and categories to present different views. For example, if Burrito Land wanted to display a pie chart showing percentages for each state, a PivotChart could display that percentage using any field such as sales per state, number of mall locations per state, or locations with play areas.

Excel creates and associates a PivotTable with every PivotChart. A **PivotTable** (Figure 9-1h) is an interactive view of worksheet data that gives you the ability to summarize the database and then rotate the table's row and column titles to show different views of the summarized data. An inexperienced user with little knowledge of formulas, functions, and ranges can employ powerful what-if analyses of the data simply by clicking a field from a list of fields in a PivotChart or PivotTable.

Other techniques introduced in this project apply to issues of multiple users of the same workbook, including routing, tracking changes, and comments. If you want several people to look at a workbook and make comments, you can **route** it, or pass the workbook around, electronically. You can **track changes** to a workbook by displaying who changed what data, in which cell, and when. **Comments**, or descriptions, which do not regularly display as part of the worksheet data, can be added to the workbook itself to alert the recipients to special instructions, and later edited or deleted.

Project Nine — Burrito Land Sales Analysis

From your meeting with José Velez, you have accumulated the following workbook specifications:

Need: Import data from the three states that have Burrito Land restaurants (Figures 9-1a, 9-1b, and 9-1c on the next page) into a worksheet containing headings and formulas, but no data (Figure 9-1d). Once the data is imported, the formulas in cells H3 and I3 must be copied to each row of data (Figure 9-1e). After the import is complete, the data in the worksheet requires verification by the state coordinators. Once the data is verified, create a data map displaying store sales and locations visually (Figure 9-1f). Finally, a PivotChart (Figure 9-1g) and its associated PivotTable (Figure 9-1h) allow interactive views of the data from the worksheet.

Source of Data: The three state coordinators for Burrito Land will submit data from their respective states via a text file (Illinois), an Access database (Texas), and a Web page (New York).

Calculations: The formulas used to calculate average sales per register in the first quarter of 2002 and 2001 are in cells H3 and I3 of the worksheet (Figure 9-1d). The formulas divide sales at the individual location by the number of registers in the store. After importing the data, the formulas need to be copied down for all rows of data.

Special Requirements: Before creating the data map, PivotChart, and PivotTable, route the workbook with the imported data (Figure 9-1e) to the three state coordinators for verification and then accept Tracked Changes.

Chart Requirements: Create a data map of the United States (Figure 9-1f) that highlights the three states. The data map also should show comparisons between the 2002 sales and the 2001 sales. Create a PivotChart (Figure 9-1g) and associated PivotTable (Figure 9-1h) that analyze sales based on any combination of states and locations.

More About

External Data

Imported data that maintains a refreshable link to its external source is called external data. When using external data, if a change is made to the original file, the worksheet will update as well. You can choose when to refresh the external data in the workbook.

More About

Importing Data

If your system contains only a minimum installation of Excel, the first time you use one of the import features, Excel may attempt to install MSQuery. MSQuery is the supplemental application included in Microsoft Office 2000 used to retrieve data from external data sources.

(a) Text File

(b) Access File

(c) HTML File

(d) Worksheet Has No Data

FIGURE 9-1

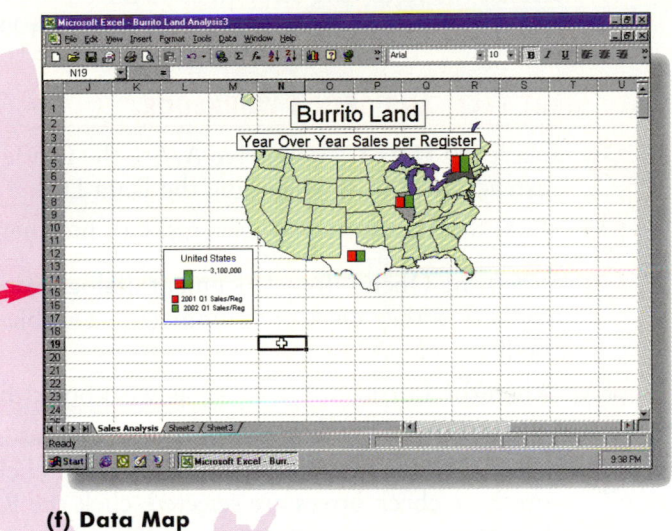

(f) Data Map

(h) PivotTable

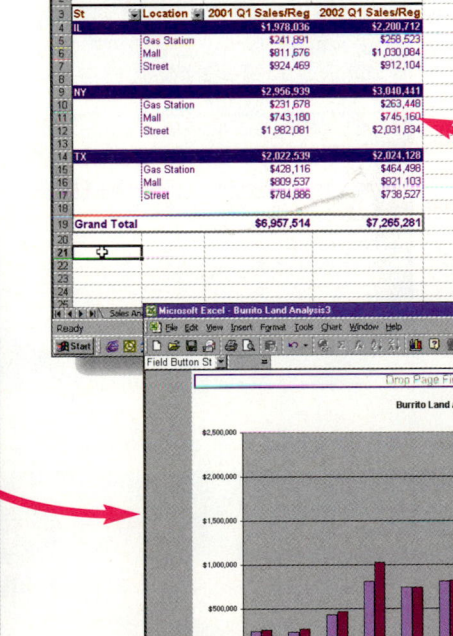

(e) Data Imported into Worksheet

(g) PivotChart

Starting Excel and Opening a Workbook

Perform the following steps to start Excel, reset the toolbars, and open the empty workbook, Burrito Land Analysis, from the Data Disk.

TO START EXCEL AND OPEN A WORKBOOK

1 Insert the Data Disk in drive A. See the inside back cover of this book for instructions for downloading the Data Disk.

2 Click the Start button on the taskbar and then click Open Office Document.

3 When the Open Office Document dialog box displays, click the Look in box arrow and then click 3½ Floppy (A:). Double-click Burrito Land Analysis in the list.

4 When the Burrito Land Analysis workbook displays, click Tools on the menu bar, and then click Customize.

5 When the Customize dialog box displays, click the Options tab, make sure the top three check boxes are selected, click the Reset my usage data button, and then click the Yes button.

6 Click the Toolbars tab. Click Standard, click the Reset button, and then click the OK button. Click Formatting, click the Reset button, and then click the OK button. Click the Close button.

The Burrito Land Analysis workbook displays in the Excel window (Figure 9-2).

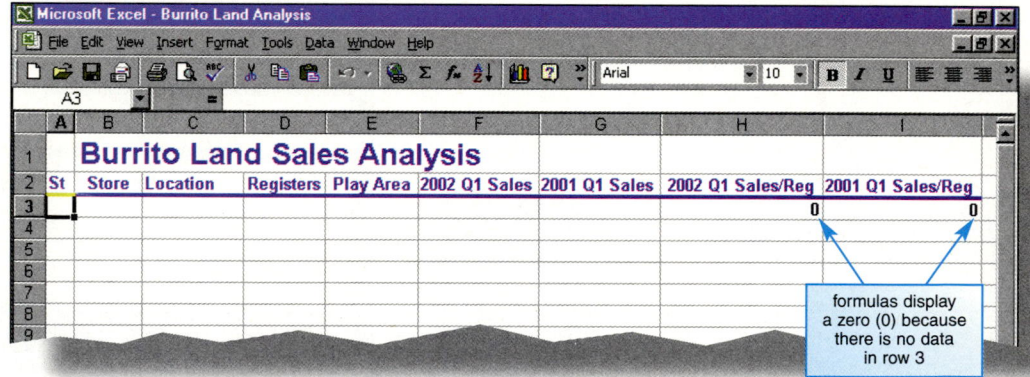

FIGURE 9-2

Table 9-1 Burrito Land Data Fields	
NAME OF FIELD	*DATA DESCRIPTION*
St	Standard postal abbreviation for the name of the state in which the store is located
Store	Store identification number - 3-digit number
Location	Physical location of store; i.e., Mall, Street, or Gas Station
Registers	Number of cash registers at the store - 1-digit number
Play Area	Logical Y or N field indicates whether or not the store has a play area for children
2002 Q1 Sales	First quarter sales in 2002 expressed in whole dollars
2001 Q1 Sales	First quarter sales in 2001 expressed in whole dollars
2002 Q1 Sales/Reg	Average sales per register for the first quarter of 2002 (2002 Q1 Sales / Registers)
2001 Q1 Sales/Reg	Average sales per register for the first quarter of 2001 (2001 Q1 Sales / Registers)

As shown in Figure 9-2, columns A through I have been resized and formatted so the imported data will be readable. Table 9-1 shows a summary of the column fields.

When you import data into a formatted worksheet, Excel formats the incoming data using the formats assigned to the cells as best it can.

Importing Files

Data may come to you from a variety of sources. Even though many users keep data in databases such as Microsoft Access, it is common to receive text files with fields of data separated by commas, especially from mainframe computer users. Also, with the increasing popularity of the World Wide Web, more companies are posting data on the Web. The ability to download data from the Web into an Excel worksheet is required. Importing data into Excel, rather than copying and pasting the data, also can create a refreshable link you may use to update data whenever the original file changes.

Importing Text Files

A **text file** contains electronic data created with little or no formatting. Many software applications such as Excel offer an option to import data from a text file, also called an ASCII text file. **ASCII** stands for the American Standard Code for Information Interchange.

In text files, commas, tabs, or other characters often separate the fields. Alternately, the text file may have fields of equal length in columnar format. Each record usually exists on a separate line. A **delimited file** contains a selected character, such as a comma, to separate data fields. A **fixed width file** contains data fields of equal length in the records. In the case of a fixed width file, a special character need not separate the data fields. During the import process, Excel provides a preview to help you identify the type of text file with which you are working.

The following steps import a comma delimited text file into the Burrito Land Analysis workbook using the **Text Import Wizard**. The text file on the Data Disk contains data about the first quarter sales in the state of Illinois (Figure 9-1a on page E 9.6).

 Steps **To Import Data from a Text File into a Worksheet**

1 **With the Burrito Land Analysis worksheet active and the Data Disk in drive A, click cell A3. Click Data on the menu bar. Point to Get External Data and then point to Import Text File on the Get External Data submenu.**

The Data menu and the Get External Data submenu display (Figure 9-3).

FIGURE 9-3

2 Click Import Text File. When the Import Text File dialog box displays, click the Look in box arrow, and then click 3½ Floppy (A:). Point to IllinoisQ1.

The text files on drive A display (Figure 9-4).

FIGURE 9-4

3 Double-click IllinoisQ1. When the Text Import Wizard - Step 1 of 3 dialog box displays, point to the Next button.

Excel displays the Text Import Wizard - Step 1 of 3 dialog box (Figure 9-5). The Text Import Wizard provides step-by-step instructions on importing text into Excel. The Preview box shows that the data from the file contains one record per line and the fields are separated by commas. The Delimited option button is selected in the Original data type area.

FIGURE 9-5

4 Click the Next button. When the Text Import Wizard - Step 2 of 3 dialog box displays, click Comma in the Delimiters area. Click Tab to clear the check box. Point to the Next button.

The Data preview area reflects the change (Figure 9-6). Excel correctly shows the fields of data in the Data preview area.

FIGURE 9-6

5 Click the Next button. When the Text Import Wizard - Step 3 of 3 dialog box displays, point to the Finish button.

The third dialog box of the Text Import Wizard displays (Figure 9-7). Step 3 allows you to select the format of each column of data. General is the default selection. The Data preview area shows the data separated based on the comma delimiter.

FIGURE 9-7

6 **Click the Finish button. When the Import Data dialog box displays, point to the Properties button.**

The Import Data dialog box displays (Figure 9-8). The **Import Data dialog box** *lets you select the location of the data in the worksheet, as well as providing a way to tailor the data before importing it. Data will be imported beginning at cell A3. A marquee displays around cell A3.*

FIGURE 9-8

7 **Click the Properties button. When the External Data Range Properties dialog box displays, click Adjust column width in the Data formatting and layout area to clear the check box. Point to the OK button.**

The **External Data Range Properties dialog box** *displays as shown in Figure 9-9.*

FIGURE 9-9

8 Click the OK button. When the Import Data dialog box displays, click the OK button. If the External Data toolbar displays on your screen, click its Close button.

Excel imports the data into the worksheet beginning at cell A3 (Figure 9-10).

	A	B	C	D	E	F	G	H	I
1		**Burrito Land Sales Analysis**							
2	St	Store	Location	Registers	Play Area	2002 Q1 Sales	2001 Q1 Sales	2002 Q1 Sales/Reg	2001 Q1 Sales/Reg
3	IL	219	Mall	4	N	1,482,019	1,214,923	370,505	303,731
4	IL	342	Street	4	N	1,795,580	1,594,039		
5	IL	347	Gas Station	5	Y	1,034,092	967,564		
6	IL	456	Mall	5	Y	1,342,332	1,039,323		
7	IL	539	Mall	5	Y	1,000,393	980,000		
8	IL	556	Mall	4	Y	1,564,453	1,200,323		
9	IL	789	Street	3	Y	789,392	989,877		

text file data imported

formulas display nonzero results because of data in row 3

FIGURE 9-10

The commas in the last two columns of numbers in the Data preview area (Figure 9-7 on page E 9.11) are not considered to be delimiters because each of these data values was surrounded by quotation marks when the text file was created.

By default, the cell that is active when you perform the text import will become the upper-left cell of the imported range. If you want to import the data to a different location, you can specify the location in the Import Data dialog box (Figure 9-8).

By importing the text file, Excel can **refresh**, or update, the data whenever the original text file changes using the **Refresh command** on the Data menu.

Importing Access Tables

When you import data from an Access database, you start by making a query of the data. A **query** is a way to qualify the data you want to import by specifying a matching condition or asking a question of a database. You may choose to import the entire file or only a portion. For example, you can make a query to import only those records that pass a certain test, such as records containing numeric fields greater than a specific amount, or records containing text fields matching a specific value.

The steps on the next page import an entire table from an Access database using the **Database Query Wizard**. The table in the Access database on the Data Disk contains data about the first quarter sales in the state of Texas (Figure 9-1b on page E 9.6).

Other Ways

1. Press ALT+D, press D, press T

More About

Dragging and Dropping a Text File

Excel allows you to drag a text file to a blank worksheet. Simply drag the file name or the icon from its location to a blank worksheet. You then can format the data easily using the Text to Columns command on the Data menu. The data does not maintain a refreshable link to the text file, however.

To Import Data from an Access Table into a Worksheet

1 Click cell A10. Click Data on the menu bar, point to Get External Data, and then point to New Database Query.

The Get External Data submenu displays (Figure 9-11).

FIGURE 9-11

2 Click New Database Query. When the Choose Data Source dialog box displays, if necessary, click the Databases tab, and then click MS Access Database* in the list. Point to the OK button.

The Choose Data Source dialog box displays several database application formats (Figure 9-12). This list may differ on your computer. A check mark displays in the Use the Query Wizard to create/edit queries check box.

FIGURE 9-12

3 Click the OK button. When the Select Database dialog box displays, click the Drives box arrow and then click a: in the list. Point to texasq1.mdb in the Database Name list.

The *Select Database dialog box* displays (Figure 9-13). Your system may not display the Connecting to data source progress box.

FIGURE 9-13

4 Double-click texasq1.mdb. When the Query Wizard – Choose Columns dialog box displays, select the Texas Q1 Sales Information table and then point to the Add Table button.

The database has one table to add to the query (Figure 9-14).

FIGURE 9-14

5 Click the Add Table button and then point to the Next button.

The fields of the Texas Q1 Sales Information table display (Figure 9-15).

FIGURE 9-15

6 **Click the Next button. When the Query Wizard - Filter Data dialog box displays, click the Next button. When the Query Wizard - Sort Order dialog box displays, click the Next button. When the Query Wizard - Finish dialog box displays, point to the Finish button (Figure 9-16).**

Since the entire table is being imported without a specific query, clicking the Next button in each of the Wizard dialog boxes accepts the preset values.

FIGURE 9-16

7 **Click the Finish button. When the Returning External Data to Microsoft Excel dialog box displays, point to the Properties button.**

The Returning External Data to Microsoft Excel dialog box displays (Figure 9-17). Data will be imported beginning at cell A10. A marquee displays around cell A10.

FIGURE 9-17

8 Click the Properties button. When the External Data Range Properties dialog box displays, click Include field names and Adjust column width in the Data formatting and layout area to clear the check boxes. Point to the OK button.

The External Data Range Properties dialog box displays (Figure 9-18). With the two check marks removed, Excel will not import the field names or adjust column widths in Excel.

FIGURE 9-18

9 Click the OK button. When the Returning External Data to Microsoft Excel dialog box (Figure 9-17) redisplays, click the OK button. If your system displays the External Data toolbar, click its Close button.

The data imported from the Access database displays in the worksheet (Figure 9-19).

St	Store	Location	Registers	Play Area	2002 Q1 Sales	2001 Q1 Sales	2002 Q1 Sales/Reg	2001 Q1 Sales/Reg
IL	219	Mall	4	N	1,482,019	1,214,923	370,505	303,731
IL	342	Street	4	N	1,795,580	1,594,039		
IL	347	Gas Station	5	Y	1,034,092	967,564		
IL	456	Mall	5	Y	1,342,332	1,039,323		
IL	539	Mall	5	Y	1,000,393	980,000		
IL	556	Mall	4	Y	1,564,453	1,200,323		
IL	789	Street	3	Y	789,392	989,877		
TX	432	Mall	4	Y	893,353	903,432		
TX	545	Street	5	N	1,893,342	1,987,687		
TX	592	Gas Station	3	Y	1,133,493	1,084,349		
TX	592	Mall	4	N	1,672,910	1,578,201		
TX	763	Street	4	Y	1,439,434	1,549,394		
TX	765	Mall	5	N	897,687	945,645		

FIGURE 9-19

Other Ways

1. Press ALT+D, press D, press N

By default, the cell that is active when you perform the database query becomes the upper-left cell of the imported range. If you want to import the data to a different location, you specify the location in the Returning External Data to Microsoft Excel dialog box (Figure 9-17).

More About 2000

Dragging and Dropping an Access File

If you have both Excel and Access open on your desktop, you can drag and drop an entire table or query from Access to Excel. Select the table or query you want to transfer in the database window and then drag it to the location in the worksheet.

The Access file, texasq1.mdb, contains only one table, Texas Q1 Sales Information. The table contains seven fields that correspond to the columns in the worksheet. The Add Table button shown in Figure 9-14 on page E 9.15 added all the columns of data. The second step of the Query Wizard allows you to **filter**, or specify, which records from the database should be included in the result set, using operators such as is-greater-than or begins-with. For example, you can filter the data in the previous example by specifying to import records that have five or more registers.

With the data from Illinois and Texas imported, the next step is to import the New York data from a Web page.

Importing Data from a Web Page

A Web page uses a file format called HTML. **HTML** stands for **Hypertext markup language**, which is a language that Web browsers can interpret. A Web page allows you to import data into preformatted areas of the worksheet. You specify which parts of the Web page you want and how much of the HTML formatting you want to keep.

Excel creates four saved **Web queries** when you first install Excel, most of which involve investment and stock market Web pages. The next sequence of steps creates a new Web query. You do not have to be connected to the Internet to perform these steps because the Data Disk includes the Web page (Figure 9-1c on page E 9.6).

 Steps To Import Data from a Web Page into a Worksheet

1 Click cell A16. Click Data on the menu bar, point to Get External Data, and then point to New Web Query.

The Data menu and Get External Data submenu display (Figure 9-20).

FIGURE 9-20

2   **Click New Web Query. When the New Web Query dialog box displays, type** `a:\newyorkq1.htm` **in the step 1 text box and then point to the OK button.**

The file location displays in the step 1 text box at the top of the New Web Query dialog box (Figure 9-21).

FIGURE 9-21

3   **Click the OK button. When the Returning External Data to Microsoft Excel dialog box displays, point to the Properties button.**

The Returning External Data to Microsoft Excel dialog box displays (Figure 9-22). Data will be imported beginning at cell A16. A marquee displays around cell A16.

FIGURE 9-22

4 **Click the Properties button. When the External Data Range Properties dialog box displays, click Adjust column width in the Data formatting and layout area to clear the check box and then point to the OK button.**

The External Data Range Properties dialog box displays (Figure 9-23).

FIGURE 9-23

5 **Click the OK button. When the Returning External Data to Microsoft Excel dialog box displays, click the OK button. If the External Data toolbar displays on your screen, click its Close button.**

The data displays in the worksheet (Figure 9-24).

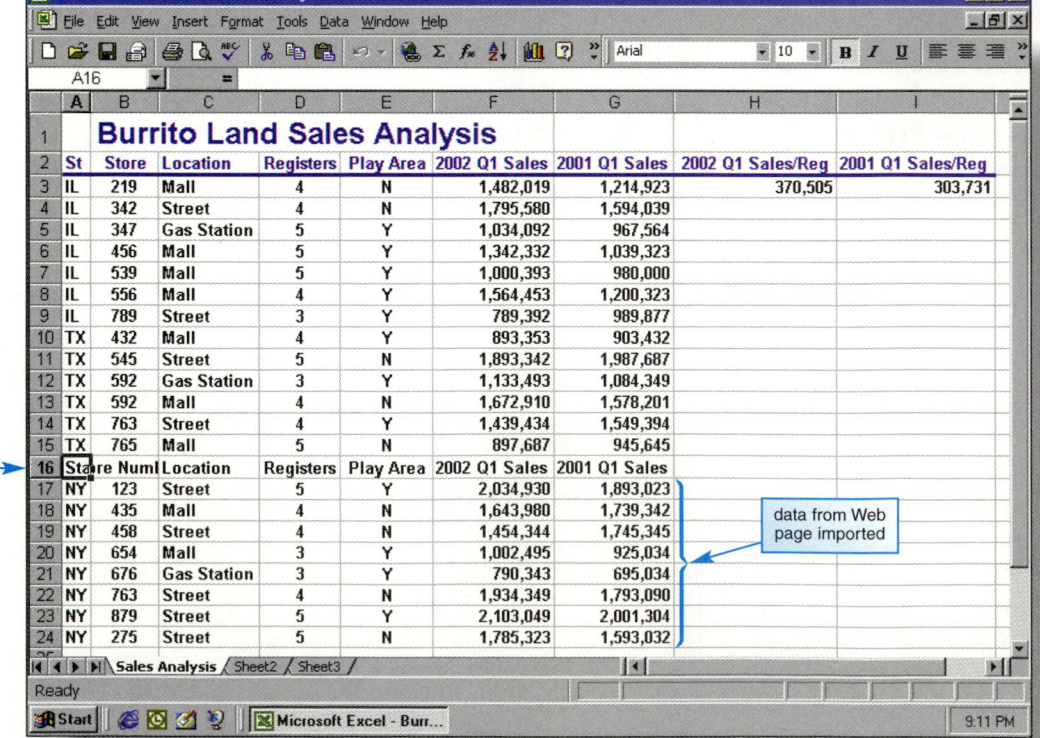

FIGURE 9-24

6 **Right-click row heading 16. Point to Delete on the shortcut menu.**

The shortcut menu for the selected row displays (Figure 9-25). You will delete these extra column headings from the Web page table.

FIGURE 9-25

7 **Click Delete.**

Excel deletes row 16, which contained the column headings from the Web page (Figure 9-26).

FIGURE 9-26

By default, the cell that is active when you perform the Web query will become the upper-left cell of the imported range. If you want to import the data to a different location, you can specify the location in the Returning External Data to Microsoft Excel dialog box (Figure 9-22 on page E 9.19).

Using a Web query has advantages over other methods of importing data from a Web page. For example, copying data from Web pages to the Clipboard and then pasting it into Excel does not maintain the formatting. In addition, it is tedious to have to highlight just the data you want in a Web page. Finally, copying and pasting does not create a link to the Web page for future updating.

Other Ways

1. Press ALT+D, press D, press S

Replicating Formulas

The workbook opened at the beginning of this project contained a worksheet title, headings for each column, and formulas in cells H3 and I3 to calculate the sales per register for 2002 and 2001. This technique of copying the formulas after completing the import is necessary because the total number of records to be imported usually is unknown. The following steps use the fill handle to copy the formulas. Some spreadsheet specialists refer to copying formulas as **replication**.

 To Replicate Formulas

1 **Select the range H3:I3 and then point to the fill handle.**

The range H3:I3 is selected (Figure 9-27). The mouse pointer changes to a cross hair when pointing to the fill handle.

FIGURE 9-27

2 **Drag the fill handle down through row 23.**

Excel copies the two formulas to the range H4:I23 and displays the new values for Sales per Register (Figure 9-28).

FIGURE 9-28

Other Ways

1. Click Copy button on Standard toolbar, click Paste button on Standard toolbar
2. On Edit menu click Copy, on Edit menu click Paste
3. Press CTRL+C, press CTRL+V
4. Click Copy on shortcut menu, click Paste on shortcut menu

Recall that when you copy, or replicate, a formula, Excel adjusts the cell references so the new formulas contain references corresponding to the new locations and perform calculations using the appropriate values. If you want an exact copy without replication, you must hold down the CTRL key while dragging the fill handle. Holding down the SHIFT key while dragging the fill handle inserts new cells rather than overwriting the existing data.

Saving the Workbook with a New File Name

Perform the following steps to save the workbook with the file name Burrito Land Analysis1.

TO SAVE THE WORKBOOK WITH A NEW FILE NAME

1 Click File on the menu bar and then click Save As.

2 When the Save As dialog box displays, Type `Burrito Land Analysis1` in the File name text box.

3 If necessary, click 3½ Floppy (A:) in the Save in list.

4 Click the Save button in the Save As dialog box.

Excel saves the workbook on the Data Disk in drive A using the file name Burrito Land Analysis1.

Preparing the Workbook for Routing

The next step is to add a routing comment and then verify the accuracy of the data by routing it to the state coordinators for review.

Inserting Comments

Comments are used to describe the function of a cell, a range, a sheet, or an entire workbook, or they may be used to clarify entries that might otherwise be difficult to understand. Multiple users or people reviewing the workbook often use comments to communicate suggestions, tips, and other messages. José suspects that the sales amount in cell F9 from Illinois is incorrect, and thus will add a comment to the cell before routing the workbook to the three state coordinators as shown in the steps on the next page.

More About 2000

Importing External Data

Excel assigns a name to each external data range. You can view these names by clicking the Name box arrow in the formula bar. External data ranges from text files are named with the text file name. External data ranges from databases are named with the name of the query. External data ranges from Web queries are named with the name of the Web page from which the data was retrieved.

More About 2000

Selecting External Data

If you want to view the part of your worksheet that is imported, or if you want to format or delete an external data range, click the Name box arrow in the formula bar, and then click the external data range name.

More About 2000

Saving a Workbook with External Data

Excel provides the option of saving the workbook without saving the external data so the workbook file size is reduced. Click Data Range Properties on the External Data toolbar and then click the Refresh data on file open. To save the workbook with the query definition but without the external data, click Remove external data from worksheet before saving in the Data Range Properties dialog box.

Steps | **To Insert a Comment**

1 Right-click cell F9. Point to Insert Comment on the shortcut menu.

The shortcut menu displays (Figure 9-29).

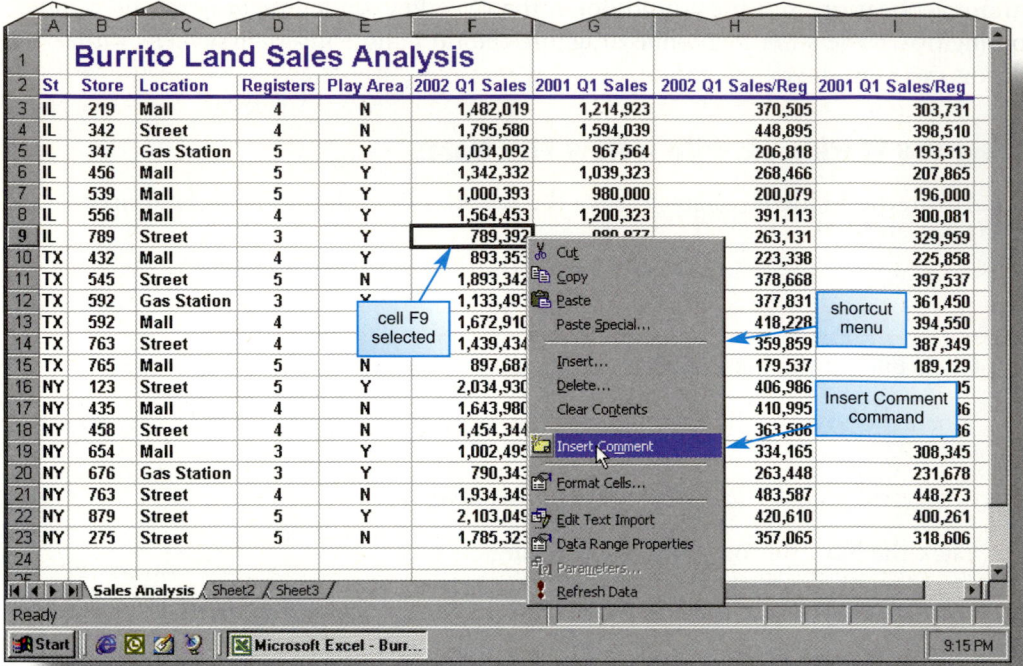

FIGURE 9-29

2 Click Insert Comment. When the comment box displays, enter the comment as shown in Figure 9-30.

*Excel opens a **comment box** next to the selected cell (Figure 9-30). The insertion point displays in the comment box below the system user name. Your system user name will differ from this figure. Excel adds a small red triangle, called a **comment indicator**, to cell F9. A small black arrow attached to the comment box points to the comment indicator.*

3 Click anywhere outside the comment box and then click the Save button on the Standard toolbar to save the workbook using the file name Burrito Land Analysis1.

Other Ways

1. On Insert menu click Comment
2. Press ALT+I, press M

FIGURE 9-30

When Excel closes the comment box and returns to the workbook window, the comment disappears from the screen. If you want to redisplay the comment, simply point to the cell containing the red comment indicator.

If you want to print the comments where they display on the sheet, click Comments on the View menu, move and resize the comments as necessary, and then print in the normal way. If you want to print the comments at the end of the worksheet, on the File menu, click Page Setup, and then click the Sheet tab. Click At end of sheet in the Comments box.

Collaborating on Workbooks

If you plan to have others edit your workbook or suggest changes, Excel provides four ways to collaborate with others. **Collaborating** means working together in cooperation on a document with other Excel users.

First, you can **distribute** your workbook to others, physically on a disk or through e-mail using the Send To command on the File menu. With the Send To command, you may choose to embed the document as part of the e-mail message or attach the file as an e-mail attachment, which allows receivers of the e-mail message to open the file if they have the application on their system.

Second, you can **route** your workbook to a list of people who pass it along from one to another on the routing list using e-mail. The Send To command on the File menu includes a Routing Recipient command. A routing slip displays in which you can specify e-mail addresses. Excel handles creating the e-mail message with routing instructions. It even reminds people who open the document to pass it along to the next person in the routing list when they are finished.

Third, you can **collaborate** interactively with other people through discussion threads or online meetings. The integration of **NetMeeting** with Microsoft Office 2000 allows you to share and exchange files with people at different sites. When you start an online meeting from within Excel, NetMeeting automatically starts in the background and allows you to share the contents of your file.

Fourth, you can collaborate by sharing the workbook. **Sharing** means more than simply giving another user a copy of your file. Sharing implies that multiple people can work independently on the same workbook at the same time if you are in a networked environment.

With any of the collaboration choices, you should keep track of the changes that others make to your workbook.

Tracking Changes

Tracking changes means that Excel, through the **Track Changes command** on the Tools menu, will display the edited cells with a comment indicating who made the change, when the change was made, and the original value of the cell that was changed. Tracking and sharing work together. When you turn on one, the other is enabled by default. The steps on then next page turn on Track Changes.

More About 2000

Collaboration

Another way to collaborate on workbooks is by using an Exchange folder. If you send the workbook to an Exchange folder, others working on the same project have a central location where they can go for project information. This method is preferential if many revisions need to be circulated because it saves time. Project members can look at what is relevant to them instead of going through numerous project-related e-mails.

More About 2000

Excel's Routing Capability

To e-mail or route a workbook as an attachment in Excel format, you need Excel 2000 and one of the following e-mail programs: Outlook, Outlook Express, Microsoft Exchange Client, Lotus cc:Mail or another compatible program with the Messaging Application Programming Interface (MAPI). To receive a routed workbook you need Excel 97 or later.

More About 2000

Shared Workbook Limitations

Some features of Microsoft Excel are not available when you use a shared workbook. Features such as merging cells; delete blocks of cells or worksheets; editing toolbars and menus; editing data validation restrictions and conditional formats; inserting tables, charts, pictures, or hyperlinks; drawing tools; scenarios; and editing macros are disabled temporarily while the workbook is shared. If you need to use these features, do so before you share the workbook, or remove the workbook from shared use.

To Turn on Track Changes

1 **Click Tools on the menu bar, point to Track Changes, and then point to Highlight Changes.**

The Track Changes submenu displays (Figure 9-31).

FIGURE 9-31

2 **Click Highlight Changes. When Highlight Changes dialog box displays, click Track changes while editing. If necessary, clear all of the check boxes in the Highlight which changes area. Point to the OK button.**

The Highlight Changes dialog box displays (Figure 9-32). Clicking the Track changes while editing check box also shares the workbook. The When, Who, and Where check boxes and list boxes play no role when you first enable Track Changes.

FIGURE 9-32

3 Click the OK button. When the Microsoft Excel dialog box displays asking if you want to continue by saving, click the OK button to save the workbook.

The title bar indicates this workbook is shared (Figure 9-33).

workbook is shared

	A	B	C	D	E	F	G	H	I
1			**Burrito Land Sales Analysis**						
2	St	Store	Location	Registers	Play Area	2002 Q1 Sales	2001 Q1 Sales	2002 Q1 Sales/Reg	2001 Q1 Sales/Reg
3	IL	219	Mall	4	N	1,482,019	1,214,923	370,505	303,731
4	IL	342	Street	4	N	1,795,580	1,594,039	448,895	398,510
5	IL	347	Gas Station	5	Y	1,034,092	967,564	206,818	193,513
6	IL	456	Mall	5	Y	1,342,332	1,039,323	268,466	207,865
7	IL	539	Mall	5	Y	1,000,393	980,000	200,079	196,000
8	IL	556	Mall	4	Y	1,564,453	1,200,323	391,113	300,081
9	IL	789	Street		Y				

FIGURE 9-33

Other Ways

1. Press ALT+T, press T, press H

Routing the Workbook

The next step is to route the workbook to the three state coordinators for Burrito Land. If you are doing this project on a PC, you will be prompted to choose the e-mail addresses of the routing recipients. If you plan actually to execute the routing, substitute the e-mail addresses shown with e-mail addresses from your address book or class. Your return e-mail contact information must be valid as well, in order to round trip the file back to you. The term **round trip** refers to sending a document to recipients and then receiving it back at some point in time.

 To Route a Workbook

1 Click File on the menu bar, point to Send To, and then point to Routing Recipient.

The File menu and Send To submenu display (Figure 9-34).

FIGURE 9-34

2 **Click Routing Recipient. If the Choose Profiles dialog box displays, choose your user profile and then click the OK button. If the Check Names dialog box displays, you may have to add your return address as a new listing to the address book. When the Routing Slip dialog box displays, point to the Address button.**

A *routing slip* displays that allows you to specify the recipient, subject, and message similar to an e-mail message (Figure 9-35). Your routing slip will display a different user profile name. If you are working on a networked system, see your instructor or network administrator for the correct user profile.

FIGURE 9-35

3 **Click the Address button. Click an address in your list and then click the To button. Repeat the process for two more recipients. Point to the OK button.**

If no addresses display in your address list, you may leave the recipients blank for the purposes of this project. To add new e-mail recipients, you would click the New button and then enter the correct information (Figure 9-36).

FIGURE 9-36

4 Click the OK button. When the Routing Slip dialog box displays again, click the Message text box. Type Please review the attached worksheet and make changes as necessary. When you are finished reviewing, route to the next recipient. Thank you. Point to the Route button.

The Routing Slip dialog box displays the addresses, subject, and message (Figure 9-37).

FIGURE 9-37

5 Click the Route button.

6 Click the Save button on the Standard toolbar to save the workbook using the file name Burrito Land Analysis1. Click the workbook Close button on the menu bar.

Excel saves a copy of the workbook on the floppy disk and closes the workbook.

Other Ways

1. Press ALT+F, press D, press R

More About 2000

Routing Slips

Since routing workbooks among team members is an important tool for most businesses, many Web magazines have begun to publish tips and tricks for helping you perform routings tasks in Excel. To look at examples, visit the Excel 2000 More About Web page (www.scsite.com/Ex2000/more.htm) and then click Routing Tips.

In the previous sequence of steps, the e-mail to the first recipient was sent immediately when you clicked **Route button**. If you had clicked the **Add Slip button** instead of the Route button, then Excel would have asked if it should send the e-mail when the workbook was closed. Figure 9-38 on the next page illustrates the e-mail received by the first recipient, Carlos Nunez. A sample message displays and Excel automatically attaches the workbook to the message and inserts instructions to the routing recipients. As each routing recipient receives the e-mail, he or she opens the workbook and looks it over, making changes as necessary. Excel reminds each recipient to forward the workbook to the next person in the list. Excel prompts the last person to forward the workbook back to the owner.

Routing Addresses

The e-mail addresses you use in the routing slip must be valid addresses from your Contacts folder. Your own name and e-mail address must be in the Contacts folder as well, if you want to round-trip the workbook. To add an address, from the Routing Slip dialog box, click the Address button, and then click the New button.

Shared Workbook Change History

Shared workbooks usually are current, active worksheets. Excel maintains a preset change history of 30 days. If you want more time to keep track of changes, you may change the number of days. For example, when you turn on change history but are not sure exactly when the merge will take place, you can pre-serve the change history by setting a large number of days to maintain the change history, up to the maximum of 32,767 days.

FIGURE 9-38

Excel keeps a **Change History file** with each shared workbook. In the case of a shared workbook in which you want to track the changes, Excel provides a way for users to make data entry changes, but does not allow them to modify the Change History file. Click the Tools menu and then point to Protection. In a shared workbook, the only available command is **Protect Shared Workbook**. This command displays a dialog box enabling you to protect the Change History file associated with a shared workbook, so no one can turn it off except the owner.

Reviewing Tracked Changes

Instead of writing suggestions and changes on a printed draft copy, Excel's Track Changes feature allows users to enter suggested changes directly on the workbook. The owner of the workbook then looks through each change and makes a decision about whether or not to accept it.

Reviewing the Routed Workbook

After a routed workbook has progressed through the entire routing list, it comes back to the owner. Because Highlight Changes was enabled for the Burrito Land Analysis1 workbook, the file has come back to you with each recipient's changes, corrections, and comments. As the owner, you review those changes and make decisions about whether or not to accept the changes. A tracked workbook named Burrito Land Analysis2 is stored on the Data Disk. The following steps use this workbook to illustrate reviewing the changes.

Steps **To Open a Routed Workbook and Review Tracked Changes**

1 **With Excel active, click the Open button on the Standard toolbar. When the Open dialog box displays, if necessary click the Look in box arrow and then click 3½ Floppy (A:). Double-click the Burrito Land Analysis2 workbook. When the workbook displays, click Tools on the menu bar, point to Track Changes, and then point to Highlight Changes.**

The Burrito Land Analysis2 workbook displays, as does the Track Changes submenu (Figure 9-39).

FIGURE 9-39

2 **Click Highlight Changes. When the Highlight Changes dialog box displays, click When to clear the check box and then point to the OK button.**

The Highlight Changes dialog box displays (Figure 9-40). Removing the check mark from the When check box indicates you want to review all changes in the history file.

FIGURE 9-40

3 Click the OK button. Click Tools on the menu bar and then click Options. If necessary, click the View tab and then click Comment & indicator in the Comments area. Click the OK button. Point to cell E21.

All comments in the work-sheet display. A description of the change made to cell E21 displays (Figure 9-41). Blue triangles represent a data change and red triangles represent comments.

FIGURE 9-41

4 Click Tools on the menu bar and then click Options. If necessary, click the View tab and then click Comment indicator only in the Comments area. Click the OK button. Click Tools on the menu bar, point to Track Changes, and then point to Accept or Reject Changes.

All comments are hidden. The Track Changes submenu again displays (Figure 9-42).

FIGURE 9-42

⑤ Click Accept or Reject Changes. When the Select Changes to Accept or Reject dialog box displays, if necessary, clear the check boxes and then point to the OK button.

The Select Changes to Accept or Reject dialog box allows you to specify the types of changes you want to review (Figure 9-43).

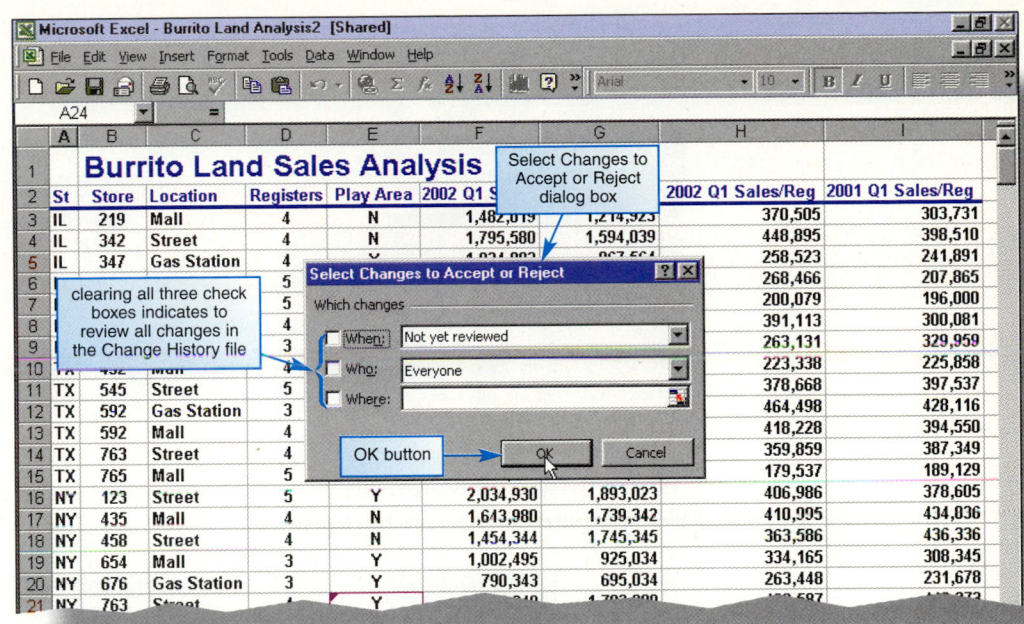

FIGURE 9-43

⑥ Click the OK button. When the Accept or Rejects Changes dialog box displays Change 1, point to the Accept button.

One change at a time displays in the Accept or Reject Changes dialog box (Figure 9-44). The cell with the change displays with a marquee. Excel allows you to accept or reject the changes one at a time, or all at once.

⑦ Click the Accept button. As each change displays, click the Accept button. Right-click cell A10 and then click Delete Comment on the shortcut menu. Right-click cell F9 and then click Delete Comment on the shortcut menu.

The process of reviewing and accepting the changes to the workbook is complete.

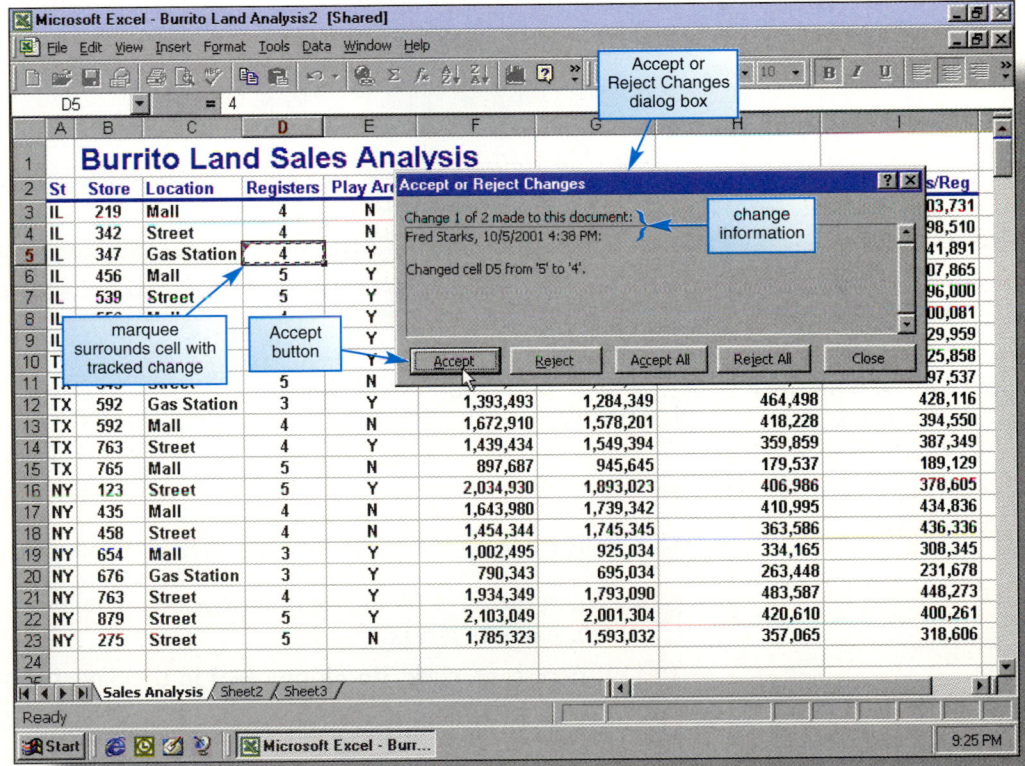

FIGURE 9-44

In Figure 9-43 on the previous page, you can select the category of changes in the Change History file you want to accept or reject. Table 9-2 summarizes the three check boxes.

Table 9-2 Categories of Changes in the Select Changes to Accept or Reject Dialog Box	
CHECK BOX	**DESCRIPTION**
When	Select when you want to review changes within a time interval; the four choices are (1) Since I Last Saved; (2) All; (3) Not Yet Reviewed; and (4) Since Date
Who	View changes based on who made them
Where	View changes made to a range of cells

For each tracked change, Excel displays the Accept or Reject Changes dialog box (Figure 9-44 on the previous page) with five buttons from which to choose. Table 9-3 summarizes the five buttons.

Table 9-3 Buttons in the Accept or Reject Changes Dialog Box	
BUTTON	**DESCRIPTION**
Accept	Accepts the current change
Reject	Rejects the current change
Accept All	Accepts all changes
Reject All	Rejects all changes
Close	Quits the Accept or Reject Changes command

With the changes accepted, the following steps save the workbook using a new file name.

TO SAVE THE TRACKED CHANGES IN A WORKBOOK WITH A NEW FILE NAME

1. Click File on the menu bar and then click Save As.

2. When the Save As dialog box displays, type `Burrito Land Analysis3` in the File name text box.

3. If necessary, click 3½ Floppy (A:) in the Save in list.

4. Click the Save button in the Save As dialog box.

Excel saves the workbook on drive A, using the file name Burrito Land Analysis3.

The next step is to turn off the Track Changes feature. Excel denies access to features such as the data map and PivotChart while the workbook is shared. Perform the following steps to turn off Track Changes, which also automatically turns off sharing and saves the workbook as an exclusive one. That is, it no longer is a shared workbook.

TO TURN OFF TRACK CHANGES

1. Click Tools on the menu bar, point to Track Changes, and then click Highlight Changes.

2. When the Highlight Changes dialog box displays, click Track changes while editing to clear the check box.

3. Click the OK button in the Highlight Changes dialog box.

4. When the Microsoft Excel dialog box displays, asking you to make the workbook exclusive, click the Yes button.

The workbook displays without the word, Shared, in the title bar. Excel disables Track Changes.

When you turn off Track Changes, you turn off sharing as well. At the same time, Excel erases the change history. The workbook automatically resaves as an exclusive workbook. An **exclusive workbook** is only available to be opened by a single user.

The imports and changes complete the Burrito Land Analysis workbook. The next step is to create a data map in preparation for the Burrito Land Board of Directors' meeting.

More About

Tracking Changes with Passwords

If you want to make sure others will not turn off the change history or reduce the number of days in the history, you can protect a shared workbook with a password. Click Protection on the Tools menu and then click Protect and Share Workbook on the Protection submenu. Passwords may be added only if the workbook is unshared at the time of protection.

Creating a Data Map

Microsoft Excel includes a mapping feature, called **Microsoft Map**, which you use to see the relationships between numbers and geographic regions. With a few clicks of the mouse, you can embed a data map of any location in the world in the worksheet and then format it. For example, you may add labels, text, and pins to a data map to display and analyze the sales by state. Figure 9-45 shows the data map required for this project. It is a data map of the United States, highlighting the three states where Burrito Land has stores. The Column chart on top of each of the three states compares the sales per register from the data columns 2002 Q1 Sales/Reg and 2001 Q1 Sales/Reg.

FIGURE 9-45

To use the mapping feature of Excel, you select a range of cells on your worksheet that includes geographic data, such as countries or states, and then click the **Map button** on the Standard toolbar. Once the Map button is clicked, the mouse pointer changes to a cross hair, and you can drag it to an open area on your worksheet to define the data map location and size.

The data you plan to use to create a data map must be in columnar form with standard names or abbreviations of the states (or countries) in a column. For example, the data shown in Table 9-4 can be used to create a data map because the first column contains the names of countries.

The state or country data does not have to be in the leftmost column. The columns need not be adjacent. You may press the CTRL key and drag to select nonadjacent multiple ranges of data, if one of the columns contains the state or country names.

If you reset the toolbars at the beginning of this project, you may not see the Map button that displays as a globe on the Standard toolbar (Figure 9-46). Clicking the More Buttons button (Figure 9-46) allows you to display the hidden buttons. If you still do not see the Map button, you need to add it using the Customize command on the Tools menu, as explained in the following steps.

Table 9-4	Sample Data for Mapping	
COUNTRY	INTERNATIONAL OFFICES	
Venezuela	7	
Colombia	5	
Brazil	12	
Peru	6	

Adding the Map Button to the Standard Toolbar

Perform the following steps if your Standard toolbar does not display the Map button.

TO ADD THE MAP BUTTON TO THE STANDARD TOOLBAR

1. Double-click the move handle on the Standard toolbar to make sure the Map button is not in a demoted state.

2. If the Map button does not display when the Standard toolbar displays in its entirety, right-click a toolbar and then click Customize on the shortcut menu.

3. Click the Commands tab and then click Insert in the Categories list.

4. Click the Commands box down scroll arrow until the Map button displays.

5. Drag the Map button to the right end of the Standard toolbar.

6. Click the Close button in the Customize dialog box.

The Map button displays on the right end of the Standard toolbar (Figure 9-46).

If the Map button is dimmed on the Standard toolbar, see your instructor about installing the Map feature.

Creating the Data Map

Follow the steps below to create a data map in the range L1:S17 using the data from columns A, H, and I in the Burrito Land Sales Analysis database. To draw a map, one of the columns must be made up of locations, such as the states in column A. The data map for Burrito Land will display the sum of the sales per register figures for all stores in all three states.

To Create a Data Map

1 **With the workbook Burrito Land Analysis3 open, select the range A2:A23. Hold down the CTRL key and then drag to select the additional range H2:I23. Point to the Map button on the Standard toolbar.**

Excel highlights the selected ranges (Figure 9-46).

FIGURE 9-46

2 **Click the Map button. Click the right scroll arrow at the bottom of the worksheet until cell J1 displays in the upper-left corner of the worksheet. Drag from the upper-left corner of cell L1 to the lower-right corner of cell S17 and hold.**

The map location range L1:S17 is surrounded by a light border (Figure 9-47).

FIGURE 9-47

3 **Release the mouse button. When the Multiple Maps Available dialog box displays, click United States in North America and then point to the OK button.**

Microsoft Map's menu bar and toolbar display at the top of the screen in place of Excel's menu bar and toolbars. A heavy gray border surrounds the map location indicating it is active, and the **Multiple Maps Available dialog box** *displays (Figure 9-48).*

FIGURE 9-48

4 **Click the OK button.**

Microsoft Map draws a map of North America and displays the **Microsoft Map Control dialog box** *(Figure 9-49). The three states with Burrito Land stores (Illinois, Texas, and New York) display in varying shades.*

FIGURE 9-49

Other Ways

1. On Insert menu click Object, on Create New tab click Microsoft Map

The basic data map is complete. The next step is to format the data map so it displays as shown in Figure 9-45 on page E 9.35. When the data map is active (the heavy gray border indicates it is active), the menu bar and toolbar at the top of the screen can be used to manipulate the data map. Figure 9-50 describes the functions of the buttons on the **Microsoft Map toolbar**. When you first create a data map, two of the buttons on the toolbar are recessed (active) — Select Objects and Show/Hide Microsoft Map Control.

FIGURE 9-50

When the **Select Objects button** is recessed, you are able to select items within the data map location, such as legends and the data map title, and move and format them. When the **Show/Hide Microsoft Map Control button** is recessed, the Microsoft Map Control dialog box displays, which allows you to format the data map. The **Grabber button** allows you to grab the data map and move it. This button is especially useful when the data map is zoomed out and you want to see hidden parts.

Changing the Map's Features

When the data map is selected with a single click, a set of handles surrounds the data map and you can resize it, move it, or delete it. When the data map is active, by using a double-click, a heavy gray border surrounds the data map and you can change its features and format it.

The **Features command** on the shortcut menu allows you to add or delete countries from the active data map. For example, Canada or Mexico can be removed from the data map, because Burrito Land stores are located only in the United States. The steps on the next page illustrate how to change the features of a data map.

The Mapstats File

If you easily want to add statistical information to your data map, Microsoft Map installs a sample workbook containing demographic and geographic information. This Mapstats file includes world demographic data by Country, United States demographic data by state, Canada demographic data by province, Mexico demographic data by state, Europe demographic data by country, United Kingdom & Republic of Ireland by county, Australia demographic data by state, and South Africa and neighboring countries by region. To locate the Mapstats file, click the Start button on the taskbar and then click Find. Search for the file named Mapstats.xls.

Drawing the Data Map Location

Holding down the ALT key while dragging to define the data map location instructs Excel to snap the data map location to the nearest gridline on the worksheet.

Data Map Features

Additional characteristics can be added to a data map, such as major highways, cities, airports, lakes, or a combination of these. Right-click the data map and then click Features on the shortcut menu.

To Change the Features of a Data Map

1 **Right-click the data map and then point to Features.**

The shortcut menu displays (Figure 9-51).

FIGURE 9-51

2 **Click Features. When the Map Features dialog box displays, click Canada, Canada Lakes, and Mexico to clear the corresponding check marks from the Visible list. Point to the OK button.**

The Map Features dialog box displays as shown in Figure 9-52. Great Lakes and United States are selected.

FIGURE 9-52

Click the OK button.

The data map displays with-out Mexico, Canada, and Canada Lakes (Figure 9-53). Only the United States and the Great Lakes display.

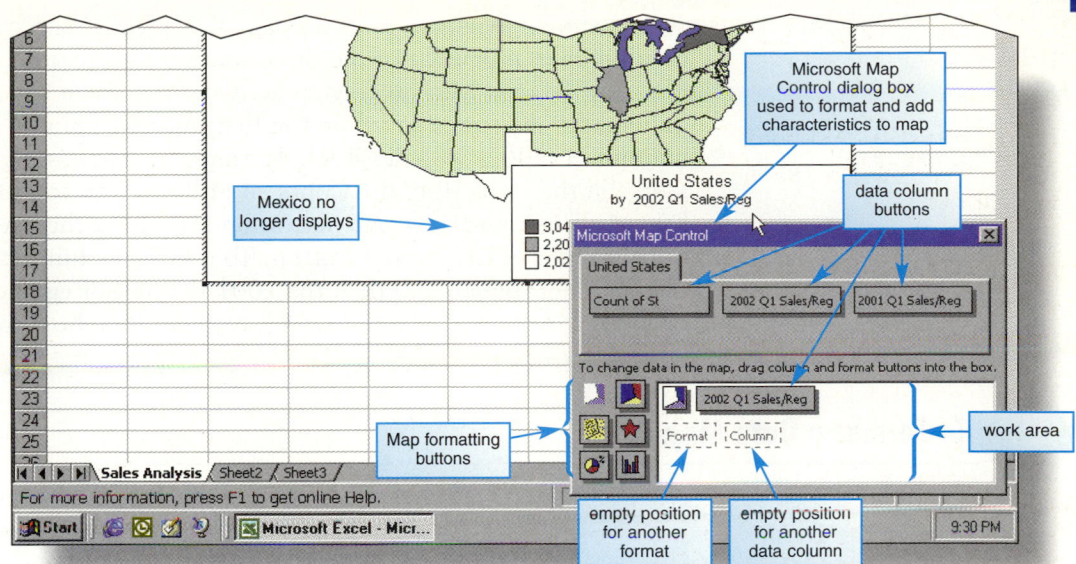

FIGURE 9-53

Formatting a Data Map and Adding Column Chart Symbols

The **Microsoft Map Control dialog box** (Figure 9-53), which displays when the data map first is created, is used to format the map and add charts. The Microsoft Map Control dialog box is divided into three areas: the Data column buttons area, the Map formatting buttons area, and the work area. The **Data column buttons area** includes a button for each column heading used to create the data map. The **Map formatting buttons area** includes six formatting buttons as described in Table 9-5. The **work area** in the Microsoft Map Control dialog box is where you drag buttons from the other two areas to format the data map.

Other Ways

1. On Map menu click Features, click categories to remove, click OK button
2. Right-click data map, click Features on shortcut menu, click map feature in Visible box in Map Features dialog box, click Remove button, click OK button

Table 9-5 Map Formatting Buttons

MAP FORMATTING BUTTON	BUTTON NAME	FUNCTION
	Value Shading	Shades each category (state) on the data map according to the value in the corresponding data column. This button is the default. Figure 9-53 shows this button in the work area; the result is the three states in different shades.
	Category Shading	Shades each category (state) on the data map differently.
	Dot Density	Displays dots within the boundaries of each category (state) on the data map. The dot density is based on the values in one column of data in the data map range.
	Graduated Symbols	Displays graduated symbols, such as varying size circles, at the center of each category (state) on the data map. The size of each symbol is based on the values in one of the columns of data in the data map range.
	Pie Chart	Displays a Pie chart for each category (state) on the data map. The slices in the Pie chart are dependent on the values of the selected column of data.
	Column Chart	Displays a column chart for each category (state) on the data map. The number of columns in the chart is dependent on the number of columns selected. The heights of the columns are dependent on the magnitude of the data for each different category (state).

As shown in Figure 9-45 on page E 9.35, the data map for this project calls for column charts for each of the three states with Burrito Land stores (IL, TX, and NY). By default, Microsoft Map activates the **Value Shading button** in the work area and shades the states based on the first numeric column in the data map range, column H (2002 Q1 Sales/Reg). To shade the three states based on the count of stores in the state, drag the Count of St button on top of the 2002 Q1 Sales/Reg button. When you drag one button on top of another in the work area, the dragged button replaces the current button. To add the column chart symbols, drag the **Column Chart button** and then the 2001 Q1 Sales/Reg and the 2002 Q1 Sales/Reg onto the work area. The following steps describe how to format the data map.

To Format a Data Map

1 **Point to the Count of St button in the Data column buttons area of the Microsoft Map Control dialog box.**

The mouse pointer changes to a hand grabbing a handle (Figure 9-54). A ScreenTip displays the complete name of the button when you point to it.

FIGURE 9-54

2 **Drag the Count of St button on top of the 2002 Q! Sales/Reg button in the work area. Point to the Column Chart button in the Map formatting buttons area.**

Microsoft Map changes the legend to display data about the number of stores instead of the 2002 Q1 Sales/Reg (Figure 9-55). The Grabber displays over the Column Chart button.

FIGURE 9-55

3 Drag the Column Chart button onto the outlined word, Format, in the work area. One by one, drag the 2001 Q1 Sales/Reg button and the 2002 Q1 Sales/Reg button from the Data column buttons area onto the outlined word, Column, in the work area.

The work area in the Microsoft Map Control dialog box displays as shown in Figure 9-56. Each of the three states with Burrito Land stores is assigned a Column chart on the data map. The leftmost column represents the first quarter sales per register for 2001 for a given state. The rightmost column represents the first quarter sales per register for 2002.

FIGURE 9-56

4 Click the Show/Hide Microsoft Map Control button on the toolbar. Click the Shade legend in the lower-right corner of the data map location.

The Microsoft Map Control dialog box closes and the data map displays with two legends in the lower-right corner of the data map location (Figure 9-57). The **Shade legend** *defines the shading; the* **Column chart legend** *defines the Column charts. The Shade legend is selected.*

FIGURE 9-57

5 Press the DELETE key to delete the Shade legend. Drag the Column chart legend to the lower-left corner of the data map location. Double-click the map title, North America. Type Burrito Land in the text box and then point to the OK button.

The new title displays and the Edit Text Object dialog box displays (Figure 9-58).

FIGURE 9-58

6 Click the OK button. Click View on the menu bar and then point to Subtitle.

The new title displays and the View menu displays (Figure 9-59).

FIGURE 9-59

7 Click Subtitle. When the Subtitle text box displays in the map, double-click it. Enter the subtitle shown in Figure 9-60. Resize and center the title and subtitle as necessary. Click cell N19 to deactivate the data map. Click the Save button on the Standard toolbar.

The data map is complete (Figure 9-60).

FIGURE 9-60

As you can see from Figure 9-60, you can create sophisticated data maps with just a few clicks of the mouse button.

Excel's Microsoft Map feature comes with a file called Mapstats.xls. The file contains demographic data such as populations and household income. You may combine your data with the data from the Mapstats file to recognize trends and perform analysis in a map.

Creating and Formatting PivotCharts and PivotTables

A **PivotChart** is an interactive chart used to analyze data graphically by varying the fields and categories to present different views. After you create a PivotChart, you may view different levels of detail, reorganize the layout of the chart by dragging its fields, or display and hide items in drop-down lists. While you usually create a PivotChart on a separate worksheet in the same workbook containing the data you are analyzing, you can create a PivotChart on the same worksheet as the data.

When you create a PivotChart, Excel creates and associates a PivotTable automatically. A **PivotTable** is an interactive view of worksheet data that gives you the ability to summarize data in the database, and then rotate the table's row and column titles to show different views of the summarized data.

Creating a PivotChart

The **PivotChart command** on the Data menu starts the **PivotTable and PivotChart Wizard**, which guides you through creating a PivotChart. The wizard does not modify the data in any way; it simply uses the data to generate information on a new worksheet.

More About

Formatting the Data Map Title

You can format the data map title in the same way you format chart titles. Right-click the data map title and then click Format Font on the shortcut menu.

The required PivotChart for this project is shown in Figure 9-61. It summarizes 2001 and 2002 first quarter sales per register information by location within state for the Burrito Land Sales Analysis worksheet. The X-axis displays categories by location within state. The Y-axis displays the series values for the total sales per register for each year. The interactive buttons allow the user to choose which fields to display. The legend displays the color coding for each year.

FIGURE 9-61

To create the PivotChart shown in Figure 9-61, perform the following steps.

 To Create a PivotChart

1 Scroll to cell A3 and click it. Click Data on the menu bar and then point to PivotTable and PivotChart Report (Figure 9-62).

FIGURE 9-62

2 Click PivotTable and PivotChart Report.
When the PivotTable and PivotChart Wizard – Step 1 of 3 dialog box displays, click PivotChart (with PivotTable). Point to the Next button.

The *PivotTable and PivotChart Wizard – Step 1 of 3 dialog box* displays (Figure 9-63). The Microsoft Excel list or database and the PivotChart (with PivotTable) option buttons are selected.

FIGURE 9-63

3 Click the Next button.

The *PivotTable and PivotChart Wizard – Step 2 of 3 dialog box* displays. The range A2:I23 automatically is selected (Figure 9-64). A marquee surrounds the data on the worksheet.

FIGURE 9-64

4 **Click the Next button. When the PivotTable and PivotChart Wizard – Step 3 of 3 displays, if necessary, click New Worksheet and then point to the Finish button.**

The Wizard will place the chart and table on separate worksheets in the workbook (Figure 9-65).

FIGURE 9-65

5 **Click the Finish Button. When the PivotChart area and the PivotTable toolbar display, drag the toolbar up and to the right in order to display all areas of the PivotChart.**

The PivotChart displays on a new worksheet (Figure 9-66). The PivotTable toolbar also displays. Fields from the list of data display as buttons on the toolbar.

FIGURE 9-66

1. Press ALT+D, press P

The four main areas of a PivotChart (Figure 9-66) are described in Table 9-6.

Table 9-6 PivotChart Drop Areas	
PIVOTCHART DROP AREA	DESCRIPTION OF DATA
Drop Page Fields Here	Data fields that categorize the entire chart
Drop Data Items Here	Data fields plotted on the chart, summarizing the detail of the database cells
Drop More Series Fields Here	Multiple data items plotted as a series, summarizing the detail columns of the database cells
Drop More Category Fields Here	Data fields to categorize on the X-axis

Adding Data to the PivotChart

The following steps create the PivotChart in Figure 9-61 on page E 9.46 by dropping four fields from the PivotTable toolbar onto the PivotChart area, two for the X-axis along the bottom of the chart and two for the data series in the chart. As shown in Figure 9-61, the X-axis displays location within state. The Y-axis includes the two data fields 2001 Q1 Sales/Reg and 2002 Q1 Sales/Reg.

To Add Data to the PivotChart

1 **Drag the St (state) button from the PivotTable toolbar to the Drop More Category Fields Here area. Drag the Location button from the PivotTable toolbar and drop it to the right of the St (state) button. Point to the 2001 Q1 Sales/Reg button.**

The State and Location field buttons display at the bottom of the PivotChart area (Figure 9-67). The sales per register buttons display to the right of the sales buttons for each year. When you point to a field button, Excel displays its full name and instructions as a ScreenTip.

FIGURE 9-67

2 Drag the 2001 Q1 Sales/Reg button to the Drop Data Items Here area. Drag the 2002 Q1 Sales/Reg button to the same area.

The data fields display in the PivotChart (Figure 9-68). Because multiple fields have been added to the chart, a field Data button displays in the categories area at the bottom of the chart.

FIGURE 9-68

3 Drag the field Data button to the Drop More Series Fields Here area.

The two data fields display stacked (Figure 9-69).

FIGURE 9-69

Other Ways

1. In PivotTable and PivotChart Wizard – Step 3 of 3 dialog box, click Layout button

Regular charts in Excel are linked directly to worksheet cells, which means that when data changes in the worksheet cell, the chart is updated automatically. PivotCharts are not linked to worksheet cells. The PivotTable toolbar contains a Refresh button (Figure 9-69) to update data when it changes on the worksheet. PivotCharts and their associated PivotTables can be based on several different types of data including Excel lists and databases, multiple data ranges that you want to consolidate, and external sources, such as Microsoft Access databases.

Formatting a PivotChart

Excel provides many ways to format PivotCharts. If you are familiar with regular charts, you will find that most formatting processes, such as choosing a chart type, displaying category or axis labels, and inserting titles, are performed the same way in PivotCharts as they are in regular charts.

The preset chart type for a PivotChart is a Stacked Column chart. PivotCharts can display any chart type except XY (Scatter), Stock, or Bubble. The following steps change the Burrito Land PivotChart from a Stacked Column chart to a Clustered Column chart that displays the two-year data side by side, adds a title, and formats the numbers along the Y-axis.

 To Change the PivotChart Type and Format It

1 **Click the Chart Wizard button** on the PivotTable toolbar. When the Chart Wizard - Step 1 of 4 - Chart Type dialog box displays, click the Clustered Column chart in the top row of the Chart sub-type box. Point to the Next button.

The Chart Type dialog box allows you to choose the type of chart and its subtype (Figure 9-70). A preview is available with the Press and Hold to View Sample button.

FIGURE 9-70

2 **Click the Next button. When the Chart Wizard - Step 3 of 4 - Chart Options dialog box displays, if necessary, click the Titles tab. Click the Chart title text box, type** Burrito Land Analysis, **and then point to the Finish button.**

The Chart Options dialog box displays as shown in Figure 9-71.

FIGURE 9-71

3 **Click the Finish button. Right-click any of the numbers along the Y-axis on the left side of the PivotChart. Point to Format Axis on the shortcut menu.**

The Chart Wizard closes and the axis shortcut menu displays (Figure 9-72). Clicking the Finish button accepted the preset values for the rest of the Chart Wizard.

FIGURE 9-72

4 Click Format Axis. When the Format Axis dialog box displays, click the Number tab, and then click Currency in the Category box. Type 0 in the Decimal places box. Point to the OK button.

The Format Axis dialog box displays as shown in Figure 9-73.

FIGURE 9-73

5 Click the OK button. Double-click the Chart1 sheet tab at the bottom of the workbook. Type PivotChart and then press the ENTER key to rename the sheet.

The numbers along the Y-axis display using the Currency format (Figure 9-74).

6 Click anywhere on the chart to deselect the Y-axis. Click the PivotTable toolbar Close button and then click the Save button on the Standard toolbar.

Excel saves the workbook with the PivotChart on drive A.

FIGURE 9-74

Other Ways

1. Click PivotChart button on PivotTable toolbar, click Options

2. Click Chart Wizard button on PivotTable toolbar, apply formatting in each step

With the chart completed and formatted appropriately, the chart can be manipulated and the data analyzed in a variety of views.

Changing the View of a PivotChart

With regular charts, you must create one chart for each view of the data summary that you want to see. With a PivotChart, you are able to create a single chart and view the summaries several ways just by using the mouse. The PivotChart provides a powerful interactive summarization of data with the visual appeal and benefits of a chart.

The Burrito Land PivotChart currently displays the sales per register data for each quarter within location within state (Figure 9-74 on the previous page).

It is easy to see common trends, such as that most locations in the three states have had increases in sales. You also can see that in general, gas station locations have a lower sum of sales per register. It might be easier to analyze that data, however, if all the gas station locations were grouped. If you want to compare the data in different combinations, you can use the interactive buttons in the categories area at the bottom of the chart.

Because Illinois and Texas have more mall locations than New York, you might want to view the data and compare only those two states rather than all three. Moving the two data ranges next to each other in the worksheet would be tedious, but in the PivotChart, you may choose which categories to display, by again using the interactive buttons at the bottom of the chart.

If you want to isolate one year versus another, for instance, you use the interactive buttons in the series area on the right of the chart.

Perform the following steps to interact with the PivotChart categories and series of data.

 Steps **To Change the View of a PivotChart**

① **Drag the St (state) button at the bottom of the chart to the right of the Location button.**

Notice the locations are grouped together now, rather than the states (Figure 9-75).

FIGURE 9-75

2 **Click the Data button arrow on the right of the chart. When the list displays, click the check box next to Sum of 2001 Q1 Sales/Reg to clear the check box. Point to the OK button.**

The list of data fields on the chart displays (Figure 9-76).

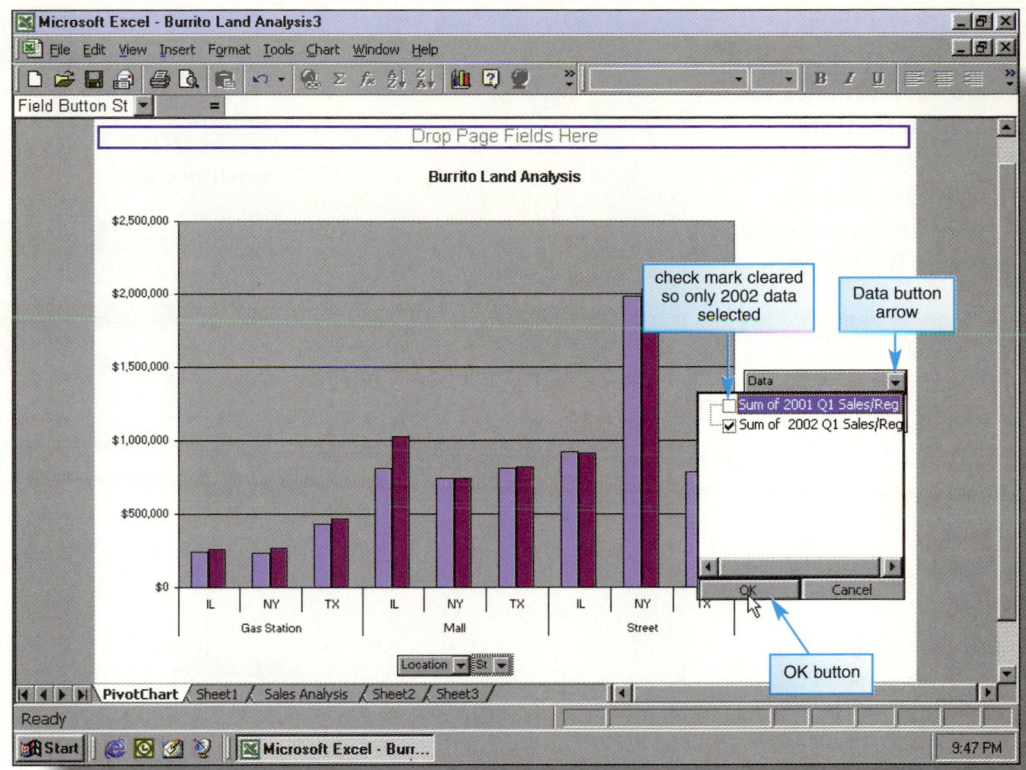

FIGURE 9-76

3 **Click the OK button in the Data list box. Point to the Undo button on the Standard toolbar.**

Only the data for 2002 displays (Figure 9-77). The Sum of 2002 Q1 Sales/Reg becomes a field for the entire page.

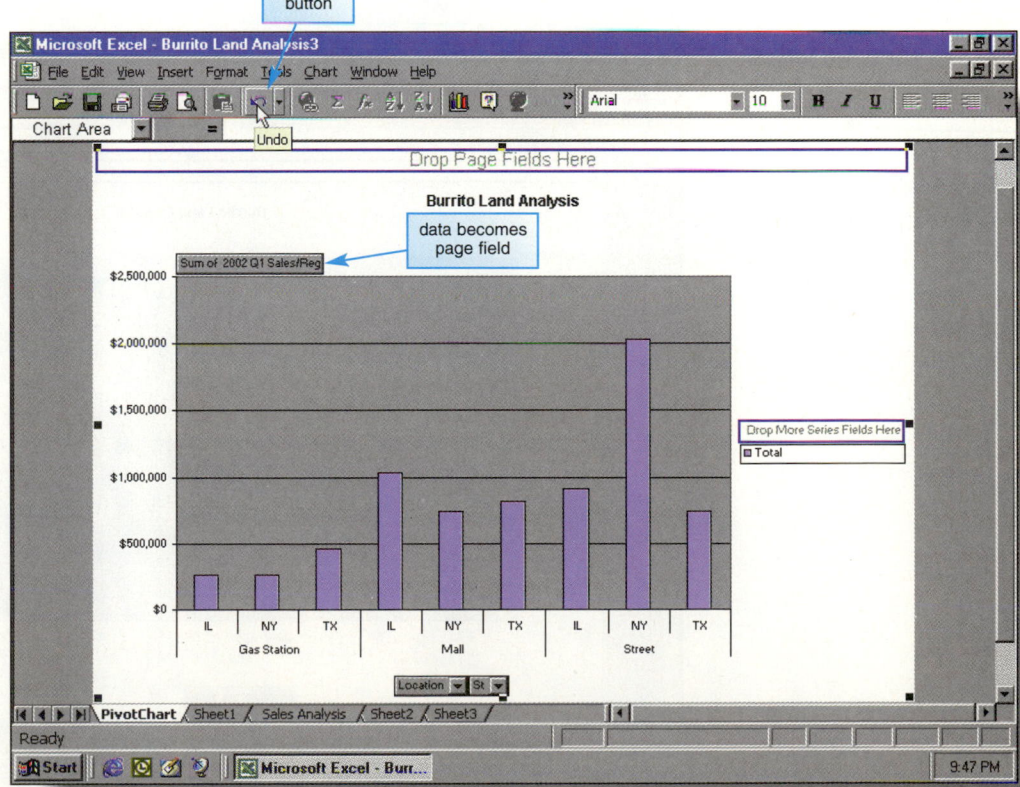

FIGURE 9-77

4 **Click the Undo button on the Standard toolbar. Click the arrow on the St (state) interactive button, click the check mark for NY so it does not display, and then point to the OK button.**

The data fields in the St (state) button display (Figure 9-78). The 2001 data again displays in the PivotChart.

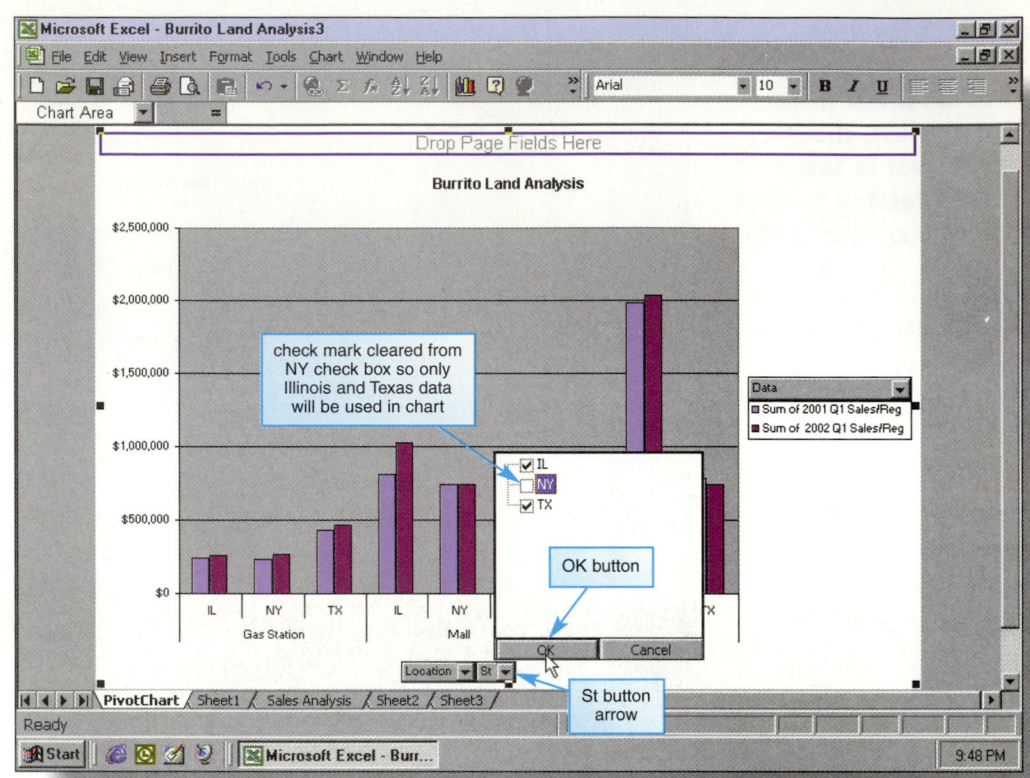

FIGURE 9-78

5 **Click the OK button.**

Only the data for Illinois and Texas displays (Figure 9-79).

6 **Click the Undo button.**

The data for all states displays (Figure 9-75 on page E 9.54).

Other Ways

1. To remove data, drag button off chart
2. To add data, drag button from PivotChart toolbar

FIGURE 9-79

You can employ powerful data summarization techniques using PivotCharts. Choosing which kinds of data best represent trends and comparisons is easy with the interactive buttons on a PivotChart.

PivotChart and PivotTable Relationships

Excel creates and associates a PivotTable on a separate sheet with every PivotChart. A PivotTable (Figure 9-80) is an interactive view of worksheet data that gives you the ability to summarize data and then rotate the table's row and column titles to show different views of the summarized data.

When you change the position of a field in a PivotChart or PivotTable, the corresponding field in the other changes automatically. **Row fields** in a PivotTable correspond to category fields in a PivotChart, while **column fields** in a PivotTable correspond to series fields in charts.

Formatting a PivotTable

When you choose to format a PivotTable, Excel displays samples in the AutoFormat dialog box with various formatting applied to the cells, borders, and numbers. You can choose from colors, patterns, alignments, fonts, and borders, which apply to the entire table. You may also apply any of the wide range of Excel's normal formats to individual cells. The following steps choose a format that contains color and borders to enhance the data.

More About

PivotTables

The PivotTable is one of the more powerful analytical tools available in Excel. PivotTables are used to show the relationships among the data in a list or a database. These tables allow you to use drag and drop to examine the data from different views.

 To Format a PivotTable

1 **Double-click the Sheet1 tab at the bottom of the workbook. Type** PivotTable **and then press the ENTER key, to rename the sheet. Right-click a toolbar and click PivotTable on the shortcut menu to display the PivotTable toolbar. Point to the Format Report button on the PivotTable toolbar.**

The PivotTable, created by Excel and associated with the PivotChart, displays (Figure 9-80). If the PivotTable toolbar does not display, right-click the menu bar and click PivotTable.

FIGURE 9-80

2 Click the Format Report button. When the AutoFormat dialog box displays, if necessary, scroll to display Report 6. Click Report 6 and then point to the OK button.

The AutoFormat dialog box displays report formats to add color and variety to the PivotTable (Figure 9-81).

FIGURE 9-81

3 Click the OK button. Double-click the border between column headings A and B to change column A to best fit. Click the Select All button. Right-click any cell and then click Format Cells. When the Format Cells dialog box displays, click Currency in the Category list, type 0 in the Decimal places box, and then click the OK button. Click cell A21 to deselect the worksheet.

The PivotTable displays as shown in Figure 9-82.

4 Click the Save button to save the workbook using the file name Burrito Land Analysis3.

FIGURE 9-82

Other Ways

1. Right-click table, click Format Report on shortcut menu

The AutoFormat dialog box shown in Figure 9-81 includes 12 customized formats. Use the scroll box to view the formats that do not display in the dialog box.

Each one of these customized formats offers a different look. The one you choose depends on the worksheet you are creating. If you want to remove the format on a PivotTable, you can click None in the list of formats.

Interacting with the PivotTable

Interacting with a PivotTable is as easy as it is with the PivotChart. You can change the way the data fields are summarized, add new fields to the analysis, or you can rotate the row and column fields.

SWITCHING SUMMARY FUNCTIONS In the Burrito Land PivotChart, you may have realized that the data created in the chart summarizes the sum of the sales per register. The fact that more mall locations exist than gas station locations in any given state will make their figures higher automatically if you look at the sums. An average might be a better way to compare the locations. To change the field setting from sum to average, you simply right-click the data field in the PivotTable, click Field Settings on the shortcut menu, and then choose Average in the Summarize by list as shown in the following steps.

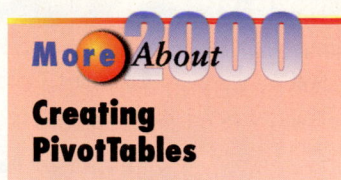

More About

Creating PivotTables

For more information about the process of creating PivotTables, visit the Excel 2000 More About Web page (www.scsite.com/Ex2000/more.htm) and then click PivotTables.

 To Switch Summary Functions in a PivotTable

1 **Right-click cell C4. Click Field Settings on the shortcut menu. When the PivotTable Field dialog box displays, click Average in the Summarize by list. Click the OK button.**

The numbers in column C change from sums to averages.

2 **Right-click cell D4. Click Field Settings on the shortcut menu. When the PivotTable Field dialog box displays, click Average in the Summarize by list box. Click the OK button.**

The numbers in column D change from location sums to location averages (Figure 9-83).

FIGURE 9-83

3 **Click the PivotTable toolbar Close button.**

Table 9-7 Summary Functions for PivotTable Data Analysis

SUMMARY FUNCTION	DESCRIPTION
Sum	Sum values. This is the default function for numeric source data.
Count	The number of items.
Average	The average of the values.
Max	The largest value.
Min	The smallest value.
Product	The product of the values.
Count Nums	The number of rows that contain numeric data.
StdDev	An estimate of the standard deviation of all the data to be summarized.
StdDevp	The standard deviation of all of the data to be summarized.
Var	An estimate of the variance of all of the data to be summarized.
Varp	The variance of the data to be summarized.

Table 9-7 lists the summary functions from which you may choose through the Field Settings command on the shortcut menu to analyze your data in PivotCharts and PivotTables.

CHANGING THE VIEW OF A PIVOTTABLE You can rotate the row and column fields around the data field by dragging the buttons to different locations on the PivotTable. For example, if you drag the St (state) button to the Drop Page Fields Here area at the top of the table (above row 1 in the worksheet), you change the view of the PivotTable as shown in the following steps.

 To Change the View of a PivotTable

 Drag the St button above row 1.

Excel displays a new, different view of the PivotTable (Figure 9-84), which is easier to read than the PivotTable shown in Figure 9-83 on the previous page.

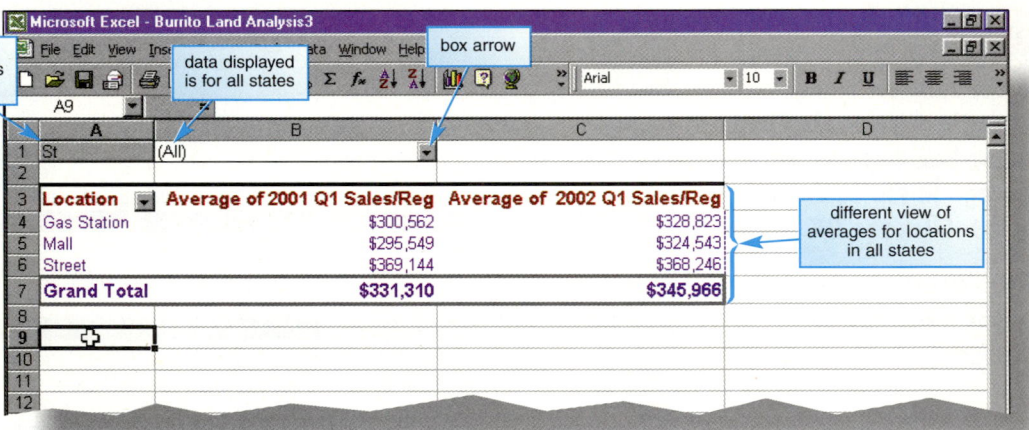

FIGURE 9-84

2 **Click the St box arrow, click IL, and then click the OK button.**

Excel displays the averages for each location type in the state of Illinois (Figure 9-85).

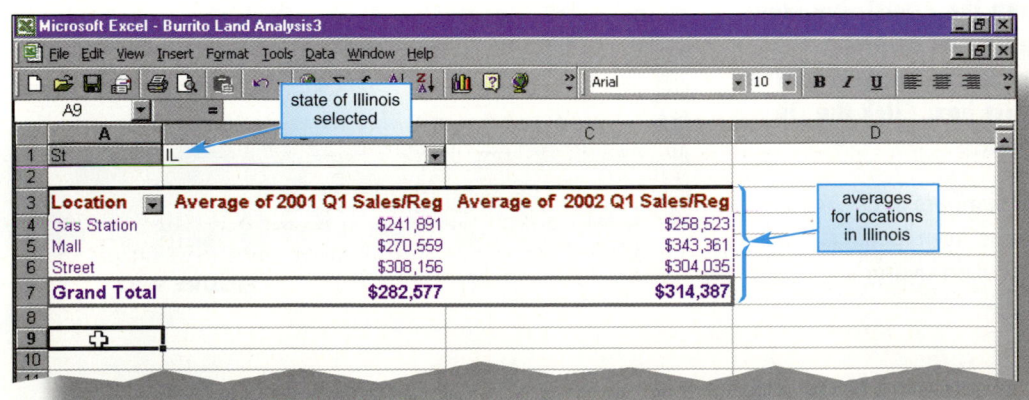

FIGURE 9-85

In Figure 9-84, the St button has a box and drop-down arrow to the right. Click the arrow to display the St list box and select the specific states whose averages you want to view.

PivotTables are powerful data analysis tools because they allow you to view the data in various ways by interchanging or pairing up the row and column fields. You can print a PivotChart or PivotTable just as you would any other worksheet. If you update the data on the Quarter 1 Sales Data sheet, click **Refresh Data** on the Data menu or click the **Refresh button** on the PivotTable toolbar to update the corresponding PivotTable and PivotChart.

Quitting Excel

The project is complete. To quit Excel, follow the steps below.

TO QUIT EXCEL

1 Click the Close button on the right side of the title bar.

2 If the Microsoft Excel dialog box displays, click the No button.

Merging Workbooks

Instead of tracking all of the changes to a single copy of a workbook, it sometimes is necessary to merge copies of the same workbook together, because either multiple users are entering data, or new data has come in from a different source. To merge the changes from one workbook into another, both workbooks must satisfy the following requirements:

- You must make the original workbook shared, before making copies, and each workbook must be a copy of the same workbook.
- When you make copies, Track Changes or sharing must be turned on (which keeps a Change History file of the workbook).
- The Share Workbook command on the Tools menu displays a dialog box with a tab for recording the number of days to record the change history. Shared workbooks must be merged within that time period.
- If you use passwords, all workbooks involved in the merge must have the same password.
- When the copies come back, each must have a different file name.

When you have all the copies of the workbook together, you open the copy of the shared workbook into which you want to merge changes from another workbook file on disk. Then, on the Tools menu, click **Merge Workbooks**, which will display choices for you to choose a workbook or workbooks to merge. Not only is the data merged, but if comments are recorded, they display one after another in the given cell's comment box.

If Excel cannot merge the two workbooks, you still can incorporate the information from one workbook into the other, by copying and pasting the information from one workbook to another.

Changing PivotTables

At any time while the workbook containing a PivotTable is active, you can click the tab of the sheet containing the PivotTable, and then click PivotTable on the Data menu to display the PivotTable Wizard - Step 3 of 3 dialog box (Figure 9-65 on page E 9.48). Use the Layout button in this dialog box as an alternative to using drag and drop to change the view of the PivotTable.

Quick Reference

For a table that lists how to complete the tasks covered in this book using the mouse, menu, shortcut menu, and keyboard, see the Excel Quick Reference Summary at the back of this book or visit the Office 2000 Web page (www.scsite.com/off2000/qr.htm), and then click Microsoft Excel 2000.

CASE PERSPECTIVE SUMMARY

With the imported data, the data map, the PivotChart, and the PivotTable developed in this project, the marketing manager for Burrito Land, José Velez, can view and analyze the sales data in a variety of ways. Links to the external data will update automatically when he refreshes his tables. During his presentation to the board of directors, he will have the ability to answer questions and clarify data by interacting with the PivotChart and PivotTable. His report will display timely, accurate, and visual data.

Project Summary

In this project, you learned how to import data in different formats into a worksheet, track changes, route workbooks, and create visual representations of the data in a worksheet. Using a preformatted worksheet, you learned how to import a text file, an Access database, and a Web table. You then learned how to Track Changes, which also shared the workbook. After routing the workbook to the coordinator from each state, you learned how to accept the changes. You then learned how to create a data map to represent data graphically according to locations. You learned how to create interactive PivotCharts and PivotTables, format them, and view them in different ways. Finally, you learned about sharing and merging workbooks.

What You Should Know

Having completed this project, you should be able to perform the following tasks:

▶ Add Data to the PivotChart *(E 9.49)*

▶ Add the Map Button to the Standard Toolbar *(E 9.36)*

▶ Change the Features of a Data Map *(E 9.40)*

▶ Change the PivotChart Type and Format It *(E 9.51)*

▶ Change the View of a PivotChart *(E 9.54)*

▶ Change the View of a PivotTable *(E 9.60)*

▶ Create a Data Map *(E 9.37)*

▶ Create a PivotChart *(E 9.46)*

▶ Format a Data Map *(E 9.42)*

▶ Format a PivotTable *(E 9.57)*

▶ Import Data from a Text File into a Worksheet *(E 9.9)*

▶ Import Data from a Web Page into a Worksheet *(E 9.18)*

▶ Import Data from an Access Table into a Worksheet *(E 9.14)*

▶ Insert a Comment *(E 9.24)*

▶ Open a Routed Workbook and Review Tracked Changes *(E 9.31)*

▶ Quit Excel *(E 9.61)*

▶ Replicate Formulas *(E 9.22)*

▶ Route a Workbook *(E 9.27)*

▶ Save the Workbook with a New File Name *(E 9.23)*

▶ Save the Tracked Changes in a Workbook with a New File Name *(E 9.34)*

▶ Start Excel and Open a Workbook *(E 9.8)*

▶ Switch Summary Functions in a PivotTable *(E 9.59)*

▶ Turn Off Track Changes *(E 9.35)*

▶ Turn On Track Changes *(E 9.26)*

Microsoft Certification

The Microsoft Office User Specialist (MOUS) Certification program provides an opportunity for you to obtain a valuable industry credential – proof that you have the Excel 2000 skills required by employers. For more information, see Appendix D or visit the Shelly Cashman Series MOUS Web page at www.scsite.com/off2000/cert.htm.

Apply Your Knowledge

Project Reinforcement at www.scsite.com/off2000/reinforce.htm

1 Creating a Data Map

Instructions: Start Excel and perform the following tasks.

1. Open the workbook, Sales Rep Database from the Data Disk. The worksheet database displays as shown in Figure 9-86a.

(a) Worksheet Database

Microsoft Excel - Sales Rep Database

	Lname	Fname	Age	Gender	Title	St	Quota 2002	Sales 2002	Quota 2001	Sales 2001
	Sales Representative Database									
3	Biagi	Linda	41	F	Manager	IL	2,073,227	2,241,750	1,983,000	2,032,575
4	Jacobs	Lucy	45	F	Telemarketer	NY	1,627,844	1,524,600	1,557,000	1,595,925
5	Groen	Jodi	35	F	Telemarketer	TX	836,451	1,536,350	800,000	820,050
6	Grodzieki	Fran	37	F	Sales Rep	IL	3,241,050	3,407,250	3,100,000	3,177,500
7	Baxter	John	35	M	Sales Rep	TX	2,456,925	2,403,750	2,350,000	2,408,750
8	Josef	Jeff	44	M	Manager	NY	2,875,125	3,307,500	2,750,000	2,818,750
9	Joseph	Albert	55	M	Manager	TX	1,568,250	1,227,500	1,500,000	1,537,500
10	Wade	Susan	54	F	Manager	CA	4,286,550	4,567,500	4,100,000	4,202,500
11	Little	Deborah	27	F	Telemarketer	IL	1,001,589	1,338,750	958,000	981,950
12	Russo	Lin	41	F	Sales Rep	CA	2,091,000	2,890,650	2,000,000	2,050,000
13	Doolittle	Jeff	34	M	Sales Rep	NY	1,306,875	1,575,000	1,250,000	1,281,250
14	James	Kevin	31	M	Telemarketer	CA	1,568,250	1,537,500	1,500,000	1,537,500

(b) Data Map

Microsoft Excel - Sales Rep Database1

$ Quota by State
2002 vs. 2001 Figures

United States
8,000,000
■ Quota 2002
■ Quota 2001

FIGURE 9-86

(continued)

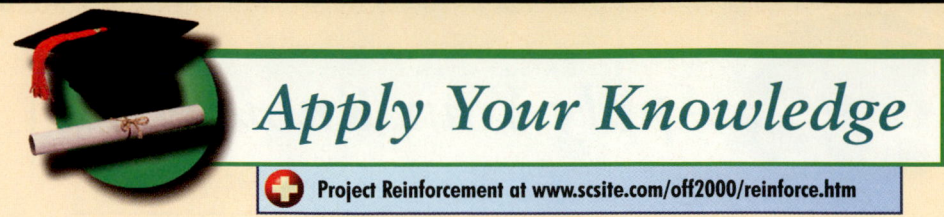

Apply Your Knowledge

Project Reinforcement at www.scsite.com/off2000/reinforce.htm

Creating a Data Map *(continued)*

2. Select the range, A2:J14. Click the Map button on the Standard toolbar. If your system does not display a Map button, see page E 9.36 for instructions on adding the Map button to the Standard toolbar. Scroll to view cell L1 in the upper-left corner of the screen. Drag the map from N1:U17. Choose the United States in North America in the Multiple Maps Available list. When the map displays, right-click the map and then click Features on the shortcut menu. Remove Canada, Canada Lakes, and Mexico from the map and then click the OK button.

3. If necessary, click the Show/Hide Microsoft Map Control button on the Microsoft Map toolbar. When the Microsoft Map Control dialog box displays, drag the Count of St button to the work area and drop it to replace the Quota 2002 button. Drag the Column Chart button to the word Format. Drag the Quota 2002 and the Quota 2001 buttons to the word Column.

4. Delete the Shade legend. Drag the Column chart legend to the lower-left corner of the map. Change the map title to $ Quota by State. Add the subtitle 2002 vs. 2001 Figures using the View menu. Move and resize the titles as shown in Figure 9-86b.

5. Click outside the map area. Enter your name, course, computer laboratory exercise (Apply 9-1), date, and instructor name in the range A19:A23. Click the Print button on the Standard toolbar. The worksheet database (Figure 9-86a) will print on page one, the data map (Figure 9-86b) will print on page two. Save the workbook using the file name Sales Rep Database1.

6. Double-click the Map to make it active, and display the Microsoft Map Control dialog box. Drag the two Quota buttons from the work area back to the Data column buttons area. Drag the Column Chart button to the word Format. Drag the two Sales buttons to the word Column in the work area.

7. Change the map headings to reflect the actual sales rather than the quotas.

8. Print the worksheet and map.

9. Save the workbook using the file name Sales Rep Database2.

In the Lab

1 Importing Data into an Excel Worksheet

Problem: You are employed as an inventory control specialist for the local school district. You have asked each of the three grade schools to send you a list of inventory they are planning to dispose of at the end of the school year, complete with inventory number, quantity, description, location, age, purchase price, and depreciation allowance. Each school has sent the required data but in a variety of formats. School A used a mainframe computer and sent a text file with fields separated by commas. School B maintains its inventory in an Access database, and queried it, creating a table to send to you. School C posted its list on the school's intranet as a Web page.

Instructions: Perform the following tasks.

1. Open the workbook Local School District Disposables (Figure 9-87a) from the Data Disk.

(a) Worksheet Prior to Import

(b) Worksheet After Import

FIGURE 9-87

(continued)

In the Lab

Importing Data into an Excel Worksheet *(continued)*

2. In cell H3, enter the formula, `=F3-G3`.

3. In cell I3, enter the formula, `=IF(H3=0,"Fully Depreciated","Not Fully Depreciated")`.

4. Click cell A3. From the Data Disk, import the text file, SchoolA. It is a comma delimited text file. In step 2 of the Text Import Wizard, click the Comma check box; otherwise accept the default settings. When the External Data Range Properties dialog box displays, click Properties, and choose not to adjust the column width.

5. Click Cell A9. From the Data Disk, import the Access database file, SchoolB. Add all the fields from the Disposable Inventory table. Accept all of the default settings. When the External Data Range Properties dialog box displays, click Properties, choose not to adjust the column width, and choose not to include the field names from the table.

6. Click cell A14. From the Data Disk, import the HTML file, SchoolC. Accept the default setting for the New Web Query. When the External Data Range Properties dialog box displays, click Properties, and choose not to adjust the column width. Manually delete the column headings imported from the HTML file.

7. Replicate the formulas from cell H3 and cell I3 to fill the range H4:I21 (Figure 9-87b).

8. Enter your name, course, computer laboratory exercise (Lab 9-1), date, and instructor name in the range A25:A29.

9. On the File menu, click Page Setup and then click Landscape Orientation on the Page tab. Print a copy of the worksheet.

10. Save the workbook using the file name Local School District Disposables1.

2 Creating a Canadian Province Population Data Map

Problem: The Canadian government would like you to create a map showing the country's 1999 population by province (right side of Figure 9-88). You have been given a worksheet database of the 1999 population by province (upper-left corner of Figure 9-88).

Instructions: Perform the following tasks:

1. Open the workbook Canadian Province Population from the Data Disk.

2. Select the data range A2:B12. Using the Map button on the Standard toolbar, draw a data map of Canada in the range C1:J23. When the Multiple Maps Available dialog box displays, choose Canada. When the Microsoft Map Control dialog box displays, click its Close button. Click the Shade legend and then press the DELETE key to delete it.

3. Click the Map Labels button on the Microsoft Map toolbar (Figure 9-50 on page E 9.39). When the Map Labels dialog box displays, click Values from and then, if necessary, choose 1999 in the list. Click each province in the data map to display its population (Figure 9-88).

4. Double-click the map title and enter `1999 Canadian Population by Province` as the new title. Right-click the new title and use the Format Font command to change the title to 14 point bold. Drag the title to center it as shown in Figure 9-88.

5. Enter your name, course, computer laboratory exercise (Lab 9-2), date, and instructor name in the range, A18:A22. Print the worksheet. Save the workbook using the file name Canadian Province Population1.

In the Lab

FIGURE 9-88

3 Creating a PivotChart and Associated PivotTable for an Order Entry Database

Problem: You are employed as a spreadsheet specialist in the order entry department of Bernita's Wholesale Restaurant Supply. You have been assigned the task of creating a PivotChart and PivotTable from the company's order entry worksheet database (Figure 9-89a on the next page). The PivotChart and PivotTable are shown in Figures 9-89b and 9-89c on page E 9.69.

Instructions: Perform the following tasks:

1. Open the workbook Bernita's Wholesale Restaurant Supply from the Data Disk.
2. Create the PivotChart shown in Figure 9-89b and PivotTable shown in Figure 9-89c on separate sheets. The PivotChart and PivotTable summarize dollar amount information by order number and order date. Use the PivotTable and PivotChart Wizard to create the PivotChart and associated PivotTable.
3. Add the title shown in Figure 9-89b.
4. Format the Y-axis labels to currency with no decimal places.
5. Rename the Chart1 tab PivotChart. Rename the Sheet1 tab PivotTable.

(continued)

In the Lab

Creating a PivotChart and Associated PivotTable for an Order Entry Database *(continued)*

6. Drag the Amount button to the Drop Data Items Here area (Y-axis). Drag the Order No and Order Date buttons to the Drop More Category Fields Here area (X-axis).

7. Select the Order Database and PivotTable sheets. Enter your name, course, computer laboratory exercise (Lab 9-3), date, and instructor name in the range A20:A24. Hold down the SHIFT key and then click the Order Database tab.

8. Print the worksheet, PivotChart, and PivotTable. Save the workbook using the file name Bernita's Wholesale Restaurant Supply1.

9. Click the Order Date box arrow to deselect the date 1/25/99. Print the PivotChart and PivotTable. Add the 1/25/99 date back in.

10. Remove the Order Number from the X-axis, and add the Description button to the right of the Order Date button. Print the PivotChart and PivotTable.

11. Close Bernita's Wholesale Restaurant Supply1 without saving changes, and then reopen it. Click the PivotTable tab. Drag the buttons to create three different views. Print the PivotTable for each view. Close the workbook without saving changes.

(a) Worksheet Database

In the Lab

(b) PivotChart

(c) PivotTable

FIGURE 9-89

Cases and Places

The difficulty of these case studies varies:
◗ are the least difficult; ◗◗ are more difficult; and ◗◗◗ are the most difficult.

1 ◗ Open Burrito Land Analysis from the Data Disk. Import data from the table in the Access database TexasQ1 beginning in row 3. Import the text file IllinoisQ1 beginning in row 9. Copy the formulas in cell H3 and cell I3 through row 15. Enter your name, course, computer laboratory exercise (Cases and Places 9-1), date, and instructor name in the range A17:A21. Turn on Track Changes. Print the worksheet. Save the workbook using the file name Case 9-1. Route the workbook to three classmates. Tell them in the e-mail to respond within a day and make at least two changes each. When the workbook comes back to you, accept the changes. Print the worksheet. Save the workbook using the file name Case 9-1a.

2 ◗ Open the Sales Rep Database. Develop a PivotChart with the two Quota and two Sales amount fields in the Drop Data Items Here area (Y-axis) and the Gender and Age fields in the Drop More Category Fields Here (X-axis). Include a title and formatted Y-axis labels. Enter your name, course, computer laboratory exercise (Cases and Places 9-2), date, and instructor name in the range A17:A21. Save the workbook using the file name Case 9-2. Print the worksheet, PivotChart, and PivotTable. Display the PivotTable sheet. Drag the buttons to display five different views. Print the PivotTable for each.

3 ◗◗ The National Tornado Project maintains a database on the Internet about tornados in each state. The tornado data for the state of Indiana can be viewed at tornadoproject.com/alltorns/intorn.htm#top. Drag and drop three different county tables into a Word document. Remove excess spaces and insert commas between fields. Save the document as a text file. Open a new workbook in Excel, add appropriate column headings, and import the data into the workbook. Format the worksheet appropriately. Create a PivotChart and PivotTable. Print the worksheet. Print the PivotChart and PivotTable for three different views.

4 ◗◗ As an independent information specialist, World-Wide Producers has approached you for help. The company is considering building a new manufacturing center in one of five states: Illinois, Texas, Virginia, South Carolina, or Kansas. To help them decide, they want demographic data from each of the five states. Use the Find command on the Start menu to locate the MapStats.xls file, a workbook that accompanies Excel 2000. Find the most recent demographic information about the states, including Total Population, Number of Households, Total Businesses, and Total Employees, and copy it to a blank workbook. Develop a PivotChart and PivotTable to obtain different views of the data. Print five different views.

5 ◗◗◗ Using your own music recording library of CDs or tapes, create a database of the artists, musical selection title, type of music, recording medium, and year of recording. Create a PivotChart and PivotTable with year and type of music as the X-axis categories and recording medium as data (Y-axis). Print the worksheet, PivotChart, and PivotTable. Display the PivotTable sheet. Drag the buttons to display three different views. Print the PivotTable for each.

Microsoft Excel 2000

Creating a PivotTable List Web Page Using Excel

<table>
<tr><td>
C
A
S
E

P
E
R
S
P
E
C
T
I
V
E
</td><td>

LifeStyle Motorcycle Clothing & Apparel sells street apparel, dirt apparel, and motorcycle accessories through a nationwide sales force. The sales force is divided into districts within zones within regions. The management team consists of a sales manager for each region, an assistant manager for each zone, and a team leader for each district.

Following a year of dismal sales, Sturgis Davis was recently hired as the national sales manager. Sturgis's primary asset is his extensive cross industry and sales automation experiences. His immediate plan calls for developing an intranet-based sales reporting system that gives his management team up-to-date sales information to help make decisions.

As the spreadsheet specialist at LifeStyle Motorcycle Clothing & Apparel, Sturgis has asked you to take sales representative information supplied in a workbook and make it available to the managers and team leaders in an easy-to-use form. From your experience with Excel 2000, you know that you can create interactive Web pages. You also know that PivotTables are an ideal tool for analyzing data. You decide the best solution is to develop an interactive PivotTable list Web page.
</td></tr>
</table>

Introduction

Excel 2000 allows you to save a workbook, a worksheet, a range of cells, or a chart as a Web page using the Save as Web Page command on the File menu. Excel also allows you to save worksheet data as a PivotTable list. A **PivotTable list** is a Web page that lets you analyze data using your Web browser, rather than Excel. Similar to a PivotTable report, a PivotTable list is an interactive table that allows you to change the view of data, filter data, and create summaries of the data. The difference between the two PivotTables is that a PivotTable report is manipulated in Excel, whereas a PivotTable list is manipulated in your Web browser.

To create a PivotTable list, you start with an Excel workbook (Figure 1a on the next page). You use the Save as Web Page command on the File menu to create the PivotTable list (Figure 1b on the next page). Once you display the PivotTable list in your Web browser, you can change the view of the data as shown in Figures 1c and 1d. Figure 1c shows the data in Figure 1b summarized by the sales representatives' education within gender. Figure 1d illustrates the filtering capabilities of a PivotTable list, showing only the rows that represent sales representatives who work in Region 1, Zone 2, District 2. The other records in the list (Figure 1b) are hidden.

For other users to interact with a PivotTable list, they must have the Office Web components installed and they must be using Microsoft Internet Explorer 4.01 or later. The Office Web components are installed automatically as part of the Office 2000 installation process.

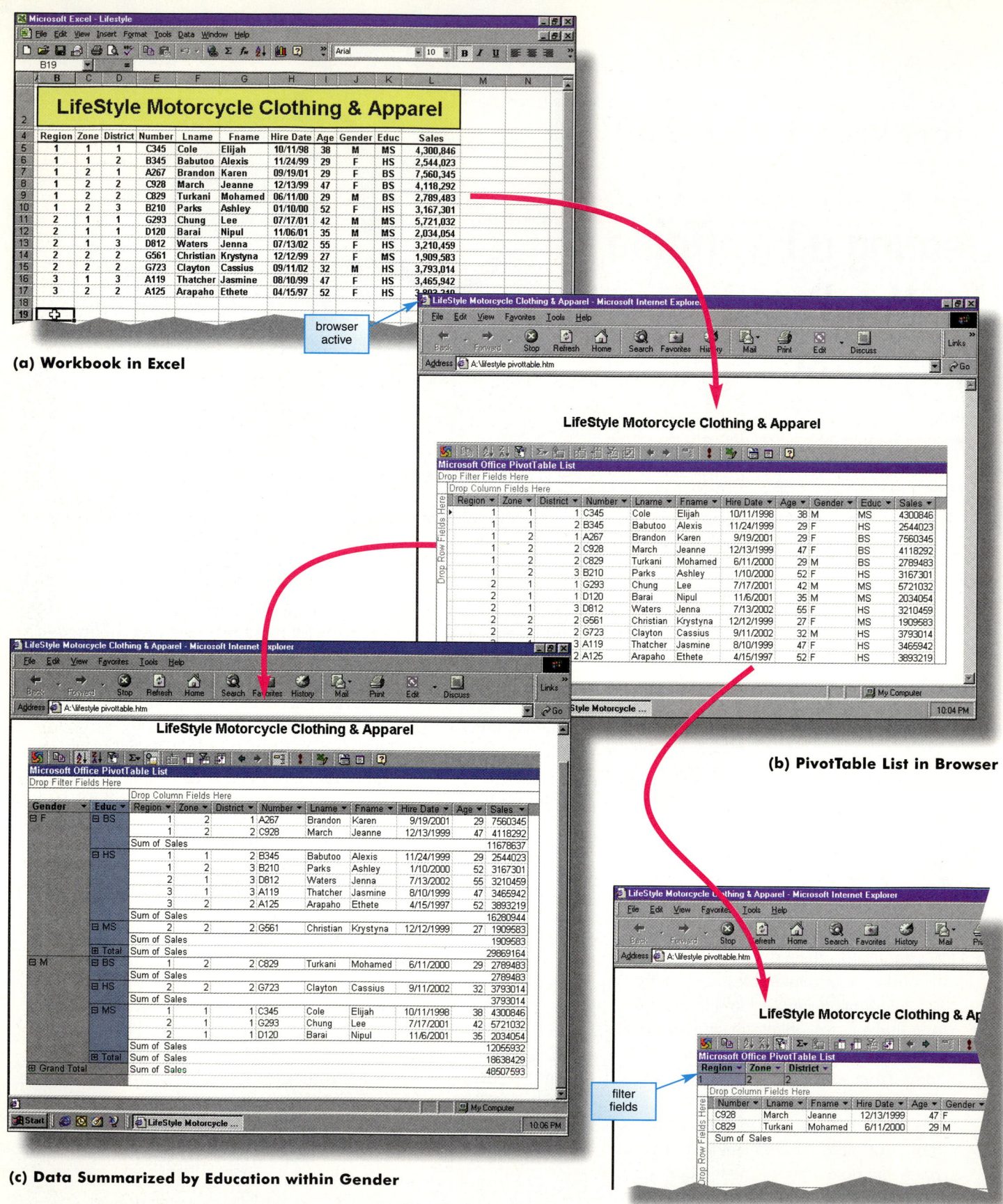

(a) Workbook in Excel

(b) PivotTable List in Browser

(c) Data Summarized by Education within Gender

(d) Only Region 1, Zone 2, District 2 Rows Display

FIGURE 1

Saving a Worksheet Database as a PivotTable List

The first step in this project is to open the Lifestyle workbook (Figure 1a) and save the database in the range B4:L17 as a PivotTable list.

More About **2000**

PivotTables

For more information on PivotTables, visit the Excel 2000 More About Web page (www.scsite.com/ex2000/more.htm) and click PivotTables.

Steps **To Save a Worksheet Database as a PivotTable List**

 Insert the Data Disk in drive A. Start Excel and then open the workbook Lifestyle on drive A. Reset your toolbars as described in Appendix C. Select the range B4:L17. Click File on the menu bar and then point to Save as Web Page.

The File menu displays (Figure 2).

FIGURE 2

 Click Save as Web Page. When the Save As dialog box displays, type lifestyle pivottable **in the File name text box. If necessary, click the Save in box arrow and then select 3½ Floppy (A:). Point to the Publish button.**

The Save As dialog box displays as shown in Figure 3.

FIGURE 3

③ **Click the Publish button. When the Publish as Web Page dialog box displays, click the Choose box arrow and then click Range of cells. Click Add interactivity with, click the Add interactivity with box arrow, and then click PivotTable functionality. Click the Change button. When the Set Title dialog box displays, type** LifeStyle Motorcycle Clothing & Apparel **in the Title text box. Point to the OK button.**

*The Publish as Web Page and Set Title dialog boxes display as shown in Figure 4. Selecting the **Add interactivity with check box** indicates that the Web page will be created with functionality.*

FIGURE 4

④ **Click the OK button. Click the Publish button. Click the Close button on the right side of the Excel title bar. Click the Yes button in the Microsoft Excel dialog box to save the changes.**

Excel saves the PivotTable list in HTML (hypertext markup language) format on drive A.

PivotTable Lists and Associated Charts

Along with a PivotTable list, you can include a chart that displays the same data graphically. If you display the PivotTable list in your browser and change the view, you will see the same changes in the chart.

If you click the Save button in Figure 3 on the previous page, Excel saves the entire workbook as a non-interactive Web page. If you click the Selection: Database option button and then click the Save button, Excel saves the selected range B4:L17 as a non-interactive Web page. Selecting the Add interactivity with check box in the Publish as Web Page dialog box (Figure 4) allows you to save the selected range as an interactive Web page. An **interactive Web page** allows you to change the values in the cells in your browser, but it does not give you the ability to rotate fields unless you add PivotTable functionality.

When you use the Publish button, you must tell Excel what you want to publish. In Figure 4, the range of cells selected on the worksheet is selected in the Choose list box. In the Viewing options area, once you select the Add interactivity with check box, the adjacent list box becomes active. The list box gives you two choices – Spreadsheet functionality or PivotTable functionality. The Change button in Figure 4 displays the **Set Title dialog box**, which allows you to add a title to the PivotTable list.

Viewing the PivotTable List Using Your Browser

With the PivotTable list saved as an HTML file, the next step is to view it using your browser as shown in the following steps.

 Steps   To View a PivotTable List Using Your Browser

1 **Click the Launch Internet Explorer Browser button on the Quick Launch toolbar.**

2 **When the Internet Explorer window displays, type** a:\lifestyle pivottable.htm **in the Address bar, and then press the ENTER key.**

The PivotTable list, lifestyle pivottable.htm, displays (Figure 5).

browser active

PivotTable list toolbar

title of PivotTable list

file name in Address bar

data field drop-down arrow allows you to hide records that do not meet a criterion

data field area

filter field area

column field area

row field area

LifeStyle Motorcycle Clothing & Apparel

Drop Filter Fields Here

Drop Column Fields Here

Region	Zone	District	Number	Lname	Fname	Hire Date	Age	Gender	Educ	Sales
1	1	1	C345	Cole	Elijah	10/11/1998	38	M	MS	4300846
1	1	2	B345	Babutoo	Alexis	11/24/1999	29	F	HS	2544023
1	2	1	A267	Brandon	Karen	9/19/2001	29	F	BS	7560345
1	2	2	C928	March	Jeanne	12/13/1999	47	F	BS	4118292
1	2	2	C829	Turkani	Mohamed	6/11/2000	29	M	BS	2789483
1	2	3	B210	Parks	Ashley	1/10/2000	52	F	HS	3167301
2	1	1	G293	Chung	Lee	7/17/2001	42	M	MS	5721032
2	1	1	D120	Barai	Nipul	11/6/2001	35	M	MS	2034054
2	1	3	D812	Waters	Jenna	7/13/2002	55	F	HS	3210459
2	2	2	G561	Christian	Krystyna	12/12/1999	27	F	MS	1909583
2	2	2	G723	Clayton	Cassius	9/11/2002	32	M	HS	3793014
3	1	3	A119	Thatcher	Jasmine	8/10/1999	47	F	HS	3465942
3	2	2	A125	Arapaho	Ethete	4/15/1997	52	F	HS	3893219

Drop Row Fields Here

data field area

data area

Launch Internet Explorer Browser button

FIGURE 5

The PivotTable list Web page in Figure 5 resembles an Excel worksheet with the column and row structure. The Address bar displays the URL. The title above the columns and rows is the same as the entry made in the Set Title dialog box shown in Figure 4. The toolbar immediately below the title includes buttons that allow you to complete tasks quickly, such as copy, sort, filter, calculate summaries, and move fields. Figure 6 identifies the buttons on the PivotTable list toolbar.

FIGURE 6

The area below the toolbar is divided into five areas as shown in Figure 5 on the previous page: (1) data area; (2) data field area; (3) row field area; (4) column field area; and (5) filter field area. The **data area** contains the data. Each entry in the data area is called an **item**. In the **data field area**, a **data field** at the top of each column identifies the data below it. For example, the Age data field identifies the ages in the same column. Each data field contains a **field drop-down arrow** that allows you to set up filters to display only records that meet a criterion. You drag data fields to the **row field area** on the left side of the PivotTable list and the **column field area** at the top of the PivotTable list to display different views of the data. You also can drag data fields to the **filter field area** to display different views of the data using filtering techniques.

More About 2000

Undoing PivotTable List Changes

If you make several changes to a PivotTable list and wish to restore it to its original view, quit your browser, launch your browser, and then display the PivotTable list again.

Changing the View of the PivotTable List

This section shows you how to change the view of the PivotTable list by (1) using the field drop-down arrows; (2) adding summary totals; (3) sorting columns of data; (4) dragging data fields to the row field area; and (5) dragging data fields to the filter field area.

Using the Field Drop-Down Arrows to Display Records That Pass a Test

You can use the field drop-down arrows at the right side of the data fields to hide rows of data that do not pass a test. This allows you to work with a subset of the data. For example, the following steps hide the rows of data representing males, leaving only the rows of data representing females displaying in the PivotTable list.

Steps: To Use Field Drop-Down Arrows to Display Records That Pass a Test

1 **Click the Gender data field drop-down arrow, click M (for male) to clear the check box, and then point to the OK button.**

The Gender drop-down list displays. The list of different items in the Gender column of data displays as check boxes along with a check box titled (Show All). The M check box does not have a check mark (Figure 7).

FIGURE 7

2 **Click the OK button.**

Only the rows of data representing females display (Figure 8). The rows of data representing males are hidden.

FIGURE 8

3 **Click the AutoFilter button on the toolbar.**

*The filter is disabled and all rows of data display (Figure 9). The **AutoFilter button** turns criteria on and off.*

FIGURE 9

When you use a field drop-down arrow to filter the data, the arrow changes to the color blue. It remains blue until you disable the filter by using the AutoFilter button or selecting the Show All check box (Figure 7 on page EW 2.6). You can add additional filters by using other field drop-down arrows. Thus, you can display a subset of a subset. If you disable the filter by clicking the AutoFilter button and then select new filters, the original disabled filter is lost.

Adding Summary Totals

A PivotTable list is more useful if you add summaries to key columns of data. For example, you can add a summary to the Sales column in Figure 9 on the previous page. Four summary functions are available through the AutoCalc button on the toolbar. The four **summary functions** are Sum, Count, Min, and Max. The following steps add the Sum summary function to the Sales column of data.

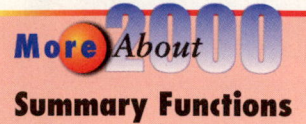

Summary Functions

The type of data in a field determines whether a summary function is available or not. For example, if a field contains dates, then the Sum function is not available. If a field contains text, you cannot use the Sum, Min, or Max function, but you can use Count.

 Steps **To Add a Summary Total to a Column of Data**

1 **Click the Sales data field to select the entire column. Click the AutoCalc button on the toolbar and then point to Sum.**

The PivotTable list displays as shown in Figure 10.

FIGURE 10

2 **Click Sum.**

A grand total displays below the Sales column of data (Figure 11).

summary data area

grand total displays in summary data area

FIGURE 11

One at a time, you can select all four of the summary functions shown on the AutoCalc button menu in Figure 10. Each time you select a summary function, a new summary line is added to the summary data area.

Sorting Columns of Data

The data in a PivotTable list is easier to work with and more meaningful if you arrange the data sequentially based on one or more fields. The sort routine available with a PivotTable list is similar to Excel in that it sorts the data using the current order of the records. Thus, if you need to sort on more than one column of data, sort the minor field first on up to the major field.

The step on the next page sorts the PivotTable list in ascending sequence by education within gender.

More *About*

Sort Order

The order in which numbers, text, and special characters are sorted depends on the source data and your regional settings in the Windows Control Panel.

Steps: To Sort Columns of Data

1 Click the Educ data field and then click the Sort Ascending button on the toolbar. Click the Gender data field and then click the Sort Ascending button on the toolbar.

The data in the PivotTable list is sorted by education within gender (Figure 12).

FIGURE 12

With the data sorted by Educ within Gender, you now can change the view of the data by moving these data fields to the drop areas to change the view of the PivotTable list.

Dragging Data Fields to the Row Field Area

Moving data fields to the drop areas changes the view. The **drop areas** are above and to the left of the data area. Actually, you can move any data field to a drop area whether or not you first sort the column of data, but moving a data field whose column data has not been sorted to a row field or column field area often results in a useless display. The following steps drag the sorted Gender and Educ data fields to the row field area on the left side of the PivotTable list to generate a new view. The last step returns the PivotTable list to its original view.

Sorting

To undo a sort and return the data to its previous order, click the recessed Sort Ascending or Sort Descending button.

To Drag Data Fields to the Row Field Area

1 **Drag the Gender data field to the row field area. Drag the Educ data field to the row field area and to the right of the Gender field.**

The PivotTable list changes dramatically, showing subtotals for each education category and each gender category (Figure 13).

2 **When you are finished viewing the PivotTable list, drag the Educ and Gender data fields to their original locations in the data area.**

FIGURE 13

When you drag a data field to a drop area, the data field is moved rather than copied. Thus, in Figure 13 the data field area no longer contains the Gender and Educ data fields. They are now in the row field area. In Figure 12, only one total displayed at the bottom of the PivotTable list. In Figure 13, after dragging the two data fields, eight subtotals and one grand total display and the rows of data are divided into categories based on their respective Educ and Gender values.

Dragging Data Fields to the Filter Field Area

Another way to manipulate the view of the PivotTable list is to drag data fields to the filter field area at the top of the PivotTable list. When you drag a data field to this drop area, the data field maintains the field drop-down arrow, which allows you to apply a filter to the data. The steps on the next page drag the Region, Zone, and District data fields to the filter field area and then apply a filter.

More About

Dragging Fields to Drop Areas

When you drag a data field to the row field area, each unique data item within the field displays down the rows of the PivotTable list. When you drag a data field to the column field area, each unique data item within the field displays across the columns of the PivotTable list.

Steps **To Drag Data Fields to the Filter Field Area and Apply a Filter**

1 Drag the Region data field to the filter field area. Drag the Zone data field to the right of the Region filter field. Drag the District data field to the right of the Zone filter field.

The PivotTable list displays as shown in Figure 14.

FIGURE 14

2 Click the Region data field drop-down arrow, click 1, and then click the OK button. Click the Zone data field drop-down arrow, click 2, and then click the OK button. Click the District data field drop-down arrow, click 2, and then click the OK button.

Only two rows of data display (Figure 15). The remaining rows of data failed to pass the test of belonging to Region 1, Zone 2, and District 2.

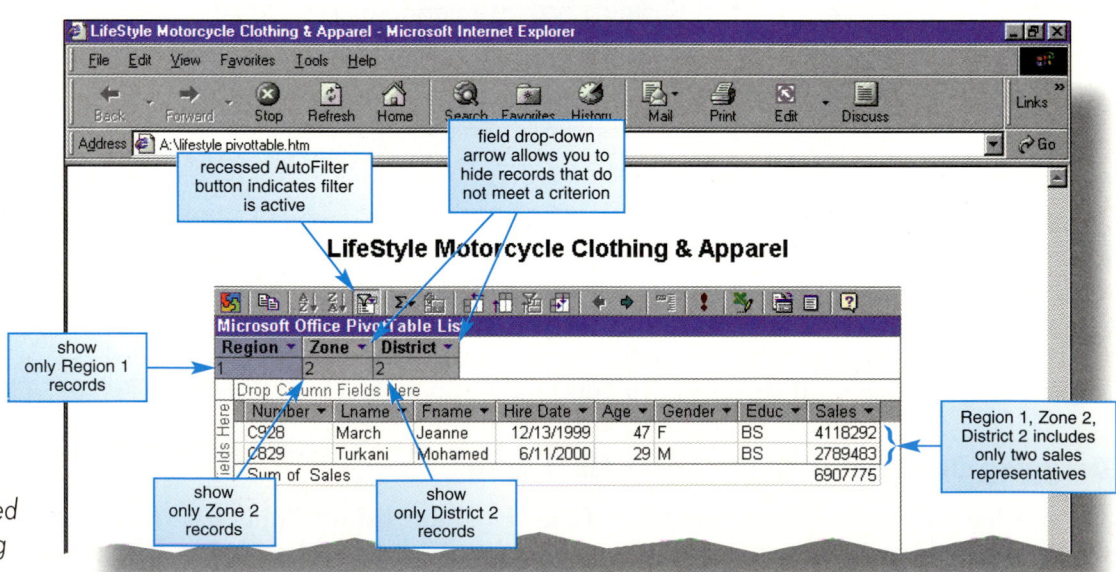

FIGURE 15

3 When you are finished viewing the PivotTable list in its current form, click the AutoFilter button on the toolbar to disable the filter. One at a time, drag the three filter fields back to their original position in the data field area.

You could have applied the filters to the data fields in the data field area, rather than dragging them to the filter field area. By dragging these fields to the filter field area, however, the rows that pass the test are cleaner and easier to read. For example, you do not have the Region, Zone, and District data fields repeating the same numbers over and over again as was the case in Figure 8 on page EW 2.7 when the filter was applied to the Gender data field.

Removing Fields and Adding Fields to a PivotTable List

The more data fields you have in a PivotTable list, the more difficult it is to interpret the data. The following steps show how to remove the Number data field and then add the field back to the data area.

Microsoft Certification

The Microsoft Office User Specialist (MOUS) Certification program provides an opportunity for you to obtain a valuable industry credential - proof that you have the Excel 2000 skills required by employers. For more information, see Appendix D or visit the Shelly Cashman Series MOUS Web page at www.scsite.com/off2000/cert.htm.

 To Remove Fields from and Add Fields to a PivotTable List

1 **Click the Field List button on the toolbar to display the PivotTable Field List window. Right-click the Number data field. Point to Remove Field on the shortcut menu.**

The PivotTable Field List window displays a list of all the data fields in the PivotTable list (Figure 16). The Number data field and its data are selected and the shortcut menu displays. Most of the commands on the shortcut menu in Figure 16 are the same as the buttons on the toolbar.

FIGURE 16

2 **Click Remove Field.**

The Number data field and its column of data are hidden. The word Number in the PivotTable Field List window is regular font style, whereas the active data fields are bold in the PivotTable Field List window. (Figure 17).

FIGURE 17

3 **Drag the Number data field from the PivotTable Field List window to its original location between the District and Lname data fields.**

The Number data field is added to the data area in the PivotTable list (Figure 18). The word Number is now bold in the PivotTable Field List window.

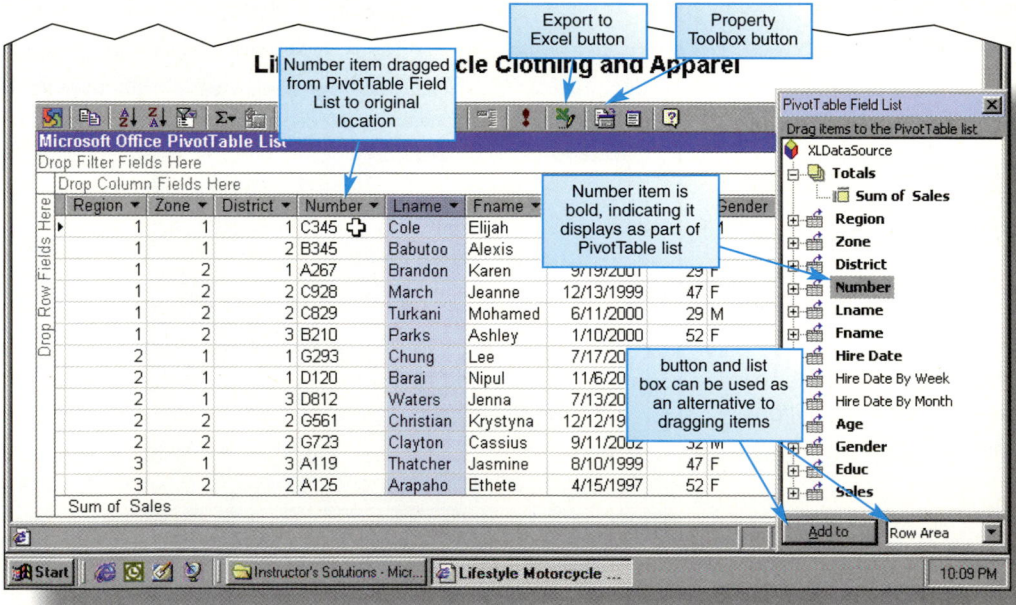

FIGURE 18

You can remove (hide) as many data fields as you want from the data area to simplify the PivotTable list. When you add data fields, you can insert them at any location. For example, you could have added the Number data field anywhere in the data area. You cannot duplicate a data field. That is, the Number data field can show up only once in the data area.

The two fields in the PivotTable Field List (Hire Date By Week and Hire Date By Month) can be used to change the view. If you click the plus signs to the left of these two fields, you can drag the date-related data fields to the drop areas and use the field drop-down arrow to establish filters.

Besides removing fields and adding fields, you can move data fields from one location in the data area to another by dragging.

Improving the Appearance of a PivotTable List

You can improve the appearance of the PivotTable list using the **Property Toolbox button** (Figure 18). For example, you can change the font, format numbers, change colors of cells, and align text. You can also increase or decrease the column width by dragging column borders as you did in Excel. Any formatting you do to the PivotTable list remains in force as long as you do not close your browser. Once you close your browser, the formats are lost.

Finally, you can export the PivotTable list to Excel by using the Export to Excel button (Figure 18). In Excel, the PivotTable list becomes a PivotTable report. You can format the PivotTable report using Excel's powerful formatting capabilities and then save it back as a PivotTable list.

The following steps close your browser.

More About 2000

Quick Reference

For a table that lists how to complete the tasks covered in this book using the mouse, menu, shortcut menu, and keyboard, see the Excel Quick Reference Summary at the back of this book or visit the Office 2000 Web page (www.scsite.com/office 2000/qr.htm), and then click Microsoft Excel 2000.

TO CLOSE YOUR BROWSER

 Click the Close button on the right side of the browser's title bar.

CASE PERSPECTIVE SUMMARY

Sturgis Davis will be pleased with the PivotTable list capabilities. It will serve as the first step towards implementing his intranet-based sales reporting system. His managers and team leaders will be able to analyze the sales data by displaying different views. More importantly, they will be able to analyze the data using their browsers, rather than using Excel.

Web Feature Summary

This Web Feature introduced you to publishing an Excel worksheet as a PivotTable list Web page. You learned how to use PivotTable lists and the terms that are used to describe them. You also learned how to enhance a PivotTable list using your browser by adding summaries, filtering data so only rows that pass a test display, sorting, changing the view, and removing and adding data fields.

What You Should Know

Having completed this Web feature, you now should be able to perform the following tasks:

▶ Add a Summary Total to a Column of Data *(EW 2.8)*
▶ Close Your Browser *(EW 2.15)*
▶ Drag Data Fields to the Filter Field Area and Apply a Filter *(EW 2.12)*
▶ Drag Data Fields to the Row Field Area *(EW 2.11)*
▶ Remove Fields from and Add Fields to a PivotTable List *(EW 2.13)*
▶ Save a Worksheet Database as a PivotTable List *(EW 2.3)*
▶ Sort Columns of Data *(EW 2.6)*
▶ Use Field Drop-Down Arrows to Display Records That Pass a Test *(EW 2.6)*
▶ View a PivotTable List Using Your Browser *(EW 2.5)*

In the Lab

1 Creating the Millennium Sports Open Orders PivotTable List

Problem: You are a spreadsheet specialist for Millennium Sports, a major sports retail company with stores throughout the United States. You recently attended an Excel seminar on creating PivotTable reports and lists. You decide to use a PivotTable list to distribute information across the company's intranet that can be analyzed using a browser.

Instructions: Start Excel and open the workbook Millennium Sports Open Orders from the Data Disk. Save the range A9:G20 as a PivotTable list on drive A using the file name Millennium Sports Open Orders. Add the title `Millennium Sports Open Orders` as shown in Figure 19 before publishing the Web page. Quit Excel and open your browser. Display the PivotTable list by entering `a:\Millennium Sports Open Orders.htm` in the Address bar and then print the PivotTable list. Print the PivotTable list for each of the following:

1. Add a summary total to the Amount column. Sort the PivotTable list on Amount in ascending sequence.
2. Sort in ascending sequence by Order Date within Order No. Drag the Order No data field to the filter field area (Figure 19). Use the Order No drop-down arrow to display rows from Order 128187.

FIGURE 19

In the Lab

2 Creating the Match Point Tennis Club PivotTable List

Problem: You are a member of your school's Match Point Tennis Club. The members would like to access online the club's database, which includes each member's name, age, gender, class, state, major, and total credit hours. You have been asked to use your Excel skills to create a PivotTable list from the database so it can be manipulated using a browser.

Instructions: Start Excel and open the workbook Match Point Tennis Club from the Data Disk. Save the range A8:H18 as a PivotTable list on drive A using the file name Match Point Tennis Club. Add the title `Match Point Tennis Club` as shown in Figure 20 before publishing the Web page. Quit Excel and open your browser. Display the PivotTable list by entering `a:\Match Point Tennis Club.htm` in the Address bar and then print the PivotTable list. Print the PivotTable list for each of the following:

1. Add a summary total to the Credit Hrs column. Display only club members majoring in EET.
2. Sort in ascending sequence by Class within Gender. Drag the Gender and Class data fields to the row field area as shown in Figure 20.

FIGURE 20

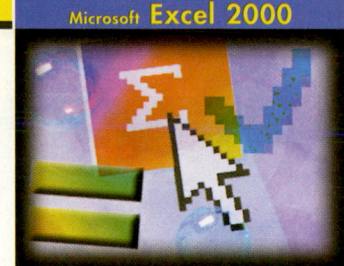
APPENDIX A
Microsoft Excel 2000 Help System

Using the Excel Help System

This appendix shows you how to use the Excel Help system. At any time while you are using Excel, you can interact with its Help system and display information on any Excel topic. It is a complete reference manual at your fingertips.

The two primary forms of Help are the Office Assistant and Microsoft Excel Help window. Which one you use will depend on your preferences. As shown in Figure A-1, you access either form of Help by pressing the F1 key, or clicking Microsoft Excel Help on the Help menu, or clicking the Microsoft Excel Help button on the Standard toolbar. Excel responds in one of two ways:

1. If the Office Assistant is turned on, then the Office Assistant displays with a balloon (lower-right side in Figure A-1).
2. If the Office Assistant is turned off, then the Microsoft Excel Help window displays (lower-left side in Figure A-1)

Table A-1 on the next page summarizes the nine categories of Help available to you. Because of the way the Excel Help system works, please review the right-most column of Table A-1 if you have difficulties activating the desired category of Help.

FIGURE A-1

Table A-1 Excel Help System

TYPE	DESCRIPTION	HOW TO ACTIVATE	TURNING THE OFFICE ASSISTANT ON AND OFF
Answer Wizard	Similar to the Office Assistant in that it answers questions that you type in your own words.	Click the Microsoft Excel Help button on the Standard toolbar. If necessary, maximize the Help window by double-clicking its title bar. Click the Answer Wizard tab.	If the Office Assistant displays, right-click it, click Options on the shortcut menu, click Use the Office Assistant to remove the check mark, click the OK button.
Contents sheet	Groups Help topics by general categories. Use when you know only the general category of the topic in question.	Click the Office Assistant button on the Standard toolbar. If necessary, maximize the Help window by double-clicking its title bar. Click the Contents tab.	If the Office Assistant displays, right-click it, click Options, click Use the Office Assistant to remove the check mark, click the OK button.
Detect and Repair	Automatically finds and fixes errors in the application.	Click Detect and Repair on the Help menu.	
Hardware and Software Information	Shows Product ID and allows access to system information and technical support information.	Click About Microsoft Excel on the Help menu and then click the appropriate button.	
Help for Lotus 1-2-3 Users	Used to assist Lotus 1-2-3 users who are learning Microsoft Excel.	Click Lotus 1-2-3 Help on the Help menu.	
Index sheet	Similar to an index in a book; use when you know exactly what you want.	Click the Microsoft Excel Help button on the Standard toolbar. If necessary, maximize the Help window by double-clicking its title bar. Click the Index tab.	If the Office Assistant displays, right-click it, click Options, click Use the Office Assistant to remove the check mark, click the OK button.
Office Assistant	Answers questions that you type in your own words, offers tips, and provides Help for a variety of Excel features.	Click the Microsoft Excel Help button on the Standard toolbar or double-click the Office Assistant icon. Some dialog boxes also include the Microsoft Excel Help button.	If the Office Assistant does not display, click Show the Office Assistant on the Help menu.
Office on the Web	Used to access technical resources and download free product enhancements on the Web.	Click Office on the Web on the Help menu.	
Question Mark button and What's This? command	Used to identify unfamiliar items on the screen.	In a dialog box, click the Question Mark button and then click an item in the dialog box. Click What's This? on the Help menu, and then click an item on the screen.	

The best way to familiarize yourself with the Excel Help system is to use it. The next several pages show examples of how to use the Help system. Following the examples are a set of exercises titled Use Help that will sharpen your Excel Help system skills.

The Office Assistant

The **Office Assistant** is an icon that displays in the Excel window (lower-right-side of Figure A-1 on page E A.1). It has dual functions. First, it will respond with a list of topics that relate to the entry you make in the text box at the bottom of the balloon. The entry can be in the form of a word, phrase, or question written as if you were talking to a human being. For example if you want to learn more about saving a file, in the balloon text box, you can type, save, save a file, how do I save a file, or anything similar. The Office Assistant responds by displaying a list of topics from which you can choose. Once you choose a topic, it displays the corresponding information.

Second, the Office Assistant monitors your work and accumulates tips during a session on how you might better do your work. You can view the tips at any time. The accumulated tips display when you activate the Office Assistant balloon. Also, if at anytime you see a light bulb above the Office Assistant, click it to display the most recent tip.

You may or may not want the Office Assistant to display on the screen at all times. You can hide it, and then show it at a later time. You may prefer not to use the Office Assistant at all. In this case, you use the Microsoft Excel Help window (lower-left-side of Figure A-1 on page E A.1). Thus, not only do you need to know how to show and hide the Office Assistant, but you also need to know how to turn the Office Assistant on and off.

Showing and Hiding the Office Assistant

When Excel is first installed, the Office Assistant displays in the Excel window. You can move it to any location on the screen. You can click it to display the Office Assistant balloon, which allows you to request Help. If the Office Assistant is on the screen and you want to hide it, you click the **Hide the Office Assistant command** on the Help menu. You also can right-click the Office Assistant to display its shortcut menu and then click the **Hide command** to hide it. When the Office Assistant is hidden, then the **Show the Office Assistant command** replaces the Hide the Office Assistant command on the Help menu. Thus, you can show or hide the Office Assistant at any time.

Turning the Office Assistant On and Off

The fact that the Office Assistant is hidden does not mean it is turned off. To turn the Office Assistant off, it must be displaying in the Excel window. You right-click it to display its shortcut menu (right-side of Figure A-2). Next, click Options. Invoking the **Options command** causes the Office Assistant dialog box to display (left-side of Figure A-2).

FIGURE A-2

The top check box in the Options sheet determines whether the Office Assistant is on or off. To turn the Office Assistant off, remove the check mark from the **Use the Office Assistant check box** and then click the OK button. As shown in Figure A-1 on page E A.1, if the Office Assistant is off when you invoke Help, then the Microsoft Excel Help window displays instead of the Office Assistant. To turn the Office Assistant on at a later date, click the Show the Office Assistant command on the Help menu.

Through the Options command on the Office Assistant shortcut menu, you can change the look and feel of the Office Assistant. For example, you can hide the Office Assistant, turn the Office Assistant off, change the way it works, choose a different Office Assistant icon, or view an animation of the current one. These options also are available by clicking the Options button that displays in the Office Assistant balloon (Figure A-3 on the next page).

The Gallery sheet (Figure A-2) in the Office Assistant dialog box allows you to change the appearance of the Office Assistant. The default is the paper clip (Clippit). You can change it to a bouncing red happy face (The Dot), a robot (F1), a professor (The Genius), the Microsoft Office logo (Office Logo), the earth (Mother Nature), a cat (Links), or a dog (Rocky).

Using the Office Assistant

As indicated earlier, the Office Assistant allows you to enter a word, phrase, or question and then it responds by displaying a list of topics from which you can choose to display Help. The following steps show how to use the Office Assistant to obtain Help on saving a workbook.

Steps To Use the Office Assistant

1 **If the Office Assistant is not turned on, click Help on the menu bar and then click Show the Office Assistant. Click the Office Assistant. When the Office Assistant balloon displays, type** save workbook **in the text box immediately above the Options button. Point to the Search button.**

The Office Assistant balloon displays as shown in Figure A-3.

FIGURE A-3

2 **Click the Search button. When the Office Assistant balloon redisplays, point to the topic, Save a workbook (Figure A-4).**

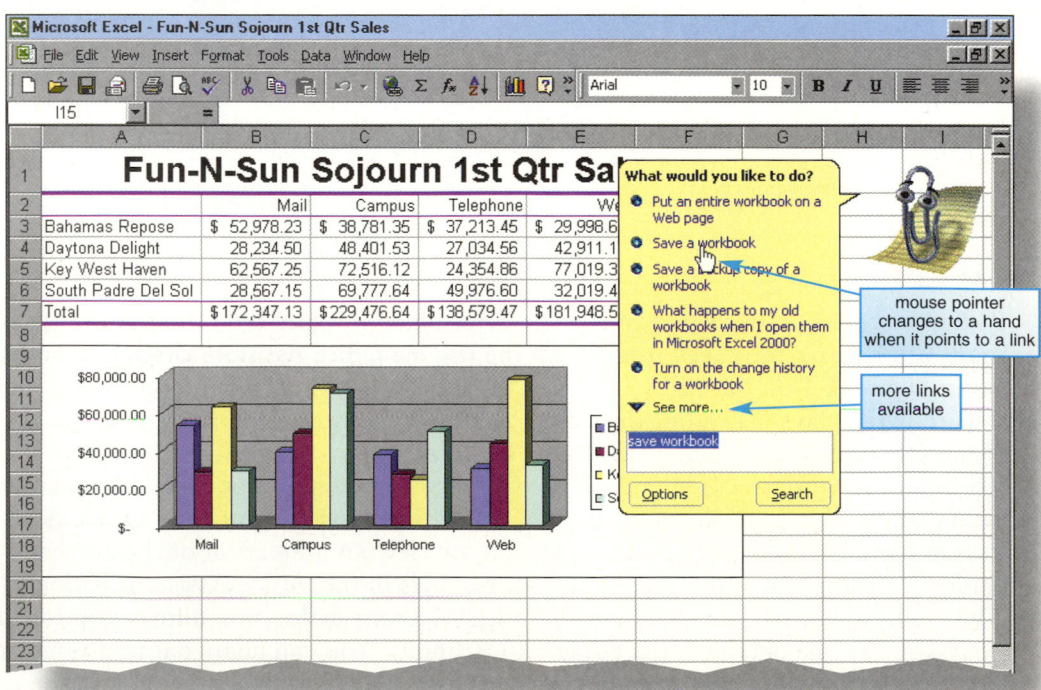

FIGURE A-4

3 **Click the topic, Save a workbook. Double-click the Microsoft Excel Help window title bar to maximize it. If necessary, move or hide the Office Assistant so you can view all of the text in the Microsoft Excel Help window.**

The Microsoft Excel Help window displays with information on how to save a workbook (Figure A-5).

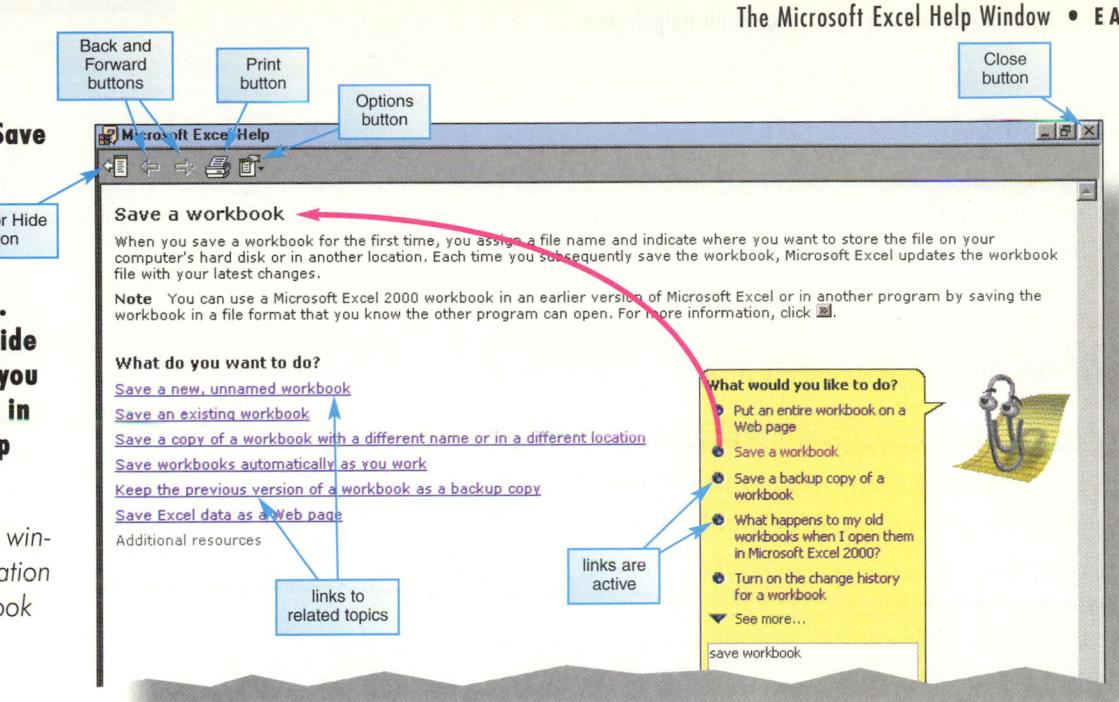

FIGURE A-5

When the Microsoft Excel Help window displays, you can read or print it. To print the information, click the Print button on the Microsoft Excel Help toolbar. Table A-2 lists the function of each button on the Microsoft Excel Help toolbar. To close the Microsoft Excel Help window shown in Figure A-5, click the Close button on the title bar.

Table A-2	Microsoft Excel Help Toolbar Buttons	
BUTTON	**NAME**	**FUNCTION**
or	Show or Hide	Displays or hides the Contents, Answer Wizard, and Index tabs
	Back	Displays the previous Help topic
	Forward	Displays the next Help topic
	Print	Prints the current Help topic
	Options	Displays a list of commands

Other Ways

1. If Office Assistant is turned on, on Help menu click Microsoft Excel Help, or click Microsoft Excel Help button on Standard toolbar to display Office Assistant balloon

The Microsoft Excel Help Window

If the Office Assistant is turned off and you click the Microsoft Excel Help button on the Standard toolbar, the **Microsoft Excel Help window** displays (Figure A-6 on the next page). This window contains three tabs on the left side: Contents, Answer Wizard, and Index. Each tab displays a sheet with powerful look-up capabilities. Use the Contents sheet as you would a table of contents at the front of a book to look up Help. The Answer Wizard sheet answers your queries the same as the Office Assistant. You use the Index sheet in the same fashion as an index in a book to look up Help.

Click the tabs to move from sheet to sheet. The five buttons on the toolbar, Show or Hide, Back, Forward, Print, and Options are described in Table A-2.

Besides clicking the Microsoft Excel Help button on the Standard toolbar, you also can click the Microsoft Excel Help command on the Help menu or press the F1 key to display the Microsoft Excel Help window to gain access to the three sheets. To close the Microsoft Excel Help window, click the Close button in the upper-right corner on the title bar.

Using the Contents Sheet

The **Contents sheet** is useful for displaying Help when you know the general category of the topic in question, but not the specifics. The following steps show how to use the Contents sheet to obtain information on collecting and pasting multiple items.

TO OBTAIN HELP USING THE CONTENTS SHEET

1 With the Office Assistant turned off, click the Microsoft Excel Help button on the Standard toolbar (Figure A-3 on page E A.4).

2 When the Microsoft Excel Help window displays, double-click the title bar to maximize the window. If necessary, click the Show button to display the tabs.

3 Click the Contents tab. Double-click the Using Shortcut Keys book on the left side of the window.

4 Click the Keyboard shortcuts subtopic below the Using Shortcut Keys book.

Excel displays Help on the subtopic, Keyboard shortcuts (Figure A-6).

FIGURE A-6

Once the information on the subtopic displays, you can scroll through and read it or you can click the Print button to obtain a hard copy. If you decide to click another subtopic on the left or a link on the right, you can get back to the Help page shown in Figure A-6 by clicking the Back button.

Each topic in the Contents list is preceded by a book icon or question mark icon. A **book icon** indicates subtopics are available. A **question mark icon** means information on the topic will display if you double-click the title. The book icon opens when you double-click the book (or its title) or click the plus sign (+) to the left of the book icon.

Using the Answer Wizard Sheet

The **Answer Wizard sheet** works like the Office Assistant in that you enter a word, phrase, or question and it responds with topics from which you can choose to display Help. The following steps show how to use the Answer Wizard sheet to obtain Help on selecting ranges.

TO OBTAIN HELP USING THE ANSWER WIZARD SHEET

1 With the Office Assistant turned off, click the Microsoft Excel Help button on the Standard toolbar (Figure A-3 on page E A.4).

2 When the Microsoft Excel Help window displays, double-click the title bar to maximize the window. If necessary, click the Show button to display the tabs.

3 Click the Answer Wizard tab. Type how do i select a range in the What would you like to do? text box on the left side of the window. Click the Search button.

4 When a list of topics displays in the Select topic to display list box, click Select ranges.

Excel displays Help on how to select ranges (Figure A-7).

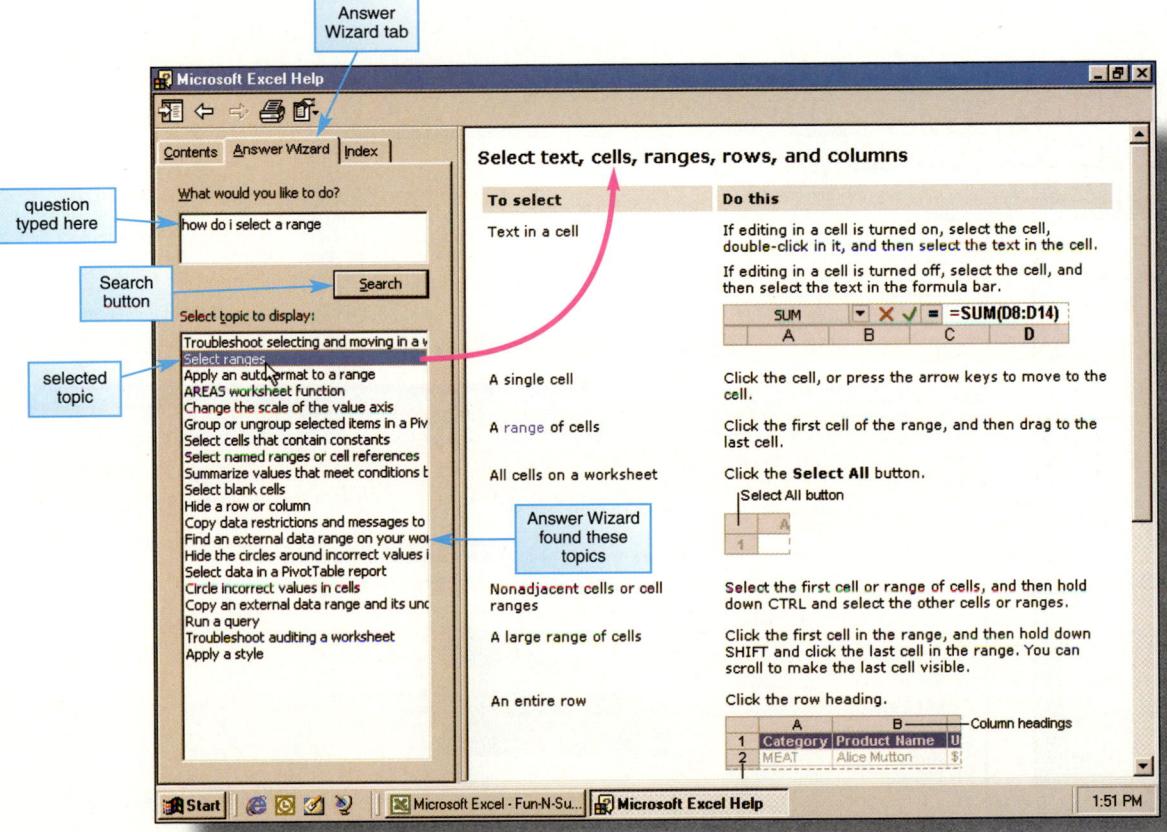

FIGURE A-7

If the topic, Select ranges, does not include the information you are searching for, click another topic in the list. Continue to click topics until you find the desired information.

Using the Index Sheet

The third sheet in the Microsoft Excel Help window is the Index sheet. Use the **Index sheet** to display Help when you know the keyword or the first few letters of the keyword you want to look up. The following steps show how to use the Index sheet to obtain Help on types of charts.

TO OBTAIN HELP USING THE INDEX SHEET

1 With the Office Assistant turned off, click the Microsoft Excel Help button on the Standard toolbar (Figure A-3 on page E A.4).

2 When the Microsoft Excel Help window displays, double-click the title bar to maximize the window. If necessary, click the Show button to display the tabs.

3 Click the Index tab. Type `chart type` in the Type keywords text box on the left side of the window. Click the Search button.

4 When a list of topics displays in the Choose a topic list box, click Examples of chart types. When the Help topic displays, click the graphic as indicated.

A second Microsoft Excel Help window displays with Help about the topic, Examples of chart types (Figure A-8).

FIGURE A-8

You can click each chart type in the second Help window to display an example of the selected chart type. In the Choose topic list box on the left side of the window, you can click another topic to display additional Help.

An alternative to typing a keyword in the Type keywords text box is to scroll through the Or choose keywords list box (the middle list box on the left side of the window). When you locate the keyword you are searching for, double-click it to display Help on the topic. Also in the Or choose keywords list box, the Excel Help system displays other topics that relate to the new keyword. As you begin typing a new keyword in the Type keywords text box, Excel jumps to that point in the middle list box. To begin a new search, click the Clear button.

What's This? Command and Question Mark Button • E A.9

APPENDIX A

What's This? Command and Question Mark Button

Use the What's This command on the Help menu or the Question Mark button in a dialog box when you are not sure what an object on the screen is or what it does.

What's This? Command

You use the **What's This? command** on the Help menu to display a detailed Screen-Tip. When you invoke this command, the mouse pointer changes to an arrow with a question mark. You then click any object on the screen, such as a button, to display the ScreenTip. For example, after you click the What's This? command on the Help menu and then click the Font box on the Standard toolbar, a description of the Font box displays (Figure A-9). You can print the ScreenTip by right-clicking it and clicking Print Topic on the shortcut menu.

FIGURE A-9

Question Mark Button

Similarly to the What's This? command, the **Question Mark button** displays a ScreenTip. You use the Question Mark button with dialog boxes. It is located in the upper-right corner on the title bar of dialog boxes, next to the Close button. For example, in Figure A-10, the Sort dialog box displays on the screen. If you click the Question Mark button, and then click the Sort by box, an explanation of the Sort by box displays in a ScreenTip. You can print the ScreenTip by right-clicking it and clicking Print Topic on the shortcut menu.

If a dialog box does not include a Question Mark button, press the SHIFT+F1 keys. This combination of keys will change the mouse pointer to an arrow with a question mark. You then can click any object in the dialog box to display the ScreenTip.

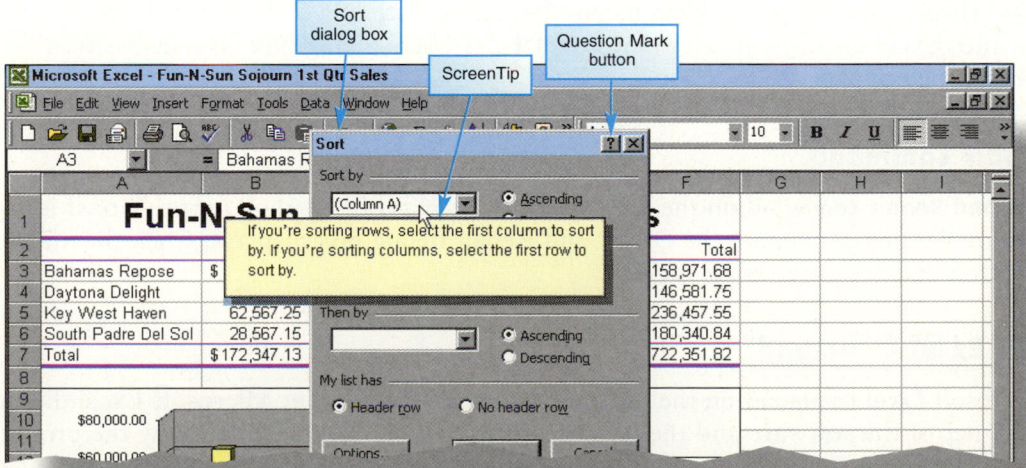

FIGURE A-10

Office on the Web Command

The **Office on the Web command** on the Help menu displays a Microsoft Web page containing up-to-date information on a variety of Office-related topics. To use this command, you must be connected to the Internet. Once the page displays, you can click the Excel link on the left side of the window and then click the Assistance link (Figure A-11). The Excel Assistance Web page contains several links such as Knowledge Base Articles about Excel and Excel Tips and Tricks.

FIGURE A-11

Other Help Commands

Three additional commands available on the Help menu are Lotus 1-2-3 Help, Detect and Repair, and About Microsoft Excel. The Lotus 1-2-3 Help command is available only if it was included as part of a Custom install of Excel 2000.

Lotus 1-2-3 Help Command

The **Lotus 1-2-3 Help command** on the Help menu offers assistance to 1-2-3 users switching to Excel. When you choose this command, Excel displays the Help for Lotus 1-2-3 Users dialog box. The instructions in the dialog box step the user through the appropriate selections.

Detect and Repair Command

Use the **Detect and Repair command** on the Help menu if Excel is not running properly or if it is generating errors. When you invoke this command, the Detect and Repair dialog box displays. Click the Start button in the dialog box to initiate the detect and repair process.

About Microsoft Excel Command

The **About Microsoft Excel command** on the Help menu displays the About Microsoft Excel dialog box. The dialog box lists the owner of the software and the product identification. You need to know the product identification if you call Microsoft for assistance. The two buttons below the OK button are the System Info button and the Tech Support button. The **System Info button** displays system information, including hardware resources, components, software environment, and applications. The **Tech Support button** displays technical assistance information.

Use Help

1 Using the Office Assistant

Instructions: Perform the following tasks using the Excel Help system.

1. If the Office Assistant is turned on, click it to display the Office Assistant balloon. If the Office Assistant is not turned on, click Help on the menu bar, and then click Show the Office Assistant.
2. Right-click the Office Assistant and then click Options on the shortcut menu. Click the Gallery tab in the Office Assistant dialog box and then click the Next button to view all the Office Assistants. Click the Options tab in the Office Assistant dialog box and review the different options for the Office Assistant. Click the Question Mark button and display ScreenTips for the first two check boxes. Right-click the ScreenTips to print them. Hand them in to your instructor. Close the Office Assistant dialog box.
3. Click the Office Assistant and then type how do i enter formulas in the text box at the bottom of the balloon. Click the Search button.
4. Click, About constructing formulas, in the Office Assistant balloon. If necessary, double-click the title bar to maximize the Microsoft Excel Help window. Read and print the information. One at a time, click the links to learn about order of precedence and calculation operators in formulas. Print the information. Hand in the printouts to your instructor. Use the Back and Forward buttons to return to the original page.
5. Click the Close button in the Microsoft Excel Help window.
6. Click the Office Assistant. If it is not turned on, click Show the Office Assistant on the Help menu. Search for the topic, formatting a chart. Click the About formatting charts link. When the Microsoft Excel Help window displays, maximize the window and then click the graphic. Read and print the information. Click the three links below More Information regarding Colors, textures, and gradient fills. Print the information on each link. Close the Microsoft Excel Help window.

2 Expanding on the Excel Help System Basics

Instructions: Use the Excel Help system to understand the topics better and answer the questions listed below. Answer the questions on your own paper, or hand in the printed Help information to your instructor.

1. Right-click the Office Assistant. If it is not turned on, click Show the Office Assistant on the Help menu. When the shortcut menu displays, click Options. Click Use the Office Assistant to remove the check mark, and then click the OK button.
2. Click the Microsoft Excel Help button on the Standard toolbar. Maximize the Microsoft Excel Help window. If the tabs are hidden on the left side, click the Show button. Click the Index tab. Type undo in the Type keywords text box. Click the Search button. Click Reset built-in menus and toolbars. Print the information. Click the Hide and then Show buttons. Click the four links below What do you want to do? Read and print the information for each link. Close the Microsoft Excel Help window. Hand in the printouts to your instructor.
3. Press the F1 key. Maximize the Microsoft Excel Help window. Click the Answer Wizard tab. Type help in the What would you like to do? text box, and then click the Search button. Click Ways to get assistance while you work. Read through the information that displays. Print the information. Click the first two links. Read and print the information for both.
4. Click the Contents tab. Click the plus sign (+) to the left of the Printing book. One at a time, click the first three topics below the Printing book. Read and print each one. Close the Microsoft Excel Help window. Hand in the printouts to your instructor.
5. Click Help on the menu bar and then click What's This? Click the AutoSum button on the Standard toolbar. Right-click the ScreenTip and click Print Topic on the shortcut menu. Click the Save As command on the File menu. When the Save As dialog box displays, click the Question Mark button on the title bar. Click the Save in box. Right-click the ScreenTip and click Print Topic. Hand in the printouts to your instructor.

APPENDIX B
Publishing Office Web Pages to a Web Server

With a Microsoft Office 2000 program, such as Word, Excel, Access, or PowerPoint, you use the **Save as Web Page command** on the File menu to save the Web page to a Web server using one of two techniques: Web folders or File Transfer Protocol. A **Web folder** is an Office 2000 shortcut to a Web server. **File Transfer Protocol (FTP)** is an Internet standard that allows computers to exchange files with other computers on the Internet.

You should contact your network system administrator or technical support staff at your ISP to determine if their Web server supports Web folders, FTP, or both, and to obtain necessary permissions to access the Web server. If you decide to publish Web pages using a Web folder, you must have the Office Server Extensions (OSE) installed on your computer. OSE comes with the Standard, Professional, and Premium editions of Office 2000.

Using Web Folders to Publish Office Web Pages

If you are granted permission to create a Web folder (shortcut) on your computer, you must obtain the URL of the Web server, and a user name and possibly a password that allows you to access the Web server. You also must decide on a name for the Web folder. Table B-1 explains how to create a Web folder.

Office adds the name of the Web folder to the list of current Web folders. You can save to this folder, open files in the folder, rename the folder, or perform any operations you would to a folder on your hard disk. You can use your Office program or Windows Explorer to access this folder. Table B-2 explains how to save to a Web folder.

Using FTP to Publish Office Web Pages

When publishing a Web page using FTP, you first add the FTP location to your computer and then you can save to it. An **FTP location**, also called an **FTP site**, is a collection of files that resides on an FTP server. In this case, the FTP server is the Web server.

To add an FTP location, you must obtain the name of the FTP site, which usually is the address (URL) of the FTP server, and a user name and a password that allows you to access the FTP server. You save and open the Web pages on the Web server using the name of the FTP site. Table B-3 explains how to add an FTP site.

Office adds the name of the FTP site to the FTP locations in the Save As and Open dialog boxes. You can open and save files on this FTP location. Table B-4 explains how to save using an FTP location.

Table B-1   Creating a Web Folder

1. Click File on the menu bar and then click Save As; or click File on the menu bar and then click Open.
2. When the Save As dialog box or the Open dialog box displays, click the Web Folders shortcut on the Places Bar along the left side of the dialog box.
3. Click the Create New Folder button.
4. When the first dialog box of the Add Web Folder wizard displays, type the URL of the Web server and then click the Next button.
5. When the Enter Network Password dialog box displays, type the user name and, if necessary, the password in the respective text boxes and then click the OK button.
6. When the last dialog box of the Add Web Folder wizard displays, type the name you would like to use for the Web folder. Click the Finish button.
7. Close the Save As or the Open dialog box.

Table B-2   Saving to a Web Folder

1. Click File on the menu bar and then click Save As.
2. When the Save As dialog box displays, type the Web page file name in the File name text box. Do not press the ENTER key.
3. Click Web Folders shortcut on the Places Bar along the left side of the dialog box.
4. Double-click the Web folder name in the Save in list.
5. When the Enter Network Password dialog box displays, type the user name and password in the respective text boxes and then click the OK button.
6. Click the Save button in the Save As dialog box.

Table B-3   Adding an FTP Location

1. Click File on the menu bar and then click Save As; or click File on the menu bar and then click Open.
2. In the Save As dialog box, click the Save in box arrow and then click Add/Modify FTP Locations in the Save in list; or in the Open dialog box, click the Look in box arrow and then click Add/Modify FTP Locations in the Look in list.
3. When the Add/Modify FTP Locations dialog box displays, type the name of the FTP site in the Name of FTP site text box. If the site allows anonymous logon, click Anonymous in the Log on as area; if you have a user name for the site, click User in the Log on as area and then type the user name. Type the password in the Password text box. Click the OK button.
4. Close the Save As or the Open dialog box.

Table B-4   Saving to an FTP Location

1. Click File on the menu bar and then click Save As.
2. When the Save As dialog box displays, type the Web page file name in the File name text box. Do not press the ENTER key.
3. Click the Save in box arrow and then click FTP Locations.
4. Double-click the name of the FTP site you want to save to.
5. When the FTP Log On dialog box displays, type your user name and password and then click the OK button.
6. Click the Save button in the Save As dialog box.

APPENDIX C

Resetting the Excel Menus and Toolbars

When you first install Microsoft Excel 2000, the Standard and Formatting toolbars display on one row. As you use the buttons on the toolbars and commands on the menus, Excel personalizes the toolbars and the menus based on their usage. Each time you start Excel, the toolbars and menus display in the same settings as the last time you used the application. The following steps show how to reset the menus and toolbars to their installation settings.

 ## To Reset My Usage Data and Toolbar Buttons

1 **Click View on the menu bar and then point to Toolbars. Point to Customize on the Toolbars submenu.**

The View menu and Toolbars submenu display (Figure C-1).

FIGURE C-1

2 **Click Customize. When the Customize dialog box displays, click the Options tab. Make sure the three check boxes in the Personalized Menus and Toolbars area have check marks and then point to the Reset my usage data button.**

The Customize dialog box displays as shown in Figure C-2.

FIGURE C-2

E C.1

3 **Click the Reset my usage data button. When the Microsoft Excel dialog box displays explaining the function of the Reset my usage data button, click the Yes button. In the Customize dialog box, click the Toolbars tab.**

The Toolbars sheet displays (Figure C-3).

4 **Click Standard in the Toolbars list and then click the Reset button. When the Microsoft Excel dialog box displays asking you if you are sure you want to reset the Standard toolbar, click the OK button. Click Formatting in the Toolbars list and then click the Reset button. When the Microsoft Excel dialog box displays, click the OK button.**

FIGURE C-3

5 **Click the Close button in the Customize dialog box.**

The toolbars display as shown in Figure C-4.

FIGURE C-4

Steps 3 and 4 display or remove any buttons that were added or deleted through the use of the Add or Remove Buttons button on the More Buttons menu.

You can turn off both the toolbars sharing a single row and the short menus by removing the check marks from the two top check boxes in the Options sheet in the Customize dialog box (Figure C-2 on the previous page). If you remove these check marks, Excel will display the toolbars on two separate rows below the menu bar and will show only full menus.

Microsoft **Excel 2000**

APPENDIX D

Microsoft Office User Specialist Certification Program

The Microsoft Office User Specialist (MOUS) Certification Program provides a framework for measuring your proficiency with the Microsoft Office 2000 applications, such as Word 2000, Excel 2000, Access 2000, and PowerPoint 2000. Three levels of certification are available — Master, Expert, and Core. The three levels of certification are described in Table D-1.

Table D-1	Three Levels of MOUS Certification		
LEVEL	*DESCRIPTION*	*REQUIREMENTS*	*CREDENTIAL AWARDED*
Master	Indicates that you have a comprehensive understanding of Microsoft Office 2000	Pass all FIVE of the required exams: Microsoft Word 2000 Expert Microsoft Excel 2000 Expert Microsoft PowerPoint 2000 Core Microsoft Access 2000 Core Microsoft Outlook 2000 Core	Candidates will be awarded one certificate for passing all five of the required Microsoft Office 2000 exams: Microsoft Office User Specialist: Microsoft Office 2000 Master
Expert	Indicates that you have a comprehensive understanding of the advanced features in a specific Microsoft Office 2000 application	Pass any ONE of the Expert exams: Microsoft Word 2000 Expert Microsoft Excel 2000 Expert	Candidates will be awarded one certificate for each of the Expert exams they have passed: Microsoft Office User Specialist: Microsoft Word 2000 Expert Microsoft Office User Specialist: Microsoft Excel 2000 Expert
Core	Indicates that you have a comprehensive understanding of the core features in a specific Microsoft Office 2000 application	Pass any ONE of the Core exams: Microsoft Word 2000 Core Microsoft Excel 2000 Core Microsoft PowerPoint 2000 Core Microsoft Access 2000 Core Microsoft Outlook 2000 Core	Candidates will be awarded one certificate for each of the Core exams they have passed: Microsoft Office User Specialist: Microsoft Word 2000 Microsoft Office User Specialist: Microsoft Excel 2000 Microsoft Office User Specialist: Microsoft PowerPoint 2000 Microsoft Office User Specialist: Microsoft Access 2000 Microsoft Office User Specialist: Microsoft Outlook 2000

Why Should You Get Certified?

Being a Microsoft Office User Specialist provides a valuable industry credential — proof that you have the Office 2000 applications skills required by employers. By passing one or more MOUS certification exams, you demonstrate your proficiency in a given Office application to employers. With nearly 80 million copies of Office in use around the world, Microsoft is targeting Office certification to a wide variety of companies. These companies include temporary employment agencies that want to prove the expertise of their workers, large corporations looking for a way to measure the skill set of employees, and training companies and educational institutions seeking Microsoft Office teachers with appropriate credentials.

The MOUS Exams

You pay $50 to $100 each time you take an exam, whether you pass or fail. The fee varies among testing centers. The Expert exams, which you can take up to 60 minutes to complete, consist of between 40 and 60 tasks that you perform online. The tasks require you to use the application just as you would in doing your job. The Core exams contain fewer tasks, and you will have slightly less time to complete them. The tasks you will perform differ on the two types of exams.

How Can You Prepare for the MOUS Exams?

The Shelly Cashman Series® offers several Microsoft-approved textbooks that cover the required objectives on the MOUS exams. For a listing of the textbooks, visit the Shelly Cashman Series MOUS Web page at www.scsite.com/off2000/cert.htm and click the Shelly Cashman Series Office 2000 Microsoft-Approved MOUS Textbooks link (Figure D-1). After using any of the books listed in an instructor-led course, you will be prepared to take the MOUS exam indicated.

How to Find an Authorized Testing Center

You can locate a testing center by calling 1-800-933-4493 in North America or visiting the Shelly Cashman Series MOUS Web page at www.scsite.com/off2000/cert.htm and then clicking the Locate an Authorized Testing Center Near You link (Figure D-1). At this Web page, you can look for testing centers around the world.

Shelly Cashman Series MOUS Web Page

The Shelly Cashman Series MOUS Web page (Figure D-1) has more than fifteen Web pages you can visit to obtain additional information on the MOUS Certification Program. The Web page (www.scsite.com/off2000/cert.htm) includes links to general information on certification, choosing an application for certification, preparing for the certification exam, and taking and passing the certification exam.

FIGURE D-1

Microsoft Excel 2000 User Specialist Certification Map

This book has been approved by Microsoft as courseware for the Microsoft Office User Specialist (MOUS) program. After completing the projects and exercises in this book, students will be prepared to take the Core level and Expert level Microsoft Office User Specialist Exam for Microsoft Excel 2000. Table D-2 lists the skill sets, activities, and page number where the activity is discussed in the book for the Core level Microsoft Office User Specialist Exam for Microsoft Excel 2000. You should be familiar with each of the activities if you plan to take the Microsoft Excel 2000 Core examination. Table D-3 on the next page lists the skill sets, activities, and page number where the activity is discussed in the book for the Expert level Microsoft Office User Specialist Exam for Microsoft Excel 2000.

Table D-2 Microsoft Excel 2000 MOUS Core Skill Sets, Activities, and Map

SKILL SETS	ACTIVITIES	PAGE NUMBERS
Working with cells	Use Undo and Redo	E 1.52, E 1.61
	Clear cell content	E 1.53
	Enter text, dates, and numbers	E 1.15, E 1.20, E 2.7, E 3.21
	Edit cell content	E 1.51, E 1.59
	Go to a specific cell	E 1.34, E 1.36
	Insert and delete selected cells	E 3.16, E 3.76
	Cut, copy, paste, paste special, and move selected cells, use the Office Clipboard	E 1.24, E 3.14, E 3.15
	Use Find and Replace	E 6.58
	Clear cell formats	E 1.53
	Work with series (AutoFill)	E 3.8-10
	Create hyperlinks	E 4.42
Working with files	Use Save	E 2.50, E 3.43
	Use Save As (different name, location, format)	E 1.41, E 3.19
	Locate and open an existing workbook	E 1.48, E 3.65
	Create a folder	E 1.44
	Use templates to create a new workbook	E 6.26
	Save a worksheet/workbook as a Web Page	EW 1.3
	Send a workbook via e-mail	E 2.62
	Use the Office Assistant	E 1.55
Formatting worksheets	Apply font styles (typeface, size, color, and styles)	E 2.28, E 2.30, E 3.36
	Apply number formats (currency, percent, dates, comma)	E 2.35, E 2.37, E 2.39, E 3.22
	Modify size of rows and columns	E 2.43, E 2.47, E 3.12
	Modify alignment of cell content	E 2.33
	Adjust the decimal place	E 2.36, E 2.39
	Use the Format Painter	E 3.10
	Apply AutoFormat	E 1.31
	Apply cell borders and shading	E 2.30, E 2.33, E 2.36
	Merge cells	E 1.33, E 2.30
	Rotate text and change indents	E 3.8
	Define, apply, and remove a style	E 6.22
Page setup and printing	Preview and print worksheets and workbooks	E 2.51, E 3.58
	Use Web Page Preview	EW 1.3
	Print a selection	E 2.54
	Change page orientation and scaling	E 2.56, E 3.58
	Set page margins and centering	E 6.49

Table D-2 Microsoft Excel 2000 MOUS Core Skill Sets, Activities, and Map

SKILL SETS	ACTIVITIES	PAGE NUMBERS
Page setup and printing (con't)	Insert and remove a page break	E 6.56
	Set print, and clear a print area	E 5.22
	Set up headers and footers	E 6.49
	Set print titles and options (gridlines, print quality, row and column headings)	E 6.55
Working with worksheets and workbooks	Insert and delete rows and columns	E 3.16
	Hide and unhide rows and columns	E 2.43, E 2.46
	Freeze and unfreeze rows and columns	E 3.19, E 3.32
	Change the zoom setting	E 3.59
	Move between worksheets in a workbook	E 2.61, E 3.58
	Check spelling	E 2.48, E 3.57
	Rename a worksheet	E 2.61, E 3.56
	Insert and delete worksheets	E 6.27
	Move and copy worksheets	E 6.28
	Link worksheets and consolidate data using 3-D References	E 6.61
Working with formulas and functions	Enter a range within a formula by dragging	E 2.17, E 2.20
	Enter formulas in a cell and using the formula bar	E 2.9, E 2.11, E 3.26
	Revise formulas	E 2.24
	Use references (absolute and relative)	E 3.24
	Use AutoSum	E 1.22, E 2.14, E 3.21, E 3.31, E 3.29
	Use Paste Function to insert a function	E 2.20
	Use basic functions (AVERAGE, SUM, COUNT, MIN, MAX)	E 1.22, E 2.16
	Enter functions using the Formula Palette	E 2.18, E 2.20, E 3.28
	Use date functions (NOW and DATE)	E 3.21
	Use financial functions (FV and PMT)	E 4.16
	Use logical functions (IF)	E 3.27
Using charts and objects	Preview and print charts	E 2.51, E 3.58
	Use Chart Wizard to create a chart	E 1.36, E 3.45
	Modify charts	E 1.36, E 1.40, E 3.49
	Insert, move, and delete an object (picture)	E 4.42
	Create and modify lines and objects	E 6.45

Table D-3 Microsoft Excel 2000 MOUS Expert Skill Sets, Activities, and Map

SKILL SETS	ACTIVITIES	PAGE NUMBERS
Importing and exporting data	Import data from text files (insert, drag and drop)	E 9.9, E 9.13
	Import from other applications	E 9.13, E 9.18
	Import a table from an HTML file (insert, drag and drop – including HTML round tripping)	E 9.18
	Export to other applications	E 9.9
Using templates	Apply templates	E 6.26
	Edit templates	E 6.16
	Create templates	E 6.7
Using multiple workbooks	Use a workspace	E 6.62
	Link workbooks	E 6.61
Formatting numbers	Apply number formats (accounting, currency, number)	E 2.35, E 2.37, E 2.39, E 3.22
	Create custom number formats	E 6.20
	Use conditional formatting	E 2.40
Printing workbooks	Print and preview multiple worksheets	E 3.58, E 5.22
	Use Report Manager	E 8.48
Working with named ranges	Add and delete a named range	E 4.12, E 5.19
	Use a named range in a formula	E 4.14
	Use Lookup Functions (HLOOKUP or VLOOKUP)	E 5.15
Working with toolbars	Hide and display toolbars	E 1.14, E 3.37, E 3.43
	Customize a toolbar	E 7.18
	Assign a macro to a command button	E 7.18
Using macros	Record macros	E 7.11
	Run macros	E 7.15
	Edit macros	E 7.16, E 7.33
Auditing a worksheet	Work with the Auditing toolbar	E 8.10, E 8.15
	Trace errors (find and fix errors)	E 8.15
	Trace precedents (find cells referred to in a specific formula)	E 2.25
	Trace dependents (find formulas that refer to a specific cell)	E 2.25
Displaying and formatting data	Apply conditional formats	E 2.40, E 4.27
	Perform single and multi-level sorts	E 5.22, E 5.25
	Use grouping and outlines	E 5.30
	Use data forms	E 5.9
	Use subtotaling	E 5.27
	Apply data filters	E 5.35
	Extract data	E 5.43
	Query databases	E 5.32, E 5.35, E 5.40
	Use data validation	E 8.15
Using analysis tools	Use PivotTable AutoFormat	E 9.51
	Use Goal Seek	E 3.65, E 4.52, E 8.21
	Create pivot chart reports	E 9.42
	Work with Scenarios	E 8.35, E 8.48
	Use Solver	E 8.23
	Use data analysis and PivotTables	E 9.59
	Create interactive PivotTables for the Web	EW 1.1
	Add fields to a PivotTable using the Web browser	EW 2.13
Collaborating with workgroups	Create, edit, and remove a comment	E 6.47
	Apply and remove worksheet and workbook protection	E 4.49
	Change workbook properties	E 8.54
	Apply and remove file passwords	E 8.32
	Track changes (highlight, accept, and reject)	E 9.25
	Create a shared workbook	E 9.25
	Merge workbooks	E 9.61

Index

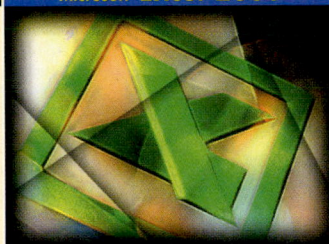
Microsoft Excel 2000

Microsoft Excel 2000
Quick Reference Summary

In Microsoft Excel 2000, you can accomplish a task in a number of ways. The following table provides a quick reference to each task presented in this textbook. You can invoke the commands listed in the MENU BAR and SHORTCUT MENU columns using either the mouse or keyboard.

Microsoft Excel 2000 Quick Reference Summary

TASK	PAGE NUMBER	MOUSE	MENU BAR	SHORTCUT MENU	KEYBOARD SHORTCUT
Advanced Filter	E 5.41		Data	Filter	Advanced Filter		ALT+D	F	A
Arrow, Add	E 6.45	Arrow button on Drawing toolbar			
AutoFilter	E 5.35		Data	Filter	AutoFilter		ALT+D	F	F
Auditing Toolbar, Display	E 8.10		Tools	Auditing	Show Auditing Toolbar		ALT+T	U	S
AutoFormat	E 1.31		Format	AutoFormat		ALT + O	A
AutoSum	E 1.22	AutoSum button on Standard toolbar	Insert	Function		ALT+=
Bold	E 1.29	Bold button on Formatting toolbar	Format	Cells	Font tab	Format Cells	Font tab	CTRL+B
Borders	E 2.30	Borders button on Formatting toolbar	Format	Cells	Border tab	Format Cells	Border tab	CTRL+1	B
Center	E 2.33	Center button on Formatting toolbar	Format	Cells	Alignment tab	Format Cells	Alignment tab	CTRL+1	A
Center Across Columns	E 1.33	Merge and Center button on Formatting toolbar	Format	Cells	Alignment tab	Format Cells	Alignment tab	CTRL+1	A
Chart	E 1.37	Chart Wizard button on Standard toolbar	Insert	Chart		F11
Clear Cell	E 1.53	Drag fill handle back	Edit	Clear	All	Clear Contents	DELETE
Close All Workbooks	E 1.46		SHIFT+File	Close All		SHIFT+ALT+F	C
Close Workbook	E 1.46	Close button on menu bar or workbook Control menu icon	File	Close		CTRL+W
Color Background	E 2.30	Fill Color button on Formatting toolbar	Format	Cells	Patterns tab	Format Cells	Patterns tab	CTRL+1	P
Column Width	E 2.44	Drag column heading boundary	Format	Column	Width tab	Column Width	ALT+O	C	W
Comma Style Format	E 2.32	Comma Style button on Formatting toolbar	Format	Cells	Number tab	Accounting	Format Cells	Number tab	Accounting	CTRL+1	N
Command Button	E 7.27	Command Button button on Control Toolbox toolbar			
Comment	E 6.47		Insert	Comment	Insert Comment	ALT+I	M
Conditional Formatting	E 2.40		Format	Conditional Formatting		ALT+O	D

(continued)

Microsoft Excel 2000 Quick Reference Summary *(continued)*

TASK	PAGE NUMBER	MOUSE	MENU BAR	SHORTCUT MENU	KEYBOARD SHORTCUT
Copy and Paste	E 3.14	Copy button and Paste button on Standard toolbar	Edit | Copy; Edit | Paste	Copy to copy | Paste to paste	CTRL+C; CTRL+V
Currency Style Format	E 2.35	Percent Style button on Formatting toolbar	Format | Cells | Number tab | Currency	Format Cells | Number tab | Accounting	CTRL+1 | N
Custom Formats	E 6.20		Format | Cells | Number tab | Custom	Format Cells | Number tab | Custom	CTRL+1 | N
Cut	E 3.16	Cut button on Standard toolbar	Edit | Cut	Cut	CTRL + X
Data Form	E 5.9		Data | Form		ALT+D | O
Data Map, Add Button	E 9.36		Tools | Customize	Customize	ALT+T | C
Data Map, Change Features	E 9.40		Map | Features	Features	
Data Map, Create	E 9.37	Map button on Standard toolbar	Insert | Object | Microsoft Map		ALT+I | O
Data Map, Format	E 9.42	In Microsoft Map Control, drag button to work area	View		ALT+V
Data Table	E 4.19		Data | Table		
Data Validation, Cell	E 8.16		Data | Validation		ALT+D | L
Date	E 3.22	Paste Function button on Standard toolbar	Insert | Function		CTRL+ SEMICOLON
Decimal Place, Decrease	E 2.36	Decrease Decimal button on Formatting toolbar	Format | Cells | Number tab | Currency	Format Cells | Number tab | Currency	CTRL+1 | N
Decimal Place, Increase	E 2.36	Increase Decimal button on Formatting toolbar	Format | Cells | Number tab | Currency	Format Cells | Number tab | Currency	CTRL+1 | N
Delete Rows or Columns	E 3.18		Edit | Delete	Delete	DELETE
Draft Quality	E 6.55		File | Page Setup | Sheet tab		ALT+F | U | S
Drop Shadow	E 3.39	Shadow button on Drawing toolbar			
Embed a Clip Art Graphic	E 4.44		Insert | Picture | Clip Art		ALT+I | P | C
E-mail from Excel	E 2.63	E-mail button on Standard toolbar	File | Send To | Mail Recipient		ALT+F | D | A
File Passwords, Saving	E 8.32		File | Save As | Tools | General Options		ALT+F | A | ALT+L | G
Find	E 6.58		Edit | Find		CTRL+F
Fit to Print	E 2.56		File | Page Setup | Page tab		
Font Color	E 2.30	Font Color button on Formatting toolbar	Format | Cells | Font tab	Format Cells | Font tab	CTRL+1 | F
Font Size	E 1.30	Font Size box arrow on Formatting toolbar	Format | Cells | Font tab	Format Cells | Font tab	CTRL+1 | F
Font Type	E 2.28	Font box on Formatting toolbar	Format | Cells | Font tab	Format Cells | Patterns tab	CTRL+1 | F
Footer	E 6.49		File | Page Setup | Header/Footer tab		ALT+F | U | H

Microsoft Excel 2000 Quick Reference Summary *(continued)*

TASK	PAGE NUMBER	MOUSE	MENU BAR	SHORTCUT MENU	KEYBOARD SHORTCUT
Formula Palette	E 2.18	Edit Formula box in formula bar	Insert | Function		CTRL+A after typing function name
Formulas Version	E 2.56		Tools | Options | View | Formulas		CTRL+ SINGLE LEFT QUOTATION MARK
Freeze Worksheet Titles	E 3.20		Windows | Freeze Panes		ALT+W | F
Function	E 2.20	Paste Function button on Standard toolbar	Insert | Function		SHIFT+F3
Gridlines	E 6.55		File | Page Setup | Sheet tab		ALT+F | U | S
Go To	E 1.36	Click cell	Edit | Go To		F5
Goal Seek	E 3.65		Tools | Goal Seek		ALT+T | G
Header	E 6.49		File | Page Setup | Header/Footer tab		ALT+F | U | H
Help	E 1.54	Microsoft Excel Help button on Standard toolbar	Help | Microsoft Excel Help		F1
Hide Column	E 2.46	Drag column heading boundary	Format | Column	Column Height	CTRL+0 (zero) to hide CTRL+SHIFT+) to display
Hide Row	E 2.48	Drag row heading boundary	Format | Row	Row Height	CTRL+9 to hide CTRL+SHIFT+(to display
Import Data from Access Table	E 9.14		Data | Get External Data | New Database Query		ALT+D | D | N
Import Data from Text File	E 9.9		Data | Get External Data | Import Text File		ALT+D | D | T
Import Data from Web Page	E 9.18		Data | Get External Data | New Web Query		ALT+D | D | W
In-Cell Editing	E 1.51	Double-click cell			F2
Insert Rows or Columns	E 3.16		Insert | Rows or Insert | Columns	Insert	ALT+I | R or ALT+I | C
Italicize	E 3.42	Italic button on Formatting toolbar	Format | Cells | Font tab	Format Cells | Font tab	CTRL+I
Link Update	E 6.63		Edit | Links		ALT+E | K
Link Worksheet to Word Document	EI 1.4		Edit | Copy; Edit | Paste Special	Copy to copy | Paste Special to paste	CTRL+C; ALT+E | S
Macro, Execute	E 7.15	Run Macro button on Visual Basic toolbar	Tools | Macro | Macros		ALT+F8
Macro, Record	E 7.11		Tools | Macro | Record New Macro		ALT+T | M | R
Macro, View Code	E 7.16		Tools | Macro | Macros | Edit		ALT+F8
Margins	E 6.49		File | Page Setup | Margins		ALT+F | U | M
Menu, Customize	E 7.22		Tools | Customize | Commands tab	Customize | Commands tab	ALT+T | C | C
Move	E 3.15	Point to border and drag	Edit | Cut; Edit | Paste		CTRL+X; CTRL+V
Name Cells	E 4.12	Click in Name box and type name	Insert | Name | Create or Insert | Name | Define		CTRL+SHIFT+F3
Name Cells, Redefine	E 5.18		Insert | Name | Define		ALT+I | N | D

(continued)

Microsoft Excel 2000 Quick Reference Summary *(continued)*

TASK	PAGE NUMBER	MOUSE	MENU BAR	SHORTCUT MENU	KEYBOARD SHORTCUT
New Workbook	E 1.54	New button on Standard toolbar	File | New		CTRL+N
Open Workbook	E 1.48	Open button on Standard toolbar	File | Open		CTRL+O
Outline a Range	E 4.9	Borders button on Formatting toolbar	Format | Cells | Border tab	Format Cells | Border tab	CTRL+1 | B
Outline a Worksheet	E 5.30		Data | Group and Outline		ALT+D | G | A
Page Break	E 6.56		Insert | Page Break		ALT+I | B
Percent Style Format	E 2.39	Percent Style button on Formatting toolbar	Format | Cells | Number tab | Percentage	Format Cells | Number | Percentage	CTRL+1 | N
PivotChart, Add Data to	E 9.49	Drag button from PivotTable toolbar to PivotChart			
PivotChart, Change View of	E 9.54	Click interactive buttons on PivotChart			
PivotChart, Create	E 9.46		Data | PivotTable and PivotChart Report		ALT+D | P
PivotChart, Format	E 9.51	Chart Wizard button on PivotTable toolbar	Chart | Chart Type	Chart Type	ALT+C | T
PivotTable List, Add Fields	EW 2.14	Drag field from PivotTable Field List window			
PivotTable List, Add Summary Totals	EW 2.6	AutoCalc button on toolbar in browser			
PivotTable List, Change View	EW 2.10	Drag data fields to Row Field area in browser			
PivotTable List, Create	EW 2.2		File | Save as Web Page		ALT+F | G
PivotTable List, Filter	EW 2.4	Click field drop-down arrow and remove check marks			
PivotTable List, Remove Field	EW 2.12			Remove Field	
PivotTable List, Sort	EW 2.8	Sort Ascending button or Sort Descending button on toolbar in browser			
PivotTable, Change View	E 9.60	Drag buttons to different locations on PivotTable			
PivotTable, Format	E 9.57	Format Report button on PivotTable toolbar	Format | AutoFormat	Format Report	ALT+O | A
Preview Worksheet	E 2.51	Print Preview button on Standard toolbar	File | Print Preview		ALT+F | V
Print Row and Column Headings	E 6.55		File | Page Setup | Sheet tab		ALT+F | U | S
Print Row and Column Titles	E 6.55		File | Page Setup | Sheet tab		ALT+F | U | S
Print Worksheet	E 2.51	Print button on Standard toolbar	File | Print		CTRL+P
Properties, Set	E 7.30	Properties button on Control Toolbox toolbar			

Microsoft Excel 2000 Quick Reference Summary *(continued)*

TASK	PAGE NUMBER	MOUSE	MENU BAR	SHORTCUT MENU	KEYBOARD SHORTCUT
Protect Worksheet	E 4.49		Tools | Protection | Protect Sheet		ALT+T | P | P
Quit Excel	E 1.46	Close button on title bar	File | Exit		ALT+F4
Redo	E 1.52	Redo button on Standard toolbar	Edit | Redo		ALT+E | R
Remove Auditing Arrows	E 2.23	Remove All Arrows button on Auditing toolbar	Tools | Auditing | Remove All Arrows		ALT+T | U | A
Remove Precedent Arrows, Audit	E 8.12	Remove Precedent Arrows button on Auditing toolbar			
Remove Splits	E 3.62	Double-click split bar	Window | Split		ALT+W | S
Rename Sheet Tab	E 2.61	Double-click sheet tab		Rename	
Replace	E 6.58		Edit | Replace		CTRL+H
Rotate Text	E 3.8		Format | Cells | Alignment tab	Format Cells | Alignment tab	ALT+O | E | A
Route Workbook	E 9.27		File | Send To | Routing Recipient		ALT+F | D | R
Row Height	E 2.47	Drag row heading boundary	Format | Row	Row Height	ALT+O | R | E
Save as Web Page	EW 1.3		File | Save as Web Page		ALT+F | G
Save Workbook – New Name	E 1.41		File | Save As		ALT+F | A
Save Workbook – Same Name	E 2.50	Save button on Standard toolbar	File | Save		CTRL+S
Scenario Manager	E 8.35		Tools | Scenarios		ALT+T | E
Scenario PivotTable	E 8.52	Summary button on Scenario Manager dialog box, choose Scenario PivotTable	Tools | Scenarios		ALT+T | E | ALT+U | ALT+P
Scenario Summary	E 8.50	Summary button on Scenario Manager dialog box, choose Scenario summary	Tools | Scenarios		ALT+T | E | ALT+U | ALT+S
Scenario, Add	E 8.45	Add button on Scenario Manager dialog box	Tools | Scenarios		ALT+T | E | ALT+A
Scenario, Show	E 8.47	Show button on Scenario Manager dialog box	Tools | Scenarios		ALT+T | E | ALT+S
Select All of Worksheet	E 1.54	Select All button on worksheet			CTRL+A
Select Multiple Sheets	E 3.57	CTRL and click tab or SHIFT and click tab	Select All Sheets		
Series	E 3.8	Drag fill handle	Edit | Fill | Series		ALT+E | I | S
Shortcut Menu	E 1.51	Right-click			SHIFT+F10
Solver	E 8.23		Tools | Solver		ALT+T | V
Solver, Solve Problem	E 8.25	Solve button in Solver Parameters dialog box	Tools | Solver		ALT+T | V | ALT+S
Sort	E 5.22	Click Sort Ascending or Sort Descending button on Standard toolbar	Data | Sort		ALT+D | S

(continued)

Microsoft Excel 2000 Quick Reference Summary *(continued)*

TASK	PAGE NUMBER	MOUSE	MENU BAR	SHORTCUT MENU	KEYBOARD SHORTCUT
Spell Check	E 2.49	Spelling button on Standard toolbar	Tools | Spelling		F7
Split Window into Panes	E 3.61	Drag vertical or horizontal split box	Window | Split		ALT+W | S
Stock Quotes	E 2.58		Data | Get External Data | Run Web Query		ALT+D | D | D
Style, Add	E 6.22		Format | Style | Add button		ALT+O | S
Style, Apply	E 6.25		Format | Style		ALT+O | S
Subtotals	E 5.27		Data | Subtotals		ALT+D | B
Subtotals, Remove	E 5.31		Data | Subtotals | Remove All button		ALT+D | B | R
Switch Summary Functions	E 9.59	Field Settings button on PivotTable toolbar		Field Settings	
Text Box, Add	E 6.45	Text Box button on Drawing toolbar			
Toolbar, Customize	E 7.18		Tools | Customize | Commands tab	Customize | Commands tab	ALT+T | C | C
Toolbar, Reset	E 1.14		View | ToolBars | Customize | Toolbars tab	Customize | Toolbars tab	ALT+V | T | C | B
Toolbar, Show Entire	E 1.28	Double-click move handle			
Toolbar, Show or Hide	E 3.38		View | Toolbars	Customize	ALT+V | T
Trace Dependents	E 2.25	Trace Dependents button on Auditing toolbar		Tools | Auditing | Trace Dependents	ALT+T | U | D
Trace Precedents	E 2.25	Trace Precedents button on Auditing toolbar	Tools | Auditing | Trace Precedents		ALT+T | U | T
Track Changes, Disable	E 9.35		Tools | Track Changes | Highlight Changes | remove check		ALT+T | T | H
Track Changes, Enable	E 9.26		Tools | Track Changes | Highlight Changes		ALT+T | T | H
Track Changes, Review	E 9.31	Point to blue triangle	Tools | Track Changes | Accept or Reject Changes		ALT+T | T | A
Underline	E 3.42	Underline button on Formatting toolbar	Format | Cells | Font tab	Format Cells | Font tab	CTRL+U
Undo	E 1.52	Undo button on Standard toolbar	Edit | Undo		CTRL+Z
Unfreeze Worksheet Titles	E 3.32		Windows | Unfreeze Panes		ALT+W | F
Unlock Cells	E 4.49		Format | Cells | Protection tab	Format Cells | Protection	CTRL+1 | SHIFT+P
Unprotect Worksheet	E 4.51		Tools | Protection | Unprotect Sheet		ALT+T | P | P
Visual Basic Editor	E 7.31	View Code button on Control Toolbox toolbar	Tools | Macro | Visual Basic Editor		ALT+F11
WordArt	E 6.41	Insert WordArt button on Drawing toolbar	Insert | Picture | WordArt		ALT+I | P | W
Web Page Preview	EW 1.3		File | Web Page Preview		ALT+F | B
Workbook Properties	E 8.54		File | Properties		ALT+F | I
Zoom	E 3.59	Zoom box on Standard toolbar	View | Zoom		ALT+V | Z